Complex Data Warehousing and Knowledge Discovery for Advanced Retrieval Development:
Innovative Methods and Applications

Tho Manh Nguyen
*Institute of Software Technology and Interactive Systems,
Vienna University of Technology, Austria*

 **INFORMATION SCIENCE REFERENCE**

Hershey • New York

Director of Editorial Content:	Kristin Klinger
Senior Managing Editor:	Jamie Snavely
Managing Editor:	Jeff Ash
Assistant Managing Editor:	Michael Brehm
Publishing Assistant:	Sean Woznicki
Typesetter:	Jeff Ash
Cover Design:	Lisa Tosheff
Printed at:	Yurchak Printing Inc.

Published in the United States of America by
Information Science Reference (an imprint of IGI Global)
701 E. Chocolate Avenue
Hershey PA 17033
Tel: 717-533-8845
Fax: 717-533-8661
E-mail: cust@igi-global.com
Web site: http://www.igi-global.com/reference

Copyright © 2010 by IGI Global. All rights reserved. No part of this publication may be reproduced, stored or distributed in any form or by any means, electronic or mechanical, including photocopying, without written permission from the publisher.
     Product or company names used in this set are for identification purposes only. Inclusion of the names of the products or companies does not indicate a claim of ownership by IGI Global of the trademark or registered trademark.

Library of Congress Cataloging-in-Publication Data

Complex data warehousing and knowledge discovery for advanced retrieval development : innovative methods and applications / Tho Manh Nguyen, editor.
     p. cm.

Includes bibliographical references and index.
Summary: "This book provides a comprehensive analysis on current issues and trends in retrieval expansion"--Provided by publisher.

ISBN 978-1-60566-748-5 (hardcover) -- ISBN 978-1-60566-749-2 (ebook) 1. Data warehousing. 2. Database searching. I. Nguyen, Tho Manh.

QA76.9.D37C67 2009
005.74--dc22
                         2009005271

British Cataloguing in Publication Data
A Cataloguing in Publication record for this book is available from the British Library.

All work contributed to this book is new, previously-unpublished material. The views expressed in this book are those of the authors, but not necessarily of the publisher.

Advances in Data Warehousing and Mining Series (ADWM)

ISBN: 1935-2646

Editor-in-Chief: David Taniar, Monash Univerisy, Australia

Research and Trends in Data Mining Technologies and Applications
David Taniar, Monash University, Australia

IGI Publishing • copyright 2007 • 340 pp • H/C (ISBN: 1-59904-271-1) • US $85.46 (our price)
• E-Book (ISBN: 1-59904-273-8) • US $63.96 (our price)

Activities in data warehousing and mining are constantly emerging. Data mining methods, algorithms, online analytical processes, data mart and practical issues consistently evolve, providing a challenge for professionals in the field. Research and Trends in Data Mining Technologies and Applications focuses on the integration between the fields of data warehousing and data mining, with emphasis on the applicability to real-world problems. This book provides an international perspective, highlighting solutions to some of researchers' toughest challenges. Developments in the knowledge discovery process, data models, structures, and design serve as answers and solutions to these emerging challenges.

The Advances in Data Warehousing and Mining (ADWM) Book Series aims to publish and disseminate knowledge on an international basis in the areas of data warehousing and data mining. The book series provides a highly regarded outlet for the most emerging research in the field and seeks to bridge underrepresented themes within the data warehousing and mining discipline.
The Advances in Data Warehousing and Mining (ADWM) Book Series serves to provide a continuous forum for state-of-the-art developments and research, as well as current innovative activities in data warehousing and mining. In contrast to other book series, the ADWM focuses on the integration between the fields of data warehousing and data mining, with emphasize on the applicability to real world problems. ADWM is targeted at both academic researchers and practicing IT professionals.

Hershey • New York

Order online at www.igi-global.com or call 717-533-8845 x 10 –
Mon-Fri 8:30 am - 5:00 pm (est) or fax 24 hours a day 717-533-8661

Editorial Advisory Board

Torben Bach Pedersen, *Aalborg University, Denmark*
Stephane Bressan, *National University of Singapore (NUS) Singapore*
Johann Eder, *University of Klagenfurt, Austria*
Mukesh Mohania, *IBM India Research Lab, India*
Zbigniew W. Ras, *University of North Carolina, USA*
Il-Yeol Song, *Drexel University, USA*
David Taniar, *Monash University, Australia*
Dimitri Theodoratos, *New Jersey Institute of Technology, USA*
A Min Tjoa, *Vienna University of Technology, Austria*
Karen Davis, *University of Cincinnati, USA*
Mohammed J. Zaki, *Rensselaer Polytechnic Institute, USA*
Stefano Rizzi, *University of Bologna, Italy*
Sourav S. Bhowmick, *Nanyang Technological University, Singapore*
Panos Vassiliadis, *University of Ioannina, USA*
Juan Trujilo, *University of Alicante, Spain*

List of Reviewers

Alberto Abello, *Universitat Politecnica de Catalunya, Spain*
Elena Baralis, *Politecnico di Torino, Italy*
Ladjel Bellatreche, *LISI/ENSMA, France*
Bettina Berendt, *Humboldt University Berlin, Germany*
Peter Brezany, *University of Vienna, Austria*
Henrik Bostrom, *University of Skovde, Sweden*
Amilcar Cardoso, *University of Coimbra, Portugal*
Ezeife Christie, *University of Windsor, Canada*
Sunil Choenni, *University of Twente and Dutch Ministry of Justice, Netherlands*
Alfredo Cuzzocrea, *University of Calabria, Italy*
Vladimir Estivill-Castro, *Griffith University, Australia*
Eduardo Fernandez-Medina, *University of Castilla-La Mancha, Spain*
Matteo Golfarelli, *DEIS - University of Bologna, Italy*
Gunter Grieser, *Technical University Darmstadt, Germany*
Eyke Hermeier, *Otto-von-Guericke-University Magdeburg, Germany*

Jaakko Hollmen, *Helsinki University of Technology, Finland*
Andreas Hotho, *University of Kassel, Germany*
Se June Hong, *RSM emeritus, IBM TJ Watson Research Center, USA*
Jimmy Huang ,*York University, Canada*
Ryutaro Ichise, *National Institute of Informatics, Japan*
Fan Jianping, *University of North Carolina, USA*
Jinyan Li, *Institute for Infocomm Research, Singapore*
Guanling Lee, *National Dong Hwa University, Taiwan*
Giuseppe Manco, *ICAR-CNR, National Research Council, Italy*
Michael May, *Fraunhofer Institut Autonome Intelligente Systeme, Germany*
Rosa Meo, *University of Turin, Italy*
Alexandros Nanopoulos, *Aristotle University of Thessaloniki, Greece*
Jaakko Peltonen, *Helsinki University of Technology, Finland*
Andrew Rau-Chaplin, *Dalhousie University, Canada*
Monica Scannapieco, *University of Rome, Italy*
Michael Schrefl, *University Linz, Austria*
Giovanni Semeraro, *University of Bari, Italy*
Alkis Simitsis, *Stanford University, USA*
Min Song, *New Jersey Institute of Technology, USA*
Jerzy Stefanowski, *Poznan University of Technology, Poland*
Ah-Hwee Tan, *Nanyang Technological University, Singapore*
Il-hoi Yoo, *University of Missouri, Columbia, USA*
Jenny Zhang, *RMIT University, Australia*
Marek Wojciechowski, *Poznan University of Technology, Poland*
Wolfram Wöß, *University of Linz, Austria*

Table of Contents

Section 3
DWH and OLAP Applications

Detailed Table of Contents

Section 1
DWH Architectures and Fundamentals

Three chapters in Section 1 present the current trends of research on data warehouse architecture, storage and implementations which towards on improving performance and response time.

Chapter 1

Todd Eavis, Concordia University, Canada
David Cueva, Concordia University, Canada

In Chapter 1, the authors propose an LBF R-tree framework for effective indexing mechanisms in multi-dimensional database environment. The proposed framework addressed not only improves performance on common user-defined range queries, but also gracefully degrades to a linear scan of the data on pathologically large queries. Experimental results demonstrating both efficient disk access on the LBF R-tree, as well as impressive compression ratios for data and indexes.

Chapter 2

Fadila Bentayeb, University of Lyon – ERIC Laboratory, France
Cécile Favre, University of Lyon – ERIC Laboratory, France
Omar Boussaid, University of Lyon – ERIC Laboratory, France

Chapter 2 addresses the issues related to the workload's evolution and maintenance in data warehouse systems in response to new requirements modeling resulting from users' personalized analysis needs. The proposed workload management system assists the administrator to maintain and adapt dynamically the workload according to changes arising on the data warehouse schema by improving two types of workload updates: (1) maintaining existing queries consistent with respect to the new data warehouse schema and (2) creating new queries based on the new dimension hierarchy levels.

Chapter 3

Songmei Yu, Felician College, USA
Vijayalakshmi Atluri, Rutgers University, USA
Nabil Adam, Rutgers University, USA

Chapter 3 presents an optimization approach for materialized view implementation in spatial data warehouse. Due to the fact that spatial data are larger in size and spatial operations are more complex than the traditional relational operations, both the view materialization cost and the on-the-fly computation cost are often extremely high. The authors propose a new notion, called preview, for which both the materialization and on-the-fly costs are significantly smaller than those of the traditional views, so that the total cost is optimized.

Section 2
Multidimensional Data and OLAP

Section 2 consists of three chapters discussing related issues and challenges in multidimensional database and online analytical processing (OLAP) environment.

Chapter 4

Guillaume Cabanac, Université de Toulouse, France
Max Chevalier, Université de Toulouse, France
Franck Ravat, Université de Toulouse, France
Olivier Teste, Université de Toulouse, France

Chapter 4 deals with an annotation-based decisional system. The decisional system is based on multidimensional databases, which are composed of facts and dimensions. The expertise of decision-makers is modeled, shared and stored through annotations. Every piece of multidimensional data can be associated with zero or more annotations which allow decision-makers to carry on active analysis and to collaborate with other decision-makers on a common analysis.

Chapter 5

Stefan Berger, University of Linz, Data & Knowledge Engineering Group, Austria
Michael Schrefl, University of Linz, Data & Knowledge Engineering Group, Austria

Chapter 5 discusses federated data warehouse systems which consist of a collection of data marts provided by different enterprises or public organizations and widen the knowledge base for business analysts, thus enabling better founded strategic decisions. The authors argue that the integration of heterogeneous data marts at the logical schema level is preferable to the migration of data into a physically new system if the involved organizations remain autonomous. They present a federated architecture that provides a global multi-dimensional schema to which the data mart schemas are semantically mapped, repairing all heterogeneities.

Jérôme Cubillé, EDF R&D, France
Christian Derquenne, EDF R&D, France
Sabine Goutier, EDF R&D, France
Françoise Guisnel, EDF R&D, France
Henri Klajnmic, EDF R&D, France
Véronique Cariou, ENITIAA, France

Chapter 6 describes algorithms to support business intelligence in OLAP databases applying data mining methods to the multidimensional environment. Those methods help end-users' analysis in two ways. First, they identify the most interesting dimensions to expand in order to explore the data. Then, they automatically detect interesting cells among a user selected ones. The solution is based on a tight coupling between OLAP tools and statistical methods, based upon the built-in indicators computed instantaneously during the end-users' exploration of the data cube.

Section 3
DWH and OLAP Applications

The chapters in Section 3 present some typical applications using data warehouse and OLAP technology as well as the challenges and issues facing in the real practice.

Svetlana Mansmann, University of Konstanz, Konstanz, Germany
Thomas Neumuth, Innovation Center Computer Assisted Surgery (ICCAS), Leipzig, Germany
Oliver Burgert, Innovation Center Computer Assisted Surgery (ICCAS), Leipzig, Germany
Matthias Röger, University of Konstanz, Konstanz, Germany
Marc H. Scholl, University of Konstanz, Konstanz, Germany

Chapter 7 presents a conceptual framework for adopting the data warehousing technology for business process analysis, with surgical workflows analysis as a challenging real-world application. Deficiencies of the conventional OLAP approach are overcome by proposing an extended multidimensional data model, which enables adequate capturing of flow-oriented data. The model supports a number of advanced properties, such as non-quantitative and heterogeneous facts, many-to-many relationships between facts and dimensions, full and partial dimension sharing, dynamic specification of new measures, and interchangeability of fact and dimension roles.

Deployment of a federated data warehouse approach for the integration of the wide range of different medical data sources and for distribution of evidence-based clinical knowledge, to support clinical decision makers, primarily clinicians at the point of care is the main topic of chapter VIII: "Data Warehouse Facilitating Evidence-Based Medicine". A real-world scenario is used to illustrate the possible application field in the area of emergency and intensive care in which the evidence-based medicine merges data originating in a pharmacy database, a social insurance company database and diverse clinical DWHs with the minimized administration effort.

Chapter 9, "Deploying Data Warehouses in Grids with Efficiency and Availability," discusses the deployment of data warehouses over Grids. The authors present the Grid-NPDW architecture, which aims at providing high throughput and data availability in Grid-based warehouses. High efficiency in situations with site failure is also achieved with the use of on-demand query scheduling and data partitioning and replication. The chapter also describes the main components of the Grid-NPDW scheduler and presents some experimental results of proposed strategies.

Section 4
Data Mining Techniques

Section 4 consists of three chapters discussing a variety of traditional data mining techniques such as clustering, ranking, classification but towards the efficiency and performance improvement.

Chapter 10, "MOSAIC: Agglomerative Clustering with Gabriel Graphs," introduces MOSAIC, a post-processing technique that has been designed to overcome these disadvantages. MOSAIC is an agglomerative technique that greedily merges neighboring clusters maximizing an externally given fitness function; Gabriel graphs are used to determine which clusters are neighboring, and non-convex shapes are approximated as the unions of small convex clusters. Experimental results are presented that show that using MOSAIC leads to clusters of higher quality compared to running a representative clustering algorithm stand-alone.

Chapter 11

Ronnie Alves, University of Nice Sophia-Antipolis, France
Joel Ribeiro, University of Minho, Portugal
Orlando Belo, University of Minho, Portugal
Jiawei Han, University of Illinois at Urbana-Champaign, USA

Chapter 11 investigates how to mine and rank the most interesting changes in a multi-dimensional space applying a promising TOP-K gradient strategy. Interesting changes in customer behavior are usually discovered by gradient queries which are particular cases of multi-dimensional data analysis on large data warehouses. The main problem, however, arises from the fact that more interesting changes should be those ones having more dimensions in the gradient query (the curse-of-dimensionality dilemma). Besides, the number of interesting changes should be of a large amount (the preference selection criteria).

Chapter 12

Manoranjan Dash, Nanyang Technological University, Singapore
Vivekanand Gopalkrishnan, Nanyang Technological University, Singapore

In Chapter 12, a method is proposed to combine feature selection and tuple selection to improve classification accuracy. Although feature selection and tuple selection have been studied earlier in various research areas such as machine learning, data mining, and so on, they have rarely been studied together. Feature selection and tuple selection help the classifier to focus better. The method is based on the principle that a representative subset has similar histogram as the full set. The proposed method uses this principle both to choose a subset of features and also to choose a subset of tuples. The empirical tests show that the proposed method performs better than several existing feature selection methods.

Section 5
Advanced Mining Applications

Section 5 introduces innovative algorithms and applications in some emerging application fields in Data Mining and Knowledge Discovery, especially continuous data stream mining, which could not be solved by traditional mining technology.

In Chapter 13, "Learning cost-sensitive decision trees to support medical," the authors discuss about diagnosis a cost-sensitive learning method. The chapter aims to enhance the understand of cost-sensitive learning problems in medicine and presents a strategy for learning and testing cost-sensitive decision trees, while considering several types of costs associated with problems in medicine. It begins with a contextualization and a discussion of the main types of costs. Then, reviews related work and presents a discussion about the evaluation of classifiers as well as explains a cost-sensitive decision tree strategy and presents some experimental results.

Chapter 14 discusses about catching the recent trend of data when mining frequent itemsets over data streams. A data representation method, named frequency changing point (FCP), is introduced for monitoring the recent occurrence of itemsets over a data stream to prevent from storing the whole transaction data within a sliding window. The effect of old transactions on the mining result of recently frequent itemsets is diminished by performing adjusting rules on the monitoring data structure. Accordingly, the recently frequent itemsets or representative patterns are discovered from the maintained structure approximately. Experimental studies demonstrate that the proposed algorithms achieve high true positive rates and guarantees no false dismissal to the results yielded.

Chapter 15 proposes a simple machine learning approach for protocol identification in network streams that have been encrypted, such that the only information available for identifying the underlying protocol of a connection was the size, timing and direction of packets. With very little information available from the network stream, it is possible to pinpoint potentially inappropriate activities for a workplace, institution or research center, such as using BitTorrent, GMail or MSN, and not confuse them with other common protocols such as HTTP and SSL.

Chapter 16

Rodrigo Salvador Monteiro, COPPE / UFRJ, Brazil
Geraldo Zimbrão, COPPE / UFRJ, Brazil
Holger Schwarz, IPVS - University of Stuttgart, Germany
Bernhard Mitschang, IPVS - University of Stuttgart, Germany
Jano Moreira de Souza, COPPE / UFRJ, Brazil

Chapter 16 introduces a calendar-based pattern mining aims at identifying patterns on specific calendar partitions in continuous data streams. The authors present how a data warehouse approach can be applied to leverage calendar-based pattern mining in data streams and how the framework of the DWFIST approach can cope with tight time constraints imposed by data streams, keep storage requirements at a manageable level and, at the same time, support calendar-based frequent itemset mining. The minimum granularity of analysis, parameters of the data warehouse (e.g., mining minimum support) and parameters of the database (e.g., extent size) provide ways to tune the load performance.

Preface

Data warehousing and knowledge discovery are established key technologies in many application domains. Enterprises and organizations improve their abilities in data analysis, decision support, and the automatic extraction of knowledge from data; for scientific applications to analyze collected data, for medical applications for quality assurance and for steps to individualized medicine, to mention just a few examples. With the exponentially growing amount of information to be included in the decision making process, the data to be processed become more and more complex in both structure and semantics. Consequently, the process of retrieval and knowledge discovery from this huge amount of heterogeneous complex data constitutes the reality check for research in the area.

The primary objective of the book *Complex Data Warehousing and Knowledge Discovery for Advanced Retrieval Development: Innovative Methods and Applications* is to give readers comprehensive knowledge on the current issues as well as the development trends of data warehousing and knowledge discovery. The book presents the latest research issues and experiences in developing and deploying data warehousing and knowledge discovery systems, applications, and solutions. The 16 book chapters, organized in 5 Sections, were contributed by authors and editorial board members from the *International Journal of Data Warehousing and Mining*, as well as invited authors who are experts in the data warehousing and knowledge discovery field.

Three chapters in **Section 1, Data Warehouse Architectures & Fundamentals**, present the current trends of research on data warehouse architecture, storage and implementations towards improving performance and response time.

In Chapter 1, "The LBF R-tree: Scalable Indexing and Storage for Data Warehousing Systems" by Todd Eavis and David Cueva (Concordia University, Canada), the authors propose an LBF R-tree framework for effective indexing mechanisms in multi-dimensional database environments. The proposed framework addressed not only improves performance on common user-defined range queries, but also gracefully degrades to a linear scan of the data on pathologically large queries. Experimental results demonstrating both efficient disk access on the LBF R-tree, as well as impressive compression ratios for data and indexes.

Chapter 2, "Dynamic Workload for Schema Evolution in Data Warehouses: A Performance Issue," by Cécile Favre, Fadila Bentayeb and Omar Boussaid (ERIC Laboratory, University of Lyon, France), addresses the issues related to the workload's evolution and maintenance in data warehouse systems in response to new requirements modeling resulting from users' personalized analysis needs. The proposed workload management system assists the administrator to maintain and adapt dynamically the workload according to changes arising on the data warehouse schema by improving two types of workload updates: (1) maintaining existing queries consistent with respect to the new data warehouse schema and (2) creating new queries based on the new dimension hierarchy levels.

Songmei Yu, Vijayalakshmi Atluri, and Nabil R. Adam (MSIS Department and CIMIC, Rutgers University, USA) in Chapter 3, "Preview: Optimizing View Materialization Cost in Spatial Data Warehouses," present an optimization approach for materialized view implementation in spatial data warehouse. Due to the fact that spatial data are larger in size and spatial operations are more complex than the traditional relational operations, both the view materialization cost and the on-the-fly computation cost are often extremely high. The authors propose a new notion, called preview, for which both the materialization and on-the-fly costs are significantly smaller than those of the traditional views, so that the total cost is optimized.

Section 2, Multidimensional Data & OLAP, consists of three chapters discussing related issues and challenges in multidimensional database and online analytical processing (OLAP) environment.

Chapter 4, "Decisional Annotations: Integrating and Preserving Decision-Makers' Expertise in Multidimensional Systems," by Guillaume Cabanac, Max Chevalier, Franck Ravat and Olivier Teste (Université de Toulouse, France), deals with an annotation-based decisional system. The decisional system is based on multidimensional databases, which are composed of facts and dimensions. The expertise of decision-makers is modeled, shared and stored through annotations. Every piece of multidimensional data can be associated with zero or more annotations which allow decision-makers to carry on active analysis and to collaborate with other decision-makers on a common analysis.

In Chapter 5, "Federated Data Warehouse*s*," Stefan Berger and Michael Schrefl (University of Linz, Austria) discuss federated data warehouse systems which consist of a collection of data marts provided by different enterprises or public organizations and widen the knowledge base for business analysts, thus enabling better founded strategic decisions. The authors argue that the integration of heterogeneous data marts at the logical schema level is preferable to the migration of data into a physically new system if the involved organizations remain autonomous. They present a federated architecture that provides a global multi-dimensional schema to which the data mart schemas are semantically mapped, repairing all heterogeneities.

Chapter 6, "Decisional Annotations: Integrating and Preserving Decision-Makers' Expertise in Multidimensional Systems," by Jérôme Cubillé, Christian Derquenne, Sabine Goutier, Françoise Guisnel, Henri Klajnmic (EDF Research and Development, France) and Véronique Cariou (ENITIAA, France), describes algorithms to support business intelligence in OLAP databases applying data mining methods to the multidimensional environment. Those methods help end-users' analysis in two ways. First, they identify the most interesting dimensions to expand in order to explore the data. Then, they automatically detect interesting cells among a user selected ones. The solution is based on a tight coupling between OLAP tools and statistical methods, based upon the built-in indicators computed instantaneously during the end-users' exploration of the data cube.

The next three chapters in **Section 3, DWH & OLAP Applications**, present some typical applications using data warehouse and OLAP technology as well as the challenges and issues facing in the real practice.

Chapter 7, "Conceptual Data Warehouse Design Methodology for Business Process Intelligence," by Svetlana Mansmann, Matthias Röger and Marc H. Scholl (University of Konstanz, Konstanz, Germany), Neumuth and Oliver Burgert (Innovation Center Computer Assisted Surgery (ICCAS), Leipzig, Germany), presents a conceptual framework for adopting the data warehousing technology for business process analysis, with surgical workflows analysis as a challenging real-world application. Deficiencies of the conventional OLAP approach are overcome by proposing an extended multidimensional data model, which enables adequate capturing of flow-oriented data. The model supports a number of advanced properties, such as non-quantitative and heterogeneous facts, many-to-many relationships between facts and dimensions, full and partial dimension sharing, dynamic specification of new measures, and interchangeability of fact and dimension roles.

Deployment of a federated data warehouse approach for the integration of the wide range of different medical data sources and for distribution of evidence-based clinical knowledge, to support clinical decision makers, primarily clinicians at the point of care is the main topic of Chapter 8, "Data Warehouse Facilitating Evidence-Based Medicine," authored by Nevena Stolba, Tho Manh Nguyen, A Min Tjoa (Vienna University of Technology, Austria). A real-world scenario is used to illustrate the possible application field in the area of emergency and intensive care in which the evidence-based medicine merges data originating in a pharmacy database, a social insurance company database and diverse clinical DWHs with the minimized administration effort.

In Chapter 9, "Deploying Data Warehouses in Grids with Efficiency and Availability," Rogério Luís de Carvalho Costa and Pedro Furtado (Departamento de Engenharia Informática, University of Coimbra, Portugal) discuss the deployment of data warehouses over Grids. The authors present the Grid-NPDW architecture, which aims at providing high throughput and data availability in Grid-based warehouses. High efficiency in situations with site failure is also achieved with the use of on-demand query scheduling and data partitioning and replication. The chapter also describes the main components of the Grid-NPDW scheduler and presents some experimental results of proposed strategies.

Section 4, Data Mining Techniques, consists of three chapters discussing a variety of traditional data mining techniques such as clustering, ranking, classification but towards the efficiency and performance improvement.

Chapter 10, "MOSAIC: Agglomerative Clustering with Gabriel Graphs," by Rachsuda Jiamthapthaksin, Jiyeon Choo, Chun-sheng Chen, Oner Ulvi Celepcikay, Christoph F. Eick (Computer Science Department, University of Houston, USA) and Christian Giusti (Department of Mathematics and Computer Science, University of Udine, Italy), introduces MOSAIC, a post-processing technique that has been designed to overcome these disadvantages. MOSAIC is an agglomerative technique that greedily merges neighboring clusters maximizing an externally given fitness function; Gabriel graphs are used to determine which clusters are neighboring, and non-convex shapes are approximated as the unions of small convex clusters. Experimental results are presented that show that using MOSAIC leads to clusters of higher quality compared to running a representative clustering algorithm stand-alone.

In Chapter 11, "Ranking Gradients in Multi-Dimensional Spaces," Ronnie Alves, Joel Ribeiro, Orlando Belo (Department of Informatics, University of Minho, Portugal) and Jiawei Han (Department of Computer Science, University of Illinois at Urbana-Champaign, USA) investigate how to mine and rank the most interesting changes in a multi-dimensional space applying a promising TOP-K gradient strategy. Interesting changes in customer behavior are usually discovered by gradient queries which are particular cases of multi-dimensional data analysis on large data warehouses. The main problem, however, arises from the fact that more interesting changes should be those ones having more dimensions in the gradient query (the curse-of-dimensionality dilemma). Besides, the number of interesting changes should be of a large amount (the preference selection criteria).

In Chapter 12, "Simultaneous Feature Selection and Tuple Selection for Efficient Classification," by Manoranjan Dash & Vivekanand Gopalkrishnan (Nanyang Technological University, Singapore), a method is proposed to combine feature selection and tuple selection to improve classification accuracy. Although feature selection and tuple selection have been studied earlier in various research areas such as machine learning, data mining, and so on, they have rarely been studied together. Feature selection and tuple selection help the classifier to focus better. The method is based on the principle that a representative subset has similar histogram as the full set. The proposed method uses this principle both to choose a subset of features and also to choose a subset of tuples. The empirical tests show that the proposed method performs better than several existing feature selection methods.

The last four chapters in **Section 5, Advanced Mining Applications** introduces innovative algorithms and applications in some emerging application fields in data mining and knowledge discovery, especially continuous data stream mining, which could not be solved by traditional mining technology.

Alberto Freitas, Altamiro Costa-Pereira, Pavel Brazdil (Faculty of Medicine, University of Porto, Portugal) discuss in Chapter 13, "Learning cost-sensitive decision trees to support medical diagnosis," a cost-sensitive learning method. The chapter aims to enhance the understand of cost-sensitive learning problems in medicine and presents a strategy for learning and testing cost-sensitive decision trees, while considering several types of costs associated with problems in medicine. It begins with a contextualization and a discussion of the main types of costs. Then, reviews related work and presents a discussion about the evaluation of classifiers as well as explains a cost-sensitive decision tree strategy and presents some experimental results.

Chapter 14, "An Approximate Approach for Maintaining Recent Occurrences of Itemsets in a Sliding Window over Data Streams," by Jia-Ling Koh, Shu-Ning Shin, and Yuan-Bin Don (Department of Information Science and Computer Engineering National Taiwan Normal University Taipei, Taiwan), discusses about catching the recent trend of data when mining frequent itemsets over data streams. A data representation method, named frequency changing point (FCP), is introduced for monitoring the recent occurrence of itemsets over a data stream to prevent from storing the whole transaction data within a sliding window. The effect of old transactions on the mining result of recently frequent itemsets is diminished by performing adjusting rules on the monitoring data structure. Accordingly, the recently frequent itemsets or representative patterns are discovered from the maintained structure approximately. Experimental studies demonstrate that the proposed algorithms achieve high true positive rates and guarantees no false dismissal to the results yielded.

In Chapter 15, "Protocol Identification of Encrypted Network Streams," Matthew Gebski, Alex Penev, Raymond K. Wong (National ICT Australia and University of New South Wales, Australia) propose a simple machine learning approach for protocol identification in network streams that have been encrypted, such that the only information available for identifying the underlying protocol of a connection was the size, timing and direction of packets. With very little information available from the network stream, it is possible to pinpoint potentially inappropriate activities for a workplace, institution or research center, such as using BitTorrent, GMail or MSN, and not confuse them with other common protocols such as HTTP and SSL.

Finally, Chapter 16, "Exploring Calendar-based Pattern Mining in Data Streams," by Rodrigo Salvador Monteiro, Geraldo Zimbrão, Jano Moreira de Souza (COPPE / UFRJ - Brazil), Holger Schwarz, Bernhard Mitschang (IPVS - University of Stuttgart - Germany) introduces a calendar-based pattern mining aims at identifying patterns on specific calendar partitions in continuous data streams. The authors present how a data warehouse approach can be applied to leverage calendar-based pattern mining in data streams and how the framework of the DWFIST approach can cope with tight time constraints imposed by data streams, keep storage requirements at a manageable level and, at the same time, support calendar-based frequent itemset mining. The minimum granularity of analysis, parameters of the data warehouse (e.g., mining minimum support) and parameters of the database (e.g., extent size) provide ways to tune the load performance.

Overall, the sixteen book chapters, contributed by recognition experts and researchers in data warehousing and knowledge discovery, cover broad research areas on both theoretical and practical aspects of the fields. They present innovative principles, methods, algorithms and solutions to challenging problems faced in the real applications with experimental results. Future trends, research challenges and opportunities are also mentioned and discussed.

Tho Manh Nguyen, Editor
Vienna University of Technology, Austria
January 2009

Section 1
DWH Architectures and Fundamentals

Chapter 1
The LBF R–Tree
Scalable Indexing and Storage for Data Warehousing Systems

Todd Eavis
Concordia University, Canada

David Cueva
Concordia University, Canada

ABSTRACT

In multi-dimensional database environments, such as those typically associated with contemporary data warehousing, we generally require effective indexing mechanisms for all but the smallest data sets. While numerous such methods have been proposed, the R-tree has emerged as one of the most common and reliable indexing models. Nevertheless, as user queries grow in terms of both size and dimensionality, R-tree performance can deteriorate significantly. Moreover, in the multi-terabyte spaces of today's enterprise warehouses, the combination of data and indexes — R-tree or otherwise — can produce unacceptably large storage requirements. In this chapter, the authors present a framework that addresses both of these concerns. First, they propose a variation of the classic R-tree that specifically targets data warehousing architectures. Their new LBF R-tree not only improves performance on common user-defined range queries, but gracefully degrades to a linear scan of the data on pathologically large queries. Experimental results demonstrate a reduction in disk seeks of more than 50% relative to more conventional R-tree designs. Second, the authors present a fully integrated, block-oriented compression model that reduces the storage footprint of both data and indexes. It does so by exploiting the same Hilbert space filling curve that is used to construct the LBF R-tree itself. Extensive testing demonstrates compression rates of more than 90% for multi-dimensional data, and up to 98% for the associated indexes.

1 INTRODUCTION

Over the past ten to fifteen years, data warehousing (DW) has become increasingly important to organi-

DOI: 10.4018/978-1-60566-748-5.ch001

zations of all sizes. In particular, the representation of historical data across broad time frames allows decision makers to monitor evolutionary patterns and trends that would simply not be possible with operational databases alone. However, this accumulation of historical data comes at a price; namely,

Copyright © 2010, IGI Global. Copying or distributing in print or electronic forms without written permission of IGI Global is prohibited.

the enormous storage requirements of the tables that house process-specific measurements.

Typically, such databases are constructed as a series of data marts, each designed around a heavily de-normalized logical model known as a Star Schema (or its normalized counterpart, the Snowflake Schema). In its simplest form, the Star schema consists of a central *fact table* and a series of peripheral dimension tables connected via standard foreign key relationships. Within the fact table, we refer to the foreign keys as *feature* attributes, while fields identifying the aggregate values for the underlying organizational process are known as *measures*.

In practice, the dimension tables are relatively small, with their record counts equivalent to the cardinality of the related entity (e.g., date, customer or product). The fact tables, by contrast, can be extremely large and comprise the bulk of the data warehouse. The enormous scale of the fact tables creates two related but distinct processing challenges. First, it is imperative that efficient indexing mechanisms be available. Given the low selectivity of common DW queries (i.e., a large percentage of all records are selected), DW designers often forego indexes altogether and rely upon simple, and expensive, linear table scans. Clearly, this approach can become cost prohibitive in enterprise environments. Second, even in the presence of effective indexing structures, the sheer volume of data can still overwhelm the storage and processing resources of contemporary systems. As such, effective domain-specific compression methods are sorely needed.

In terms of indexing and access methods, it is important to note that the majority of Decision Support queries are *multi-dimensional* in nature. In other words, the most common access pattern tends to be some form of *range query*, in which the user submits a request that specifies a range restriction on one or more dimensional columns. Such queries are not well supported by traditional single-dimensional indexes such as the B-tree.

While a significant number of true multi-

dimensional techniques have been presented in the literature, the R-tree has emerged as perhaps the most rigorously studied and consistently implemented model. However, while numerous R-tree variations have been presented, none fully support all three of the simple but crucial features of the data warehousing fact table; namely, that it supports medium dimensionality range queries (i.e., 2-10 dimensions), that it is relatively *static*, and that it is extremely large in practice. The third point, in particular, tends to be under-appreciated in theoretical treatments on the topic.

In this chapter, we discuss the Linear Breadth First R-tree. The LBF R-tree builds directly upon the traditional R-tree model but optimizes its construction and tree traversal in order to consistently reduce the number of costly seeks associated with arbitrary user-defined range queries. Specifically, we utilize a space filling curve to pre-pack the R-tree and then carefully arrange the associated blocks on disk to allow a breadth first traversal pattern to map directly to the physical storage layout. Perhaps more importantly, this *linearization* model also provides graceful performance degradation in the face of arbitrarily large queries. Experimental results demonstrate a 30% — 50% reduction in the number of seeks relative to existing R-tree packing and query strategies.

As noted, however, indexing alone is not enough to guarantee appropriate performance in practical DW settings. Specifically, given a finite amount of storage space, we are limited in both the number of fact tables that can be constructed, as well as the length of the historical period. Moreover, as fact tables grow in size, real time query costs may become unacceptable to end users. A partial solution to the latter constraint is the materialization of summary views that aggregate the fact table data at coarser levels of granularity. But even here, the space available for such views is limited by the size of the underlying fact tables. As a result, we can conclude that a reduction in fact table size not only improves space utilization but it allows for the construction of additional summary views that may dramatically improve real time performance on common user queries.

To address this issue, we have proposed a DW-specific compression model that is based upon the notion of tuple *differentials*. Unlike previous work in which the compression of tables and indexes has been viewed as separate processes, we present a framework, fully integrated with the LBF R-tree, that provides a model for the compression of both elements. Specifically, we employ a Hilbert space filling curve to order data points in a way that allows for the subsequent construction of pre-packed, Hilbert ordered R-tree indexes. Experimental results demonstrate compression rates of 80%-95% on both skewed and uniform data and up to 98% compression on multi-dimensional R-tree indexes.

The remainder of the chapter is organized as follows. In Section 2 we discuss related work in the areas of database indexing and compression. Section 3 presents relevant supporting material, while Section 4 describes the new algorithms for index construction, searching, and updates. The integrated compression model is then introduced in Section 5, with experimental results presented in Section 6. Finally, concluding remarks are offered in Section 7.

2 RELATED WORK

Gaede and Gunter provide a comprehensive survey of multi-dimensional indexing methods in (Gaede & Gunther, 1998). However, while many of these techniques are quite interesting, few have actually found their way into practical systems. Of this latter group, the R-tree and its numerous variations have been targeted by commercial vendors and academics alike. The seminal R-tree paper was presented by Guttman (Guttman, 1984), who described the structure, processing model, and algorithms for node splitting. The R+-tree alters the basic model by prohibiting box overlap at the same level of the tree (Sellis, Roussopoulos, &

Faloutsos, 1987), while the R*-tree uses an object re-insertion technique to reduce overlap during node splitting (Beckmann, Kriegel, Schneider, & Seeger, 1990). In static environments, R-tree *pre-packing* has been proposed in order to improve storage utilization and object clustering properties. Primary approaches include the original lexicographic coordinate order (Roussopoulos & Leifker, Direct spatial search on pictorial databases using packed R-trees, 1985), as well as improved methods based on the Hilbert curve (Faloutsos & Kamel, On packing R-trees, 1993) and Sort Tile Recursion (Leutenegger, Lopez, & Eddington, 1997).

In terms of R-tree traversal patterns, most implementations employ the more resource efficient depth first (DF) approach. Nevertheless, researchers have also used breadth first (BF) searches to exploit optimizations not possible with DF search. In (Kim & Cha, 1998), Kim and Cha describe a *sibling clustering* technique that tries to at least partially order spatially related nodes so that a breadth first traversal can more efficiently retrieve query blocks. Breath first traversal is also employed by Huang et al. to globally optimize the join processing for pairs of spatial data set (Huang, Jing, & Rundensteiner, 1997).

Subsequent to the early work on node splitting and packing, researchers turned to the creation of theoretical models for analyzing performance and predicting worst case behaviour. Kamel and Faloutsos used the idea of fractals to identify a lower bound for multi-dimensional point data (Faloutsos & Kamel, Hilbert R-tree: An improved R-tree using fractals, 1994). In terms of spatial data, Theodoridis and Sellis describe a model for predicting optimal R-tree range query performance in dynamic environments (Theodoridis & Sellis, 1996), while Pagel et al. provide a similar result for static data (Pagel, Six, & Winter, 1995). In each case, the models' estimates are shown to fall within 10% — 20% of actual results. Arge et al. also define an asymptotic lower bound on the number of blocks retrieved, and provide the

Figure 1. R-tree partitioning for a maximum node count of four

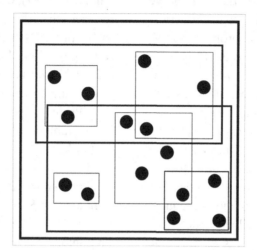

PR-tree as a mechanism for improving the I/O efficiency of hyper-rectangular objects (Arge, de Berg, Haverkort, & Yi, 2004). In all of these cases, the underlying assumption is that performance is strictly a function of the number of blocks retrieved, rather than a function of the number and size of the *seeks* required.

In the data warehousing context, fact table indexing is of crucial importance. In (Gupta, Harinarayan, Rajaraman, & Ullman, 1997), Gupta et al. propose a simple indexing model composed of a collection of B-trees. Roussopoulos et al. describe the *cube tree* (Roussopoulos, Kotidis, & Roussopoulos, Cubetree: Organization of the bulk incremental updates on the data cube, 1997), a *data cube* indexing model based upon the concept of a packed R-tree (Roussopoulos & Leifker, Direct spatial search on pictorial databases using packed R-trees, 1985). The data cube, first described by Gray et al. (Gray, Bosworth, Layman, & Pirahesh, 1996), refers to an OLAP (Online Analytical Processing) data model representing the materialization of the $O(2^d)$ group-bys or *cuboids* in a *d*-dimensional space.

In commercial environments, designers often utilize *join* or *bitmap* indexes (O'Neil & Graefe, 1995; O'Neil & Quass, 1997). In the former case, multi-table joins are pre-computed and stored as

<key, rowID> pairings. In the latter case, we use bit strings to represent low cardinality domains so that fact table record locations can be resolved by way of standard binary operators. Wu and Buchanon extend the bitmap mechanism for higher cardinalities, though the general technique can still require an excessive number of binary operations for higher dimension and cardinality counts (Wu & Buchmann, 1998).

General compression algorithms have been well studied in the literature and include *statistical* techniques, such as Huffman Coding (Huffman, 1952) and Arithmetic Compression (Rissanen, 1976), as well as *dictionary* techniques like LZ77 (Ziv & Lempel, 1977). Database-specific methods are presented by Ray and Harista, who combine column-specific frequency distributions with arithmetic coding (Ray, Haritsa, & Seshadri, 1995). Westmann at al. propose a model that utilizes integer, float, and string methods, as well as simple dictionaries (Westmann, Kossmann, Helmer, & Moerkotte, 2000).

Ng and Ravishankar propose a technique called Tuple Differential Coding (TDC), in which the records of the data set are pre-ordered so as to identify tuple *similarity* (Ng & Ravishankar, 1997). Tuple difference values are then calculated and compactly stored with Run-Length Encoding

(Golomb, 1966). A second differential technique, hereafter referred to as GRS, was subsequently presented by Goldstein et al (Goldstein, Ramakrishnan, & Shaft, 1998). GRS computes and stores column-wise rather than row-wise differentials. In contrast to TDC, the authors of GRS also discuss the use of indexes in conjunction with their compressed data sets. Both techniques are particularly relevant in the DW setting as they specifically target multidimensional spaces.

The concept of representing a multi-dimensional space as a single dimensional, non-differentiable curve began with Peano (Peano, 1890). Jagadish provides an analysis of four such curves --- snake scan, gray codes, z-order, and Hilbert --- and identifies the Hilbert curve as providing the best overall clustering properties (Jagadish, 1990), a result duplicated in (Faloutsos & Roseman, 1989).

Finally, we note that more recent research in the data warehousing context has focused on the development of structures for the compact representation of the data cube (Sismanis, Deligiannakis, Roussopoulos, & Kotidis, 2002), (Lakshmanan, Pei, & Zhao, 2003). For example, Sismanis et al. present the Dwarf cube, a tree-based data structure that represents the 2^d *group-bys* found in the *d*-dimensional data cube (Sismanis, Deligiannakis, Roussopoulos, & Kotidis, 2002). However, while the Dwarf is certainly an interesting option when data cube queries are heavily utilized, we note that it may still be sig, where *M* is the maximum *branching factor* and *n* is equivalent to the number of points in the data set. A user query Φ may be defined as $\{r_1, r_2 \ldots, r_d\}$ for $(r_{min(i)}, r_{max(i)})$, $1 \le i \le d$ and is answered by comparing the values on $\{r_1, r_2 \ldots, r_d\}$ with the coordinates of the rectangle $\aleph$ that surrounds the points in each data page. The search algorithm descends through levels *l* = *1, 2,…, H* of the index until valid leaf nodes are identified. A simple R-tree hyper-rectangle decomposition can be seen in Figure 1.

For *static* environments, it is possible to improve space utilization by using bulk insertion methods *pre-pack* points into disk blocks. As such, it is possible to avoid the half-filled boxes that often result from dynamic node splitting. Run-time query performance may also be improved as the packing process typically reduces box overlap and improves point clustering. Regardless of the packing strategy employed, the basic approach is as follows:

1. Pre-pro. $\left\lceil \frac{n}{M} \right\rceil$
2. Associate each of the *M* leaf node pages with an ID that will be used as a file offset by parent bounding boxes.
3. Construct the remainder of the index by recursively packing the bounding boxes of lower levels until the root node is reached.

Clearly, the sort order is the key requirement and, in fact, several approaches have been taken. Previous research has shown that both STR (Leutenegger, Lopez, & Eddington, 1997) and Hilbert ordering (Faloutsos & Kamel, Hilbert R-tree: An improved R-tree using fractals, 1994) improve upon simple lexicographic ordering, though there does not appear to be a clear winner when evaluated across a variety of data sets.

Hilbert ordering, however, is particularly interesting in the current context as it can be used to provide a relative effective linear ordering of points in a *d*-dimensional space. First proposed in (Hilbert, 1891), the Hilbert curve is a non-differentiable curve of length s^d that traverses all s^d points of the *d*-dimensional grid having side length *s*, making unit steps and turning only at right angles. We say that a *d*-dimensional cubic space has order *k* if it has a side length $s = 2^k$ and use the notation to denote the kth order approximation of a *d*-dimensional curve, for $k \ge 1$ and $d \ge 2$. Figure 2 illustrates a $\left\lceil \frac{n}{M} \right\rceil$ curve.

Figure 2. A H_3^2 Hilbert curve

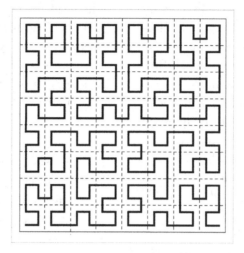

4 A NEW I/O EFFICIENT MODEL FOR DW ENVIRONMENTS

As noted, R-trees have been used in one form or another for the indexing of multi-dimensional data. Extensions to the basic model have been used to minimize bounding box overlap and/or reduce bounding box size, thereby reducing the number of blocks retrieved from disk. For this reason, previous work in the area of disk-based indexing has focused on blocks retrieved as a metric of index performance (Leutenegger, Lopez, & Eddington, 1997) (Faloutsos & Kamel, On packing R-trees, 1993), and (Arge, de Berg, Haverkort, & Yi, 2004).

However, a "raw" count of accessed blocks can be quite misleading since the true response time is dependant not just upon the number of accesses but upon the *type* of access. In particular, we must be able to distinguish between (i) blocks that are read following an independent seek — denoted here as *intra-file* seeks — and (ii) blocks that are read following an access of the previous (contiguous) physical block. While the *read ahead* caching mechanism employed on modern disks tends to hide the penalty associated with very short seeks, intra-file movements can, and do, have a very real effect upon query performance in production scale environments.

4.1 The Linear Breadth First R-tree

We now present the **LBF R-tree,** an indexing model first introduced in (Eavis & Cueva, The LBF R-tree: Efficient Multidimensional Indexing with Graceful Degradation, 2007). Our primary objective is to reduce the occurrence of intra-file seeks by structuring the blocks of both index and data so as maximize the number of contiguous blocks associated with an arbitrary query. Conceptually, this is similar to the B$^+$-tree model, where records of the data set are maintained in sorted order so that the index is able to identify contiguous record clusters. In fact, this notion of building upon tthe B$^+$-tree was also discussed in (Kim & Cha, 1998), where the authors construct an R-tree for dynamic spatial environments. There, pre-allocated blocks are used to form *sibling clusters*. As nodes reach capacity they are split, so that points are distributed into the pre-allocated cluster blocks. Of course, there are limits on the degree of pre-allocation and, in practice, sibling clustering deteriorates with increased query size and complexity.

In effect, our model employs an extreme form

Figure 3. LBF R-tree Construction

INPUT: An arbitrarily ordered multi-dimensional data set S of size n, with branching factor M

OUTPUT: A packed R-tree index R_{ind} and associated Hilbert-ordered data set R_{data}

1: Sort records of S as S' in terms of their Hilbert ordinal index

2: In a linear pass, partition the n records of S' into $\left\lceil \frac{n}{M} \right\rceil$ blocks

3: Write the base level to disk as R_{tmp}^1

4: **WHILE** we have not reached the index root

5: Linearly partition the q blocks of R_{tmp}^i into the $\left\lceil \frac{q}{M} \right\rceil$ parent boxes at level $i + 1$

6: Write the blocks of level $i + 1$ to disk as R_{tmp}^{i+1}

7: Concatenate the H temporary index files into R_{ind} in the order R_{tmp}^H, R_{tmp}^{H-1}, ... R_{tmp}^2.

of linear clustering for static environments. Like other R-tree frameworks targeting such spaces, we exploit a packing strategy to improve storage and run-time query performance. In our case, we utilize the Hilbert curve so as to most effectively map the multi-dimensional points to a linear order. Figure 3 describes the construction technique. Though similar to the basic packing strategies previously discussed, the key feature in our method is the combination of the **WHILE** loop in Step 4 and the concatenation of temporary files in Step 7. As each successive level H_3^2, $1 \leq i \leq H$, in the index tree is constructed, its blocks are written in a strictly linear fashion to disk (i.e., a logical left-to-right traversal). A series of H temporary *level* indexes is created. Once the root level H_3^2 is reached, we produce a final index by arranging the levels of

the indexes by reverse order of creation, H_3^2, R_{tmp}^i ,..., R_{tmp}^i. Note that this process is composed of a series of streaming operations and therefore can be executed with minimal buffer space.

Figure 4 illustrates the final structure of a small LBF R-tree, with $n = 15$, $M = 3$, and $H = R_{tmp}^i = 3$. We see how the ordering of data points (B3—B8) is dictated by the order of the R_{tmp}^H Hilbert curve. Index boxes (B0—B2) are then constructed as per the creation order of their children (note that B0 is simply the box that encloses the full d-dimensional space). In Figure 5 we see the physical disk arrangement, consisting of an independent index and data set. Note the purely sequential block ID sequence represented by the direct concatenation of index and data components. Specifically, let us assume that for R_{ind} and R_{data}

Figure 4. The logical partitioning of a small R_{tmp}^H Hilbert space

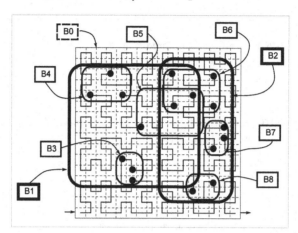

we have block counts C_{ind} and C_{data} respectively. We can therefore guarantee a disk resident mapping of the consecutive block ID sequence $ID_{ind(0)}$, $ID_{ind(1)}$, ..., $ID_{ind(C\_ind - 1)}$, $ID_{data(C\_ind)}$, $ID_{data(C\_ind + 1)}$, ..., $ID_{data(C\_ind + C\_data)}$.

4.2 The Search Strategy

In all previous R-tree clustering algorithms, the primary motivation has been a reduction in the number of blocks *touched* by a user query. As such, implementations rely upon a conventional Depth First Search (DFS) and seek to measure performance via a count of accessed blocks. However, the application of DFS is poorly suited to data warehousing fact tables. Specifically, by repeatedly moving between index and data set in order to resolve multi-block range queries, we introduce dramatic growth in intra-file seek time. As the size of the underlying data set increases, the growing number of random head movements can lead to a significant degree of *thrashing*. Because the previous packing algorithms were evaluated (i) on very small data sets (100,000 records or less), and (ii) with the unrealistic assumption that all indexes would be entirely cached in memory, this fact would have been completely obscured. In Tera-scale data warehousing environments, it would certainly not be.

Figure 6 describes an alternative search strategy that is tailored to the unique structure of the packed R-tree. We refer to this strategy as Linear Breadth First Search to emphasize the mapping to the physical linearization on disk. In general, the algorithm follows the standard BFS technique of traversing the tree level-by-level in a left-to-right fashion. Queries are resolved as follows. For the current level i of the tree, the query engine successively identifies the j nodes at level $i - 1$ whose bounding boxes intersect the query $\Phi = \{r_1, r_2, ..., r_d\}$. It places these page IDs into a *working list W*. We note that because of the way the LBF

Figure 5. The physical layout on disk

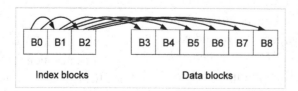

Figure 6. Linear Breadth First R-tree

INPUT: A packed R-tree index, its associated data, and a user query ψ

OUTPUT: Fully resolved query.

1:   Initialize *pageList* with ID of first index block
2:   **WHILE** not at the leaf level
3:     *childList* = new empty list
4:     **FOR** each range node k in the *pageList*
5:       **FOR** each page ID $i \geq$ pageList[k]$_{min}$ AND $\leq$ pageList[k]$_{max}$
6:         Using i as a block offset, read the relevant disk block B into memory.
7:         **FOR** each child block j of B that intersects ψ
8:           **IF** for the current range node l in the *childList*, we have *childList[l]* $_{max} = j - 1$
9:             set *childList[l]* $_{max} = j$
10:          **ELSE**
11:            create new range node $l + 1$ and set *childList[l + 1]* $_{min}$ = *childNode[l + 1]* $_{max} = j$
12:    *pageList* = *childList*
13: **FOR** each page ID i in the current *pageList*
14:   Using i as an offset, read the relevant disk block B into memory.
15:   Process B for records matching ψ

R-trees are built, the page IDs of W are, by definition, sorted in ascending order. Using the list of j page IDs, the query engine traverses the blocks at level $i - 1$ and replaces the current working list W with a new child list W' containing the relevant blocks for level $i - 2$. It repeats this procedure until it has reached the data blocks (R_{data}) at the base of the tree. At this point, the algorithm simply identifies and returns the d-dimensional records encapsulated by Φ.

We note that one of the primary reasons for the use of a Depth First search strategy in most R-tree implementations is its more modest memory requirements. Specifically, it must store no more than

$0 (\log_M n) = H$ nodes to traverse the length of a path from root to leaf, while for an m-block data set a standard Breadth First traversal is $O(m)$ in the worst case (i.e., Φ fully encapsulates block B0). Recall, however, that the primary purpose of the Hilbert order is in fact to identify point and/or box clusterings in the d-dimensional space. As such, hyper-rectangular range queries consist primarily of one or more *contiguous* clusters of disk blocks. In this context, it is extremely inefficient to store individual block IDs. Instead, the *monotonically increasing* ID lists (i.e., *pageList* and *childList*) for Linear BFS consist of a sequence of min/max *range nodes* that identify contiguous block clusters in the linearized disk layout. The lists themselves are constructed in lines 7—11 as a given level is sequentially accessed. Figure 7 provides an illustration of how the combination of range nodes and Linear BFS would be utilized. Note how the selected nodes of the index and data set consist of a strictly increasing set of block

Figure 7. Mapping Linear Breadth First search to the physical block order

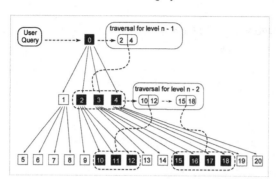

IDs, a sequence that maps directly to the physical disk ordering.

In the case of a query that encloses the entire space, for example, the total memory requirement for Linear BFS is just one range/node. Asymptotically, of course, the worst case complexity remains $O(m)$ as we could have every other leaf node included in the result. We note, however, that this is clearly a pathological case and is quite difficult to actually produce with a linearized Hilbert-ordered space.

4.3 Analysis of Performance Degradation

As previously noted, researchers have worked under the assumption that all block retrievals are equally costly, a notion that is simply not accurate for large data sets. In fact, for queries of sufficient size (typically 5% — 15% of the data set), a straight sequential scan of the data set will outperform a multi-dimensional index due to the degree of disk thrashing introduced by the latter. It is therefore useful to look at the practical impact for the LBF R-tree for very large queries. In fact, it is possible to show that the worst case I/O of a packed R-tree using Linear BFS is equivalent to $LS(R\text{-}tree_{ind}) + LS(R\text{-}tree_{data})$, where LS implies a linear scan.

Recall that the construction mechanism of the LBF R-tree implies that block IDs run consecutively from $ID_{ind(0)} \dots ID_{data(C\_ind + C\_data)}$.

Consequently, while traversing $[R_{ind} + R_{data}]$, we can guarantee for a given level l that (i) a block $b_{l(i)}$ *must* be visited before $b_{l(j)}$ for $i < j$, and (ii) any block $b_{l(i)}$ *must* be visited before $b_{l-1(j)}$ for any i, j. The worse case I/O performance is therefore equivalent to the time taken to sequentially scan the index, followed by the time taken to sequentially scan the data set.

To illustrate the impact of the previous observation, we issued a query on a pair of ten dimensional data sets, the first containing one million records (43,479 blocks) and the second housing 10,000,000 records (434,783 blocks). The hyper-rectangle of the query was designed to encapsulate the full space. A sequential scan on the first set resulted in 43,478 contiguous reads and a resolution time of 1.04 seconds. The time for the LBF search on the same set was 1.17 seconds, with the 12.9% increase associated with the additional scan of the R-tree index. A standard Depth First strategy, however, ran in 1.33 seconds, with the 28.3% increase being generated by 3925 non-contiguous reads. On the larger dataset, however, intra file seeks produced a much more dramatic effect. With the sequential traversal, read time on the larger file was 11.2 seconds. Linear BFS — gracefully degrading to a linear scan of the index and the data file — was once again competitive with an I/O time of 12.8 seconds. The standard Depth First Traversal, on the other hand, generated 39,228 non-contiguous reads and caused the read time to explode to 61.73 seconds, a 550%

increase over the sequential scan.

As a final point, it should be obvious that Linear BFS is only effective if the logically linearized order of disk blocks is equivalent to the physical ordering of blocks. This would not be true in the general R-tree/B-tree case because the dynamic updates of the tree would permute the original order of the blocks. In the data warehousing context, however, this is not the case. Recall that bulk loading/updating is typically used in such environments. In practice, we can in fact adapt the bulk update technique first proposed by Roussopoulos et al. (Roussopoulos, Kotidis, & Roussopoulos, Cubetree: Organization of the bulk incremental updates on the data cube, 1997) in which the update set is first sorted and then merged with the current LBF R-tree in a single linear pass. Complete details are provided in (Eavis & Cueva, The LBF R-tree: Efficient Multidimensional Indexing with Graceful Degradation, 2007). As such, we are able to guaranteed persistent equivalency between the logical and physical ordering of data and index blocks.

5 COMPRESSING THE LBF R-TREE

Though the LBF R-tree represents an effective approach to improving data warehouse query performance, additional storage and performance benefits can be realized by extending the basic model so as to permit effective compression of the data and indexing mechanisms associated with both the primary fact tables and the largest aggregates. In so doing, we not only reduce I/O demands on the system, but we dramatically increase the space available for the storage of supporting aggregates and summary structures. In practice, the use of such aggregates can transform the end user interface from a sluggish, "brute force" batch environment to a nimble, much more interactive form. In the following section, we therefore present an integrated compression architecture that builds upon the underlying Hilbert space filling curve to

allow robust compression of both data and indexes. Before discussing the new methods, however, we begin with a brief review of the concepts and terminology relevant to this area.

5.1 Preliminaries

As noted in Section 2, Ng and Ravishankar presented a compression technique called Tuple Differential Coding (TDC) that was specifically targeted at multi-dimensional data sets (Ng & Ravishankar, 1997). The algorithm works as follows. Given a relation R, we may define a schema $<A_1, A_2,...,A_d>$ as a sequence of attribute domains $A_i = \{1,2,...,|A_i|\}$ for $1 \leq i \leq d$. A d-dimensional tuple in this space exists within a *bounding box* of size $|A_1| \times |A_2| \times ... \times |A_d|$. In addition, the points in R may be associated with an *ordering rule*. This rule is defined by a mapping function that converts each tuple into a unique integer representing its ordinal position within the space. In the case of TDC, the mapping function utilizes a standard lexicographic ordering defined as φ: $R \rightarrow \mathcal{N}R$ where $\mathcal{N}R = \{0, 1,...||R||-1\}$ and $||R|| = R_{tmp}^H : \varphi(a1, a2... ad) = R_{tmp}^H$

In effect, the TDC ordering algorithm converts a series of tuple attributes into a single integer that uniquely identifies the position of the associated tuple in the multi-dimensional space. Consequently, it is possible to convert the ordinal representation of each tuple into a differential value that represents the distance between successive ordinals, with the full sequence relative to a single reference value stored in each disk block. Simple RLE techniques can then be used to minimize the number of bits actually required to store the difference values themselves.

While the lexicographic orderings utilized in TDC (and GRS) allow us to uniquely order the values of the point space prior to differential calculation, space filling curves represent a more sophisticated approach to this same general problem. In fact, such curves, have been investigated in the database context as they allow for the conversion of a multi-dimensional space to the linear representation of disk blocks. This feature, in fact, is central to the LBF R-tree methods described below.

5.2 Hilbert Space Differential Compression

We now provide the details of a new compression model first presented in (Eavis & Cueva, A Hilbert Space compression architecture for data warehouse environments, 2007). We note at the outset that our primary objectives are (i) to provide an intuitive tuple-oriented model that can be easily integrated into current RDBMS servers, and (ii) to offer competitive compression facilities coupled with the most efficient indexing methods available for *primarily* static environments (e.g., batch oriented updates).

5.3 Compressing the Point Data

To begin, we assume the existence of a d-dimensional space and a fact table R consisting of n tuples of $d + 1$ fields. The first d fields represent the feature attributes of R, having cardinalities $\{|A_1|, |A_2|, ..., |A_d|\}$, while the final field provides the *measure* value. Note that our focus in this chapter is upon compression of the d feature attributes, not the floating point measure (the same is true of previous research in the area).

Recall that the TDC algorithm converts a multi-dimensional tuple into a unique integer via a lexicographic ordering rule. This *invertible* mapping function is at the heart of differential encoding. The Hilbert curve, however, is completely incompatible with lexicographic ordering. That being said, the Hilbert traversal path can be exploited in order to form a new invertible ordering rule. Specifically, the s^d-length Hilbert curve represents a unique, strictly increasing order on the s^d point positions, such that $C_{HIL}: \{1,...,s^d\} \rightarrow \{1,...,s\}^d$. We refer to each such position as a *Hilbert*

ordinal. Figure 8(a) provides a simple illustration of the 16 unique point positions in R_{tmp}^{H-1}. Here, for example, we would have $C_{HIL}(2,2) = 3$.

Figure 9 presents the method for providing point compression based upon this Hilbert ordering rule. We begin by first converting the multi-dimensional records into their Hilbert ordinal representation and then sorting the result. Our immediate objective is to fill page size units with compressed tuples, where each page is equivalent to some multiple of the physical block size. As each new page is created, we initialize the first record as the uncompressed *ordinal reference value* that represents the starting differential sequence. Next, we compute ordinal differentials $h_{i+1} - h_i$ until the page has been filled to capacity. We determine saturation by dynamically adjusting the *minimal bit count* δ required to represent the largest differential ρ in the running sequence. Once the capacity has been reached, the bit compacted indexes and their measures are written to a physical disk block.

To illustrate the concept, Figure 8(b) displays two *2-d* points along the same simple R_{tmp}^{H-1} Hilbert curve. The initial point represents the reference ordinal stored in the block header, while the second point is the ordinal corresponding to the next tuple. In Figure 8(c) we see the Bit Compacted Differential form for the second point. Storage required is now just $\rho = 9 - 6 = 3_{10}$, or 11_2 in binary form. This is 62 bits less that the default encoding for a two dimensional value (assuming 32-bit integers).

In addition to the tuple count and the uncompressed reference, the block's meta data includes the ρ value that indicates the minimum number of bits required to represent the highest tuple difference seen in the block. Each block has a unique ρ value, and therefore includes a varying number of compressed tuples. Note that differences are stored across byte or word boundaries, so as to maximize the compression rate. To de-compress, the query engine need only retrieve the reference tuple and then consecutively add each of the differences to obtain the original Hilbert ordinals. Subsequently, the ordinals are transformed back to multi-dimensional tuple form as required.

Finally, we note that in multi-dimensional environments, difference values can exceed the capacity of standard 32-bit or even 64-bit registers. Specifically, for a d-dimensional space, the maximum differential value is equivalent to R^1_{tmp} for dimension cardinalities $|A_1|, |A_2|,...,|A_d|$. In a

Figure 8. (a) The ordinal mapping on a R^{H-1}_{tmp} curve. (b) Basic differentials (c) Compressed form

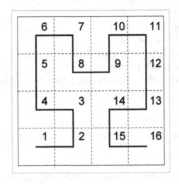

(a)

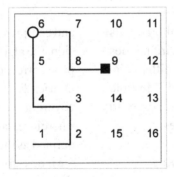

(b)

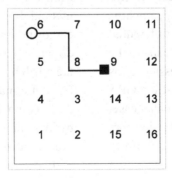

(c)

Figure 9. Data compression

INPUT: An aggregated and arbitrarily sorted relation R, with n tuples consisting of k feature attributes and one measure. A temporary buffer P. A required block disk block size B.

OUTPUT: A fully compressed cuboid R' with page level granularity.

```
1:   FOR all n tuples of R
2:       convert each k-tuple to its Hilbert ordinal value
3:   re-sort the n indexes of R
4:   FOR each tuple i, with i ≤ n
5:       read next Hilbert ordinal hᵢ
6:       WHILE estimated page size Pₑₛₜ < B
7:           IF P is currently empty
8:               record hᵢ as the uncompressed reference value
9:               set the page bit count ρ = 0
10:          ELSE
11:              calculate differential δ as hᵢ₊₁ - hᵢ
12:              compute bit count β required to represent δ
13:              IF β > ρ
14:                  ρ = β
15:      write page P to disk, appending the measures as required
```

10-dimensional space, for example, differentials can reach 100 bits, assuming uniform cardinalities of just 1000. Consequently, the Hilbert differential model has been extended with the GNU Multiple Precision Arithmetic Library (GMP) in order to support arbitrarily large Hilbert spaces.

5.4 Compression of the Indexes

One of the primary advantages of the use of the Hilbert curve is that it allows for the clean integration of data and index compression. Specifically, the same Hilbert order that provides the differential based mapping for point compression can also be used to support extremely high compression ratios for the associated indexes. Recall that the GRS method also provides indexing but, in this case, relies on a very simple linearization of points that ultimately depends upon an unrealistic uniform distribution assumption. As we will see in Section 6, indexing efficiency suffers as a result.

Figure 10 illustrates the method for generating and compressing the index. As with data compression, the algorithm fills page size units, with each page corresponding to a node n of the R-tree. Geometrically, a node constitutes a *hyper-rectangle* covering a delimited section of the point space. Therefore, compressed data blocks are naturally defined as the leaf nodes of the R-tree. The rest of the index structure is built bottom-up from level-0 (i.e., the leaf level) to the root.

We start with a relation R', which has already been compressed using our Hilbert Differential method. For each of the leaf nodes, we record its enclosing level-0 hyper-rectangle as a pair of d-dimensional vertexes. These two points represent the attribute values corresponding to the block's local minima, which we refer to as the *pivot*, and the maxima. Next, we create the nodes in *level - 1* by including each hyper rectangle from *level - 0*. We initialize the pivot of the node in *level - 1* with the one located in the current leaf. For each dimension, we calculate the bits β necessary to represent the difference between the maxima

Figure 10. Index compression

> **INPUT**: A cuboid C' containing b blocks and compressed with the Hilbert Differential method. Temporary buffers P and T. A required disk block size B.
>
> **OUTPUT**: A fully compressed R-tree index I with one node per page.
>
> ```
> 1:    FOR all b blocks of R'
> 2:        calculate Vmin and Vmax vertexes of b, V = {A1,
>           A2,...,Ak}
> 3:        write node N₀ᵇ = {Vmin ,Vmax} to T
>           uncompressed
> 4:    REPEAT
> 5:        retrieve number of nodes nN from level L
> 6:        FOR each i, with i ≤ nN
> 7:          read one node NL = {Vmin ,Vmax} from level L
> 8:          IF page P is empty
> 9:            create node NL+1 in level L+1
> 10:           initialize NL+1 = NL
> 11:          ELSE
> 12:           include vertexes of NL in NL+1
> 13:           recalculate pivot of NL+1: G = minL+1
> 14:           recalculate bit count β needed to represent
>                Vmax in NL+1
> 15:          IF estimated page size Pest > B
> 16:            rollback last inclusion
> 17:            write NL+1 to page P uncompressed
> 18:            FOR all NL nodes of level L
> 19:              FOR all k attribute of each vertex VL of
>                     NL
> 20:                calculate differential ψ as VL(k) - G(k)
> 21:                write ψ to P using Bit Compaction
> 22:   UNTIL number of nodes nN = 1
> ```

and minima. For each new hyper-rectangle, the pivot and bit strings are updated, along with the point count, until saturation is achieved. Once the page is full, the vertexes are bit compacted and written to a physical block that simply stores the *per-dimension* differences with respect to the pivot value. This process is then repeated until we reach a single root node at the tree's apex.

Index block meta data includes the following values: the number of child nodes, the bit offset of the first child, and an array indicating the number of bits ψ used to represent each dimension in the current block. As with the data compression, blocks may house a varying number of compressed vertexes. Note that the *pivot* value is not included in the block, but rather compressed in the node immediately above. Because searching the index always requires traversing its nodes top down, we can guarantee that the pivots required to uncompress nodes in level L have already been decompressed in level $L+1$.

To retrieve data the query engine performs a standard top-down index traversal. Each time a node is visited, exactly one page P is read and decompressed. To decompress P we read each hyper-rectangle N formed by the two vertexes

(V_{min}, V_{max}), adding to every dimension attribute the value of its corresponding attribute in the current pivot vertex G_L. If the query lies inside the boundary formed by V_{min} and V_{max}, a new *task* is created. The task is included in a FIFO queue as $\{G_{L+1}, o\}$, where V_{min} becomes the pivot G_{L+1} when the task is to be resolved on the next tree level, and o is the offset of N in the disk file. When the query engine reaches a leaf node, a data page is loaded. At that point, tuple decompression is performed as per the description in Section 5.3

5.5 Optimization for Massive Data Sets

Given the size of contemporary data warehouses, practical compression methods must concern themselves not only with expected compression ratios, but with performance and scalability issues as well. As such, the framework supports a comprehensive buffering subsystem that allows for *streaming* compression of arbitrarily large data sets. This is an *end-to-end* model that consists of the following *pipelined* stages: generation of Hilbert indexes from multi-dimensional data, secondary memory sorting, Hilbert index alignment, Hilbert differential data compression, and R-tree index compression.

To minimize sorting costs during the initial compression phase, we note the following. Given an

$O(n \log n)$ comparison based sort, we can assume an average of $\log n$ *Hilbert* comparisons for each of the n tuples. Since tuple conversions are identical in each case, significant performance improvements can be realized by minimizing the number of Hilbert transformations. Consequently, our framework uses a pre-processing step in which the n tuples of R are converted into ordinal form *prior* to sorting. This single optimization typically reduces costs by a factor of 10 or more, depending on dimension count. To support larger data sets, we extend the compression pipeline with an external memory sorting module that employs a standard P-way merge on intermediate partial runs. P is maximized as $\left\lceil \dfrac{m}{b} \right\rceil$, where b is the available in-memory buffer size and m is the size of the disk resident file. With the combination of the streaming pipeline, ordinal pre-processing, and the P-way sort, there is currently no upper limit on the size of the files to be compressed other than the limitations of the file system itself.

6 EXPERIMENTAL RESULTS

In this section, we provide experimental results that assess the query performance and compression characteristics of the LBF R-tree relative to a number of practical indexing alternatives. All tests are conducted on a 3.2 GHz workstation, with 1 GB of main memory and a 160 GB disk drive operating at 7200 RPM. The majority of individual tests utilize synthetic data sets so that we may vary key test parameters in a precise fashion. For completeness, results for a real data set that is commonly employed in the DW literature are also provided. For the performance evaluations, we use the standard approach of timing queries in batch mode. In our case, an automated query generator constructs batches of range queries, in which high/low ranges are randomly generated for each of k attributes, randomly selected from the d-dimensional space, $k \subseteq d$. To more closely reflect the characteristics of real world query environment, queries are restricted to subsets of 3 attributes or less (users tend not to use a large number of attributes in the same query). To minimize the interference of OS caching, we utilize the page deletion mechanism offered by the 2.6.x line of the Linux kernel to completely clear the page caches between individual queries. Finally, for the compression tests, results are expressed as a percentage indicating the effective size reduction with respect to the original table, where the fields of each record are initially represented as 32 bit integers. High numbers are therefore better.

6.1 Data Set Size

To assess the impact of data set size on index performance, we ran a series of tests on synthetically generated data sets with record counts from 100,000 to 10 million records. The data sets consist of 6 dimensions, with cardinalities randomly chosen in the range 4 — 400 and a data distribution skewed with a zipfian value of one. The data itself is uncompressed (compression tests are performed separately). Batches of 50 queries per run were used, with the results averaged across five independent runs. In total, five distinct index forms were created: a linear breadth first R-tree (LBF), a linear depth first R-tree (LDF), a standard depth first Hilbert packed R-tree (HDF), a bitmap index on unordered data (U-BMP), and a bitmap index on the Hilbert ordered data set (H-BMP).

In Figure 11(a), we see a count of the total number of blocks accessed during the query runs (note the logarithmic y axis). The results are as expected, with a close to linear increase in blocks processed as the data set grows in size. Counts are virtually identical for each of the Hilbert ordered data sets, with a small increase for the unordered bitmap index. Note that we do not plot the values for the bitmaps at 10 million records due to the excessive memory requirements in larger spaces.

In Figure 11(b), we examine the actual seek counts on the same queries. Here, the "seek count" refers to the total number of seeks across the full query set. The results paint a clear picture of the effect of linearization on both R-trees and the bitmap models. The new LBF form produces the lowest seek counts, followed closely by LDF. In contrast, the conventional packed R-tree, HDF, generates almost twice as many seeks on the largest data set. H-BMP is comparable to the standard R-tree (it is using the same underlying data set and its index must be paged from disk), while the unordered U-BMP bitmap produces almost 3 times as many seeks due to its lack of point clustering.

Figure 11(c) provides a partial illustration of the effect of seek count on run-time performance. Again, we can see that the linearized r-trees, LBF and LDF, produce the lowest query times. Performance for the standard R-tree and the bitmaps are demonstrably slower. For example, the bitmaps are 10%-20% slower than LBF at 1 million records, while at 10 million records, we see than the run-time of the standard R-tree is approximately 20% higher than that of LBF. We note that this is smaller than the gap for the raw seek count. There are two reasons for this. First, due to the interleaving of I/O and post processing (e.g., sorting, aggregation, and presentation) our query times include both components. In fact, post processing costs typically account for close to half of total query resolution costs and, moreover, are identical for all methods. Consequently, if post processing contributions were removed, we would expect the relative difference in run-time to almost double for the data set with 10 million records.

Second, as noted previously, smaller seeks can be "absorbed" by the read-ahead caching mechanism of modern disks, thereby partially hiding the degree of improvement we would expect to see on the Terabyte-scale fact tables found in production environments. To demonstrate how this issue might affect larger tables, we created a data set of 70 million records with the same basic parameters of our previous test. This data set was approximately 2 GB in size, and is the largest fact table that we can create on a 32-bit file system. LBF and HDF indexes were then created. Figure 11(d) displays the head-to-head comparison for the run-time of the two methods. Note that the run-time does not represent a seven-fold increase over the times for 10 million records. Due to the fact that an external memory version of the index methods was required, we utilized our full framework which includes the R-tree compression algorithms. As a result, the final data set is only 28% larger than the set of 10 million records. Still, we can see an increase of almost 30% in run-time for the HDF index relative to LBF, a significant

Figure 11. For data sets of 100K to 10M records: (a) Blocks accessed (b) seeks performed (c) run time. (d) Run-time for 70 million records.

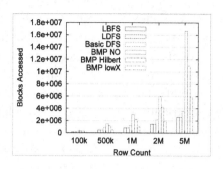

(a)

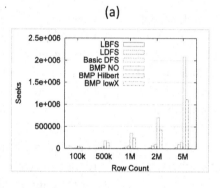

(b)

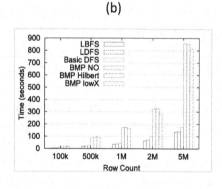

(c)

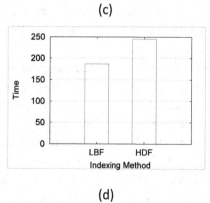

(d)

Figure 12. (a) seeks by dimension count (b) run-time by dimension count

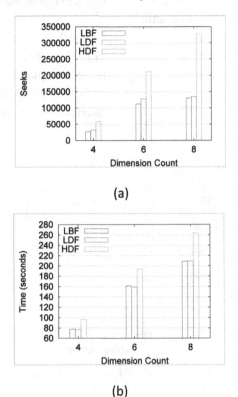

(a)

(b)

difference versus the smaller data sets. Again, we would expect this growth to be far more dramatic on data sets that might in practice be an order of magnitude larger.

6.2 Dimension Count

Figure 12(a) and Figure 12(b) illustrate the impact of an increase in dimensions on seek count and performance, respectively. We specifically evaluate the R-trees in this test, using data sets with 10 million records, mixed cardinalities and a zipfian skew of one. In Figure 12(a), we clearly see that as dimensions increase, there is rapid growth in seek count. In fact, by 8 dimensions, the seek count for HDF has more than tripled that of LBF. This is reflective of the fact that higher dimension spaces tend to produce shorter clusters, thereby producing frequent tree traversals for HDF. The same general trend is illustrated in the performance results of

Figure 12(b). By 8 dimensions, the HDF query stream takes about 25% longer to execute than the linearized trees. Again, the relative penalty will grow significantly in practical environments where we see much larger data sets.

6.3 Real Data

While we have utilized a zipfian skew in all of our synthetic tests, real data sometimes has skew patterns that are difficult to mimic programmatically. We have therefore evaluated the R-tree methods on a weather pattern data set that is regularly used in the DW literature (Hahn, Warren, & Loudon). It consists of 1.2 million records, nine dimensions, and cardinalities ranging from 2 to 7,037. Figure 13(a) depicts the growth in seek times for the three tree methods, demonstrating a 60% rise in seeks in HDF relative to LBF. The associated query times are shown in Figure 13(b), with a 29% increase in cost for HDF. The results for the real data set are therefore consistent with those of the synthetic data sets of comparable size.

6.4 LBF versus Sequential Scans

Recall that as the size of a query approaches 10% to 15% of the full data set, no index can improve upon a sequential scan. However, with Linear BFS, the penalty associated with unusually large queries is so small that sequential scans would

Figure 13. (a) seek count, real data (b) run-time, real data (c) time versus sequential scans

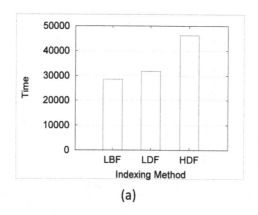

(a)

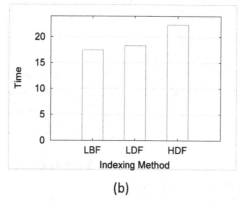

(b)

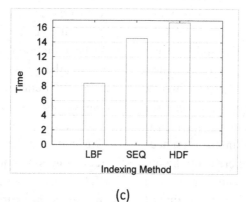

(c)

almost never be necessary. Figure 13(c) illustrates the relative cost of LBF and HDF versus sequential scans of the real data set described above (again with random query batches). Here, the queries have been defined so as to represent "large" result sets, in this case averaging approximately 7% of the full data set. The results are quite interesting. First, we see here a more extreme difference between the linearized LBF R-tree and the standard HDF R-tree. In fact, the cost of HDF is essentially twice that of LDF. Second, we see that since the average query size is about half that of the "index usefulness threshold", the LBF indexes do indeed significantly outperform a simple sequential scan. Specifically, the scan requires about 75% more time on the same queries (though it still outperforms the standard packed R-tree).

6.5 Compression Ratios by Table Size

We begin our evaluation of the compression framework by looking at the effect of compression on data sets of one million records, with cardinalities randomly chosen in the range 4 — 10000, as dimension count increases from two to ten. The methods evaluated include TDC, GRS, and our own Hilbert Space Compression methods, referred to as HSC. Figure 14(a) displays the results for a fairly typical zipfian skew of one, while Figure 14(b) illustrates the effect of more extreme clustering produced by a zipfian value of three. Several observations can be made. First all differential algorithms demonstrate compression ratios in excess of 80%, with TDC slightly above the Hilbert method. This difference is primarily attributable to the fact that the Hilbert axes must be rounded up to the nearest "power of two", thereby sacrificing a half bit on average. Second, the increased clustering produced by data skew leads to extremely high compression rates. TDC and HSC, in particular, hover between 95% and 98%. GRS trails the other two methods, largely due to its unrealistic uniformity assumption. Third,

there is a general decline in the compression ratio as dimensions increase due to the point space becoming significantly larger.

6.6 Scalability

In practice, record counts in data warehouse environments are extremely large. Figure 15(a), therefore illustrates the effect of increasing the data set size from 100,000 to 10 million. Here we see a marked increase in compression ratios as record count grows. Again, this is expected for differential methods as increased record count leads to elevated density that, in turn, reduces the distance between points. For TDC and HSC in particular, compression rates reach approximately 90% percent at just 10 million rows. We also performed a single HSC compression test on a data set of four dimensions and 100 million rows (skew = 1, mixed cardinalities). The rows occupied approximately 1.6 GB in uncompressed form, but were reduced to just 58 MB with the Hilbert methods. The final compression rate was 96.36%. Again, the very high compression rates are heavily influenced by the increased density of large sets. We note that the associated compressed index occupied just 553 KB.

6.7 Compression of Real Data

Figure 15(b) provides another direct comparison, this time on the aforementioned weather data set. In this case, the positions of TDC and GRS are reversed, a result reflective of the fact that the modest skew of the real data set closely models the uniformity assumption of GRS. The compression for HSC is almost completely consistent with Figure 14(a), as one would expect with the Hilbert curve.

6.8 Comparison with the Dwarf

In Figure 16(a), we see a direct compression comparison with HSC and the Dwarf cube show-

Figure 14. (a) typical skew (b) dramatic skew

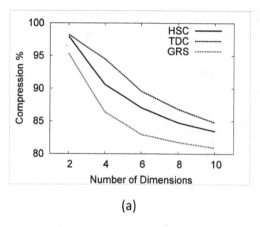

(a)

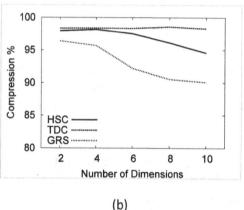

(b)

ing the two techniques on data sets of varying record counts. We note that we use a smaller data set here due to a limited Dwarf implementation. Given the current parameters, we see a simple trend indicating improved performance for the Hilbert methods at higher record counts. This is likely due to the increased ability to exploit space density. We note that additional testing did show advantages for the Dwarf in very high dimensions, though again we stress that users seldom issue queries in this region of the space.

6.9 Index Compression

Figure 16(b) illustrates the compression rates for the index components for record counts varying from 100000 to 10 million (zipf = 1, mixed cardi-

nalities). Here, we can see ratios from 94.90% up to 99.20% for the largest data sets. We note that comparable index compression numbers for GRS were never provided. Figure 16(c) examines the effect of varying the dimension count. As dimensions increase from two to 12, the compression ratio varies from 96.64% to 98.50%. In contrast to data compression, increased dimension count is not a problem for the indexing methods. Specifically, the compact pivot-based representation for the bounding boxes does not deteriorate as we increase the number of axes of the enclosing hyper-rectangle.

Figure 15. (a) data set size (b) real data

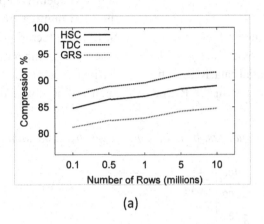

(a)

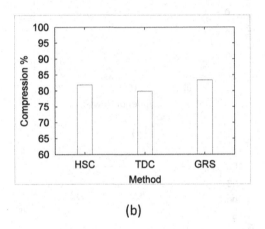

(b)

6.10 Query Performance

Finally we examine the impact of compression on query performance (using the data sets of Figure 14(a)). Figure 17(a) indicates that the average number of disk blocks retrieved during a query batch when using compressed Hilbert R-trees is about 10% of the number retrieved when using uncompressed data. Recall the GRS is the only other differential method that describes a possible indexing approach. In (Goldstein, Ramakrishnan, & Shaft, 1998), the authors indicate that IO costs for their compressed methods are approximately 40%-50% of the costs of the uncompressed benchmark. The elevated I/O costs, relative to HSC, likely result from a linearization strategy that less effectively exploits the increased fan-out of the compressed blocks. This is a crucial observation with respect to practical implementations.

Finally in Figure 17(b), we look at the time taken during these same query runs to uncompress records and place them into the result set, versus the time to do so with completely uncompressed records. Here, we see the ratio increase from about a factor of two in low dimensions to about a factor of 4 in higher dimensions. We note, however, that we currently working with a simple Hilbert library and that further performance optimizations would almost certainly reduce the decompression costs. We expect that even modest improvements would eventually allow the decompression methods to keep pace with the raw IO.

7 CONCLUSION

In multi-dimensional environments, R-trees have been used extensively and successfully to provide efficient access to point and spatial data. Researchers have also shown great interest in the R-tree and have identified packing methods that reduce the total number of blocks accessed per query. Still, these techniques do not optimize (or even assess) the number or size of the seeks required to retrieve relevant disk blocks. For large data sets, such as those found in data warehousing systems,

Figure 16. (a) Dwarf Cube (b) indexes, by rows (c) indexes, by dimensions

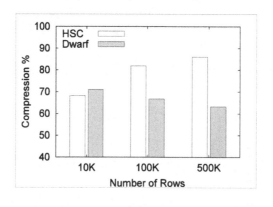

(a)

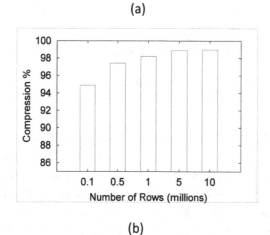

(b)

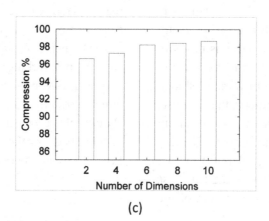

(c)

Figure 17. (a) query blocks (b) query decompression

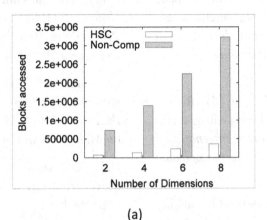

(a)

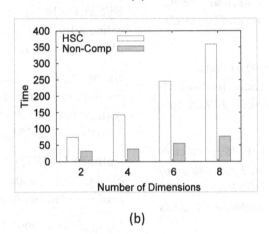

(b)

this disk head movement can have a significant impact on overall query performance. In this chapter, we discuss the linearization of R-tree indexes and data, a technique that significantly reduces the number of seeks required for common range queries. We then describe extensions to the basic model that utilize record differential calculations to dramatically compress the native point space. Most importantly, the Hilbert ordering logic is fully incorporated into the index compression process so as to create a single coordinated framework. Experimental results support our design decisions, demonstrating both efficient disk access on the LBF R-tree, as well as impressive compression ratios for data and indexes. Taken as a whole, we believe the current model represents the most effective and comprehensive storage and access framework for today's vast multi-dimensional environments.

8 REFERENCES

Arge, L., de Berg, M., Haverkort, H., & Yi, K. (2004). The priority r-tree: A practically efficient and worst case optimal r-tree. In *Proceedings of the Dagstuhl Seminar.*

Beckmann, N., Kriegel, H. P., Schneider, R., & Seeger, B. (1990). The R*-tree: An efficient and robust method for points and rectangles. In *Proceedings of the 1990 ACM SIGMOD International Conference on Management of Data* (pp. 322-331).

Eavis, T., & Cueva, D. (2007). A Hilbert Space compression architecture for data warehouse environments. In *Proceedings of the International Conference on Data Warehousing and Knowledge Discovery* (pp. 1-12).

Eavis, T., & Cueva, D. (2007). The LBF R-tree: Efficient multidimensional indexing with graceful degradation. In *Proceedings of the International Database Engineering & Applications Symposium* (pp. 241-250).

Faloutsos, C., & Kamel, I. (1993). On packing R-trees. In *Proceedings of the second international conference on Information and knowledge management* (pp. 490-499).

Faloutsos, C., & Kamel, I. (1994). Hilbert R-tree: An improved R-tree using fractals. In *Proceedings of the 20th Annual Conference on VLDB* (pp. 500-509).

Faloutsos, C., & Roseman, S. (1989). Fractals for secondary key retrieval. In *Proceedings of the Eighth ACM SIGACT-SIGMOD-SIGART Symposium on Principles of Database Systems (PODS)* (pp. 247-252).

Gaede, V., & Gunther, O. (1998). Multidimensional access methods. *ACM Computing Surveys, 30*(2), 170–231. doi:10.1145/280277.280279

Goldstein, J., Ramakrishnan, R., & Shaft, U. (1998). Compressing relations and indexes. In *Proceedings of the Fourteenth International Conference on Data Engineering* (pp. 370-379).

Golomb, S. W. (1966). Run-length encodings. *IEEE Transactions on Information Theory, 12*(3), 399–401. doi:10.1109/TIT.1966.1053907

Gray, J., Bosworth, A., Layman, A., & Pirahesh, H. (1996). Data cube: A relational aggregation operator generalizing group-by, cross-tab, and sub-totals. In *Proceedings of the Twelfth International Conference on Data Engineering* (pp. 152-159).

Gupta, H., Harinarayan, V., Rajaraman, A., & Ullman, J. (1997). Index selection for OLAP. In *Proceedings of the Thirteenth International Conference on Data Engineering* (pp. 208-219).

Guttman, A. (1984). R-trees: A dynamic index structure for spatial searching. In *Proceedings of the 1984 ACM SIGMOD international conference on Management of data* (pp. 47-57).

Hahn, C., Warren, S., & Loudon, J. (n.d.). Retrieved from http://cdiac.esd.ornl.gov/cdiac/ndps/ndpo26b.html

Hilbert, D. (1891). Ueber die stetige abbildung einer line auf ein flchenstck. *Mathematische Annalen, 38*(3), 459–460. doi:10.1007/BF01199431

Huang, Y., Jing, N., & Rundensteiner, E. (1997). Spatial joins using r-trees: Breadth first traversal with global optimizations. In *Proceedings of the VLDB* (pp. 322-331).

Huffman, D. (1952). A method for the construction of minimum redundancy codes. *Proceedings of the Institute of Radio Engineers, 40*(9), 1098–1101.

Jagadish, H. (1990). Linear clustering of objects with multiple attributes. *SIGMOD Record, 19*(2), 332–342. doi:10.1145/93605.98742

Kim, S., & Cha, S. (1998). Sibling clustering of tree-based indexes for efficient spatial query processing. In *Proceedings of the ACM Intl. Conf. Information and Knowledge Management* (pp. 322-331).

Lakshmanan, L., Pei, J., & Zhao, Y. (2003). QC-trees: An efficient summary structure for semantic OLAP. In *Proceedings of the 2003 ACM SIGMOD international conference on Management of data* (pp. 64-75).

Leutenegger, S., Lopez, M., & Eddington, J. (1997). STR: A simple and efficient algorithm for R-tree packing. In *Proceedings of the Thirteenth International Conference on Data Engineering* (pp. 497-506).

Lo, M., & Ravishankar, C. (1995). Towards eliminating random I/O in hash joins. In *Proceedings of the Twelfth International Conference on Data Engineering* (pp. 422-429).

Moon, B., Jagadish, H., Faloutsos, C., & Saltz, J. (2001). Analysis of the clustering properties of the Hilbert space-filling curve. *Knowledge and Data Engineering, 13*(1), 124–141. doi:10.1109/69.908985

Ng, W., & Ravishankar, C. V. (1997). Block-oriented compression techniques for large statistical databases. *IEEE Transactions on Knowledge and Data Engineering, 9*(2), 314–328. doi:10.1109/69.591455

O'Neil, P., & Graefe, G. (1995). Multi-table joins through bitmapped join indices. *SIGMOD Record, 24*(3), 8–11. doi:10.1145/211990.212001

O'Neil, P., & Quass, D. (1997). Improved query performance with variant indexes. *SIGMOD Record, 26*(2), 38–49. doi:10.1145/253262.253268

Pagel, B., Six, H., & Winter, M. (1995). Window query-optimal clustering of spatial objects. In *Proceedings of the fourteenth ACM SIGACT-SIGMOD-SIGART symposium on Principles of database systems* (pp. 86-94).

Peano, G. (1890). Sur une courbe, qui remplit toute une aire plane. *Mathematische Annalen, 36*(1), 157–160. doi:10.1007/BF01199438

Ray, G., Haritsa, J. R., & Seshadri, S. (1995). Database compression: A performance enhancement tool. In *Proceedings of the International Conference on Management of Data (COMAD)*.

Rissanen, J. (1976). Generalized Kraft inequality and arithmetic coding. *IBM Journal of Research and Development, 20*(3), 198–203.

Roussopoulos, N., Kotidis, Y., & Roussopoulos, M. (1997). Cubetree: Organization of the bulk incremental updates on the data cube. In *Proceedings of the 1997 ACM SIGMOD international conference on Management of data* (pp. 89-99).

Roussopoulos, N., & Leifker, D. (1985). Direct spatial search on pictorial databases using packed R-trees. *SIGMOD Record, 14*(4), 17–31. doi:10.1145/971699.318900

Sellis, T., Roussopoulos, N., & Faloutsos, C. (1987). The R+-tree - a dynamic index for multidimensional objects. In *Proceedings of the 13th International Conference on Very Large Data Bases* (pp. 507-518).

Sismanis, Y., Deligiannakis, A., Roussopoulos, N., & Kotidis, Y. (2002). Dwarf: Shrinking the PetaCube. In *Proceedings of the 2002 ACM SIGMOD Conference* (pp. 464-475).

Theodoridis, Y., & Sellis, T. (1996). A model for the prediction of R-tree performance. In *Proceedings of the 15th ACM Symposium on Principles of Database Systems (PODS)* (pp. 161-171).

Westmann, T., Kossmann, D., Helmer, S., & Moerkotte, G. (2000). The implementation and performance of compressed databases. *SIGMOD Record, 29*(3), 55–67. doi:10.1145/362084.362137

Wu, M., & Buchmann, B. (1998). Encoded bitmap indexing for data warehouses. In *Proceedings of the Fourteenth International Conference on Data Engineering* (pp. 220-230).

Ziv, J., & Lempel, A. (1977). A universal algorithm for sequential data compression. *IEEE Transactions on Information Theory, 23*(3), 337–343. doi:10.1109/TIT.1977.1055714

Chapter 2
Dynamic Workload for Schema Evolution in Data Warehouses
A Performance Issue

Fadila Bentayeb
University of Lyon – ERIC Laboratory, France

Cécile Favre
University of Lyon – ERIC Laboratory, France

Omar Boussaid
University of Lyon – ERIC Laboratory, France

ABSTRACT

A data warehouse allows the integration of heterogeneous data sources for identified analysis purposes. The data warehouse schema is designed according to the available data sources and the users' analysis requirements. In order to provide an answer to new individual analysis needs, the authors previously proposed, in recent work, a solution for on-line analysis personalization. They based their solution on a user-driven approach for data warehouse schema evolution which consists in creating new hierarchy levels in OLAP (on-line analytical processing) dimensions. One of the main objectives of OLAP, as the meaning of the acronym refers, is the performance during the analysis process. Since data warehouses contain a large volume of data, answering decision queries efficiently requires particular access methods. The main issue is to use redundant optimization structures such as views and indices. This implies to select an appropriate set of materialized views and indices, which minimizes total query response time, given a limited storage space. A judicious choice in this selection must be cost-driven and based on a workload which represents a set of users' queries on the data warehouse. In this chapter, the authors address the issues related to the workload's evolution and maintenance in data warehouse systems in response to new requirements modeling resulting from users' personalized analysis needs. The main issue is to avoid the workload generation from scratch. Hence, they propose a workload management system which helps the administrator to maintain and adapt dynamically the workload according to changes arising on the data warehouse schema. To achieve this maintenance, the authors propose two types of workload updates: (1) maintaining existing queries consistent with respect to the new data warehouse

DOI: 10.4018/978-1-60566-748-5.ch002

Copyright © 2010, IGI Global. Copying or distributing in print or electronic forms without written permission of IGI Global is prohibited.

schema and (2) creating new queries based on the new dimension hierarchy levels. Their system helps the administrator in adopting a pro-active behaviour in the management of the data warehouse performance. In order to validate their workload management system, the authors address the implementation issues of their proposed prototype. This latter has been developed within client/server architecture with a Web client interfaced with the Oracle 10g DataBase Management System.

INTRODUCTION

Research in data warehousing and OLAP (On-Line Analytical Processing) has produced important technologies for the design, management and use of information systems for decision support. Nevertheless, despite the maturity of these technologies, there are new data and analysis needs in companies. These needs not only demand more storage capacity, but also new methods, models, techniques or architectures. Some of the hot topics in data warehouses include schema evolution, versioning and OLAP operators for dimension updates.

To be an effective support of OLAP analysis, data warehouses store subject-oriented, integrated, time-variant and non-volatile collection of data coming from heterogeneous data sources in response to users' analysis needs. In a data warehouse, data are organized in a multidimensional way. The objective is then to analyse facts through measures, according to dimensions which can be divided into hierarchies, representing different granularity levels of information. The granularity levels of each dimension are fixed during the design step of the data warehouse system. After deployment, these dimensions remain static because schema evolution is poorly supported in current OLAP models.

To design a data warehouse, several approaches exist in the literature. Inmon, W.H. (2002) argues that the data warehouse environment is data-driven, in comparison to classical systems which are requirements-driven. Anahory, S., & Murray, D. (1997) propose a catalogue for conducting users interviews in order to collect end-user requirements while Kimball, R. (1996) and Kimball, R. et al. (1998) state that the main step of the design

process in data warehousing is based on a business process to model. User requirements describe the tasks that the users must be able to accomplish with the help of the data warehouse system. They are often collected in the design step of the data warehouse. Thus some new requirements are not satisfied and some trends are not explored. Indeed, data sources and requirements are often changing so that it is very important that the data warehouse schema evolves according to these changes. In business environment, several changes in the content and structure of the underlying data sources may occur and individual analysts' needs can emerge and grow in time. Thus, a data warehouse schema cannot be designed in one step since it evolves over the time.

To consider this problem, two categories of research emerged: (1) temporal multidimensional data models that manage and keep the evolutions history by time-stamping relations over hierarchy levels proposed by Morzy, T., & Wrembel, R. (2004), Morzy, T., & Wrembel, R. (2003), Mendelzon, A.O., & Vaisman, A.A. (2000) and Bliujute, R. et al. (1998); and (2) extending the multidimensional algebra with a set of schema evolution operators proposed by Pourabbas, E., & Rafanelli, M. (2000), Hurtado, C.A. et al. (1999) and Blaschka, M. et al. (1999).

In the context of data warehouse evolution, we proposed in a previous work a new data warehouse architecture which takes into account personalized user's analyses independently of the data sources. More precisely, in Bentayeb, F. et al. (2008) and Favre, C. et al. (2007a) we designed a user-driven data warehouse model in which schema evolves according to new user's analysis needs. In this case, new dimension hierarchies are then created based on personalized user's analyses in an interactive way. The user becomes then one of the key points of the data warehouse incremental evolution process. To validate our model, we followed a relational approach and implemented our data warehouse model inside Oracle DataBase Management System (DBMS). Furthermore, we also applied our approach on banking data of the French bank Le Crédit Lyonnais[1] (LCL).

In the other hand, when designing a data warehouse, choosing its architecture is crucial. We can find in the literature three classical main types of data warehouse models, namely star, snowflake, and constellation schemas presented by Inmon, W.H. (2002) and Kimball, R., & Ross, M. (1996) and implemented in several environments such as ROLAP (Relational OLAP), MOLAP (Multidimensional OLAP) or HOLAP (Hybrid OLAP). Moreover, in the case of data warehouse schema evolution, other data modelling possibilities exist such as data warehouse versions that are also based on the above classical data warehouse models.

Hence, the choice of data warehouse architecture is not neutral: it always has advantages and drawbacks and greatly influences the response time of decision-support queries. Once the architecture is selected, various optimization techniques such as indexing or materializing views further influence querying and refreshing performance. This is especially critical when performing tasks, such as computing data cubes or performing data mining.

Generally, to evaluate the efficiency of performance optimization techniques, (such as index and materialized view techniques), one should design a data warehouse benchmark. This latter may be defined as a database model and a workload model (set of queries to execute on the database). Different goals can be achieved by using a benchmark: (1) compare the performance of various systems in a given set of experimental conditions (users); (2) evaluate the impact of architectural choices or optimization techniques on the performance of one given system (system designers). In a

data warehouse benchmark, the workload may be subdivided into: (1) decision-support queries, mostly OLAP queries such as cube, roll-up, drill down and slice and dice; (2) queries used during the ETL (Extract Transform Load) process.

In the context of the data warehouse evolution approach, the workload of the benchmark should follow the evolution of the data warehouse schema. In Favre, C., et al. (2007b), we proposed a comprehensive automatic approach to reflect the data warehouse schema evolutions on the workload. Then, in this chapter, we propose a workload management system for controlling the execution of queries used to select optimization strategies, based on data warehouse schema evolution model. Our objective is to define a dynamic workload. Thus, we design a workload as a generic query model defined by a grammar, which introduces much-needed analytical capabilities to relational database querying. This increases the ability to perform dynamic, analytic SQL queries. So, given an initial workload, our objective is to update the workload with respect to the new data warehouse schema in an incremental way. The workload update consists then in: (1) creating new decision-support queries based on new hierarchy levels in dimensions, representing users' personalized analyses; (2) maintaining the existing queries consistent with regard to the new data warehouse schema. It allows the administrator to adopt a pro-active behaviour in the data warehouse performance management.

The remainder of this chapter is organized as follows. The following section is devoted to the related work on data warehouse evolution, including schema evolution, performance evaluation and query evolution. Then, we present our general framework for schema evolution in data warehouses. After that, we detail our approach to help the data warehouse administrator to update an existing workload, as a support for optimization dynamic strategy. Next, we present an example of our approach applied to a real simplified case study of LCL French bank, before providing implementation issues. We finally conclude and provide future research directions.

RELATED WORK

In this section, we present researches that are most closely related to our work, namely: (1) data warehouses' model evolution, (2) performance evaluation and (3) query evolution.

Data Warehouses' Model Evolution

We can distinguish in the literature two types of approaches regarding model evolution in data warehouses: model updating and temporal modelling.

The first approach consists in transforming the data warehouse schema and proposes to enrich data warehouses with adapted evolution operators that allow schema updates, such as proposed by Blaschka, M. (1999), Blaschka, M. et al. (1999), Hurtado, C.A. et al. (1999a) and Hurtado, C.A. et al. (1999b). In Hurtado, C.A. et al. (1999a) and Hurtado, C.A. et al. (1999b) dimensions are modeled as an acyclic graph, where nodes represent dimension attributes and arcs represent hierarchical links between these attributes. Evolution operators are then defined under the form of algebraic functions, which are able to modify the graph structure. Blaschka, M. (1999) and Blaschka, M. et al. (1999) propose elementary operators for schema evolution, which can be combined to define more complex operators. We note that these two methods support only one schema and do not keep the history of evolutions.

On the contrary, the second approach keeps track of the schema evolution, by using temporal validity labels. These labels are affixed either on dimension instances such as proposed by Bliujute, R. et al. (1998), or on aggregation links such as proposed by Mendelzon, A.O., & Vaisman, A.A. (2000), or on schema versions such as proposed by Morzy, T., & Wrembel, R. (2004), Bebel, B.

et al. (2004) and Body, M. et al. (2002). Let us detail these different methods. Mendelzon, A.O., & Vaisman, A.A. (2000) propose a temporal multidimensional model and a query language supporting it (namely TOLAP). Dimension elements are timestamped at the schema or instance level (or both) in order to keep track of the updates that occur. The regular star schema treats all dimensions, one of them being the Time dimension, equally and assumes them to be independent. Bliujute, R. et al. (1998) propose a temporal star schema, where time is not a separate, independent dimension table, but is a dimension of all tables and is represented via one or more time-valued attributes in all tables. Another promising approach to handling changes in data warehouse structure and content is based on a multiversion data warehouse such as proposed by Morzy, T., & Wrembel, R. (2004), Bebel, B. et al. (2004) and Body, M. et al. (2002). In such a data warehouse, each version describes a schema and data at certain period of time. In order to appropriately analyse multiversion data, an extension to traditional SQL language is required.

Both of these approaches do not directly involve users in the data warehouse evolution process, and thus constitute a solution rather for data sources evolution than for users' analysis needs evolution. Indeed, once the data warehouse is created, users can only carry out analyses provided by the model. Thus these solutions make the data warehouse schema evolve, ignoring new analysis needs driven by users' knowledge. A personalization process is then required in order to provide answers to users' emergent individual needs. Furthermore, the personalization of the data warehouse becomes crucial for expanding its use to the most of users. It is a research perspective, which emerges in the data warehouse community. Works in this domain are particularly focused on the visualization of data, based on users' preferences modelling and exploitation with the profile concept such as proposed by Bellatrèche, L. et al. (2005). It consists in refining queries to show a part of data, which meets user's preferences.

To achieve analyses personalization, whatever it is, the data warehouse should be more flexible. Works aimed at bringing flexibility within the data warehouse use mostly rule-based languages. Firstly, to define the data warehouse schema in a flexible way, two approaches are possible: using rules either to express the analysis needs such as proposed by Kim, H.J. et al. (2003) or the knowledge about data warehouse construction such as proposed by Peralta, V. et al. (2003). Secondly, the data warehouse administrator could use rules to define some integrity constraints in order to ensure the consistency of the data and the analyses as a consequence. For Carpani, F., & Ruggia, R. (2001) and Ghozzi, F. et al. (2003), the expressed integrity constraints use the data semantic to manage data inconsistency within the analysis. Thirdly, in order to make the analysis more flexible, a rule-based language has been developed by Espil, M.M., & Vaisman, A.A. (2001) to manage exceptions during the aggregation process. This language allows to intentionally expressing redefinitions of aggregation hierarchies. Thus, rule-based languages allow flexibility within data warehouses in different works. We want to introduce such flexibility in the analysis evolution process. However, the flexibility of the analysis evolution depends on the flexibility of the schema evolution, in particular dimension hierarchies updates, as we present thereafter.

Performance Evaluation

One of the most important issues in data warehouse physical design is to select an appropriate set of materialized views and indices, which minimizes total query response time, given a limited storage space.

A judicious choice in this selection must be cost-driven and influenced by the workload experienced by the system. Indeed, it is crucial to adapt the performance of the system according to

its use as Gallo, J. (2002) says. In this perspective, the workload should correspond to a set of users' queries. The most recent approaches syntactically analyse the workload to enumerate relevant candidates (indices or views) such as proposed by Agrawal, S. et al. (2000). The selection is based on cost models that evaluate the cost of accessing data using optimization structures (views, indices) and the cost of storing and maintaining these structures.

The workload is supposed to represent the users' demand on the data warehouse. In the literature, most of the proposed approaches rely on the existence of a reference workload that represents the target for the optimization such as Theodoratos, D., & Sellis, T. (2000). However, Golfarelli, M., & Saltarelli, E. (2003) argue that real workloads are much larger than those that can be handled by these techniques and thus view materialization and indexing success still depends on the experience of the designer. Thus, they propose an approach to build a clustered workload that is representative of the original one and that can be handled by views and indices selection algorithms.

query evolution

Workload evolution. In views selection area, various works concern their dynamical selection such as those proposed by Kotidis, Y., & Roussopoulos, N. (1999), Theodoratos, D., & Sellis, T. (2000) and Lawrence, M., & Rau-Chaplin, A. (2006). The dynamic aspect is an answer to workload evolution. However, workload evolution can also be considered from different points of views. Lawrence, M., & Rau-Chaplin, A. (2006) consider that the view selection must be performed at regular maintenance intervals and is based on an observed or expected change in query probabilities. Kotidis, Y., & Roussopoulos, N. (1999), Theodoratos, D., & Sellis, T. (2000) suppose that some queries are added to the initial workload. Thus these works assume that previous queries are always correct. However, we affirm that it is not always the case. That is why we interested in the problem of query evolution.

The query evolution problem. The problem of query evolution in data warehouses has been addressed in an indirect way. We evoked briefly the problem of materialized view maintenance. However, we have to consider the duality of views, which are both sets of tuples according to their definition of extension and queries according to their definition of intention. Indeed, a view corresponds to the result of a query. Thus the question of view evolution can be treated as the query evolution problem. This perspective is followed by Bellahsène, Z. (2002), where the impact of data sources schema changes is examined to each of the clauses of the view query (structural view maintenance).

However, in data warehousing domain, the issue of query evolution has not yet been addressed as a problem in itself. This point is important because queries are not only used to define views; for instance, in a decisional architecture, queries are also used in reporting (predefined queries) or to test the performance of the system when they form a workload.

The problem of query maintenance has been evoked in the database field. Some authors think that model management is important for the entire environment of a database. Indeed, queries maintenance should also involve the surrounding applications and not only be restricted to the internals of a database such as explained by Vassiliadis, P. et al. (2007). Traditional database modelling techniques do not consider that a database supports a large variety of applications and provides tools such as reports, forms. A small change like the deletion of an attribute in this database might impact the full range of applications around the system: queries and data entry forms can be invalidated; application programs accessing this attribute might crash.

Thus, Papastefanatos, G. et al. (2005) first introduce and sketch a graph-based model that captures relations, views, constraints and queries.

Then, Papastefanatos, G. et al. (2006) extend their previous work by formulating a set of rules that allow the identification of the impact of changes to database relations, attributes and constraints. They propose a semi-automated way to respond to these changes. The impact of the changes involves the software built around the database, mainly queries, stored procedures, triggers. This impact corresponds to an annotation on the graph, requiring a tedious work for the administrator.

In this chapter, we focus on the query evolution aspect in data warehousing context. More particularly, we focus on the performance optimization objective through the evolution of the workload. As compared to previous presented work, we do not consider annotations for each considered model. We propose a general approach to make any workload evolve. These evolutions are made possible by using the specificity of multidimensional model that encapsulates semantic concepts such as dimension, dimension hierarchy. Indeed, these concepts induce roles that are recognizable in any model.

GENERAL FRAMEWORK FOR SCHEMA EVOLUTION IN DATA WAREHOUSES

The issue we consider in this section is how to provide features to support schema evolution of data warehouses. In earlier work, namely in Bentayeb, F. et al. (2008), we investigated the use of data warehouse schema evolution to provide an answer to changes and extensions of business requirements. More precisely, our approach supports schema changes of data warehouses independently of the data sources. These changes should not be propagated to the data sources since they are autonomous. Indeed, they represent new users' needs in terms of OLAP analyses. Thus, we presented an original approach for users' personalized analyses in data warehouses, following a schema updating approach. In this section, we present the

Figure 1. Data warehouse schema for the NBI analysis

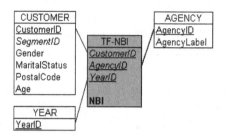

main aspects of our approach that constitutes our framework for schema evolution. Firstly, we present the framework of the personalization process. Then, we detail the metamodel used to achieve the schema evolution management.

Illustrative Example

To illustrate our approach, we use a simplified example of the LCL French bank, and more particularly an extract of the data warehouse concerning the annual Net Banking Income (NBI). The NBI is the profit obtained from the management of customers account. It is a measure observed according to three dimensions: CUSTOMER, AGENCY and YEAR (Figure 1).

The presented schema is an answer to the global analysis needs on NBI. However, LCL is a large company, where the data warehouse users work in various departments, and thus have different points of view. Then, they need specific analyses, which depend on their own knowledge and their own objectives.

Let us take now the case of the man in charge of student products. He knows that there are three types of agencies: "student" for agencies which gather only student accounts, "foreigner" for agencies whose customers do not leave in France, and "classical" for agencies without any particularity. Thus he knows the various types of agencies and the corresponding agency identifiers. However, this knowledge is not included in the existing data warehouse. It therefore cannot be used to carry out an analysis about student dedicated agencies.

Our idea consists then in considering this specific users' knowledge, which can provide new aggregated data, to generate a new analysis axis by dynamically creating a new granularity level: the agency type.

Data Warehouse Schema Updates for Analysis Personalization

To achieve analyses personalization, we propose a global approach that allows the integration of new analysis needs into the existing data warehouse. This personalization corresponds to a user-driven data warehouse schema evolution (Figure 2).

Our approach can be represented as a global architecture. The first step is the *acquisition* of the users' knowledge under the form of "if-then" rules. Then, in the second step, these rules are integrated within the DBMS, which implements the current data warehouse. This *integration* consists in transforming "if-then" rules into mapping tables. Then the *evolution* step is achieved by creating a new granularity level inside an existing dimension hierarchy or defining a new one. Finally, the *analysis* is carried out on the updated data warehouse. It is an incremental evolution process, since each time new analysis needs may occur. In the following, we detail the first three steps of our architecture.

Users' knowledge acquisition. In our approach, we consider a specific users' knowledge, which determines the new aggregated data to integrate into the underlying data warehouse. More precisely, our idea consists in involving

Figure 2. Data warehouse user-driven evolution process

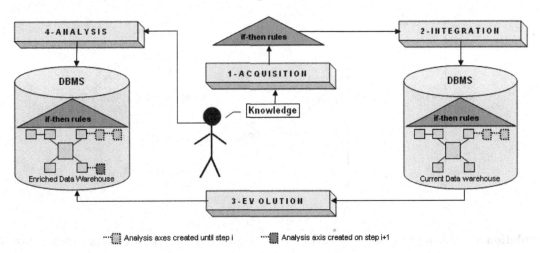

⋯▦ Analysis axes created until step i   ⋯▦ Analysis axis created on step i+1

users in the data warehouse schema evolution, to create new granularity levels according to their own knowledge. Thus, we define the concept of "Aggregation Data Knowledge" (ADK), which defines how to aggregate data from a given level to another one to be created.

The ADK is represented in the form of "if-then" rules. These rules have the advantage of being very intelligible for users since they model information explicitly such as explained by Holland, J.H. et al. (1986), and are well adapted to define the aggregation link between two successive granularity levels. The *if*-clause contains conditions on the attributes of the lower level. The *then*-clause contains the definition of a higher level, and more precisely the values of the attributes, which characterize the new level to create.

For instance, let us assume that the person in charge of students' products needs to define the level AGENCY TYPE from the lower level AGENCY, since he knows that there is three types of agencies: some agencies host only student accounts, some others deal with foreigners, and other agencies are said to be classical. The following rules define the level AGENCY TYPE, by defining the values of the attributes AgencyTypeLabel and AgencyTypeCode, which characterize this level. The conditions expressed in the *if*-clause concern

the attribute Agency_ID of the level AGENCY.

(R1) *if* AgencyID ∈ {`01903´, `01905´, `02256´}
    then AgencyTypeCode = `STU´ and AgencyTypeLabel = `student´
(R2) *if* AgencyID = `01929´
    then AgencyTypeCode = `FOR´ and AgencyTypeLabel = `foreigner´
(R3) *if* AgencyID ∈ {`01903´, `01905´, `02256´, `01929´}
    then AgencyTypeCode = `CLA´ and AgencyTypeLabel = `classical´

Knowledge integration. After the acquisition of the ADK under the form of "if-then" rules, these rules are integrated within the DBMS, which implements the current data warehouse. This integration consists in transforming "if-then" rules into mapping tables and storing them into the DBMS, by means of relational structures.

For a given set of rules which define one new granularity level, we associate one mapping table, which contains the conditions expressed on attribute(s) of the lower level, the corresponding value(s) for the attribute(s) in the created level, and some others useful information.

Figure 3. AGENCY dimension schemas

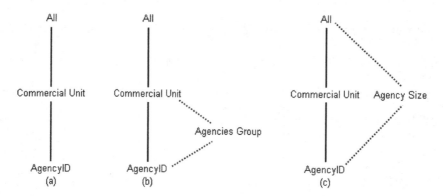

Evolution. The data warehouse schema evolution consists in updating the current schema by creating a new granularity level in a dimension hierarchy. The created level can be added at the end of a hierarchy or inserted between two existing ones; we thus speak of adding and inserting a level, respectively. In the two cases, the rules have to determine the aggregation link between the lower and the created levels. But, in the second case, it is also necessary to determine the aggregation link between the inserted level and the existing higher level in an automatic way.

A user makes the choice to insert a level between two existing ones only if it is possible to semantically aggregate data from the inserted level to the existing higher level. For instance, let us suppose the AGENCY dimension schema of Figure 3(a). In this case, it is possible to aggregate data according to Commercial Unit that is a set of agencies, according to their geographical localization. Let us suppose that we create a new level called Agencies Group, which is also a set of agencies, according to their geographical localization, but smaller than a commercial unit. Agencies Group level could be inserted between the AGENCY and Commercial Unit levels, where a commercial unit can be seen as a set of Agencies Groups (Figure 3(b)). Now, let us suppose that we add a new level that aggregates data according to the "size" of agencies: small, medium and large. It is semantically impossible to create an

aggregation link between the Agency Size and the existing level Commercial Unit. In this case, the user cannot insert the created level between Agency and Commercial Unit, but he can create it to define a new hierarchy (Figure 3(c)).

With this user-centered architecture, users can create new analysis possibilities by creating new dimension hierarchy levels. Since this creation impacts the model, these analysis possibilities are shared with the whole of users. Note also, that the user can delete a level that he/she has created before.

Metamodel for Data Warehouse Model Management

To manage the schema update of a data warehouse according to our approach, we propose the UML model presented in Figure 4.

A data warehouse is defined as a set of tables. The `DATA WAREHOUSE´ and `TABLE´ classes are linked with a composition link. These tables could be dimension or fact tables. Thus a generalization link connects `FACT´ and `DIMENSION´ classes to the `TABLE´ class.

Each dimension table has a `DIMENSION PRIMARY ID´ and various `DIMENSION ATTRIBUTES´. Moreover, fact tables present one or more `MEASURES´ and a `PRIMARY ID´, which is an aggregation of foreign keys referencing `DIMENSION PRIMARY ID´.

Figure 4. Data warehouse metamodel

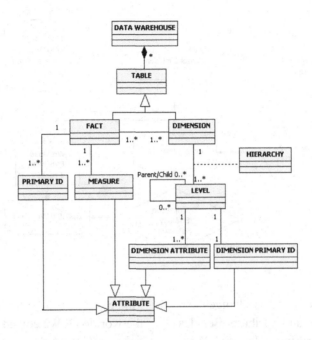

There is an association between the `LEVEL´ class and the `DIMENSION´ class called `HIERARCHY´, to represent the fact that each dimension table corresponds to one or more granularity levels that constitute a dimension hierarchy.

The metamodel we propose allows ensuring genericity capabilities to our approach. Indeed it can generate every evolving data warehouse model.

Note that the main aspect of this metamodel to ensure the personalization process is the `LEVEL´ class. Indeed, this class allows the user to add new levels representing the new analysis needs.

WORKLOAD EVOLUTION: OUR APPROACH

General Architecture

To support the workload adaptation after changes in data warehouse schema, we propose the global architecture depicted in Figure 5. According to an initial data warehouse schema, a first work-load is defined, containing the users' queries. A selection of optimization strategy can be carried out, based on this workload. When the data warehouse model evolves, according to the personalization process in our case, the workload has to be maintained.

Taking into account both the initial workload and the changes applied on the data warehouse schema, a workload evolution process is applied. This allows for the creation of an updated workload that contains queries which can be executed on the updated data warehouse. This workload contains not only queries that have been updated but also new queries if the data warehouse changes induce new analysis possibilities.

Data Warehouse Schema Evolution: Changes and Consequences

In this section, we discuss changes arising in the data warehouse schema independently of the data sources, following the ROLAP (Relational OLAP) approach.

Figure 5. Architecture for workload updating

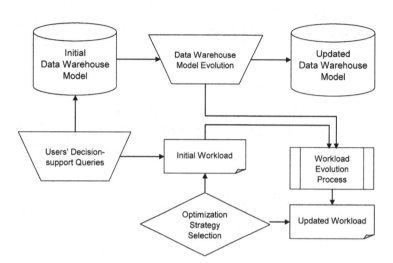

In a relational context, schema changes can occur at two levels: table and attribute. Besides classical concepts describing relational databases (table, attribute, foreign key, etc.), in data warehouses other specific concepts have to be considered (fact, dimension, level, measure, etc.). Indeed, changes occurred in a fact table or in a dimension table have different impacts.

In Table 1, we represent a typology of the main changes applied to the data warehouse schema and what their possible impacts on the workload are. We define what "concept" is modified, what kind of modification it is and its consequence on the workload. We consider three types of consequences: (1) updating queries; (2) deleting queries; (3) creating queries.

First, we note that we do not deal with the creation or the deletion of a fact table. In this case, there is an impact on dimension tables also. We think that these changes make the data warehouse schema evolve in an important way, so that the previous queries expressing analysis needs are no longer coherent or we are not able to define analysis needs due to a large number of possibilities.

Table 1. Typology of required changes for workload maintenance

Role in the DW model	Type	Operation	Query Updating	Query Deleting	Query Creating
Dimension	*Table*	*Creating*			*YES*
Dimension and level	*Table*	*Deleting*	*YES*	*YES*	
Dimension and level	*Table*	*Updating (Renaming)*	*YES*		
Fact	*Table*	*Updating (Renaming)*	*YES*		
Measure	*Attribute*	*Creating*			*YES*
Measure	*Attribute*	*Deleting*	*YES*	*YES*	
Measure	*Attribute*	*Updating (Renaming)*	*YES*		
Dimension descriptor	*Attribute*	*Creating*			*YES*
Dimension descriptor	*Attribute*	*Deleting*	*YES*	*YES*	
Dimension descriptor	*Attribute*	*Updating (Renaming)*	*YES*		

Query updating consists in propagating the change on the syntax of the implied queries. More precisely, the syntax of the queries' clauses has to be rewritten when they use a concept that has changed. For the creation of a level, several possible queries can be created.

For the deleting operation, we can observe two consequences: propagation and deletion. This means that if rewriting (propagation) is not possible, the query is deleted.

Thereafter, we focus more precisely on query deleting and query creating that are required in the personalized context we defined previously.

Workload Maintenance

In our context of personalization, we mainly investigated two types of workload maintenance: (1) query deleting and (2) query creating. Indeed, it is an answer to the fact that a user can add a granularity level or delete one (when he/she created it).

Query deleting. When a user deletes a level (that he/she created), we have to detect queries based on this level in order to delete them. Thus we define an evolution detection context in order to achieve the detection. We must be able to capture the concepts used in each query and to detect which query is concerned by the deletion of a concept.

In a relational context, decision support queries are based on clauses that exploit tables and attributes. Thus, we propose to represent this detection context by two matrices: one "queries-tables" matrix and one "queries-attributes" matrix. The "queries-tables" matrix has the various workload queries as lines and the various data warehouse tables as columns. The presence of a table in a clause of the query is marked by a "1" and the absence by a "0". The "queries-attributes" matrix has the various workload queries as lines and the various attributes as "columns". The use of an attribute in one of the query clauses is represented by a "1" and the absence by a "0".

Note that this context can also be used for an evolution of attributes themselves. In our case, we say that we just delete queries that use the level that will be deleted. Thus we have just to consider the "queries-tables" matrix since a level corresponds to a table in the relational context. Then, when a level is deleted, we have just to find the queries where there is "1" for the table to be deleted.

Query creating. When a user creates a granularity level, the idea is to guide the administrator to create new queries according to this level. Concerning the definition of new queries exploiting the new analysis possibilities, we use the grammar that we defined in Darmont, J. et al. (2007). This grammar is a subset of the SQL-99 standard, which introduces much-needed analytical capabilities to relational database querying (Figure 6). Moreover, the idea is to exploit the metamodel defined previously, in order to guide the query creation.

CASE STUDY

To illustrate our approach, let us consider the case study of the LCL French bank. Let us recall that the data warehouse concerns data about the annual Net Banking Income (NBI). Let us consider the following schema (Figure 7). In this schema, the NBI is analysed according to three dimensions: CUSTOMER, AGENCY and YEAR. The dimension AGENCY comprises a hierarchy with the level COMMERCIAL_DIRECTION that has been created by a user.

According to the use of the data warehouse, a workload is defined from users' queries. Usually, in an OLAP environment, queries require the computation of aggregates over various dimension levels. Indeed, given a data warehouse, the analysis process allows to aggregate data by using (1) aggregation operators such as SUM or AVG; and (2) GROUP BY clauses (GROUP BY CUBE, GROUP BY ROLLUP also). Here, we consider a simple example with an extract of a workload

Figure 6. Decision-support queries grammar

```
Query ::-

Select              ![<Attribute Clause> | <Aggregate Clause>
                    | [<Attribute Clause>, <Aggregate Clause>]]
From                !<Table Clause> [<Where Clause>
                    || [<Group by Clause> * <Having Clause>]]

Attribute Clause ::-   Attribute name [[, <Attribute Clause>] | ⊥]
Aggregate Clause ::-   ![Aggregate function name (Attribute name)] [As Alias]
                       [[, <Aggregate Clause>] | ⊥]

Table Clause ::-       Table name [[, <Table Clause>] | ⊥]

Where Clause ::-       Where ![<Condition Clause> | <Join Clause>
                       | [<Condition Clause> And <Join Clause>]]
Condition Clause ::-   ![Attribute name <Comparison operator> <Operand Clause>]
                       [[<Logical operator> <Condition Clause>] | ⊥]
Operand Clause ::-     [Attribute name | Attribute value | Attribute value list]
Join Clause ::-        ![Attribute name i = Attribute name j]
                       [[And <Join Clause>] | ⊥]

Group by Clause ::-    Group by [Cube | Rollup] <Attribute Clause>
Having Clause ::-      [Alias | Aggregate function name (Attribute name)]
                       <Comparison operator> [Attribute name | Attribute value list]

Key:                   The [ and ] brackets are delimiters.
                       !<A>: A is required.
                       *<A>: A is optional.
                       <A || B>: A or B.
                       <A | B>: A exclusive or B.
                       ⊥: empty clause.
                       SQL language elements are indicated in bold.
```

comprising five queries that analyse the sum or the average of NBI according to various dimensions at various granularity levels (Figure 8).

The evolution detection context for this workload extraction is represented with the queries-tables matrix (Figure 9) and with the queries-attributes matrix (Figure 10).

Due to the personalization process, the following changes are applied on the data warehouse,

resulting an updated schema (Figure 11):

• creation of the COMMERCIAL_UNIT level ;

• deletion of the COMMERCIAL_DIRECTION level.

After the schema evolution, our approach is applied and an updated workload is provided

Figure 7. Initial data warehouse schema for the NBI analysis

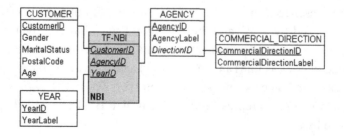

Figure 8. Initial workload for the NBI analysis

Q1: **SELECT** Gender, Agency Label, YearLabel, AVG (NBI) **FROM** AGENCY, YEAR, TF-NBI WHERE AGENCY.AgencyID=TF-NBI.AgencyID AND YEAR.YearID=TF-NBI.YearID **GROUP BY CUBE** (Gender, Agency Label, YearLabel);

Q2: **SELECT** CommercialDirectionLabel, YearLabel, AVG (NBI) **FROM** AGENCY, COMMERCIAL_DIRECTION, TF-NBI WHERE AGENCY.AgencyID=TF-NBI.AgencyID AND COMMERCIAL_DIRECTION.CommercialDirectionID= AGENCY.DirectionID **GROUP BY CUBE** (CommercialDirectionLabel, YearLabel);

Q3: **SELECT** MaritalStatus, YearLabel, SUM (NBI) **FROM** CUSTOMER, TF-NBI WHERE CUSTOMER.CustomerID=TF-NBI.CustomerID **GROUP BY CUBE** (MaritalStatus, YearLabel);

Q4: **SELECT** CommercialDirectionLabel, AgencyLabel, SUM (NBI) **FROM** AGENCY, COMMERCIAL_DIRECTION, TF-NBI WHERE AGENCY.AgencyID=TF-NBI.AgencyID AND COMMERCIAL_DIRECTION.CommercialDirectionID=AGENCY.DirectionID AND YearLabel='2000' **GROUP BY ROLLUP** (CommercialDirectionLabel, AgencyLabel);

Q5: **SELECT** AgencyLabel, AVG (NBI) **FROM** AGENCY, COMMERCIAL_DIRECTION, TF-NBI WHERE AGENCY.AgencyID=TF-NBI.AgencyID AND COMMERCIAL_DIRECTION.CommercialDirectionID=AGENCY.DirectionID AND YearLabel='2000' AND CommercialDirectionLabel='Lyon' **GROUP BY** AgencyLabel;

Figure 9. Queries-tables matrix

	t1	t2	t3	t4	t5
q1	1	1	1	0	0
q2	1	1	0	0	1
q3	1	0	0	1	0
q4	1	1	0	0	1
q5	1	1	0	0	1

t1	TF-NBI
t2	AGENCY
t3	YEAR
t4	CUSTOMER
t5	COMMERCIAL_DIRECTION

Figure 10. Queries-attributes matrix

	a1	a2	a3	a4	a5	a6	a7	a8	a9	a10	a11	a12	a13	a14
q1	1	1	0	0	0	0	1	0	1	0	1	1	1	1
q2	1	0	1	1	1	0	0	0	1	0	1	0	0	1
q3	0	0	0	0	0	1	0	1	0	1	1	0	0	1
q4	1	1	1	1	1	0	0	0	1	0	1	0	0	1
q5	1	1	1	1	1	0	0	0	1	0	1	0	0	1

a1	AGENCY.AgencyID
a2	AGENCY.AgencyLabel
a3	AGENCY.DirectionID
a4	COMMERCIAL_DIRECTION.CommercialDirectionID
a5	COMMERCIAL_DIRECTION.CommercialDirectionLabel
a6	CUSTOMER.CustomerID
a7	CUSTOMER.Gender
a8	CUSTOMER.MaritalStatus
a9	TF-NBI.AgencyID
a10	TF-NBI.CustomerID
a11	TF-NBI.NBI
a12	TF-NBI.YearID
a13	YEAR.YearID
a14	YEAR.YearLabel

Figure 11. Updated data warehouse schema for the NBI analysis

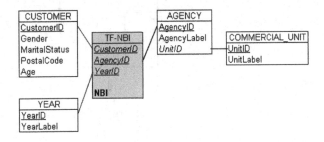

Figure 12. Updated workload for the NBI analysis

Q1: **SELECT** Gender, AgencyLabel, YearLabel, AVG (NBI) **FROM** AGENCY, YEAR, TF-NBI WHERE AGENCY.AgencyID=TF-NBI.AgencyID AND YEAR.YearID=TF-NBI.YearID **GROUP BY CUBE** (Gender, AgencyLabel, YearLabel);

Q3: **SELECT** MaritalStatus, YearLabel, SUM (NBI) **FROM** CUSTOMER, TF-NBI WHERE CUSTOMER.CustomerID=TF-NBI.CustomerID **GROUP BY CUBE** (MaritalStatus, YearLabel);

Q6: *SELECT AgencyLabel, UnitLabel, AVG (NBI) FROM AGENCY, COMMERCIAL_UNIT, TF-NBI WHERE AGENCY.AgencyID=TF-NBI.AgencyID AND COMMERCIAL_UNIT.UnitID=AGENCY.UnitID GROUP BY ROLLUP (UnitLabel, AgencyLabel);*

Q7: *SELECT UnitLabel, YearLabel, AVG (NBI) FROM AGENCY, COMMERCIAL_UNIT, TF-NBI WHERE AGENCY.AgencyID=TF-NBI.AgencyID AND COMMERCIAL_UNIT.UnitID=AGENCY.UnitID GROUP BY CUBE (UnitLabel, YearLabel);*

Q8: *SELECT AgencyLabel, AVG (NBI) FROM AGENCY, COMMERCIAL_UNIT, TF-NBI WHERE AGENCY.AgencyID=TF-NBI.AgencyID AND COMMERCIAL_UNIT.UnitID=AGENCY.UnitID AND YearLabel='2000' AND UnitLabel='Ardèche' GROUP BY AgencyLabel;*

(Figure 12). Firstly, the queries-tables matrix is used to detect that queries 2, 4 and 5 used the COMMERCIAL_DIRECTION level which has been deleted. Thus, these queries are deleted. Then the administrator is guided to create new queries on the COMMERCIAL_UNIT created level. In our example, he creates three queries (Q6, Q7 and Q8) with various clauses (GROUP BY, GROUP BY CUBE, GROUP BY ROLLUP) that exploit the new level.

Note that once the workload has been modified, the two matrices are also updated to represent properly the workload.

IMPLEMENTATION ISSUES

To validate our workload management system, we developed a prototype. We implemented our approach according to client/server architecture, with the Oracle 10g DBMS interfaced with PHP scripts in a platform named WEDriK (data Warehouse Evolution Driven by Knowledge).

The personalization process can be achieved by applying different algorithms, whose result is an evolution of the data warehouse schema. The sequence of these algorithms is represented in the Figure 13. The starting point of the algorithms sequence is a set of rules expressed by a user to create a granularity level. First an algorithm is used to check the validity of the rules. If the rules

Figure 13. Algorithms sequence

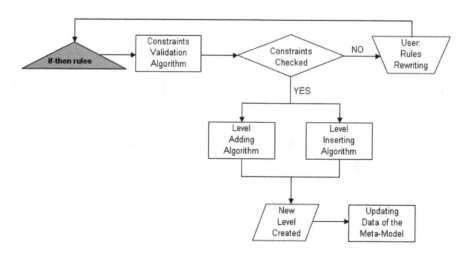

are not correct, the user has to modify them. This process is repeated until the rules are correct. If they are correct, the addition at the end of a hierarchy or the insertion between two existing successive levels of a new level is made according to the addition or the insertion algorithms respectively, by generating the corresponding queries. These algorithms are presented in Bentayeb, F. et al. (2008).

Once the data warehouse schema has evolved, we can consider the performance issue in the evolving context. Thus we are currently adding a module named WEPerf (data Warehouse Evolution Performance) to the WEDriK platform.

To achieve the whole process, we exploit the data warehouse metamodel presented previously, which is stored in a relational way. For instance, it allows for determining what the dimension hierarchies are, the links between tables in order to write new queries. This metamodel contains the semantic induced by the data warehouse model, particularly for the dimension hierarchies.

In one hand, we implemented a procedure that takes as input a workload and the data warehouse schema. This procedure builds the two matrices that represent the evolution detection context. These matrices are implemented under the form of relational tables.

In the other hand, changes on the data warehouse schema are stored into two relational tables: one for changes on tables, and one for changes on attributes. These tables present some useful information such as the evolution type, the name of the object that has changed. When changes occur, the two matrices are exploited to detect which ones of the queries are impacted. The workload is then modified according the required evolutions.

CONCLUSION

To consider an analysis personalization process in data warehouses, we proposed to involve users in data warehouse schema evolution. The idea

was to integrate their knowledge to create new granularity levels. Thus, considering this evolving context and the OLAP objectives, what about performances? Indeed, to evaluate the efficiency of performance optimization techniques (such as index and materialized view techniques), we usually use a workload which is a set of representative (in terms of users' analysis needs) queries, consistent with the data warehouse. With the data warehouse schema evolution, queries may be not representative anymore and the consistency can be corrupted. Thus, in this chapter, we designed a workload management system for data warehouse schema evolution model. Our workload model is dynamic, maintained incrementally and dynamically when data warehouse schema evolves, particularly in response to analysis personalization. The main advantage of our approach is to support the administrator task by providing him with a pro-active method to manage the data warehouse performances. Firstly it ensures that the existing queries remain consistent according to the data warehouse schema. Secondly it adds new queries to the existing workload based on new hierarchy levels in order to analyse performances on the whole data warehouse.

This work opens several perspectives. First of all, we plan to extend the possibilities of the workload maintenance. We want to consider not only structure evolution but also data evolution, such as evoked by Rizzi, S., & Golfarelli, M. (2006), since this type of changes may induce changes in queries. More particularly, changes may require updates on WHERE clauses of the queries. For instance, we can consider value evolution of a foreign key.

In addition, we can investigate the possibilities of a semi-automatic process for creating new queries. For instance, it would be interesting to create automatically queries considering some parameters given by the administrator (number of queries to be created, constraints on the join numbers, etc.).

Moreover, we have to apply our proposal on other data warehouses more voluminous. Thus, we will be able to study the performance in a pro-active way since it is the final aim of our proposal. For instance, it may be interesting to study the impact of parameters such as the number of queries in the workload, the importance of changes in the data warehouse on our approach. And we have to determine the context in which the workload evolution has a real impact on the optimization strategy by testing algorithms that select optimization structures.

ACKNOWLEDGMENT

We would like to thank the anonymous referees for their helpful suggestions and comments on the previous draft of this chapter.

REFERENCES

Agrawal, S., Chaudhuri, S., & Narasayya, V. R. (2000). Automated selection of materialized views and indexes in SQL databases. In *Proceedings of the 26ᵗʰ International Conference on Very Large Data Bases (VLDB 00)*, Cairo, Egypt (pp. 496-505).

Anahory, S., & Murray, D. (1997). *Data warehousing in the real world: A practical guide for building decision support systems*. Reading, MA: Addison-Wesley Longman Publishing.

Bebel, B., Eder, J., Koncilia, C., Morzy, T., & Wrembel, R. (2004). Creation and management of versions in multiversion data warehouse. In *Proceedings of the 19ᵗʰ ACM Symposium on Applied Computing (SAC 04)*, Nicosia, Cyprus (pp. 717-723).

Bellahsène, Z. (2002). Schema evolution in data warehouses. *Knowledge and Information Systems*, *4*(3), 283–304. doi:10.1007/s101150200008

Bellatrèche, L., Giacometti, A., Marcel, P., Mouloudi, H., & Laurent, D. (2005). A personalization framework for OLAP queries. In *Proceedings of the 8ᵗʰ ACM International Workshop on Data Warehousing and OLAP (DOLAP 05)*, Bremen, Germany (pp. 9-18).

Bentayeb, F., Favre, C., & Boussaid, O. (2008). A user-driven data warehouse evolution approach for concurrent personalized analysis needs. *Journal of Integrated Computer-Aided Engineering*, *15*(1), 21–36.

Blaschka, M. (1999). FIESTA: A framework for schema evolution in multidimensional information systems. In *Proceedings of the 6ᵗʰ Doctoral Consortium*.

Blaschka, M., Sapia, C., & Höfling, G. (1999). On schema evolution in multidimensional databases. In *Proceedings of the 1ˢᵗ International Conference on Data Warehousing and Knowledge Discovery (DaWaK 99)*, Florence, Italy (LNCS 1676, pp. 153-164).

Bliujute, R., Saltenis, S., Slivinskas, G., & Jensen, C. (1998). Systematic Change Management in dimensional data warehousing. In *Proceedings of the 3ʳᵈ International Baltic Workshop on Databases and Information Systems*, Riga, Latvia (pp. 27-41).

Body, M., Miquel, M., Bédard, Y., & Tchounikine, A. (2002). A multidimensional and multiversion structure for OLAP applications. In *Proceedings of the 5ᵗʰ ACM International Workshop on Data Warehousing and OLAP (DOLAP 02)*, McLean, Virginia, USA (pp. 1-6).

Carpani, F., & Ruggia, R. (2001). An integrity constraints language for a conceptual multidimensional data model. In *Proceedings of the 13ᵗʰ International Conference on Software Engineering & Knowledge Engineering (SEKE 01)*, Buenos Aires, Argentina (pp. 220-227).

Darmont, J., Bentayeb, F., & Boussaid, O. (2007). Benchmarking data warehouses. *International Journal of Business Intelligence and Data Mining, 2*(1), 79–104. doi:10.1504/IJBIDM.2007.012947

Espil, M. M., & Vaisman, A. A. (2001). Efficient intensional redefinition of aggregation hierarchies in multidimensional databases. In *Proceedings of the 4th ACM International Workshop on Data Warehousing and OLAP (DOLAP 01)*, Atlanta, Georgia, USA (pp. 1-8).

Favre, C., Bentayeb, F., & Boussaid, O. (2007a). Dimension hierarchies updates in data warehouses: A user-driven approach. In *Proceedings of the 9th International Conference on Enterprise Information Systems (ICEIS 07)*, Funchal, Madeira, Portugal (pp. 206-211).

Favre, C., Bentayeb, F., & Boussaid, O. (2007b). Evolution of data warehouses' optimization: A workload perspective. In *Proceedings of the 9th International Conference on Data Warehousing and Knowledge Discovery (DaWaK 07)*, Regensburg, Germany (LNCS 4654, pp. 13-22).

Gallo, J. (2002). Operations and maintenance in a data warehouse environment. *DM Review Magazine.* Retrieved from http://www.dmreview.com/article sub.cfm?articleId=6118

Ghozzi, F., Ravat, F., Teste, O., & Zurfluh, G. (2003). Constraints and multidimensional databases. In *Proceedings of the 5th International Conference on Enterprise Information Systems (ICEIS 03)*, Angers, France (pp. 104-111).

Golfarelli, M., & Saltarelli, E. (2003). The workload you have, the workload you would like. In *Proceedings of the 6th ACM International Workshop on Data Warehousing and OLAP (DOLAP 03)*, New Orleans, Louisiana, USA (pp. 79-85).

Holland, J. H., Holyoak, K. J., Nisbett, R. E., & Thagard, P. R. (1986). *Induction: Processes of inference, learning, and discovery.* Cambridge, MA: MIT Press.

Hurtado, C. A., Mendelzon, A. O., & Vaisman, A. A. (1999a). Maintaining data cubes under dimension updates. In *Proceedings of the 15th International Conference on Data Engineering (ICDE 99)*, Sydney, Australia (pp. 346-355).

Hurtado, C. A., Mendelzon, A. O., & Vaisman, A. A. (1999b). Updating OLAP dimensions. In *Proceedings of the 2nd ACM International Workshop on Data Warehousing and OLAP (DOLAP 99)*, Kansas City, Missouri, USA (pp. 60-66).

Inmon, W. H. (2002). *Building the data warehouse* (3rd ed.). Hoboken, NJ: John Wiley & Sons.

Kim, H. J., Lee, T. H., Lee, S. G., & Chun, J. (2003). Automated data warehousing for rule-based CRM systems. In *Proceedings of the 14th Australasian Database Conference, Database Technologies (ADC 03)*, Adelaide, Australia (pp. 67-73).

Kimball, R. (1996). *The data warehouse toolkit: Practical techniques for building dimensional data warehouses.* Hoboken, NJ: John Wiley & Sons.

Kimball, R., Reeves, L., Ross, M., & Thornthwaite, W. (1998). *The data warehouse lifecycle toolkit: Expert methods for designing, developing and deploying data warehouses.* Hoboken, NJ: John Wiley & Sons.

Kimball, R., & Ross, M. (1996). *The data warehouse toolkit: The complete guide to dimensional modeling* (2nd ed.). Hoboken, NJ: John Wiley & Sons.

Kotidis, Y., & Roussopoulos, N. (1999). DynaMat: A dynamic view management system for data warehouses. *SIGMOD Record, 28*(2), 371–382. doi:10.1145/304181.304215

Lawrence, M., & Rau-Chaplin, A. (2006). Dynamic view selection for OLAP. In *Proceedings of the 8th International Conference on Data Warehousing and Knowledge Discovery (DaWaK 06)*, Krakow, Poland (LNCS 4081, pp. 33-44).

Mendelzon, A. O., & Vaisman, A. A. (2000). Temporal queries in OLAP. In *Proceedings of the 26th International Conference on Very Large Data Bases (VLDB 00)*, Cairo, Egypt (pp. 242-253).

Morzy, T., & Wrembel, R. (2003). Modeling a multiversion data warehouse: A formal approach. In *Proceedings of the 5th International Conference on Enterprise Information Systems (ICEIS 03)*, Angers, France (pp. 120-127).

Morzy, T., & Wrembel, R. (2004). On querying versions of multiversion data warehouse. In *Proceedings of the 7th ACM International Workshop on DataWarehousing and OLAP (DOLAP 04)*, Washington, Columbia, USA (pp. 92-101).

Papastefanatos, G., Kyzirakos, K., Vassiliadis, P., & Vassiliou, Y. (2005). Hecataeus: A framework for representing SQL constructs as graphs. In *Proceedings of the 20th International Workshop on Exploring Modeling Methods for Systems Analysis and Design (EMMSAD 05), in conjunction with the 17th International Conference on Advanced Information Systems Engineering (CAiSE 05)*, Porto, Portugal.

Papastefanatos, G., Vassiliadis, P., & Vassiliou, Y. (2006). Adaptive query formulation to handle database evolution. In *Proceedings of the 18th International Conference on Advanced Information Systems Engineering (CAiSE 06), CAiSE Forum*, Luxembourg, Grand-Duchy of Luxembourg.

Peralta, V., Illarze, A., & Ruggia, R. (2003). On the applicability of rules to automate data warehouse logical design. In *Proceedings of the 15th International Conference on Advanced Information Systems Engineering (CAiSE 03), CAiSE Workshops*, Klagenfurt, Austria.

Pourabbas, E., & Rafanelli, M. (2000). Hierarchies and relative operators in the OLAP environment. *SIGMOD Record, 29*(1), 32–37. doi:10.1145/344788.344799

Rizzi, S., & Golfarelli, M. (2006). What time is it in the data warehouse? In *Proceedings of the 8th International Conference on Data Warehousing and Knowledge Discovery (DaWaK 06)*, Krakow, Poland (LNCS 4081, pp. 134-144).

Theodoratos, D., & Bouzeghoub, M. (2000). A general framework for the view selection problem for data warehouse design and evolution. In *Proceedings of the 3rd ACM International Workshop on Data Warehousing and OLAP (DOLAP 00)*, Washington, Columbia, USA (pp. 1-8).

Theodoratos, D., & Sellis, T. (2000). Incremental design of a data warehouse. *Journal of Intelligent Information Systems, 15*(1), 7–27. doi:10.1023/A:1008773527263

Vassiliadis, P., Papastefanatos, G., Vassiliou, Y., & Sellis, T. (2007). Management of the evolution of database-centric information systems. In *Proceedings of the 1st International Workshop on Database Preservation (PresDB 07)*, Edinburgh, Scotland, UK.

ENDNOTE

[1] Collaboration with the Management of Rhône-Alpes Auvergne Exploitation of LCL-Le Crédit Lyonnais within the framework of an Industrial Convention of Formation by Research (CIFRE).

Chapter 3
Preview
Optimizing View Materialization Cost in Spatial Data Warehouses

Songmei Yu
Felician College, USA

Vijayalakshmi Atluri
Rutgers University, USA

Nabil Adam
Rutgers University, USA

ABSTRACT

One of the major challenges facing a data warehouse is to improve the query response time while keeping the maintenance cost to a minimum. Recent solutions to tackle this problem suggest to selectively materialize certain views and compute the remaining views on-the-fly, so that the cost is optimized. Unfortunately, in the case of a spatial data warehouse, both the view materialization cost and the on-the-fly computation cost are often extremely high. This is due to the fact that spatial data are larger in size and spatial operations are more complex than the traditional relational operations. In this chapter, the authors propose a new notion, called preview, for which both the materialization and on-the-fly costs are significantly smaller than those of the traditional views. Essentially, to achieve these cost savings, a preview pre-processes the non-spatial part of the query, and maintains pointers to the spatial data. In addition, it exploits the hierarchical relationships among the different views by maintaining a universal composite lattice, and mapping each view onto it. The authors present a cost model to optimally decompose a spatial query into three components, the preview part, the materialized view part and the on-the-fly computation part, so that the total cost is minimized. They demonstrate the cost savings with realistic query scenarios, and implement their method to show the optimal cost savings.

1 INTRODUCTION

One of the major challenges facing a data warehouse is to improve the query response time while keep-ing the maintenance cost to a minimum. Recently, selectively materializing certain views over source relations has become the philosophy in designing a data warehouse. While materialized views incur the space cost and view maintenance cost, views that

DOI: 10.4018/978-1-60566-748-5.ch003

Copyright © 2010, IGI Global. Copying or distributing in print or electronic forms without written permission of IGI Global is prohibited.

are not materialized incur on-the-fly computation cost. One has to balance both these costs in order to materialize the optimal views that incur minimum cost. This problem is exasperated when we consider a spatial data warehouse (SDW). This is because, spatial data are typically large in size (e.g., point, line, region, raster and vector images), and the operations on spatial data are more expensive (e.g., region merge, spatial overlay and spatial range selection). As a result, often, both on-the-fly computation cost and the view materialization cost are prohibitively expensive.

In this chapter, we take a novel approach to resolve this issue. In particular, we introduce an intermediary view, called preview, for which both the materialization and on-the-fly costs are significantly smaller than those of the traditional views. Essentially, the idea of a preview is to pre-process the non-spatial part of the query and materialize this part, but leave the spatial part for the on-the-fly computation and maintain pointers to the spatial data on which the spatial operation should be performed. In addition, a preview also exploits the hierarchical relationships among different views.

The process of computing a preview is as follows. We first capture the relationships among the general and specific concepts of each dimension in the data warehouse, which, in general can form a partial order. By considering all the dimensions together, one can construct a *universal composite lattice* (UCL). Basically, every query that can be posed to the data warehouse will be represented in the UCL. Then we decompose each query into a set of *atomic spatial queries*. An atomic spatial query contains only one spatial operation, but may contain many non-spatial operations. UCL is instantiated by mapping all the atomic spatial queries, which could be either materialized, computed on-the-fly or built for a preview based on certain cost conditions, such that their inter-dependent relationships are retrieved. If we decide to build a preview for a specified atomic spatial query, we extract the *spatial projection* of this atomic spatial

query, which is nothing but the part containing the spatial operation. A preview for a spatial atomic query contains: its spatial projection, pointers to the spatial objects on which the spatial operation is performed, materialized non-spatial part, and pointers to the lower level previews or materialized views in the UCL. Essentially, by materializing previews, we are in some sense pre-executing the non-spatial part of the query and compute its spatial projection. As a result, the on-the-fly computation part of a preview or an atomic query computed on-the-fly could be done more efficiently from the existing lower level views than starting from the base tables.

Obviously, storing previews in a data warehouse introduces overhead because it requires additional storage and process efforts to maintain the data sets during updates. However, in this chapter, we demonstrate that, the performance gain achieved through preview more than offsets this storage and maintenance overhead. Our ultimate goal is to optimize the total cost of a spatial data warehouse, which is the sum of the space cost of materialized views, the online computation cost of queries if not materialized, and the online computation and space cost of previews, if any.

Generally, there are two categories of modes of processing a spatial query: (1) *display-mode,* where the spatial objects are retrieved and simply displayed, but no real spatial operations are performed on them, and (2) *operation-mode*, in which certain spatial operations are performed to produce the result specified in the query. For example, retrieving the existing population maps within certain areas and certain time frames is a display-mode query, but finding the boundary of these maps is an operation-mode because there is a spatial operation *boundary(maps)* involved. We distinguish these two modes because the cost associated with each mode varies significantly, even within each mode, the cost varies depending on the specific operation. For a specific query, if preview cannot optimize its total cost, we either materialize it or compute it on-the-fly. Therefore, we need to select an appropriate subset of spatial queries for preview construction in order to minimize the cost of the whole spatial data warehouse.

Our approach begins with decomposing a spatial query into atomic queries, and then instantiating a UCL to build inter-dependency relationships among these atomic queries, and finally categorizing them into three groups: view materialization, on-the-fly computation, and pre-view materialization. The above categorization is done in such a way that the total cost of a given spatial query is minimal.

This rest of the chapter is organized as follows. We present the motivation example in Section 1. We present some preliminaries in Section 2. We introduce the Universal Composite Lattice in section 3. We define preview in Section 4. We outline the cost model and decomposition method with associated algorithm for a spatial query in Section 5. We describe how a spatial query can be effectively evaluated using previews in Section 6. We conduct implementation and simulation study in Section 7. We discuss the related works in Section 8. We conclude our work in Section 9.

1.1 Motivating Example

In this section, we present an example that demonstrates that, for certain spatial queries, our approach to maintaining previews results in lower cost than optimally choosing a combination of on-the-fly and view materialization. Assume the spatial data warehouse comprising of a set of maps with their alphanumeric counterparts such as the area, the population amount and the temperature degree, as well as three basic metadata: location, time, and resolution. Assume that these maps specify different subjects of interest such as weather, precipitation, vegetation, population, soil, oil, or administrative region.

Now consider the following query that shows interests on a specific region: find the administrative boundary change of New Jersey area over last

10 years at 1m resolution level, and shows the vegetation patterns and population distributions within the same area, time frame and resolution level, and finally overlay the population maps and vegetation maps to deduce any relationships between them. The relation to store these data is called Map. An SQL-like query to specify this could be as follows:

SELECT boundary(M.admin_map),
    M.vegetation_map, M.population_
    map, overlay(M.vegetation_map,
    M.populationa_map)
FROM Map
WHERE Map.resolution = 1m AND Map.location = 'NJ' AND 1994 < Map.year < 2005

For the purposes of execution, this query p can be visualized as having four parts, q_1, q_2, q_3 and q_4, where q_1 and q_4 are in operation-mode, q_2 and q_3 are in display-mode:

(i) q_1: a spatial selection that retrieves boundaries of administrative maps in the New Jersey area for last ten years on 1m resolution level.

(ii) q_2: a spatial selection that retrieves vegetation maps in the New Jersey area for last ten years on 1m resolution level.

(iii) q_3: a spatial selection that retrieves population maps in the New Jersey area for last ten years on 1m resolution level.

(iv) q_4: a spatial join that overlays the results of q_2 and q_3. Hence q_2 and q_3 are intermediate views for q_4.

Assume the following cost tables (Table 1 and 2). Given a query q, we assume S(q) denotes the space cost, C(q) denotes the on-the-fly computation cost, and T(q) = S(q) + C(q) denotes the total cost. For the sake of this example, we assume $S(q)$ is measured in Mega Bytes, and $C(q)$ in seconds. When computing $T(q)$, we assume 1MB translates into 1 cost unit and 1sec translates into 1 cost unit.

Now let us consider the cost of the above query in the two extremes:

(i)   The entire query p is materialized. In other words, we materialize the result of q1 and q4. T(p) = S(q1) + S(q4) = 5.0 × 10 + (7.2+6.0) × 10 = 50 + 132 = 182.

(ii) The entire query p is computed on-the-fly. In which case, T(p) = C(q1) + C(q2) + C(q3) + C(q4) = (4 × 10) + (2 × 10) + (2 × 10) + (10 × 10) = 40 + 20 + 20 + 100 = 180.

However, complete materialization and complete on-the-fly computation are two extreme cases. A more optimal solution would be to selectively materialize certain views while computing the remaining on-the-fly. For this specific example, there are the following two possible combinations.

(i)   Materialize q_1 and perform on-the-fly computation of q_4. Then the total cost is $T(p)$ = $S(q_1)$ + $C(q_4)$ = 50 + (20 + 20 + 100) = 190.

(ii) Materialize q_4 and perform on-the-fly computation of q_1. Then the total cost is $T(p)$ = $S(q_4)$ + $C(q_1)$ = 132 + 40 = 172.

Obviously one can choose the one among the alternatives that provides the highest cost savings. Now let us examine how using previews can reduce the view materialization cost. Let us assume we store the preview of q_1 and materialize q_4. Specifically, for q_1, "SELECT boundary(M.admin_maps) FROM Map M WHERE M.resolution = 1m AND M.location = 'NJ' AND 1994 < M.year < 2005", we store the metadata(NJ, 1995-2004, 1m) and pointers to the New Jersey administrative maps from year 1995 to year 2004 in the preview and leave the spatial operation *boundary* on-the-fly. Hence the query process engine first searches the preview representing this query, then retrieves and performs the spatial operation on the images accordingly. This basically pre-processes the

Table 1. On-the-fly computation cost

Operation	Query Response Time (s/image)
q_1	4
q_2	2
q_3	2
q_4	10

query by performing the traditional projection and selection operations of the query, and the spatial operator will be executed at the run time. Compared to materializing 10 years' boundaries of administrative maps, the space and maintenance cost of storing preview is much cheaper than storing the spatial view itself. Compared to perform on-the-fly computation of retrieving 10 years' boundaries of administrative maps, the query response time will be reduced by adding pointers. In another word, we reduce some on-the-fly computation cost of q_1 by paying price of storing its preview, so that the overall cost is optimized. For q_4, we still materialize it due to the very expensive *overlay* operation.

The total cost of building a preview is the space cost of storing the preview and the on-the-fly computation cost starting from the preview. In this real example, the space of using one row to store the preview is 0.01MB and the online boundary retrieval takes 2 second for each map. We use $PC(q)$ to denote the preview cost of query q, therefore:

(i) $PC(q_1) = S(q_1) + C(q_1) = (0.01 × 10) + (2 × 10) = 0.1 + 20 = 20.1$

(ii) $S(q_4) = 132$

Table 2. Space cost

Subject	Size (MB)
admin_map boundary	5.0
vegetation_map	7.2
population_map	6.0

(iii) $T(p) = PC(q_1) + S(q_4) = 20.1 + 132 = 152.1$

Compared to the costs of previous methods, the total cost of query p is further optimized by constructing previews of q1. In the next sections, we will present the definition of preview, and how we select appropriate set of queries for preview to optimize the total cost of a spatial data warehouse.

2 SPATIAL QUERIES

In this section, we briefly present several important concepts. First, we define the basic algebra expression that is needed for constructing a *spatial query*. We then define an *atomic spatial query*, which serves as the smallest cost unit by decomposing a spatial query. We finally introduce a process denoted as *spatial projection*, which will be used to generate a preview.

The *hybrid algebra*, including hybrid relations R, hybrid operators *op* and hybrid operands X, constitutes the basis for defining a spatial query in a spatial data warehouse. Within an SDW, a base relation is a *hybrid relation* that includes attributes and tuples from both alphanumeric relations and spatial relations. For spatial relations, we adopt the definitions from the standard specifications of Open Geospatial Consortium (OGC). The spatial data types supported by this standard are from Geometry Object Model (GOM), where the geometry class serves as the base class with sub-classes for *Point*, *Curve* (*line*) and *Surface* (*Polygon*), as well as a parallel class of *geometry collection* designed to handle geometries of a collection of points, lines and polygons. Conceptually, spatial entities are stored as relations with geometry valued attributes as columns, and their instances as rows. The hybrid operators *op* combine a complete set of relational operators *rop* (σ, π, $\cup$, -, $\times$), comparison operators *cop* (=, <, $\leq$,

$\geq$, >, $\neq$), aggregate operators *aop* (distributive functions, algebraic functions, holistic functions) and spatial operators *sop* defined by OGC (Spatial Basic Operators, Spatial Topological Operators, Spatial Analysis Operators), or *op* $\in$ (*rop* $\cup$ *cop* $\cup$ *aop* $\cup$ *sop*). Examples of spatial operators include: Spatial Basic Operators = {area, envelope, export, isEmpty, isSimple, boundary}, Spatial Topological Operators = {equal, disjoint, intersect, touch, cross, within, contains, overlap, relate}, and Spatial Analysis Operators = {distance, buffer, convexHull, intersection, union, difference, symDifference}. A *hybrid algebra operand* is a distinct attribute of a hybrid relation, which could be either spatial operand or non-spatial operand.

Now we define a spatial query based on the hybrid algebra.

Definition 1: Spatial Query. A spatial query is a hybrid algebra expression F, which is defined as: (i) a single formula f, can be either unary ($op(X_1)$), binary ($op(X_1, X_2)$), or n-nary ($op(X_1, X_2, ...X_n)$), where *op* is a hybrid algebra operator and each X_i is a hybrid operand, (ii) if F_1 is a hybrid algebra expression, then $F = op(X_1, X_2, ..., X_m, F_1)$ is a hybrid algebra expression, and (iii) if F_1 and F_2 are two hybrid algebra expressions, then $F_1 \wedge F_2, F_1 \vee F_2, \neg F_1$ and (F_1) are hybrid algebra expressions.

In our motivating example, the spatial query is to retrieve the boundaries of administrative maps and overlaid results of vegetation maps and population maps under certain conditions from the hybrid relation Map: $p_1 = \pi_{boundary(admin\_map),\ overlay(vegetation\_map,\ population\_map)}(\sigma_{(1994<year<2005)\ \wedge\ (region\ =\ NJ)\ \wedge\ (resolution\ =1m)}$ Map)

Each spatial query is composed of one or more atomic spatial queries, or $p = \{q_1, q_2, ..., q_n\}$, which is defined as follows:

Definition 2: Atomic Spatial Query. Given a spatial query p, an atomic spatial query q is a component query within p, which is a hybrid algebra expression aF such that it contains only a single spatial operator *sop*.

An atomic spatial query essentially is nothing but an atomic formula that serves as the smallest unit for the spatial operation cost measurement purpose. For example, p_1 can be decomposed into the following two atomic spatial queries where each query includes only one spatial operator *boundary* and *overlay* separately:

$q_{11} = \pi_{\text{boundary (admin\_map)}}$
$(\sigma_{(1994 < \text{year} <2005) \wedge (\text{region} = \text{NJ}) \wedge (\text{resolution} = 1\text{m})} \text{Map})$

q12 = πoverlay(vegetation_map, population_map)($\sigma_{(<1994\text{year}<2005)}$
∧ (region=NJ) ∧ (resolution = 1m) Map)

As we can see, an atomic spatial query q can be composed of two parts, the spatial part and the non-spatial part. The spatial part includes a single well-defined spatial operator, and the non-spatial part could include the traditional selection-projection-join operations, comparison operations and aggregate operations. For each q, if we want to construct a preview for it, we need to perform spatial projection defined as follows:

Definition 3: Spatial Projection. Let q be an atomic spatial query. The spatial projection of q, denoted as q^s, is such that all operators in it are only spatial operators.

Essentially, a spatial projection of an atomic spatial query is computed by simply removing all non-spatial operations as well as all the operands associated with these operators. It comprises of only one spatial operation since by definition, the preview contains one spatial operation to begin with. For example, the spatial projection of q_{11} and q_{12} are as follows: $q_{11}^s = \pi_{\text{boundary(admin\_map)}} \text{Map} q_{12}^s = \pi_{\text{overlay(vegetation\_map, population\_map)}} \text{Map}$

3 THE UNIVERSAL COMPOSITE LATTICE

In this section, we define the Universal Composite Lattice (UCL), which captures the hierarchical relationships among all the possible queries in a given spatial data warehouse. UCL is essentially constructed by composing all its dimension hierarchies together. We first introduce a single dimension hierarchy.

3.1 The Single Dimension Hierarchy

For any given data warehouse, each attribute or dimension may vary from more general to more specific; the relationships thus mapped are called the dimension hierarchies or attribute concept hierarchies (Gupta, H., & Mumick, I. 2005). Now we formally define the single dimension hierarchy, following the lines in (Gupta, H., & Mumick, I. 2005).

Definition 4: Single Dimension Hierarchy. Given an attribute d, we say there exists an edge from node h_i to node h_j, $h_i \rightarrow h_j$, in the dimension hierarchy H of d, if h_i is a more general concept than h_j, denoted as $h_i > h_j$.

Here h_i and h_j are two nodes in the dimension hierarchy of d. Generally an attribute could have as many nodes as the user specified to capture the relationships among the different levels of the generalization of the dimension. The resultant dimension hierarchy may be a partial order. The most general concept is the NULL description, whereas the most specific concept corresponds to the specific values of attributes in the base relations.

Considering once again our motivating example, we have three dimensions: location, time and resolution, which serve as three dimensions for the spatial views. The location shows the coverage or the spatial areas of the map that could be defined by location name or determinate coordinates. The time indicates when the map is composed. The resolution shows the area covered by a pixel within the image. Each metadata serves as one dimension of the spatial views. A concept hierarchy for each dimension can be created by users or experts or generated automatically by data analysis. For example, we could have a partial or total order as a concept hierarchy for each dimension, i.e., Year → {Month, Week} → Day for Time; Country →

State → County for Location; and \$1000m\$(low) → \$30m\$(mid) → \$1m\$(high) for Resolution. In figure 1, we present this single dimension hierarchy for each metadata as follows. Here the arrow indicates the dependency relationship, for example, the view built on Year depends on the view built on Month. We assume the concept hierarchy for each dimension is given at the data warehouse design level.

The concept hierarchy provides a basic framework for the query dependency relationship. Given two nodes hi and hj in H, we say there exists a dependency relationship between hi and hj if there exists hi → hj. The dependency relationship indicates that the query represented at node hi can be built by that represented at hj. In other words, if one materializes the view at hj, the query at hi can be answered by simply generalizing the view at hj. For example, we could generate a map of a country by combining maps of each state in that country, hence we say the query on the country depends on the query on the states. Another example could be that a query with lower resolution images depends on a query with higher resolution images because we can perform certain transformation on higher resolution images to produce lower resolution ones to cover more regions. In this way, we can use the lower level query result to answer higher level queries instead of computing from scratch, which has been demonstrated to be an efficient query optimization technique (Gupta, H., & Mumick, I. 2005).

3.2 The Universal Composite Lattice

The Universal Composite Lattice (UCL) is built by integrating all the dimension concept hierarchies from a set of attribute domains $D = \{d_1, d_2, ..., d_k\}$. Therefore, we can use the UCL to represent the hierarchical relationships for all the queries in this data warehouse, and any input query can be mapped into this composite lattice and be evaluated based on its sub-queries.

Suppose N_i be the set of nodes in the dimension hierarchy of d_i. Assuming a spatial data warehouse comprises of dimensions $D = \{d_1, ..., d_k\}$ of the spatial measures, then the UCL could at most have $(N_1 \times N_2 \times ... \times N_k)$ nodes. We define a universal composite lattice as follows.

Definition 5: Universal Composite Lattice. Let $D = \{d_1, ..., d_k\}$ be the set of dimensions in SDW. Each node u in UCL is of the form $u = (n_1, ... n_k)$ such that $n_1 \in N_1$ or null, $n_2 \in N_2$ or null, ..., $n_k \in N_k$ or null. There exists an edge $u_i \rightarrow u_j$, iff every $n_{ik} > n_{jk}$.

Essentially, a universal composite lattice (UCL) is a directed graph that describes the query dependency relationships for a given spatial data warehouse. Every node in UCL is comprised of at least one node from the each dimension

Figure 1. The single dimension hierarchy

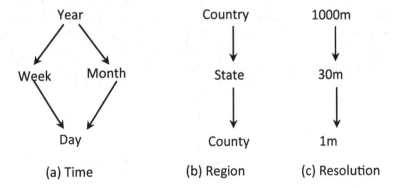

(a) Time   (b) Region   (c) Resolution

hierarchy or a null. The edge in UCL, as in the single dimension hierarchy represents that the higher level view represented by that node can be constructed from lower level views. Figure 2 shows the UCL constructed by combining the three dimension hierarchies of in figure 1. For the sake of simplicity, we have used the total order for the "Time" dimension.

Generally, for any data warehouse, one can construct such a lattice to indicate the dependency relationships among different queries. The big advantage of this lattice is that every atomic spatial query can be mapped to some node on UCL. We call such mapping process UCL instantiation. We will introduce our notion of previews and how UCL instantiation help us to exploit the existing views when computing certain queries on-the-fly.

4 THE PREVIEW

Essentially, the preview of an atomic query comprises of the materialized view of the pre-processed non-spatial part of the query, and the information necessary to compute the spatial part on-the-fly. As such it maintains pointers to

Figure 2. A sample universal composite lattice

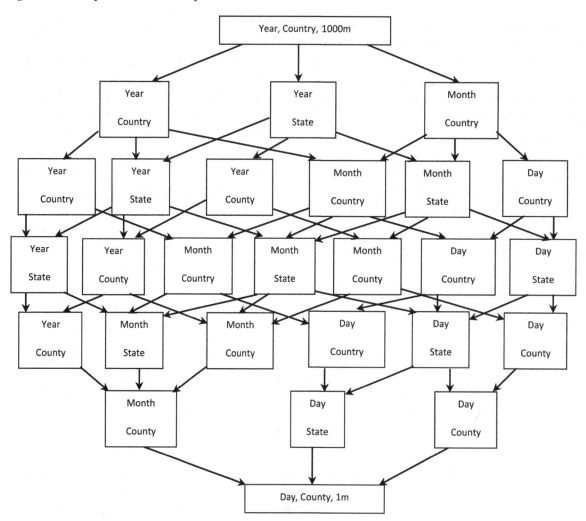

the spatial objects on which the spatial operation should be performed. In addition, a preview also exploits the dependency relationships among different previews.

A preview is formally defined as follows:

Definition 5: Preview. Let q be an atomic spatial query. The preview of q, denoted as $pre(q)$, is a 4-tuple $\langle M, sop, O, V \rangle$, where:

(i) M is materialized non-spatial parts of q,

(ii) sop is the spatial operator

(iii) O is a set of pointers to spatial objects, and

(iv) V is a set of pointers to all the sub-views that q depends on.

By constructing a preview, we need to first do spatial projection of an atomic spatial query by separating spatial and non-spatial parts. In other words, if we decide to build a preview for a specific q, we first perform non-spatial operations of q to get M, and keep O, the set of pointers to the spatial objects. Then we extract spatial operator sop, which will be computed on the fly when q is executed. Finally we construct the pointer set V which points to all views or previews at the lower dependent level by instantiating the given UCL.

For example, in the motivating example, we perform the traditional selection and projection on q_1 and store $\langle$(1995-2004), New Jersey, 1m), (boundary), (ptr$_1$-ptr$_{10}$), $V\rangle$ as its preview $pre(q_1)$, where the non-spatial part $M = \langle$1995-2004, New Jersey, 1m$\rangle$ is materialized by SPJ operations, the pointers (ptr$_1$-ptr$_{10}$) to maps are projected out based on certain conditions. Since there is one spatial operator involved and the query is in operation-mode, we put *boundary* in the operator position for the on-the-fly spatial operation purpose. V could include one or more pointers depending on how many sub-views are available. This preview is stored as a tuple in the data warehouse for further query evaluations.

4.1 UCL Instantiation

Now we show how a preview can be mapped onto a UCL, and the pointer set pointing to the sub-views can be constructed accordingly. Generally, for any atomic spatial query, it will be either materialized, computed on-the-fly or built for a preview. UCL instantiation includes not only mapping the previews but also mapping the materialized views or the views computed on-the-fly. For simplicity, we only show mapping a preview onto UCL, and other mappings of a materialized view or a view computed on-the-fly can be conducted similarly with straightforward extensions.

As we introduced before, an SDW comprises of a dimension set $(d_1, ..., d_k)$ with dimension hierarchies set $(N_1, ..., N_k)$ for each dimension. Each specific node $u = (n_1, ... n_k) (n_i \in N_i, i=1,...,k)$ has corresponding actual values stored in the base tables of the data warehouse, which is denoted as VL_i. For example, Year is one hierarchy in dimension Time, and its corresponding actual value in the data warehouse is a complete set or subset of (1980-2005). Generally, we denote $u = VL_i$ $(i =1,...,k)$ iff VL_i is the set of actual values associated to u. For example, in the figure 2, $\langle$Year, State, resolution 1m$\rangle = \langle$(1995-2004), New Jersey, 1m$\rangle$.

Given a UCL, now we present a simple linear search algorithm to map a preview of an atomic spatial query q, denoted as $pre(q)$, onto a given UCL.

Algorithm 1: Query Mapping Algorithm. The query mapping algorithm maps $pre(q)$, a preview of an atomic spatial query q, onto the given UCL.

```
Method:
    for j = 1 to n
        for i = 1 to k
            if u_j = VL_{ij}pre(q) is
mapped onto u
            end if
        end for
    end for
```

This algorithm basically performs linear search from the lowest level node to the highest level node in the UCL, and see if the *M* of a *pre(q)* includes the actual hierarchy values of certain node. If we find this match, we add a pointer from that node to the *pre(q)*. Therefore we map a preview to an actual node in the UCL. In addition to the previews, we assume the materialized views and views that computed on-the-fly are also mapped onto the UCL, which instantiate the UCL for a spatial data warehouse.

In figure 3, we revisit our motivation example and show how we build *V* (the pointer set of a preview pointing to its sub-views) for $pre(q_1)$. We map $pre(q_1)$ to the node (Year, State, 1m) in the lattice of figure 2. In figure 3, this node has two directed edges to its lower level nodes, which means the queries mapped to this node will be dependent on views mapped to those directed two nodes. Hence if there are any materialized views or previews mapped there, we add a pointer from $pre(q_1)$ to those lower level views, or sub-views. Basically, $V = (t_1, t_2, ..., t_n)$ where $t_i, i \in (1, n)$ is a pointer to one sub-view of $pre(q_1)$.

5 THE EXTENDED COST MODEL OF A SPATIAL DATA WAREHOUSE

In this section, we define the cost model of a spatial data warehouse. The following three factors should be considered to decide the execution cost of an atomic spatial query *q* as *C(q)*, where *P(q)*, *fr(q)* and *S(q)* are the on-the-fly computation cost, frequency and size of *q* respectively, and assume given the maximum space capacity of the SDW is *L*.

$$C(q) = (P(q) \times fr(q)) / (S(q)/L) \qquad (5.1)$$

We extend the cost model in (Yu, S., Atluri, V., & Adam, N. 2005) as follows: we set two thresholds, δ and θ, to control the cost of executing a *q* where δ is the lower bound and θ is the upper bound. We assume that δ and θ have been chosen at the data warehouse design level. The general rule is as follows:

(1) if $C(q) \leq \delta$, we compute it on-the-fly,
(2) if $C(q) \geq \theta$, we materialize it,
(3) if $\delta < C(q) < \theta$, we construct the preview of *q* and materialize the preview.

Figure 3. Mapping pre(q1) to UCL

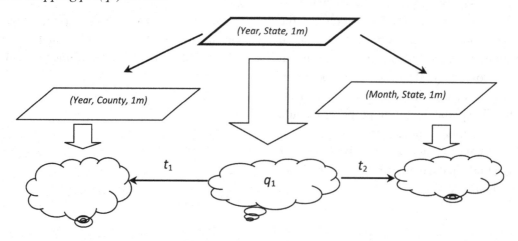

Obviously, if we materialize the preview of q, then the on-the-fly computation cost will be less than that from the scratch because in the preview, we pre-process any other non-spatial operations except spatial ones. This will certain reduce query evaluation time. On the other hand, the size of a preview that stores traditional alphanumeric data in a relational data warehouse is normally measured by the number of rows to store these datasets, which will be much less than the size of materializing the spatial objects such as images or maps, and the maintenance cost is reduced accordingly.

By controlling the execution cost of each q within a spatial query p, we divide p into three subsets, one is denoted as $p_{m,}$ for materialization, one is denoted as p_p for preview construction, and the other one is denoted as p_o, for on-the-fly computation. Then we use p_o, p_p and p_m to re-write p. Since the on-the-fly computational cost is the major part of the spatial query evaluation cost, and the maintenance cost is analogous to the space of materialized views (Gupta, H., & Mumick, I. 2005), we compute the total cost of a spatial query p as:

$$T(p) = P(p_o) + P(p_p) + \lambda S(p_m) + \mu S(p_p) \qquad (5.2)$$

Here $T(p)$ is the total cost of a given spatial query p, $P(p_o)$ is the sum of the on-the-fly computation cost of p ($P(p_o) = \sum P(q)$ for each $q \in p_o$), $P(p_p)$ is the sum of the on-the-fly computation cost of previews ($P(p_p) = \sum P(q)$ for each $q \in p_p$), $S(p_m)$ is the total space to store p_m, $S(p_p)$ is the total space to store p_p, and λ and μ are parameters between 0 and 1 indicating the relative importance of the spatial query computational cost vs. the space cost. In formula (5.2), the on-the-fly computation cost is monotonically decreasing as the number of materialized views increases, and the space cost is monotonically increased as more views or previews are materialized.

Our goal is to achieve an optimal point to balance the on-the-fly computation cost and space

cost thus the total cost for each spatial query is minimized. Given the set of spatial queries $Q = \{p_1, ..., p_n\}$ and a set of materialized views V and previews PV from Q, the total cost of an SDW is defined as:

$$T(Q, V, PV) = \sum\nolimits_{i=1}^{n} C(p_i) \qquad (5.3)$$

6 SPATIAL QUERY DECOMPOSITION AND EVALUATIONS

Based on the cost value associated with each atomic spatial operation, we decompose a spatial query into three different categories, such that the total cost of the spatial data warehouse is optimized. In this section we describe the greedy algorithms to decompose spatial queries into three parts for a given spatial data warehouse, and the technique to evaluate the query from these three parts accordingly.

As we introduced before, a spatial query p is first identified with several atomic spatial operations $\{q_1, ..., q_n\}$ within it, then based on the cost associated with each q, we decompose p into three categories, i.e., materialized view, preview and on-the-fly computation. The main objective of this technique is to optimize the space-time tradeoff when developing a set of views for materialization or pre-processing. This optimization problem is NP-complete, which is a straightforward reduction from Set-Cover (Gupta, H., & Mumick, I. 2005). Thus, we are motivated to look at heuristics to produce approximated solutions. The obvious choice of heuristic is a greedy algorithm, where we select a set of views for either materialization or building preview or performing on-the-fly computation that demonstrate to be the best choice based on what have been given so far. This approach is always fairly close to optimal and in some cases can be shown to produce the best possible selection of materialized views given an SDW.

We first define a *benefit function* to monitor the

cost savings for an SDW given an input query set Q. Let q be an arbitrary atomic operation decomposed from a spatial query, the benefit of q with respect to V/PV that is an already selected set of materialized views/previews, denoted as $B(q,V)/B(q,PV)$, is defined as: if $C(Q,V \cup q, PV) < C(Q,V,PV)$, then $B(q,V) = C(Q,V,PV) - C(Q,V \cup q,PV)$, otherwise $B(q,V) = 0$; or if $C(Q,V,PV \cup q) < C(Q,V,PV)$, then $B(q,PV)=C(Q,V,PV)-C(Q,V,PV \cup q)$, otherwise $B(q,PV) = 0$. Specifically, we assume all spatial queries will be computed on the fly at the beginning, then we compute the benefit of q by considering how it can reduce the total cost of a given SDW. For each q we choose to materialize or build preview, we compare the total cost of the SDW with the one before the transformation. If q helps, i.e., the current cost is less than before, then the difference represents the benefit of selecting q for materialization or for preview, otherwise, there is no benefit. Now we present the greedy decomposition algorithm as follows:

Algorithm 2: Greedy Query Decomposition Algorithm. The greedy query decomposition algorithm decomposes input queries and selects a set of q as either materialized views or previews, which minimizes the total cost of a spatial data warehouse.

```
Method:
1. V = ∅, PV = ∅
2. for each q in Q:
      if (P(q) × fr(q) / S(q)) ≥ θ
      if B(A,V) is maximized
            while S(Q,V,PV) ≤ LV =
V ∪ A
      end if
   end if
      if δ < (P(q) × fr(q) / S(q))
< θ
      if B(A,PV) is maximized
            while S(Q,V,PV) ≤ LPV =
PV ∪ q
      end if
   end if
   if (P(q) × fr(q) / S(q)) ≤ δ
      keep q in Q
```

```
   end if
end for
3. Materialize all q in V, and
build preview of all q in PV.
```

Essentially, in the beginning we assume all the queries in Q are computed on-the-fly. Step 2 computes the cost associated with each atomic operation in Q, and does categorization accordingly to maximize the benefit function. Specifically, if the cost is higher than the upper bound of the threshold, we materialize it; if the cost is between the upper bound and lower bound of the threshold, we build the preview of it; if the cost is less than the lower bound of the threshold, we keep it for on-the-fly computation. This spatial greedy algorithm is a cost driven technique deriving a sub-optimal solution for a given SDW because it commits to a local maximum cost benefit at each iteration of step 2, although not every locally maximum choice can guarantee the global maximality.

Next, we discuss how we actually evaluate a given spatial query in a spatial data warehouse by using previews. Having the decomposed parts of each input query, and their inter-dependent relationship with each other, now we come to the query evaluation part by taking all the decomposed parts of a spatial query to answer the query. The goal is to reduce the query response time as much as possible.

Let's revisit the motivating example. We build preview for q_1 and materialize q_4 to minimize the total cost and also get their dependency relationship by mapping to the UCL accordingly. In order to execute the query, we need to execute q_1 and retrieve the materialized q_4. However, we don't execute q_1 from the base tables, instead we look for its sub-views first at the lower level. In other word, if there is one materialized sub-view or preview that q_1 depends on, we can start from that view and perform one single aggregate function, denoted as f with associated cost as $c(f)$, which will obviously reduce the query processing time compared to aggregating from the scratch. We can recursively searching from the lower levels until we reach the lowest level that is the base tables stored in the data warehouse.

Given an instantiated UCL, now we formally present the query evaluation algorithm as follows.

Algorithm 3: Query Evaluation Algorithm. The query evaluation algorithm processes a spatial query p using its decomposed parts V, PV and Q, by considering the materialized views or previews of its lower levels first to reduce the query evaluation time.

```
Method:
1. for each q ∈ Q mapped to node u_i
   for i = (k-1) to 1
       if exist q' ∈ V or q' ∈ PV
that q depends on
                   q = f(q') such
that c(f) is minimized
       end if
   end for
end for
2. for each q ∈ PV with pre(q)
mapped to node u_i
   for i = (k-1) to 1
       if exist q' in V that q de-
pends on
                   q = f(q')
such that c(f) is minimized
       end if
   end for
end for
```

Generally, this algorithm executes a spatial query p by looking at all the decomposed atomic queries in Q, V and PV at certain dependency levels. For all q in V, we retrieve the materialized views directly from the memory. For a q in PV or Q, we search recursively for the views or previews associated with the lower dependency levels that q depends on, until we get to the lowest level where we have to start from the base tables. If we find some materialized views or previews in the middle, we start from there. This algorithm makes use of

the UCL to integrate the query dependency level into the query evaluation process to achieve the quick query response time.

7 IMPLEMENTATIONS AND SIMULATION STUDY

We have shown the cost savings by constructing the preview in the motivation example. In this section, we conduct the simulation study for a class of 1000 spatial queries with varied space consumption and online computational cost for each simple atomic spatial query within each query. Since the goal to build previews (PV) is to save the total cost of a spatial data warehouse, we are interested in knowing generally how much cost can be saved by comparing to other methods such as pure materialization (PM), pure on-the-fly (PO) computation and selective materialization (SM).

The comparison is performed in terms of the following factors: (1) the complexity of the input query set, and (2) the relative importance of the query on-the-fly computation cost and space cost, i.e., parameter λ and μ. The complexity of the query set is expressed by spatial selection/join operations with varied cost assumption for each operation within the input queries. In the following we describe the various experiments performed and show the results in figure 4.

Experiment 1: *the space cost varies*. We study the cost savings when the space cost varies for the spatial objects within the input queries. We consider that there is no space constraint, the number of spatial operations per query is constant, and the online computation cost for each spatial query is relatively small (50% of space cost) (Figure 4(a)).Experiment 2: *the online computation cost varies*. We study the cost savings when the online computation cost varies for the spatial operations within the input queries. We consider that the number of spatial operations per query is constant, and the space cost of input queries is

Figure 4. Experimental Results of Cost Savings for Previews (a) total cost vs. space cost; (b) total cost vs. online computation cost; (c): total cost vs. product of space cost × online computational cost, (d): total cost vs. parameter λ; (e) total cost vs. parameter μ

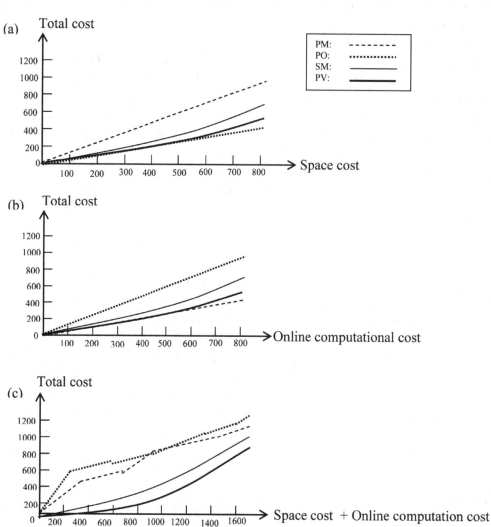

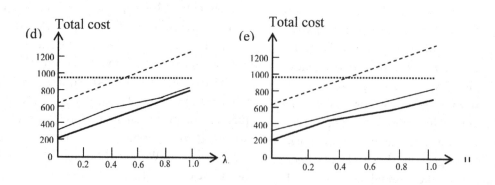

relatively small (50% of online computation cost). (Figure 4(b)). Experiment 3: *both the space cost and the online computation cost vary*. We study the cost savings when the space cost and the online computation cost vary for the spatial operations within the input queries. For simplicity, we use the varied sum of the space cost and online computation cost of input queries, with randomly assigned space cost and online computation cost for each atomic spatial query. We consider that there is no space constraint. (Figure 4(c)). Experiment 4: *parameter λ and μ vary*. We ran the algorithm 2 (the greedy query decomposition algorithm) for a set of queries with varied λ and μ. We consider the query set is given with randomly assigned space cost and online computational cost for each atomic spatial query, and there is no space constraint (Figure 4(d) and 4(e)).

From all the experiments (a, b, c, d, e), we could conclude that building previews within spatial queries wins in case (c, d, e), which maximizes the cost savings for a spatial data warehouse in a general case. However, in case (a, b), it is not a winner because those are two extreme cases and two extreme solutions win. Specifically, in case (b), the space cost counts 2/3 of the total cost hence the PO method wins; in case (c), the online computational cost counts 2/3 of the total cost hence the PM method wins. In other words, preview provides an optimal solution in terms of the cost benefit in a spatial data warehouse, where the space cost and the online computational cost are statistically equal. Note here we consider the space cost of a preview is very small compared to that of storing spatial objects.

8 RELATED WORKS

A lot of work has been done in the area of optimizing cost of a data warehouse. As we discussed before, most of their work deal with selective materialization to reduce the total cost. In the initial research done on the view selection problem,

Harinarayan et al. in (Harinarayan, V., Rajaraman, A., & Ulman, J. 1996) present algorithms for the view-selection problem in data cubes under a disk-space constraint. Gupta et al. extend their work to include indexes in (Gupta, H., & Mumick, I. 2005). Stefanovic et al. in (Stefanovic, N., Han, J., & Koperski, K. 2000) introduce the spatial data warehouse concept and object based selective materialization techniques for construction of spatial data cubes. There have also some negative theoretical results on the problem of selection of views. In particular, Karlo et al. (Karlo, H., & Mihail, M. 1999) show that the variation of the view-selection problem where the goal is to optimize the query cost is inapproximable for general partial orders. Furthermore, Chirkova et al. in (Chirkova, R. 2002; Chirkova, R., Halevy, A., & Suciu D. 2001) show that the number of views involved in an optimal solution for the view-selection problem may be exponential in the size of the database schema, when the query optimizer has good estimates of the sizes of the views.

Besides the theoretical research, there has been a substantial amount of effort (Yang, J., Karlapalem, K., & Li, Q. 1997; Yu, S., Atluri, V., & Adam, N. 2005) on developing heuristics for the view-selection problem that may work well in practice. Most of the work done in this context has developed various frameworks and heuristics for selection of views in order to optimize the query response time and/or view maintenance time with or without a resource constraint. The heuristics developed are either exhaustive searches or do not have any performance guarantees on the quality of the solution delivered. In the similar vein, Kalnis et al. in (Kalnis, P., Mamoulis, N., & Papadias, D. 2002) show that randomized search methods provide near-optimal solutions and can easily be adapted to various versions of the problem, including existence of size and time constraints. Recently, certain works have been done on how to materialize views for some specific systems or to answer queries more efficiently. Specifically, Karenos et al in (Karenos, K., Samaras,

G., Chrysanthis, P., & Pitoura, E. 2004) propose view materialization techniques to deal with mobile computing services, Liu et al in (Liu, Z., Chrysanthis, P., & Tsui, F. 2004) compare two view materialization approaches for medical data to improve query efficiency, Theodoratos et al in (Theodoratos, d., Ligoudistianos, S., & Sellis, T. 2001) build a search space for view selections to deal with evolving data warehousing systems, and Wu et al in (Wu, W., & Ozsoyoglu, Z. 2005) work on Web data to rewrite queries using materialized views.

However, all of their methods fall into two categories, i.e. either materialize a view or compute it on the fly. Our work presented in this chapter differs from the above works in that given the specialty of spatial operations involved in a query, we design a third technique, *preview*, between view materialization and on-the-fly computation, which delivers a provably good solution with cost minimization for a spatial query and eventually a whole spatial data warehouse. We also show that previews demonstrate the hierarchical relationship with each other so that a query can be efficiently processed to use existing views and reduce the query response time.

9 CONCLUSION

A spatial data warehouse integrates alphanumeric data and spatial data from multiple distributed information sources. Compared to a traditional one, a spatial data warehouse has a distinguished feature in that both the view materialization cost as well as the on-the-fly computation cost are extremely high, which is due to the fact that spatial data are larger in size and spatial operations are more expensive to process. Therefore, the traditional way of selectively materializing certain views while computing others on the fly does not solve the problem of spatial views.

In this chapter we have dealt with the issue of minimizing the total cost of a spatial data ware-

house while at the same time improve the query response time by considering their inter-dependent relationships. We first use a motivation example in realistic query scenarios to demonstrate the cost savings of building a preview. We then formally define preview, for which both the materialization and on-the-fly costs are significantly smaller than those of the traditional views. Specifically, a preview pre-processes the non-spatial part of the query, leaves the spatial operation on the fly, and maintains pointers to the spatial data. In addition, we show that a preview exploits the hierarchical relationships among the different views by maintaining a Universal Composite Lattice built on dimension hierarchies, and mapping each view onto it. We present a cost model with associated greedy algorithms to optimally decompose a spatial query into three components, the preview part, the materialized view part and the on-the-fly computation part, so that the total cost is minimized and the query can be efficiently evaluated from the dependent views. We finally conduct simulation analysis to see how preview optimizes the materialization cost of a spatial data warehouse.

REFERENCES

Chirkova, R. (2002). The view selection problem has an exponential bound for conjunctive queries and views. In *Proceedings of the ACM Symposium on Principles of Database Systems 2002*.

Chirkova, R., Halevy, A., & Suciu, D. (2001). A formal perspective on the view selection problem. In *Proceedings of the International Conference on Very Large Database Systems 2001*.

Gupta, H., & Mumick, I. (2005). Selection of views to materialize in a data warehouse. [TKDE]. *Transactions of Knowledge and Data Engineering, 17*(1), 24–43. doi:10.1109/TKDE.2005.16

Han, J., & Kamber, M. (2001). *Data mining: Concepts and techniques.* San Francisco: Morgan Kaufman Publishers.

Harinarayan, V., Rajaraman, A., & Ulman, J. (1996). Implementing data cubes efficiently. In *Proceedings of SIGMOD 1996.*

Kalnis, P., Mamoulis, N., & Papadias, D. (2002). View selection using randomized search. *Data & Knowledge Engineering, 42*(1). doi:10.1016/S0169-023X(02)00045-9

Karenos, K., Samaras, G., Chrysanthis, P., & Pitoura, E. (2004). Mobile agent-based services for view materialization. *ACM SIGMOBILE Mobile Computing and Communications Review, 8*(3).

Karlo, H., & Mihail, M. (1999). On the complexity of the view-selection problem. In *Proceeding of PODS 1999.*

Liu, Z., Chrysanthis, P., & Tsui, F. (2004). A comparison of two view materialization approaches for disease surveillance system. In *Proceedings of SAC 2004.*

Stefanovic, N., Han, J., & Koperski, K. (2000). Object-based selective materialization for efficient implementation of spatial data cubes. *IEEE Transactions on Knowledge and Data Engineering, 12*(6). doi:10.1109/69.895803

Theodoratos, D., Ligoudistianos, S., & Sellis, T. (2001). View selection for designing the global data warehouse. *Data & Knowledge Engineering, 11*(39).

Theodoratos, D., & Sellis, T. (1999). Dynamic data warehouse design. In *Proceedings of DaWaK 1999.*

Theodoratos, D., & Xu, W. (2004). Constructing search spaces for materialized view selection. In *Proceedings of the 7th ACM international workshop on Data warehousing and OLAP 2004.*

Wu, W., & Ozsoyoglu, Z. (2005). Rewriting XPath queries using materialized views. In *Proceedings of VLDB 2005.*

Yang, J., Karlapalem, K., & Li, Q. (1997). Algorithms for materialized view design in data warehousing environment. In *Proceedings of the Intl. Conference on Very Large Database Systems 1997.*

Yu, S., Atluri, V., & Adam, N. (2005). Selective view materialization in a spatial data warehouse. In *Proceedings of Data Warehouse and Knowledge Discovery (DaWak 2005).*

Section 2
Multidimensional Data
and OLAP

Chapter 4
Decisional Annotations
Integrating and Preserving Decision-Makers' Expertise in Multidimensional Systems

Guillaume Cabanac
Université de Toulouse, France

Max Chevalier
Université de Toulouse, France

Franck Ravat
Université de Toulouse, France

Olivier Teste
Université de Toulouse, France

ABSTRACT

This chapter deals with an annotation-based decisional system. The decisional system the authors present is based on multidimensional databases, which are composed of facts and dimensions. The expertise of decision-makers is modeled, shared and stored through annotations. These annotations allow decision-makers to carry on active analysis and to collaborate with other decision-makers on a common analysis.

INTRODUCTION

Multidimensional data analysis consists in manipulations through aggregations of data drawn from various transactional databases. This approach is often based on *multidimensional databases* (MDB). MDB schemas are composed of facts (subjects of analysis) and dimensions (axes of analysis) (Ravat

DOI: 10.4018/978-1-60566-748-5.ch004

et al., 2008). Decision-making consists in analysing these multidimensional data. Nevertheless, due to its numeric nature it is difficult to interpret business data. This work requires decision-makers to achieve a tedious cognitive effort, which is an *immaterial capital*. To take relevant decisions this required expertise is very valuable but it cannot be expressed, stored, and exploited in traditional multidimensional systems. Such an expertise can be qualified as ephemeral from the organization

Copyright © 2010, IGI Global. Copying or distributing in print or electronic forms without written permission of IGI Global is prohibited.

standpoint.

As paper annotations convey information between readers (Marshall, 1998), we argue that *annotations* can also support this immaterial capital for MDB. We consider an annotation as a high value-added component of MDB from the users' standpoint. Such components can be used for a *personal use* to remind any information concerning the data under study, as well as for a *collective use* to share information that makes complex analyses easier. This collective use of annotations would serve as a basis for building an expertise memory that stores previous decisions and commentaries. Moreover as Foshay et al. (2007) state "Metadata helps data warehouse end users to understand the various types of information resources available from a data warehouse/business intelligence environment." As a consequence, in our proposition, annotations and their contents enable end users to analyse, discuss and share knowledge in context during the decision making process.

This chapter addresses the problem of integrating the annotation concept into MDB management systems. Annotations are designed to assist decision-makers and to turn their expertise persistent and reusable.

Related works and discussion. To the best of our knowledge, integrating annotations in the MDB context has not been studied yet. The closest works are related to annotation integration in Relational DataBase Management Systems (RDBMS). First, in the DBNotes system (Bhagwat et al. 2004, 2005; Chiticariu et al., 2005; Tan, 2003) zero or several annotations are associated with a relation element. Annotations are transparently propagated along as data is being transformed (through SQL queries). This annotation system traces the origin and the flow of data. Second, the authors in (Cong et al., 2006) and (Geerts et al., 2006) specify an annotation-oriented data model for the manipulation and the search of both data and annotations. This model is based on the concept of block to annotate both a single value and a set of values. A prototype, called MONDRIAN,

supports this annotation model. Third, similar to the previous systems, the works presented in (Bhatnagar et al., 2007a) and (Bhatnagar et al., 2007b) consist in annotating relational data. DBNotes and MONDRIAN use relational data to express annotations whereas this last work models annotations using eXtensible Markup Language (XML). The model allows users to cross-reference related annotations.

As conceptual structures of a MDB are semantically richer, the outlined works cannot be directly applied to our context.

- Contrary to RDBMS where a unique data structure is used to both store and display data, in our MDB context, the storage structures are more complex and a specific display is required.
- In the RDBMS framework, annotations are straightforwardly attached to tuples or cell values (Bhagwat et al., 2004). Due to the MDB structures, annotations must be attached to more complex data; *e.g.* dimension attributes are organised according to hierarchies and displayed decisional data are often computed from aggregations.

To annotate a MDB we define a specific model having the following properties:

- An annotation is characterised by a type, an author, and a creation date.
- Each annotation is associated with an anchor, which is based on a path expression tying the annotations to the MDB components (structure or value). Thanks to this anchor, annotations can be associated with different data granularities.
- Annotations can spark off debates called "discussion threads," which enables asynchronous communication during collaborative work.
- To facilitate user interactions, annotations are defined and displayed through a

conceptual view of the MDB where they are transparently propagated and stored into R-OLAP structures.

Chapter outline. Section 2 extends the conceptual multidimensional model defined in (Ravat et al., 2008) for integrating annotations. Section 3 describes the R-OLAP implementation of an annotated MDB. Section 4 presents a system for managing annotations on a MDB.

AN ANNOTATION-FEATURED MULTIDIMENSIONAL MODEL

In this section, we describe the multidimensional model concepts. First, we define basic concepts like fact, dimension, hierarchy and constellation. The conceptual model we define is close to the user's standpoint and independent of implementation choices. This model intends to facilitate correlations between several subjects of analysis through a constellation of facts and dimensions, and it supports several data granularities according to which subjects may be analyzed. Second, we extend the model by integrating annotations. Annotations are used both to comment multidimensional data and to share various user standpoints during the analysis processes.

MULTIDIMENSIONAL CONCEPTS

Concept of Constellation.

The conceptual model we define represents data as a constellation (Kimball, 1996) gathering several subjects of analysis (facts), which are studied according to several axes of analysis (dimensions).

Definition. A constellation C is defined as $(N^C, F^C, D^C, Star^C, Annotate^C)$ where

- N^C is the constellation name,

- F^C is a set of facts,
- D^C is a set of dimensions,
- $Star^C$: $F^C \rightarrow 2^{DC}$ associates each fact to its linked dimensions,
- $Annotate^C$ is a set of *global annotations* of the constellation elements (see section 3).

Example. The case study is a business example. The multidimensional database supports the analysis of sales through quantities and amounts of products sold to a customer at a specific date. The constellation is composed of three dimensions named *time*, *customer*, and *product*, and an unique fact named *order*; i.e. the constellation is formally defined by ("SALES", $\{F^{ORDER}\}$, $\{D^{TIME}, D^{PRODUCT}, D^{CUSTOMER}\}$, $Star^{SALES}$, $Annotate^{SALES}$) where $Star^{SALES}(F^{ORDER}) = \{D^{TIME}, D^{PRODUCT}, D^{CUSTOMER}\}$.

Concept of Dimension and Hierarchy.

A dimension reflects information according to which subjects will be analysed. A dimension is composed of parameters organised through one or several hierarchies.

Definition. A dimension D_i is defined by $(N^{Di}, A^{Di}, H^{Di}, Ext^{Di})$ where

- N^{Di} is the dimension name,
- $A^{Di} = \{a_1, ..., a_q, All\}$ is a set of dimension attributes,
- $H^{Di} = \{H^{Di}_1, ..., H^{Di}_w\}$ is a set of hierarchies,
- $Ext^{Di} = \{i^{Di}_1, ..., i^{Di}_Y\}$ is a set of dimension instances.

Example. The dimension $D^{PRODUCT}$ is defined by ("D_PRODUCT", {IdP, Product_Desc, Brand_Desc, Category_Name, Sector_Name, All}, $\{H^{Brand}, H^{Sector}\}$, $Ext^{DProduct}$).

The dimension $D^{CUSTOMER}$ is defined by ("D_CUSTOMER", {IdC, Firstname, Lastname, City, Country, All}, $\{H^{Country}\}$, $Ext^{DCustomer}$). The

Table 1. Some dimension instances of ExtDCustomer.

IdC	Firstname	Lastname	City	Country	All
$i^{\text{DCUSTOMER}}_1$	Pierre	Dupond	Paris	France	All
$i^{\text{DCUSTOMER}}_2$	Paul	Durand	Paris	France	All
$i^{\text{DCUSTOMER}}_3$	Jean	Martin	Toulouse	France	All
$i^{\text{DCUSTOMER}}_4$	Marie	Martin	Toulouse	France	All
$i^{\text{DCUSTOMER}}_5$	John	Smith	London	United Kingdom	All

following table (Table 1) gives some dimension instances.

Analysis axes are dimensions seen through a particular perspective, namely a hierarchy. This hierarchy of dimension attributes organises the different graduations of the analysis axis.

Definition. A hierarchy $H^{Di}j$ is defined by $(N^{HDi}_j, P^{HDi}_j, WA^{HDi}_j)$ where

- N^{HDi}_j is the hierarchy name,
- $P^{HDi}_j = <Id, p_1,..., p_s, All>$ is an ordered set of dimension attributes, called parameters, $\forall k \in [1..s]$, $p_k \in A^{Di}$. Each parameter specifies a granularity level of the analysis.
- The $WA^{HDi}_j: P^{HDi}_j \rightarrow 2^{ADi}$ function associates each parameter to a set of *weak attributes* for adding semantic information to the parameter.

Entire hierarchies in one dimension start with a same parameter, noted Id called root parameter. Entire hierarchies end with a same parameter, noted All called extremity parameter.

Example. The dimension $D^{PRODUCT}$ is composed of two hierarchies, which are defined as ("H_Brand", <IdP, Brand_Desc, All>, $WA^{HBrand}(IdP) = \{Product\_Desc\}$) and ("H_Sector", <IdP, Category_Name, Sector_Name, All>, $WA^{HSector}(IdP) = \{Product\_Desc\}$).

Concept of Fact

A fact regroups indicators called measures that have to be analysed.

Definition. A fact F_i is defined by $(N^{Fi}, M^{Fi}, Ext^{Fi}, IStar^{Fi})$ where

- N^{Fi} is the fact name,
- $M^{Fi} = \{f_1(m_1),..., f_p(m_p)\}$ is a set of measures $m_1,..., m_p$ associated with aggregation functions $f_1,..., f_p$,
- $Ext^{Fi} = \{i^{Fi}_1,..., i^{Fi}_x\}$ is a set of fact instances.
- $IStar^{Fi}: Ext^{Fi} \rightarrow Ext^{Star(Fi)}$ associates each fact instance to its linked dimension instances.

Example. The fact F^{ORDER} is defined by ("F_ORDER", {SUM(Quantity), SUM(Amount)}, Ext^{FOrder}, $IStar^{FOrder}$). Table 2 gives some fact instances. Note that these instances refer to six products, three dates and the four customer instances, which are defined in the above section. More precisely:

- i^{DTIME}_1 refers to a date in April, 2007,
- i^{DTIME}_2 refers to a date in May, 2007,
- i^{DTIME}_3 refers to a date in June, 2007.

GRAPHICAL NOTATIONS

We introduce graphical notations to design multidimensional databases. These notations extend the notations introduced in (Golfarelli et al., 1998). Figure 1 describes graphical notations of facts and dimensions with their hierarchies.

Example. Figure 2 shows the multidimensional schema of the previous examples. The illustrated constellation schema is composed of one fact

Table 2. Some fact instances of Ext^{FOrder}

IdC	IdT	IdP	Quantity	Amount
$i^{DCUSTOMER}_{1}$	i^{DTIME}_{1}	$i^{DPRODUCT}_{1}$	5	5000
$i^{DCUSTOMER}_{1}$	i^{DTIME}_{1}	$i^{DPRODUCT}_{2}$	3	697
$i^{DCUSTOMER}_{2}$	i^{DTIME}_{1}	$i^{DPRODUCT}_{1}$	5	5000
$i^{DCUSTOMER}_{1}$	i^{DTIME}_{2}	$i^{DPRODUCT}_{1}$	2	2000
$i^{DCUSTOMER}_{2}$	i^{DTIME}_{2}	$i^{DPRODUCT}_{3}$	1	100
$i^{DCUSTOMER}_{2}$	i^{DTIME}_{3}	$i^{DPRODUCT}_{4}$	1	3868
$i^{DCUSTOMER}_{3}$	i^{DTIME}_{1}	$i^{DPRODUCT}_{1}$	2	2000
$i^{DCUSTOMER}_{4}$	i^{DTIME}_{1}	$i^{DPRODUCT}_{5}$	1	693
$i^{DCUSTOMER}_{4}$	i^{DTIME}_{2}	$i^{DPRODUCT}_{4}$	1	3868
$i^{DCUSTOMER}_{3}$	i^{DTIME}_{3}	$i^{DPRODUCT}_{1}$	4	4000
$i^{DCUSTOMER}_{4}$	i^{DTIME}_{3}	$i^{DPRODUCT}_{6}$	1	293

Figure 1. Graphical notations of multidimensional concepts

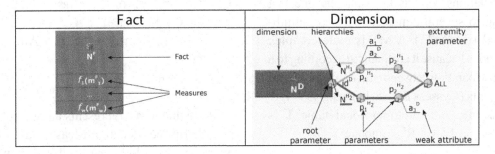

named F_ORDER and three dimensions respectively named D_PRODUCT, D_CUSTOMER and D_TIME. This constellation supports analyses of sales through quantities and amounts of products sold to customers at several dates.

The dimension attributes are organised according to one or several hierarchies; i.e. each path starting from Id and ending by All represents a hierarchy. Note that the extremity parameter (All) is not displayed in the graphical representation as this parameter tends to confuse users (Malinowsky & Zimányi, 2006).

Figure 2. Example of constellation schema

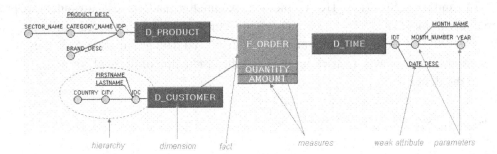

Figure 3. Example of MT. © 2009 Guillaume Cabanac, Max Chevalier, Franck Ravat, and Olivier Teste. Used with permission.

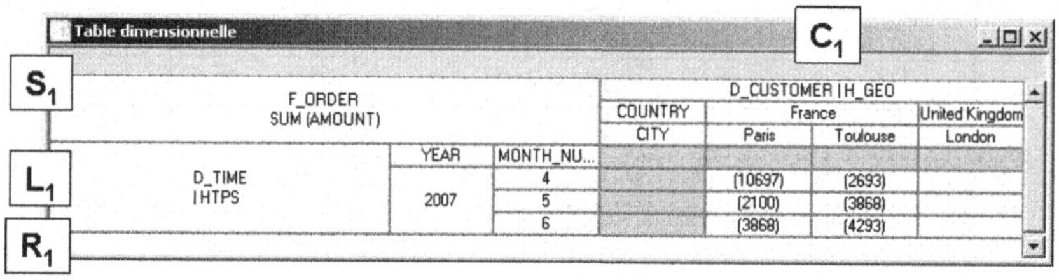

MULTIDIMENSIONAL TABLE

Constellation schemas depict MDB structures whereas user analyses are based on tabular representations (Gyssens & Lakshmanan, 1997) where structures and data are displayed. The visualisation of constellations consists in displaying one fact according to several dimensions into a multidimensional table (MT). A MT is more complex than relations because it is organised according to a non-clear separation between structural aspects and data contents (Gyssens & Lakshmanan, 1997).

Definition. A multidimensional table T is defined as $(S^T, L^T, C^T, R^T, \text{Annotate}^T)$

- $S^T = (F^T, \{f_1(m_1), \ldots, f_p(m_p)\})$ is the subject of analysis, which is represented by a fact and its displayed measures $f_1(m_1), \ldots, f_p(m_p)$,
- $L^T = (DL, HL, PL)$ is the horizontal analysis axis where $PL=<p^{HL}_{max}, \ldots, p^{HL}_{min}>$ are displayed parameters of $DL \in \text{Star}^C(F)$ and $HL \in H^{DL}$ is the *current hierarchy*,
- $C^T = (DC, HC, PC>)$ is the vertical analysis axis where $PC=<p^{HC}_{max}, \ldots, p^{HC}_{min}>$, $HC \in H^{DC}$ and $DC \in \text{Star}^C(F^T)$, HC is the *current hierarchy* of DC,
- $R^T = \text{pred}_1 \wedge \ldots \wedge \text{pred}_s$ is a normalised conjunction of predicates restricting the scope of the dimensions.
- Annotate^T is a set of *local annotations* of the MT elements (see the following section).

Example. Figure 3 depicts an example of MT that displays amount orders according to the temporal axis and the customer axis. $T_1 = (S_1, L_1, C_1, R_1, \varnothing)$ with

- $S_1 = (\text{F\_ORDER}, \{\text{SUM}(\text{Amount})\})$,
- $L_1 = (\text{D\_TIME}, \text{HTPS}, <\text{All}, \text{YEAR}, \text{MONTH\_NUMBER}>)$,
- $C_1 = (\text{D\_CUSTOMER}, \text{HGEO}, <\text{All}, \text{COUNTRY}, \text{CITY}>)$,
- $R_1 = \text{true}$.

Note that a MT represents an excerpt of data recorded in a constellation. Measures are displayed according to a bidimensional space, which is defined through two dimensions.

Example. Figure 4 shows the previous MT and the corresponding constellation elements from which the MT is extracted. S_1 is extracted from the fact named F_ORDER ($F^{ORDER} \in F^C$) whereas L_1 and C_1 are derived from two linked dimensions of F^T ($D^{TIME} \in \text{Star}^C(F^{ORDER})$ and $D^{CUSTOMER} \in \text{Star}^C(F^{ORDER})$). Along each current dimension, a current hierarchy is fixed ($H^{TPS} \in H^{TIME}$ and $H^{GEO} \in H^{CUSTOMER}$) according to which some parameters (and/or weak attributes) are projected in the MT. These projected attributes fixed the displayed data granularities; *i.e.* they represents the graduation of the analysis axes.

Figure 4. Example of MT. © 2009 Guillaume Cabanac, Max Chevalier, Franck Ravat, and Olivier Teste. Used with permission.

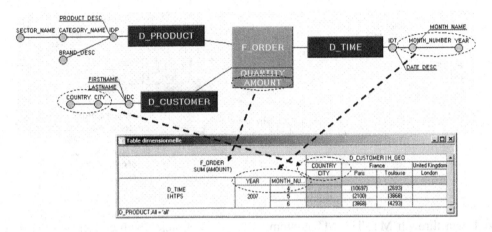

AN INTEGRATED ANNOTATION MODEL

In order to annotate a MDB, we provide a specific annotation model that is incorporated into the multidimensional model. As for paper-based and digital document annotations (Cabanac et al., 2007), a MDB annotation is twofold; it consists in:

- *subjective* information that corresponds to its content (e.g. a text typed in by decision-makers) and at least one "annotation type" to understand its content easier, i.e. without having to read its content. We define some basic types (a comment, a question, an answer to an existing annotation, a conclusion…) which can be extended with domain-specific types.
- *objective* data (also called meta-data) that correspond to the annotation unique identifier, its creation date, its creator identifier, a link to the parent annotation (when answering to another annotation) and an anchor to annotated data.

The system automatically generates the set of objective data whereas the annotation creator formulates the set of subjective data.

The proposed annotation model is collaboration-oriented. It provides functionalities that allow users/designers to share information that is relevant to analyses/designs and to discuss and debate directly in the context of any MT through discussion threads (thanks to the link to the parent annotation). Figure 5 shows an example of such discussion between two analysts (users). Annotations and discussions/debates may concern a single analysis or may be more general as they concern every analysis containing the annotated elements. In addition annotating schema elements enables designers and users to share comments, in order to improve their understanding of the annotated elements. Thus, in our approach we define an annotation at two levels:

- A *local* annotation is **only** displayed in a specific context corresponding to a specific MT.
- A *global* annotation is shown in **any** MT displaying the globally annotated element(s).

As a result various global and local annotations can be associated with a unique element according to the annotator's need.

During an analysis, decision makers visualize

Figure 5. Example of a real-life discussion (thread) in the context of a MT. © 2009 Guillaume Cabanac, Max Chevalier, Franck Ravat, and Olivier Teste. Used with permission.

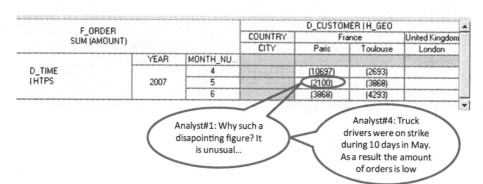

synthesized data through MT. The MT content can be modified by the use of commands associated with a related algebra (Ravat et al., 2008). Annotations should follow these changes. As a consequence annotation anchors cannot be specified with a coordinate-based system. That is why we define a unique anchoring notation. This later relies on a path-like notation that allows the anchoring of any annotation to any element displayed in a MT or existing in a constellation. Moreover, the proposed anchoring notation takes into account local and global levels associated with annotations.

In the following definitions, λ denotes the empty path. Let us consider *CONS* as a constellation, *MT* as a multidimensional table, *Fact* as a fact, *measure* as a measure, *f(m)* as an aggregation function applied to a measure *m*, *val* as a specific measure value, *Dim* as a dimension, *Hier* as a hierarchy, *param* as a dimension attribute (parameter or weak attribute) and *valueP* as a value of a dimension attribute.

Definition. An anchor is defined as (S, D_1, D_2) where[1]:

- S = λ | [CONS | MT][.Fact "(" (/measure | /f(m) ")" [=val])*] denotes a path to any fact or measure used in a constellation or in a MT.
- D_1 = λ | Dim[.Hier(/param[=valueP])*]

denotes a path concerning the first dimension of the MT.
- D_2 = λ | Dim[.Hier(/param[=valueP])*] denotes a path concerning the second dimension of the MT.

If the two dimensions D_1 and D_2 are given, the system is able to identify a specific cell in the MT. Thanks to this anchoring notation and to the different combinations of values that it allows, annotations can be easily stored in the MDB, retrieved, and displayed in a specific MT for instance.

Example. In Figure 6, two users annotate elements related to the constellation C1 and elements displayed in the multidimensional table MT1. User U1 creates the annotations A7, A8, A9, and A10. The annotation A9 is a question that corresponds to the root of a discussion thread. User U2 creates the annotations from A1 to A6. He also answers A9 through the A11 annotation. Figure 6 only shows elements concerned by every annotation: it does not show the way annotations are displayed in the MT.

The anchor for each annotation is:

- *A1*: (λ,D_CUSTOMER,λ) or (λ,λ,D_CUSTOMER) which are equivalent paths[2]. This anchor implies that the annotation concerns the D_CUSTOMER dimension in any

Figure 6. Example of annotations on a MT as well as on the MDB schema. © 2009 Guillaume Cabanac, Max Chevalier, Franck Ravat, and Olivier Teste. Used with permission.

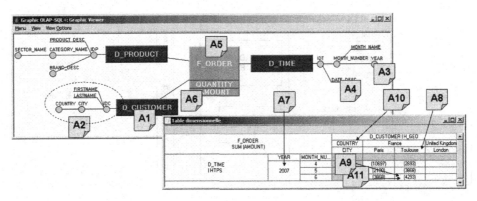

constellation associated with this dimension. The annotation will be displayed every time D_CUSTOMER is used. To limit the scope of this annotation and to display it only when the constellation C1 and the F_ORDER fact are used together for instance, one has to transform the anchor into (C1.F_ORDER,D_CUSTOMER,λ) or (C1.F_ORDER,λ,D_CUSTOMER).

- **A2**: (λ,D_CUSTOMER.HGEO,λ).
- **A3**: (λ,D_TIME.HTPS/YEAR,λ).
- **A4**: (λ,D_TIME.HTPS/IDT/DATE_DESC,λ).
- **A5**: (C1.F_ORDER,λ,λ). This annotation will only be displayed when the fact F_ORDER is associated with the constellation C1.
- **A6**: (C1.F_ORDER/AMOUNT,λ,λ).Previous anchor paths refer to global annotations since they do not contain any element specific to any MT. These annotations will be displayed every time annotated elements are used. If needed, we can limit the scope to a specific MT (local annotation) of the annotation A5 for instance by transforming its anchoring path into (MT1.F_ORDER,λ,λ). This means that this annotation will only be displayed in MT1. Most of the following annotations are local ones.
- **A7**: (MT1, D_TIME.HTPS/YEAR='2007',λ).
- **A8**: (MT1, D_CUSTOMER.HGEO/ COUNTRY='France'/CITY='Toulouse',λ).

- **A9**: (MT1.F_ORDER/SUM(AMOUNT),D_TIME. HTPS/YEAR='2007'/MONTH_NUMBER='6',D_ CUSTOMER.HGEO/COUNTRY='France'/ CITY='Toulouse'). This latter anchoring path refers to the potentially evolving measure value contained in the specified MT1 cell. To annotate the specific value of this measure one have to include it into the anchoring path: (MT1.F_OR-DER/SUM(AMOUNT)='4293', D_TIME.HTPS/ YEAR='2007'/MONTH_NUMBER='6',D_ CUSTOMER.HGEO/COUNTRY='France'/ CITY='Toulouse'). This means that the corresponding annotation will only be displayed if this value is unchanged.
- **A10**: (MT1, D_CUSTOMER.HGEO/COUNTRY, λ).
- **A11**: The anchoring path of A11 is identical to A9, only its content is different. The link between A9 and A11 is stored as an objective meta-data in A11.

The anchoring path we propose is suitable to express any kind of annotation that users may link to any multidimensional element (schema, multidimensional table). Even if the notation used complies with the EBNF notation, concretely users may not express themselves such anchoring paths. On the contrary, this anchoring path is automatically generated by the system according

Figure 7. Threefold annotation management system for MDB s architecture. © 2009 Guillaume Cabanac,Max Chevalier, Franck Ravat, and Olivier Teste. Used with permission.

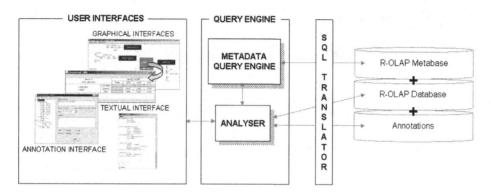

to the elements selected by the user.

R-OLAP IMPLEMENTATION

In order to validate the solution that we presented in this chapter, we developed an annotated multidimensional management system. As mentioned in Figure 7, the architecture of our annotation management system is composed of three main modules:

- The display interfaces (GUI) enable decision-makers (1) to annotate the constellation schema and the MT via global and local annotations, and (2) to display analyses through annotated MT.
- The query engine translates user interactions into SQL queries. Correctness of query expressions is validated through meta-data. These SQL queries are sent to the databases; results are sent back to the GUI.
- The R-OLAP data warehouse is an RDBMS storing multidimensional data, meta-data and annotations.

METABASE STRUCTURE

Constellations are implemented in an R-OLAP context. To store the multidimensional structures, we have defined meta-tables that describe the constellation (META_FACT, META_DIMENSION, META_HIERARCHY…). For example, Figure 8 describes the constellation structure illustrated in Figure 1; this example presents metatables of one constellation.

SNOWFLAKE DATABASE

An important challenge for storing annotations is the implementation of anchors. To associate each annotation with a unique row in the R-OLAP database, we opted for a snowflake data schema (Kimball, 1996). It consists in normalising dimensions according to hierarchies so as to eliminate redundancy; the annotation anchors point towards a unique data.

Example. Figure 9 shows the R-OLAP implementation of the constellation illustrated in Figure 1 according to a snowflake modelling.

Note that these tables of the snowflake schema must be completed with pre-aggregated tables for improving query performances. Moreover, as argued in (Bhagwat et al., 2004), adding and propagating annotations in RDBMS must drop

Figure 8. Metabase for storing a constellation

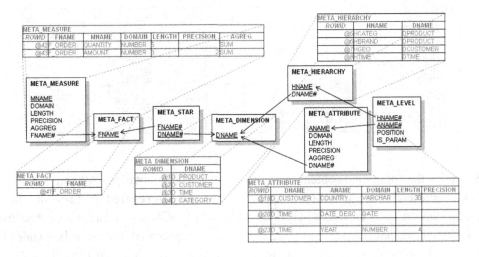

performances down. Their experimental results show that for large databases (500MB and 1GB), the queries integrating annotations took only about 18% more time to execute than their corresponding SQL queries.

ANNOTATION STORAGE

We provide a mechanism for storing global and local annotations into the same structure. The main problem consists in implementing the formal anchoring notation while providing a homogeneous way of managing the annotations that may be anchored to detailed data, aggregated data or meta-data.

Our solution consists in storing annotations into a single table whose schema is composed of the following columns:

- PK is the annotation identifier,
- NTABLE is the table or a meta-table where the annotated data is stored,
- ROWID is an internal row identifier used in the database system related to the annotated data of the NTABLE,
- COL stores the attribute name of annotated data. If the annotation is anchored to the multidimensional structure, it is anchored to a row in a meta-table (COL is null) whereas if the annotation is associated with a value, COL is valued.

Figure 9. R-OLAP snowflake schema

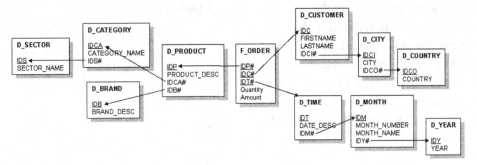

Figure 10. Storage of the annotations

PK	NTABLE	ROWID	COL	DESC	LOCAL	TYPE	DATE	PARENT	AUTHOR
	ANNOTATION								
1	META_DIMENSION	@2		A1		Comment	02/04/2007		U2
2	META_HIERARCHY	@7		A2		Comment	02/04/2007		U2
3	META_ATTRIBUTE	@23		A3		Comment	02/04/2007		U2
4	META_ATTRIBUTE	@20		A4		Comment	02/04/2007		U2
5	META_FACT	@41		A5		Comment	02/04/2007		U2
6	META_MEASURE	@43		A6		Comment	02/04/2007		U2
7	D_YEAR	@100	YEAR	A7		Comment	02/04/2007		U1
8	D_CITY	@101	CITY	A8	V1	Question	02/04/2007		U1
9	MV1	@200	AMOUNT	A9	V1	Comment	02/04/2007		U1
10	META_ATTRIBUTE	@18		A10	V1	Comment	02/04/2007		U1
11	MV1	@200	AMOUNT	A11	V1	Answer	03/04/2007	9	U2

- DESC stores the annotation content.
- LOCAL represents the annotation scope. When the annotation is local to a MT, then this attribute is valued.
- TYPE describes the annotation type (comment, question, answer...).
- DATE stores the creation date of the annotation.
- PARENT represents a relationship between annotations. This attribute is used to keep the discussion thread structure (for example, an answer following a question).
- AUTHOR is the author of the annotation.

Example. The following table (Figure 10) stores annotations defined in section 2.2.

These annotations are anchored to three levels.

- Annotations A1 to A6 as well as A10 are associated with the **meta-data tables**; *e.g.* A1, stored in the 1st row and conceptually noted (λ, D_CUSTOMER,λ), is anchored to the row identified by @2 into the META_DIMENSION table.
- The global annotation A7 and the local annotation A8 are anchored to **detailed values** (of parameters). The attributes named ROW and COL are used to locate these annotated data. In Figure 8 we assume that D_YEAR and D_CITY contain respectively the rows [@100, y1, 2007] and [@101, ci1, Toulouse, co1].

- The annotations A9 and A11 are anchored to **aggregated values** of the measure AMOUNT. In order to define the anchor, aggregated data must be materialised. The MT is calculated from the following SQL query, noted V1:

```
SELECT year, month_
number,country,city,SUM(amount)
AS amount
FROM F_ORDER or,D_CUSTOMER cu,D_CITY
ci,D_COUNTRY co,D_TIME ti,D_MONTH
mo,D_YEAR ye
WHERE or.idc=cu.idc AND
cu.idci=ci.idci AND ci.idco=co.
idco
    AND or.idt=ti.idt AND
ti.idm=mo.idm AND mo.idy=ye.idy
GROUP BY year,month_
number,country,city;
```

To store these annotations we define the materialized view of V1, noted MV1 that stores only annotated aggregated values as illustrated in Figure 11.

Figure 11. Storage of annotated aggregated values

MV1					
ROWID	year	month_number	country	city	amount
@200	2007	6	France	Toulouse	4293

AN ANNOTATED MULTIDIMENSIONAL DATABASE MANAGEMENT SYSTEM

Our annotated multidimensional database management system is based on several GUI (Graphical User Interface) implemented in Java 6 on top of the Oracle 10g RDBMS (see Figure 7). It allows the definition, manipulation, and querying of constellation and their annotations.

The constellation schema is defined through SQL-like commands. The textual interface allows users to express these orders. The system generates R-OLAP structures to store decisional data and it populates its metabase where multidimensional structures are depicted. Figure 12 shows the command for creating the dimension named D_PRODUCT and the command for creating the

fact named F_ORDER.

The constellation schema is displayed through a specific GUI:

- The displayed constellation schema is composed of facts, dimensions and hierarchies. The graphical notations are based on the conceptual notations that we presented in section 2.1.4.
- Users analyze decisional data through multidimensional tables. These multidimensional tables are computed from extracted data of the R-OLAP database.

In order to improve their decision-making process, the system provides annotation features to users. The annotations are defined from the constellation schema and/or from the multidi-

Figure 12. Example of SQL-like commands © 2009 Guillaume Cabanac, Max Chevalier, Franck Ravat, and Olivier Teste. Used with permission.

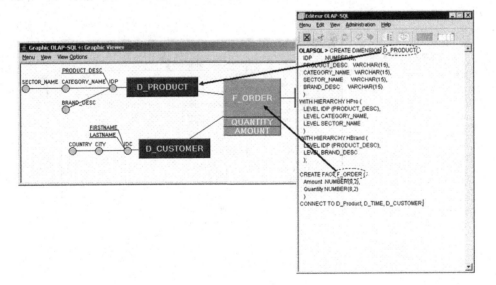

Figure 13. Example of annotation definition. © 2009 Guillaume Cabanac, Max Chevalier, Franck Ravat, and Olivier Teste. Used with permission.

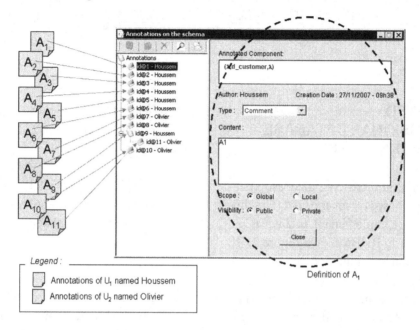

mensional tables. Figure 14 shows an example of annotation creation.

Our current annotated multidimensional database management system provides interfaces to display annotations by authors, by types, or by MDB concepts. The following figure gives an example of annotations by types; note that users can display questions as well as their answers.

Figure 14. Annotations by types. © 2009 Guillaume Cabanac, Max Chevalier, Franck Ravat, and Olivier Teste. Used with permission.

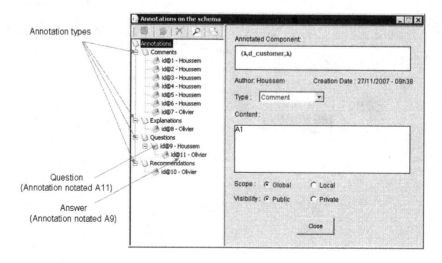

CONCLUDING REMARKS AND FUTURE WORKS

This chapter described the implementation of an MDB integrating annotations. Every piece of multidimensional data can be associated with zero or more annotations. We conceive annotations as a means of storing decision-makers remarks about multidimensional data that would otherwise not be kept in a traditional database. Indeed every annotation contains high value information since it the annotation content is contextualized within a specific analysis context. Thus, from the organization standpoint, it is worth to store and reuse them. In our proposition annotations are provided for a personal use to remind any information concerning the analyzed data, as well as for a collective use to materialize and to share decision-makers' expertise, thus facilitating collaborative analyses and decisions. The model we propose allows end-users to point troubles related to any schema element (hierarchy reorganisation, need for attribute details, wrong/missing values...) through annotations, which can be exploited by designers so that they can modify the database accordingly.

Our solution enables decision-makers to annotate multidimensional data at various levels of granularities—fact, dimension, hierarchy, attributes, detailed or aggregated values. Annotations assist users in understanding MDB structures and decisional analysis expressed through MT. Global annotations are displayed into all MT integrating the annotated data, whereas local annotations are displayed according to a analysis context, *i.e.* a specific MT.

We investigated how global and local annotations can be stored into a homogeneous data structure. We developed a relational meta-database describing constellation components; these metadata are associated with global annotations. We also described an R-OLAP environment where multidimensional data are stored into snowflake relations. The normalized dimensions enable the system to annotate detailed multidimensional data. In this normalized framework, we are interested in determining which aggregated information to materialize annotated values. The implementation solution we describe provides straightforward, uniform and efficient storage structures of decisional annotations over multidimensional data.

In the proposed model, annotations can only be "public" or "private". Unfortunately, these simple security levels are not suitable to the real-life context. Thus, we have to develop security management policies in order to better fit the enterprise needs. It would be interesting to prospect how to detect similarities between analyses in order to propagate annotations from the local analysis context to any similar analysis contexts. We also investigate opportunities for integrating annotations into the lattice of materialized views to improve query computation in our current approach. Future works will revisit materialized view selection algorithms for determining relevant materialized views according to annotations. A new challenge raised compared to the RDBMS context is the annotation propagation along aggregated data. To do this, an interesting trail can be seen through the aggregation of annotations content (text) with specific aggregation functions (Ravat et al., 2007).

REFERENCES

Bhagwat, D., Chiticariu, L., Tan, W.-C., & Vijayvargiya, G. (2004). An annotation management system for relational databases. In *Proceedings of the 30th VLDB International Conference on Very Large Databases*, Toronto, Canada (pp. 900-911).

Bhagwat, D., Chiticariu, L., Tan, W.-C., & Vijayvargiya, G. (2005). An annotation management system for relational databases. *The VLDB Journal, 14*(4), 373–396. doi:10.1007/s00778-005-0156-6

Bhatnagar, N., Juliano, B. A., & Renner, R. S. (2007a). Data annotation models. In *Proceedings of the 3rd ICICIS International Conference on Intelligent Computing and Information Systems*, Cairo, Egypt.

Bhatnagar, N., Juliano, B. A., & Renner, R. S. (2007b). Data annotation models and annotation query language. In *Proceedings of the ICKM International Conference on Knowledge Mining*, Bangkok, Thailand (pp. 440-445).

Cabanac, G., Chevalier, M., Chrisment, C., & Julien, C. (2007). Collective annotation: Perspectives for information retrieval improvement. In *Proceedings of the 8th RIAO International Conference on Information Retrieval and its Applications*, Pittsburgh, PA, USA. Retrieved from http://riao.online.fr/papers/99.pdf

Chiticariu, L., Tan, W.-C., & Vijayvargiya, G. (2005). DBNotes: A post-it system for relational databases based on provenance. In *Proceedings of the ACM SIGMOD International Conference on Management of Data*, Baltimore, MD, USA (pp. 942-944).

Cong, G., Fan, W., & Geerts, F. (2006). Annotation propagation revisited for key preserving views. In *Proceedings of the 15th ACM CIKM International Conference on Information and Knowledge Management*, Arlington, VA, USA (pp. 632-641).

Foshay, N., Mukherjee, A., & Taylor, A. (2007). Does data warehouse end-user metadata add value? *Communications of the ACM, 50*(11), 70–77. doi:10.1145/1297797.1297800

Geerts, F., Kementsietsidis, A., & Milano, D. (2006). MONDRIAN: Annotating and querying databases through colors and blocks. In *Proceedings of the 22nd IEEE ICDE International Conference on Data Engineering*, Atlanta, GA, USA (pp. 82).

Golfarelli, M., Maio, D., & Rizzi, S. (1998). Conceptual design of data warehouses from E/R schemes. In *Proceedings of the 31st HICSS Annual Hawaii International Conference on System Sciences*, Hawaii, USA (pp. 334).

Gyssens, M., & Lakshmanan, L. V. S. (1997). A foundation for multi-dimensional databases. In *Proceedings of the 23rd VLDB International Conference on Very Large Databases*, Athens, Greece (pp. 106-115).

Kimball, R. (1996). *The data warehouse toolkit: Practical techniques for building dimensional data warehouses*. Hoboken, NJ: John Wiley & Sons.

Malinowski, E., & Zimányi, E. (2006). Hierarchies in a multidimensional model: From conceptual modeling to logical representation. *Journal of Data & Knowledge Engineering, 59*(2), 348–377. doi:10.1016/j.datak.2005.08.003

Marshall, C. C. (1998). Toward an ecology of hypertext annotation. In *Proceedings of the 9th ACM HYPERTEXT International Conference on Hypertext and Hypermedia*, Pittsburgh, PA, USA (pp. 40-49).

Ravat, F., Teste, O., & Tournier, R. (2007). OLAP aggregation function for textual data warehouse. In *Proceedings of the 9th ICEIS International Conference on Enterprise Information Systems*, Funchal, Ravat, F., Teste, O., Tournier, R., & Zurfluh, G. (2008). Algebraic and graphic languages for OLAP manipulations. *International Journal of Data Warehousing and Mining, 4*(1), 17–46.

Tan, W.-C. (2003). Containment of relational queries with annotation propagation. In *Proceedings of the 9th DBPL International Workshop on Database and Programming Languages*, Potsdam, Germany (LNCS 2921, pp. 37-53).

ENDNOTES

[1]   This notation complies with the Extended Backus-Naur Form (EBNF) notation (ISO-14977).

[2]   To improve readability we do not specify every equivalent anchoring paths in the examples.

Chapter 5
Federated Data Warehouses

Stefan Berger
University of Linz, Data & Knowledge Engineering Group, Austria

Michael Schrefl
University of Linz, Data & Knowledge Engineering Group, Austria

ABSTRACT

Federated data warehouses are a collection of autonomous and often heterogeneous data marts (DM). When attemping to integrate autonomous DMs, data designers commonly face numerous conflicts that must be repaired. This chapter analyzes and classifies the conflicts at the schema and instance level among dimensions and cubes in a systematic way, based on a formal data model. It shows the dependencies between dimension and cube integration and presents a methodological DM integration approach. A running example demonstrates how to repair the various heterogeneities. Moreover, the chapter introduces a federated DW reference architecture enabling tightly coupled integration of autonomous DMs.

INTRODUCTION

Data Warehouses (DWs) are sophisticated, highly specialized database systems optimized for analytical workload (strategic decision making) rather than transactional data processing. An organization's DW collects and consolidates data from disparate sources on all subject areas that are helpful for decision making. In that sense, the DW represents the "corporate memory" in which historical business data is collected and reconciled on a fine grained detail level. Typical DWs host huge amounts of data, up to several terabytes (Inmon, 2005).

DOI: 10.4018/978-1-60566-748-5.ch005

Data Marts (DMs) are specific repositories, designed on top of the DW to deliver some data subset to a particular group of users, e.g. the managers of the sales division. Sometimes the detail level of a DM is coarser compared to the underlying DW data (e.g. sales by product group vs. sales transactions by customer receipt) to reduce storage requirements. Nevertheless, the amount of data in DMs is still very large. Both the DW and DMs typically conform to the multidimensional data model, arranging the items of interest (*"measures"*) as *data cubes*, i.e. within an analysis space having several axes (*"dimensions"*) that represent different business perspectives (Inmon, 2005).

Copyright © 2010, IGI Global. Copying or distributing in print or electronic forms without written permission of IGI Global is prohibited.

DWs and OLAP systems are widely used by both public and private organizations to enable better strategic business decisions. Data analysts utilize spreadsheet based reports, visualization graphs, OLAP operations, and so forth to drill into the collected data and analyze the performance of their business processes. Traditionally, DWs have been designed as stand-alone systems that are operated by the centralized IT department of the organization.

Nowadays, medium-sized to large organizations commonly integrate their business activities by means of strategic cooperations or mergers and acquisitions. Data integration across autonomous organizations is a necessary prerequisite for any business cooperation. The traditional approach of database systems integration has been researched for several decades. (Halevy, Rajaraman, & Ordille, 2006) survey recent progress achieved by the data integration community and list future challenges. Federated Database Systems (Sheth & Larson, 1990) are a prominent example of systems applying these techniques.

Lately, due to the advent of more processing power and network capacity, the integration of data stemming from independent DWs is becoming increasingly interesting and important. The integration of autonomous DWs allows the cooperating organizations to mutually share their "corporate memories". Successful DW integration offers exciting additional opportunities for the decision makers since it opens up a larger pool of information in all participating organizations, broadening the knowledge base.

Without the appropriate methodology and tool support, DW/DM integration is a tedious and error-prone task, though. As an illustrative example of the practical difficulties consider the conceptual multi-dimensional schema of a fictitious health insurance organization, consisting of independent sub-organizations within several Federal States governed by a federal association. For simplicity, our scenario considers only two sub-organizations, both of which autonomously operate a Data Mart, as depicted in Figure 1. The schema is instantiated at two distinct nodes, named dwh1 and dwh2.

The schemas in Figure 1 are specified in the *"Dimensional Fact Model" (DFM)* proposed by (Golfarelli, Maio, & Rizzi, 1998). DFM is a graphical notation for conceptual multi-dimensional models. It visualizes the *facts* and *dimensions* of data cubes as well as the dependencies within a cube. Notice that the DFM allows to "reuse" or "share" dimensions among multiple facts (e.g. date_time).

The example schema defines two cubes, treatment and medication, each with three dimensions describing the facts. An example instantiation of the conceptual DW schema at both sites dwh1 and dwh2 is specified in Figures 2–3, showing possible dimension and fact instances.[1] We assume the conceptual schema be implemented as so-called relational *star schema* (Thomsen, 2002), (Inmon, 2005). This means, that the physical multi-dimensional schema consists of one "fact table" per cube plus one "dimension table" for each dimension, containing all the level and non-dimensional attributes.

The sample DM instantiations (see Figures 2–3) demonstrate a situation commonly found in practice. Obviously, both DMs model a similar part of the real world. Nevertheless, the medication and treatment fact tables are difficult to integrate due to several heterogeneities among dwh1 and dwh2. On the one hand, the schemas of the medication cubes are identical, but their instances are heterogeneous, as shown in Figure 2. On the other hand, the treatment cubes do not even match in their schemas, as Figure 1 reveals at one glance.

Throughout this chapter, we will use the case study to illustrate the fundamental problems in DM integration and discuss possible solutions. We use two distinct cubes only for presenting different conflicts—in practice, all conflicts could easily occur in a single cube. For an easier presentation, we intentionally kept the example at the minimum

Figure 1. Health insurance conceptual schemas of local Data Marts

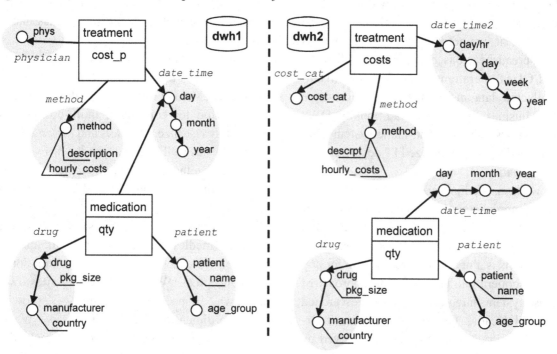

possible size. This does not mean that the problems it contains are trivial to solve, as the forthcoming examples shall demonstrate.

The remainder of this chapter will introduce the state-of-the-art reference architecture of Federated DW Systems and explain how to integrate local autonomous Data Marts. For that purpose, we will introduce a formal model of multi-dimensional data, classify the possible heterogeneities among dimensions and cubes, and describe a methodology resolving these conflicts appropriately. Moreover, the chapter briefly addresses the *query language SQL-MDi* ("SQL for multi-dimensional integration") as one possible technology for the

Figure 2. "Medication" fact tables and "drug" dimensions—[ALL] levels omitted—of the local Data Marts dwh1, dwh2

dwh1::medication (patient [l_patient], drug [l_drug], date_time [day], qty, costs)

patient	drug	date_time	qty	costs
p1	'A'	25-01-06	1	68.4
p2	**'A'**	**03-02-06**	5	342.0
p3	'B'	17-02-06	4	728.0

dwh2::medication (patient [l_patient], drug [l_drug], date_time [day], qty, costs)

patient	drug	date_time	qty	costs
p5	'AA'	03-02-06	2	148.0
p6	'B'	14-02-06	3	624.3
p2	**'A'**	**03-02-06**	1	70.8

dwh1::drug_dim

[drug]	pkg_size	↦ [maufct.]	Country
'A'	**25 pcs.**	'Roche'	CH
'B'	40 pcs.	**'Novartis'**	CH
'C'	250 ml.	'Merck'	US

dwh2::drug_dim

[drug]	pkg_size	↦ [maufct.]	Country
'A'	**30 pcs.**	'Roche'	CH
'B'	40 pcs.	**'Bayer'**	DE

Figure 3. "Treatment" fact tables and "time" dimensions of the local Data Marts dwh1, dwh2

dwh1::treatment (method [l_method],

day [l_day], phys [l_phys], cost_p, cost_m)

method	day	phys	cost_p	cost_m
X-ray	23-02-06	'Dr. A'	356.0	425.0
CT	23-02-06	'Dr. C'	125.2	1742.0
CT	25-02-06	'Dr. F'	473.0	903.8

dwh1::date_time

[day] $\mapsto$	[month] $\mapsto$	[year] $\mapsto$	[All]
23-02-06	02-2006	2006	All
25-02-06	02-2006	2006	All

dwh2::treatment (method [l_method],

day/hr [l_day/hr], cost_cat [l_cost_cat], costs)

method	day/hr	cost_cat	costs
X-ray	23-02-06 08:00	personnel	480.0
X-ray	23-02-06 09:00	material	613.0
CT	25-02-06 14:00	material	624.5

dwh2::date_time2

[day/hr] $\mapsto$	[day] $\mapsto$	[week] $\mapsto$	[year] $\mapsto$ [All]
23-02-06 08:00	23-02-06	w08/06	2006	All
25-02-06 09:00	23-02-06	w08/06	2006	All
24-02-06 14:00	24-02-06	w08/06	2006	All

implementation of the FDW approach. We start by reviewing the relevant literature in the next section.

APPROACHES AND CHOICES OF DW INTEGRATION

In order to reduce the complexity of DW integration, a Federated DW System is usually established at the DM level, not the DW or enterprise level. Using this strategy, the efforts of integration projects may concentrate on a single, relatively small DM instead of complete DWs. Current research on DM integration is inspired by several previous approaches, mainly in the field of distributed databases.

The simplest solution is the migration of existing DMs into a common system with an integrated schema. Basically, this means establishing a "DW of local DMs"—physically copying the data from the distributed, autonomous DMs, and converting it to the integrated schema. Obviously, the migration approach is appropriate for very close and permanent business relationships, e.g. for merged companies. The complexity of data migration projects is very high, though, easily reaching a time-frame between several months or even years (Kimball, 2002). An important challenge posed by DM migration is finding a feasible solution how to access all data before the integrated DM is fully operational.

If the cooperating enterprises retain their organizational autonomy, however, the integration of DMs is better performed at the logical level by building a federation. The advantages of such an approach are well known from the field of databases. Federated Database Systems establish a dedicated access layer (denoted as "federation layer") on top of autonomous data sources to hide data heterogeneity from the applications and users (Özsu & Valduriez, 1999), (Sheth & Larson, 1990), (Litwin, Mark, & Roussopoulos, 1990). The local systems participating in the federation can be queried by a uniform language, which facilitates access to the data.

Two different strategies for describing an integrated schema over heterogeneous data sources are known: global-as-view (GAV) and local-as-view (LAV). In both approaches, the actual data is physically stored among distributed autonomous sources. While GAV systems specify the global schema as view expressions over the sources, LAV systems conversely describe the sources as views over the global schema (Halevy, Rajaraman, & Ordille, 2006). According to database theory GAV mappings facilitate query processing, whereas LAV mappings are easier to maintain and evolve.

The tutorial of (Lenzerini, 2002) and the survey of (Halevy, 2001) discuss the challenges and possible solutions in these contexts in detail.

The use of well-established Federated Database (FDB) architectures for autonomous DMs has a major shortcoming. Data integration techniques employed in FDBs were developed for the relational data model. As such, they are optimized for dealing with heterogeneity among relational entities. However, DMs are typically based on the multi-dimensional data model—the relevant information being modelled as *measure variables* in cubes, contextualized by several *dimension variables* representing the business perspectives (Inmon, 2005). The complex properties specific to facts and dimensions—e.g. grain levels, roll-up hierachies—cannot be represented properly in current FDB Systems. In order to solve DM integration, additional functionality is necessary.

Instead, *Federated Data Warehouse Systems* (FDWS) provide a global multi-dimensional schema and a common query language, "unifying" the users' and applications' view and access methods on its component DMs. Such architectures overcome heterogeneity across distributed data cubes without changing the component systems. So-called *mappings* specify the operations necessary for each local DM to convert local data to the global schema. At query time, the FDWS uses these mappings to generate a query plan and to compute homogeneous query results from the local result data. Notably, a FDWS permits the local DMs to retain their decision and data management autonomy. In contrast, systems in which the local Data Marts are not autonomous but depend on some global authority are denoted *Distributed* DW Systems.

The global schema is expressed in the so-called *canonical data model* of the FDWS (see Figure 4). It represents the formal model of the global application domain, containing the common elements of all local multi-dimensional schemas. Evidently, the presence of the global schema is very comfortable for the end users

since the schema and data heterogeneity among the federated DMs remain transparent from the OLAP applications. Moreover, a stable global schema secures the federated system against local schema evolution. Thus, FDWS architectures adopt an improved version of the "global-as-view" data integration paradigm (Lenzerini, 2002) by eliminating the main disadvantage in current GAV systems—their high sensitivity to schema changes at local sites.

Several approaches in the direction of Federated DW Systems were proposed in literature, e.g. the "DaWaII" tool (Cabibbo & Torlone, 2004), the "Skalla" architecture (Akinde, Böhlen, Johnson, Lakshmanan, & Srivastava, 2003), drill-across relationships between cubes (Abelló, Samos, & Saltor, 2002), or the medical federated DW of (Banek, Tjoa, & Stolba, 2006). Conceptually, these systems do not support a global schema. The loosely-coupled integration of local DMs provided by these systems does not hide schema and data heterogeneity from the OLAP applications. Consequently, the users are responsible for the ad-hoc integration of the distributed multi-dimensional data, which is often a laborious task.

Dimension integration, a subproblem of DW integration, has been addressed by several recent works in the fields of distributed and federated Data Warehousing. For example, "DaWaII", a visual dimension integration tool, allows the user to specify mappings between dimensions and check them for correctness (Torlone & Panella, 2005) based on the notion of dimension compatibility (Cabibbo & Torlone, 2004). Hurtado et al. used a graph model of dimensions in order to detect similar levels and hierarchies in heterogeneous dimensions (Hurtado, Gutiérrez, & Mendelzon, 2005). Mangisengi et al. (2003) and Binh et al. (2003) proposed an architecture using XML tools for dimension integration and query processing in a federation of DMs.

OLAP query processing in distributed DW systems with homogeneous schemas and without a federated layer is addressed by the Skalla sys-

Figure 4. Federated Data Warehouse reference architecture

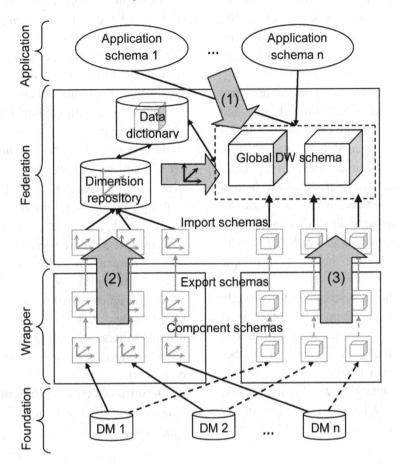

tem and DWS-AQA approach. "Skalla" (Akinde, Böhlen, Johnson, Lakshmanan, & Srivastava, 2003) provides a strong framework for the complete evaluation of distributed queries, whereas "DWS-AQA" (Bernardino, Furtado, & Madeira, 2002) investigates approximate query answering, a strategy to optimize response time at the cost of some accuracy of the result. An interesting idea of both approaches is the replication of dimension data at all local sites to improve query performance.

Existing approaches do no adequately regard conflicts that are specific to the multi-dimensional data model. In this chapter we therefore systematically classify the possible heterogeneities in multi-dimensional data, based on a formal conceptual model. The subsequent discussion of

the conflict taxonomy and integration methodology also emphasizes the dependencies between dimension and cube integration, an issue often not properly solved in previous works.

MULTI-DIMENSIONAL CANONICAL DATA MODEL

The FDW reference architecture (see Figure 4) requires a conceptual, i.e. system-independent multi-dimensional data model to act as the FDW System's "canonical model" (Sheth & Larson, 1990). It provides the formal foundation for modeling the global and local DM schemata. The semantics of the canonical model must be rich enough to represent all the complex properties of facts and dimensions. The multi-dimensional model introduced in (Berger & Schrefl, 2008) supports the essential concepts *dimension* and *cube* and provides sufficient expressivity to meet this requirement.

Each DM defines one or more measure variables within cubes, categorized by some dimensions that are organized in hierarchies of aggregation levels. A cube is a data structure linking a fact table to dimensions, comprising a multi-dimensional space that stores the factual data. To denote dimension instances we use the commonly accepted term *dimension members* or *members* for short (Vassiliadis & Sellis, 1999). Each "cell" of the cube associates a unique combination of members to values of measure variables. Thus, the analyst is able to correctly interpret the *context* of numerical information stored in the cube cells. A measure value disconnected from any members is merely a number with no semantics whatsoever.

Definition 1 (Data Mart): *A Data Mart DM = $\{C_1...,C_n; D_1...,D_m\}$ consists of a non-empty set of Cubes C_i and a non-empty set of dimensions D_i.*

Example 1: As depicted in Figure 1, our case study defines two Data Marts: dwh1 and dwh2. Each DM contains two Cubes, named treatment and medication. Moreover, the DMs define seve *of DM has the dimension schema $S_D = (L_D, S(L_D), H_D)$ containing (I) the finite, non-empty set of Levels $L_D = \{l_1,...,l_j,...,l_m,l_{all}\}$ with level schemas $S(L_D) = \{S_{l_1},...,S_{l_m}\}$ and (II) a roll-up hierarchy $H_D \subseteq L_D \times L_D$, where H_D forms a lattice. If $l_1, l_2 \in H_D$, we write $l_1 \mapsto l_2$ and we say that l_1 "rolls-up to" l_2. The level schema $S_{l_j} \in S(L_D)$ is an attribute schema $l_j (K_j, N_{j1},...N_{jk})$ with name l_j, key K_j (the dimensional or "roll-up" attribute) and optional non-dimensional attributes $N_{j1},... N_{jk}$, alternatively denoted as $l_j.K, l_j.N_1,...,l_j.N_k$ or "N-attributes". Every attribute has a data type τ as domain, denoted $dom(K_j) = dom(\tau_{K_j})$ and $dom(N_{ji}) = dom(\tau_{N_{ji}})$.*

Example 2: Dimension schema drug in DM dwh1 consists of (1) L_{drug} = *{drug, manufacturer}*, (2) $S(L_{drug})$ = *{l_drug (drug, pkg_size), l_manufacturer (manufacturer, country)}* and (3) H_{drug} = *{drug $\mapsto$ manufacturer}* (see Figure 1; notice that level names are omitted there).

Definition 3 (Dimension instance): *A dimension instance $d(S_D)$ over schema S_D consists of (I) its name d, identifying the instance set, and (II) its set of members V_d with each $v \in V_d$ being a tuple over a level schema S_{l_j}, and (III) the family of "roll-up" functions ρ_d among the members according to H_D.*

Example 3: Dimension instance drug in DM dwh1 is named dwh1::drug. Its member set V_{drug} contains the tuples ('A', ...), ('B', ...), ('C', ...) shown in Figure 2. This corresponds to the union of all tuples over *l_drug(drug,pkg_size)* (the drug-members) with all tuples over *l_manufacturer (manufacturer,country)* (the manufacturer-members).

Definition 4 (roll-up functions): *Let l, k $\in$ L_D be two levels, l $\neq$ k, of a dimension D. The roll-up function $\rho_D^{l \to k} : l \to k$ is defined for each pair l, k $\in H_D$. It associates every l-member with a unique k-member. The family of roll-up functions ρ_d contains all $\rho_D^{l \to k}$ defined in this way.*

Example 4: dwh1::drug only defines two levels, [l_manufacturer] and [l_drug] (example 2). Thus, its hierarchy H_{drug} is simple: {drug $\mapsto$ manufacturer}. Thus, ρ_{drug} contains only roll-up function $\rho_{dwh1::drug}^{drug \mapsto manufacturer}$.

Definition 5 (base level of hierarchy): *The base level of hierarchy H_D, denoted l_0^D, representing the finest grain of the dimension's members, is the bottom element of the lattice H_D. The all-level, denoted l_{all}^D or l_{all} for short, is the top element of the lattice H_D.*

Example 5: The base level of hierarchy $H_{dwh1::drug}$ (see the previous example 2) is [l_ drug]. Accordingly, the base level of hierarchy $H_{dwh1::date\_time}$ is [l_day] and so forth. Every hierarchy in dwh1 and dwh2 contains the implicit all-level

l_{all} (not shown in Figure 1).

Next we specify the concept of "dimension functions" and the family of roll-up functions ρ_d of a dimension instance $d(S_D)$.

Definition 6 (dimension functions): *Let D be a dimension with schema S_D, level schema $S(L_D)$ and instance $d(S_D)$. We define the following functions over D:*

- *level: $V_d \rightarrow L_D$ returns the level l_i corresponding to a given $v_i \in V_d$.*
- *members: $L_D \rightarrow 2^{V_D}$ returns the set $T_i = \{v \in V_d \mid level(v) = l_i\}$ containing all members $v \in V_d$ belonging to level l_i.*

Example 6: Function expression *members(dwh1::drug)* returns all $v \in V_{drug}$ that belong to level l_drug, i.e. all tuples over level schema *l_drug(drug,pkg_size)*. Evaluating this function over dwh1::drug_dim (Figure 2), we obtain three members: ('A', '25 pcs.'), ('B', '25 pcs.'), ('C', '250 ml.'). Intuitively, the *level* function is the inverse of the *members* function. Accordingly, the result of function expression *level('A', '25 pcs.')* is level *l_drug*.

Definition 7 (Cube schema): *A Cube C has the cube fact schema $S_C = \{A_C, M_C\}$ that is composed of (I) a set of dimension attributes $A_C = \{A_1[l_1],... A_n[l_n]\}$, (II) a set of measure attributes $M_c = \{M_1,...,M_k\}$. Each $A_i[l_i]$ is linked with a level $l_i \in L_{D_i}$ of the dimensions $D_i \in \{D_1,...,D_m\}$ of the Data Mart, each $M_j \in M_C$ with a data type τ_j. The domain of the attributes in S_C is defined as $dom(A_i) = members(l_i)$ and $dom(M_j) = dom(\tau_j)$. The number n of dimensions in D_C is referred to as the dimensionality of C, whereby $n \leq m$.*

Example 7: Cube schema medication in dwh1 is defined as (1) $A_{medication}$ = {patient [l_patient], drug [l_drug], date_time [day]} (dimension attributes) and (2) $M_{medication}$ = {qty, costs} (measure attributes). As indicated by the resemblance of names, the dimension attributes associate the dwh1::medication-cells to the levels given in

square brackets of dwh1::patient, dwh1::drug and dwh1::date_time, respectively. Whenever it is clear from the context that level l_i is referred by $A_i[l_i]$, we simply write A_i instead of $A_i[l_i]$.

Definition 8 (Cube instance): *The cube instance $c(S_C)$ over schema S_C consists of (I) its name c, identifying the instance set, and (II) a set of tuples over $\{[dom(A_1) \times ... \times dom(A_n)], [dom(M_1) \times ... \times dom(M_m)]\}$. A tuple $f \in c(S_C)$ is called a "cell" or "fact". Moreover, we call the values $[f(A_1),...,f(A_n)]$ the "coordinates" of a cell, modeling the multi-dimensional context for the measures $[f(M_1),...,f(M_m)]$.*

Example 8: The cube instance of cube medication in Data Mart dwh1 is named dwh1::medication and consists of all the cells defined as tuples over the fact schema, as depicted in Figure 2.

Finally, we define consistency between a roll-up function and its associated hierarchy and specify "finer/coarser than" relationships between aggregation levels.

Definition 9 (roll-up consistency): *Let $l, k \in L_D$ be two levels, $l \neq k$, of a dimension D, and $T_l = members(l)$, $T_k = members(k)$. Roll-up function $\rho_D^{l \rightarrow k}$ is consistent with the hierarchy H_D iff all members of level l roll-up to a member of level k, such that $\forall v \in T_l : \rho_D^{l \rightarrow k}(v) \in T_k$.*

Example 9: Roll-up function $\rho_{dwh1::drug}^{drug \mapsto manufacturer}$ of dimension dwh1::drug is consistent because it maps every [l_drug]-member unambiguously to one member of level [manufacturer]. Assuming that we merge dwh1::drug and dwh2::drug, however, the roll-up function would become inconsistent because it is ambiguous for member 'B' among dwh1 and dwh2: $\rho_{dwh1::drug}^{drug \mapsto manufacturer}('B') = 'Novartis'$ versus $\rho_{dwh2::drug}^{drug \mapsto manufacturer}('B') = 'Bayer'$.

Definition 10 (Fineness and coarseness of levels) *Let $l_i, l_j \in H_D$ be two levels in some dimension D and operator $\mapsto^+$ denote the transitive closure of operator $\mapsto$ (rolls-up to, see definition 2). If $l_i \mapsto^+ l_j$, we say that l_i is "finer than" or "more fine-grained than" l_j, and that l_j is "coarser than"* *or "more coarse-grained than" l_i .*

Example 10: In dimension dwh1::date_time (see Figure 1), level [day] is finer than [month] and [year]. Level [year] is coarser than [month] and [day], etc.

The multi-dimensional data model described here extends the so-called *MD* model (Cabibbo & Torlone, 2004), introducing additional properties of the *dimension* construct in order to cope with *all* heterogeneities analyzed in (Berger & Schrefl, 2006). Moreover, its conceptual nature does not restrict the technology used for implementation. Thus, several platforms for a preferred DW tool and query language are supported, e.g. relational systems with the query languages SQL (ISO, 1992) and SQL-MDi.

In particular, the model's distinguishing features are the following (Berger & Schrefl, 2008): (1) the support for non-dimensional attributes in a dimension's level schema (Def. 2), and (2) the functions *level* and *members* specifying the relationship between the schema and instances of dimensions (Def. 6). Generally, the model concepts *data mart*, *cube* and *dimension* define a local DM as a *universe of discourse* for the declaration of dimensions.

TAXONOMY OF CONFLICTS IN MULTI-DIMENSIONAL DATA

This section introduces a taxonomy of heterogeneity in the multi-dimensional data model, based on the definitions given in the previous section. The basic classification of conflicts at the schema and instance level of the relational data model was introduced by (Kim & Seo, 1991). They defined conflict classes affecting relations, the conceptual entity behind relational data. For example, "table versus table" conflicts occur when different table definitions are used to represent the same relation(s) in different databases.

The multi-dimensional model is semantically richer than the relational model, since it

distinguishes two conceptual entities, namely *dimensions* and *cubes*. In particular, the hierarchies of aggregation levels in dimensions and the dependencies between dimensions and facts cause additional classes of heterogeneity. Consequently, the possible conflicts at the schema and the instance level of multi-dimensional data are not only more numerous, but may also be more complex.

Heterogeneities among Data Marts covering the same application domain (e.g. sales figures of grocery stores) result from (1) different modeling patterns and methodologies, and/or (2) ambiguous domain vocabularies. Based on the multi-dimensional data model of the previous section, which defined schemas and instances of dimensions and cubes, we classify heterogeneities at the following levels: (i) schema-instance conflicts, (ii) schema conflicts among dimensions or cubes, and finally (iii) instance conflicts among dimensions or cubes. The conflict classifiction forms the basis for obtaining homogeneous dimensions and cubes, as will be explained in the next section.

Schema versus Instance Conflicts

Schema-instance conflicts among cubes are the result of using different modelling elements to represent the facts and/or their context (see Table 1). Sometimes, part of the context is modelled in two different cubes using once elements at the schema and once elements at the instance level. As a result, the modelled context information is directly visible as a dimension in one cube, but hidden in the cells of the other data cube.

Schema Level Conflicts

This subsection categorizes and explains the conflicts that may occur at the schema level among dimensions and facts of autonomous data cubes. The taxonomy concentrates on conflicts specific to the multi-dimensional model. We omit naming conflicts (i.e. synonyms and/or homonyms among dimension and cube schemas) since these

Table 1. Schema-instance-conflicts in multi-dimensional data

Conflict	Description	Example
#1: Fact context vs. members	Part of the fact context is modelled differently: in one DM as measure variables (cube schema), whilst in another DM as dimension members (cube instance).	In both treatment cubes (Figure 3) the categories of costs figures belong to the context. In dwh1, the measure variables cost_m and cost_p represent these categories. In dwh2, however, the cost_cat members inform about the costs category.

are rather trivial and well addressed in literature (Dhamankar, Lee, Doan, Halevy, & Domingos, 2004).

Conflicts among Dimension Schemas

The basic concept underlying our classification of possible conflicts among dimension schemas is the *equivalence* of levels, as defined below. Intuitively, equivalent levels represent the same real-world entities in a uniform schema. However, if dimension schemas use different precision for modeling the entities, the sets of aggregation levels and/or the hierarchy among semantically similar dimensions may not match.

Heterogeneities among autonomous dimension schemas—classified in Table 2—may affect all schema elements, i.e. (1) the level sets, (2) the hierarchy between the levels, and (3) the attributes within levels (see Definition 7). Dimension schemas among which no conflicts exist are denoted *homogeneous* (Definition 12). For the following definition, let D_1 and D_2 denote two dimensions in autonomous Data Marts.

Definition 11 (Equivalence of levels): *Two levels* $l_1 \in D_1$ *and* $l_2 \in D_2$ *are called equivalent, denoted* $l_1 \equiv l_2$, *iff* $l_1.k = l_2.k$, *i.e. the key attributes of the level schemas* S_{l_1} *and* S_{l_2} *are the same.*

Example 11: Levels [l_drug] and [manufacturer] of both drug dimensions are equivalent because their key attributes, drug resp. manufacturer, are the same in both schemas (see Figure 2).

Correspondence among dimension schemas refers to the extent of identical level attributes (see Table 2). Non-corresponding dimensions do not have any common levels, so they cannot

be integrated in a meaningful way. Partially corresponding dimension schemas match only in subsets of their levels. In contrast, the levels of corresponding dimension schemas model exactly the same entities. If additionally their hierarchies match exactly, and the names and domains of their attributes are the same, they match "perfectly". We denote such pairs of dimension schemas *homogeneous*:

Definition 12 (Homogeneous dimension schemas): *Two dimension schemas* S_{D_1} *and* S_{D_2} *are called homogeneous, iff the following conditions hold:* (1) S_{D_1} *and* S_{D_2} *are free of naming conflicts,* (2) S_{D_1} *and* S_{D_2} *are corresponding* $(L_{D_1} = L_{D_2} \wedge l_0^{D_1} \equiv l_0^{D_2})$, (3) *the hierarchies in* L_{D_1} *and* L_{D_2} *are exactly the same (i.e.* $H_{D_1} = H_{D_2}$) *and (4) the level attributes of* S_{D_1} *and* S_{D_2} *are free of domain conflicts, such that* $\forall l_{j1} \in L_{D_1}, l_{j2} \in l_{D2} : dom(l_{j1}.K) = dom(l_{j2}.K)$.

Non-dimensional attributes of a level schema S_{l_j} complement the key attribute K_j representing additional properties of the l_j-members (Definition 2). Notice that non-corresponding N-attributes need not be repaired, since they do not affect an aggregation hierarchy. Instead, N-attributes can simply be removed from the import schemas.

Example 12: Dimension schemas dwh1::drug and dwh2::drug are homogeneous because their levels and hierarchies match exactly, and the names and domains among their level- and N-attributes are identical.

Table 2. Conflict classes in dimension schemas

Conflict	Description	Example
Non-equivalent sets of levels in S_{D_1} and S_{D_2}: **#2**: disjoint levels	Non-corresponding dimension schemas: $L_{D_1} \cap L_{D_2} = \varnothing$, *i.e. the level sets* L_{D_1} *and* L_{D_2} do not have any level in common.	Dimension schemas dwh1::drug and dwh2::date_time2 do not have common aggregation levels, i.e. $L_{dwh1::drug} \cap L_{dwh2::date\_time2} = \varnothing$
Non-equivalent sets of levels in S_{D_1} and S_{D_2}: **#3**: overlapping levels	Partially corresponding dimension schemas: $L_{D_1} \cap L_{D_2} = \varnothing$, *i.e.* S_{D_1} *and* S_{D_2} have at least one, but not all level attributes in common: *a. Inner-level corresponding:* $l_0^{D_1} \not\equiv l_0^{D_2}$, i.e. both base levels are different. *b. Base-level corresponding:* $l_0^{D_1} \equiv l_0^{D_2}$, i.e. both base levels are the same.	dwh1::date_time and dwh2::date_time2 are inner-level corresponding because the level sets of both schemas commonly define [day] and [year], but their base levels differ: [day] versus [day/hr]. If the base levels matched, say [day], the schemas would be base-level corresponding.
#4: Equivalent levels, different hierarchies among S_{D_1} and S_{D_2}	Flat-corresponding dimension schemas: $L_{D_1} = L_{D_2} \wedge l_0^{D_1} \equiv l_0^{D_2}$, *i.e. the levels in* L_{D_1} *and* L_{D_2} match exactly and their base levels are the same. However, $H_{D_1} \neq H_{D_2}$, i.e. the hierarchies in D_1 and D_2 are different.	dwh1::date_time and a fictious dimension schema calendar with identical levels and level schemas, but different hierarchies: $H_{calendar} = \{day \mapsto year \mapsto month\}$ (recall that $H_{dwh1::date\_time} = \{day \mapsto month \mapsto year\}$).
Domain conflicts: **#5**: level attributes	Levels in hierarchies: the domain of two levels l_1 and l_2, with $l_1 \equiv l_2$, is heterogeneous if $dom(l_1.k) \neq dom(l_2.k)$, i.e. if the domain of the level schemas' key attribute is different.	**(Inner level domain conflict):** Assuming the [manufacturer] levels of both drug_dim dimensions contain exclusively Swiss respectively German manufacturers in dwh1 and dwh2, the domains of the inner level [manufacturer] are different.
	Domain conflicts among base levels:. since cube schemas associate measure variables with base levels in dimensions (def. 7), such conflicts affect all associated cube schemas.	**(Base level domain conflict):** date_time dimensions in both treatment cubes: level [day] in dwh1::date_time represents days of years, whereas level [day/hr] in dwh2::date_time2 additionally models the time of day.
Domain conflicts: **#6**: N-attributes	The domain of two overlapping N-attributes $N_{l_1 i}$ and $N_{l_2 i}$ is heterogeneous iff $dom(N_{l_1 i}) \neq dom(N_{l_2 i})$.	Assuming that hourly_costs of the [method] level records costs figures in US-$ at dwh1::method respectively € in dwh2::method, the domains of the hourly_costs attributes are heterogeneous.

Conflicts among Cube Schemas

In order to correctly recognize conflicts among autonomous cube schemas, we now assume two prerequisites. Firstly, no schema-instance conflicts exist among the cube schemas. Secondly, all dimension schemas associated with the cubes are homogeneous (Definition 12).

The basic concept underlying our classification of the possible conflicts among cube schemas is *correspondence* of dimension attributes, as defined below. Intuitively, corresponding cube schemas model the same context for the measure values in their cells. Heterogeneities among cube schemas—classified in Table 3—may affect both schema parts, i.e. (1) the set of dimension attributes, and (2) the set of measure attributes (see Definition 7).

Cube schemas among which no conflicts exist are denoted homogeneous (see Definition 15). In what follows, let C_1 and C_2 denote two cubes in autonomous Data Marts.

Definition 13 (Corresponding cube schemas): *Iff* $A_{C_1} = A_{C_2}$, *i.e. the dimension attributes of cube schemas* S_{C_1} *and* S_{C_2} *match exactly,* S_{C_1} *and* S_{C_2} *are called corresponding.*

Example 13: The cube schemas dwh1::medication and dwh2::medication are cor-

Table 3. Conflict classes in cube schemas

Conflict	Description	Example
#7: Non-equivalent dimension attributes	Non-corresponding cube schemas: $A_{C_1} \cap A_{C_2} = \varnothing$, *i.e.* S_{C_1} and S_{C_2} do not have any common dimension attribute.	dwh1::treatment and ficticious cube schema dwh3::sales with $A_{dwh3::sales}$ = *{store, product}* and arbitrary measures $M_{dwh3::sales}$ are non-corresponding since $A_{dwh3::sales} \cap A_{dwh1::treatment} = \varnothing$
#8: Dimensionality conflict	Partially corresponding cube schemas: $A_{C_1} \cap A_{C_2} \neq \varnothing$, *i.e.* S_{C_1} and S_{C_2} have at least one, but not all dimension attributes in common: *a. Iff* $A_{C_1} \setminus A_{C_2} \neq \varphi \wedge A_{C_2} \setminus A_{C_1} \neq \varnothing$ *the cube schemas* S_{C_1} *and* S_{C_2} *are dimension intersecting, denoted* $S_{C_1} \between S_{C_2}$. *b. Iff* $A_{C_1} \setminus A_{C_2} = \varphi \wedge A_{C_2} \setminus A_{C_1} \neq \varnothing$, *the cube schema* S_{C_1} *is contained in* S_{C_2} *denoted* $S_{C_1} \subset S_{C_2}$.	treatment cube schemas in dwh1 and dwh2 are partially-corresponding because $A_{dwh1::treatment} \cap A_{dwh2::treatment} = \{method\}$ and dimension-intersecting because the dimension attributes day, day/hr, phys and cost_cat are defined in only one of the schemas.

Now, let $A_i[l_{i1}]$, $A_i[l_{i2}]$ denote one of the dimension attributes in S_{C_1} and S_{C_2}, associated with levels l_{i1} and l_{i2}, respectively.

Conflict	Description	Example
#9: Equivalent dimension attributes, but associated with different levels	Roll-up corresponding cube schemas: $A_{C_1} = A_{C_2}$, *i.e. the dimension attributes of* S_{C_1} *and* S_{C_2} match exactly. Iff $l_{i1} \mapsto^+ l_{i2}$, *i.e. level* l_{i1} *is finer than level* l_{i2} *(def. 10), the cube schemas are called roll-up corresponding, denoted* $S_{C_1} \rightarrow S_{C_2}$.	dwh1::medication (see Figure 2) and fictitious cube schema dwh3::med (patient [l_patient], drug [l_drug], date_time [month], amount): the only difference among their dimension attributes is level [month] in dwh3 (in which, however, the roll-up [day] $\mapsto$ [month] is possible).
#10: Measure attribute domain conflicts	The domain of two overlapping measure attributes M_1 and M_2 with associated data types τ_1 resp. τ_2, is heterogeneous iff $dom(\tau_1) \neq dom(\tau_2)$.	Assuming that dwh2::treatment records costs figures in US-$ (attribute costs) but dwh1 in € (attributes cost_p and cost_m), the costs attribute domains in both treatment cubes schemas differ.

responding because $A_{dwh1::medication} = A_{dwh2::medication}$.

Correspondence among cube schemas refers to the extent to which their dimension attributes—modeling the context of measures in the fact entities—match. If also the aggregation levels associated with the dimension attributes of corresponding cube schemas match exactly, we call these schemas *dimension-homogeneous*:

Definition 14 (Dimension-homogeneity): *Iff for all A_i of the corresponding cube schemas* S_{C_1}

and S_{C_2} *(i.e.* $A_{C_1} = A_{C_2}$ *) condition* $l_{i1} \equiv l_{i2}$ *holds, i.e. level* l_{i1} *is equivalent to level* l_{i2} *(Definition 11), the cube schemas* S_{C_1} *and* S_{C_2} *are called dimension-homogeneous, denoted* $S_{C_1} \equiv S_{C_2}$.

Example 14: Cube schemas dwh1::medication and dwh2::medication are dimension-homogeneous because $A_{dwh1::medication} = A_{dwh2::medication}$ and the patient, drug and date_time dimension attributes are associated to equivalent levels in both schemas.

Dimension-homogeneous cube schemas match "perfectly" only if the names and domains of their attributes are also the same, as defined below. Disparate domains among cube schemas may affect both the dimension and measure attributes. Notice, however, that Table 3 only considered conflicting domains among measures since the previous discussion of correspondence between cube schemas (see Definition 13) entirely covered domain conflicts among dimension attributes.

Definition 15 (Homogeneous cube schemas): *Two cube schemas S_{C_1} and S_{C_2} are called homogeneous, iff the following conditions hold:* (1) S_{C_1} and S_{C_2} are free of naming conflicts, (2) S_{C_1} and S_{C_2} are dimension-homogeneous (Def. 14), and (3) S_{C_1} and S_{C_2} are free of domain conflicts.

Instance Level Conflicts

This subsection categorizes and explains the conflicts that may occur at the instance level among members and cube cells of autonomous DMs. In contrast to the schemas of dimensions and cubes, we do not define the notion of *homogeneous* instances. Instead, dimension or cube instances are denoted either *overlapping* or *disjoint*. In what follows, we assume instances of dimensions and cubes with homogeneous schemas. If schemas (of dimension or facts) are not homogeneous, their instances are always *incompatible*.

Conflicts among Dimension Instances

Even if the schemas of dimensions are homogeneous, further heterogeneity may occur among their sets of members. Possible reasons for conflicts among member sets are either non-disjoint member extensions, the roll-up functions between the members, or heterogeneous single members (see Table 4).

The basic concept to determine and classify heterogeneities among member sets is equivalence between members, as defined below. For what follows, let $l_1 \in L_{D_1}$ and $l_2 \in L_{D_2}$ denote two equivalent dimension levels ($l_1 \equiv l_2$, see Definition 11) with common parent level l_p (i.e. $l_1 \mapsto l_p$ and $l_2 \mapsto l_p$) in the two dimensions D_1 and D_2 with homogeneous schemas $S_{D_1} \equiv S_{D_2}$ (Definition 12). Moreover, $m_1 \in members(l_1)$ and $m_2 \in members(l_2)$ denote sample members of l_1 and l_2, respectively.

Definition 16 (Equivalent members): *Iff $m_1(l_1.K) = m_2(l_2.K)$, i.e. the key values of both members are the same, m_1 and m_2 are called equivalent, denoted $m_1 \equiv m_2$.*

Conflicts among Cube Instances

Even if the schemas of cubes are homogeneous, further heterogeneity may occur among the cube cells. In what follows, we examine the semantic correspondence between cells of homogeneous cube schemas based on the notions of *overlapping* and *disjoint* cube instances (see Table 5). Notice that cells with identical coordinates may occur in overlapping and disjoint cube instances alike. The difference is, however, that conflicting measure *values* among these cells can only occur if the measure *attributes* of the cube schemas overlap.

Let $c_1(S_{C_1})$ and $c_2(S_{C_2})$ denote two instances of homogeneous cube schemas ($S_{C_1} \equiv S_{C_2}$, Definition 15) in autonomous Data Marts. Moreover, $f_1 \in c_1$ and $f_2 \in c_2$ denote two sample cells of $c_1(S_{C_1})$ and $c_2(S_{C_2})$, respectively.

FEDERATED DW REFERENCE ARCHITECTURE

The reference architecture—depicted in Figure 4—represents the state-of-the-art of multidimensional data integration. It gives an outline of the concepts and components of Federated DW (FDW) systems. The architecture does not constrain the technology used to implement the FDW system.

Table 4. Conflict classes in dimension instances (with homogeneous dimension schemas)

Conflict	Description	Example
#11: Overlapping extensions	Given some pair of levels $l_1 \equiv l_2$, *members*(l_1) and *members*(l_2) overlap if the value sets of $l_1.K$ and $l_2.K$ are non-disjoint: i.e. $\exists\, m_1, m_2 : m_1 \equiv m_2$ (see def. 16).	The extensions of the drug dimensions overlap, e.g. the [l_drug]members: {'A', 'B', 'C'} in dwh1, {'A', 'B'} in dwh2. Both members 'A' and 'B' are "equivalent".
#12: Heterogeneous roll-up functions $\rho_{D_1}^{l_1 \mapsto l_p}, \rho_{D_2}^{l_2 \mapsto l_p}$	The roll-up functions of equivalent members $m_1 \equiv$ define ambiguous parent members: $$\rho_{D_1}^{l_1 \mapsto l_p}(m_1) \neq \rho_{D_2}^{l_2 \mapsto l_p}(m_2)$$	In dwh1::drug_dim, the member with drug-value 'B' rolls-up to manufacturer 'Novartis' ($\rho_{dwh2::drug\_dim}^{drug \mapsto manufact.}(B) = Novartis$), where-as in dwh2 drug-member 'B' rolls-up to 'Bayer' ($\rho_{dwh1::drug\_dim}^{drug \mapsto manufact.}(B) = Bayer$).
#13: Overlapping non-dimensional values	The equivalent members $m_1 \equiv m_2$ cause overlapping non-dimensional values, if the *N*-attributes of S_{l_1}, S_{l_2} overlap ($N_{l_1 \cap l_2} = \{N_{l_1 1}, ..., N_{l_1 k}\} \cap \{N_{l_2 1}, ..., N_{l_2 k}\}$ $\neq \varnothing$ and the values of some common *N*-attribute(s) N_0 differ among both members, i.e. $\exists N_0 \in N_{l_1 \cap l_2}$: $m_1(N_0) \neq m_2(N_0)$.	The values of attribute pkg_size for the drug_dim members with drug-value 'A' are inconsistent (see Figure 2): '25 pieces' in dwh1::drug_dim versus '30 pieces' in dwh2::drug_dim.

In order to abstract from the heterogeneities among the autonomous DMs, the FDW reference architecture provides a global multi-dimensional schema. The global schema is independently defined, whereby *mappings* specify the necessary transformations from each of the autonomous DM to the global schema. Thus, the reference architecture describes a FDW system as tightly coupled with the autonomous and probably distributed component DMs.

The FDW reference architecture combines the advantages of GAV and LAV data integration. On the one hand, the direction of mappings "from source to global" (as in the GAV strategy) facilitates query processing since the query plan can be computed straightforwardly from the mapping. On the other hand, the stable global schema (as in LAV) secures the federation layer against local schema changes (Lenzerini, 2002), (Halevy, 2001). Figure 4 shows the five levels known from (Sheth & Larson, 1990) on four *system layers* (we combine the "component" and "export" schema layers into the "wrapper layer").

Compared to "classical" and well-established Federated Database systems, the Federated DW

architecture defines an additional component, the so-called *dimension repository*. It stores the consolidated dimension schemas and mirrors the dimensional data such that copies of all dimension members are present in the repository. When answering queries, the dimensional data and metadata (members, hierarchies, etc.) are available directly from the dimension repository.

This approach reduces the complexity of distributed query processing in the FDWS by eliminating the sub-queries necessary to retrieve dimensions from the local component DMs, thus improving overall query response time. It is motivated by the basic idea behind the Skalla (Akinde, Böhlen, Johnson, Lakshmanan, & Srivastava, 2003) and DWS-AQA approaches (Bernardino, Furtado, & Madeira, 2002) indicating that local dimension replicates improve query performance. Moreover, dimensions—similar to domain ontologies—typically evolve slowly and are relatively small in size (Kimball, 2002).

The following concepts build the cornerstones of the proposed FDW reference architecture. Together, these concepts provide a comprehensive framework that allows to tackle the interrelated

Table 5. Conflict classes in cube instances (with homogeneous cube schemas)

Conflict	Description	Example
#14: Overlapping cube instances	If S_{c_1} and S_{c_2} have overlapping or identical measure attributes ($M_{C_1} \cap M_{C_2} \neq \emptyset$ or $M_{C_1} = M_{C_2}$), the cell sets $c_1(S_{c_1})$ and $c_2(S_{c_2})$ "*potentially overlap*". For brevity, we simply say that $c_1(S_{c_1})$ and $c_2(S_{c_2})$ *overlap*.	The cell sets of the medication cubes overlap because both cube schemas are homogeneous with identical measures. Therefore, identical coordinates of cells in both cube instances may occur, as happens in our case study (see the cells with coordinates ('p2', 'A', '03-02-06') in Figure 2).
#15: Disjoint cube instances	If S_{c_1} and S_{c_2} have disjoint measure attributes ($M_{C_1} \cap M_{C_2} \neq \emptyset$), the cell sets $c_1(S_{c_1})$, and $c_2(S_{c_2})$ are called *disjoint* and the cubes C_1, C_2 are called *mergecompatible*.	Assuming that the measure attributes of the medication cubes were named "qty1" and "cost1" in dwh1, cube instances dwh1::medication and dwh2::medication would be disjoint (see Figure 2). In this case, the two cells with coordinates ('p2', 'A', '03-02-06') could easily be merged into a cube with measure attributes qty, costs, qty1 and cost1.

problems of dimension integration and fact integration in a systematic way:

- *Global schema modelling* (label (1) in Figure 4) and *user requirements modelling*: in the first place, the FDW designer defines the global multi-dimensional schema. The global cube definitions should correspond to the information needs of the applications and users. Object oriented modelling techniques, e.g. the UML, are the common solution to modeling the user requirements (Luján-Mora, Trujillo, & Song, 2006). In our architecture, for example, UML use case diagrams can be used to express the "desired" cubes of the global schema. In general, requirements modelling is well researched (for example, refer to Nuseibeh (2000) for an overview) and out of the scope of this chapter.

- *Dimension integration* (label (2) in Figure 4): the system's federation layer needs to correctly interpret the global context of distributed fact data. Therefore, the FDW designer represents the dimensions found in the component DMs in terms of the canonical model, removing all existing heterogeneities. The result of the dimension integration process is the consolidated, global dimension schema. Moreover, it is necessary to design *mappings* from the local DMs to the consolidated dimensions. Each mapping associates transformation operators with one of the local dimensions, specifying how to represent its members in the consolidated schema. The *dimension repository* is the "dictionary" of the global dimension schema: it hosts the integrated consolidated schemas, the mappings and copies of the dimension members.

- *Cube integration* (label (3) in Figure 4): the local DMs participating in the federated system may autonomously define their multi-dimensional schemas. In order to globally consolidate the local fact entities, the FDW designer represents the autonomous cube schemas in terms of the canonical model, removing the existing heterogeneities. The result of the cube integration process is a *mapping* from each local DM to the global schema. Every mapping associates a sequence of transformation operators with one local cube, specifying how to represent its cells in the global schema. Both the meta-data of the global schema and the mappings are stored in the *data dictionary*. When processing a user query over the global schema, the federated layer uses the mappings both to generate a query plan—decomposing the query to a set of queries to local DMs—and to transform all result data to the global schema.

Summarizing, the main benefits of the FDW approach presented herein are the following: (1) it allows the integration of autonomous DMs to a global schema, whilst the DMs retain schema and data autonomy; (2) the global schema remains stable, so that the federated layer is secure against schema changes in the local DMs; (3) the tightly coupled federation of DMs allows the users and applications to operate on the global schema, providing transparacy from possible heterogeneities; and (4) the architecture supports different DM implementation platforms.

INTEGRATION METHODOLOGY OF DATA MARTS

The integration of autonomous Data Marts pursues the goals of (1) defining homogeneous import schemas of both the dimensions and facts, and (2) resolving overlapping sets among both members and facts. Importantly, the analyst must be an expert of the application domain and the vocabularies underneath the conflicting autonomous DMs in order to correctly identify the conceptual entities behind the local schemas and instances. Only then the analyst will correctly recognize the conflicts between the local DMs and the global schema and, consequently, set the adequate actions repairing these heterogeneities. In this section, we introduce an integration methodology for heterogeneous and autonomous DMs, based on the taxonomy of conflicts discussed in the previous section.

For example, let us assume the health insurance's federal association defines its global multi-dimensional schema as depicted in Figure 5. The analysts wants to access the data of both DMs in dwh1 and dwh2 (introduced in Figure 1) through the global schema.

Only having repaired all conflicts that exist among the schemas and instances of dwh1 and dwh2, the global schema can be instantiated successfully. In that case, the medication and treatment fact tables are computed from the local DMs dwh1 and dwh2 as depicted in Figure 6. Notice that the global cubes g::medication and g::treatment would be available for analytical queries then, but not necessarily be physically stored by the federated system. Instead, a federated DW may compute global cubes "on the fly".

The general paradigm behind the integration methodology is viewing the federated layer as the *"privileged hub"* on top of the local DMs. In this hub architecture, the FDW administrates the global schema and collects mappings for each autonomous cube participating in the federation. The mappings define how to convert dimension and fact data from local schemas to the global schema. This way, the applications accessing the global schema are secured against schema changes in the local DMs and the federated system remains extensible.

The integration methodology consists of three consecutive phases, in which the autonomous data cubes are harmonized step by step.[2] Starting with the removal of schema-instance conflicts in the first phase, the proposed approach systematically follows the conflict taxonomy (see previous section). During the second phase, the analyst overcomes heterogeneities at the schema level of dimensions and facts. The third and final phase considers the remaining conflicts at the instance level. In general, heterogeneities among dimensions are repaired before those among cubes since cube schemas logically depend on dimension schemas in the multi-dimensional data model.

Resolve Schema-Instance Conflicts

The goal of the first phase of DM integration is to repair any heterogeneous representation of the application domain using modeling elements at the schema and the instance level. The resolution of

Figure 5. Global conceptual schema of health insurance DM federation

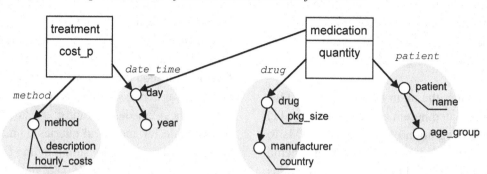

schema-instance conflicts (#1) is possible in two directions, depending on the desired schema of the global cube. In both cases, the import schemas of one or more of the autonomous local cubes are restructured with *pivoting* operations:

- The conversion of *dimension members into contextualized facts* creates new measure variables that are more specific than in the original schema. Part of the context information represented at the instance level by dimension members is transformed into additional measure variables of the cube schema. Hence, the cube's dimensionality

decreases, while its number of measure variables increases. Thus, the augmented expressivity of the multi-dimensional schema leads to "deflation" of cells.

- The conversion of *implicit fact context into dimension members* generates a new context dimension. Part of the context information hidden within the measure variables at the schema level is transformed into the members of the new context dimension. Hence, the cube's dimensionality increases, while its number of measure variables decreases. Thus, the diminished expressivity of the multi-dimensional schema leads

Figure 6. Global fact tables and dimensions—[ALL] levels omitted—computed from the local Data Marts dwh1, dwh2

g::medication

patient	drug	date	SUM (qty)	SUM (cost)
p1	'A'	25-01-06	1	68.4
p2	**'A'**	**03-02-06**	**6**	**412.8**
p3	'B'	17-02-06	4	728.0
p5	'A'	03-02-06	2	148.0
p6	'B'	14-02-06	3	624.3

g::treatment

method	date	SUM (cost_p)	SUM (cost_m)
X-ray	23-02-06	676.0	833.6
CT	23-02-06	125.2	1742.0
CT	24-02-06	416.3	0.0
CT	25-02-06	473.0	903.8

g::drug_dim

[drug]	pkg_size	$\mapsto$ [manufct.]	Country
'A'	**25 pcs.**	'Roche'	CH
'B'	40 pcs.	**'Bayer'**	**DE**
'C'	250 ml.	'Merck'	US

g::date

[day] $\mapsto$ [year] $\mapsto$ [All]
23-02-06   2006   All
25-02-06   2006   All

Integrate Dimension and Cube Schemata

In the second phase of the integration methodology the analyst defines homogeneous schemas for both the dimensions and facts. Recall that the integration of dimension schemas has priority over the integration of cube schemas. Therefore, the dimension schemas should reach a "fixed" homogeneous state before examining the cube schemas for heterogeneities.

In general, the schema integration process in our methodology follows the *minimum match strategy*, i.e. the reduction of import schemas to the common parts. This strategy copes with the comparative nature of typical OLAP analysis where comparison among compatible measures is desired. In order to utilize as much of the source data as possible, several slices of some local cube can be defined as import schemas. Alternatively, a *maximum use strategy* would try to fully import the local schemas, allowing to retain elements that do not match with other schemas.

The *dimension schema integration* process among the DMs consists of the following steps. Let D_1 and D_2 be two dimensions in autonomous DMs:

1. Check the dimension schemas for naming conflicts. If necessary, change ambiguous names of following schema elements: (1) dimension names, (2) levels L_D in hierarchies, (3) level attributes in level schemas, and (4) non-dimensional attributes in level schemas.

    Having revised the dimension names, repeat the following steps 2.–4. for all pairs of dimensions D_1 and D_2 in the DM with identical names.

2. Check the correspondence among the sets of levels L_D. If necessary, eliminate conflicts among the level sets L_{D_1}, L_{D_2} and hierarchies H_{D_1}, H_{D_2} as follows:

    a. If L_{D_1} and L_{D_2} are non-corresponding (#2), stop the integration process for D_1 and D_2. In this case, D_1 and D_2 do not have common semantics. Proceed to the next pair of dimensions.

    b. If L_{D_1} and L_{D_2} are inner-level corresponding (#3), (1) identify the most fine-grained, common level $l_0{}' \in H_{D_1}, H_{D_2}$, and (2) identify all common levels $L_{D_1} \cap L_{D_2}$; delete all other levels.

    c. If L_{D_1} and L_{D_2} are base-level corresponding (#3), identify all common levels $L_{D_1} \cap L_{D_2}$ and delete all other levels.

    d. If L_{D_1} and L_{D_2} are flat corresponding (#4), keep only the base level $l_0 \in H_{D_1}, H_{D_2}$ and delete all other levels.

3. Next, check every pair of levels $l_1 \in L_{D_1}, l_2 \in L_{D_2}$ $(l_1 \equiv l_2)$ for heterogeneous non-dimensional attributes: identify the common N-attributes $\{N_{l_1 1}, ... N_{l_1 k}\} \cap \{N_{l_2 1}, ... N_{l_2 k}\}$; delete all other N-attributes.

4. Finally, check the attribute domains among the level schemas $S(L_{D_1})$ and $S(L_{D_2})$. Inspect the following schema elements for heterogeneities (see #5, #6):

    a. For all level attributes $l_0^{D_1}.k, l_0^{D_2}.k$, of the base levels $l_0^{D_1} \in H_{D_1}, l_0^{D_2} \in H_{D_2}$ check if $dom\left(l_0^{D_1}.k\right) = dom\left(l_0^{D_2}.k\right)$.

    b. For the level attributes $l_1.k, l_2.k$, of all levels $l_1 \in H_{D_1}, l_2 \in H_{D_2}$, coarser than the base level (i.e. $\forall l_1 \in H_{D_1} : l_0^{D_1} \mapsto^+ l_1 \wedge \forall l_2 \in H_{D_2} : l_0^{D_2} \mapsto^+ l_2$ holds), check if $dom(l_1.k) = dom(l_2.k)$.

    c. For the overlapping N-attributes $N_{l_1 i} \in S_{l_1}, N_{l_2 i} \in S_{l_2}$ of all levels

$l_1 \in L_{D_1}$, $l_2 \in L_{D_2}$ check if the attribute domain is the same among the equivalent levels $(l_1 \equiv l_2)$, i.e. $dom(N_{l_i i}) = dom(N_{l_i i})$.

If domain conflicts among any of the above attributes are detected, identify a common domain and specify appropriate conversion functions.

Now, the dimension schemas S_{D_1} and S_{D_2} are homogeneous (Def. 12) and their integration is complete. Proceed with the *cube schema integration* process among the two cubes C_1 and C_2, consisting of the following steps:

1. Check the cube schemas for naming conflicts. If necessary, change ambiguous names in the following schema elements: (1) cube name C, (2) dimension attributes A_C, (3) measure attributes M_C.

2. Check the correspondence among the cube schemas S_{C_1} and S_{C_2}, based on both sets of dimension attributes A_{C_1} and A_{C_2}. If S_{C_1}, S_{C_2} are not dimension-homogeneous (Definition 14), eliminate heterogeneities among the dimension attribute sets as follows:

   a. If C_1 and C_2 are non-corresponding (#7), stop the integration process. In this case, C_1 and C_2 do not have common semantics. Proceed to the next pair of cubes.

   b. If S_{C_1} and S_{C_2} are partially corresponding (#8), identify (1) the common dimension attributes $A_{C_1} \cap A_{C_2}$, and (2) the appropriate aggregation functions for rolling-up all other dimension attributes to the [all]-level.

   c. If S_{C_1} and S_{C_2} are roll-up corresponding (#9), (1) identify all dimension attributes $A_0[l_1] \in A_{C_1}, A_0[l_2] \in A_{C_2} : l_1 \mapsto^+ l_2 \vee l_2 \mapsto^+ l_1$, and (2) determine appropriate aggregation functions and roll-up to the

common levels.

3. Determine the subsets of disjoint and overlapping measure variables: $\{M_{C_1} \setminus M_{C_2}\} \cup \{M_{C_2} \setminus M_{C_1}\}$, respectively $M_{C_1} \cap M_{C_2}$. Notice that—in contrast to non-overlapping N-attributes during dimension integration—non-overlapping measure attributes are not eliminated from the cube import schemas since all measures may contain potentially valuable information, whereas N-attributes deliver only auxiliary information on members.

4. By now, the cube schemas S_{C_1} and S_{C_2} are dimension-homogeneous. Next, inspect the domains of all measure attributes (#10): for all overlapping measures $M_1, M_2 \in \{M_{C_1} \cap M_{C_2}\}$ check if $dom(M_1) = dom(M_2)$. If domain conflicts among the measure attributes are detected, identify a common domain and specify appropriate conversion functions.

Now, the cube schemas S_{C_1} and S_{C_2} are homogeneous (Defnition 15). Thus, the schema integration phase is complete.

Consolidate Dimension and Fact Instances

The goal of the third and final phase of DM integration is converting the instances of dimensions and facts into the common schema defined previously. Initially, both the dimension and cube schemas are homogeneous among the autonomous data cubes. All heterogeneities that still reside among the dimension members and cube cells are now resolved. Again, the removal of the conflicts among members has priority over the conflicts among cells.

The *member integration process* consists of the following steps, that are repeated for every pair of dimension instance $d_1(S_{D_1})$ and $d_2(S_{D_2})$ of the autonomous DMs. Let *members*(l_1) and *members*(l_2) denote the member sets of two equivalent levels $l_1 \equiv l_2$.

1. For all pairs of levels $l_1 \equiv l_2$ check the correspondence among their member extensions (#11):

   a. If *members*(l_1) and *members*(l_2) overlap, decide which set operation to apply on the overlapping member subsets (e.g. UNION, MINUS, INTERSECT, etc.). Any disjoint member subsets are merged using the UNION operator.

   b. If *members*(l_1) and *members*(l_2) are disjoint, always merge the member sets using the UNION operation.

   Apply the **same** set operation chosen before on the remaining pairs of levels $l_1' \equiv l_2'$ (with $l_1 \mapsto^+ l_1'$ and $l_2 \mapsto^+ l_2'$) in order to maintain valid roll-up functions.

2. In all pairs of levels $l_1 \equiv l_2$ repair value conflicts among their members:

   a. Only if both member extensions overlap (#11), check for heterogeneous roll-up functions. If the roll-up functions of two members $m_1 \in$ *members*(l_1) and $m_2 \in$ *members*(l_2) differ (#12), decide which roll-up function gives the appropriate parent member. Overwrite the wrong roll-up function accordingly.

   b. Only if the N-attributes of the level schemas S_{C_1}, S_{l_1} overlap, check for non-dimensional value conflicts. If two members $m_1 S_{l_2}$ *members*(l_1) and $m_2 \in$ *members*(l_2) have different values of some non-dimensional attribute $\in$, i.e. $m_1(N_0) \neq m_2(N_0)$, decide which value is the correct one and overwrite the other value (#13).

Now, the dimensions D_1, D_2 are homogeneous since all conflicts among their schemas $N_0 \in S_{l_1} \cap S_{l_2}$, $N_0 \in S_{l_1} \cap S_{l_2}$ and instances $d_1(S_{C_2})$, $d_2(S_{C_2})$ have been removed. The dimen-

sion integration process is complete.

The subsequent *cells integration process* consists of the following steps, that are repeated for every pair of cube instances $c_1(S_{C_1})$ and $c_2(S_{C_1})$ of the autonomous DMs.

1. In case that the cube instances $c_1(S_{C_1})$ and $c_2()$ overlap (#14) and their cells should be merged using the UNION set operation, determine the correspondence among the entities of the application domain that are modelled by the cubes. Characterize the overlapping facts as either identical-related or context-related:

   a. *Identical-related*: the measures of overlapping, identical-related facts describe the same real-world entity in the same context (e.g. stock-market prices for a particular day and company share). In most cases, identical-related measure values cannot be meaningfully summarized. Thus, identical-relationship is similar to measures with stock semantics (Lenzerini, 2002).

   In case of overlapping cube instances with identical-related cells either (1) prefer the measure values of either $c_1(S_{C_2})$ or $c_2()$, or alternatively (2) extend the cells of both instances with a new dimension, called the *context dimension*.

   b. *Context-related*: the measures of overlapping, context-related facts describe either (1) the same real-world entity in different contexts (e.g. stock-market prices for a particular company share on different stock exchanges), or (2) different real-world entities in similar contexts (e.g. sales figures of several subsidiaries). The challenge with these overlapping cells is to correctly recognize *what* they describe. Only an expert of the underlying application domain can correctly decide whether the measures are summarizable or not, depending on the semantic context among the overlapping cells. As such, context-relationship is similar to measures with flow semantics (Lenzerini, 2002).

In case of overlapping cube instances with context-related cells either (1) specify the aggregation function used to merge the measure values of $c_1(S_{D_2})$ and if the aggregated value is the interesting information for the analyst; or (2) extend the cells with the context dimension if the original cell context is important for the analyst.

Alternatively, overlapping cube instances may be merged using some set operation other than UNION (e.g. OUTER JOIN, MINUS) between the cells of the cube instances $c_1()$ and . In that case, it is not necessary to determine whether the cells of the overlapping cube instance are identical-related or context-related.

2. If the cube instances $c_1()$ and are disjoint (#15), the UNION operation is applied on the cells. As stated in Table 5, disjoint cube instances are merge-compatible. This means that the UNION operation, applied on disjoint cube instances, computes a cube instance $c(C)$ with cube schema S_{D_2}, S_{D_2}. This cube schema accommodates all measure values (recall that S_{C_2} so the measure variables cannot overlap), but the cells will contain NULL values.

Now, the cubes C_1, C_2 are homogeneous since all conflicts among their schemas S_{C_2}, S_{C_1} and instances , have been removed. The cube integration process is complete.

SQL-MDI—THE DISTRIBUTED OLAP LANGUAGE

The query language SQL-MDi (*SQL for multidimensional integration*) allows the integration of several autonomous Data Marts by supporting distributed OLAP queries (Berger & Schrefl, 2006). As its name suggests, SQL-MDi is based on the well-known SQL standard. An SQL-MDi query forms the prologue of a standard SQL query with grouping and aggregation operations, as commonly used for analytical queries in OLAP. The cube definition clauses of the SQL-MDi language precede the basic SELECT – FROM – WHERE – GROUP BY – HAVING structure of SQL (ISO, 1992).

Using the query clauses provided by SQL-MDi, the OLAP analyst specifies a sequence of conversion operators computing a "virtual" global cube from two or more corresponding local and autonomous cubes. Subsequently, the OLAP queries are evaluated against the global cube schema, using the data distributed across the local cubes. This section explains the rich set of query clauses and operators that the language provides to overcome heterogeneity among cubes.

The basic structure of an SQL-MDi query consists of the following three main clauses:

```
1  DEFINE [GLOBAL] CUBE
<cube-declarations>
2  MERGE DIMENSIONS    <merge-
dim-subclauses>
3  MERGE CUBES    <merge-cubes-
subclauses>
```

Succeeding the SQL-MDi clauses the OLAP analyst formulates the business question that refers to the global cube schema, using the following well-known syntax (ISO, 1992):

```
1  SELECT  <dimension attri-
butes>, <aggregated measures>
2  FROM     <fact tables>, <di-
mension tables>
3  WHERE    <selection criteria>
4  GROUP BY<dimension attri-
butes>
5  [HAVING <group selection cri-
teria>]
```

Notably, the output cube schema is not explicitly specified in the SQL-MDi query, but rather composed from schemas of the local source or "input" cubes. This is why we denote the output cube "virtual"—it is not necessarily materialized physically. Of course, SQL-MDi query tools may implement a result cube materialization or "data caching" mechanism to optimize performance.

In general, SQL-MDi matches the corresponding schema elements of dimensions or facts on *name equality* across the input cubes. Consequently, within the DEFINE clauses the analyst unifies the names of all corresponding elements that should be merged in the result. Using this approach, it is easier to integrate more than two input cubes in setwise manner, avoiding awkward pairwise mappings between schema elements.[3]

Firstly, the DEFINE clauses are used to specify both the source cubes and the target cube. Every cube is assigned a mandatory *alias name* to be used later for referencing its properties (e.g. measure attributes). Each DEFINE CUBE clause describes the *import schema* of a local cubes by explicitly listing all dimension and fact attributes that are required. SQL-MDi provides the import operators MEASURE and DIM as sub-clauses of DEFINE CUBE for this purpose. Elements of local schemas not mentioned within any import operator are ignored. The optional WHERE sub-clause allows selective predicates on the cube cells (i.e. slice and dice). In order to repair domain and naming heterogeneities among local cubes, the conversion operators CONVERT MEASURES, ROLLUP and PIVOT as well as the renaming operators MAP LEVELS, '->' (for attribute names) and '>>' (for attribute values) are available under DEFINE CUBE. Figure 7 splits measure c2.costs based on the cost_cat-members (line 11) and removes the phys dimension of dwh1 (dimensionality conflict, lines 1–5). Moreover, the DEFINE CUBE clauses convert the costs-attribute domain in dwh2 from US-\$ to € (domain conflict, line 12) and repair the time-hierarchies (lines 5, 9, 12).

The DEFINE GLOBAL CUBE clause declares only the name of the output cube, but no elements of its schema. Instead, the DEFINE CUBE and MERGE DIMENSIONS clauses refer, respectively, to the fact and dimension attributes of the input cubes and specify their conversion to the output schema in detail. Therefore, it is essential to carefully reconcile the number and names of local dimensions and measure attributes, using the rename operators in order for the MERGE CUBES clause to work (as explained later). Figure 7 illustrates the DEFINE GLOBAL CUBE clause in line 14.

Secondly, for each dimension in the input schemas, one MERGE DIMENSIONS clause specifies the renaming and conversion operators obtaining a homogeneous dimension in the output cube. All dimensions created this way are automatically added to the global cube schema and available within the MERGE CUBES clause (explained in the next paragraph). In order to repair heterogeneity among local dimensions, the conversion operators CONVERT ATTRIBUTES and RELATE LEVELS as well as the renaming operators RENAME (with '->' for attribute names) and '>>' (for attribute values) are available as sub-clauses. Figure 7 contains a MERGE DIMENSIONS clause for the two common dimensions method and calendar_date (lines 15–17).

Thirdly and finally, the MERGE CUBES clause completes the definition of the output cube. It determines the cells of the global cube as "superset" of the local cube cells—recall that both the intersection of *overlapping* cells (#14 in Table 5) and the union of *disjoint* cells (#15 in Table 5) are computed. The measure attributes of the import schemas specified in the DEFINE CUBE clauses must match exactly regarding both their number and names. If necessary, the conversion operators PREFER, AGGREGATE MEASURE and TRACKING SOURCE AS DIMENSION are available as sub-clauses of MERGE CUBES to repair heterogeneity among the local cube cells. In Figure 7 we assume that the treatment-cells are context-related and summarizable. Thus we merge both cubes summarizing their measures

Figure 7. **(SQL-MDi query):** *The following SQL-MDi code computes the global cube g::treatment (as given in Figure 6) from the local treatment cubes (see Figure 3):*

```
1   DEFINE CUBE dwh1::treatment AS c1
2     (MEASURE c1.cost_p -> costs_personnel,
3      MEASURE c1.cost_m -> costs_material,
4      DIM c1.method, DIM c1.date -> calendar_date
5      (MAP LEVELS dwh1::date_time ([ day ], [ year ]) )
       )
6   CUBE dwh2::treatment AS c2
7     (MEASURE c2.cost-$,
8      DIM c2.method, DIM c2.date_time -> calendar_date
9       (MAP LEVELS dwh2::date_time2 ([ day ], [ year ]) ),
10     DIM c2.cost_cat,
11     PIVOT SPLIT MEASURE c2.cost-$ BASED ON c2.cost_cat
       )
12     (ROLLUP c2.calendar_date TO LEVEL [day] WITH SUM() FOR c2.costs)
13     (CONVERT MEASURES APPLY usd2eur() FOR c2.cost-$ DEFAULT)

14  GLOBAL CUBE g::treatment AS c0

15  MERGE DIMENSIONS c1.method AS md1, c2.method as md2
    INTO c0.method AS md0

16  MERGE DIMENSIONS c1.calendar_date AS cd1, c2.calendar date AS cd2
    INTO c0.calendar_date AS cd0
17  (ATTRIBUTE cd2.descrpt -> description )

18  MERGE CUBES c1, c2 INTO c0 ON method, calendar_date
19  AGGREGATE MEASURE costs_personnel IS SUM OF costs_personnel
20  AGGREGATE MEASURE costs_material IS SUM OF costs_material
```

in the global cube cells on the dimensions method and calendar_date (lines 18–20).

Each of the main clauses available in SQL-MDi provides numerous conversion operators that repair the conflicts we presented in the taxonomy (see Figure 7). Due to space limitations, however, we omit an in-depth discussion of the SQL-MDi language. We refer the interested reader to (Berger & Schrefl, 2006).

In order to demonstrate the practical validity of the FDW approach, we implemented prototypes of several system components of the reference architecture. The *Visual Schema Integration Tool* allows the user to define (1) the global multi-dimensional schema and (2) mappings from the local, autonomous DM schemas to the global schema (Maislinger, 2009). The *SQL-MDi Query Tool* accepts a query string written in the SQL-

MDi language (Brunneder, 2008), computes the result of the query and displays the result to the user (Rossgatterer, 2008).

SUMMARY

This chapter gave a comprehensive overview on the current state of Federated DW approaches and discussed a multi-dimensional canonical data model for FDWs. We illustrated the essential concepts of DW integration and defined a reference architecture for the components and processes in FDW systems independent of the technology used for implementation. A significant part of the chapter dealt with the problem of deriving a consolidated, global DM from autonomous and heterogeneous local DMs. We introduced a taxonomy of conflicts in multi-dimensional data and presented a general methodology to repair these conflicts during DM integration. Moreover, we demonstrated how to merge autonomous DMs using SQL-MDi, a language based on SQL.

ACKNOWLEDGMENT

We are grateful to our colleagues Bernd Neumayr, Christian Eichinger and Katharina Grün for the fruitful discussions and for proof-reading the chapter.

REFERENCES

Abelló, A., Samos, J., & Saltor, F. (2002). On relationships offering new drill-across possibilities. In D. Theodoratos (Ed.), *Proceedings of the DOLAP* (pp. 7-13). New York: ACM.

Akinde, M. O., Böhlen, M. H., Johnson, T., Lakshmanan, L. V., & Srivastava, D. (2003). Efficient OLAP query processing in distributed data warehouses. *Information Systems, 28*(1-2), 111–135. doi:10.1016/S0306-4379(02)00051-0

Banek, M., Tjoa, A. M., & Stolba, N. (2006). Integrating different grain levels in a medical data warehouse federation. In A. M. Tjoa & N. Tho (Ed.), *Proceedings of the DaWaK* (pp. 185-194). Krakow, Poland: Springer.

Berger, S., & Schrefl, M. (2006). Analysing multi-dimensional data across autonomous data warehouses. In A. M. Tjoa & N. Tho (Ed.), *Proceedings of the DaWaK* (pp. 120-133). Krakow, Poland: Springer.

Berger, S., & Schrefl, M. (2008). From federated databases to a federated data warehouse system. In *Proceedings of the HICSS*. Kona, Hawaii: IEEE Computer Society.

Bernardino, J., Furtado, P., & Madeira, H. (2002). DWS-AQA: A cost effective approach for very large data warehouses. In M. A. Nascimento, T. M. Özsu, & O. R. Zaïane (Eds.), *Proceedings of the IDEAS* (pp. 233-242). Washington, DC: IEEE Computer Society.

Binh, N. T., Tjoa, A. M., & Mangisengi, O. (2003). Metacube XTM: A multidimensional metadata approach for Semantic Web warehousing systems. In Y. Kambayashi, M. M. Mohania, & W. Wöss (Eds.), *Proceedings of the DaWaK* (pp. 76-88). Berlin, Germany: Springer.

Brunneder, W. (2008). *Parsing and transformation of SQL-MDi queries in federated data warehouses* (In German). Linz, Austria: Johannes Kepler University.

Cabibbo, L., & Torlone, R. (2004). On the integration of autonomous data marts. In *Proceedings of the SSDBM* (pp. 223-234). Washington, DC: IEEE Computer Society.

Cabibbo, L., & Torlone, R. (2005). Integrating Heterogeneous Multidimensional Databases. In J. Frew (Ed.), *Proceedings SSDBM* (pp. 205-214). IEEE Computer Society.

Dhamankar, R., Lee, Y., Doan, A., Halevy, A., & Domingos, P. (2004). iMAP: Discovering complex semantic matches between database schemas. In *Proceedings of the SIGMOD* (pp. 383-394). Paris, France: ACM.

Gingras, F., & Lakshmanan, L. V. (1998). nD-SQL: A multi-dimensional language for interoperability and OLAP. In A. Gupta, O. Shmueli, & J. Widom (Eds.), *Proceedings of the VLDB* (pp. 134-145). San Francisco: Morgan Kaufmann.

Golfarelli, M., Maio, D., & Rizzi, S. (1998). The dimensional fact model: A conceptual model for data warehouses. *Int. J. Cooperative Information Systems, 7*(2-3), 215–247. doi:10.1142/S0218843098000118

Halevy, A. Y. (2001). Answering queries using views: A survey. *The VLDB Journal, 10*(4), 270–294. doi:10.1007/s007780100054

Halevy, A. Y., Rajaraman, A., & Ordille, J. J. (2006). Data integration: The teenage years. In U. Dayal, K.-Y. Whang, D. B. Lomet, G. Alonso, G. M. Lohman, M. L. Kersten, et al. (Eds.), *Proceedings of the VLDB* (pp. 9-16). New York: ACM.

Hurtado, C. A., Gutiérrez, C., & Mendelzon, A. O. (2005). Capturing summarizability with integrity constraints in OLAP. *ACM Transactions on Database Systems, 30*(3), 854–886. doi:10.1145/1093382.1093388

Hurtado, C. A., & Mendelzon, A. O. (2001). Reasoning about summarizability in heterogeneous multidimensional schemas. In J. Van den Bussche, & V. Vianu (Eds.), *Proceedings of the ICDT* (pp. 375-389). Berlin, Germany: Springer.

Inmon, W. (2005). *Building the data warehouse* (4th ed.). New York: John Wiley & Sons.

ISO. (1992). ISO/IEC 9075:1992: Information technology -- database languages -- SQL.

Kim, W., & Seo, J. (1991). Classifying schematic and data heterogeneity in multidatabase systems. *IEEE Computer, 24*(12), 12–18.

Kimball, R. (2002). *The data warehouse toolkit: Practical techniques for building dimensional data warehouses* (2nd ed.). New York: John Wiley & Sons.

Lenz, H.-J., & Shoshani, A. (1997). Summarizability in OLAP and statistical data bases. In Y. E. Ioannidis, & D. M. Hansen (Eds.), *Proceedings of the SSDBM* (pp. 132-143). Washington, DC: IEEE Computer Society.

Lenzerini, M. (2002). Data integration: A theoretical perspective. In L. Popa (Ed.), *Proceedings of PODS* (pp. 233-246). New York: ACM.

Litwin, W., Mark, L., & Roussopoulos, N. (1990). Interoperability of multiple autonomous databases. *ACM Computing Surveys, 22*(3), 267–293. doi:10.1145/96602.96608

Luján-Mora, S., Trujillo, J., & Song, I.-Y. (2006). A UML profile for multidimensional modeling in data warehouses. *Data & Knowledge Engineering, 59*(3), 725–769. doi:10.1016/j.datak.2005.11.004

Maislinger, L. (2009). *Grafisches Werkzeug zur Integration von Data Marts* (in German). Linz, Austria: Johannes Kepler University.

Mangisengi, O., Essmayr, W., Huber, J., & Weippl, E. (2003). XML-based OLAP query processing in a federated data warehouse. In *Proceedings of the ICEIS*, (pp. 71-78).

Nuseibeh, B., & Easterbrook, S. (2000). Requirements engineering: A roadmap. In *Proceedings of the ICSE* (pp. 35-46). New York: ACM Press.

Özsu, T. M., & Valduriez, P. (1999). *Principles of distributed database systems* (2nd ed.). Upper Sadle River, NJ: Prentice Hall.

Rizzi, S., Abelló, A., Lechtenbörger, J., & Trujillo, J. (2006). Research in data warehouse modeling and design: Dead or alive? In I.-Y. Song & P. Vassiliadis (Eds.), *Proceedings of the DOLAP* (pp. 3-10). New York: ACM.

Rossgatterer, T. (2008). Entwicklung eines Query Prozessors in einem Föderierten Data Warehouse System (in German). Linz, Austria: Johannes Kepler University.

Sheth, A. P., & Larson, J. A. (1990). Federated database systems for managing distributed, heterogeneous, and autonomous databases. *ACM Computing Surveys, 22*(3), 183–236. doi:10.1145/96602.96604

Thomsen, E. (2002). *OLAP solutions -- building multidimensional information systems* (2nd ed.). New York: John Wiley & Sons.

Torlone, R., & Panella, I. (2005). Design and development of a tool for integrating heterogeneous data warehouses. In A. M. Tjoa, & J. Trujillo (Ed.), *Proceedings of the DaWaK* (pp. 105-114). Berlin, Germany: Springer.

Vassiliadis, P., & Sellis, T. K. (1999). A survey of logical models for OLAP databases. *SIGMOD Record, 28*(4), 64–69. doi:10.1145/344816.344869

Vetterli, T., Vaduva, A., & Staudt, M. (2000). Metadata standards for data warehousing: Open information model vs. common warehouse metamodel. *SIGMOD Record, 29*(3), 68–75. doi:10.1145/362084.362138

of the output schema in the SELECT clause. Moreover, the "mappings" between the tables have to be done in pair wise manner by giving "join" conditions in the WHERE clause. Although this approach has its own merits, the specification of pair wise joins for queries involving a large number of tables is quite awkward.

ENDNOTES

[1]   In the example, we use the postfix '_dim' to name dimension tables to avoid confusion with identical level attribute names. Moreover, we use the prefix 'l_', denoting level names, in order to avoid confusion between identical dimension *level* names and level *attribute* names.

[2]   In the description of the methodology we give the conflict number addressed by each step in brackets. These numbers (#...) refer to the definitions and examples of the conflict taxonomy in the previous section.

[3]   In contrast, the standard database query language SQL (ISO, 1992) employs exactly the opposite paradigm. In an SQL query, the user explicitly specifies the attributes

Chapter 6
Built–In Indicators to Support Business Intelligence in OLAP Databases

Jérôme Cubillé
EDF R&D, France

Christian Derquenne
EDF R&D, France

Sabine Goutier
EDF R&D, France

Françoise Guisnel
EDF R&D, France

Henri Klajnmic
EDF R&D, France

Véronique Cariou
ENITIAA, France

ABSTRACT

This chapter is in the scope of static and dynamic discovery-driven explorations of a data cube. It presents different methods to facilitate the whole process of data exploration. Each kind of analysis (static or dynamic) is developed for either a count measure or a quantitative measure. Both are based on the calculation, on the fly, of specific statistical built-in indicators. Firstly, a global methodology is proposed to help a dynamic discovery-driven exploration. It aims at identifying the most relevant dimensions to expand. A built-in rank on dimensions is restituted interactively, at each step of the process. Secondly, to help a static discovery-driven exploration, generalized statistical criteria are detailed to detect and highlight interesting cells within a cube slice. The cell's degree of interest is determined by the calculation of either test-value or Chi-Square contribution. Their display is done by a color-coding system. A proof of concept implementation on the ORACLE 10g system is described at the end of the chapter.

DOI: 10.4018/978-1-60566-748-5.ch006

Copyright © 2010, IGI Global. Copying or distributing in print or electronic forms without written permission of IGI Global is prohibited.

Figure 1. Simplified cube representation based on the three dimensions TARIFF, CONTRACT *and* ENERGY HEATING

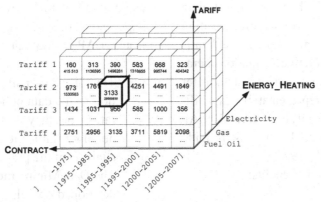

INTRODUCTION

Context

Most of large companies have identified the importance and the strategic value of the information contained in their Data Warehouses. But these Data Warehouses are of interest only if the knowledge they contain, is correctly extracted, formatted, summarized, presented and shared by business analysts in order to create added value. Different technologies exist that can organize, present and make data available, from simple request or visualization tools to simulation applications or multidimensional analysis.

In particular, On-Line Analytical Processing (OLAP) applications are powerful decision support tools. They offer a multidimensional view of the data, by calculating and displaying indicators either in detail or with some level of aggregation. Given the fact table of a cube, the multidimensional model consists in dimensional attributes (dimensions) and measures attributes (measures) defined using an aggregate function like sum, count or average.

In practice, a data cube is built from a single large table which contains the most detailed data and we assume that the structure of this underlying table (called DETAIL) is the following:DETAIL(#ID,

$d_1, d_2, ..., d_z, M_1, M_2, ..., M_q, W_1, W_2, ..., W_l$)where $d_1, d_2, ..., d_z$ are called *dimension attributes* and form the dimensions of the data cube, $M_1, M_2, ..., M_q$ are called *measure attributes* and form the measures, and $W_1, W_2, ..., W_l$ are a set of *weights* of each tuple. Usually one of them equals 1 and is used for the count measure. Tuples of this detailed table are called *statistical units*.

The measures functionally depend on the set of dimensions they are associated with. In this chapter, we consider a sales data cube example[1] in order to analyze customers energy consumption per year and market segmentation according to the following relation scheme:CUSTOMER(#Cust, TARIFF, DWELLING, HEATING, OCCUPATION, WATER HEATING, OLDNESS OF HOUSE, DATE OF CONTRACT SUBSCRIPTION, TYPE OF DWELLING, CONSUMPTION)

Figure 1 presents, in a simplified data cube, the mean electrical consumption (per year) and the number of customers according to three characteristics.

In the underlined cell on Figure 1, 3 133 corresponds to the number of customers with **Tariff 2** subscribed between **1985** and **1995** and using **fuel oil** for their energy heating. These customers have consumed 29 560 930 KWh per year.

In many company departments, such as Marketing, Sales or Human Resources, business analysts take advantage of OLAP products for market segmentation, customers analysis or sales forecasting activities. This multidimensional view is easily understandable by business analysts who can become direct end-users of the corresponding commercial software. Exploration of the data is performed thanks to interactive navigation operators. Moreover, OLAP management systems offer reporting and graphical representations capabilities to analyze more efficiently data. Several OLAP products, for instance ORACLE 10g, also provide a web restitution for end-users.

This fact has interesting benefits:

- Business analysts can directly interact with data instead of relying on computer scientists,
- The development cost of computer-based decision systems decreases since business analysts build interactively the reports they desire.

Nevertheless, as soon as multidimensional databases become very large, the number of cells of the cube dramatically increases. Business analysts are rapidly confronted to a difficult and tedious task in order to analyze such multidimensional databases with multiple criteria. They would like to answer such type of questions:

- How to quickly find which cell of the multidimensional table contains an atypical value for the measure (that is which cell contains a value very different from expected)?
- How to rapidly discover the dimensions which are the most correlated or associated one to another?
- How to automatically detect that a measure with specific selection criteria has an abnormal temporal evolution compared to the others?

Commercial OLAP products do not provide such intelligent analysis operators to help business analysts in the browsing of their data. Indeed, Data Mining methods which allow to carry out complex exploration and to discover useful information in huge amount of data are generally used separately from OLAP technologies:

- The OLAP systems give an efficient solution to the data cubes building and exploration, but they do not offer any statistical nor algorithmic method in order to help the analysis of the presented aggregated data,
- The Data Mining methods are traditionally developed on "classical" individuals-variables table or on relational databases and are not extended to multidimensional databases. Even if Data Mining algorithms are more and more integrated in relational database management systems (for instance Oracle 10g or Sql Server 2005), direct implementations are only done on detailed data and not on aggregated one.

This chapter describes methods to support business intelligence in OLAP databases based on:

- A dynamic analysis in order to guide end-users' navigation. The aim is to identify the most interesting dimensions to expand, given a current slice under study. The built-in indicators, we developed, help the user by proposing him or her at each step of the process the dimension to expand first.
- A static analysis of a multidimensional cube, coupled with the previous one, in order to help end-users' analysis. The aim is to automatically detect interesting cells among a user selected cells. In this chapter, interesting cells mean cells containing a measure very different from the other selected ones. We propose two different algorithms depending on the nature of the measure displayed in the cells (a count measure or a quantitative one).

The originality of this work is the adaptation of Data Mining methods to multidimensional environment where detailed data are no more available and only aggregated ones can be used. Our solution is based on a tight coupling between OLAP tools and statistical methods. Methods are performed thanks to built-in indicators computed instantaneously during exploration without any pre-computation. They constitute an add-in OLAP tool providing a support to decision making.

Related Work

Since the last decade, there have been growing interests in coupling Data Mining methods and OLAP tools. In this scope, different problems have been investigated:

- How to perform Data Mining techniques on a data cube?
- How to facilitate the user-exploration of a data cube?
- How to enrich OLAP tools with statistical operators?

Historically, researches focused on the first aspect. In 1997, Han et al. proposed a new tool, DB Miner, which aimed at mining multidimensional data at different levels of aggregation. Several functions were investigated such as association rules, classification or clustering. Nevertheless, most of the other contributions in this domain focused on the association rules algorithms. (Zhu, 1998 and Nestorov et al., 2003) proposed an adaptation of the Apriori algorithm while considering multidimensional data. (Kamber et al., 1997) defined a metarule-guided mining algorithm. It aimed at extracting matched patterns from data cubes, with regard to some user-defined meta-rules. Closely related to the association rules problem, (Imielinski et al., 2002) and (Dong et al., 2001) defined the cubegrade query. Instead of extracting all kinds of association rules, their goal was to explain main trends in the data cube.

It resulted in the capture of rules that describe significant measure changes associated with changes in dimension description (e.g. values of dimensions).

The second aspect concerns discovery-driven exploration of a data cube. Analyzing multidimensional data with a huge number of dimensions rapidly becomes a tedious and difficult task for the analyst. To facilitate user exploration, some authors have introduced specific operators (Chen, 1999, Sarawagi, 1998). These ones enable to detect automatically relevant cells in a data cube (SELFEXP operator). They also provide the user to identify the "best" path in exploring data by highlighting the most relevant dimensions to drill-down. All these operators are based on the notion of degree of exception of a cell. A cell measure is said to be an exception if it differs significantly from the value predicted with statistical models. These ones are based either on log-linear models (for count measures) or on analysis of variance (for measures based on the average aggregate function). Models are saturated ones, since dimensions and all their interactions are taken into account. The model is fitted using the OLS (ordinary least squares) estimation. The exception of the cell is then defined as the standardized residual between the aggregated value and the predicted one. Going on this approach, Sarawagi proposed other discovery-driven operators. The DIFF operator (Sarawagi, 1999) is used to explain differences between two cell values. The INFORM operator (Sarawagi, 2000) intends to find the parts of the cube a user will find most surprising given a-priori knowledge. Finally, the RELAX operator (Sathe et al., 2001) tries to find the most aggregated level where an exception can be observed. These operators lead to a two stages algorithm implementation.

More recently, some authors have studied how to enrich the data cube manipulation by new statistical operators. The aim is to enable the user a better visualization of the data thanks to data model reorganization. This is achieved by values permutation within a dimension (Ben Messaoud et al., 2006) or by dimension hierarchy building (Ben Messaoud et al., 2004). These methods are closely related to the generalized association plots concept (Chen, 2002).

This chapter is in the scope of discovery-driven exploration of a data cube. In our approach, two analyses are considered. The first one consists in analyzing rapidly a slice, by highlighting the most significant cells. The second one facilitates the whole process of exploration of the data cube by giving the most relevant dimensions to drill-down. In this chapter, we focus on the first kind of analysis. Given a user-defined dimensions drill-down, it consists in identifying which cells are the most "interesting". This problem is similar to the SelfExp operator of Sarawagi. Nevertheless, we stress two main contributions compared to the previous approach. Here, the degree of exception of a cell is not based on a saturated model. Indeed, such models lead to unstable solution especially considering sparse data and using OLS estimation. The way we compute the degree of exception is detailed in the next section. We study the use of Chi-Square contribution and the use of test-value (Morineau, 1984) to highlight relevant cells. Since no hypothesis is made on the exploration path, the degree of interest is computed without regard to interactions between dimensions. This guarantees the business analyst an easier and more robust interpretation of the most interesting cells.

The other contribution lies in the way indicators are built. We take advantages of OLAP functionalities so that indicators can be computed instantaneously according to the dimensions interactively chosen to structure the slice. It offers a compromise between computation performance and model complexity. The approach leads to an enriched OLAP tool without any need of pre-computation task.

Working Example

We illustrate our approach with an example based on a database issued from a marketing context. In this example, we consider a simplified detailed table with the following relation scheme:CUSTOMER(#Cust, TARIFF, DWELLING, HEATING, OCCUPATION, WATER HEATING, OLDNESS OF HOUSE, DATE OF CONTRACT SUBSCRIPTION, TYPE OF DWELLING, CONSUMPTION)

One tuple of Table 1 is related to one customer and will be called a *statistical unit* in this chapter. From this detailed table, the corresponding data cube is structured by 8 dimensions: type of contract, type of dwelling, type of heating, … and by the following measures: number of customers and mean of electrical consumption.

On our snapshots, the category 'TOT' stands for the common value 'ANY' or 'ALL' which represents the total aggregated level of a dimension. All displayed measures are structured by the dimensions "TARPUI" (*Tariff*), "CONTRAT" (*Date_Of_Contract_Subscription*), "TYPRES" (*Type_Of_Dwelling*), "TYPHAB" (*Dwelling*), "CONSTRUCT" (*Oldness_Of_House*), "STOC" (*Occupation*), "CHFP" (*Heating*), "EAUCHA" (*Water_Heating*).

A global methodology is proposed to facilitate the browsing of a data cube for business intelligence activities. Firstly, a dynamic discovery-driven exploration aims at identifying the most relevant dimensions to expand. Thereafter, interesting cells are detected and highlighted in order to help a static analysis of the current cube slice derived from the set of dimensions already chosen.

DYNAMIC ANALYSIS

We propose a method to guide end-users navigation through the multidimensional data by proposing them at each step of the process the

Table 1. Example of a customers detailed table

# Cust	Tariff	Dwelling	Heating	...	Consumption
1	Tariff 1	House	Electrical		212
2	Tariff 2	Flat	Gas		153
3	Tariff 1	Flat	Electrical		225
4	Tariff 2	Flat	Gas		142
5	Tariff 3	House	Fuel Oil		172
...	...	...	...	...	...

dimensions to expand first.

Data-driven built-in indicators, calculated on the fly, measure the degree of interest of each expandable dimension.

At each step, the adopted approach for guided navigation includes two distinct tasks:

- First, the sorting of the expandable dimensions by decreasing order of interest (this order could be displayed as a gray scale) (see Figure 2).
- Then, once a dimension has been chosen and expanded, the identification and the display of the most atypical cells of the current slice could be done.

Insofar as it is supposed that, at each step, the user interprets a new table, the method aims to only emphasize new information conditionally to the information already highlighted in the slice displayed at the previous step.

In this work, we suppose that the dimensions have simple hierarchies (two levels: the first one with only the position "ALL" and the second one with all the categories).

Two methods are developed to measure the degree of interest of each expandable dimension: one for a count measure (such as the number of customers) and the other for a quantitative measure (such as electric consumption). They differ from the kind of built-in indicators used to sort the expandable dimensions:

- In the case of a count measure, the method is based on the deviation of the observed cells values against the assumption of the independence model. Deviation is computed for each possible dimension with a kind of Tschuprow's T indicator (Bishop et al., 1975).
- In the case of a quantitative measure, the method is based on the calculation of the variation among the cells means given by the sum of squares among cells (denoted SSA in classical analysis of variance in Jobson, 1991).

The restitution is done by a color scale applied on each dimension which proposes to the end-user the dimensions rank. In both case, the algorithm is built on the following general idea.

Figure 2.

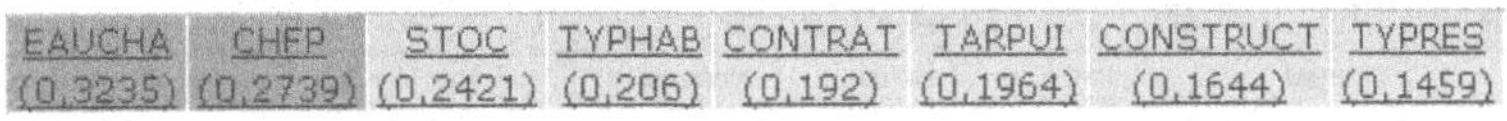

EAUCHA	CHEP	STOC	TYPHAB	CONTRAT	TARPUI	CONSTRUCT	TYPRES
(0,3235)	(0,2739)	(0,2421)	(0,206)	(0,192)	(0,1964)	(0,1644)	(0,1459)

Figure 3. Application snapshot at the beginning of the process © 2009 [Françoise Guisnel] Used with permission.

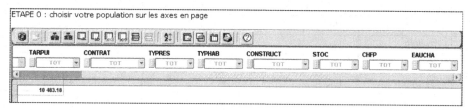

Initialization: Choice of the Population under Study

The process starts from the most aggregated level, i.e. all the available dimensions are still in page axes and none of them have been expanded to structure a table. Let us note D={all structuring dimensions} (see Figure 3).

In our example, D={Tarpui, Contrat, Typres, Typhab, Construct, Stoc, Chfp, Eaucha}.

First of all, the end-user can define a data selection (also called subpopulation in the statistical formalism) on which he wants to perform his analysis. The method allows him to select positions on a set of dimensions called D_{popu} in order to restrict the subpopulation of study. After this initialization step, no further selection will be possible during the navigation process and those axes will not be expandable anymore. This potentially defines a new set D^* of expandable dimensions. If no subpopulation is selected $D^*=D$. That is to say D^*={potential expandable dimensions}=$D \setminus D_{popu}$ (see Figure 4).

In the example, a data selection has been performed to restrict the analysis to customers having a given tariff (Tarpui='DT<=6'). In this case, D_{popu} = {Tarpui} and D^*={Contrat, Typres, Typhab, Construct, Stoc, Chfp, Eaucha}.

Step 1: Choice of the First Dimension

When the process is executed for the first time, an indicator is calculated for each expandable dimension. The value taken by this indicator for each dimension of D^* enables to classify those dimensions depending on their degree of interest. The choice of the first dimension to unfold remains to the user who can decide to choose another dimension which seems more relevant according to his data knowledge and to the purpose of his analysis. This first dimension will then be noted $d_{(1)}$ and the data are displayed to the user according to this dimension (see Figure 5).

The two subsets of dimensions are updated: $D^* = D^* \setminus d_{(1)}$ and $D_1=\{d_{(1)}\}$

In the example, $d_{(1)}$= Typhab involving D^*={Contrat, Typres, Construct, Stoc, Chfp, Eaucha } and D_1={Typhab}.

Figure 4. Application snapshot after the subpopulation selection © 2009 [Françoise Guisnel] Used with permission.

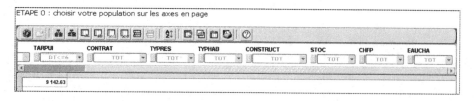

Figure 5. Application snapshot at the end of the first step © 2009 [Françoise Guisnel] Used with permission.

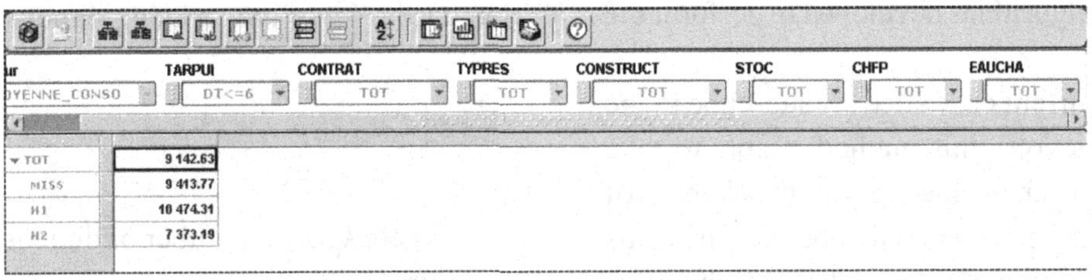

Step s: Choice of the sth Dimension

For all the dimensions expanded until the s-1th step ($D_{s-1}=\{d_{(1)}, d_{(2)},...,d_{(s-1)}\}$), the idea is to build a virtual dimension $d_{(v)}$ resulting from the crossing of all dimensions in D_{s-1}. So, the problem to solve at the sth step is to find which dimension of D^* will provide the best partition when crossed with the virtual dimension $d_{(v)}$.

The quality of the resulting partition is measured by a second built-in indicator calculated for each dimension of D^*. The value of this indicator allows to order the dimensions of D^* relating to their degree of interest. As at the first step, a sorting of the dimensions is performed according to this indicator and the choice of the dimension to unfold remains to the user. This dimension will then be noted $d_{(s)}$ and the data are displayed to the user according to the s dimensions $d_{(1)}, d_{(2)},..., d_{(s-1)}$ and $d_{(s)}$. At the end of this step, D^* is updated as $D^* = D^* \setminus d_{(s)}$ and $D_s=\{d_{(1)}, d_{(2),}...,d_{(s)}\}$.

This step is repeated until $card(D^*)=0$ (see Figure 6).

In the example on Figure 6, $d_{(2)}=$ EAUCHA, so we have $D^*=\{$CONTRAT, TYPRES, CONSTRUCT, STOC, CHFP$\}$ and $D_2=\{$TYPHAB, EAUCHA$\}$.

The way built-in indicators are defined to identify the most significant dimension to expand (Cariou et al., in press) is beyond the scope of this chapter. In the sequel, we focus on the second part, i.e., once the dimensions have been expanded, how to highlight interesting cells of such a given slice data cube. In the following paragraphs, we will present the notations before describing the built-in indicators corresponding to the static analysis for a count measure and a quantitative one.

STATIC ANALYSIS

The dynamic analysis helps the end-user to determine which dimensions have to first be expanded in order to discover the most interesting cells.

Figure 6. Application snapshot at the end of the second step © 2009 [Françoise Guisnel] Used with permission.

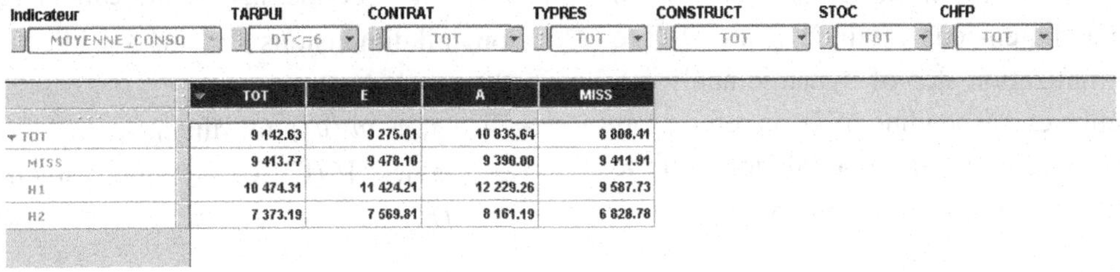

Once this step performed, the static analysis will highlight those interesting cells. This paragraph presents the algorithms developed to perform the static analysis.

Given a current cube slice (or sub-cube in the case of restriction), this method is able to take into account, in an interactive way, the changes of criteria that the end-user could operate during his analysis (definition of subpopulations, choice of the dimensions in line and column). Indeed, static analysis is based on the computation of built-in indicators. These ones are generic since they can be computed whenever any OLAP operations are performed (*roll-up*, *drill-down*, *restriction*, *slice* ...).

Two methods are developed depending on the kind of the measure that is a count measure (such as the number of customers) or a quantitative one (such as electric consumption):

- The first one is based on the computation of the cell contribution to the total Chi-Square of the cube slice.
- The second one is based on the calculation of the test-value (Morineau, 1984)

The restitution of these methods is done by a color-coding system which proposes to the end-user several exploration levels according to the number of colored interesting cells (e.g. for expert exploration, only the cells with the most important level of interest are colored; in that case a method of detection of different thresholds is applied).

Notations

We recall that D is the set of all structuring dimensions of the cube while $D*$ is the set of all expandable dimensions retained from D (see section initialization step of dynamic analysis). The sub-cube corresponding to $D*$ is referred as subpopulation E issued from population P of the cube. If no selection is made on the page axes, $E=P$.

Once E is fixed, we call t the current slice of the sub-cube and $\tilde{X}$ one measure under study. Let us note D_t the set of the crossing dimensions of t:

$$D_t = \left\{ d_1, ..., d_r, ..., d_{k_t} \right\}$$

- where k_t is the number of dimensions structuring t
- and d_r is one dimension structuring t.

We also denote n_E the size of the subpopulation E and M_{d_r} the number of distinct values on the dimension d_r at the current aggregated level of d_r hierarchy ('TOT' is excluded).

A line or a column of the resulting table where the value is TOT, is called a margin (it corresponds to the "ANY" position). The margins of the table are not included in this slice t.

For any cell i of the current slice t, we define $m_i(d_r)$ as the position of the dimension d_r corresponding to the cell i. We notice that the cell $i \in t$ is at the crossing of k_t dimensions for the values $m_i(d_1), ..., m_i(d_r), ..., m_i(d_{k_t})$.

Let us note:

- n_i the size of the cell $i \in t$ which is the number of statistical units in the cell $i \in t$, $\forall t, n_E = \sum_{i \in t} n_i$

- f_i the relative frequency of cell i in the subpopulation E: $f_i = \dfrac{n_i}{n_E}$

- $x_j^{(i)}$ the value of $\tilde{X}$ for the statistical unit j in the cell i of the slice t.

Let $n_i^{[d_r]}$ be the size of the cell i aggregated along all dimensions $D_t \setminus \left\{ d_r \right\}$ with:

- value $m_i(d_r)$ for dimension d_r
- value "TOT" for all other dimensions in $D_t \setminus \left\{ d_r \right\}$

Figure 7. Definition of subpopulations and slice t © 2009 [Françoise Guisnel] Used with permission.

Indicateur	STOC	TARPUI	CONTRAT	TYPRES	TYPHAB	CONSTRUCT
MOYENNE_CONSO ▼	O ▼	TOT ▼	TOT ▼	P ▼	TOT ▼	TOT ▼

▼	TOT	MISS	E	A	G
▼ TOT	12 751.47	11 790.12	13 647.57	12 853.37	12 136.80
E	13 187.41	12 450.31	13 685.03	12 789.66	12 155.36
A	12 840.30	9 390.00	13 452.47	13 508.27	12 124.08
MISS	11 908.18	11 776.87	13 489.88	10 603.62	12 178.38

$n_i^{[d_r]}$ corresponds to the number of statistical units with value $m_i(d_r)$ in subpopulation E.

In addition, we will denote:

- $f_i^{[d_r]}$ the relative frequency of value $m_i(d_r)$ in the subpopulation E

$$f_i^{[d_r]} = \frac{n_i^{[d_r]}}{n_E}$$

- $\bar{X}_i$ the average of the variable $\tilde{X}$ for the cell i of the slice t

$$\bar{X}_i = \frac{1}{n_i} \sum_{j=1}^{n_i} x_j^{(i)}$$ while $\bar{X}_E$ is the overall average of subpopulation E.

Example 1

On the example presented Figure 7, E is the subpopulation corresponding to home owners (STOC=O) living in their main home (TYPRES=P). In this table with two dimensions, t is framed by a dotted line.

For the cell i such as
$i = d_1$ 'A' $\times d_2$ ']1975 $-$ 1985]' :

- $m_i(d_1)$= 'A'
- $m_{i(d2)=}$ ']1975 $-$ 1985]'

Case 1: Count Measure

The problem we are interested in is, for each cell of a given table, to compute an indicator that expresses the "level of interest" of the cell according to a count measure. In the case of a count measure, $x_j^{(i)} = 1$ for all statistical units j in the cell i of the slice t.

Basic Idea

Our framework may be related to a log-linear modeling as far as each slice defines a contingency table where the associated dimensions correspond to the categorical variables. The method, we propose, is based on the comparison between the value of the observed measure in the cell and the expected value under the independence model that is a homogeneous distribution among the cells, with regard to the margin values.

For a two-dimensional case, two dimensions d_1 and d_2 are independent if the frequency in the cells at each crossing of a value of d_1 and a value of d_2 only depends on the "margins" of the table.

We recall that n_i is the observed number. Let us define $\hat{n}_i$ the estimated frequency, i.e. the expected number of statistical units in a cell i with regard to the independence model.

For a cell i defined by the crossing of d_1 and d_2, $\hat{n}_i$ is estimated under the assumption of independence. It is equal to (Agresti, 2002):

$$\hat{n}_i = n_E f_i^{[d_1]} f_i^{[d_2]}$$

Table 2. Count measure with two dimensions

d_2 \ d_1	A	B	C	D	Total
H	12 034	716	24 398	370	37 518
F	*19 062*	20 973	2 759	401	**43 195**
G	16 532	11 800	10 368	52 662	91 362
Total	**47 628**	33 489	37 525	53 433	**172 075**

The standardized residual for cell i is then defined as:

$$e_i = \frac{n_i - \hat{n}_i}{\hat{n}_i^{1/2}}$$

Let us illustrate this idea with the following example.

Example 2

In this example based on the detailed Table 1, Table 2 can be built where the measure of the data cube represents the number of customers whose specific characteristics are organized by dimensions d_1 and d_2.

Let us focus on the pointed-out cell (d_1 'A' et d_2 'F'). If d_1 and d_2 were independent, instead of the observed value 19 062 in italic on Table 2, we should have a value close to the product of the two margins values (underlined bold values) (43 195 and 47 628) divided by the size of the subpopulation (here 172 075). So, in the case of independence between the two dimensions, that given cell should contain a value close to 11 956, instead of 19 062.

We can generalize the independence concept to several dimensions $d_1, ..., d_r, ..., d_{k_t}$ as following:

$$\hat{n}_i = n_E \prod_{r=1}^{k_t} f_i^{[d_r]} = n_E \prod_{r=1}^{k_t} \frac{n_i^{[d_r]}}{n_E}$$

Construction of the Indicator

Let us now precise the theoretical framework of this formulation. In two-way contingency tables, the null hypothesis of independence can be tested with the Pearson chi-squared statistic (Agresti, 2002):

$$\chi^2 = \sum_{i \in t} \frac{\left(n_i - \hat{n}_i\right)^2}{\hat{n}_i}$$

The higher the χ^2 is, the more different, compared to the null hypothesis of independence, the cells are. So to identify the most atypical cells, we use the contribution of a cell i, denoted $C_{\chi 2}(i)$, to the table chi-square χ^2. In the general case of k_t dimensions, the contribution can be written:

$$C_{\chi 2}(i) = \frac{\left(n_i - \hat{n}_i\right)^2}{\hat{n}_i} = e_i^2$$

With regard to the model of independence, our approach thus consists in identifying the cells having the most important standardized residuals.

In order to detect interesting cells, we define the level of interest of the cell i by the following built-in indicator $IC(i)$:

$$IC(i) = \frac{C_{\chi 2}(i)}{\sum_{i \in t} C_{\chi 2}(i)}$$

Table 3. Indicator of contribution of Chi-Square

d_2 \ d_1	A	B	C	D
H	0.00	0.05	0.27	0.09
F	0.04	0.15	0.04	0.11
G	0.03	0.02	0.04	0.16

We notice that $\sum_{i \in t} IC(i) = 1$.

Example 3

Table 3 contains the values of indicator *IC* of the example in Table 2.

General Interpretation of the Indicator IC

By definition, *IC* is included between 0 and 1 ($0 \leq IC(i) < 1$). If $IC(i) = 0$, the cell *i* corresponds to an homogeneous distribution of the statistical units with regard to the margins values. The closer to 1 $IC(i)$ is, the farther the distribution of the statistical units from the situation of independence is. It thus means that the cell *i* abnormally either attracts or rejects the statistical units of slice *t*.

Identifying Interesting Cells

At this stage, the indicator *IC(i)* is calculated for each cell. The problem to be solved now is to select the cells for which indicator's values are the highest, in order to color them in a suitable way. To perform that, two ways have been investigated

in parallel: a statistical approach based on a clustering of *IC(i)* values and an analytical approach based on the detection of gaps on the distribution curve of the *IC(i)* as shown on Figure 8.

In our experiments, the results of both approaches are very close. With regard to time performance, the second approach gives better results while implemented in the OLAP management system. So the latter solution has been retained to detect thresholds and to color interesting cells.

In our method, two thresholds (labeled 1 and 2 on Figure 8) are actually defined in order to distinguish two levels of interest for the cells. Cells having an indicator value greater than threshold 1 are colored in dark color; those having an indicator value between threshold 1 and threshold 2 are colored in light color. The other cells are not colored. The color will be specified in the following paragraph.

Example 4

In the working example, the curve for the distribution of *IC(i)* has been built from the selection of two dimensions (as shown on Table 2).

One cell is colored in dark color and two cells in light color. We precise that the margin cells are shaded in order to indicate that they are not analyzed.

Definition of Attraction and Repulsion Zones

For a business analyst, it may be relevant to know whether a highlighted cell corresponds to

Figure 8. Research of threshold for IC(i)

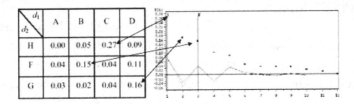

Table 4. Colored cells

d_2 \ d_1	A	B	C	D	Total
H	12 034	716	24 398	370	37 518
F	19 062	**20 973**	2 759	401	43 195
G	16 532	11 800	10 368	52 662	91 362
Total	47 628	33 489	37 525	53 433	172 075

an attraction or a repulsion case. Each computed contribution can be signed:

- If $n_i - \hat{n}_i > 0$ then the cell is an attraction zone of the statistical units, i.e. where the statistical units are "abundant" (it means that the cell contains more statistical units than expected in the independence case). These cells are colored in green with two levels of intensity: light green and dark green), according to the level of atypicity.

- If $n_i - \hat{n}_i < 0$ then the cell is a repulsion zone of the statistical units, i.e. where the statistical units are "rare" (it means that the cell contains less statistical units than expected in the independence case). These cells are colored in red with two levels of intensity: light red and dark red, according to the level of atypicity.

Example 6

In Table 4, in the cell defined by $\{d_1=$'C' and $d_2=$'H'$\}$, $n_i = 24\ 398$ and $\hat{n}_i = 8\ 181.7$, so, this cell will be colored in dark green, while two other ones will be colored in light green (cells defined by $\{d_1=$'B' and $d_2=$'F'$\}$ and by $\{d_1=$'D' and $d_2=$'G'$\}$).

Case 2: Quantitative Measure

Studying a quantitative measure $\tilde{X}$ such as electric consumption, the test-value (Morineau, 1984) is chosen to detect interesting cells.

Basic Idea

The basic idea is to compare the real value of the measure $\tilde{X}$ in a cell with the mean on the whole subpopulation for the given slice t. The test-value enables us to identify and to order the significant difference between the estimated value (i.e. the mean value) and the cell aggregated one. It consists in standardizing the difference between the two values by taking into account the variance of the measure within the cell (under a later precised hypothesis).

It makes possible to compare the gap between:

- the average on a subpopulation, e.g. the average consumption of all the customers whatever their central heating energy is,
- and the average for a combination of dimensions values, e.g. the average consumption of the customers with an electric heating system and hot water system.

With regard to the measure $\tilde{X}$, the more important this variation is, the more different the cell is. The test-value thus provides an indicator of exception of a cell.

Construction of the Indicator

The assumption for the use of the test-value is that the n_i statistical units of cell i are randomly sampled without replacement from the subpopulation E. The measure $\bar{X}_i$ represents the average of the measure in the cell with $\mathbf{E}(\bar{X}_i) = \bar{X}_E$ and $V(\bar{X}_i) = \tilde{S}_i^2$. $\tilde{S}_i^2$ denotes the variance of $\bar{X}_i$ under the assumption of a random sampling of n_i elements from the subpopulation E, while S_E^2 is the empirical variance of the variable X on E:

$$\tilde{S}_i^2 = \frac{n_E - n_i}{n_E} \frac{S_E^2}{n_i} \text{ with } \tilde{S}_i^2 = \frac{n_E - n_i}{n_E} \frac{S_E^2}{n_i}$$

$$S_E^2 = \frac{1}{n_E - 1} \left[\sum_{i \in t} \sum_{j=1}^{n_i} \left[x_j^{(i)} \right]^2 - n_E \bar{X}_E^2 \right] \text{ with}$$

$$S_E^2 = \frac{1}{n_E - 1} \left[\sum_{i \in t} \sum_{j=1}^{n_i} \left[x_j^{(i)} \right]^2 - n_E \bar{X}_E^2 \right]$$

According to the previous formula, the test-value is defined as:

$$vt(i) = \frac{\bar{X}_i - \bar{X}_E}{\tilde{S}_i}$$

Thus, if the test-value is high (corresponding to a low probability of equality between the studied averages), we can consider that the average in the cell significantly differs from the average of the population under study. This indicator is used to order the cells according to their degree of interest.

IMPLEMENTATION WITH ORACLE 10G

In this paragraph, we present the implementation performed on real data. The aim is to show, as a proof of concept, the easiness of the implementation on an existing OLAP Management System.

The experiment has been performed on data issued from a marketing context. The data model has been presented previously in the motivating example. Currently, OLAP databases have been built with Oracle 10g. End users data browsing is provided thanks to a web application.

The whole discovery driven exploration of a data cube, including the dynamic and the static analysis, has been implemented under Oracle 10g since this software is opened enough to develop our own scripts. Algorithms are implemented in a data independent way and can be applied for hyper cubes with a great number of dimensions (in the motivating example, eight dimensions are studied). The implementation consists in a set of programs implemented in the Oracle L4G (Language 4th generation) language which also allows a web restitution.

When a user connects on the multidimensional application, the page shown in Figure 9 is displayed.

After a possible restriction of the browsing on a subpopulation, the first step of the drill-through can be processed by means of the extra-button *Navigation*. This consists first in solving the kind of measure associated with the slice. Then the corresponding built-in indicator program is executed. The results are displayed with a color's scale and hypertext links (see Figure 10).

Thereafter, the analyst makes its own dimension choice in order to analyze the data:

- At Step 1, no dimension has already been selected. The dimension chosen by the end-user will be displayed as a line axis.
- At Step 2, one dimension has already been expanded. The dimension chosen by the analyst will be displayed as a column axis.
- At Step s ($s>2$) of the process, s-1 dimensions have already been expanded and the dimension $d_{(s-1)}$ chosen at the previous step s-1 will be moved from column axis to row axis. The chosen dimension $d_{(s)}$ will then be put as a column axis.

Figure 9.

Navigation

Step 0: Choose your studied population

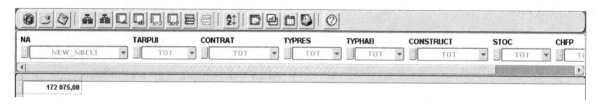

Once an axis was chosen and the slice of the cube displayed, the extra-button *Navigation* is again available. The drill-through process can be re-run for further steps. Furthermore, in the same time, the degree of exception of each cell of the current slice is calculated. It is restituted by means of a color-coding of the most interesting cells depending on the value of the indicator. If the user wants to see the added information, he may be helped using the extra "Detect and color" button.

When the business analyst has chosen the dimensions of interest, the display of the table with colored cells is instantaneous. Nevertheless, two factors can influence the processing time. As the system is based on a client-server architecture, computation is dependent on network performance. Furthermore, the number of expandable dimensions influences the system response time but it never exceeds 5 seconds in our experiments.

In the example depicted on Figure 11 below, the number of customers according to central heating energy and hot water energy is considered.

Cells are red (resp. green) colored since they correspond to an abnormally low (resp. high) number of customers.

For example, a green color indicates an unexpected large number of consumers having simultaneously electrical energy for central heating and for water heating. It means that the two values are highly "interacting" within the slice crossing the two dimensions.

All computations are done after the user has defined his data view. An example is given on Figure 12 where the shaded margins help understanding the slice defined by the three dimensions.

The implementation (Figure 13) of the discovery-driven exploration is based on the definition of different *Analytical Workspaces* (OLAP data cube in Oracle 10g):

- one *Technical Analytic Workspace* contains all the generic built-in indicators algorithms.
- different *Data Analytic Workspaces* contain the specific data (sales, marketing, human resources). They can query the Technical Analytical Workspace on demand.

Figure 10.

EAUCHA	CHFP	STOC	TYPHAB	CONTRAT	TARPUI	CONSTRUCT	TYPRES
(0,3235)	(0,2739)	(0,2421)	(0,206)	(0,192)	(0,1964)	(0,1644)	(0,1459)

Figure 11. Data View with 2 dimensions © 2009 [Françoise Guisnel] Used with permission.

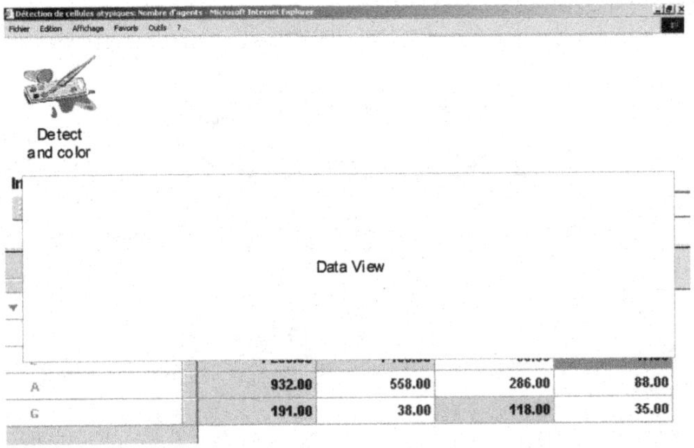

No pre-computation is required in the Data Analytical Workspace since all the computations are performed on the fly.

A facsimile of the Oracle schema is shown in the Figure 14. This corresponds to the technical analytical workspace presented previously. The program OM_CC_MARGE first detects the table's margins and shades those cells in order to facilitate the reading of the table. Then the program OM_DETECT_CAS is executed to choose the

Figure 12. Data View with 3 dimensions © 2009 [Françoise Guisnel] Used with permission.

		TOT	P	S	MISS
TOT	TOT	172 075.00	138 281.00	8 835.00	24 959.00
	MISS	106 672.00	78 452.00	5 423.00	22 797.00
	N	28 903.00	28 213.00	331.00	359.00
	O	36 500.00	31 616.00	3 081.00	1 803.00
E	TOT	43 195.00	35 923.00	2 831.00	4 441.00
	MISS	16 078.00	11 735.00	854.00	3 489.00
	N	11 167.00	10 847.00	173.00	147.00
	O	15 950.00	13 341.00	1 804.00	805.00
A	TOT	37 518.00	34 505.00	676.00	2 337.00
	MISS	13 627.00	11 370.00	161.00	2 096.00
	N	13 020.00	12 846.00	72.00	102.00
	O	10 871.00	10 289.00	443.00	139.00
MISS	TOT	91 362.00	67 853.00	5 328.00	18 181.00
	MISS	76 967.00	55 347.00	4 408.00	17 212.00
	N	4 716.00	4 520.00	86.00	110.00
	O	9 679.00	7 986.00	834.00	859.00

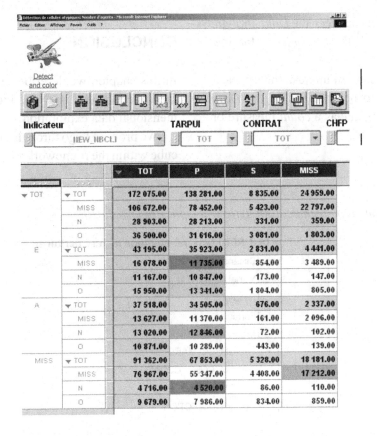

Figure 13. Principle of implementation

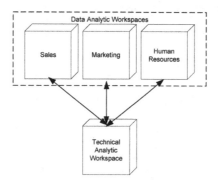

appropriate algorithm, whether the measure is a count or a quantitative one. The computation of all indicators (test-value or Chi-Square contribution) is done by the OM_DETECTION program. Finally, the program OM_COLORCODING is run to return the right color.

Processing guided navigation on a new *Data Analytical Workspace is straightforward* since only two tasks have to be done:

- to define the link between the *Data Analytic Workspace* and the *Technical Analytic Workspace*
- to tag the measures of interest. Indeed, each measure has to be specified in the *Data Analytic Workspace* as a *count* measure or a *quantitative* one.

Furthermore, a referential in the *Technical Analytic Workspace* has been defined in order to simplify the maintenance of the system. It consists in linking each measure with its type.

More generally, the implementation of our framework presented above would make it possible to integrate these built-in indicators in different OLAP Management Systems as functions already existing like mean, median or forecast.

CONCLUSION

In this chapter, we describe an original work to facilitate business analysts' interactive multidimensional data exploration.

We propose to go through a multidimensional cube within the framework of a dynamic analysis

Figure 14. Facsimile of the technical Analytic Workspace in Oracle 10g

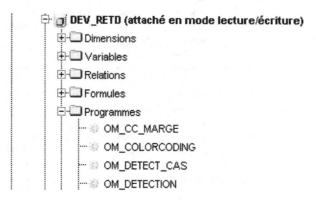

of the cube, given a users' data selection to study. Selection is materialized by the choice of page axes to define this subpopulation.

From a dynamic point of view, guided navigation is provided by the calculation of indicators which enables to order expandable dimensions by degree of interest.

From a static point of view, the detection and the highlighting of interesting cells within a data cube slice are addressed.

Our approach substantially differs from previous works. In our work, the degree of exception of a cell is not based on a saturated model but on the fast computation of straightforward statistical built-in indicators.

We consider two cases depending on the kind of measure. For a count measure, the indicator is based on the computation of the cell contribution to the total Chi-Square of the analyzed data cube slice. For a quantitative measure, we use test-value. The restitution is done by a color-coding system.

In both cases, without any pre-computation of the data cube, those indicators are evaluated instantaneously according to the user-defined subpopulation choice. These methods have been implemented, in a data independent way, as a proof of concept under Oracle 10g system and made it possible to validate the feasibility of the implementation of the suggested methods. The tests have been carried out in parallel with the statistical SAS® System software which also validated our work from traditional statistical data tables rather than on aggregated data as detailed in this chapter. The way we have defined the different built-in indicators would make it possible to enrich existing OLAP Management Systems with a new business intelligence tool that is discovery-driven exploration.

This work will be extended in several directions.

With regard to multidimensional model, it is necessary to take into account hierarchical dimensions. Firstly, the way to expand a hierarchical dimension at a current step should be studied. Indeed, several strategies can be considered depending on whether drill-down is restricted to the directly lower level or not. Secondly, the way a hierarchical level is unfolded (globally or partially) may impact the way built-in indicators are defined.

We are currently studying which indicator will be the most adapted one in the case of a ratio measure. For instance in the marketing domain, this could be used in data cubes to explore marketing campaign efficiency. A possible measure could be the ratio between the number of questionnaires filled and the number of questionnaires sent to a targeted market segment.

Further investigations are also needed for a dynamic analysis. The expand of a great number of dimensions during the exploration of the data cube often involves the display of cells with low size. Statistical indicators are not robust faced to these ones. A way may be examined, to prevent users from going on further in the drill-through process when the number of already expanded dimensions (implying a huge number of cells) is large. Insofar as discovery process on aggregated data does not intend to highlight rare events but rather important tendencies, this limitation may also be interpreted as a support to restrict the analysis to the most understandable slices.

REFERENCES

Agresti, A. (2002). *Categorical data analysis* (2nd ed.). New York: John Wiley & Sons.

Ben Messaoud, R., Boussaid, O., & Rabaseda, S. (2006). Efficient multidimensional data representations based on multiple correspondence analysis. In *Proceedings of the Twelfth ACM SIGKDD International Conference on Knowledge Discovery and Data Mining (KDD 2006)*, Philadelphia, Pennsylvania, USA (pp. 662-667). New York: ACM Press.

Ben Messaoud, R., Rabaseda, S., Boussaid, O., & Bentayeb, F. (2004). OpAC: A new OLAP operator based on a data mining method. In *Proceedings of the 6th International Baltic Conference on Databases and Information Systems (DB&IS04)*, Riga, Latvia.

Bishop, Y. M. M., Fienberg, S. E., & Holland, P. W. (1975). *Discrete multivariate analysis*. Cambridge MA: The MIT Press.

Cariou, V., Cubillé, J., Derquenne, C., Goutier, S., Guisnel, F., & Klajnmic, H. (2007). Built-in indicators to automatically detect interesting cells in a cube. In *Proceedings of the 9th International Conference on Data Warehousing and Knowledge Discovery (DaWaK 2007)*, Regensburg, Germany (pp. 123-124). Berlin, Germany: Springer.

Cariou, V., Cubillé, J., Derquenne, C., Goutier, S., Guisnel, F., & Klajnmic, H. (in press). Built-in indicators to discover interesting drill paths in a cube. In *Proceedings of the 10th International Conference on Data Warehousing and Knowledge Discovery (DaWaK2008)*, Torino, Italy.

Caron, E. A. M., & Daniels, H. A. M. (2007). Explanation of exceptional values in multi-dimensional business databases. *European Journal of Operational Research*. doi:.doi:10.1016/j.ejor.2007.04.039

Chen, C. H. (2002). Generalized association plots: Information visualization via iteratively generated correlation matrices. *Statistica Sinica, 12*, 7–29.

Chen, Q. (1999). *Mining exceptions and quantitative association rules in OLAP data cube*. Unpublished doctoral dissertation, School of Computing Science, Simon Fraser University, British Columbia, Canada.

Dong, G., Han, J., Lam, J., Pei, J., & Wang, K. (2001). Mining multi-dimensional constrained gradients in data cubes. In *Proceedings of the 27th Very Large Data Bases conference, (VLDB2001)*, Roma, Italy.

Fayyad, M., Piatetsky-Shapiro, G., Smyth, P., & Uthurusamy, R. (1996). *Advances in knowledge discovery and data mining*. Menlo Park, CA: The AAAI Press.

Han, J. (1997). OLAP mining: An integration of OLAP with data mining. In *Proceedings of the 1997 IFIP Conference on Data Semantics (DS-7)*, Leysin, Switzerland (pp. 1-11).

Imielinski, T., Khachiyan, L., & Abdulghani, A. (2002). Cubegrades: Generalizing association rules. *Data Mining and Knowledge Discovery, 6*(3), 219–258. doi:10.1023/A:1015417610840

Jobson, J. D. (1991). *Applied multivariate data analysis. Volume I: Regression and experimental design*. New York: Springer Verlag.

Kamber, M., Han, J., & Chiang, J. (1997). Metarule-guided mining of multi-dimensional association rules using data cubes. In *Proceedings of the 3rd International Conference on Knowledge Discovery and Data Mining (KDD 1997)*, Newport Beach, CA, USA (pp. 207-210). Menlo Park, CA: The AAAI Press.

Morineau, A. (1984). Note sur la caractérisation statistique d'une classe et les valeurs-test. *Bulletin technique Centre Statistique Informatique Appliquées, 2*(1-2), 20-27.

Nestorov, S., & Jukic, N. (2003). Ad-hoc association-rule mining within the data warehouse. In *Proceedings of the 36th Hawaii International Conference on System Sciences (HICSS-36)*.

Palpanas, T., & Koudas, N. (2005). Using datacube aggregates for approximate querying and deviation detection. *IEEE Transactions on Knowledge and Data Engineering, 17*(11), 1–11. doi:10.1109/TKDE.2005.187

Sarawagi, S. (1999). Explaining differences in multidimensional aggregates. In *Proceedings of the 25th International Conference On Very Large Databases (VLDB1999)*, Edinburgh, Scotland, UK.

Sarawagi, S. (2000). User-adaptative exploration of multidimensional data. In *Proceedings of the 26th International Conference On Very Large Databases (VLDB2000)*, Cairo, Egypt.

Sarawagi, S., Agrawal, R., & Megiddo, N. (1998). *Discovery-driven exploration of OLAP data cubes* (Tech. Rep.). IBM Almaden Research Center, San Jose, USA.

Sathe, G., & Sarawagi, S. (2001). Intelligent rollups in multidimensional OLAP data. In *Proceedings of the 27th International Conference On Very Large Databases (VLDB2001)*, Roma, Italy.

Zhu, H. (1998). *On-line analytical mining of association rules*. Unpublished doctoral dissertation, Simon Fraser University, Burnaby, British Columbia V5A 1S6, Canada.

ENDNOTE

[1]   This motivating example will be detailed later.

Section 3
DWH and OLAP Applications

Chapter 7
Conceptual Data Warehouse Design Methodology for Business Process Intelligence

Svetlana Mansmann
University of Konstanz, Konstanz, Germany

Thomas Neumuth
Innovation Center Computer Assisted Surgery (ICCAS), Leipzig, Germany

Oliver Burgert
Innovation Center Computer Assisted Surgery (ICCAS), Leipzig, Germany

Matthias Röger
University of Konstanz, Konstanz, Germany

Marc H. Scholl
University of Konstanz, Konstanz, Germany

ABSTRACT

The emerging area of business process intelligence aims at enhancing the analysis power of business process management systems by employing performance-oriented technologies of data warehousing and mining. However, the differences in the assumptions and objectives of the underlying models, namely the business process model and the multidimensional data model, aggravate straightforward and meaningful convergence of the two concepts. The authors present an approach to designing a data warehousing for enabling the multidimensional analysis of business processes and their execution. The aims of such analysis are manifold, from quantitative and qualitative assessment to process discovery, pattern recognition and mining. The authors demonstrate that business processes and workflows represent a non-conventional application scenario for the data warehousing approach and that multiple challenges arise at various design stages. They describe deficiencies of the conventional OLAP technology with respect to business process modeling and formulate the requirements for an adequate multidimensional presentation of process descriptions. Modeling extensions proposed at the conceptual level are verified by implementing them in a relational OLAP system, accessible via state-of-the-art visual frontend tools. The authors demonstrate the benefits of the proposed modeling framework by presenting relevant

DOI: 10.4018/978-1-60566-748-5.ch007

Copyright © 2010, IGI Global. Copying or distributing in print or electronic forms without written permission of IGI Global is prohibited.

analysis tasks from the domain of medical engineering and showing the type of the decision support provided by our solution.

INTRODUCTION

Modern enterprises increasingly integrate and automate their business processes with the objective of improving their efficiency and quality, reducing costs and human errors. Business Process Management Systems (BPMS) are employed to optimize process design and execution. These systems track business processes by logging large volumes of data related to their execution and provide basic functionality for routine analysis and reporting. However, conventional BPMS focus on the design support and simulation functionality for detecting performance bottlenecks, with rather limited, if any, analysis capabilities to quantify performance against specific business metrics. Deficiencies of the underlying business process modeling approaches in terms of supporting comprehensive analysis and exploration of process data have been recognized by researchers and practitioners (Dayal, et al., 2001; Grigori, et al., 2004).

The ability to analyze process execution has become indispensable for eliminating the gaps in decision making. Last decade witnessed immense technological advancements in application integration, business rules and workflows, Business Intelligence (BI), and BPMS. Forward-thinking organizations are beginning to realize that process intelligence goes beyond simple automation of business processes and that the convergence of BI and business process management technologies would create value beyond the sum of their parts (Smith, 2002). The fundamental technology of BI is referred to as OLAP (*On-line Analytical Processing*), a term coined by Codd, et al. (1993). Data warehousing and OLAP are aimed at providing key people in the enterprise with access to whatever level of information they need for decision making.

BUSINESS PROCESS INTELLIGENCE

"*Business Process Intelligence* (BPI) refers to the application of business intelligence techniques (including for example OLAP analysis and data mining) in business process management, with the goal of providing a better understanding of a company's processes and of devising ways to improve them." (Castellanos & Casati, 2005). Recent advances in the above techniques as well as in business process and business performance management have come together to enable a near real-time monitoring and measurement of business processes as to identify, interpret, and respond to critical business events.

According to Hall (2004), BPI can help companies improve their process management initiatives by:

- providing a consistent, process-based view of the company,
- facilitating real-time business process monitoring,
- aligning execution with strategy,
- managing enterprise performance.

The BPI approach overcomes the deficiencies of standard BPMS by storing process execution data in a data warehouse in a cleansed, transformed, and aggregated form (Dayal, et al., 2001). Such data can be analyzed using OLAP and data mining tools to support various knowledge extraction tasks that can be subdivided into the following subareas (Castellanos & Casati, 2005):

- *Process discovery* is done by analyzing enterprise operations in order to derive the process model that can be used for automating process execution or increasing its efficiency.

- *Process mining and analysis* seeks to identify interesting correlations helpful for forecasting, planning, or explaining certain phenomena.
- *Prediction* is important for anticipating or preventing occurrence of certain situations.
- *Exception handling* assists the analyst in addressing specific problems, for instance, by retrieving the data on how similar problems were handled in the past.
- *Static optimization* is concerned with optimizing the process configuration against previously identified optimization areas.
- *Dynamic optimization* is an intelligent component for supervising process instances at runtime in order to influence their execution as to maximize certain business objectives.

The employment of BI within the BPI framework has also caused companies to rethink the ways they use data warehouses by blurring the traditional separation of operational systems from BI applications (Hall, 2004). Traditionally, data warehouses store consolidated historical data and, thus, provide a retrospective analysis. In BPI scenarios, data warehouses are fed with current transactional data that has to be available for near real-time analysis. This requirement of supporting day-to-day decision-making has triggered the emergence of a new branch called *Operational BI*, which links BI with business processes and enables process-oriented perspective of the analysis.

"*Operational BI* combines real-time operational transaction data with historical information to let decision-makers move beyond the "point-in-time" analysis associated with traditional BI and data warehousing applications" (Hall, 2004).

Within our research, the terms *Business Process Intelligence* and *Operational Business Intelligence* are treated interchangeably.

CONTRIBUTION AND OUTLINE

The area of BPI is still immature and controversial, with many open issues and very few examples of existing solutions. One of the major BPI challenges is finding a meaningful solution for converging business process and workflow modeling techniques with the multidimensional data model that lies at the heart of the OLAP technology. The task of unifying the flow-oriented process specification and the snapshot-based multidimensional design for quantitative analysis is by far not trivial due to differing and even conflicting prerequisites and objectives of the underlying approaches.

Concepts and proposals presented in this work have been inspired by practical challenges encountered in the ongoing project on designing and implementing a BPI platform for a specific domain of Surgical Workflow Analysis (SWA). The project is hosted by the Innovation Center Computer Assisted Surgery (ICCAS)[1] and involves collaborators from multiple scientific disciplines, such as medicine, medical engineering, databases and data warehousing, web technologies, scientific visualization, etc. Surgical Workflows will be used as a real-world usage scenario for demonstrating the applicability of the presented solution.

The contribution of this work is to design a methodological framework for enabling business process analysis. The fundamental challenge of invoking the OLAP approach in the BPI context is a conceptual one, namely, gaining an adequate multidimensional perspective of process execution data. We demonstrate that the classical data warehouse design steps are not feasible in this scenario due to general unavailability of pre-defined measures of interest. As a solution, we propose a cardinality-based approach of transforming existing process models and process execution schemes into a set of facts and dimensions in a unified multi-dimensional space. The multidimensional model itself had to be extended to handle complex patterns encountered in the data. These extensions are reflected in terms of formal concepts as well as a graphical notation *X*-DFM, which extends the popular DF Model of Golfarelli, et al. (1998). We expect the proposed extended model to be applicable to a variety of data warehouse scenarios dealing with complex data. As a proof of concept, we demonstrate its usage of our model for solving typical SWA tasks.

The remainder of the chapter is structured as follows: Section 2 provides an overview of the related work in the field of BPI in general and Surgical Workflow Analysis in particular. The case study and its analysis requirements is presented in Section 3. Section 4 contains the background information on the relevant conceptual data models, followed by Section 5 featuring the challenges of business process data warehouse design. In Sections 6 and 7 we present an extended conceptual model in terms of its fundamental elements and advanced concepts, respectively. Section 8 describes the overall approach to obtaining a multi-dimensional business process model from existing process descriptions, based on analyzing and refining the cardinalities of the relevant relationships between process components. Section 9 contains some considerations regarding the implementation and demonstrates the use of the presented framework for solving exemplary tasks from the field of SWA. Concluding remarks are given in Section 10.

RELATED WORK

Due to multidisciplinarity of our research, the related work falls into several categories, such as (a) enhancing business process analysis by employing the data warehousing approach, (b) extending OLAP to support complex scenarios, and (c) medical informatics research related to our application field of SWA.

Grigori, et al. (2004) present a comprehensive BPI tool suite for managing business process quality that was developed at Hewlett-Packard and implemented on top of HP Process Manager BPMS. The suite includes three main components: 1) the PDW loader for transferring the process log data into a Process Data Warehouse (PDW), 2) the Process Mining Engine for deriving sophisticated models from the data, and 3) the Cockpit, which is a graphical reporting tool of the end-user. The data warehousing approach was employed for structuring the relevant process data according to the star schema, with process, service, and node state changes as facts and the related definitions as well as temporal and behavioral characteristics as dimensions. This approach enables analysis of process execution and system state evolution in the environments where processes have a uniform and well-defined scheme.

Hao, et al. (2006) proposed an approach to visual analysis of business process performance metrics (impact factors) using *VisImpact*, a visualization interface especially suitable for aggregating over large amounts of process-related data and based on analyzing process schemes and instances to identify business metrics of interest. The selected impact factors and the corresponding process instances are presented using a symmetric circular graph to display the relationships and the details of the process flows.

Medical applications are frequently encountered in the data warehousing literature in the role of motivating case studies. Pedersen, et al. (2001) proposed an extended multidimensional data model for meeting the needs of non-standard application domains at the example of accumulated patient diagnosis data. Golfarelli, et al. (1998) demonstrate the methodology of obtaining multidimensional schemes from existing E/R schemes using hospital admission as a usage scenario. Song, et al. (2001) use patient diagnosing and billing case study to demonstrate various strategies of handling many-to-many relationships between facts and dimensions. Mansmann, et al. (2007a) describe how Surgical Process Modeling, used as a non-conventional data warehousing application scenario, results in the necessity to extend the conceptual foundations of the multidimensional data model. Implications of conceptual extensions for implementing a data warehouse and frontend tools for interactive analysis are given in (Mansmann, et al., 2007b).

Another category of related works refers to the modeling of Surgical Workflows. An approach to facilitating the complex task of surgery preparation by employing the workflow technology to automate and optimize the surgical process was presented by Qi, et al. (2006). Münchenberg, et al. (2000) designed instruction graphs to drive a surgical assist system for application in Frontal Orbital Advancements. Jannin, et al. (2003) used a ontologically designed scheme to model activities in the context of image-guided surgery. Ahmadi, et al. (2006) proposed an approach to automatic surgical workflow recovery without explicit models of surgery types. A more recent work of Padoy, et al. (2007) presents a model-based recovery approach based on automatics segmentation of surgeries into phases using hidden Markov models.

A pioneering interdisciplinary research on designing scientific methods for Surgical Workflows is carried out at ICCAS. Major directions of their projects are surgical workflow formalization (Neumuth, et al., 2006), semantics (Burgert, et al., 2006), analysis (Neumuth, et al., 2007), standardization (Burgert, et al., 2007), and visualization (Neumuth, Schumann, et al., 2006).

MOTIVATING CASE STUDY

Medical applications are frequent suppliers of motivating usage scenarios in workflow management research. Patient treatments, diagnostic investigations, hospitalization, surgical interventions, and the overall hospital operation are examples of complex processes where the workflow technology promises significant performance gains. Our case study is concerned with an emerging interdisciplinary field of SWA.

Surgical Workflows foster intelligent acquisition of process descriptions from surgical interventions for the purpose of their clinical and technical analysis, as defined by Neumuth, Strauß, et al. (2006). This type of analysis is crucial for developing surgical assist systems for the operating room of the future. Besides, it provides a framework for evaluating new devices or surgical strategy evolution. The medical informatics term *Surgical Workflows* describes the methodological concept of the data acquisition and consolidation procedure. Process data is obtained manually or semi-automatically by monitoring and recording the course of a surgical intervention. The manual part is carried out either in the real-time mode, i.e., by observing the surgical intervention live in the operating room, or retrospectively, e.g., from a video recording.

REQUIREMENTS OF SURGICAL WORKFLOW ANALYSIS

Surgeons, medical researchers, and engineers are interested in obtaining a well-defined formal recording scheme of a surgical process that would lay a foundation for a systematic accumulation of the obtained process descriptions in a centralized data warehouse to enable its comprehensive analysis and exploration. Whatever abstraction approach is adopted, there is a need for an unambiguous description of concepts that characterize a surgical process in a way adequate for modeling a wide range of workflow types and different surgical disciplines.

Applications of SWA are manifold: support for the preoperative planning by retrieving similar precedent cases, clinical documentation, postoperative exploration of surgical data, formalization of the surgical know-how, analysis of the optimization potential with respect to the instruments and systems involved, evaluation of ergonomic conditions, verification of medical hypotheses, gaining input for designing surgical assist systems and workflow automation. Obviously, such high diversity of potential applications

Figure 1. Vertical (de-)composition of a surgical process

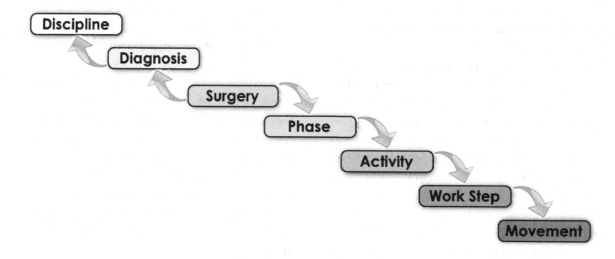

results in the diversity of expected query types. We distinguish the following major categories of analytical queries:

1. *Quantitative* queries are concerned with performance indicators and other measurements occurrences, frequencies, duration, or availability of various events or objects.
2. *Qualitative* queries aim at discovering relationships, patterns, trends, and other kind of additional knowledge from the data.
3. *Ergonomic* queries evaluate the design of the workspace, ergonomic limitations, positions and directions of involved participants and objects.
4. *Cognitive* queries attempt to assess such "fuzzy" issues as usefulness, relevance, satisfaction, etc.

Considering the expected query types, the multidimensional database technology seems a promising solution as it allows the analyst to view data from different perspectives, define various business metrics, and aggregate the data to the desired granularity.

STRUCTURING SURGICAL WORKFLOWS

Surgical Workflows provide an abstraction of surgical interventions by capturing the characteristics of the original process that are relevant for the analysis. A common approach to structuring a process is to decompose it vertically, i.e., along the timeline, into logical units, such as sub-processes, stages, work steps, etc. Figure 1 shows a possible decomposition hierarchy of a surgery.

From the logical point of view, surgical processes consist of phases, which, in their turn, consist of activities, i.e., work steps performing a certain action. Both phases and activities may overlap. Technically, an action may be executed by multiple participants using multiple instruments. To account for this observation, we refine the granularity to a "movement", which refers to a part of an action performed by a body part of a participant on a structure of a patient using a surgical instrument. In the upward direction, surgical instances can be grouped into classes by the diagnosis or therapy, which, in their turn, are associated with particular surgical disciplines. The above decomposition is called *logical*, or *task-driven* as it relies on the reasoning of a human expert for recognizing the constituent elements of a process.

An alternative decomposition practice is a *state-based* one, aimed at automated data acquisition. This approach uses the concepts *system*, *state*, and *event* to capture state evolution of involved systems and events that trigger state transitions. The concept of a *system* is very generic and may refer to a participant or his/her body part, a patient or a treated structure, an instrument or a device, etc. For instance, surgeon's eyes can be considered a system, their gaze direction can be then modeled as states, while surgeon's directives to other participants may be captured as events.

Both data acquisition practices can be used as complementary ones to benefit from combining a human perspective with a systemic one. We introduce a superordinate concept *component*, synonymous to the term *flow object* defined in BPMN (2006), to enable uniform treatment of logical (i.e., activities) and technical (i.e., states and events) units of a process with regard to their common properties. Thereby, the analyst is able to retrieve a unified timeline for the whole course of a surgery.

With respect to the vertical decomposition depicted in Figure 1, we propose to distinguish between two major granularity levels of the acquired data:

- *Workflow level* refers to the characteristics of a surgical intervention as a whole, such as patient, location, date, etc. This data is normally supplied by other clinical information systems. Workflow-level data is useful for high-level analysis, such as hospital utilization, patient history, etc.
- *Intra-workflow level* refers to the properties of process components (e.g., events, activities), such as instrument and device usage or treated structures. Detailed data is acquired from running surgical interventions and used for analyzing workflow execution within as well as across multiple instances.

Figure 2 shows a simplified approximation of Surgical Workflows structure, expressed in the E/R (Entity-Relationship) modeling notation. This scheme will be refined in the upcoming sections. To identify the major design challenges, we proceed by inspecting the fundamentals of the involved modeling techniques.

CONTROL FLOWS VS. MULTIDIMENSIONAL CUBES

As mentioned in the introductory section, BPI aims at converging the techniques of business process modeling and business intelligence. More precisely, business process models serve as the input whereas the multidimensional data model builds the foundation of a BPI framework. In this section, we overview the main concepts of both models as a preparation step for finding ways of their meaningful convergence.

BUSINESS PROCESS MODELING

Business process models are employed to describe business activities in the real world. Business processes are typically described in terms of their objects, activities, and resources. WfMC (1999) defines *business process* as "a set of one or more linked procedures or activities which collectively realize a business objective or policy goal, normally within the context of an organizational structure defining functional roles and relationships" and proposes to distinguish between manual and workflow activities. *Activities* are the work units of a process that have an objective and change the state of the objects. *Resources* are consumed to perform activities. Relationships between the entities may be specified using *control flow* (consecutive, parallel, or alternative execution) and/ or hierarchical decomposition.

There is an important distinction between the conceptual and the actual manifestation of a

Figure 2. Recording scheme of a surgical process model as an E/R diagram

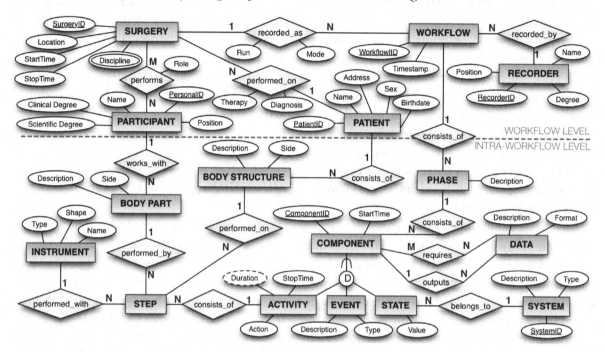

process: the term "process" refers to a conceptual, or abstract, way of organizing work and resources whereas process executions, or "instances", involving real resources and actors are the actual manifestation of a business process (Reijers, 2003). An example from the medical domain could be a surgery of type discectomy. Abstract process description of discectomy is "removal of all or part of an intervertebral disc (the soft tissue that acts as a shock absorber between the vertebral bodies)" (SRS, n.d.). This description may further define a typical cause of a surgery, major work steps, and the types of instruments and devices used at each step. Instances of discectomy as a surgical process are actual surgeries carried out by particular surgeons.

Another distinction has to be made between the concepts *process* and *workflow*. While these two terms are used interchangeably by some authors (Aalst & Hee, 2002), diverse workflow definitions can be found in the literature. One popular interpretation is that business processes output products while workflows deliver services (Reijers, 2003).

Another use of the term "workflow" is to denote the control flow, i.e., dependencies among tasks during the execution of a business process (Sharp & McDermott, 2001). In this work, we adopt the differentiation in the levels of abstraction proposed by Muth, et al. (1998): while business processes are mostly modeled in a high-level and informal way, workflow specifications serve as a basis for the largely automated execution and are derived by refining the business process specification. Figure 3, adopted from (WfMC, 1999) with some adjustments, summarizes the relationships between the basic terms related to business processes.

Coexistence of different workflow specification methods is common in practice. We restrain ourselves to naming a few techniques and refer the interested reader to the book of Matoušek (2003) for a detailed overview. *Net-based*, or *graph-based*, methods enjoy great popularity due to their ability to visualize processes in a way understandable even for non-expert users. Especially the *activity and state charts* are frequently used to specify a process as an oriented

Figure 3. Relationships in the basic business process terminology

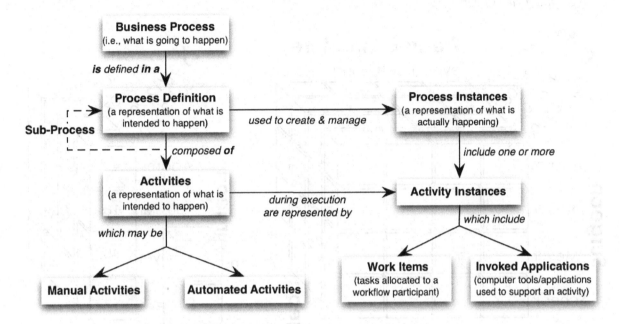

graph with nodes representing the activities and arcs defining the ordering in which these are performed. *Logic-based* methods use temporal logic to capture the dynamics of the system. Finally, *Event-Condition-Action* rules are used for specifying the control flow between activities in the conditional form.

MULTIDIMENSIONAL DATA MODEL AND OLAP

OLAP technology draws its analytical power from the underlying *multidimensional data model*. The data is modeled as cubes of uniformly structured *facts*, consisting of analytical values, referred to as *measures*, uniquely determined by descriptive values drawn from a set of *dimensions*. Each dimension forms an axis of a cube, with dimension members as coordinates of the cube cells storing the respective measure values. Figure 4 shows a simplified example of a 3-dimensional data cube, storing instrument usage statistics (measure number of instruments) determined by

dimensions Surgeon, Treated Structure, and Date. Besides the original cube storing the data at the finest granularity, Figure 4 also displays the results of two "roll-up" operations totaling the measure over all treated structures and, subsequently, over all dates. In real-world applications, data cubes may have arbitrarily many dimensions, and are therefore denoted *hypercubes*.

Member values within a dimension are further organized into *classification hierarchies* to enable additional aggregation levels. For example, dates can be aggregated into months, quarters, years, and so on. Dimension hierarchies are strictly structured, i.e., values at each hierarchy level must be of the same *category*. Multiple hierarchies may be defined within a dimension and can be mutually exclusive (e.g., dates can be aggregated by month or by week, but not both), denoted *alternative*, or non-exclusive, or *parallel* (e.g., surgeons can be grouped by qualification and, subsequently, by the level of expertise, or vice versa). Within a dimension, the attributes that form the hierarchy are called *dimension levels*, or *categories*. Other descriptive attributes belonging to a particular

Figure 4. A sample 3-dimensional cube (fragment) storing surgical instrument usage statistics (left) and its aggregated views (right)

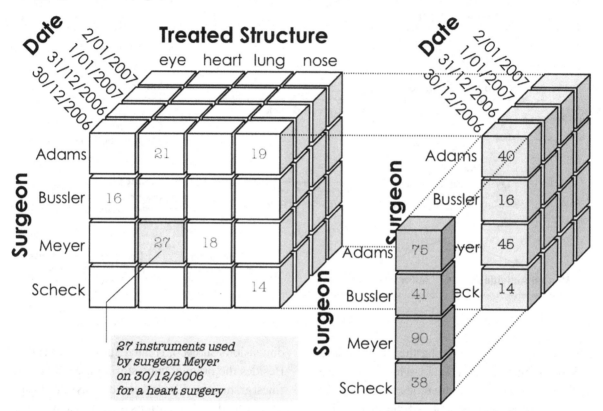

BUSINESS PROCESS DATA WAREHOUSE DESIGN: CHALLENGES

category are *property attributes*. For instance, Hospital and City are categories of the dimension Location, whereas hospital name and city code are properties of the respective categories. Categories along with parent-child relationships between them represent the *intension*, or *scheme*, of a dimension whereas the hierarchy of its members, i.e., the actual data tree, forms its *extension*.

Desired subsets and views for analysis can be retrieved from the "raw" data by applying OLAP operations, such as *slice-and-dice* to reduce the cube, *drill-down* and *roll-up* to perform aggregation and disaggregation, respectively, along a hierarchical dimension, *drill-across* to combine multiple cubes, *ranking* to find the outlier values, and *rotating* to see the data grouped by other dimensions (Pedersen& Jensen, 2001).

Transformation of semantically rich business process models into multidimensional data structures can be seen as a reduction of the complete set of extensible process elements, such as various types of flow objects and relationships between them, to a rigid format, which forces the former to be decomposed into a set of uniformly structured facts with associated dimensions.

Three abstraction levels recommended by ANSI/X3/SPARC, namely *conceptual*, *logical* and *physical* design, are widely accepted as a sound framework to guide the database modeling process. There is a general acknowledgement of this framework's validity for data warehouse design (Hüsemann, et al., 2000). In addition to the above three phases, Golfarelli & Rizzi, (1998) identify two phases preceding the conceptual design, namely, *i) analysis of the information system* for obtaining the (conceptual or logical) scheme of the pre-existing information system, and *ii) requirement specification* for defining the type of analysis and indicating the preliminary workload. Back to the Surgical Workflows scenario, the E/R scheme in Figure 2 may be taken as a model of the pre-existing system, whereas the expected types of queries and applications given in Section 3 correspond to the output of the requirement specification phase.

STAGES OF THE CONCEPTUAL MODELING

The convergence of the business process model and the multidimensional data model takes place primarily at the conceptual level. Therefore, the conceptual design phase is the central issue of this work. Conceptual modeling provides a high level of abstraction for capturing relevant relationships in the application domain and the data to be stored and analyzed, in an implementation independent fashion. The output of this phase is a set of *fact schemes* and the prevailing techniques are based on graphical notations, such as E/R diagrams, UML and their variants, understandable by both designers and target users.

According to Hüsemann, et al., (2000), conceptual data warehouse design process evolves in the following consecutive phases:

1.   Context definition of *measures*,
2.   *Dimensional hierarchy* design,
3.   Definition of *summarizability constraints*.

The versatility of feasible application areas and analysis tasks of BPI imposes multiple challenges on the conventional data warehouse design methodology. Back to the kinds of queries in the SWA

context, the same data field may serve as a measure, i.e., input of an aggregate function, in one query and as a dimension, i.e., a grouping criterion for aggregation, in another query. As an example, let us consider entity types SURGERY and PATIENT in Figure 2. In order to decide whether those entity types should be mapped to facts or to dimensions, one has to consider the types of queries referring to those elements. However, some scenarios, such as hospital utilization assessment, may define number of surgeries as a measure with hospital as one of its dimensions, whereas other scenarios, such as surgical discipline analysis, may be interested in the number of hospitals offering surgical support in a specified discipline. This example shows the necessity of symmetric treatment of measure and dimension roles. Similar examples can be specified for virtually any other entity of the case study. In order to support all kinds of expected queries, the detailed data, i.e., without pre-aggregation to any of the expected measures of interest, should be available in the data warehouse.

Apparently, the classical approach to designing multidimensional schemes based on the three previously mentioned phases is not adequate for BPI. Kimball proposes a slightly different approach to structuring the conceptual design process, which appears more applicable in the context of BPI. According to Kimball (1996), the design process undergoes the stages of:

1.   choosing a business process,
2.   choosing the grain of the process,
3.   identifying the dimensional characteristics,
4.   defining the measured facts.

One major advantage of the latter approach is its ability to abstract the data model from the expected measures of analysis. This abstraction is realized by proposing to reason in terms of the business process itself and its grain and by putting measure definition into the last stage of the design. At this final step, the transformation of the "raw" process data into cubes of specified measures takes place. It is by "pushing" the measure definition from the initial step, as proposed by Hüsemann, et al. (2000), to a final step, as in the approach of Kimball (1996), that the support of operational BI scenarios can be achieved.

Quantitative queries represent just a fraction of SWA. Some BPI tasks go beyond mere aggregation and may address more complex issues, such as pattern recognition, relevance assessment, and process discovery. These tasks require the original process data in the warehouse to be stored without aggregation.

FUNDAMENTAL CONSTRAINTS OF THE MULTIDIMENSIONAL DATA MODEL

Further modeling challenges come from the inherent constraints of the multidimensional model itself, such as prohibition of many-to-many relationships and NULL values, homogeneity of the fact's characteristics and their grain, and a requirement of summarizability for all dimension hierarchies. Many of these constraints are fundamental and, as such, may not be violated or trivially overcome. We proceed by enumerating some of such fundamental issues that aggravate straightforward applicability of OLAP to business process data:

- *"Rolls-up-to" as the only relationship type*. This relationship expresses inclusion between facts and dimensions as well as between hierarchy levels. It is impossible to explicitly model any other relationship types.
- *Any many-to-many relationship must be modeled as a fact*. This "law" of Kimball (1996) prohibits non-strict hierarchies and many-to-many relationships between facts and dimensions.
- *Fact homogeneity* implies that all fact

entries fully adhere to the fact scheme, i.e., have the same dimensional characteristics and uniform granularity in each dimension.

- *Homogeneous aggregation* requires that all entries within the same fact type roll up along the same set of aggregation paths. This requirement implies prohibition of partial "roll-up" relationships.
- *Prohibition of* NULL *values* is an important guarantee for correct aggregation behavior.
- *Duality of facts and dimensions* forces to distinguish between fact and dimension schemes and statically assign each characteristic to a particular scheme.
- *Absence of object-oriented features*, such as generalization or inheritance.
- *Isolation of fact schemes* means that each scheme is modeled separately from other schemes. Whenever multiple fact or dimension schemes have identical or semantically related attributes, those are maintained redundantly. Besides, scheme isolation prevents from supporting advanced OLAP operators, such as drill-across, at the conceptual level.
- *Summarizability* requires distributive aggregate functions and dimension hierarchy values, or informally, that *i)* facts map directly to the lowest-level dimension values and to only one value per dimension, and *ii)* dimensional hierarchies are balanced trees (Lenz & Shoshani, 1997).
- *Duality of measure and dimension roles*. Measures reflect the focus of the analysis and, therefore, they should be known at design time and be explicitly specified in the fact scheme.
- *Duality of category and property roles*. A dimension category consists of a single category attribute and may have further attributes, called *properties*. Properties may not be used as aggregation levels, even

though the relationship between a category attribute and its property is equivalent to "roll-up".

In the next section we present our approach to mapping business process schemes to multidimensional schemes and show how the above limitations of the multidimensional data model can be handled.

CONCEPTUAL DATA WAREHOUSE DESIGN: TERMINOLOGY AND FORMALIZATION

In the previous section we showed that the classical data warehouse design approach, based on identifying the measures of interest and their dimensional context, is not adequate for modeling business process schemes. Instead, we propose to derive a multidimensional scheme from a pre-existing conceptual model of the process, available as E/R or UML class diagrams. Entity-Relationship model structures data in terms of *entity types* and their *attributes* as well as *relationship types* between entity types and the cardinality of each entity type's participation in a given relationship. UML class notation uses the concepts of a *class*, *property*, *relationship* and *multiplicity* to express the same concepts as entity type, attribute, relationship type, and cardinality, respectively. Therefore, it is sufficient to provide a mapping for either of these two models. We use E/R model as the input graphical notation and consider the model depicted in Figure 2 to be the starting point of the data warehouse design for our usage scenario. The transformation task consists in mapping semantic constructs of the E/R model to those of the multidimensional data model.

Two major components of semantic models are formalization and graphical notation. Existing multidimensional data models tend to focus either on the formalism or on the graphical toolkit, but not both. Formal models either adopt

some existing notation (e.g., ER, UML or their variants) or do not employ any. For the purpose of completeness, we provide both the formalism and the graphical model that is fully aligned with the proposed formal concepts, i.e., that correctly captures its semantics.

Our conceptual model relies on the popular Dimensional Fact Model (DFM) proposed by Golfarelli, et al. (1998). DFM is based on a pragmatic scientific approach, in which the graphical framework emanates from the formal conceptual framework. The authors also provide a methodology for deriving multidimensional schemes from E/R diagrams. In the abundance of notations proposed in the literature, DFM stands out for its simplicity, elegance, and expressiveness for representing the concepts introduced in our work. However, we use an extended variant of DFM, called *X*-DFM (e_xtended _Dimensional _Fact _Model), which provides an adequate mapping for a broader set of semantic elements. The formalization is adopted from our previous works (Mansmann & Scholl, 2007; Mansmann, et al., 2007a) with some modifications and builds upon the semantic models of Pedersen, et al. (2001) and Golfarelli, et al. (1998).

A UNIFIED MULTIDIMENSIONAL SPACE

One fundamental definitional issue in the conceptual model is whether global semantics, i.e., relationships across fact schemes, should be captured. A conventional approach would be to design each *n*-dimensional data cube in its own isolated *n*-dimensional space. The output of such model is a set of unrelated fact schemes. However, advanced models, such as DFM, support inter-factual semantics by allowing facts to share dimensions. The major advantage of the latter approach is given by the explicit support for a drill-across operation, which allows to compare measures of related data cubes or even to derive new measures.

A set of dimensions is merged into one shared dimension, if they are defined on a related semantic domain For example, dimensions StartTime and StopTime, both of type *date*, could be modeled as a common dimension time, containing the union of values from both dimensions. In addition to such full dimension sharing, our model recognizes further types of sharing by considering semantic compatibility at category level. The resulting conceptual schema is called *inter-stellar*, or *galaxy*. Inter-factual relationships are useful not only for the analysis, but also for the design itself as their recognition helps to reduce maintenance overhead and automatically detect valid operations. To fully capture these relationships, our model employs the concept of a *unified multi-dimensional space*, in which categories with semantically related value domains are represented in a non-redundant fashion.

FACTS AND DIMENSIONS

The output of the conceptual data warehouse design is a *multidimensional scheme*, i.e., a set of *fact schemes* composed of facts, measures, dimensions, and hierarchies. Golfarelli, et al. (1998) define a *fact scheme* to be a structured quasi-tree, which is a directed, acyclic, weakly connected graph, in which multiple directed paths may converge on the same vertex. Path convergence is the result of non-redundant dimensional modeling enforced by the constraint of the unified multidimensional space.

Definition 1. A *fact F* is a collection of uniformly structured data entries over a fact scheme F. **An *n*-dimensional fact scheme is defined as a pair** F = (M^F, D^F), **where** M^F = {M$_j$, $j = 1, ..., m$} **is a set of measures and** D^F = {D$_i$, $i = 1, ..., n$} **is a set of corresponding dimension schemes.**

Definition 2. A *dimension D* is defined by its aggregation scheme (intension) *D* and the associated data set (extension) E, so that *Type*(E) = D.

The samle data cube from Figure 4 can now be formally defined as a fact scheme INSTRUMENTS-CUBE with a set of measures M$^{INSTRUMENTS-CUBE}$ = {num_instruments}, characterized by a set of dimensions D$^{INSTRUMENTS-CUBE}$ = {Surgeon, Treated Structure, Date}.

A dimension scheme is a connected, directed graph, in which each vertex corresponds to an aggregation level and each edge represents a full or partial roll-up relationship between a pair of levels, or formally:

Definition 3. A *dimension scheme* is a quadruple D = (C^D, $\sqsubseteq_D$, T$_D$, $\perp_D$), **where** C^D = {C$_k$, $k = 1, ..., p$} **is set of category types, or dimension levels, in** D, $\sqsubseteq_D$ **is a partial order in** C, **and** T$_D$ **and** $\perp_D$ **are distinguished as the top and the bottom element of the ordering, respectively.**

$\perp_D$ corresponds to the finest grain of D, i.e., the one at which D is connected to the fact scheme. T$_D$ corresponds to an abstract root node of the dimension's hierarchy that has a single value referred to as ALL.

Relation $\sqsubseteq_D$ captures the containment relationships between category types. This containment may be *full*, denoted $\sqsubseteq_D^{(full)}$, or *partial*, denoted $\sqsubseteq_D^{(part)}$. Therefore, relation $\sqsubseteq_D$ indicates the union of the two orders. Admission of partial containment between category types is crucial for specifying heterogeneous dimension hierarchies. Predicates $\sqsubseteq$ and $\sqsubseteq^*$ specify *direct* and *transitive* containment relationship, respectively, between a pair of category types in C^D. Partial and full direct containment predicates are denoted $\sqsubseteq^{(part)}$ and $\sqsubseteq^{(full)}$, respectively. Thereby, predicates $\sqsubseteq$ and $\sqsubseteq^*$ without fullness/partiality indication imply that the containment is either full or partial, or formally: C$_i \sqsubseteq$ C$_j \Rightarrow$ (C$_i \sqsubseteq^{(full)}$ C$_j \vee$ C$_i \sqsubseteq^{(part)}$ C$_j$). Partial containment between two categories C$_i \sqsubseteq^{(part)}$ C$_j$ occurs when members of C$_i$ are not required to have parent members in C$_j$.

A pair of partial containment relationships of the same category C$_i$ (i.e., C$_i \sqsubseteq^{(part)}$ C$_j \wedge$ C$_i \sqsubseteq^{(part)}$ C$_k$) are *exclusive*, if each member of C$_i$ rolls up either to C_j or C_k, but never to both. A set of exclusive partial roll-up relationships is denoted $C_i \sqsubseteq^{(part)} (C_j | C_k)$.

C_j is said to be a category type in C, denoted $C_j \in C$. Dimension scheme defines a skeleton of the associated data tree, for which the following conditions hold:

1. $\forall C_j \in \mathbf{C^D} \setminus \{\mathbf{T_D}\}: C_j \sqsubseteq^{*(full)} \perp_D$ (a non-top category type is fully contained in the top category type).
2. $\forall C_j \in \mathbf{C^D} \setminus \{\perp_D\}: \perp_D \sqsubseteq^* C_j$ (bottom category rolls up, fully or partially, to all upper category types).
3. $\exists C_j \in \mathbf{C^D}: C_j \sqsubseteq \perp_D$ (the bottom category type is childless).

In the simplest case, a dimension consists solely of the bottom and the top category types. A scheme of a single hierarchy is a lattice, whereas dimension schemes of multiple or parallel hierarchies may result in rather complex graph structures. Multiple hierarchies in D exist whenever there exists a category type at which at least two paths converge, or formally: $\nexists C_i, C_j, C_k \in D: C_i \sqsubseteq^{(full)} C_k \wedge C_j \sqsubseteq^{(full)} C_k$.

Definition 4. A *dimension category type* is a pair $C = (A^C, A)$ where A^C is the distinguished dimension level attribute and $A = \{A_r, r = 1, ..., x\}$ is a set of property attributes associated with A^C.

Definition 5. An *aggregation path* in D is given by a pair of category types C_i, C_j such that $(C_i, C_j) \in C^D \wedge C_i \sqsubseteq^* C_j$.

Having defined the scheme elements of the model, we proceed to dimension instances and their properties.

Definition 6. An *instance*, or *extension*, E associated with dimension scheme D is a pair $(C^E, \sqsubseteq_E)$, where $C^E = \{C_j, j = 1, ..., m\}$ is a set of categories such that $Type(C_j) = C_j$ and $\sqsubseteq_E$ is a partial order on $\cup_j C_j$, the union of all dimensional values in the individual categories.

Definition 7. A *dimension category* C of type

C is a set of member values $\{e_i, i = 1, ..., n\}$ such that $Type(e_i) = C$.

Distinction between the concepts *category* and *category type* is made in order to support modeling of fully and partially shared dimensions, in which the same category type, e.g., city, may be used as categories patient city, hospital city, etc.

Partial order $\subseteq_E$ on $\cup_j C_j$ is understood as follows: given $(e_1, e_2) \in \cup_j C_j, e_1 \subseteq e_2$, if e_1 is logically contained in e_2. Predicates $\subseteq$ and $\subseteq^*$ specify direct and transitive containment relationship, respectively, between a pair of member values. Apparently, containment relationships at the instance level are always full. The total number of members in category C_j is denoted $|C_j|$.

Figure 5 demonstrates the use of *X*-DFM for graphical modeling of multidimensional schemes. In this example, fact scheme SURGERY contains single surgical interventions as its fact entries. In *X*-DFM, each fact scheme is mapped to a box-shaped node holding the scheme's name, its measures, and degenerate dimensions. Dimension schemes are shown as directed graphs with categories as nodes and containment relationships between them as edges. Labeled circles represent dimension level attributes, while property attributes are terminal nodes shown as labeled lines and attached to their respective categories. Each dimension's graph finally converges at its top category (shaded circular nodes). A directed edge connecting a pair of nodes represents a many-to-one, i.e., a roll-up, relationship between them. Optional properties of a category, such as degree within the category diagnosis, are marked by placing a dash across their edges.

X-DFM provides unambiguous graphical constructs for all semantic elements of the model. An overview of the *X*-DFM constructs is given in the Appendix. Explanations of the constructs not yet mentioned will be provided as we proceed with the definitions of the corresponding formalisms. Further details of *X*-DFM can be found in (Mansmann & Scholl, 2008).

Figure 5. Multidimensional scheme fragment in X-DFM

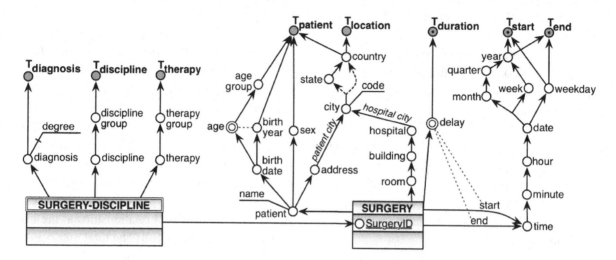

ADVANCED ELEMENTS OF THE CONCEPTUAL MODEL

Classical designation of facts is to contain relevant measures of a business process. Normally, facts are modeled by specifying the measures of interest and the context (dimensions) for their analysis. Consequently, facts schemes are expected to have a non-empty set of measures.

Definition 8. A fact scheme F **is** *measurable*, **if it has a non-empty set of measures, i.e.,** $M^F \neq \varnothing$.

Technically, a fact type is given by a many-to-many relationship between a set of attributes. According to Kimball (1996), any many-to-many relationship is a fact by definition. Some scenarios require storing many-to-many mappings in which no attribute qualifies as a measure. Typical cases include recording of some events, where an event is given by a combination of simultaneously occurring dimensional characteristics. Such scenarios result in so-called *factless fact tables* – a term introduced by Kimball (1996). However, *fact table* is a logical design construct corresponding to the semantic concept of a *fact type*. We define a conceptual equivalent of factless fact tables.

Definition 9. A fact scheme F **is** *non-measurable*, **if its set of measures is empty, i.e.,** $M^F = \varnothing$.

As explained in the previous section, non-measurable fact schemes are crucial for warehousing business process data as the former provide support for *event tracking* and *coverage* fact types. Event tracking facts model events as a robust set of many-to-many relationships between multiple dimensions, whereas coverage facts are used to track events that were eligible but did not happen (Kimball, 1996). Back to the fragment depicted in Figure 5, SURGERY is an example of a non-measurable event tracking fact type.

Whenever the fact's grain corresponds to actual events, there may exist a dimensional attribute with identifier properties, i.e., whose values are unique for each fact entry. For example, each SURGERY instance has a unique SurgeryID. Kimball, R. (1996) uses the concept of a *degenerate dimension* to handle such *id*-like attributes, while DFM treats them as *non-dimension attributes* of a fact. *Fact identifier* attribute is a special case of a degenerate dimension.

Definition 10. Dimension D **is** *degenerate*, **if it has a single category** C **consisting of a single attribute, i.e.,** $C^D = \{C, T_D\} \wedge C = \{A^C, \varnothing\}$.

Definition 11. A degenerate dimension D **is a** *fact identifier* **in** F, **if all values of** D **in** F **are unique.**

Since a degenerate dimension is only valid in the context of its fact, *X*-DFM places the former inside the fact's node as shown in Figure 5. Fact identifiers, shown with a double-underlined name, provide the foundation for modeling multi-fact schemes, as discussed later in this section.

TYPES OF MULTI-FACT SCHEMES

There may exist a many-to-many mapping of a fact with some of its dimensional characteristic or even with another fact. Giovinazzo (2000) proposes a concept of a *degenerated fact*, defined as a measure recorded in the intersection table of a many-to-many relationship between a pair of facts or a fact and a dimension. We suggest distinguishing between the following types of fact degeneration:

- *Satellite fact* scheme F ' extracts a many-to-many relationship between a fact scheme F and a dimension scheme D_i along with the corresponding measure characteristics of this relationship into a separate fact. Thereby, F acts as a dimension of F '. The term *satellite* reflects the accompanying nature of this fact with respect to its base fact.
- *Association fact* scheme F '' extracts a many-to-many relationship between a pair of fact schemes F and F ' along with the corresponding measure characteristics of this relationship into a separate fact.
- *Self-association fact* F ' extracts a recursive relationship within a fact scheme F, converting the latter into two different dimensions in F '.

Consider a many-to-many relationship between SURGERY and PARTICIPANT in the E/R diagram (Figure 2). An attempt to map this relationship to a multidimensional scheme would yield a satellite fact SURGERY-PARTICIPANT, shown in Figure 6(a), with fee as a measure referring to that mapping. As an example of an association fact, consider a trigger relationship between the facts of type EVENT and ACTIVITY (e.g., event *X* triggered activity *Y*). Figure 6(b) shows the resulting EVENT-ACTIVITY association fact and its base facts acting as dimensions of the former. Similarly, a self-association of EVENT can be defined to store a trigger relationship between pairs of events and is also represented in Figure 6(b) as EVENT-EVENT scheme.

Similarly to dimension levels, facts may display a roll-up behavior, i.e., be in a many-to-one relationship with each other.

Definition 12. A pair of fact schemes F **and** F ' **form a** *fact hierarchy*, **or a** *fact roll-up*, F ⊑* F ', **if** F **has a dimension containing fact identifier of** F ' **as one of its categories at any level of the hierarchy.**

Intuitively, fact schemes form a roll-up if they represent different grains of the same process. Fact roll-up is *direct*, if fact identifier of F' serves as a bottom category in F, and is *transitive* otherwise. Hierarchical relationships between facts typically arise between event tracking schemes that model events at different grain. In our example, there is a transitive fact roll-up of ACTIVITY to SURGERY depicted in Figure 7(a), as category phase of ACTIVITY rolls up to SurgeryID, which is a fact identifier of SURGERY.

An object-oriented concept of *inheritance* is helpful for dealing with heterogeneity of fact entries. A surgical process consists of different types of components, such as activities and events, which have a subset of common properties as well type-specific ones. A *fact generalization* is obtained when heterogeneous fact types are extracted into a superclass fact type in part of their common characteristics.

In our example, EVENT and ACTIVITY are made subclasses of COMPONENT, as shown

Figure 6. Examples of satellite fact schemes

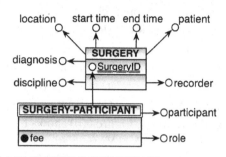

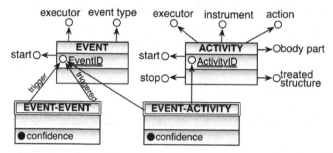

(a) *SURGERY-PARTICIPANT as a*
satellite fact of SURGERY

(b) *EVENT-ACTIVITY as an association and EVENT-EVENT*
as a self-association fact

in Figure 8. The superclass extracts all those dimensions, which are shared by all its subclasses. Moreover, fact generalization enables modeling of the degenerate facts, common for all subclasses, at the superclass level. In our example, COMPONENT-DATA could be modeled as a satellite of the generalized fact scheme COMPONENT.

Finally, fact types can be divided into *homogeneous* and *heterogeneous*. A fact scheme is homogeneous, if it disallows partial roll-up relations between the fact and any of its dimensions, and is heterogeneous otherwise. Heterogeneous fact types result from mapping non-uniformly structured facts to the same type, i.e., avoiding specialization. Figure 7(b) shows a variant of COMPONENT modeled as a heterogeneous fact scheme storing all characteristics of both subclass-

es EVENT and ACTIVITY. Relationships with dimensions, not common for all subclasses, have to be modeled as optional (dashed-line edge).

Fact types considered so far are called *primary* as they store non-derived data. Facts derivable from other facts are called *secondary*. The latter can be further categorized according to the way they were obtained:

- *Summary* fact type contains measures from the base fact type, aggregated to a coarser granularity.
- *Drill-across* fact type contains measures obtained by combining multiple related fact types.
- *Partition* fact type contains a subset of fact entries from its base fact type.

Figure 7. Examples of hierarchical relationships between fact schemes

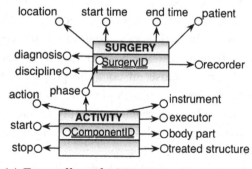

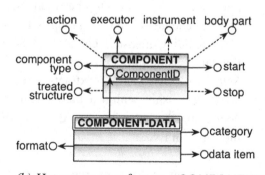

(a) *Fact rollup of ACTIVITY to SURGERY*

(b) *Heterogeneous fact type COMPONENT*

*Figure 8. Fact generalization of classes **EVENT** and **ACTIVITY** as a superclass **COMPONENT***

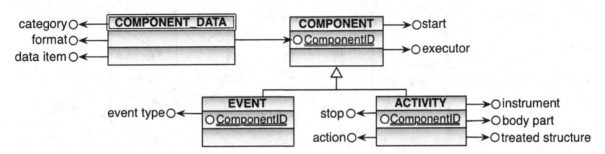

- *Conversion* fact type is obtained by applying a *push* and/or a *pull* operator.

MODELING DIMENSION HIERARCHIES

In the context of OLAP, only *structured* data hierarchies, i.e., those whose instances adhere to a certain scheme, qualify as dimensions. Values in a dimension may be organized into one or multiple hierarchies to provide additional levels of aggregation.

Definition 13. A *hierarchy scheme* H within D is a 5-tuple $(C^H, \sqsubseteq_C, \sqsubseteq_D, T_D, \perp_D)$ **for which holds:** $\nexists (C_i, C_j, C_k) \in C^H: C_i \sqsubseteq^{(full)} C_j \wedge C_i \sqsubseteq^{(full)} C_k$, **i.e., no category has more than one full roll-up relationship.**

Definition 14. A *hierarchy instance* H associated with hierarchy scheme H is a pair $(C^H, \subseteq_H)$, **where** $C^H = \{C_j, j = 1, ..., m\}$ **is a set of categories such that** $Type(C_j) = C_j, C_j \in C^H$, **and** $\subseteq_H$ **is a partial order on** $\cup_j C_j$, **the union of all dimensional values in the individual categories.**

Decomposition of complex dimension schemes into their constituting hierarchy schemes is crucial for determining valid aggregation paths within a dimension. Consider the dimension scheme patient in Figure 9(a). Apparently, it is composed of multiple hierarchy schemes with the following sets of category types:

1. $\{\perp_{patient}, sex, T_{patient}\}$,

2. $\{\perp_{patient}, birth\ date, birth\ year, T_{patient}\}$,
3. $\{\perp_{patient}, birth\ date, age, age\ group, T_{patient}\}$,
4. $\{\perp_{patient}, address, city, state, country, T_{patient}\}$,
5. $\{\perp_{patient}, address, city, country, T_{patient}\}$.

Multiple hierarchies in a dimension exist whenever its scheme contains a category that rolls up to more than one destination. We distinguish between heterogeneous and truly multiple hierarchies. In heterogeneous hierarchies, multiple paths result from partial related roll-up edges, such as in patient address hierarchy, in which the members of city have parent members either in state or directly in the state's parent category country. Therefore, the last two hierarchies in the above enumeration can be considered parts of a single heterogeneous hierarchy. Further elaborations on heterogeneous hierarchies can be found in (Mansmann & Scholl, 2007; Malinowski & Zimányi, 2006; Hurtado & Mendelzon, 2002).

Multiple hierarchies in a dimension are of type *alternative* or *parallel* with respect to one another. *Multiple alternative* hierarchies are based on the same analysis criterion with at least one shared level in the dimension scheme. Time dimension is a classical example of multiple alternatives. In start time dimension in Figure 9(a), alternative paths emerge from the category date: date values can be grouped by month or by week. However, these two aggregation levels may not be used in combination due to an implicit many-to-many

Figure 9. Modeling shared dimensional elements in X-DFM

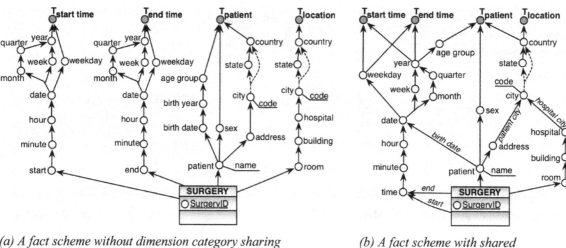

(a) *A fact scheme without dimension category sharing categories*

(b) *A fact scheme with shared*

relationship between the members of those categories: each month consists of multiple weeks and a week belongs to one or two months. *Parallel* hierarchies in a dimension account for different analysis criteria, such as the following patient hierarchies from the above list: the first hierarchy is based on the sex criterion, the third one groups patients by age, whereas the forth one is a hierarchy of patients' addresses. These three criteria have no relation to one another and, therefore, can be used in combination for aggregation. For instance, patient members can be first grouped by sex, and then by birth year, or vice versa.

Another important concept in the dimensional modeling is that of *derived* categories and dimensions. New categories may be derived as functions of the existing ones. For example, category age in Figure 5 is derived from birth year (by subtracting the birth year from the current year). Derived categories can be used in dimension schemes on the same terms as basic categories, as they provide additional aggregation levels. A category, derived from a bottom category or a set of bottom categories in a fact scheme, qualifies to be treated as a derived dimension of that fact scheme, since the former represents a derived characteristic of the

fact itself. For instance, dimension duration in Figure 5 is a derived one, as its bottom category delay is derived from the bottom categories start and end (by subtracting start values from those of end).

UNIFICATION OF THE MULTIDIMENSIONAL SPACE

A set of dimensions of any given fact scheme represents the multidimensional space of that scheme. Intuitively, the common multidimensional space of a set of fact schemes encompasses all dimensions of those schemes. For proper modeling of multifact relationships as well as of the convergence of dimension hierarchies, isolated multidimensional spaces have to be unified by replacing each set of redundant categories with a single shared category. Our approach to the unification of the multidimensional space is based on distinguishing between the concepts of a *dimension category* and a *category type*. Since a category type describes the value domain of a category, it is possible to define multiple categories of the same type. In terms of the unified space S, categories are considered redundant, if they belong to the same category type. To formalize the above idea, we introduce the concepts of *compatible, conformed,* and *related* elements.

Definition 15. Categories C_i **and** C_j **are** *compatible*, **if they belong to the same category type:** $Compatible(C_i, C_{jj}) \Leftarrow (C_i \neq C_j \land Type(C_i) = Type(C_{jj}))$.

Top-level categories are considered distinct for each dimension to account for the fact that compatible dimensions may have different member sets and that the abstract root value ALL covers only the respective dimension's data subset. Therefore, top level categories are exempted from the compatibility test. In a unified space S, each set of compatible categories is modeled as one *shared* category type.

Definition 16. Compatible categories C_i **and-** C_j **are** *conformed*, **if they roll up along the same paths:** $Conformed(C_i, C_{jj}) \Leftarrow Compatible(C_i, C_{jj})$ $\land (\forall C_m, C_i \sqsubseteq C_m: \exists C_n, C_j \sqsubseteq C_n \land Conformed(C_m, C_n))$.

Conformed categories are fully compatible because they roll-up along the same path. Back to Figure 9(a), start and end categories in start time and end time, respectively, are conformed, whereas date in start time and birth date in patient are compatible (the same value domain), but not conformed (different roll-up paths).

From category compatibility, the notions of *related dimensions* and *related fact schemes* are inferred:

Definition 17. A pair of dimensions D_i **and-** D_j **are** *related*, **if their schemes share at least one category type:** $Related(D_i, D_j) \Leftarrow \exists C_m \in D_i,$ $\exists C_n \in D_j: C_m = C_n$.

Definition 18. A pair of fact schemes F **and** F ' **are** *related*, **if they have at least one pair of related dimensions:** $Related(F, F') \Leftarrow \exists D_i \in F,$ $\exists D_j \in F': Related(D_i, D_j)$.

With respect to dimension sharing, *X*-DFM can be used in different modes, such as (a) *non-shared*, (b) *partially shared*, and (c) *fully shared* mode. In a non-shared mode, categories are not

examined for compatibility, i.e., each category is presented by a distinct node, as in a scheme shown in Figure 9(a). In the partially shared mode, only conformed categories are considered shared. This mode was applied in the scheme shown in Figure 5, where compatible yet non-conformed categories birth date and date along with their aggregation paths were not merged. In the fully shared mode all compatible categories are represented as shared nodes, thus complying with the requirements of the unified multidimensional space.

In the fully shared *X*-DFM mode, compatible categories are represented as follows:

1. Proceeding from the bottom-level categories upwards, each set of conformed categories is merged into a single category type node. Subsequently, the same is done for the remaining compatible categories.
2. Shared nodes are labeled by the name of their category types.
3. The actual names of single categories behind the shared node are shown as labels of the respective incoming roll-up edges.
4. Edge labels are obligatory in the existence of multiple unrelated incoming roll-up edges of a node and may be omitted otherwise. In the latter case, the category name is equal to its category type name.
5. To resolve ambiguities, fully qualified edge labels can be used (or displayed on demand). Such labels follow the naming convention *<fact-name>.<dimension-name>.<category-name>*.

Figure 9 pictures the concept of modeling shared dimensions at the example of the fact scheme SURGERY. Figure 9(a) shows the initial state of the model, in which each category is represented by a distinct node in the scheme. Applying the above rules of presenting shared categories in a unified multidimensional space, we derive a scheme depicted in Figure 9(b). Dimensions start time and end time now appear fully merged as their schemes are identical. The bottom categories are merged into a node of type time, whereas category names start and end are shown as edge labels. Dimensions patient and location are partially shared as both of them contain a category of type city.

In case of conformed categories, the entire roll-up graphs rooted at those categories can be merged in a single step. In case of non-conformed categories, graph merging may appear less trivial. Let us consider the example of merging birth date and date. Originally, birth date was modeled with the only parent category birth year of type year. Category date also rolls up to year, however via multiple alternative hierarchies. At this stage, the designer has to decide, whether these roll-up relationships should also be made available for birth date. In that case, the category birth year is simply mapped to year, as shown in Figure 9(b).

Category age group, however, which is a parent of year in patient, does not appear feasible as an aggregation level in start time or stop time dimensions, and, therefore, it is not added to their schemes.

With respect to the degree of convergence, three levels of dimension sharing can be identified, namely (a) *conformance*, (b) *inclusion*, and (c) *overlap*. Any of these patterns may occur between dimensions belonging to the same or to different fact schemes.

Definition 19. A pair of dimensions D **and** D' **are** *conformed***, if their bottom categories are conformed:** *Conformed(D, D')* $\Leftarrow \exists C_i \in D$, *Type($C_i$)* $= \perp_D, \exists C_j \in D'$, *Type($C_j$)* $= \perp_{D'}$: *Conformed(C_i, C_{if})*.

Since category conformance is defined as a recursive property, dimension conformance implies the identity of the respective dimension schemes, or formally: *Conformed(D, D')* $\Leftrightarrow C \setminus \{T_D\} = C' \setminus \{T_{D'}\} \wedge \sqsubseteq_D = \sqsubseteq_{D'}$. As an example of conformed dimensions, consider start time and end time of SURGERY in Figure 9(b).

Kimball & Ross (2002) introduced the term

conformed dimensions to refer to dimensions, which are not physically centralized but which have identical schemes. Our definition differs from the latter one in that we do not regard logical design issues (e.g., centralization and normalization) at the stage of conceptual modeling. Therefore, in our model, a unified multidimensional space approach does not impose any particular logical or physical design scheme. On contrary, this approach is beneficial for generating semantically rich metadata to support advanced OLAP operators and data navigation options in frontend tools irrespective of the implementation.

Inclusion pattern of dimension sharing occurs when some category in a dimension fully rolls-up to the bottom-level category of another dimension, i.e., when two dimensions represent different grain of the same characteristic. In our scenario, this is the case with the dimensions patient of SURGERY and treated structure of ACTIVITY. Bottom-level category of patient serves as an upper aggregation level in treated structure. As a result, ACTIVITY facts, if grouped by treated structure, can be further aggregated along the entire dimension scheme of patient.

Definition 20. Dimension D **is** *included* **in dimension** D'**, if its scheme is a sub-graph in the scheme of** D'**:** *Included(D, D')* $\Leftarrow C \setminus \{T_D\} \subset C' \setminus \{T_{D'}\} \wedge \sqsubseteq_D \subset \sqsubseteq_{D'}$.

Dimensions are said to be *overlapping*, if their schemes converge only partially.

Definition 21. A pair of dimensions D **and** D' **are** *overlapping***, if they are related via a category, non-bottom for either of them:** *Overlapping(D, D')* $\Leftarrow \exists C_i \in C \setminus \{\perp_D\}, \exists C_j \in C' \setminus \{T_{D'}\}$: $C_i = C_j$.

Overlapping dimensions may belong to the same or to different fact schemes. The latter provides inherent support for a drill-across operation. Dimensions patient and location in Figure 9(b) overlap as they contain hierarchies that converge in city.

Notice how presence of distinct top-level categories helps to distinguish between seemingly and truly converging paths. The former case occurs in case of category sharing between dimensions. For instance, even though country is the highest aggregation level in both location and patient, each of these dimensions ends at its own top-level node. True path convergence occurs in multiple and heterogeneous hierarchies within a dimension, as in the case of start time and end time, where multiple paths converge in year.

"FADING" DUALITY OF FACT AND DIMENSION ROLES

Throughout this section we encountered multiple examples of fact schemes acting as dimensions in other fact schemes. That might seem paradox, but it has its legitimacy. Structurally, both facts and dimensions are given by a graph of "rolls-up-to" relationships between their categories. The difference is that the aggregation graph of a dimension depends on its proper semantics, while the aggregation graph of a fact depends on the aggregation hierarchies of its analysis dimensions (Abelló, Samos, & Saltor, 2001). Fact and dimension roles are fixed only in the context of isolated fact schemes. What happens to those roles in the context multidimensional multi-fact schemes? Apparently, these roles are determined by the focus of a given analytical task, which may vary from one query to another. For example, a query focusing on a measure of an association fact treats the base fact schemes of this association as dimensions. Altogether, multidimensionality implies that what is considered a fact in one task could be considered a dimension by another one, and vice versa.

The first interchangeability case is concerned with a fact scheme acting as dimension of another fact scheme. Fact scheme F can be treated as a dimension in fact scheme F' while querying its measures when F' contains the fact identifier dimension of F. This relationship may be encountered in satellite facts and hierarchies of event

tracking facts. One implication of this interchangeability is that it results in multiple focus-dependent conceptual schemes for the same data fragment. Figure 10 illustrates the example of two conceptual views of the satellite fact relationship between SURGERY-PARTICIPANT and SURGERY. A focus-independent view of both fact schemes is shown in Figure 10(a) and a perspective focused on SURGERY-PARTICIPANT and its valid aggregation paths is given in Figure 10(b).

Thereby, fact scheme SURGERY is transformed into a dimension surgery, in which all dimensions of the original fact scheme turn into parallel hierarchies, diverging from the bottom category SurgeryID. The validity of treating the fact identifier of SURGERY as a bottom category in surgery is given by the fact that the latter has the same grain as SURGERY fact entries, and thus, has a many-to-one (i.e., a rolls-up) relationship to all other dimensions.

Another kind of interchangeability is related to treating dimensions as measures, and vice versa. Support of advanced OLAP operators, such as *push* for converting a dimension category into a measure and *pull* for converting a measure into a dimension, as well as *drill-across* for combining measures from multiple related fact schemes, is a challenge not handled by conventional conceptual models. The output of these operators is a new conceptual multidimensional scheme. Our solution for supporting scheme-transforming operators at the conceptual level is straightforward - to explicitly model their output schemes. Figure 11 exemplifies this idea by showing the conceptual consequences of "pushing" a dimension category hospital in SURGERY (see Figure 9(b)) into a measure attribute (e.g., to query a measure COUNT(DISTINCT hospital)).

The "pushed" category hospital itself as well as all categories below it are removed from the output dimension scheme of location as their granularities become available. Dashed lines connecting the measure attribute hospital with all dimensions indicate its non-additivity.

*Figure 10. Fact **SURGERY** as a dimension in its satellite fact **SURGERY-PARTICIPANT***

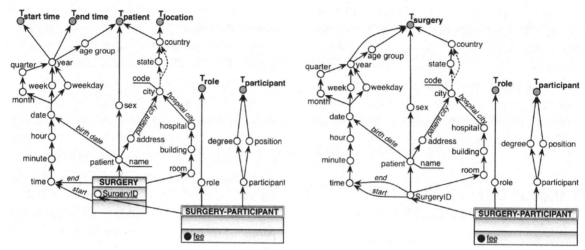

(a) Focus-independent view of a satellite fact scheme   *(b) A base fact as a dimension of its satellite fact*

OBTAINING A MULTIDIMENSIONAL SCHEME OF A PROCESS

In the two preceding sections we formalized the properties of the advanced multidimensional conceptual model that overcomes the restrictions of the conventional OLAP technology. The presented formalisms were illustrated using relevant multidimensional fragments from the cases study. However, we did not elaborate on how those frag-

*Figure 11. Transformation of the original fact scheme **SURGERY** caused by a push operation*

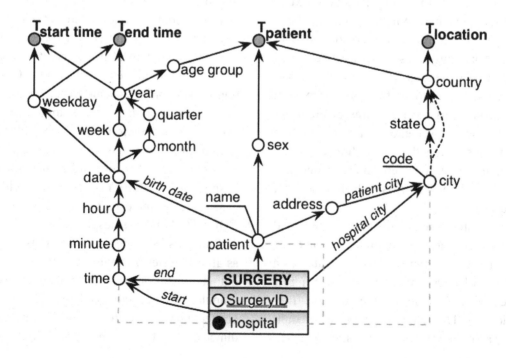

ments had actually been obtained. The algorithm of acquiring the multidimensional model of a process is the subject of this section.

The idea of developing methods for systematic acquisition of multidimensional models from E/R diagrams is well represented in the data warehouse research. Most of the existing business information management systems are relational, and, therefore, it appears feasible to derive the conceptual model of a data warehouse from that of the existing system, typically available in form of E/R or UML class diagrams. Outstanding contributions in this field were made by Cabibbo & Torlone (1998), Golfarelli, et al. (1998), Franconi & Sattler (1999), Tryfona, et al. (1999), Phipps & Davis (2002). Some of the approaches, such as the ones proposed by Cabibbo & Torlone (1998) and Franconi & Sattler (1999), are based on "encoding" the multidimensional semantics into the original E/R constructs, while others provide extended variants of the E/R model. Prominent examples of the latter class are are starER of Tryfona, et al. (1999) and *Multidimensional Entity Relationship (ME/R) Model* of Sapia, et al. (1999). Yet another group of works provides mapping of E/R schemes to ad-hoc multidimensional models. The DFM approach of Golfarelli, et al. (1998), which is the predecessor of our proposed *X*-DFM model, is an example of such methodology.

The above methods proceed by determining the facts and subsequently refining their dimensional context. However, none of those methods is directly applicable in our scenario due to their fundamental assumption that the measures of interests are known at design time. Dealing with a "factless" event-tracking data warehouse application scenario implies the necessity for a different procedure of identifying the facts.

Our approach to identifying candidate fact entities in an E/R scheme is based on analyzing the set of each entity's relationships with other entities by looking at the cardinalities and structural constraints of those relationships. From the basic definitions of facts, dimensions, and dimension

hierarchies provided in Section 6, as well as the definitions of degenerate facts and dimensions in Section 7, the following cardinality information with respect to the fact scheme structure can be deduced:

- A fact scheme is given by a set of dimension categories that have an *n*-ary relationship to each other or where a distinguished category, representing the grain of the fact, has a binary relationship with each other category in the set.
- In measurable schemes, each measure attribute has an *n*:1 relationship with any of its dimensions.
- Non-measurable schemes correspond to an entity type that represents some event, along with the set of entity types, related to the former via a 1:*n* relationship.

With respect to dimension hierarchies, the cardinality constraints are straightforward:

- Each category corresponds to an entity type and a set of its single-valued attributes.
- A homogeneous dimension hierarchy is given by a lattice of categories, in which each category is connected to at most one parent category via an *n*:1 relationship.
- Heterogeneous hierarchy contains categories involved in a generalization relationship, with the subclass as a parent category of the subclasses.

The above observations provide valuable guidance for automatic recognition of fact and dimensions candidates in E/R schemes, subject to the condition that the input scheme accurately and fully maps all required attributes as well as relationships and dependencies between attributes.

VERIFICATION AND REFINEMENT OF THE E/R SCHEME

In most cases, pre-existing conceptual models of the system are tailored towards specific application needs and are thus focused on the properties and relationships relevant in the application context. Besides, the level of detail, accuracy and completeness of the model may not be adequate to meet the requirements of the analysis. Therefore, the actual transformation of the E/R scheme into a multidimensional one is preceded by the transformation of the E/R scheme itself. This transformation evolves in two phases: (a) pruning / enriching the data set and (b) refining the relationships in the data.

The data set is pruned as to eliminate parts of the model, irrelevant for the analysis. For instance, private data of the patients, such as name, address, and birth date, may have to be removed to comply with data privacy regulations. Subsequently, the model is enriched to include further data available for the analysis. This data is obtained by integrating additional data sources. Most of the enhancements are concerned with enabling additional granularity levels. For example, a geographic database may be added to be able to aggregate address data by zip code, city, region, and so on.

The aim of the refinement phase is to have an accurate mapping of all relationships between all entities and attributes in the scheme. There is a fundamental difference in the way the E/R model and the multidimensional data model handle relationships: the former admits relationships only between entity types, whereas the latter specifies relationships between attributes. In the E/R model, each attribute is associated with a single entity or relationship type implying a one-to-many relationship in the general case, a one-to-one relationship in case of an identifier property, and a many-to-one or many-to-many relationship in case of a multivalued attribute. Thereby, it is impossible to specify dependencies between attributes. A legitimate way to overcome this penalty is to re-arrange attributes

into additional entities and explicitly specify the relationships between the newly defined entities.

The only constructs of the multidimensional model that fully correspond to that of an *attribute* in the E/R model, are *dimension level* attribute, *property* attribute, and *measure* as each of them is related to one element in the scheme. Other constructs, such as facts, dimensions, and dimension categories, participate in relationships and, therefore, have to be represented by entity types. As for relationship types, it is insufficient to specify cardinalities as simple ratios ($1{:}1$, $1{:}n$, or $m{:}n$) as this notation does not reveal whether the relationship is optional for any of participating entity types. Therefore, representation of cardinality by structural constraints in (min, max) notation is a crucial requirement of E/R scheme refinement. The above considerations of the multidimensional modeling constraints with respect to attributes and relationships are fundamental for formulating the ultimate goal of approximating an E/R scheme to a multidimensional one.

Definition 22. An E/R scheme is accurate, if the structural constraints are fully specified for each relationship type R and each entity type E participating in R, if all generalization / specialization relationships are made explicit, and if for each attribute A_i in the scheme holds:

1. *A_i is simple (i.e., non-composite),*
2. *A_i is single-valued,*
3. **A_i is either a key property (or a part of the key) or is functionally dependent on the key property,**
4. *A_i is not related (i.e., has no functional dependency) to any other attribute apart from the key of its entity type.*

To achieve the above accurate state, we propose the transformation procedure that evolves as follows:

1. Identify implicitly composite attributes (i.e., consisting of multiple data fields) and replace

Figure 12. Examplesof presenting complex attributes as composite ones and re-modeling multivalued attributes into related entity types

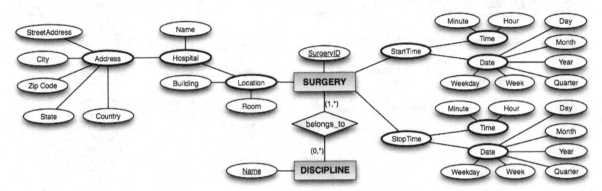

them by explicit composite attributes.

2. Similarly, re-shape explicit composite attributes into entity types consisting of simple attributes.

3. Multivalued attributes are reshaped into entity types, related to that attribute's original entity type.

4. Identify dependencies and relations between attributes, not explicit in the scheme. Each attribute, involved into such relations, is transformed into an entity type and the relationship between newly created entity types is specified.

5. Identify implied generalization/specialization relationships and make them explicit in the scheme.

6. Redundant fragments of the scheme are merged into shared fragments.

7. Elements of the scheme that became obsolete are eliminated.

The above sequence of steps is chosen as to complete the transformation of the scheme in a single iteration. As an example of refining the E/R scheme according to the above procedure, let us consider the case of SURGERY attributes in Figure 2.

In the first step, attribute Location was identified as implicitly composite, as its values are full addresses of respective operating theatres speci-

fied as the room, the building, the name of the hospital and its full address. The address values, in their turn, are also decomposable into multiple fields. Similarly, attributes of type date and time should be decomposed into their constituent fields. Figure 12 shows the results of re-structuring implicitly composite attributes Location, StartTime, and StopTime.

In the second step, composite attributes are transformed into related entity types. Figure 13 shows the results of translating composite attributes Location, StartTime, and StopTime into a set of entity types and aggregation relationships between them. Notice that both temporal attributes could be represented by the same entity type TIMESTAMP due to their identical structure. As a result, these two attributes are replaced by two respective relationships between SURGERY and TIMESTAMP.

Multivalued attributes are handled in the third step. Each multivalued attribute is transformed into an entity type linked to the hosting entity type of that attribute via a $1{:}n$ or an $m{:}n$ relationship. As an example, consider the result of transforming Discipline attribute into an entity type, depicted in Figure 12.

The fourth step of identifying "hidden" relationships between attributes is primarily concerned with revealing candidate roll-up, or "part-of", relationships. Explicit modeling of those relationships

Figure 13. Transforming composite attributes into related entity types

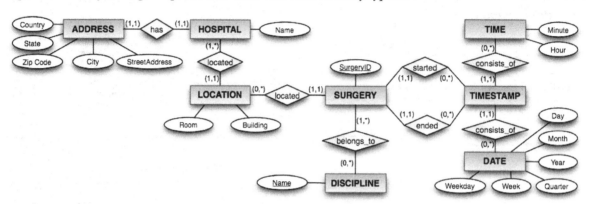

facilitates recognition of dimension hierarchies at a later stage. Back to our example, aggregation relationships exist between Room and Building, between Building and Hospital, between Hospital and City, and so on. Figure 14 shows the results of revealing the hierarchical structure behind the attributes of surgery location.

In the next step, the scheme is verified with respect to implied generalization/specialization relationships. Our original model (see Figure 2) already contains a generalization of heterogeneous process components, such as ACTIVITY, EVENT, and STATE into a superclass COMPONENT. However, the scheme can be further refined by adding a specialization relationship to the entity type SYSTEM. In our scenario, the notion of a system is heterogeneous and may refer to an in-

strument, a body part of a participant, or a treated structure of a patient. Figure 15 shows the affected part of the scheme.

The last two transformation steps finalize the refined scheme by identifying redundant fragments, merging them, and removing obsolete elements. Redundant fragments emerge in the course of transforming attributes into entity types. For instance, decomposition of the Address attribute in PATIENT will yield the same scheme as the one produced by transforming the Address attribute in HOSPITAL. This redundancy is eliminated by relating all entity types, which have an address property, with the same entity type ADDRESS. Some elements become obsolete at different stages of refinement. For example, entity type LOCA-TION (Figure 13) gets dissolved into ROOM and

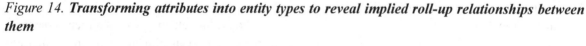

Figure 14. **Transforming attributes into entity types to reveal implied roll-up relationships between them**

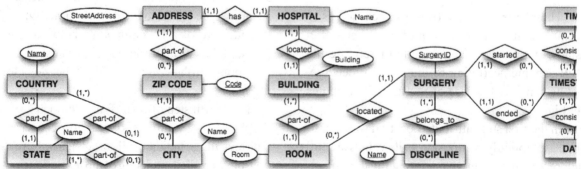

Figure 15. Adding specialization to the heterogeneous entity type **SYSTEM**

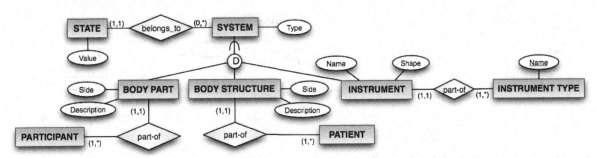

IDENTIFYING FACTS AND DIMENSIONS

BUILDING along with a "part-of" relationship between them (Figure 14). In the final step, the scheme is verified to ensure that it contains no obsolete elements.

Once the transformation of the E/R scheme is complete, a cardinality-based transformation into a multidimensional scheme can be applied. Essentially, the task consists in determining for each entity type whether it maps to a fact, a bottom-level or an upper level dimension category.

Since facts build the focus of a multidimensional scheme, the first step is concerned with identifying fact candidates. Remember that, technically, a fact structure is a collection of properties, which have many-to-many relationship to each other and a one-to-many relationship to the fact's measure(s). Therefore, there exist just three structures in terms of the E/R model, which satisfy this cardinality constraint:

- an entity type that has n:1 relationships with multiple other entity types,
- an n-ary relationship between a set of entity types,
- an m:n relationship between a pair of entity types.

For the sake of simplicity, the first two cases can be merged into one, since any n-ary relationship is convertible into an entity type by replacing each branch with a binary relationship towards the respective participating entity type. Besides, the concept of an entity type is generally superior to that of a relationship as the former may participate in other relationships. The third case is typical for a fact degeneration, i.e., an m:n relationship between a fact and a dimension, but may also occur in a non-strict dimension hierarchy.

IDENTIFYING FACTS

Generally, a fact is given by an entity type E_f involved into multiple n:1 relationships with other entity types (whereas existence of 1:n, m:n or 1:1 relationships between E_f and other entity types is not prohibited). E_f corresponds to the fact's granularity, and the set of the related entity types along with the attributes of E_f define the fact's dimensional context. To investigate the properties of E_f as a candidate fact scheme, all relationships of E_f are arranged into the following mutually disjoint sets:

- $E^{<rec>}(E_f)$ is a set of recursive (i.e., connecting the entity type to itself) relationships of E_f,
- $E^{<n:1>}(E_f)$ is a set of E_f's candidate dimensions, i.e., a set of its non-key attributes and entity types with which E_f has an n:1 relationship,

*Figure 16. Transforming entity type **STEP** (left) to a fact scheme (right)*

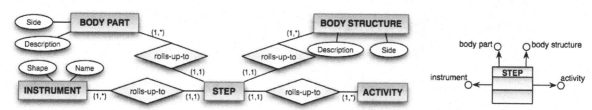

- $E^{(<super>)}(E_f)$ is a set of superclasses, i.e., direct generalizations, of E_f,
- $E^{(<sub>)}(E_f)$ is a set of subclasses, i.e., direct specializations, of E_f,
- $E^{<1:1>}(E_f)$ is a set of E_f's identifier dimensions, i.e., a set of entity types and attributes with which E_f has a 1:1 relationship,
- $E^{<1:n>}(E_f)$ is a set of E_f's candidate sub-facts, i.e., a set of entity types with which E_f has a 1:n relationship,
- $E^{<m:n>}(E_f)$ is a set of E_f's candidate degenerate facts, i.e., a set of entity types with which E_f has an m:n relationship.

Convergence of an E/R scheme into a multidimensional one evolves in a bottom-up fashion, starting with entity types that qualify as terminal facts, i.e., the elements of the finest grain, and proceeding to coarser grained elements.

Definition 23. Entity type E_f corresponds to a *terminal* fact, if it is not involved into any decomposition or specialization relationship, i.e., $E^{<1:n>}(E_f) = E^{(<sub>)}(E_f) = \varnothing$.

A 1:n relationship between E_f and some other entity type E_k indicates a composition or an aggregation relationship and, thus, existence of a fact roll-up pattern (E_k rolls up to E_f). A specialization relationship of E_f implies that each subclass inherits all characteristics of E_f and may have further characteristics of its own.

In our surgical workflow model, entity types STEP, EVENT, and STATE qualify as terminal facts. Figure 16 shows the part of the E/R diagram referring to STEP and its relationships types as well as its mapping to a 4-dimensional fact

scheme. For consistency, n:1 relationship with full participation, i.e., with (1,1) and (1,*) as its structural constraints, are all renamed to "rolls-up-to". The transformation appears straightforward as the only non-empty set of related categories $E^{<n:1>}(STEP) = \{INSTRUMENT, BODY PART, BODY STRUCTURE, ACTIVITY\}$ maps seamlessly to a set of the fact's dimensions.

As an example of a more complex fact candidate at a coarser granularity level, let us consider the entity type ACTIVITY, depicted in Figure 17, with its non-empty sets $E^{<n:1>}(ACTIVITY) = \{TIME-OFFSET, ACTION\}$, $E^{<super>}(ACTIVITY) = \{COMPONENT\}$, and $E^{<1:n>}(ACTIVITY) = \{STEP\}$. As STEP has already been mapped to a fact scheme, the 1:n relationship is interpreted as fact roll-up. COMPONENT as a superclass of ACTIVITY is also represented as a fact, yielding a fact generalization pattern.

Finally, let us consider an example of identifying and modeling degenerated facts. Once entity type E_f has been converted to a fact, its degenerated facts correspond to the relationships in $E^{<m:n>}(E_f)$ (satellite facts and fact associations) and $E^{<rec>}(E_f)$ (fact self-associations). Figure 18 shows a fragment of the E/R diagram modeling a generalized entity type COMPONENT and its relationships. COMPONENT's m:n relationship with DATA and a recursive relationship triggers are converted to a satellite fact COMPONENT-DATA and a self-association COMPONENT-TRIGGER, respectively, as depicted in Figure 18.

Having considered various examples of identifying parts of the E/R scheme that qualify to be converted into facts, we are ready to provide an

*Figure 17. Transforming entity type **ACTIVITY** (left) to a fact scheme (right)*

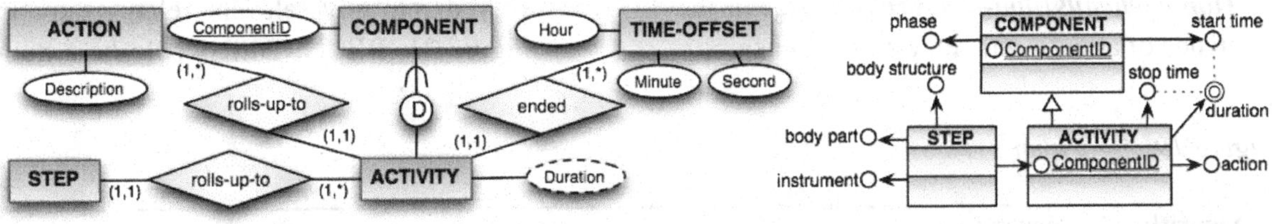

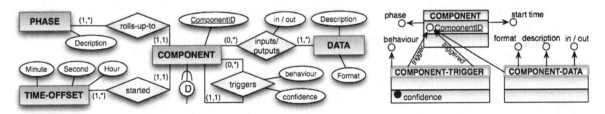

algorithmic description of acquiring fact schemes from accurate E/R schemes. Algorithm 1 (Figure 19) is invoked on each "terminal" entity type E_f, outputting a set of fact schemes, obtained by recursively applying itself to each entity type identified as a fact candidate. Sets $\mathbf{E}^{(<sub>)}(E_f)$ and $\mathbf{E}^{(<1:n>)}(E_f)$ used for identifying "terminal" entity types become obsolete inside the algorithm as it proceeds in the bottom-up fashion. In the first step, Algorithm 1 (Figure 19) creates an empty fact type and converts the attributes of the underlying entity into measures and degenerate dimensions, as shown in the subroutine Algorithm 2 (Figure 20).

IDENTIFYING DIMENSIONS

Fact schemes produced by Algorithm 1 (Figure 19) are incomplete in a sense that fact's dimensions are defined solely in terms of their bottom categories. Therefore, the next step consists in constructing complete dimension hierarchies implied by the E/R scheme. Once the E/R scheme has been brought into an accurate state, as defined in the previous subsection, dimension hierarchies become easily identifiable: each category corresponds to an entity type and the partial order on the category types is given by the hierarchical, i.e., many-to-one, relationships between categories. Similarly to the fact conversion procedure, dimension schemes are constructed in a bottom-up fashion by rooting the dimension's graph at the bottom category and recursively adding roll-up relationships until the top level is reached. In the presence of multiple and heterogeneous hierarchies, the resulting dimension scheme will contain diverging and converging paths.

Roll-up behavior of an entity type is determined by its relationships. As dimension categories are identified bottom-up, the set of *relevant* relationships is reduced to 1:1, n:1, and m:n. Let us consider the process of hierarchy modeling at the example of phase dimension in COMPONENT. The corresponding part of the E/R diagram (simplified for presentation purposes) is given in Figure 21.

From the perspective of a candidate dimension category given by the entity type E_d, possible roll-up behaviors of E_d can be categorized based on the number of its relevant relationships, their

*Figure 18. Transforming m:n and recursive relationships of **COMPONENT** (left) to degenerated facts (right)*

structural constraints and inter-dependencies:

Homogeneous (non-)hierarchy emerges in the existence of at most one relevant relationship:

- *Non-hierarchy* is given, if E_d is not involved into any relevant relationship. In Figure 21, RECORDER would be a non-

Figure 19. Algorithm 1

Algorithm 1: ConvertToFact

Data: Entity type E_f, Set of previously identified fact schemes $\mathcal{F}$
Result: Updated set of fact schemes $\mathcal{F}$
begin
  $\mathcal{F} \longleftarrow ConvertAttributes(E_f, \mathcal{F})$;
  $\mathcal{E}^{<rec>} \longleftarrow \varnothing$;
  $\mathcal{E}^{<super>} \longleftarrow \varnothing$;
  $\mathcal{E}^{<1:1>} \longleftarrow \varnothing$;
  $\mathcal{E}^{<n:1>} \longleftarrow \varnothing$;
  $\mathcal{E}^{<m:n>} \longleftarrow \varnothing$;
  $Rel \longleftarrow getRelationships(E_f)$;
  foreach $E_f \diamond E_i \in Rel$ **do**
    if $E_f = E_i$ **then**
      $append(E_f \diamond E_i, \mathcal{E}^{<rec>})$;
    else if $E_i = Generalization(E_f)$ **then**
      $append(E_i, \mathcal{E}^{<super>})$;
    else
      $c = Cardinality(E_f \diamond E_i)$;
      switch c **do**
        case $1:1$
          $append(E_i, \mathcal{E}^{<1:1>})$;
        case $n:1$ $append(E_i, \mathcal{E}^{<n:1>})$;
        otherwise
          $append(E_i, \mathcal{E}^{<m:n>})$;
  foreach $E_i \in \mathcal{E}^{<1:1>}$ **do**
    $addDimension(E_i, \mathcal{F}, \text{"shadow"})$;
  foreach $E_i \in \mathcal{E}^{<n:1>}$ **do**
    $addDimension(E_i, \mathcal{F}, \text{"normal"})$;
    if $qualifiesAsFact(E_i)$ **then**
      $\mathcal{F} \longleftarrow ConvertToFact(E_i, \mathcal{F})$;
  foreach $E_i \in \mathcal{E}^{<super>}$ **do**
    $addDimension(E_i, \mathcal{F}, \text{"superclass"})$;
    $\mathcal{F} \longleftarrow ConvertToFact(E_i, \mathcal{F})$;
  foreach $E_f \diamond E_i \in \mathcal{E}^{<rec>}$ **do**
    $\mathcal{F}_k \longleftarrow CreateFactSelfAssociation(\mathcal{F}, E_f \diamond E_i)$;
    $append(\mathcal{F}_k, \mathcal{F})$;
  foreach $E_i \in \mathcal{E}^{<m:n>}$ **do**
    $\mathcal{F}_k \longleftarrow CreateDegenerateFact(\mathcal{F}, E_i)$;
    $append(\mathcal{F}_k, \mathcal{F})$;
  foreach $E_i \in \mathcal{E}^{<1:n>}$ **do**
    $addDimension(E_i, \mathcal{F}, \text{"normal"})$;
  $append(\mathcal{F}, \mathcal{F})$;
  return $\mathcal{F}$;
end

Figure 20. Algorithm 2

Algorithm 2: ConvertAttributes

Data: Entity type E_f
Result: Fact type $\mathcal{F}$ corresponding to E_f
begin
  $\mathcal{F} \longleftarrow createFact(E_f)$;
  $Attr = getAtributes(E_f)$;
  foreach $A \in Attr$ **do**
   if $isMeasure(A)$ **then**
    | $addMeasure(A, \mathcal{F})$;
   else if $isIdentifier(A)$ **then**
    | $addDimension(A, \mathcal{F}, \text{``identifier''})$;
   else
    | $addDimension(A, \mathcal{F}, \text{``degenerated''})$;
  return $\mathcal{F}$;
end

---

hierarchical dimension in the fact scheme WORKFLOW.

- *Simple hierarchy* is given by an *n*:1 relationship between E_d and some other entity type E_i with (1,1) as the structural constraint on E_d's participation as this relationships produces a full roll-up of E_d to E_i. For instance, PHASE and WORKFLOW yield a simple hierarchy.
- *Non-strict hierarchy* is given by an *m*:*n*

relationship between E_d and some other entity type.

Heterogeneous hierarchy emerges in the existence of an optional roll-up or a single set of relevant mutually exclusive relationships:

- *Optional hierarchy* is given by an *n*:1 relationship between E_d and some other entity type E_i with (0,1) as the structural

*Figure 21. **Fragment of the E/R scheme relevant for building the dimension scheme phase in COMPONENT***

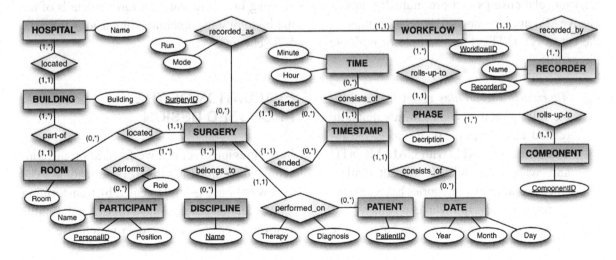

*Figure 22. Multiple alternative and parallel hierarchies in **DATE** dimension*

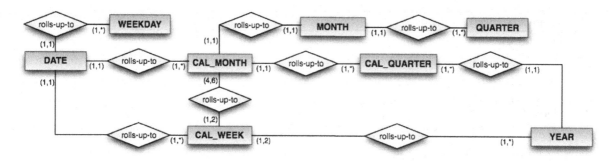

constraint on E_d's participation as this relationship produces a partial roll-up of E_d to E_i.

- *Non-covering hierarchy* results from a set partial related *n*:1 relationships. The partiality is given by (0,1) as the structural constraint on E_d's participation in each relationship. Besides, the diverging roll-up paths of E_d ought to converge at a later stage. Example of such partial related roll-up is the relationship between CITY, STATE, and COUNTRY in Figure 14.

- *Specialization hierarchy* emerges from a specialization relationship of E_d into multiple subclass categories. As an example, consider a generalized category SYSTEM in Figure 15.

Multiple hierarchies correspond to multiple relevant relationships that are mutually nonexclusive. Figure 22 shows the relationships of the category DATE as an example of multiple hierarchies.

- *Alternative hierarchies* result from multiple roll-up relationships towards mutually related entity types. For instance, the relationships of DATE with CAL_MONTH and with CAL_WEEK are alternative, since the latter two categories have a many-to-many relationship with each other.
- *Parallel hierarchies* correspond to multiple

roll-up relationships towards mutually unrelated entity types. For instance, the relationship of DATE with CAL_MONTH is parallel to that of DATE and WEEKDAY.

Figure 23 shows the results of converging the fragment of the E/R model from Figure 21 into a dimension. Additionally, the structure of the hierarchical category DATE is shown corresponding to the E/R model shown in Figure 20.

Once the construction of the dimension scheme is complete, an abstract top-level category is added as a root node at which all dimension's hierarchies converge. In case of a unified multidimensional space, redundant elements of dimension schemes have to be eliminated by merging compatible categories.

Since dimension hierarchy modeling techniques are well highlighted in the data warehousing literature, we omit further details of the methodology for obtaining dimensions from the E/R schemes.

EVALUATION OF THE PROPOSED DESIGN

In the previous sections we focused on the conceptual data modeling for BPI applications. The data warehouse is implemented by transforming the conceptual scheme into a logical and, finally, a physical one. Once the data warehouse is set

*Figure 23. The resulting dimension scheme of the **PHASE** dimension in **COMPONENT***

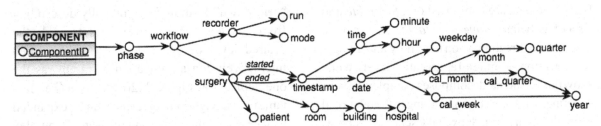

up and running, end-users access the data using so called OLAP tools. Advanced tools offer a user-friendly visual interface for interactive data analysis by implementing OLAP operators in form of interactive events, such as browsing, clicking, marking regions of interest, drag-&-drop, zooming, panning, etc., and by providing a set visual layouts (pivot tables, business charts, scatter-plots, dash boards, etc.) for convenient exploration of the retrieved data.

IMPLEMENTATION REMARKS

OLAP tools do not indicate how the data actually has to be stored. Hence, there exist multiple ways to implement a data warehouse, with the following two prominent architectures:

- *Relational OLAP (ROLAP)* systems store data in relational DBMS and employ SQL extensions and specialized access structures to efficiently implement OLAP operations.
- *Multidimensional OLAP (MOLAP)* systems directly store data in specialized multidimensional data structures (such as arrays or cubes) and implement OLAP operations over these structures.

Apart from the fundamental distinction in data storage and processing capabilities, there is a conceptual difference between MOLAP and ROLAP databases: MOLAP pursues a top-down approach

by first focusing on business problems, then identifying measures and dimensions of interest, so that the metadata model may be built prior to the acquisition of the relevant data sources; ROLAP, in contrast, encourages a bottom-up analysis to identify candidate facts and dimensions in the relational data models of existing data sources (Dodds, et al., 1999). Both paradigms have their benefits and weaknesses – the latter, however, being rapidly addressed by the respective vendors. Currently, data warehouses are predominantly built using ROLAP, especially when dealing with very large data volumes. ROLAP attributes its success to the established and proven technology, good scalability in terms of the number of facts and their dimensionality, flexibility for cube redefinitions, and support for frequent updates (Pedersen & Jensen, 2001).

Considering the complexity of the conceptual modeling for BPI applications, the relational technology appears an adequate option. Especially the bottom-up design approach relying on the existing models and data sources and the ability to adjust and modify cube definitions at runtime make ROLAP an attractive option. Besides, the relational data model with its normalization techniques, integrity constraints and object-relational features has the necessary flexibility to adequately map advanced concepts of the semantic model.

The classical way to obtain a logical model is by means of mapping the conceptual model to logical constructs, such as relations, keys, and constraints. *Star schema* and *snowflake schema –* both introduced by Kimball (1996) – are the two options of the relational data warehouse design. Both schemata are composed of a *fact table* and a set of associated *dimension tables*. Star schema places the entire dimension hierarchy into a single relation by pre-joining all aggregation levels, while snowflake schema decomposes complex dimensions into separate tables according to the relational normalization rules. Snowflake schema becomes the only option when dimensional hierarchies are prone to irregularities, such as heterogeneity, non-strictness, missing values, mixed granularity etc. Multiple fact tables with dimensions modeled using either star schema or snowflake schema may be arranged into a *galaxy* (Kimball, et al., 1998), also referred to as *fact constellation*. This schema is constructed by allowing dimension tables to be shared amongst many fact tables: each fact table is explicitly assigned to the dimensions, relevant for that fact table. This solution is very flexible and powerful as it offers a logical equivalent of a unified multidimensional space. A comprehensive methodology for obtaining a fact constellation schema from semantic schemes was proposed by Lechtenbörger (2001).

Relational concepts of virtual tables (known as *"views"*) and *materialized views* are helpful for modeling derived elements in fact and dimension schemes. Foreign key constraints are used to link related schemes. Object-relational feature of inheritance enables intuitive handling of heterogeneous facts and dimensions.

VISUAL ANALYSIS

Visual exploration has evolved into the prevailing method of modern data analysis at end-user level. Therefore, the ultimate value of the proposed conceptual and relational model extensions is determined by the easiness of incorporating those extensions into visual OLAP tools. In this subsection we sketch a prototypical implementation of an end-user interface for multidimensional business process analysis.

Analysts interact with data in a predominantly "drill-down" fashion, i.e., gradually descending from coarsely grained overviews towards the desired level of detail. Queries are specified interactively via a navigation hierarchy, as the one depicted in Figure 242(b): a cube (i.e., fact table) is a navigation object that can be expanded to access its dimensions and measures. Complex dimensions are represented as hierarchical nodes that can be expanded to access their aggregation levels (child levels are nested in their parent levels). Compulsory elements of any analytical query are 1) a measure specified as an aggregation function (e.g., sum, average, maximum etc.) and its input attribute and 2) a set of dimension categories defining the granularity of the aggregation. In addition to the pre-configured measures, the navigation hierarchy supports derivation of user-defined measures from any attribute of the scheme at query time.

New measures are defined through a wizard, as depicted in Figure 24(a), by providing the following input:

1.   The aggregation function is selected from the drop-down menu;
2.   The attribute of the measure is dragged from the navigation into the wizard.
3.   The DISTINCT option allows activating duplicate elimination.
4.   The newly defined measure may be supplied with a user-friendly name.

Each new measure has to be defined just once and remains available for further analysis. Let us consider an example of analyzing the distribution of hospitals by discipline. Intuitively, the measure of interest is the number of hospitals that has to be created from the category Hospital of the dimension Location. Figure 24(a) shows the process of creating this measure by dragging Hospital node into the wizard. Obviously, to support this measure, fact entries in SURGERY need to be aggregated to the Hospital level, the category Hospital and

Figure 24. Example of interactively defining a new measure (i.e., invoking PUSH operator) © 2009 University of Konstanz. Used with permission.

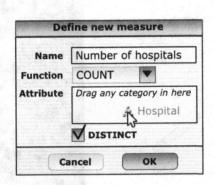

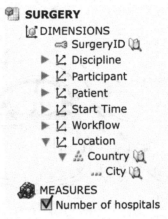

(a) Defining a measure   (b) Data cube navigation

all categories below it, i.e., Room and Building, must be removed from the navigation tree of the dimension Location, as they are invalid in the context of the specified measure. The navigation fragment of SURGERY containing a new measure is shown in Figure 24(b).

SAMPLE USAGE SCENARIOS

We demonstrate the use of the proposed analysis framework by considering an application case from the area of instrument usage analysis in surgical interventions of type discectomy, which is an intervention at the spine. The intervention goal of a discectomy is the partial removal of the herniated intervertebral disc. The objective of this sample analysis itself is to estimate the potential benefit of modifying the surgery by introducing an alternative surgical assist system. Typical expert queries in this scenario focus on the use of different conventional surgical instruments that have the same surgical objective.

During a discectomy, parts of the vertebra are removed to assess the underlying intervertebral disc. Figure 25 should give the reader some insight into the affected anatomic structure. The

main elements of vertebra are depicted in Figure 25(a), adopted from Wikimedia Commons (2007), and Figure 25(b) shows a computer-tomographic image of a rapid prototyping model of the human spine (cross-section). The intervertebral disc is hidden from surgical access in the center angle under the bone material (white segments in Figure 25(b)). The red-marked area represents the volume of the vertebra to be removed by the surgeon to gain access to the intervertebral disc in order to remove it.

To minimize invasiveness at the patient's body, the access area to the spine is spatially restricted. The two steps of ablating vertebra material and removing the disc are performed iteratively, i.e., the surgeon ablates only a small part of the vertebra, subsequently removing as much tissue of the intervertebral disc as he can reach, and then decides whether further access is needed. If so, he ablates the next portion of the vertebra and removes the tissue again, and so on.

The conventional bone ablation at the vertebra is performed using different surgical instruments, such as surgical punch, trephine, and/or surgical mallet/chisel. Each of the instrument types are available in different sizes and has different properties regarding invasiveness or handedness.

Figure 25. Human spine as the treated structure of a discectomy

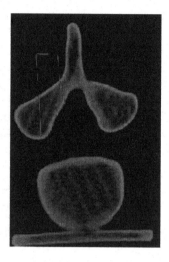

(a) Annotated diagram of vertebra   (b) Spine cross-section view

Instrument usage patterns in terms of frequency and duration of usage during a discectomy can be obtained by aggregating the corresponding data from the protocols of surgical intervention.

In a visual OLAP tool, end-users can obtain the required aggregates in few simple interaction steps. Figure 26 contains the results of the first two of the following four queries, arranged into a pivot table. **Query I**. *For each intervention of type discectomy and each of the specified bone ablating instruments, return the number of those*

work steps, in which the respective instrument was used by the surgeon.

The query is answered by specifying a new measure Occurrence, defined as COUNT(*), i.e., simple counting of qualifying fact entries, in fact table STEP. The aggregates are then computed by a roll-up of Occurrence by Surgery and Instrument with selection conditions on Instrument Type ('bone ablating') and on Participant ('surgeon'). **Query II**. *For each intervention of type discectomy and each of the specified bone*

Figure 26. Instrument usage statistics as a pivot table

Dimensions		Measures							
		● Occurrence				● Average duration			
		SurgeryID							
Instrument Group	Instrument	A	B	C	D	A	B	C	D
- bone ablating	mallet/chisel	0	3	1	1	00:00	00:23	00:34	00:50
	punch	9	22	10	9	02:38	00:35	00:46	01:27
	trephine	3	0	7	0	02:18	00:00	00:43	00:00
bone ablating Total		12	25	18	10	02:33	00:33	00:45	01:24

Figure 27. Occurrence and duration of bone ablation work steps in discectomy interventions as bar-charts

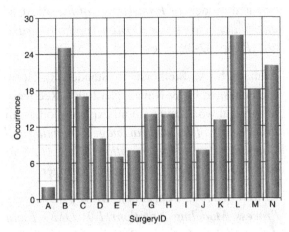

(a) *Total number of bone ablation steps (Query III)*   (b) Total timespan of bone ablation phase (Query IV)

ablating instruments, return the average duration of a work step, in which the respective instrument was used by the surgeon.

The query is answered by specifying a new measure Average Duration, defined as AVG(Duration), in fact table STEP and performing the same roll-up as in Query I. **Query III**. *For each intervention of type discectomy, return the number of those work steps, in which a surgeon used any bone ablating instrument.*

The result of this query is obtained from the results of Query I as a rollup step (by removing Instrument from the GROUP BY clause). The results of the query, arranged into a bar-chart, are shown in Figure 27(a). **Query IV**. *For each intervention of type discectomy, calculate the total time span between the begining of the first and the end of the last 'bone ablating' activity.*

The query is answered by specifying a new measure Timespan, defined as MAX(StopTime) - MIN(StartTime), in fact table ACTIVITY. The aggregates are computed as a roll-up of Timespan by Surgery with a selection condition on Action ('bone ablation'). A bar-chart with the results of this query is shown in Figure 27(b).

The above queries describe a real-world example from the field of medical engineering. The aggregates obtained in the above queries reveal the usage pattern for bone ablating instruments and provide crucial information for predicting the success of a new surgical instrument in this field (Neumuth, et al., 2007). This new system is a power driven milling system, whose evolution speed is controlled by its spatial position in relation to the patient's body (Jank, et al., 2006). This system is intended to replace the conventional bone ablating instruments and to enable the surgeon to perform the entire removal procedure in a single work step.

CONCLUSION

Motivated by the growing research interest to the evolving area of business process intelligence, we proposed a conceptual framework for providing OLAP support to business process analysis. Conventional BPMS are rather limited in the types of supported analytical tasks, whereas the data warehousing techniques appear more suitable when it comes to managing large amounts of data, defining various business metrics and running complex queries. As a challenging real-world application, we chose a case study from the innovative and promising domain of Surgical Workflows Analysis, aimed at designing a recording scheme for acquiring process descriptions from surgical interventions for their subsequent analysis and exploration.

We demonstrated the deficiencies of the standard relational OLAP approach with respect to the requirements of our case study and proposed an extended multidimensional data model that addresses multiple challenges, such as non-quantitative and heterogeneous facts, many-to-many relationships between facts and dimensions, full and partial dimension sharing, dynamic specification of new measures, and interchangeability of fact and dimension roles. We also presented a prototypical implementation of the enhanced conceptual model in a relational OLAP system where the data is stored according to the fact constellation schema and can be queried with standard SQL. The work is concluded by presenting a relevant analytical task from the domain of the case study and its sample solution, obtained interactively using an advanced visual OLAP frontend tool that supports dynamic measure definition.

ACKNOWLEDGMENT

The authors would like to thank Christos Trantakis and Jürgen Meixensberger from the Neurosurgery Department at the University Hospital of Leipzig for the valuable domain expertise.

REFERENCES

Aalst, W. M. P. van der, & Hee, K., van. (2002). *Workflow management: Models, methods, and systems (cooperative information systems)*. Cambridge, MA: The MIT Press.

Abelló, A., Samos, J., & Saltor, F. (2001). Understanding facts in a multidimensional object-oriented model. In *Proceedings of the 4th ACM international workshop on Data Warehousing and OLAP* (pp. 32-39). New York: ACM Press.

Ahmadi, S.-A., Sielhorst, T., Stauder, R., Horn, M., Feussner, H., & Navab, N. (2006). Recovery of surgical workflow without explicit models. In *Proceedings of the Medical Image Computing and Computer-Assisted Intervention (MICCAI 2006)* (pp. 420-428). Berlin, Germany: Springer.

BPMN. (2006, February). *BPMN (Business Process Modeling Notation) 1.0: OMG Final Adopted Specification*. Retreived from http://www.bpmn.org

Burgert, O., Neumuth, T., Gessat, M., Jacobs, S., & Lemke, H. U. (2007). Deriving DICOM surgical extensions from surgical workflows. *Medical Imaging 2007: PACS and Imaging Informatics, 8*(35), 651604.1-651604.11.

Burgert, O., Neumuth, T., Lempp, F., Mudunuri, R., Meixensberger, J., & Strauß, G. (2006). Linking top-level ontologies and surgical workflows. *International Journal of Computer Assisted Radiology and Surgery, 1*(1), 437–438. doi:10.1007/s11548-006-0032-x

Cabibbo, L., & Torlone, R. (1998). A logical approach to multidimensional databases. In *EDBT'98: Proceedings of the 6th International Conference on Extending Database Technology* (Vol. 1377, pp. 183-197). Berlin, Germany: Springer.

Castellanos, M., & Casati, F. (2005). Is there anything new about business process intelligence? [panel]. In *ICDE 2005: Proceedings of the 21st International Conference on Data Engineering* (pp. 1141-1141). Los Alamitos, CA: IEEE Computer Society.

Codd, E. F., Codd, S. B., & Salley, C. T. (1993). *Providing OLAP (on-line analytical processing) to user-analysts: An IT mandate* (Tech. Rep.). E. F. Codd & Associates.

Dayal, U., Hsu, M., & Ladin, R. (2001). Business process coordination: State of the art, trends, and open issues. In *VLDB 2001: Proceedings of the 27th International Conference on Very Large Data Bases* (pp. 3-13). San Francisco, CA: Morgan Kaufmann Publishers Inc.

Dodds, D., Hasan, H., & Gould, E. (1999). Relational versus multidimensional databases as a foundation for online analytical processing. In *IRIS 22: Proceedings of the 22nd Information Systems Research Seminar in Scandinavia* (pp. 281-288).

Franconi, E., & Sattler, U. (1999). A data warehouse conceptual data model for multidimensional aggregation. In *DMDW'99: Proceedings of the International Workshop on Design and Management of Data Warehouses* (Vol. 19, pp. 13.1-13.10). Retrieved from http://www.CEUR-WS.org

Giovinazzo, W. A. (2000). *Object-oriented data warehouse design: Building a star schema.* Upper Saddle River, NJ: Prentice Hall PTR.

Golfarelli, M., Maio, D., & Rizzi, S. (1998). The dimensional fact model: A conceptual model for data warehouses. *International Journal of Cooperative Information Systems, 7*(2/3), 215–247. doi:10.1142/S0218843098000118

Golfarelli, M., & Rizzi, S. (1998). A methodological framework for data warehouse design. In *DOLAP '98: Proceedings of the 1st ACM International Workshop on Data Warehousing and OLAP* (pp. 3-9). New York: ACM Press.

Grigori, D., Casati, F., Castellanos, M., Dayal, U., Sayal, M., & Shan, M.-C. (2004). Business process intelligence. *Computers in Industry, Special Issue on Process/Workflow Mining, 53*(3), 321-343.

Hall, C. (2004, June). Business process intelligence. *BP Trends Newsletter.* Retrieved from http://www.bptrends.com/publicationfiles/06%2D04%20NL%20BPI%20-%20Hall%20PH-2.pdf

Hao, M. C., Keim, D. A., Dayal, U., & Schneidewind, J. (2006). Business process impact visualization and anomaly detection. *Information Visualization, 5*, 15–27. doi:10.1057/palgrave.ivs.9500115

Hurtado, C. A., & Mendelzon, A. O. (2002). OLAP dimension constraints. In *PODS 2002: Proceedings of the 21st ACM Symposium on Principles of Database Systems* (pp. 169-179).

Hüsemann, B., Lechtenbörger, J., & Vossen, G. (2000). Conceptual data warehouse design. In *DMDW'2000: Proceedings of the 2nd International Workshop on Design and Management of Data Warehouses at CAiSE'00* (Vol. 28, pp. 6.1-6.11). Retrieved from http://www.CEUR-WS.org

Jank, E., Rose, A., Huth, S., Trantakis, C., Korb, W., & Strauss, G. (2006). A new fluoroscopy based navigation system for milling procedures in spine surgery. *International Journal of Computer Assisted Radiology and Surgery, 1*(Supplement 1), 196–198.

Jannin, P., Raimbault, M., Morandi, X., Riffaud, L., & Gibaud, B. (2003). Model of surgical procedures for multimodal image-guided neurosurgery. *Computer Aided Surgery, 8*(2), 98–106. doi:10.3109/10929080309146044

Kimball, R. (1996). *The data warehouse toolkit: Practical techniques for building dimensional data warehouses.* New York: John Wiley & Sons, Inc.

Kimball, R., Reeves, L., Ross, M., & Thornwaite, W. (1998). *The data warehouse lifecycle toolkit: Expert methods for designing, developing and deploying data warehouses.* New York: John Wiley & Sons, Inc.

Kimball, R., & Ross, M. (2002). *The data warehouse toolkit: The complete guide to dimensional modeling.* New York: John Wiley & Sons, Inc.

Lechtenbörger, J. (2001). Data warehouse schema design (Doctoral dissertation, Westfälische Wilhelms-Universität Münster). *Dissertations in database and information systems, 79.*

Lenz, H.-J., & Shoshani, A. (1997). Summarizability in OLAP and statistical data bases. In *SS-DBM 1997: Proceedings of the 9th International Conference on Scientific and Statistical Database Management* (pp. 132-143).

Malinowski, E., & Zimányi, E. (2006). Hierarchies in a multidimensional model: From conceptual modeling to logical representation. *Data & Knowledge Engineering, 59*(2), 348–377. doi:10.1016/j.datak.2005.08.003

Mansmann, S., Neumuth, T., & Scholl, M. H. (2007a). Multidimensional data modeling for business process analysis. In *ER 2007: Proceedings of the 26th International Conference on Conceptual Modeling* (pp. 23-38). Berlin, Germany: Springer.

Mansmann, S., Neumuth, T., & Scholl, M. H. (2007b). OLAP technology for business process intelligence: Challenges and solutions. In *DaWaK'07: Proceedings of the 9th International Conference on Data Warehousing and Knowledge Discovery* (pp. 111-122). Berlin, Germany: Springer.

Mansmann, S., & Scholl, M. H. (2007). Empowering the OLAP technology to support complex dimension hierarchies. *International Journal of Data Warehousing and Mining, 3*(4), 31–50.

Mansmann, S., & Scholl, M. H. (2008). Extending the multidimensional data model to handle complex data. *Journal of Computer Science and Engineering, 1*(2).

Matoušek, P. (2003). Verification of business process models (Doctoral dissertation, VŠB - Technická Univerzita Ostrava). In *Kolekce vysokoškolských kvalifikačních prací zpracovaných do konce 1. pololetí 2006.* VŠB-TUO.

Münchenberg, J., Brief, J., Raczkowsky, J., Wörn, H., Hassfeld, S., & Mühling, J. (2000). Operation planning of robot supported surgical interventions. In *IROS 2000* []. Washington, DC: IEEE.]. *Proceedings of Intelligent Robots and Systems, 1,* 547–552.

Muth, P., Wodtke, D., Weißenfels, J., Weikum, G., & Kotz-Dittrich, A. (1998). Enterprise-wide workflow management based on state and activity charts. In *Workflow management systems and interoperability* (Vol. 164, pp. 281-303). Berlin, Germany: Springer.

Neumuth, T., Schumann, S., Strauß, G., Jannin, P., Meixensberger, J., & Dietz, A. (2006). Visualization options for surgical workflows. *International Journal of Computer Assisted Radiology and Surgery, 1*(1), 438–440.

Neumuth, T., Strauß, G., Meixensberger, J., Lemke, H. U., & Burgert, O. (2006). Acquisition of process descriptions from surgical interventions. In *DEXA 2006: Proceedings of the 17th International Conference on Database and Expert Systems Applications* (pp. 602-611). Berlin, Germany: Springer.

Neumuth, T., Trantakis, C., Eckhardt, F., Dengl, M., Meixensberger, J., & Burgert, O. (2007). Supporting the analysis of intervention courses with surgical process models on the example of fourteen microsurgical lumbar discectomies. *International Journal of Computer Assisted Radiology and Surgery, 2*(Supplement 1), 436–438.

Padoy, N., Horn, M., Feußner, H., Berger, M.-O., & Navab, N. (2007). Recovery of surgical workflow: A model-based approach. In *CARS 2007: Proceedings of the 21ˢᵗ International Congress and Exhibition on Computer Assisted Radiology and Surgery*. Berlin, Germany: Springer.

Pedersen, T. B., & Jensen, C. S. (2001). Multidimensional database technology. *IEEE Computer, 34*(12), 40–46.

Pedersen, T. B., Jensen, C. S., & Dyreson, C. E. (2001). A foundation for capturing and querying complex multidimensional data. *Information Systems, 26*(5), 383–423. doi:10.1016/S0306-4379(01)00023-0

Phipps, C., & Davis, K. C. (2002). Automating data warehouse conceptual schema design and evaluation. In *DMDW'2002: Proceedings of the 4ᵗʰ International Workshop on Design and Management of Data Warehouses* (Vol. 58, pp. 23-32). Retrieved from http://www.CEUR-WS.org

Qi, J., Jiang, Z., Zhang, G., Miao, R., & Su, Q. (2006). A surgical management information system driven by workflow. In *SOLI '06: Proceedings of the IEEE International Conference on Service Operations and Logistics, and Informatics* (pp. 1014-1018). Washington, DC: IEEE.

Reijers, H. A. (2003). *Design and control of workflow processes: Business process management for the service industry* (Vol. 2617). Berlin, Germany: Springer.

Sapia, C., Blaschka, M., Höfling, G., & Dinter, B. (1999). Extending the E/R model for the multidimensional paradigm. In *ER 1998: Proceedings of the Workshops on Data Warehousing and Data Mining* (pp. 105-116).

Sharp, A., & McDermott, P. (2001). *Workflow modeling: Tools for process improvement and application development*. Norwood, MA: Artech House, Inc.

Smith, M. (2002, December, 5). Business process intelligence. *Intelligent Enterprise*. Retrieved from http://www.intelligententerprise.com/021205/601feat2 1.jhtml

Song, I.-Y., Rowen, W., Medsker, C., & Ewen, E. F. (2001). An analysis of many-to-many relationships between fact and dimension tables in dimensional modeling. In *DMDW'01: Proceedings of the 3ʳᵈ International Workshop on Design and Management of Data Warehouses* (Vol. 39, pp. 6.1-6.13). Retrieved from http://www.CEUR-WS.org

SRS. (n.d.). *SRS glossary: Definitions of scoliosis terms*. Retrieved from from http://www.srs.org/patients/glossary.asp

Tryfona, N., Busborg, F., & Christiansen, J. G. B. (1999). starER: A conceptual model for data warehouse design. In *DOLAP '99: Proceedings of the 2ⁿᵈ ACM International Workshop on Data Warehousing and OLAP* (pp. 3-8). New York: ACM Press.

WfMC. (1999, February). *Terminology & glossary*. Retrieved from http://www.wfmc.org/standards/docs/TC-1011 term glossary v3.pdf

Wikimedia Commons. (2007). *Category: Vertebra*. Retrieved from http://commons.wikimedia.org/wiki/Category:Vertebra

APPENDIX A.

*Figure 28. **Graphical node type constructs of X-DFM***

Element	Description
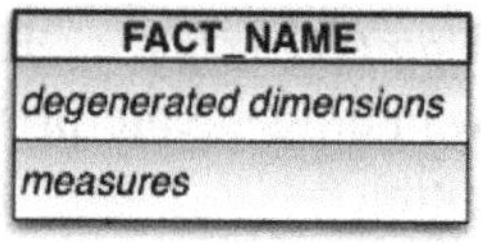 **FACT_NAME** *degenerated dimensions* *measures*	A **fact** is a box-shaped node labeled by the fact name and containing two sets of elements: 1) **degenerated dimensions** and 2) **measures**. Both sets are allowed to be empty.
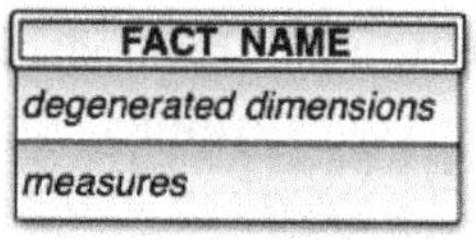 **FACT_NAME** *degenerated dimensions* *measures*	A **degenerated fact** is a many-to-many fact-dimensional mapping extracted into a separate fact, shown by placing a double-lined frame around the cell of the fact name.
● measure_name	A **measure attribute** is shown as a black circle-shaped node labeled by the measure's name. Measure nodes appear in the designated area of the fact node.
○ attribute_name	A **dimension category** corresponding to a non-abstract hierarchy level is a circle-shaped node labeled by the category's name.
◎ attribute_name ◉ measure_name	A **derived dimension/measure attribute** is shown as a double-lined circle-shaped node. Optionally, a dashed-line annotated with the derivation formula connects the derived element with its base element(s).
○ <u>attribute_name</u>	A **fact identifier** is a degenerated dimension with a one-to-one relationship to the fact, shown by underlining the attribute's name with a double line.
⬤ category_name ⬤T category_name	An **abstract dimension category** is a circle-shaped node filled with grey color and labeled by the attribute's name. In case of a top-level category, the name is shown as a subscript of the T symbol.
⊙ attribute_name ⊙T category_name	A **totally ordered dimension category** is marked by a dot in the node's center. A totally ordered dimension can be specified by placing a dot in the top category's node.
<u>attribute_name</u>	A **property attribute** is a characteristic associated with some dimension category, shown as an underlined attribute's name, connected by an undirected edge to its category node.
<u>attribute_name</u>	A **"degree-of-belonging" attribute** is a property associated with a child category of a non-strict weighted roll-up relationship.

Figure 29. Graphical node type constructs of X-DFM

Element	Description
	An **association relationship** is an undirected edge connecting a property attribute with its category or connecting a fact with a dimension in case of a one-to-one relationship between the two.
	An **optional association relationship** is shown by putting a dash across the edge.
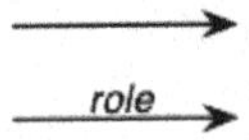 *role*	A **full strict roll-up** is a many-to-one relationship between a fact and a category or between a pair of categories, shown as a edge directed towards the parent category. In case the same category is a target of multiple roll-up relationships, each roll-up edge can be labeled by the respective role of that category.
	A **complete roll-up** is a many-to-one relationship within a complete hierarchy, shown by a diamond at the outgoing end of the roll-up edge.
	A **fuzzy roll-up** relationship, in which child elements are assigned to parent elements dynamically based on some rules, is marked as a double-pointed arrow.
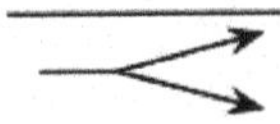	**Multiple alternative roll-up relationships** are alternative, i.e., mutually incompatible, aggregation paths of the same child category, shown by bundling the roll-up edges into a common edge at the outgoing end.
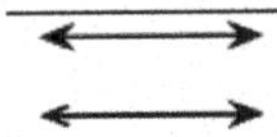	A **many-to-many relationship** between categories is shown as a bi-directed edge. In case of a **non-strict roll-up** relationship, the direction of the roll-up is indicated by a stronger arrowhead.
	A **partial roll-up** is an optional roll-up relationship of the child category, shown as a directed dotted-line edge.
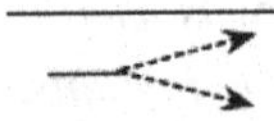	**Related partial roll-ups** are a set of mutually exclusive roll-up relationships in a heterogeneous hierarchy, shown by bundling the outgoing parts of the edges into a single solid-line edge.
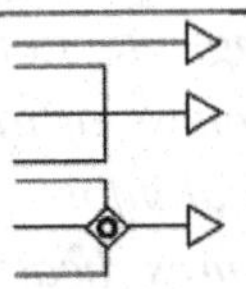	**Generalization / specialization** is shown as a solid-line edge with a hollow triangle at the superclass end. The edges of related specializations are shown in a shared-target style. By default, specialization is disjoint. Overlapping subclasses are specified by placing a diamond with "o" symbol onto the edge at the point where it branches into subclass edges.
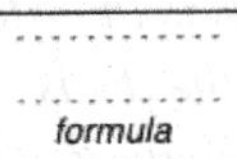 *formula*	**Derivation** relationship is a dotted-line connecting a derived element to its input element(s).
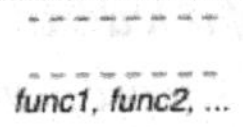 *func1, func2, ...*	**Non-aggregability/non-additivity** edge is adopted from DFM.

Chapter 8
Data Warehouse Facilitating Evidence–Based Medicine

Nevena Stolba
Vienna University of Technology, Austria

Tho Manh Nguyen
Vienna University of Technology, Austria

A Min Tjoa
Vienna University of Technology, Austria

ABSTRACT

In the past, much effort of healthcare decision support systems were focused on the data acquisition and storage, in order to allow the use of this data at some later point in time. Medical data was used in static manner, for analytical purposes, in order to verify the undertaken decisions. Due to the immense volumes of medical data, the architecture of the future healthcare decision support systems focus more on interoperability than on integration. With the raising need for the creation of unified knowledge base, the federated approach to distributed data warehouses (DWH) is getting increasing attention. The exploitation of evidence-based guidelines becomes a priority concern, as the awareness of the importance of knowledge management rises. Consequently, interoperability between medical information systems is becoming a necessity in modern health care. Under strong security measures, health care organizations are striking to unite and share their (partly very high sensitive) data assets in order to achieve a wider knowledge base and to provide a matured decision support service for the decision makers. Ontological integration of the very complex and heterogeneous medical data structures is a challenging task. The authors' objective is to point out the advantages of the deployment of a federated data warehouse approach for the integration of the wide range of different medical data sources and for distribution of evidence-based clinical knowledge, to support clinical decision makers, primarily clinicians at the point of care.

DOI: 10.4018/978-1-60566-748-5.ch008

Copyright © 2010, IGI Global. Copying or distributing in print or electronic forms without written permission of IGI Global is prohibited.

INTRODUCTION

Since it is a challenge task for clinicians to gather all necessary knowledge about given diseases, the practice of evidence-based medicine would not be imaginable without IT support. With rapid changes taking place in the field of healthcare, decision support systems play an increasingly important role. Healthcare institutions are deploying DWH applications as decision-support tools for strategic decision-making.

The combination of data warehousing technology and evidence-based medicine opens an innovative application field of information technology in healthcare industry. Medical institutions, as well as health insurance companies, are primarily interested in increasing the patient healing rate and reducing treatment costs. In the long term, the application of DWH in the area of evidence-based medicine could prove economical by avoiding the duplication of examinations, saving time through automation of routine tasks, and simplifying the accounting and administrative procedures.

Caused by the growing and aging population, chronic illnesses are going to become the major concern of the healthcare industry. Diseases of elderly people, like Diabetes, Alzheimer's disease, cardiac insufficiency, and sight loss (macular degeneration) will cause more treatment effort and therapy costs than the treatment of most difficult illnesses (cancer and heart attack) generate nowadays. Since these diseases can be treated more efficiently and more cost-effectively when detected in the early stages, the mission of modern medicine is to become able to recognize the patterns of disease formation and development. Evidence-based medicine deals with the analyses of the existing medical records, clinical studies etc., and searches for the recurring samples of disease symptoms. Data warehousing and data mining techniques play a crucial role in acquisition and gathering of existing medical experience from diverse data sources and in statistical analysis of that data. The extracted experience values and for-

mulated knowledge (evidence-based guidelines) are used for more efficient prediction, discovery, and treatment of diseases.

In this chapter, we present some application fields which are relevant to the clinical knowledge management, especially:

- Developing new knowledge – the data warehouse-supported creation of evidence-based guidelines and clinical pathways
- Knowledge sharing – the data warehouse as an easy to use platform for knowledge dissemination among healthcare decision makers.

The rest of this chapter is organized as follows. In the next section we introduce Evidence-based Medicine and its use in clinical decision support system, followed by a guideline of deploying an evidence-base data warehouse. The process of controlling clinical treatment pathways with data warehouses incorporating EBM 32 will be introduced afterward. Then we review the healthcare standard for message exchanges. After that, we discuss the semantic integration in federated Data Warehouse Model. Finally, we introduce a running example using Federated DWH supporting clinicians at the Point of Care and point out some future work.

EVIDENCE-BASED MEDICINE

Testing the outcome of medical interventions has been performed for hundreds of years. During last century, this effort started to impact all fields of welfare and healthcare. One of the founders of evidence-based practice was professor Archie Cochrane, a Scottish epidemiologist, whose engagement in this field resulted in an increased acceptance of the concepts behind evidence-based medicine. He was the first one to point out and promote the vital importance of use of medical evidence resp. randomized controlled trials for improving the effectiveness of treatments. A randomized controlled trial (RCT) is a scientific procedure most commonly used in testing medicines or medical procedures. It is a trial that uses randomized control. This is considered the most reliable form of scientific evidence because it eliminates all forms of spurious causality (Wikipedia, 2007a).

Cochrane's work was honored through naming of centers of evidence-based medical research — The Cochrane Centers — and an international organization, The Cochrane Collaboration, after him. The Cochrane Centers coordinate activities, primarily in language-defined regions, and are the main contact point for the public. The Cochrane Collaboration (Cochrane_Collaboration, 2007) is a world-wide endeavour dedicated to tracking down, evaluating, and synthesising RCTs in all areas of medicine. It is a major force in the EBM movement. The Cochrane Collaboration provides the Cohrane Library (Cochrane_Library, 2007), a collection of medical databases that contain high-quality, regularly updated independent evidence to support healthcare decision-making. It includes reliable evidence from Cochrane and other systematic reviews, clinical trials, and more.

The explicit methodologies used to determine "best evidence" were largely established by the McMaster University (Canada) research group led by David Sackett and Gordon Guyatt. According to this group, evidence-based medicine is the conscientious, explicit, and judicious use of current best evidence in making decisions about the care of individual patients. The practice of evidence-based medicine means integrating individual clinical expertise with the best available external clinical evidence from systematic research. By individual clinical expertise we mean the proficiency and judgement that individual clinicians acquire through clinical experience and clinical practice (Sackett et al., 1996)

Since 1992, when the evidence-based medicine research group at McMaster University was founded, the number of articles about evidence-based practice has grown exponentially (from 1 publication in 1992 to about a thousand in 1998) and international interest has led to the development of 6 evidence-based journals (published in up to 6 languages) that summarize the most relevant studies for clinical practice and have a combined world-wide circulation of over 175.000 (CEBM, 2004).

Concepts of Evidence-Based Medicine

Most clinical practice is based on limited evidence, like textbook information, sometimes defective research or case studies, unverified reviews, and personal experiences. In their everyday practice, clinicians constantly strive to offer the best suitable treatment to their patients. Traditionally, they would consult their manuals, textbooks or their senior, more experienced colleagues in order to solve the problem. With time, they would gain a lot of expert knowledge themselves and would act as advice-givers to their junior colleagues. This way of developing medical expertise is natural, but not always the most optimal for the patients.

The evidence-based medicine is built on another idea. Its task is to complement the existing clinical decision-making process with the most accurate and most efficient research evidence (Figure 1). For example, when treating a Diabetes patient suffering from a progressive liver disease, his (her) clinician has to find the most efficient therapy which does not conflict with the patient's ongoing Diabetes treatment. The clinician searches through evidence-based guidelines to find current best evidence for treating liver diseases, and verifies whether the proposed method fits into the Diabetes patient's health risks.

Evidence-based guidelines explicitly define the decision points to which this valid evidence needs to be integrated with the individual clinical experience in deciding on a course of action. Thus, they don't inform the clinician which decision to make and take away his (her) authority for

Figure 1. Basis of Evidence-Based Care

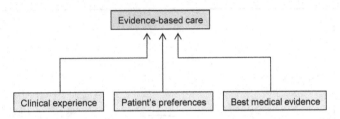

decision-making. Instead, they identify the range of potential decisions and provide the physicians with the evidence which, when added to individual clinical judgement and patient's values and expectations, will help them make their own decisions in the best interest of the patient (Audiimoolam et al., 2005).

Although it is always stated that evidence-based medicine is based on evidence, this does not mean that traditional medicine does not rely on it. The traditional medicine uses both research experience and evidence as well, but the quality

of this information (in terms of accuracy and timeliness) is much lower than of one electronically stored in the EBG repositories.

One of the greatest achievements of evidence-based medicine has been the development of systematic reviews and meta-analyses, methods by which researchers identify multiple studies on a certain topic, separate the best ones and then critically analyse them to come up with a summary of the best available evidence (White, 2004). The quality and the reliability of evidence can be classified as shown in Figure 2.

Figure 2. Hierarchy of Evidence (Carner®, 2007)

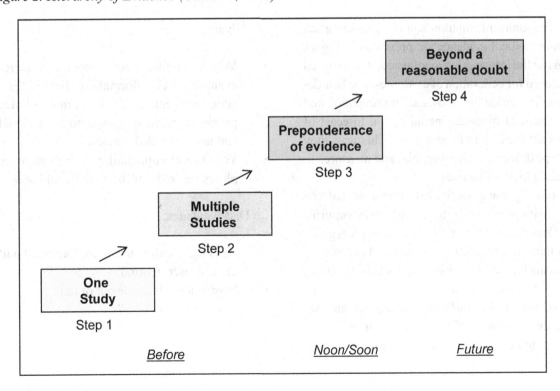

Figure 3. Data Flow in Evidence Based Medicine

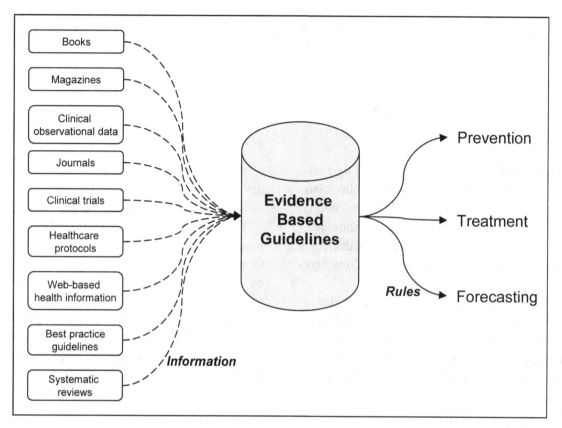

The main information sources providing accurate medical evidence are presented in Figure 3. After the information is collected, it is analysed and used for generation of evidence-based guidelines. The guidelines are used for prevention and treatment of diseases, including the forecast of relevant patient state parameters. This way, they will push for effective therapies and measures to replace ineffective ones.

Usually, the guideline can be represented as a tree, with choice nodes based on tests or inquiries and leaves describing actions. An example is given in Figure 4, representing a selection of pacemaker systems for patients with sinus node dysfunction. (AV = atrioventricular).

(Craig et al., 2001) summarizes advantages and disadvantages of the adoption of evidence-based guidelines in decision-making process as follows:

Advantages:

• Very comprehensive: summarizes all relevant research information about all possible interventions for a common clinical problem; improved power to detect small and important differences.
• Very useful applicability information, explores the trade-off of benefit and harm.

Disadvantages:

• Can be difficult to use if not formatted with the end-user in mind.
• May quickly become out of date.

Figure 4. Example EBG: Selection of Pacemaker Systems (Gregoratos et al., 1998)

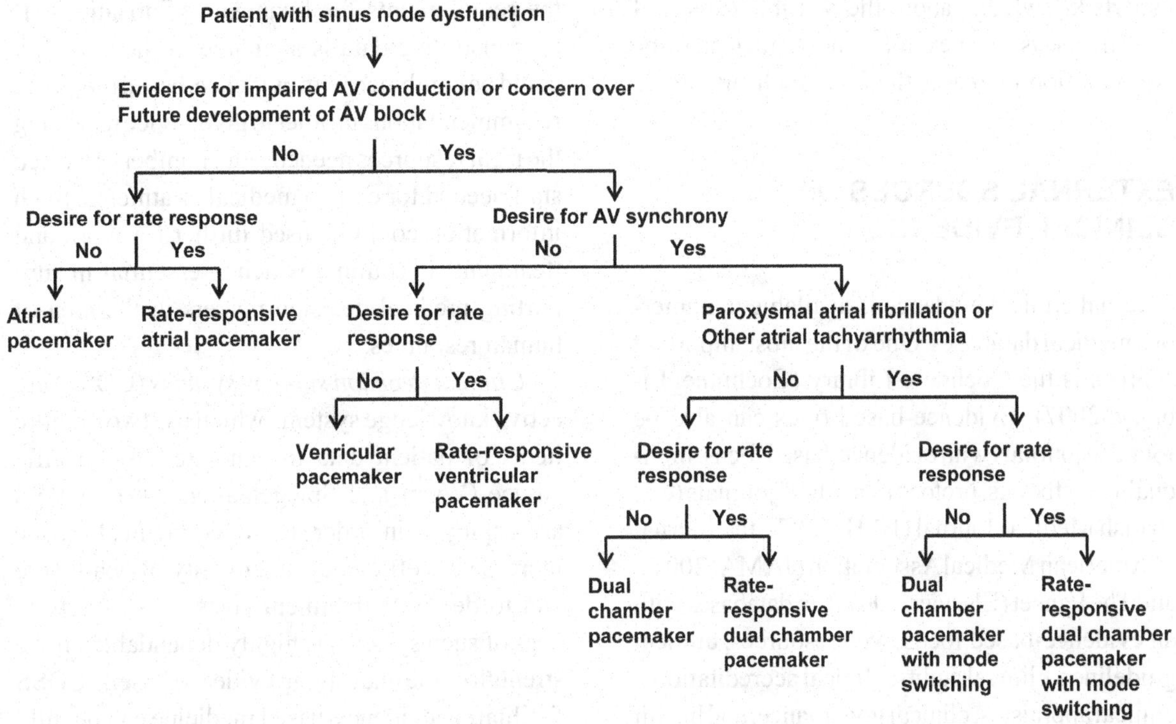

Practicing Evidence-Based Medicine

The major steps in practising evidence-based medicine are:

1. Formulate answerable questions
2. Find the best evidence
3. Evaluate the evidence for validity and usefulness under concrete circumstances
4. Apply the evidence
5. Evaluate the performance

Evidence-based medicine is required when:

- *A diagnosis needs to be established*

A clinician, who may be overwhelmed with the variety of symptoms, can consult evidence-based rules to determine the right diagnosis.

- *A patient needs to get appropriate therapy*

Here, a clinician is searching for the best-fitting therapy that is proven to be efficient. Evidence-based guidelines will usually offer a few treatments, but only those that do not conflict with the patient's preferences and health risks will be considered.

- *A prognosis is needed*

The external knowledge about the patient's future health state is provided. For example, if an elderly patient is suffering from osteoporosis, a prognosis of his (her) quality of life can be generated comparing the option of patient undergoing a surgery to them deciding to take medications.

- *A etiology needs to be clarified*

In this case, evidence-based medicine provides experts knowledge about the possible causes of a given disease. For example, how much nicotine consumption increases the risk of a heart attack.

EXTERNAL SOURCES OF CLINICAL EVIDENCE

External clinical evidence is available in numerous medical databases. One of the most important sources is the Cochrane Library (Cochrane_Library, 2007). Evidence-based rules can also be found in journals with evidence-based focus, high-quality textbooks, protocols, medical journals (e.g. British Medical Journal (BMJ, 2007), the Journal of American Medical Association (JAMA, 2007), and The Lancet (Elsevier, 2007)), in databases with an evidence-based focus, web resources, clinical guidelines, clinical audits, clinical accreditations, clinical appraisals, clinical governance, and health technology assessments.

Table 1 (White, 2004) shows some of the leading clinical evidence resources available to clinicians.

CLINICAL DECISION SUPPORT SYSTEMS EMBRACING EVIDENCE-BASED GUIDELINES

The simplest version of a clinical data warehouse facilitating evidence-based medicine is presented in Figure 5.

The medical DWH above unifies data from diverse departments as well as evidence-based guidelines. Ideally, in such a DWH, data is prepared to be queried and analysed in any way required. Clinical management is often interested in finding out which treatments and medications led to more rapid and more economic patient convalescence. Data mining and OLAP functions would support business decision-makers in creating the most effective business strate-

gies that satisfy both patients' expectations and the requirements for financial optimisations. If administrative data is available in the DWH, it could be combined with evidence-based medicine recommendations in order to give advice regarding the right resources needed, e.g., number of skilled staff needed for certain medical treatments. Such information could be used further for work and treatment scheduling, which is essential in supporting medical decision-makers in the area of human resources.

Clinical decision support systems (CDSS) are active knowledge systems which use two or more items of patient data to generate case-specific advice (Wyatt and Spiegelhalter, 1991). CDSS are deployed in order to reduce medical errors, increase the efficiency and quality of healthcare and to decrease treatment costs. The effectiveness of such systems is highly dependable on the strength of the underlying evidence base. A CDSS facilitating evidence-based medicine can be fully successful only if it is able to follow and integrate the changes coming out of the clinical research. This means that CDSS should be capable of:

1. monitoring the literature for high quality research findings,
2. extracting the best clinical evidence,
3. incorporating new knowledge into the existing decision support knowledge base.

The tasks listed above are still not fully automated. It is an open research issue to create machine-interpretable sources of evidence and thus automate the whole process of clinical evidence integration into a CDSS. (Perreault and Metzger, 1999) outline the four functions of electronic clinical decision-support systems:

- *Administrative*: Supporting clinical coding and documentation, authorization of procedures, and referrals.
- *Managing clinical complexity and details*: Keeping patients on research protocols;

Table 1. Clinical Evidence Resources (White, 2004)

Name	Description	Publisher/Sponsor
JOURNALS		
ACP Journal Club http://www.acpjc.org	Bimonthly journal that analyzes the content of over 100 clinical journals and summarizes those articles found to have scientific merit and relevance to medical practice.	American College of Physicians
American Family Physician http://www.aafp.org/afp	Twice monthly clinical review journal that contains evidence-based components, such as POEMs (patient-oriented evidence that matters), Cochrane for Clinicians and Point-of-Care Guides.	American Academy of Family Physicians
Bandolier http://www.jr2.ox.ac.uk /bandolier	Monthly journal that searches PubMed and the Cochrane Library for systematic reviews and meta-analyses published in the recent past and summarizes those that "are both interesting and make sense."	Produced from Pain Research at Oxford University with multiple sponsors
The Journal of Family Practice http://www.jfponline.org	Monthly clinical review journal that contains evidence-based components, such as its online archives of POEMs.	Dowden Health Media
EVIDENCE SUMMARIES		
Clinical Evidencehttp://www.clinicalevidence.com	A compendium of systematic reviews, gathered from Cochrane, MEDLINE and other sources, updated and expanded every six months.	BMJ Publishing Group
The Cochrane Database of Systematic Reviews http://www.cochrane.org/cochrane/revabstr/mainindex.htm	Arguably the most extensive collection of systematic reviews.	The Cochrane Collaboration
DynaMed http://www.dynamicmedical.com	A database of summaries of the evidence drawn from sources such as Clinical Evidence and the Cochrane Library.	DynaMed
FIRSTConsult http://www.firstconsult.com (formerly PDxMD)	A database of evidence summaries drawn from Cochrane, Clinical Evidence, the National Guideline Clearinghouse and others.	Elsevier
InfoRetriever http://www.infopoems.com	A search engine with access to evidence-based sources such as POEMs, Cochrane, clinical rules, a diagnostic test database, practice guideline summaries and Griffith's Five-Minute Clinical Consult; subscribers also receive Daily POEMs via e-mail.	InfoPOEMs Inc.
SUMSearch http://sumsearch.uthscsa.edu/	A search engine that gathers evidence-based clinical information from MEDLINE, DARE and the National Guideline Clearinghouse.	The University of Texas Health Science Center
TRIP Database (Turning Research Into Practice) http://www.tripdatabase.com	A search engine that gathers evidence-based clinical information from MEDLINE, DARE, the National Guideline Clearinghouse and many other evidence-based Web sites.	Gwent, Wales
The York Database of Abstracts of Reviews of Effects (DARE) http://www.york.ac.uk/inst/crd/darehp.htm	A collection of abstracts of systematic reviews.	Centre for Reviews and Dissemination, University of York
CLINICAL GUIDELINES		
Institute for Clinical Systems Improvement (ICSI) http://www.icsi.org/knowledge/	Guidelines for preventive services and disease management developed by ICSI, an independent, nonprofit collaboration of healthcare organizations, including the Mayo Clinic, Rochester, Minn.	Institute for Clinical Systems Improvement
National Guideline Clearinghouse http://www.guidelines.gov	Comprehensive database of evidence-based clinical practice guidelines.	The Agency for Healthcare Research and Quality

Name	Description	Publisher/Sponsor
U.S. Preventive Services Task Force (USPSTF) Recommendations http://www.ahrq.gov/clinic/uspstfix.htm	Recommendations for clinical preventive services based on systematic reviews by the U.S. Preventive Services Task Force.	USPSTF
OTHER		
DailyPOEMs http://www.infopoems.com	Daily e-mail update with approximately 30 POEMs per month; subscription includes InfoRetriever access online or via PDA (above).	InfoPOEMs Inc.

Figure 5. Sources and Users for Clinical DWH

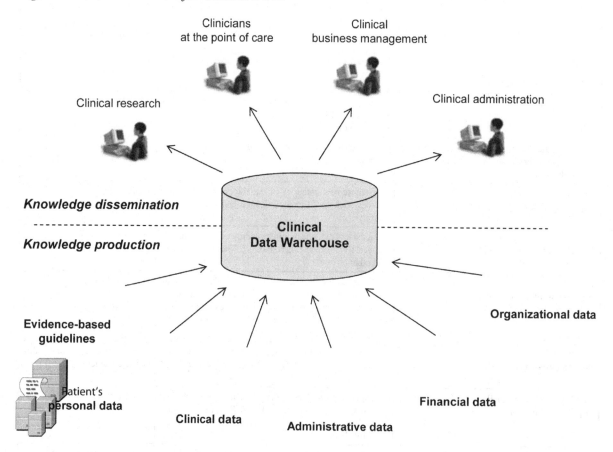

tracking orders, referrals follow-up, and preventive care.

- *Cost control*: Monitoring medication orders; avoiding duplicate or unnecessary tests.
- *Decision support*: Supporting clinical diagnosis and treatment plan processes, promoting use of best practices, condition-specific guidelines, and population-based management.

Systems Integration

The DWH is one major part of CDSS, providing an easy to use platform to support decision-making processes of care-givers and clinical managers.

EBM-oriented CDSS can vary in their scope. The simplest systems would be fed by data about diseases and best practice guidelines to support care delivery. More sophisticated systems additionally include various clinical internal and external data sources. In order to build a DWH to support evidence-based medicine, two basic operations need to be assured:

- Properly integrated source information systems
- Easy access to data and decision support tools for the wide area of users.

Here we give a more detailed list of the relevant data sources for the CDSS, based on the high-level overview shown in Figure 11:

- **Evidence-based guidelines**
- **Clinical data**
  - patient data
  - pharmaceutical data
  - medical treatments
  - length of stay
- **Patient's personal data**
  - Demographic data (age, gender, height, weight…)
  - Health risks (allergies, insufficiencies, …)
  - Personal preferences
- **Administrative data**
  - staff skills
  - overtime
  - nursing care hours
  - staff sick leave
- **Financial data**
  - treatment costs
  - drug costs
  - staff salaries
  - accounting
  - cost-effectiveness studies
- **Organisational data**
  - Room occupation
  - Facilities
  - Equipment

Decision-Support Tools

Decision-support tools support the practitioner's ability to correctly identify the problem when examining the patient and to formulate that problem in a clear question. When the answer to a defined problem is retrieved from the CDSS, decision support tools represent the result in an understandable manner. In order to find the best-fitting treatment, it is essential to assess the health differences between the examined patient and those involved in the study.

An important concern of evidence-based practice is that the guidelines could not be applied to patients without checking if they fit into the patient's health risks. Problems faced so far in practice are that the physicians often avoid evidence-based approaches because they feel forced to apply recommended treatments and not free to create personalised, tailored care. The most efficient way to diminish this resistance is by proving that the evidence-based medicine significantly helps to achieve better results and by providing the practitioners with easy-to-use decision-support tools. In this sense, the Internet is becoming an innovative way to easily extract and mine data.

Apart from just being queried on demand, decision-support tools can act proactively, for example by alerting physicians when a change in a patient's condition occurs or when duplicate medications are issued. Another example is that they can send an alert when a physician prescribes a drug that doesn't fit into the entire range of patient's health risks (Briggs, 2005).

Application Fields

The most relevant functions of DWH in the area of evidence-based medicine are marked by the ability:

Figure 6. Generation of Evidence-Based Guidelines

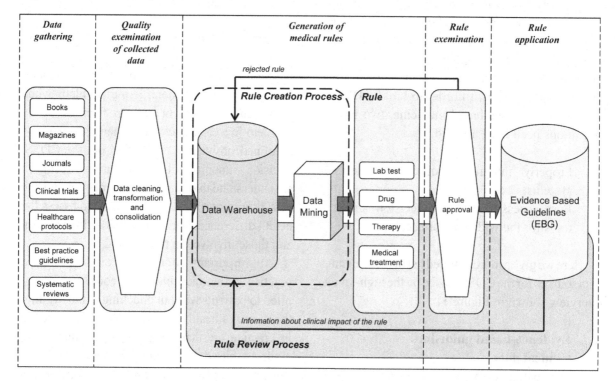

1. To support the generation process of the evidence-based guidelines,
2. To support the clinicians at the point of care delivery, by making evidence-based rules available,
3. To support the control of clinical treatment pathways,
4. To support the administrative and management tasks, by providing evidence-based knowledge as well as diverse organizational and financial data.

Beside these most common application fields, it could be used for processing huge amounts of medical data in the area of epidemiology. In the following subchapters, we are going to explain these ideas in more detail.

DEPLOYING DATA WAREHOUSES IN GENERATION OF EVIDENCE-BASED GUIDELINES

For practitioners treating patients it is not feasible to access and evaluate all primary studies applicable to an individual patient. Given the volumes and complexity of the clinical data, creation of evidence-based guidelines requires a computer-based information management system.

Data warehousing and data mining can support creation of evidence-based rules by providing a platform and tools for knowledge discovery and pattern recognition. Large amounts of data are analysed to confirm known or discover unknown trends and correlations. The discovery process in medical research would benefit enormously from data mining facilities.

Figure 6 represents our rule-generation process based on clinical evidence. In our model, data originating from different medical sources is extracted, transformed, and prepared for loading into the existing DWH structure. The DWH contains diverse patient, clinical, and pharmaceutical data. Supported by a DWH, medical knowledge workers are able to analyse and mine a vast quantity of available data.

Data mining techniques enable identification of trends and recognition of best practices for different disease treatments. Knowledge workers are interested in finding new associations and rules which are hidden in the data. The new rules need to be exhaustively checked for their correctness before being declared valid.

After a rule (in form of laboratory tests, recommended drugs, therapies, or medical treatments) has been created, it needs to be examined and approved by a higher authority. In case of rejection, the proposed rule is sent back to the DWH for further development. If the rule is approved, it is added to the database holding evidence-based guidelines. Once added to the evidence-based guidelines, rules undergo a systematic review process.

Schuerenberg describes the governance process to develop and review clinical guidelines, as it is practiced at the University Health Network (Toronto), as follows: The IT clinical advisory committee starts the process by recommending which lab tests should be ordered for which patient conditions, and why. Its recommendations are sent to an enterprise-wide medical advisory committee that has the final approval on which evidence-based rules and alerts are programmed into the decision support system. University Health's IT department then enters the new rule and its supporting evidence into the application. The medical advisory committee measures the clinical impact of each new automated rule six months after it is programmed. Rules are often modified during the review process and then reviewed again in another six months (Schuerenberg, 2003).

Development of evidence-based guidelines using DWH and data mining goes far beyond just reviewing the literature. These guidelines are a unification of best evidence with clinical expertise and patient values. They are reported in sufficient detail to allow clinicians to make judgements about the validity of their recommendations and to improve patient care.

CONTROLLING CLINICAL TREATMENT PATHWAYS WITH DATA WAREHOUSES INCORPORATING EBM

Healthcare organisations are searching for methods to rationalise their processes, to improve healthcare and ultimately also to reduce costs. As stated by the Health Informatics Research (HIR) group (HIR-group, 2006), traditional business process modelling tools and business process execution tools, such as workflow management systems, lack support for the complex, multi-organisation, dynamic, and large scale patient treatment processes that exist within the healthcare system. New research programs are launched to develop methodologies, tools, and techniques that can be applied to the more complex clinical pathway process.

Clinical Pathways are structured, multidisciplinary plans of care which are designed to support the implementation of clinical guidelines and protocols. They are built to support the overall clinical management, the clinical and non-clinical resource allocations, and last but not least the clinical audit and financial management (Open_Clinical, 2006).

Clinical practice guidelines, which often underlie clinical pathways, are primarily the responsibility of professionals, while chain management is that of managers. Therefore, clinical pathways can be considered to be a joint effort designed with the motive to improve the patient outcomes and enhance the quality of diagnosis, interventions, and management (Audiimoolam et al., 2005).

An example of improved effectiveness of the healthcare delivery during last few years are

Australian hospitals, which have been increasing application, standardisation and observation of clinical pathways (Uni_Münster, 2001), (Dowsey et al., 1999).

In the area of clinical pathways, the DWH facilitating evidence-based medicine could be used for controlling the clinical processes, from patient's admission to his (her) release. For frequently occurring diseases (like Diabetes mellitus, pneumonia, hernia etc.), the whole treatment process, from diagnosis to therapy, could be verified against clinical pathways. By analysing all relevant data stored in the DWH, it would be possible to find out if prescribed levels (operation, recovery duration) were reached on time. In case of a significant delay, the DWH could alert the responsible clinician. The discrepancy between the clinical pathway and the actual treatment can be caused by unnecessary modifications of the therapy, by management problems, but also by an incorrect rule. Clinical pathways are reviewed on a regular basis (once or twice a year). Frequently occurring deviations of a pathway are analysed, and, in case of legitimate causes, the pathway may be reformulated. This consequently contributes to the pathway refinement process.

The deployment of data-mining techniques in discovery of patterns within historically applied treatment processes would be an efficient method for clinical pathway development. Based on patient record data, administrative data, clinical log data, and evidence based rules, the mining process could be applied. This way the structure of clinical paths and the sequence of activities could be detected, a task that could hardly be done manually.

The development of clinical pathways is knowledge-intensive and it requires the cooperation among knowledge workers, clinicians, nurses, and clinical management. Data miners aim to combine the experience from the evidence-based guidelines with the concrete clinical data and to identify (time) dependency patterns. Lin et al. (Lin et al., 2000) state that by obtaining the time dependency patterns, the paths for new patients can be predicted when they are admitted to a hospital, and, in turn, the care procedure can be designed more effectively and more efficiently.

The goal of the use of DWH, data mining, and evidence-based medicine in the domain of clinical pathways is to improve the coordination of care between different clinical departments and therefore to improve the quality of care and to reduce the length of patient's hospitalisation. Apart from this, deploying clinical pathways for negotiations with cost units proved to be very effective, since they represent a detailed description of the range of services and benefits for a given patients' group. Cost units get a better view of activities offered and hospitals can better support the argument about the estimated costs of treatments. For this reason, clinical pathways represent the perfect foundation for discussions between clinical management and sponsors. Consequently, they oblige the clinical economist to take responsibility for clinical decisions, since the financial factors influence the quality of treatments and procedures proposed by a clinical pathway.

Open investigation areas include the development of new clinical pathway transformation frameworks, pathway modelling techniques, and new clinical pathway process management systems.

EVIDENCE-BASED DECISION SUPPORT AT THE POINT OF CARE

Figure 7 illustrates our idea to use a DWH facilitating EBM at the point of care. In this scenario, the clinician is querying the DWH while examining the patient, so the answers he (she) is expecting must come quickly and be presented clearly. The clinician is interested in finding the best-fitting treatment for the given patient and given disease.

The clinical question will be defined based on the patient's disease. The clinician uses an OLAP tool in order to query the DWH. Standard, pre-

Figure 7. Decision Support at the Point of Care

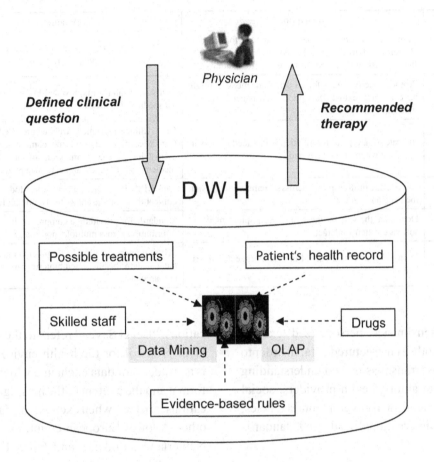

defined reports, as well as ad-hoc queries, may be used. After this, selected tables would be joined inside the DWH on the fly.

The clinician wants to analyse patient's historical health data stored in the DWH (entities *diagnosis* and *therapy*), as well as the *drugs* which were prescribed in the past. Patient's clinical dossier, accompanied by patient's age and lifestyle habits (originating from entity *patient*), would than be combined with evidence-based guidelines. Supported by the DWH functionality (aggregation, slice and dice etc.) as well as by OLAP and data mining techniques, those treatments which proved to be the most efficient in similar cases would be detected. It is important to point out that the guidelines are only suggestions and not obligatory steps in patient's treatment. The prac-

titioner has the choice of acting differently from the proposed guidelines. Having all necessary information, the clinician can decide how the patient will be treated.

Since the DWH in our scenario integrates clinic-wide data from different departments, the clinician would be able to immediately check if the proposed treatments can be carried out (if necessary facilities (entity *equipment*) or skilled stuff are available).

HEALTHCARE STANDARDS FOR MESSAGE EXCHANGE

Patient records contain not only well arranged and concise lab test results or hospital admission

Table 2. Summary of Healthcare Standards, adopted from (Kim, 2005)

Category	Description	Examples
Data Exchange/ Messaging Standards	Contain instructions (or specifications) for format, data elements, and structure and therefore allow transactions to flow consistently between systems or organizations	HL7 for administrative data, DICOM for radiology images, NCPDP for electronic prescriptions
Terminology Standards	Provide specific codes for clinical concepts that might have varying textual descriptions in a paper chart or a transcription.	LOINC for lab results, SNOMED for clinical terms, ICD for medical diagnoses
Document Standards	Indicate what type of information is included in a document and where it can be found.	CDA (Clinical Document Architecture), CCR (Continuity of Care Record) for inter-provider communication, including: patient identifying information, medical history, current medications, allergies, and care plan recommendation.
Conceptual Standards	Allow data to be transported across systems without losing meaning and context.	HL7 RIM (Reference Information Model) for describing clinical data and the context surrounding it.
Application Standards	Determine the way business rules are implemented and software systems interact.	Standards for providing a comprehensive way of viewing information across multiple, non-integrated databases.
Architecture Standards	Define the process involved in data storage and distribution.	PHIN components of an electronic surveillance and management system for integrated bioterrorism and public health preparedness.

forms, but often images, personalized text descriptions and other unstructured data. In order to enable seamless transmission and understanding of medical data among health providers, social insurance companies, and governmental agencies, application of internationally adopted standards is necessary.

Categories of Standards

Current international standards used for healthcare data exchange, like HL7, ENV 13606, and openEHR have been developed in parallel since early 1990s, some of them adopting certain concepts from others. The deployment of standards allows for consistent communication between heterogeneous healthcare information systems, without losing meaning or context. Table 2 gives the basic overview of the major standard categories.

HL7

Health Level Seven (HL7, 2007), is a standard for exchanging information between medical appli-

cations. "Level Seven" refers to the seventh OSI layer protocol for the health environment. HL7 is a protocol for data exchange which defines the format and the content of the messages that applications must use when exchanging data with each other. A lot of European countries (for instance Netherlands, Finland, and Great Britain) have chosen HL7 as a strategic concept for a nationwide healthcare communication standard.

HL7 specifies the contents and the formats of the exchanged messages at the application level. It is widely independent from the underlying hardware and network infrastructure as well as the database and applications used.

Since 1997, the HL7 organization has been developing version 3.0 of the protocol. HL7 Version 3 (HL7 V3) is a complete redefinition of the HL7 standard that is intended to try and overcome some of the issues with the current standard. Version 3 will change not only the content of the messages and fields, but also the encoding rules, LLP (low level communication protocols), base data types, and even the roles of the applications participating in HL7 communications. XML is the planned medium for HL7 interchange instead

Table 3. The Six Backbone Classes of RIM

Class name	Definition	Example	Subclasses
Act	action that is being done, has been done, can be done, or is intended or requested to be done.	clinical observation, discharging a patient	yes
Entity	physical thing, group of physical things or an organisation capable of participating in Acts	person, animal, medical device	yes
Role	competency of an Entity participating in an Act	patient, doctor, nurse	yes
Participation	association between an Act and a Role, with Entity playing that Role	Dr. Smith prescribes a therapy for patient Doe	no
ActRelationship	directed association between a source Act and a target Act.	a biopsy procedure as a result of an observation	no
RoleLink	connection between two roles expressing a dependency between those roles	clinician (employee)– hospital (employer)	no

of the simple ASCII text that is currently in use (InterfaceWare, 2007).

Unlike 2.X versions, which have been implemented only for hospitals, HL7 V3 is being designed to suit the needs of all healthcare network participants. HL7 V3 is based largely on a single formal object-oriented model called the Reference Information Model (RIM). The goal of RIM is to reduce the implementation costs of HL7-enabled solutions and further standardize the HL7 communication specifications between healthcare systems.

HL7 RIM Foundation Classes

HL7 RIM follows the general principles of UML. However, it cannot be regarded as a UML extension or to be totally UML-compliant. The backbone of RIM consists of six classes: Act, Entity, Role, Participation, RoleLink, and ActRelationship. Their detailed description (for RIM version 2.10) is given in Table 3. The UML class diagram containing the relationships between them is shown in Figure 8.

Participation represents the many-to-many relationship between Roles and Acts. This relationship is binary: each Participation joins a

Figure 8. Class Diagram Showing the Backbone Classes of HL7 RIM

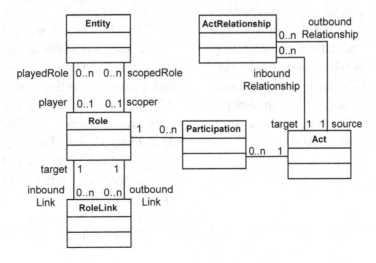

Figure 9. Structure of CDA Document Header (Beyer et al., 2004)

```
<Cli  nicalDocument>
    <!-- Header-->
        <recordTarget>       <! -- (1..*)     -- >
            <patientRole>
                <id extension="12345" root="2.16.840.1.113883.19.5"/>
                <patient>
                    <name>
                        <given>Henry</given>
                        <family>Levin</family>
                    </name>
                    <ad ministrativeGenderCode code="M"
                                        codeSystem="2.16.840.1.113883.5.1"/>
                    <birthTime value="19320924"/>
            </patient>
                </patientRole>
        </ recordTarget>
        <author>  <! -- (1..*),sub      - elements similar to recordTarget              -- ></ author>
    <custodian><!         -- (1..1),sub       - elements    -- ></custodian>
    <legalAuthenticator>              <! -- (0..1),sub      - elements  -- ></legalAuthenticator>
    <!    -- other ro    les: dataEnterer, informant, participant                      -- >
    <!-- Body -->
</ClinicalDocument>
```

single Role (and the Entity performing it) to a single Act. In reality, healthcare procedures are complex interactions, the most common examples involving several people (Entities playing Roles) participating in a "complex" Act. For instance, a patient is examined by a clinician and a diagnosis is stated. RIM splits complex events into one-role-one-act Participations.

The patient being examined participates in a PatientEncounter Act (a subclass of Act). The clinician, examining the patient, participates in an Act of Observation (also a subclass of Act). An ActRelationship joins the two Acts and may express a composition, sequence, source-target, or condition relationship. There is also a set of HL7 data types associated to RIM.

Clinical Document Architecture (CDA)

The structure and the semantic of clinical documents for the purposes of their exchange is specified by the HL7 Clinical Document Architecture (CDA), which is an XML-based document markup standard. CDA follows the concepts of RIM and uses HL7 data types.

CDA XML document can be easily converted into a human-readable document using XSLT style sheets. CDA focuses on Acts, Entities, and Roles. Their interaction is defined in a more flexible manner than in RIM, corresponding to the great structure freedom of XML. CDA data types describing RIM Acts, Entities, and Roles conform to the RIM model but the attribute matching is not complete. Those data types simplify the RIM model eliminating some of its optional attributes and, occasionally, introducing some new ones.

A CDA document consists of a header and a

Figure 10. Structure of CDA Document Body (Beyer et al., 2004)

```
<ClinicalDocument>
    <!-- Header -->
    <!-- Body -->
      <component>
          <structuredBody>
              <component>
                  <section>
                        <code code="10153    - 2"
                  codeSystem="2.16.840.1.113883.6.1" codeSystemName="LOINC"/>
                        <title>    Body temperature        </title>
                        <text>
                            <list>
                                <item> 36.9 C   </item>
                            </list>
                        </text>
      <entry>
                            <observation classCode="OBS" moodCode="EVN">
                                <code code="386725007"
                                    codeSystem="2.16.840.1.113883.6.96"
                                    codeSystemName="SNOMED CT"
                                    displayName="Body temperature"/>
                                <statusCode code="completed"/>
                                <effectiveTime value="200004071430"/>
                                <value   xsi:type="PQ" value="36.9" unit="Cel"              / >
                            </observation>
                        </entry>
      </section>
      <!                -- other sections        -- >
          </ component>
        </ structuredBody>
      </ component>
</ClinicalDocument>
```

body. Structure of the header is shown in Figure 29. The header gives information about the roles participating in the described medical events: the owner of the patient record the document is attached to (normally a patient), the author (a clinician), legal authenticator of the document (a senior clinician, head of the department), and the custodian - organization that is in charge of the document (a hospital or social insurance institution). Entity is specified as a sub-element of the role element. Elements recordTarget and patientRole in Figure 29 describe the RIM Role

Patient. Sub-elements of patient conform to the attributes of Person, a sub-class of RIM Entity. The example has been taken from CDA Specification (Beyer et al., 2004) and then simplified.

The body of the document contains CDA representation of RIM Acts. As shown in Figure 30 (again the simplified example from CDA Specification from (Beyer et al., 2004)), it is a set of recursively organized components and sections that form the structure of a human-readable document. Each section is a pair of human-readable text and a number of entry elements wrapping descriptions of acts. The entry in Figure 10 describes the process of body temperature measurement. The topic of the Observation is uniquely stated by the code sub-element of observation. Here, terminology standards LOINC (Regenstrief_Institute, 2007) and SNOMED CT (SNOMED, 2007) have been used, but other approved coding systems may also be applied. (Terminology standards are vocabularies which provide specific codes for clinical concepts such as disease, problem lists, allergies, medications, diagnoses etc. (Kim, 2005))

Relationships between acts (which are instances of RIM ActRelationship class) are generally expressed by grouping Acts into sections and components. Still, in rare cases when an explicit specification of different RIM ActRelationships types is needed, additional CDA XML tags can be used, which nest the dependent Act structure into the structure of the source Act as its sub-element.

openEHR, ENV 13606 and xDT

openEHR and ENV 13606 also introduce object-oriented reference models and a modular structure of healthcare documents. The general information model of openEHR (openEHR, 2007) describes only the nested hierarchical structure of healthcare records. Clinical data is defined separately for each healthcare domain using an ontology-defining constraint language.

ENV 13606 (proposed by the European Committee for Standardization) is currently under substantial revision due to its unnecessary complexity, which even led to some ambiguity and non-interoperability (EHCRSupA, 2007).

xDT (KBV, 2006) is a de-facto standard in Germany, used by social insurance organisations, pharmacists, and primary healthcare providers. Meanwhile, German hospitals have adopted HL7 standards. A comprehensive integration of xDT and HL7 standard has been performed by Sciphox company (SCIPHOX, 2006). The previously used octet-encoded xDT

messages have been abandoned and HL7 CDA and XML introduced. There is no general object model for xDT and its document structure is domain-dependent.

We chose to use HL7 RIM and CDA for the conceptual model of our federated DWH. Apart from HL7 RIM, no other standard offers an integrated model for all healthcare domains that can precisely define the basic structure of facts and dimensions, preventing any semantic or structural ambiguity. Fact and dimension attributes can be understood as feature descriptions having a domain precisely defined by RIM, but might actually consist of several attributes in a real database (easily defined by XML structures of CDA).

SEMANTIC INTEGRATION IN A FEDERATED DWH MODEL

During the last few years, healthcare organizations have been confronted with massive knowledge processing challenges. The primary cause for this is the increasing amount of complex medical data, but also the need to integrate wide range of data sources into a unique knowledge repository which could be used for EBM. Although willing to share their data with other healthcare providers, healthcare institutions prefer keeping their existing systems and metadata in place and participating in the federation in which integrated metadata is build on demand.

When several healthcare institutions try to consolidate their typically diverse metadata schemas, it is very likely that semantic conflicts will occur. Getting back to our running example, we illustrate semantic heterogeneity between two records corresponding to distinct metadata schemas in Figure 11.

Our goal is to create a metadata integration model, which will provide a uniform view and congeneric access to the wide range of heterogeneous data sources. Building such a model requires:

- common semantic representation (preferably by an ontology language)
- common data model
- query language that operates on this data model.

(Haslhofer, 2006) suggests the use of:

- OWL (W3C, 2004a) language for modelling ontologies, because it provides all the constructs and the expressiveness for describing the semantics of data,
- RDF data model (W3C, 2004b), because it is simple and yet powerful enough to allow

Figure 11. Semantic Heterogeneity of Two Metadata Records

Element	Value
Patient_ID	4029275
Name	John Smith
Date_of_birth	10.03.1942
Gender	M
Citizenship	A
Additional_insurance	N
Private_insurance	N
Prescription_remission	N
Relativ_flag	N
Ins._begin_date	01.04.1986
Ins._end_date	NULL

DWH1 record

Element	Value
Patient_Nr	4029275
Name	John Smith
Date_of_birth	10.03.1942
Gender	0
Citizenship	A
Additional_insurance	0
Age	65
Private_insurance	0
Relativ_flag	0
Disabled	0
Co_insired_from	01.04.1986
Co_insured_till	NULL

DWH2 record

DWH1	DWH2
Patient_ID	Patient_Nr
Name	Name
Date_of_birth	Date_of_birth
Gender	Gender
Citizenship	Citizenship
Additional_insurance	Additional_insurance
Private_insurance	Private_insurance
Relativ_flag	Relativ_flag
Ins._begin_date	Co_insired_from
Ins._end_date	Co_insured_till

Mapping DWH1 ⋈ DWH2

the description of metadata of any kind originating from various heterogeneous sources,

- SPARQL (W3C, 2007c), a query language which operates on the RDF data model.

Given that wrappers can translate between RDF and native data modes, SPARQL can be used for accessing data sources in an integrated fashion.

Figure 12. Heterogeneous Data Source Integration Layers

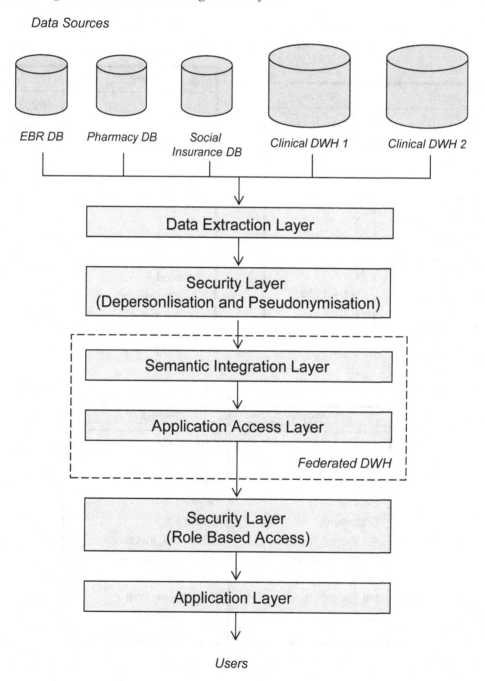

MEDICAL FEDERATED DWH INTEGRATION WORKFLOW

The model we are describing in this subchapter is based on a mediated federated DWH architecture, with a carefully designed semantical infrastructure (Figure 12). In our federated DWH model, the different healthcare domains, i.e. the social insurance domain, the pharmaceutical domain, and the evidence-based guidelines repository are participating in one federation. The existence of the federation is invisible to users of the source systems.

The clinical DWH contains data that originates from a wide variety of data sources, such as: clinical data, administrative data, financial data, and organizational data.

The health insurance company stores information about patient encounters, treatments, therapies, and drug prescriptions it supports. It communicates with the federation via web services.

Both clinical DWHs and the health insurance companies transfer their sensitive data to the federation, in case of a federated query. At this time, we assume that depersonalization and pseudonymization techniques are used to protect the confidentiality of patient data.

The pharmaceutical sector provides the federation with drug information such as medication description, packaging size, pharma-id number, indication group, pharmaceutical form (pills, juice etc.), and medication fee. In an analogous way to the social insurance company, it uses web services to provide the federation with the necessary data.

The evidence-based rules repository is a collection of most accurate and most efficient research evidence. It provides the federation with the best fitting guidelines "on demand" for a given patient and a given disease through web services.

Since only a "single version of evidence" and a unique interpretation of the joined data should exist, it is necessary to have a unique singular common federated schema, as described in previous chapter. For building the conceptual model of the federated DWHs, just data relevant to further analyses and reporting are considered. In this phase, business users (from the domain of clinical/social insurance management) have to specify the respective sensitivity levels of data. The data modeller incorporates the specified privacy restrictions into the resulting logical data model.

MEDIATED QUERY SYSTEM IN AN HEALTHCARE ENVIRONMENT

The essential part of integration of logical schemas of the underlying DWHs as well as of data structures originating on the diverse participating legacy systems (such as relational or XML databases) is the semantic integration layer (Figure 13). Our model includes wrappers and mediator, which are two main architectural components of a mediated query system.

Ontology

Ontologies are common methods of representing knowledge for interacting with heterogeneous data sources. In the DataFoundry research project (Critchlow et al., 1998), the authors focus on the use of ontologies as a formal method for storing and using the metadata required to perform automatic mediator generation.

The DataFoundry ontology represents four different concepts for mediator generation:

1. *Abstractions* of domain specific concepts - they represent knowledge about the concepts contained within the data sources being integrated.
2. *Database descriptions*, which consist of language independent class definitions that closely mirror the physical layout of a relational database.

Figure 13. Medical Federated DWH Integration Workflow

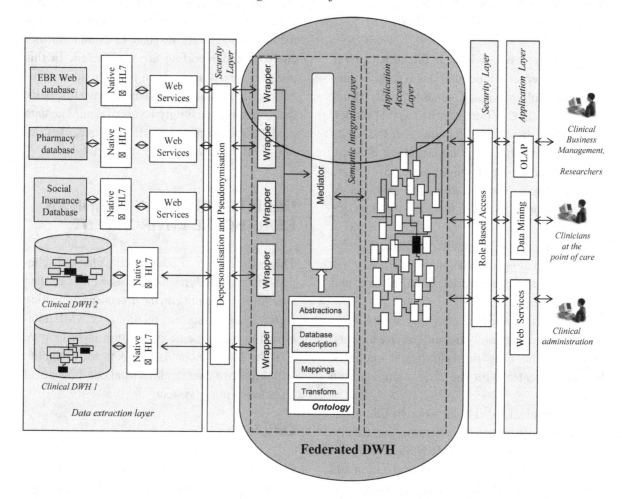

3. *Mappings,* used to identify the correspondence between database and abstraction attributes.

4. *Transformations,* which identify methods for conversion among different representations of the same characteristics.

Wrapper

Wrappers (Haslhofer, 2006) encapsulate local data sources and export their functionality and the metadata stored therein. They accept queries in a certain language and return metadata in a united form. The wrapper keeps the data schema locally for the specific data source it deals with. It trans-

lates the semantics of the metadata between the exported schema and the native data descriptions. Depending on the data source, a wrapper can be a default DBMS interface (for relational databases) or custom-built for specific sources.

By integrating wrappers, we can cope with technical heterogeneities among local systems without having to modify them.

Mediator

The mediator (Haslhofer, 2006) handles the global queries from the application layer, unfolds them into sub-queries and disperses these sub-queries to the relevant local data sources via their wrappers.

Figure 14. Mediated Query System in Healthcare Environment

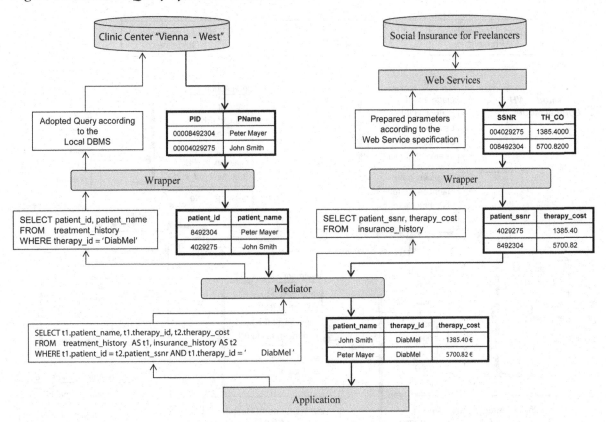

The local results will be returned by wrappers; the mediator finally combines and presents the result to the client. Hence, the mediator will keep the global data schema and the mapping between global and local schemas. To maintain the dynamic mapping between local and global schemas, an semantic-based mediator/wrapper is one of most interesting problem solving approaches.

Query Handling

Figure 14 shows an example of how a user's query is handled by wrappers and a mediator, from the query submission to the presentation of the result. On receiving the SQL query, the system performs the following:

1. DWH-Application invokes the mediator.

Query unfolding:

2. The mediator resolves the submitted query into partial queries, according to the exported schemas previously exposed by the wrappers. It determines which wrappers are relevant to the corresponding sub-queries.
3. The mediator passes the sub-queries to the affected wrappers.
4. A wrapper receives its sub-query and translates it into the format that can be understood by the underlying data source (database, web service etc.).
5. The wrapper forwards the adapted sub-query to the local DBMS or to the responsible Web Service for execution.

Query answering:

Figure 15. Extract from Federated DWH LDM with Corresponding Data Sources

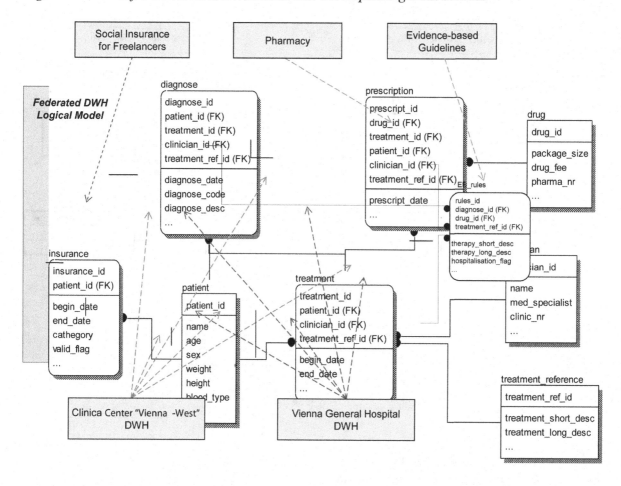

1. The wrapper retrieves the answer data set, translates it into its exported schema.
2. The wrapper passes its answer data set to the mediator.
3. The mediator integrates partial query results into one answer set, transforms and formats it so that it can be processed by the application.
4. The mediator passes the answer set to the application so that it can be presented to the user.

The users of a federated DWH are not aware of the fact that the data they are querying may be distributed across the network. Through data mining tools, web services, ad-hoc queries, and predefined reports (OLAP tools), users are able to analyse data as if they were physically stored in a centralized DWH. A role-based access model guarantees that each user gets access only to those data which are necessary for performing his (her) tasks.

RUNNING EXAMPLE: FEDERATED DWH SUPPORTING CLINICIANS AT THE POINT OF CARE

In order to illustrate the described federated DWH-based approach, we build upon our running example, introduced in previous chapters. Here, we assume that the emergency room clinician is

Figure 16. A Group of Tables Involved in Finding the Best Fitting Evidence-Based Rule

Patient

patient_id	name	age	sex	blood_type	blood_press_h	blood_press_l	...
8492304	Peter Mayer	32	M	A	110	65	...
4029275	John Smith	65	F	AB	140	80	...

Diagnoses

diagnose_id	patient_id	treatment_id	diagnose_date	diagnose_code	diagnose_desc	...
DM114	4029275	178756	10.04.1998	DiabMel	Diabetes Mellitus	
LD323	4029275	556802	22.10.2004	LeavDis	Leaver Disease	

Treatment

treatment_id	patient_id	treat_ref_id	treat_code	begin_date	end_date	cathegory	...
178756	4029275	0770	339025	12.01.2000	12.01.2000	4	
321321	4029275	1035	920572	04.02.2000	03.08.2000	3	

EBrule

EBG_id	diag_id	probl_treat_code	drug_incomp	bp_high_lim	bl_low_lim	reco_treat_code	...
4450241	DM114	920572	857215	NULL	NULL	222435	...
4450242	DM114	592688	NULL	150	60	823044	...

querying the federated DWH while examining the patient. The following scenario depicts the starting point of our example: The Diabetes patient suffering from a progressive liver disease is complaining about itchy rash on his hands. Since the attending physician is not familiar with the patient's medical history and needs to act quickly, he(she) is using federated DWH facilitating EBM to find the most efficient therapy, which does not conflict with the patient's ongoing Diabetes and liver disease treatment.

The clinician is using an OLAP tool which is set up on the federated DWH. One small but representative part of the federated DWH LDM is shown in Figure 15. Dashed arrows show the data flow between underlying data sources and resulting tables.

The clinician is querying the patient's healthcare record, containing all existing anamnesis/diagnostic data and all of patient's past treatments. Further, he(she) is interested in the patient's overall health condition (allergies and medication incompatibilities) as well as the personal data (age, weight, family predisposition to some diseases etc.). In addition, the clinician has to find out what kind of therapies will be covered by the patient's social insurance. Finally, he(she) is aiming to find the treatment which proved to be the most effective under given conditions. The answering procedure takes place in two phases:

1. The user (the clinician) is querying the federated DWH by providing only the patient's name and the corresponding social insurance number. In the first step, the mediator sends queries containing these two parameters to all relevant participating sources (in this case study, these are: clinical DWHs, pharmacy, and social insurance company). The aim of this step is to retrieve all patient data, which might be interesting as input for the second step, namely querying EBG database. Responsible wrappers return the corresponding data to the mediator, which in sequel joins them and produces a result data set.

2. In the second step, the resulting data set (containing patient's age, blood pressure, blood type, diseases history, list of received treatments and medications, social insurance categorisation etc.) is used as the input parameter for querying of the evidence-based guidelines database. The mediator forwards a new query to the EBG- database wrapper and retrieves the final data set.

As shown in Figure 16, some of the existing treatment rules are disqualified due to medication or treatment incompatibilities. Since the proposed treatments must be adjusted to the patient's health risks, parameters like blood pressure may play the determining role in the treatment verification process. Nevertheless, the scope of a patient's social insurance contract (refers to treatment categorization) is significant for the determination of applicable treatment.

In our example, the evidence-based guideline with identification: EBG_id = '4450241' is not applicable for reasons of treatment incompatibility. Namely, in the past, Mr. Smith has received a treatment with treatment_code = '920572', which is listed as a problem treatment for this guideline.

The evidence-based guideline with identification: EBG_id = '4450242' is the best fitting guideline for Mr. Smith's medical condition, so

it is forwarded to the federated DWH.

In the last step, an OLAP tool presents the result to the clinician in an understandable and illustrative way.

CONCLUSION

Interoperability between medical IS is necessary for building sustainable healthcare decision-support systems. Federated DWH has been increasingly proposed as an alternative to conventional centralized approaches, with a high transformative potential role within healthcare structures. Although the relevance and use of federated DWH within the healthcare domain is obvious, there are still many technical and organizational open issues. In this chapter we have presented, that a federated clinical DWH that facilitates EBM is a reliable and powerful platform for production and dissemination of clinical knowledge. Knowledge originating from evidence-based medicine represents a valuable resource for healthcare policy makers. Integration of knowledge management into clinical decision support system enables strategic decision making for both clinical business management and for the caregivers at the point of care, which results in a better service for the patient, the medical personal and administrative staff. A real-world scenario is used to illustrate the possible application field in the area of emergency and intensive care in which the evidence-based medicine merges data originating in a pharmacy database, a social insurance company database and diverse clinical DWHs. Our universal, simple and flexible common conceptual model enables potential future integrations of other health care organizations to be done seamlessly and with a minimum effort.

REFERENCES

W3C. (2004a, Febrauary 10). *OWL Web ontology language overview*. Retrieved July 18, 2007, from http://www.w3.org/TR/owl-features/

W3C. (2004b). *Resource description framework (RDF)*. Retrieved July 18, 2007, from http://www.w3.org/RDF/

W3C. (2007c, June 14). *SPARQL query language for RDF*. Retrieved July, 18, 2007, from http://www.w3.org/TR/rdf-sparql-query/

Abidi, S. S. R., & Abdigi, S. R. (2001). A case of supplementing evidence base medicine with inductive clinical knowledge: Towards technology enriched integrated clinical evidence system. In *Proceedings of the 14th IEEE Symposium on Computer-Based Medical Systems, (CBMS'2001)*, Bethesda, MD, USA. Washington, DC: IEEE.

AERZTE_ZEITUNG. (2005). *Briten stellen auf elektronische patientenakten um*.

Agrawal, R., Grandison, T., Johnson, C., & Kiernan, J. (2007). Enabling the 21st century health care information technology revolution. *Communications of the ACM, 50*(2), 34–42. doi:10.1145/1216016.1216018

Al-Kahtani, M. A., & Sandhu, R. (2000). Access control meets public key infrastructure, or: Assigning roles to strangers. In *Proceedings of the 2000 Symposium on Security and Privacy*.

Al-Kahtani, M. A., & Sandhu, R. (2003). Induced role hierarchies with attribute-based RBAC. In *Proceedings of the SACMAT'03*, Como, Italy. New York: ACM Press.

Audiimoolam, S., Nair, M., Gaikwad, R., & Qing, C. (2005, February 7). The role of clinical pathways in improving patient outcomes. Retrieved July 18, 2007, from http://www.healthsolve.com.au/wp-content/uploads/2008/05/role-of-clinical-pathways.pdf

Beyer, M., Kuhn, K. A., Meiler, C., Jablonski, S., et al. (2004). Towards a flexible, process oriented IT architecture for an integrated healthcare network. In *Proceedings of the 2004 ACM Symposium on Applied Computing, Special Track on Computer Applications in Health Care (CAHC)*, Nicosia, Cyprus (pp. 264-271). New York: ACM Press.

BIOPATTERN. (2007). *BIOPATTERN network of excellence*. Retrieved August 20, 2007, from http://www.biopattern.org

BMJ. (2007). *The British Medical Journal*. Retrieved September 19, 2007, from http://www.bmj.com/

Briggs, B. (2005). Decision support software matures. *Health Data Management*.

Britt, P. (2005, November 1). A warehouse of opportunity. *Finance Tech*. Retrieved September 24, 2007, from http://www.financetech.com/showArticle.jhtml?articleID=173402279

Brobst, S., & Rarey, J. (2001). The five stages of an active data warehouse evolution. *Teradata Magazine*.

Bundesgesetz. (2004). 179. Bundesgesetz, Gesundheitsreformgesetz 2005, 7. Unterabschnitt, § 84a. (5). Bundesgesetztblatt für die Republik Österreich, Teil I: 12.

Carner®. (2007). *An introduction to the evidence based decision support center (EBDSC)*. Retrieved September 26, 2007, from http://www.cerner.com/public/filedownload.asp?LibraryID=12130

CEBM. (2004). *Why the sudden interest in EBM?* Retrieved July 18, 2007, from http://www.cebm.utoronto.ca/intro/interest.htm

Clifton, C., Doan, A., Elmagarmid, A., Kantarcioglu, M., et al. (2004). Privacy-preserving data integration and sharing. In *Proceedings of the DMKD'04*, Paris, France. New York: ACM.

Cochrane_Collaboration. (2007). *Cochrane centres*. Retrieved July 18, 2007, from http://www.cochrane.org/contact/entities.htm

Cochrane_Library. (2007). *Evidence for healthcare decision-making*. Retrieved July 18, 2007, from http://www.theCochraneLibrary.com

Codd, E. F. (1985). How relational is your database management system? *Computerworld.*

Craig, J. C., Irwig, L. M., & Stockler, M. R. (2001). Evidence-based medicine: Useful tools for decision making. *The Medical Journal of Australia, MJA, 174*, 248–253.

Critchlow, T., Ganesh, M., & Musick, R. (1998). Automatic generation of warehouse mediators using an ontology engine. In *Proceedings of the 5th International Workshop on Knowledge Represenation Meets Databases (KRDB '98)*, Seattle, Washington, USA. Retrieved from http://www.CEUR-WS.org

dbMotion. (2005). *The dbMotion™ solution* [white paper].

Docobo®. (2006). doc@HOME. Retrieved August, 16, 2007, from http://www.docobo.co.uk/products_docathome.htm

Donovan, M. (2005). *Real-time connections*. Retrieved September 25, 2007, from http://www.teradata.com/t/page/131974/index.html

Dowsey, M. M., Kilgour, M. L., & Santamaria, N. M. (1999). A clinical pathway reduced length of stay, time to ambulation, and complications after hip and knee arthroplasty. *The Medical Journal of Australia, 170*, 59–62.

Duftschmid, G., Dorda, W., & Gall, W. (2003). MAGDA-LENA versus HIPAA: Two national frameworks for healthcare data exchange. In *Proceedings of the a-telemed 2003* (pp. 25-33).

Dutch_DPA. (2006). *Handling of your medical data*. Retrieved August 29, 2007, from http://www.dutchdpa.nl/documenten/en_inf_subj_Handling_Medical_Data.shtml

Eckhardt, A. (2000). *Data abuse and what can be done to prevent it*. The Patient in the Data Network.

EHCRSupA. (2007). *Introduction to ENV 13606 version 1.0*. Retrieved September 27, 2008, from http://www.chime.ucl.ac.uk/work-areas/ehrs/EHCR-SupA/13606v1_8/sld003.htm

eHealth. (2006b). *Impact of emerging ICT on patient safety*. Retrieved September 27, 2007, from http://www.ehealth-for-safety.org/workshops/bio_medical%202006/bio_medical_index.html

Eichelberg, M., Aden, T., Riesmeier, J., & Dogac, A. (2005). A survey and analysis of electronic health care record standards. *ACM Computing Surveys, 37*(4), 277–315. doi:10.1145/1118890.1118891

Elsevier. (2007). *The Lancet*. Retrieved September 19, 2007, from http://www.thelancet.com/

Elsmari, R., & Navathe, S. (2004). *Fundamentals of database systems*. Reading, MA: Addison Wesley.

EU. (1995). EU data protection directive. *Official Journal of the European Communities, 31.*

Ferraiolo, D. F., Kuhn, D. R., & Chandramouli, R. (2003). Access control policy, models, and mechanisms - concepts and examples. In *Role-based access control* (pp. 27-49). Norwood, MA: Artech House.

Ferrell, K. (2007). *Continental Airlines - landing the right data*. Retrieved September 25, 2007, from http://www.teradata.com/t/page/133723/index.html

Gorenberg, M., Marmor, A., & Rotstein, H. (2005). Detection of chest pain of non-cardiac origin at the emergency room by a new non-invasive device avoiding unnecessary admission to hospital. *Emergency Medicine Journal, 22*, 486–489. doi:10.1136/emj.2004.016188

Gregoratos, G., Cheitlin, M. D., & Conill, A. (1998). ACC/AHA guidelines for implantation of cardiac pacemakers and antiarrhythmia devices: Executive summary. *Circulation, 97*, 1325–1335.

GVG©. (2004). *Pseudonymisierung/anonymisierung*. Aktionsforum Telematik im Gesundheitswesen.

HL7. (2007). *Health level seven*. Retrieved September 26, 2007, from http://www.hl7.org

Hashmi, N., Myung, D., Gaynor, M., & Moulton, S. (2005). A sensor-based, Web service-enabled, emergency medical response system. In *Proceedings of the EESR '05: Workshop on End-to-End, Sense-and-Respond Systems, Applications and Services*, Seattle, WA. New York: ACM.

Haslhofer, B. (2006). A service oriented approach for integrating metadata from heterogeneous digital libraries. In *Proceedings of the 1st International Workshop Semantic Information Integration on Knowledge Discovery (SIIK 2006)*, Yogyakarta, Indonesia. Austrian Computer Society.

Hauptverband. (2007). *Österreichische sozialversicherung*. Retrieved September 27, 2007, from http://www.sozialversicherung.at

Hein, A., Nee, O., Willemsen, D., Scheffold, T., et al. (2006). SAPHIRE - intelligent healthcare monitoring based on semantic interoperability platform - the homecare scenario. In *Proceedings of the European Conference on eHealth 2006*, Fribourg, Switzerland (pp. 191-202).

Heitmann, K. U. (2006). Kommunikation mit HL7 version 3 – aspekte der interoperabilität im gesundheitswesen. *Datenbank Spektrum*, (17), 12-16.

HIPPA. (1996). *HIPPA.ORG*. Retrieved September 27, 2007, from http://www.hipaa.org/

HIR-group. (2006). *Health informatics research*. Retrieved September 26, 2007, from http://www.cit.uws.edu.au/hir/

IHE. (2006, June). *IHE cardiology technical framework year 2: 2005-2006. Volume I: Integration profiles*. Retrieved August 26, 2007, from http://www.ihe.net/Technical_Framework

IHE. (2007a). *IHE changing the way healhtcare connects*. Retrieved September 27, 2007, from http://www.ihe.net/

IHE. (2007b). *IHE connectathons present a unique testing opportunity*. Retrieved September 26, 2007, from http://www.ihe.net/Connectathon/

IHE. (2007c). *IHE in Europe 2007*. Retrieved September 27, 2007, from http://ihe.univ-rennes1.fr/europe2007/

Infoway, C. H. (2007a). *Transforming health care*. Retrieved September 20, 2007, from http://www.infoway-inforoute.ca/

Infoway, C. H. (2007b). *Advancing Canada's next generation of healthcare*. Retrieved October, 11, 2007, from http://www.infoway-inforoute.ca/en/pdf/Vision_2015_Advancing_Canadas_next_generation_of_healthcare.pdf

Inmon, W. H. (1992). *Building the data warehouse*. New York: John Wiley & Sons.

InterfaceWare. (2007). *HL7 standard*. Retrieved from http://www.interfaceware.com/manual/hl7.html

JAMA. (2007). *The Journal of the American Medical Association*. Retrieved September 19, 2007, from http://jama.ama-assn.org/

Jindal, R., & Acharya, A. (2004). *Federated data warehouse architecture, Wipro Technologies* [white paper]. Retrieved September 19, 2007, from http://hosteddocs.ittoolbox.com/Federated%20data%20Warehouse%20Architecture.pdf

Kalra, D., Singleton, P., Ingram, D., & Milan, J. (2004). Security and confidentiality approach for the clinical e-science framework (CLEF). *HealthGrid, 44*(2), 193–197.

KBV. (2006). *xDT - synonym für elektronischen datenaustausch in der arztpraxis*. Retrieved September 27, 2007, from http://www.kbv.de/ita/4274.html

KFF. (2006). *Comparing projected growth in health care expenditures and the economy*. Retrieved October 22, 2007, from http://www.kff.org/insurance/snapshot/chcm050206oth2.cfm

Kim, K. (2005). Clinical data standards in health care: Five case studies. *ihealh reports*.

Kimball, R. (1996). *The data warehouse toolkit*. New York: John Wiley & Sons.

Kirkgoze, R., Katic, N., Stolba, M., & Tjoa, A. M. (1997). A security concept for OLAP. In *Proceedings of the 8th International Workshop on Database and Expert System Application 1997* (pp. 619-626). Washington, DC: IEEE Computer Press.

Krenn, F. (2006). *IT-platforms help to improve efficiency in health care*. Retrieved September 27, 2007, from www.ehealth-bg.org/images/Siemens_Franz%20Krenn_1.ppt

Lampson, B. W. (1974). Protection. *ACM Operating Systems, 8*(1), 18–24. doi:10.1145/775265.775268

Lin, F., Chou, S., Pan, S., & Chen, Y. (2000). Mining time dependency patterns in clinical pathways. IN *Proceedings of the 33rd Hawaii International Conference on System Sciences*.

Loos, C. (2006). *E-health with mobile Grids: The Akogrimo heart monitoring and emergency scenario* [white paper].

Lujan-Mora, S., Trujillo, J., & Song, I. Y. (2002). Multidimensional modeling with UML package diagrams. In *Proceedings of the 21st International Conference on Conceptual Modeling (ER 2002)* (pp. 199-213). Berlin, Germany: Springer Verlag.

Malan, D., Jones, T., Welsh, M., & Moulton, S. (2004). CodeBlue: An ad hoc sensor network infrastructure for emergency medical care. In *Proceedings of the International Workshop on Wearable and Implantable Body Sensor Networks, BSN 04*.

Moron, M. J., Casilari, E., Luque, R., & Gazquez, J. A. (2005). A wireless monitoring system for pulse-oximetry sensors. In *Proceedings of the 2005 Systems Communications (ICW'05)* (pp. 79-84).

National_Research_Council. (1997). *For the record: Protecting electronic health information*. Washington, DC: The National Academies Press.

Nguyen, T. M., Schiefer, J., & Tjoa, A. M. (2005). Sense & response service architecture (SARESA): An approach towards a real-time business intelligence solution and its use for a fraud detection application. In *Proceedings of the 8th ACM international workshop on Data warehousing and OLAP (DOLAP '05)*, Bremen, Germany (pp. 77-86). New York: ACM Press.

NHS. (2005, June). *The spine*. Retrieved September 15, 2007, from http://www.connectingforhealth.nhs.uk/resources/comms_tkjune05/spine_factsheet.pdf

NHS. (2007). *Connecting for health*. Retrieved September 15, 2007, from http://www.connectingforhealth.nhs.uk/

Open_Clinical. (2006). *Knowledge management for medical care*. Retrieved September 27, 2007, from http://www.openclinical.org/clinicalpathways.html

openEHR. (2007). *The openEHR foundation*. Retrieved September 27, 2007, from http://www.openehr.org

Patient Care Technologies®, I. (n.d.). *Well@home device*. Retrieved August 16, 2007, from http://www.ptct.com/wah_device.html

Perreault, L. E., & Metzger, J. B. (1999). A pragmatic framework for understanding clinical decision-support. *Journal of Healthcare Information Management, 13*(2), 5–21.

PIPEDA. (2006). *Pipeda info*. Retrieved February 10, 2006, from http://www.pipedainfo.com/

Pommerening, K., & Reng, M. (2004). Secondary use of the EHR via pseudonymisation. *Studies in Health Technology and Informatics, 103*, 441–446.

Regenstrief_Institute. (2007). Logical observation identifiers names and codes (LOINC®). Retrieved September 20, 2007, from http://www.regenstrief.org/medinformatics/loinc/

RESolutionLtd. (2007). *Resolution xCase™*. Retrieved September, 25, 2007, from http://www.xcase.com/

Rindfleisch, T. (1997). Privacy, information technology and healthcare. *Communications of the ACM, 40*(8), 92–100. doi:10.1145/257874.257896

Sackett, D. L., Rosenberg, W. M., Gray, J. A., & Haynes, R. B. (1996). Evidence-based medicine: What it is and what it isn't. [editorial]. *BMJ (Clinical Research Ed.), 312*(7023), 71–72.

Sartipi, K., Yarmand, M. H., & Down, D. G. (2007). Mined-knowledge and decision support services in electronic health. In *Proceedings of the International Workshop on Systems Development in SOA Environments*. Washington, DC: IEEE Computer Society.

Schanner, A. (2006, September). *NÖ am weg zur elektronischen gesundheitsakte*. Retrieved September 20, 2007, from http://www.lknoe.at/

Schuerenberg, B. K. (2003). Clearing the hurdles to decision support. *Health Data Management*.

SCIPHOX. (2006). *Dokumenten-kommunikation im gesundheitswesen*. Retrieved September 27, 2007, from http://sciphox.hl7.de/ueber_uns/flyerallgemein.pdf

Sheth, A. P., & Larson, J. A. (1990). Federated database systems for managing distributed, heterogeneous, and autonomous databases. *ACM Computing Surveys, 22*(3), 183–236. doi:10.1145/96602.96604

SNOMED. (2007). *Systematized nomenclature of medicine (SNOMED)*. Retrieved September 20, 2007, from http://www.snomed.org/

Spronk, R. (2007). *The spine, an English national programme*. Retrieved September 15, 2007, from http://www.ringholm.de/docs/00970_en.htm

Stolba, N., Banek, M., & Tjoa, A. M. (2006c). The security issue of federated data warehouses in the area of evidence-based medicine. In *Proceedings of the First International Conference on Availability, Reliability and Security (ARES 2006)*, Vienna, Austria (pp. 329-339). Washington, DC: IEEE Computer Society Press.

Stolba, N., Nguyen, T. M., & Tjoa, A. M. (2007a). Towards a data warehouse based approach to support healthcare knowledge development and sharing. In *Proceedings of the 2007 Information Resources Management Association (IRMA) International Conference*, Vancouver, Canada. Hershey, PA: Idea Group Publishing.

Stolba, N., Nguyen, T. M., & Tjoa, A. M. (2007c). Towards sustainable decision-support system facilitating EBM. In *Proceedings of the 29th Annual International Conference of the IEEE Engineering in Medicine and Biology Society (EMBC 2007)*, Lyon, France.

Stolba, N., & Schanner, A. (2007). eHealth integrator - clinical data integration in lower Austria. In *Proceedings of the Third International Conference on Computational Intelligence in Medicine and Healthcare (CIMED 2007)*, Plymouth, England.

Stolba, N., & Tjoa, A. M. (2006a). An approach towards the fulfilment of security requirements for decision support systems in the field of evidence-based healthcare. In *Proceedings of the Knowledge Rights - Legal, Societal and Related Technological Aspects (KnowRight2006)*, Vienna; Austria (pp. 51-59). Austrian Computer Society.

Stolba, N., & Tjoa, A. M. (2006b). The relevance of data warehousing and data mining in the field of evidence-based medicine to support healthcare decision making. In *Proceedings of the International Conference on Computer Science (ICCS 2006)*, Prague, Czech Republic.

Stolba, N., Tjoa, A. M., Mueck, T., & Banek, M. (2007b). Federated data warehouse approach to support the national and international interoperability of healthcare information systems. In *Proceedings of the 15th European Conference on Information Systems (ECIS 2007)*, St. Gallen, Switzerland.

Strategis. (2005). *PIPEDA Overview*. Retrieved August, 29, 2007, from http://privacyforbusiness. ic.gc.ca/epic/site/pfb-cee.nsf/en/hc00005e.html

STRING-Kommission. (2000). *Rahmenbedingungen für ein logisches österreichisches Gesundheitsdatennetz ("MAGDA-LENA"), Teil 2: Hauptteil, Version 2.0.*

Sun, L., Hu, P., Goh, C., Hamadicharef, B., et al. (2006). Bioprofiling over Grid for early detection of dementia. In *Proceedings of the 1st international conference on Scalable information systems (INFOSCALE '06)*, Hong Kong. New York: ACM Press.

SYBASE. (2007a). *Elisa mobiilsideteenused. Customer success story*. Retrieved September 25, 2007, from http://www.sybase.com/ detail?id=1040227

SYBASE. (2007b). *China Telecom. Customer success story*. Retrieved September 25, 2007, from http://www.sybase.com/detail?id=1036771

Symmetry_Corporation. (2007). *ADAPT*. Retrieved September 19, 2007, from http://www. symcorp.com/

T-Systems. (2007). *Innovatives design*. Retrieved September 20, 2007, from http://www.t-systems. at/

Taweel, A., Rector, A., Kalra, D., Rogers, R., et al. (2004). CLEF – joining up healthcare with clinical and post-genomic research. In *Proceedings of the HEALTHCARE COMPUTING* (pp. 203-212). British Computer Society.

Teradata. (2003, October). *ONE GmbH. Industry solutions > communications*. Retrieved September 25, 2007, from http://www.teradata.com/t/pdf. aspx?a=83673&b=107494

Teradata. (2004, July). *Office Depot. Industry solutions > retail*. Retrieved September 25, 2007, from http://www.teradata.com/t/pdf. aspx?a=83673&b=166244

Teradata. (2006, April). *Teradata solutions methodology*. Retrieved September 24, 2007, from http://www.teradata.com/t/pdf.aspx?a=83673&b=92291

Tsui, F.-C., Espino, J. U., Dato, V. M., & Gestelnad, P. H. (2003). Technical description of RODS: A real-time public health surveillance system. [JAMIA]. *Journal of the American Medical Informatics Association, 10*(5), 399–408. doi:10.1197/jamia.M1345

Uni_Münster. (2001). *Medizincontrolling/DRG research group*. Retrieved September 20, 2007, from http://drg.uni-muenster.de/de/behandlungspfade/cpathways/clinicalpathways_reisebericht.php

Walters, T. (2003). *TELE.RING dialing up customized services*. Retrieved September 25, 2007, from http://www.teradata.com/t/page/114954/index.html

White, B. (2004). *Making evidence-based medicine doable in everyday practice*. American Academy of Family Physicians, Family Practiced Management.

Wikipedia. (2007a). *Randomized controlled trial*. Retrieved July 18, 2007, from http://en.wikipedia.org/wiki/Randomized_controlled_trial

Wikipedia. (2007b). *Data protection act*. Retrieved August 29, 2007, from http://en.wikipedia.org/wiki/Data_Protection_Act

Wikipedia. (2007c). *Personal information protection and electronic documents act*. Retrieved August 29, 2007, from http://en.wikipedia.org/wiki/Personal_Information_Protection_and_Electronic_Documents_Act

Wikipedia. (2007d). *Directive 95/46/EC on the protection of personal data*. Retrieved August, 29, 2007, from http://en.wikipedia.org/wiki/Directive_95/46/EC_on_the_protection_of_personal_data#Scope

Wikipedia. (2007e). *Pseudonymity*. Retrieved August, 30, 2007, from http://en.wikipedia.org/wiki/Pseudonymity

Wikipedia. (2007f). *Dementia*. Retrieved September 20, 2007, from http://en.wikipedia.org/wiki/Dementia

Wyatt, J. C., & Spiegelhalter, D. J. (1991). Field trials of medical decision-aids: potential problems and solutions. In *Proceedings of the Annual Symposium Computer Applications in Medical Care* (pp. 3-7).

Chapter 9
Deploying Data Warehouses in Grids with Efficiency and Availability

Rogério Luís de Carvalho Costa
University of Coimbra, Portugal

Pedro Furtado
University of Coimbra, Portugal

ABSTRACT

Many global organizations are generating huge volumes of data, which are stored in highly distributed databases. These databases can be put together through a Grid infrastructure in order to form a large virtual data warehouse, which is physically distributed but can be transparently queried by Grid participants. But in Grids the system environment is heterogeneous and resource availability may vary over time, which may lead to performance degradation and data unavailability. In this chapter, the authors present Grid-NPDW which uses specialized data placement and job scheduling strategies in order to construct a Grid-based data warehouse with high performance and availability.

INTRODUCTION

In traditional data warehouses, distributed operational data is transferred to a central site where a data warehouse is built. This data warehouse may be physically placed in parallel machines in order to provide an efficient environment over which users submit complex analytical OLAP queries. As global (real and virtual (Foster, 2001)) organizations are generating huge volumes of data which is geographically distributed but that should be efficiently and transparently queried by organiza-

tion's participants, the use of such a *central* data warehouse model may be inadequate. Constructing such a centralized data warehouse environment for global organizations, while simultaneously providing scalability and high levels of Quality of Service (QoS), may be much more expensive and both resource and time consuming than deploying a decentralized grid-enabled solution.

On the other hand, during the last decades, network systems have gone through significant bandwidth and scalability advances and the use of networked off-the-shelf computers replaced cumbersome centralized solutions in many tasks. In fact, the use of widely distributed computer

DOI: 10.4018/978-1-60566-748-5.ch009

Copyright © 2010, IGI Global. Copying or distributing in print or electronic forms without written permission of IGI Global is prohibited.

power as if it were a single powerful resource turns out to be a great opportunity and also a great challenge. In such context, the Grid (Foster, 2001) has emerged as an infra-structure that connects highly distributed and possible heterogeneous resources and makes them transparently available to users as if they are just a single but powerful computational resource. Therefore, the Grid may be used as an underling infra-structure that supports the development of a data warehouse which is distributed over several sites while simultaneously being queried efficiently and transparently by the global organizations' participants.

In order to construct the *grid-based data warehouse*, distributed WAN-connected shared resources (which may belong to different real organizations) are used. Such resources may be very heterogeneous and may become unavailable over large time periods (either due to changes in network conditions or for domain specific resource usage constraints). Therefore, special data allocation strategies must be used in order to construct a highly available and efficient environment.

Besides that, special query scheduling strategies must also be used, not only to provide high availability but also in order to generate adequate load balancing between computing resources, which is of special interest in the heterogeneous Grid environment.

In this chapter we discuss the extension of *traditional* parallel and distributed data allocation and query scheduling techniques to the grid-based data warehouse. We present the Grid-NPDW strategy, which uses data partitioning and replication together with a dynamic query scheduling policy in order to provide a highly available and efficient grid-based data warehouse environments.

This chapter is organized as follows: in the next Section, we discuss some background on parallel and distributed data warehouses, including grid-based implementations. Then, we present the Grid-NPDW data allocation strategy and its use together with a dynamic demand-driven query al-

location policy. Experimental results are presented to validate the Grid-NPDW architecture.

FROM PARALLEL TO GRID-BASED DATA WAREHOUSES

In this section we review concepts and previous work on parallel and distributed data warehouses, and also on grid-based resource management systems, which are central concepts to our grid-enabled data warehouse approach.

Data warehouses (DW) are huge databases which store historical data and are mainly used for decision support purposes. They are commonly organized as *star schemas* (Chaudhuri & Dayal, 1997), which means they have one or more large *facts tables* and some smaller *dimension tables*. A sample star schema is represented in Figure 1. In such example, table *Revenue* is a fact table and the other relations are dimension tables linked to the fact table by foreign keys.

In order to provide good response times for the complex analytical queries that are usually submitted in DWs, some special operators and techniques have been proposed in the literature, like the use of special index structures (O'Neil et Graefe, 1995), materialized views (Baralis et al, 1997) and parallelism (Akal et al, 2002; Furtado, 2004; Röhm et al, 2000; Stöhr et al, 2000).

Next, we will present some background on the implementation of parallel and distributed data warehouses.

Parallel and Distributed Data Warehouses

The implementation of parallel and distributed databases has been investigated for some decades. Several works have been done, especially in the data allocation and query scheduling fields.

There are several factors that may affect the performance of parallel and distributed databases. Walton et al (1991) made a classification of those

Figure 1. Sample Star Schema Model

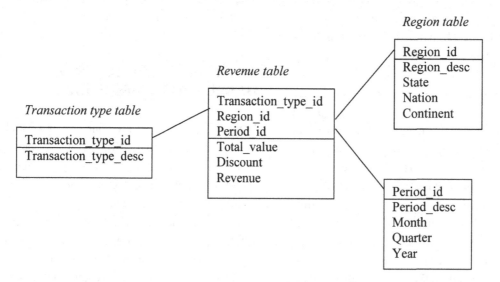

factors, which was expanded by Lerner & Lifschitz (1998). In such classification, *Tuple placement*, *Selectivity* and *Heterogeneity* skews are among the most relevant skew factor categories that affect parallel database performance in heterogeneous environments. In order to reduce the effect of such skew factors on the systems' performance, some specialized data partitioning and placement strategies were proposed.

Parallel data allocation and processing approaches typically rely on partitioning the data. Stöhr et al (2000) propose a *multi-dimensional hierarchical fragmentation* strategy called MDHF for use in shared-disk parallel systems. In MDHF, fact tables are partitioned based on a set of dimension attributes. The authors show that OLAP queries performance benefits from the use of dimension-based partitioned fact tables, even when the submitted queries are over hierarchical levels different from the ones that were used to generate the facts table's fragments.

Röhm et al (2000) discuss the execution of parallel OLAP queries in the PowerDB system, which is composed by a set of independent processing nodes (off-the-shelf computers) and a *coordinator* node. Each processing node has its

own DBMS. The coordinator node is responsible for scheduling query execution between the processing nodes and to collect results, sending them back to the user. The authors compare the use of two data placement strategies: (i) fully replicating the database into all nodes, and (ii) an hybrid approach where the largest table is partitioned across all nodes and the other tables are fully replicated at all nodes. The presented experimental results stand for the use of the hybrid approach in order to obtain higher throughput.

Virtual Partitioning (Akal et al, 2002) is another database allocation scheme experimentally tested in PowerDB. Its goal is to achieve intra-query parallelism in cluster-based data warehouses. In such a strategy, all data is fully replicated into all processing nodes. Clustered primary key indexes are created on the facts table, and one (or more) of the primary key attributes is chosen to be a *partitioning attribute*. Assuming that the possible values on the partitioning attribute are know, virtual partitions are created, considering each one a range of values in the partitioning attribute. Submitted queries are transformed into several subqueries each one addressing a virtual partition. This strategy can lead to performance

Figure 2. NPDW data partitioning and allocation strategy

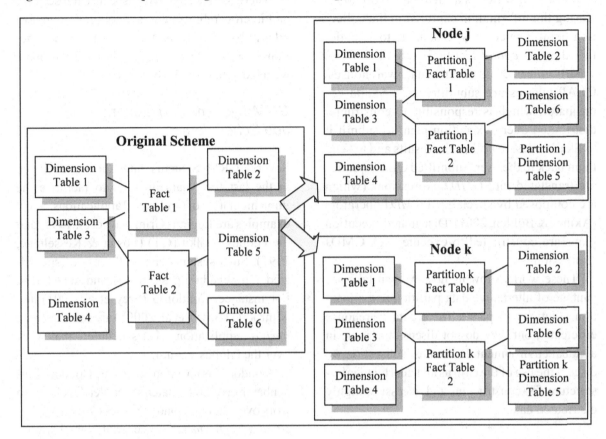

gains if the underlying DBMS considers the range predicates very selective and uses the clustered index to access only a fragment of the fact table (reducing I/O) instead of doing a full table scan in such table.

Hence, one great challenge on Virtual Partitioning is to properly choose partitions' bounds (determining its sizes). Akal et al (2002) claim that they should be chosen so that the duration of parallel subqueries execution is approximately equal, while (Lima et al, 2004) stands that the number of virtual partitions should be higher than the number of processing nodes. Performance problems can occur when a great number of transformed queries access non-partitioned tables. Besides that, there is no guarantee that the underlying DBMSs will not execute a full table scan for each transformed subquery.

The Node-Partitioned Data Warehouse (NPDW) (Furtado, 2004; Furtado, 2004b) is another strategy for the implementation of parallel data warehouses in shared-nothing systems. In NPDW, facts and large dimension tables are hash-partitioned and the resulting partitions are placed on different nodes. In order to minimize repartitioning costs, the most frequently used equi-join attribute should be used to generate facts tables' partitions. Small dimension tables are replicated at all nodes, while large dimension tables are hash-partitioned as well. NPDW data allocation strategy is illustrated in Figure 2.

The Skalla System (Akinde et al, 2002) enables the use of OLAP tools in order to analyze distributed network trace data. IP flow data[1] is obtained in several *data collection points*. Next to each data collection point is placed a *Skalla site*, which is a local data warehouse storing the information captured in the collection point. Hence, it is reasonable to consider that the *conceptual* fact table (about IP flow) is partitioned across the local data warehouses. OLAP queries are submitted to a Skalla coordinator, which is responsible to construct a distributed query execution plan, to submit it to Skalla sites, to collect the results and to send them back to the user. Submitted OLAP queries are translated into *GMDJ* expressions (which are composed by specialized *GMDJ* operators (Akinde & Böhlen, 2001). Distributed execution plans are constructed to execute each GMDJ expression.

These works show us how we can take advantage of alternative data partition and allocation solutions to parallelize a data warehouse efficiently, but they do not discuss the issue in a global environment. In the next subsection we discuss the use of the Grid as an underlying infrastructure for constructing and accessing highly distributed data.

Data Grids and Grid-Based Data Warehouses

The Grid is an infra-structure that enables transparent access to possibly heterogeneous shared resources (e.g. storages, computers, clusters and supercomputers) in multi-domain environments (Foster, 2001).

With the Grid, widely distributed resources can be used to cooperatively (or not) execute a job (or parts of it). In such context, the term *Data Grid* is commonly used in situations where large volumes of data are involved. Such data may be generated or consumed by grid applications, or even stored across different grid sites that can be viewed together as if they were a huge mass storage system (Baker et al, 2002). In data grids, geographically distributed users should transparently access widely distributed data with high levels of Quality of Service (QoS).

There are several *basic* aspects (like security and interoperability) that are common to almost all grid-based systems. Many of such basic functionalities were put together in Grid Resource Management (GRM) Systems.

GRM Systems and Generic Job Schedulers

Several GRM Systems have been developed in the last few years in order to facilitate the implementation of Grid-based applications. Some examples are Legion (Grimshaw et al, 1997) and the Globus Toolkit (GT) (Foster & Kesselman, 1997). Such systems enable the use of specialized job scheduling strategies and schedulers. For instance, Condor-G (Frey et al, 2001) and Nimrod-G (Buyya et al, 2000b) are some *general purpose* application level schedulers that work over the Globus Toolkit.

Condor-G is an extension of the Condor (Tannenbaum et al, 2002) batch scheduler developed to work over Globus. Condor-G uses *ClassAds* (*classified advertisements*) to schedule jobs between available resources. In such strategy, each resource has a ClassAd indicating its characteristics and usage constraints. Jobs also have their ClassAds, which indicate the resource requirements to execute them. Resources and jobs ClassAds are scanned by a matchmaker process, which looks forward to find compatible job's requirements and resource characteristics. After the matchmaker finds an appropriate resource to execute a job, any final details are negotiated with the resource agent and job execution may start.

In Nimrod-G, users specify jobs' deadlines. Each job is assigned to the resource that can execute it with the lowest cost, among those that commit to execute it by the specified deadline. Initially, Nimrod-G has used static information in order to choose the least expensive resource. Such static information was replaced by dynamic information with the introduction of the Grace (*GRid Architecture for Computational Economy*)

(Buyya et al, 2000) system. Grace provides a set of APIs that enable the implementation of auctions and negotiations between the scheduler and available resources. The auctions' results are used by Nimrod-G to choose the resource that can execute the job with the lowest associated cost. Nimrod-G also uses the GT to discover available resources and to manage remote job execution.

Although most grid schedulers are oriented to execute jobs according to users' expectations or requirements, some kind of load balancing strategy is usually useful in grids (Yagoubi & Slimani, 2007). The use of load balancing strategies for computational grids is discussed in (Cao et al, 2005; Koenig & Kale; 2007, Yagoubi & Slimani, 2007).

Cao et al (2003;2005) proposes the use software agents to schedule grid jobs and obtain good load balancing. Software agents are used to represent workstation clusters or multiprocessor machines that are available at the grid. All the existent agents have the same basic functionalities: (i) schedule job execution by the resource its represents; (ii) publish the resources computational capabilities, and (iii) cooperate with other agents in order to find a resource that cannot be executed locally. Each agent schedule job execution by the resource its represents considering a job execution time prediction (the PACE system (Nudd et al, 2000) is used to predict the resources' performance). For each new job, the agent verifies if the resource it represents can execute the job by its deadline. If so, then local job scheduling tries to reorder job execution in order to meet each job's deadline and to minimize the finish time of the last finished job. If it is predicted that the job cannot be locally executed by its deadline, then the agent searches between its *neighbors* agents for one that can execute the job by its deadline. The final job assignment may not be the optimal one, as the agent does not do exhaustive searches between available resources for the one that would finish job execution earlier.

Load-balancing for grid-enabled applications with high volumes of inter-processor communica-

tion is discussed in (Koenig & Kale, 2007). The available resources are hierarchically organized into clusters according to measured inter-processor communication latency. The proposed model comprises two phases. In the first phase jobs are allocated into processing nodes in order to minimize inter-cluster communication. Then, intra-cluster job assignment is done according to the processing capacity of each node: more work is assigned to nodes with faster processors than it is assigned to slower processor's nodes.

Although such job scheduling and load balancing policies fit well for the computational general-purpose grids, they do not consider some database specific factors, like data placement and skews that may happen during query execution. We discuss in the following subsection some database-oriented query scheduling and load balancing techniques that have been proposed. But it is important to notice that Grid Resource Managers (e.g. Legion and GT) should be used together with grid-based implementations of query schedulers, as GRM systems implement several *generic* functionalities (e.g. related to security and data replication) that are necessary for the grid-based DW.

Query Scheduling in Data Grids and Grid-Based Data Warehouses

Smith et al (2002) present the use of the Polar* distributed query processor in the Grid. For each submitted query, the Polar* processor generates a distributed query plan composed by operations are executed by different nodes. Alpdemir et al (2003) present the OGSA-DQP (*Distributed Query Processor based on the Open Grid Services Architecture* – OGSA (Foster et al, 2002)) architecture which is composed by a set of grid-services in order to enable the use of Polar* in a OGSA-compliant system. Gounaris et al (2005) discuss load balancing in OGSA-DQP, proposing data redistribution during query execution in order to reduce load misbalancing.

On the other hand, Ranganathan et al (2004)

have shown that grid-based data centric jobs' execution has a significantly better performance if no data movement is necessary during job execution (latency in Grids is not negligible). Ranganathan et al propose that in several situations it is worth to execute jobs in nodes that already have the necessary data to execute them even if such nodes are not idle (instead of moving data to idle nodes and start job execution on such nodes). Doing asynchronous data replication and job scheduling increases the number of alternative sites to execute incoming jobs with little effect on the performance of executing jobs.

Wehrle et al (2007) present architecture to implement grid-based data warehouses using the Globus Toolkit. Fact tables are fragmented and distributed over grid nodes. Dimension tables are all replicated on each grid node. A chunk identifier is used to refer to each tuple in the database (and its replicas). Chunks are organized in chunk blocks in order o facilitate data referencing and management. The query execution starts with the localization phase, when the submitted query is transformed into several queries each one accessing one or more chunk blocks. Then, the existence of local data that can answer the query is verified. In the case that the necessary data (in terms of chunk blocks) is not found locally, a global catalog is queried in order to identify remote nodes that have the necessary data to answer the query (or part of if). A cost function is used to construct a distributed query execution plan over available nodes.

Lawrence and Rau-Chaplin (2006) present a two-tiered query processing model for the grid-based data warehouse. The first tier is composed by cached data. OLAP servers are in the second tier. An R-Tree is used to index cached data and which data is stored at each server. At each site, a local scheduler searches for cached data that can totally or partially answer each submitted query. Then, the submitted query is re-written into a set of queries over the data fragments that cannot be obtained locally. Each *new* query (belonging to

the set of re-written queries) is sent to all server sites that may answer it (second tier). At each server site, a resource optimizer searches for the fastest way of answering the query (i.e. accessing the database server or computing the results from cached data at the server site) and, then, executes the query according to the alternative that have the lowest estimated execution cost.

In (Lawrence & Rau-Chaplin, 2006; Wehrle et al, 2007), local data is searched before remote data is queried. This strategy can be used in Grid-NPDW as well, but we discuss data placement and query scheduling, which are crucial for efficiency and availability when remote grid-based data warehouse must be used to answer a user query. In (Lawrence & Rau-Chaplin, 2006; Wehrle et al, 2007), cost models are used to predict the site that can execute a query faster. Besides the difficulty in obtaining a good execution time prediction model (that considers the available resource heterogeneity and data skews), such strategies do not take into account the changes in resource performance that can occur in the grid. In addition, it is important to notice that always scheduling the incoming queries to the node that executes each query faster without considering the actual node workload may lead to a great load unbalance, which reduces the system's throughput.

In the next Section, we present the Grid-NPDW strategy, which combines data partitioning and replication with a dynamic query scheduling model in order to obtain efficient availability when querying remote data over a grid-based data warehouse.

LOAD BALANCING AND HIGH AVAILABILITY IN GRID-NPDW

In the last years, huge volumes of data are being generated by global (real and virtual) organizations and global collaborations are becoming the norm. As data volumes increase, moving all the data across wide-area networks and build centralized data warehouses while also providing high Quality of Service levels for geographically distributed users may not be the best choice.

On the other hand, the available distributed resources (i.e. storage and computers) can be used to provide the desirable QoS levels. Distributed sites can be put together in order to execute user requests in parallel or cooperatively, reducing the network and hardware requirements that would exist if the data warehouse were stored at a single site. The Grid is the infra-structure that interconnects such distributed sites and provides transparency to users.

Hence, a generic grid-based DW is formed by various sites, which may be highly distributed and may belong to different real organizations (like the situations where industrial consortiums are formed to develop new products or where different scientific organizations come together in order to participate in a common investigation project forming a single *virtual* organization (Foster, 2001)). At each site one can have data warehouse users, data or both of them.

Data Placement and High Availability

Data placement is a key issue in grid-based systems (especially data warehouses), as moving data across different sites during query execution, can heavily depreciate query's performance (Ranganathan & Foster, 2004).

One straightforward approach to data placement in grid-based data warehouses is to consider ownership and access patterns. Placing data near the users that mostly access it is a reasonable start point. But other factors should be considered in order to generate a grid-based system with high availability and performance.

In Grid environments, shared resources may belong to different organizations. For this reason, domain controllers usually have some degree of autonomy to restrict remote access to local resources (Foster, 2001). Restriction rules on resource usage may be imposed, considering several security policies, like limiting resource access based on users profiles, on time frames or on usage limits. Hence, a domain's resource usage restrictions policy can make the locally stored data unavailable to other site's users (during certain time periods, for example). Besides that, it should be considered that network conditions in grids are somewhat unpredictable. In the general case, latency can affect query execution performance and, once in a while, a link between sites can go down.

In order to reduce the impact of these issues, we use data replication across different sites. But simply placing the entire DW at one machine and replicating it to other sites' servers may not be the wisest choice. We apply the NPDW strategy in the Grid environment using the idea of *Partitioned Replica Groups* (PRG) (Furtado, 2005b) to obtain efficient data allocation.

NPDW and Data Replication

In NPDW, data replication can be used to improve performance and availability. The first straightforward approach is to fully replicate (FR) a node's data into another processing node (that already has its own data). In such situation if a node (*Node I*) goes down, another processing node (*Node II*) can take its place and process the incoming requests that were directed to the unavailable node.

Although simple, FR can lead to a great drop in the system's performance if a node goes down: the *virtual* spare node (e.g. *Node II*) may have to process twice as many data when the original node (Node I) goes down. If we consider, for simplicity, that *Node I* and *Node II* are homogeneous, the system may take almost twice the time to complete a task even though a single node goes down. FR data allocation with no offline nodes and with one offline node is represented in Figure 3.

On the hand, the *Partitioned Replica Groups* (PRG) strategy can lead to a high availability configuration without such huge loss in performance when a node (or site) goes down. In PRG,

Figure 3. Sample FR configuration with all nodes online and with one node offline

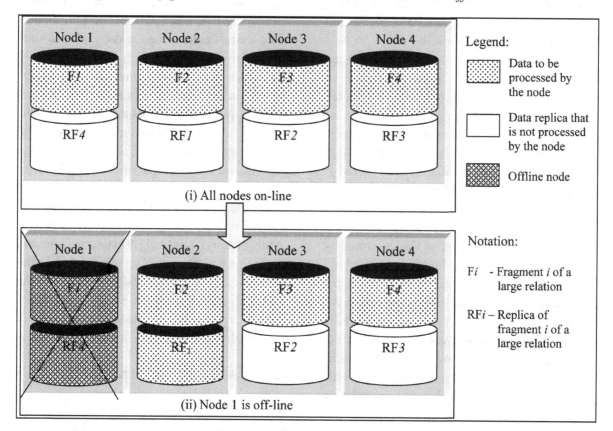

each node's partitions[2] are sliced and each slice is replicated in another processing node. Small dimension tables are already present in several nodes. Hence, if a node goes down, each of the online processing nodes would process its own data and a *slice* of the unavailable node's data. For example, let's consider a homogeneous system composed by X nodes and that takes t time units to process a request: if one node goes down, the system should take about $t + (\frac{t}{(X-1)})$ time units to process the request.

Figure 4 represents PRG data allocation with no offline nodes and with one offline node.

PRG and Grid-DPDW

In order to efficiently allocate replicas' slices, grid nodes can be grouped in order to form the *partitioned replica groups*. Partitions' replica slices from nodes of a group are placed at nodes of other groups. No partition replication is done in nodes from the same group.

As in the Grid it is somewhat more susceptible that a site become unavailable (e.g. domain specific policies or network conditions, as discussed before in this chapter) to nodes from other sites than two nodes from the same site become unavailable to each other, we consider each site to be a *partitioned replica group*. Therefore, large table's partitions replicas are sliced and placed at nodes of sites different from the one of the original node. No partition replicas are placed within the nodes of the same site.

This strategy aims at providing high availability (if an entire site does down, the system remains online) with high performance (the fall down of one site does not duplicate the necessary time to

Figure 4. Sample PRG configuration with all nodes online and with one node offline

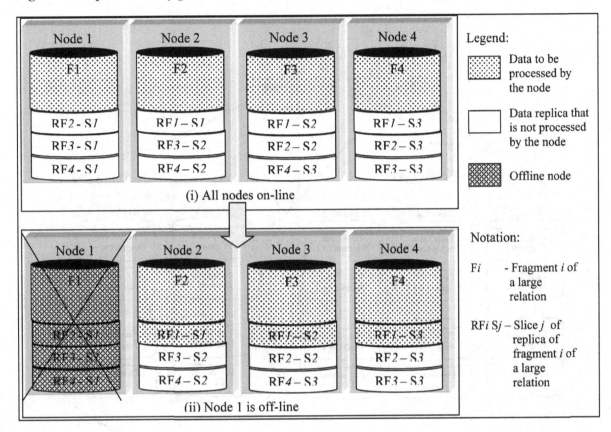

process a request).

An example of Grid-NPDW data allocation strategy is illustrated in Figure 5. A fact table is partitioned into *z* fragments that are placed in sites *i* and *j*. Grid sites with different numbers of processing nodes are considered. All fragments are replicated between the two represented replication groups.

Dynamic Scheduling for High Throughput

The Grid environment may be very heterogeneous: different number of processing nodes may be available at each site and processing nodes may have different computing and storage capacities; sites may be unreachable to remote users due to local policies; network conditions may vary over time and links between sites may be slow or broken during certain time periods. In such environment, a dynamic job scheduling policy is extremely important.

For high throughput-oriented Grid-NPDW environments, we use an on-demand task allocation policy. The used strategy aims at maximizing processing power usage: a new task is assigned to each node as soon as it becomes ready to execute it.

As in the dynamic on-demand task allocation strategy no task is pre-assigned to a node, it does load balancing even when extremely heterogeneous processing nodes are involved. Besides that, if a link goes down or if a site or node becomes unavailable for any reason, the system only has to re-schedule the task that the current unavailable node was executing just before it falls off: there is no need to re-schedule other pending or already assigned tasks.

Figure 5. Sample Grid-NPDW data allocation

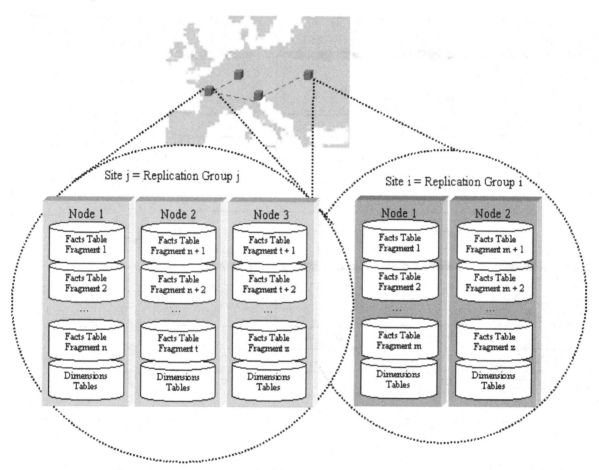

Task Generation and Job Execution

We call *jobs* to submitted queries. Each incoming job is placed in a job queue at a query scheduler node and receives a job identifier. Incoming jobs are sequentially processed, each job being transformed into a set of tasks. Tasks are re-written queries over distinct tables' fragments, whose results may be combined to generate the same result as the original query (query transformation is discussed in (Furtado, 2005)). Each task has an unique global identification (composed by the job identification and the task sequential number in the job). Besides that, each task maintains the identification of the data fragments over which it should be executed.

Once tasks are generated, each idle node receives one task to execute. No other tasks are pre-assigned to nodes. Task execution starts. At each node, a task execution is a SQL execution against the fragment that is identified in the task.

Every time a node finishes its task and becomes idle, it asks the query scheduler for a new task to execute. Then, if a pending task exists, it is assigned to the requester processing node. When an offline node becomes online, it also asks the scheduler for a task to execute. This dynamic demand-driven task allocation policy is similar to the one that has been used before in the parallel join operation (Lerner & Lifschitz, 1998).

The dynamic demand-driven strategy fits well with the Grid's site autonomy concept: any domain specific policy that limits the availability of a processing node can be easily implemented. For this, a processing node should not ask for new tasks when executing new tasks is not permitted by its domain specific policies (e.g. either for time frame constraints or for having reached the remote query execution limit).

Finally, the execution results of all tasks from the same job are merged in order to generate the job's result. This could be done by a central node, but more efficient results are obtained if distributed merging is used (Furtado, 2005).

Grid-NPDW Main Components

In order to implement the proposed approaches, a node must be used as a *Global Query Scheduler*. The main components of such *Global Query Scheduler* are:

- *Client Interface* – Implemented as a Grid Service, the *Client Interface* is responsible to accept *clients'* queries (both ad-hoc users' queries submitted through a simple Web page or queries submitted by a complex client application). Incoming queries are placed at a job queue in the *Execution Manager*;
- *Execution Manager* – This component manages the jobs queue, transforming each job into tasks and placing them at the *Task Manager's* tasks queue. In order to transform the incoming job into the necessary tasks, the *Execution Manager* must query for the information on the used data partitioning ranges. Such information is stored in a *Partition Meta-Base* stored at the *Global Query Scheduler;*
- *Partition Meta-Base* – Stores information about the global partitions, including partition attributes and the used partition criteria. Each partition has a unique global identification number. When local schedulers are used at each site, each global partition can be sliced into smaller fragments.

In this case, the matchmaking between the global partition schema and the locally used partition schema is done by a local scheduler;
- *Task Manager* – Pending tasks are at a task queue residing at *Task Manager*. When a processing node asks for a new task to execute, the *Task Manager* selects one that may be executed at the requester node. In order to select an adequate task, the *Task Manager* consults a global *Replica Catalog*. Then, *Task Manager* invokes the start of the scheduled query execution (for a Globus-based implementation of Grid-NPDW, it uses the GRAM (Czajkowski et al, 1998) service to start remote task execution). The *Task Manager* is also responsible to coordinate the generation of the job's result by the merge of its tasks results (in Globus-based implementations, GRAM is used to monitor remote task execution finish);
- *Processing Node Interface* – It is the API used by processing nodes in order to request for new tasks to execute. It can be implemented as a web service. Incoming requests are sent to *Task Manager*;
- *Replica Catalog* – It maintains information about the partition replicas existent at different sites. The used replica catalog must provide location information for each partition identifier;
- *Data Manager* – Although data warehouses are mostly read-only databases, periodic loads may occur. *Data Manager* coordinates the process of data partitioning and replication across different sites. Basic functionalities of GRM systems are used to provide efficient data transfer between sites. For instance, GridFTP (Allcock et al, 2005) may be used when Grid-NPDW runs over the Globus Toolkit. The Global Query Scheduler components are represented in Figure 6.

Figure 6. Global Query Scheduler Main Components

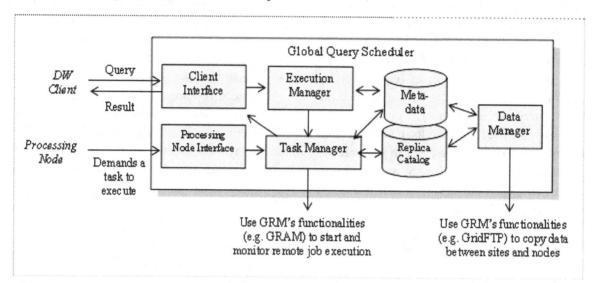

The Global Query Scheduler is capable to schedule query execution for *Processing Nodes*. Each *Processing Node* stores a (partial) copy of the data warehouse and is capable to execute SQL queries over such database. A *Processing Monitor Agent* also runs at each *Processing Node*. Such Agent periodically verifies if the node is capable to execute new tasks according to any domain specific resource usage constraints and asks for a new task to execute (invoking *Global Query Scheduler's Processing Node Interface*) whenever it is idle and resource usage constraints are fulfilled.

A *Processing Node* may represent any local shared computing resource, like a multiprocessor database server or a workstation cluster. It can also represent the entire set of shared machines at a single site. When a set of real computers is used as a single *Processing Node*, a local domain query scheduler should be used to schedule task execution between such machines.

In Figure 7, two possible simplified Grid-NPDW configurations are presented. Figure 7-a represents a site composed by several processing nodes with no local domain scheduler. In Figure 7-b, all the available resources from a site are or-

ganized in a single processing node: local domain schedulers are used. In the former configuration, the *Processing Monitor Agent* monitors the local scheduler queue in order to verify when a new task can be requested for the Central Scheduler. In case of more than one local resource managed by a local scheduler, the *Processing Monitor Agent* should also inform to Central Scheduler the available fragments over which the new task may run (the ones that are in the local resource that is idle).

The scheduling model composed by the use of local domain schedulers together with a central scheduler is known as *Hierarchical Scheduling* (Krauter et al, 2002). Such scheduling model is commonly used in Grid systems to improve scalability and to implement domain specific scheduling policies. Although the local scheduler is not necessary in Grid-NPDW to implement local domain resource usage constraints, its use can still improve the system's scalability (as all the local shared resources are seen as a single resource by the Central Scheduler). But the use of local schedulers also enables that each sites use large tables' partitioning methods different from the ones used by the Central Scheduler. In such

Figure 7. Possible Processing Nodes Organizations

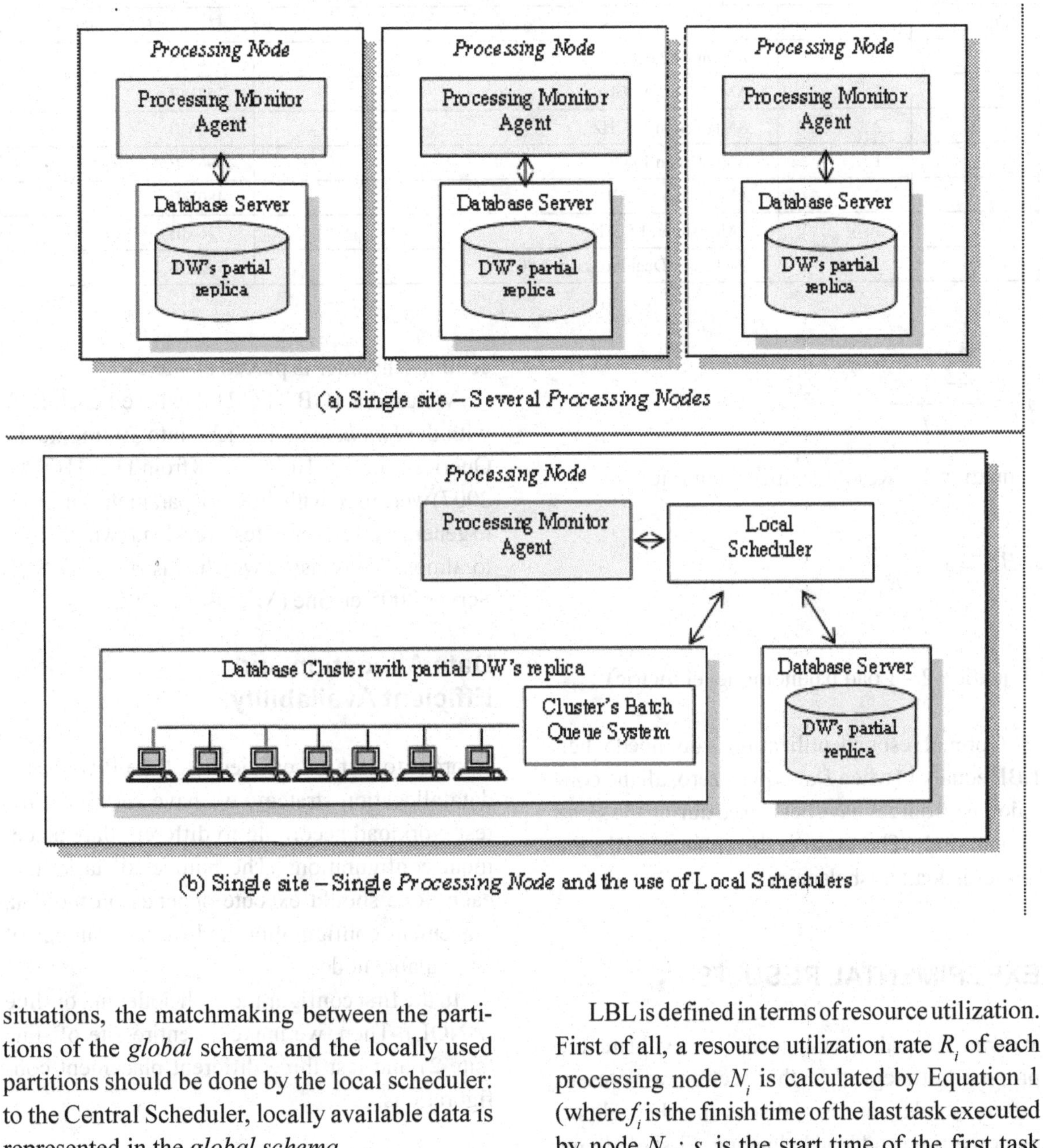

(a) Single site – Several *Processing Nodes*

(b) Single site – Single *Processing Node* and the use of Local Schedulers

situations, the matchmaking between the partitions of the *global* schema and the locally used partitions should be done by the local scheduler: to the Central Scheduler, locally available data is represented in the *global schema*.

Load Balancing Level Metric

In order to evaluate the benefits of any scheduling model, some metrics, like throughput and job's response time, can be used. Besides such metrics, we consider here the use of a metric called *Load Balancing Level* (LBL) (Cao et al, 2003).

LBL is defined in terms of resource utilization. First of all, a resource utilization rate R_i of each processing node N_i is calculated by Equation 1 (where f_i is the finish time of the last task executed by node N_i ; s_i is the start time of the first task executed by node N_i ; and t is the total execution time of the entire workload). Then, the average resource utilization rate R_A is computed as the quotient between R_i and the number of nodes. The LBL metric is obtained by Equation 2, where *Dev* represents the mean square deviation of R_i.

Table 1. Experimental Environment Description

Site	Node	Processor	RAM Memory
1	1	Pentium 4 2.66Ghz	448MB
2	1	AMD Duron 1.4Ghz	752MB
2	2	AMD Duron 1.6GHz	752MB
3	1	AMD Duron 1.6GHz	496MB
3	2	AMD Athlon 1.5GHz	480MB
4	1	AMD Athlon 1.5GHz	736MB
4	2	Intel Xeon Dual Processor 2.8Ghz	3.86GB

$$R_i = \frac{\sum_i f_i - s_i}{t}$$

(Equation 1 – Resource utilization rate)

$$LBL = 1 - \frac{Dev}{R_A}$$

(Equation 2 – Load balancing level metric)

Optimal resource utilization is obtained when LBL equals 1 (when *Dev* equals zero, all the considered resources have been used during the same time period). The lower is the value of LBL, the higher is load misbalancing.

EXPERIMENTAL RESULTS

We ran several tests in order to evaluate the proposed strategies. In this section we present the most relevant ones, discussing throughput, response time and load balancing. First of all, we present results that show the efficient availability of Grid-NPDW. Then, we show the benefits that can be obtained by the use of the proposed dynamic query scheduling policy.

Our experimental environment is composed by several nodes which are organized in four different sites. Nodes are briefly described in Table 1 (the central scheduler is placed at site 1).

We used a 1GB TPC-H database benchmark with the *Lineitem* table sliced into 30 fragments. Queries 1,5,7,8,9,10,14 and 18 from TPC-H (TPC, 2007) were used with different parameters in order to generate a 42 queries test workload (which leads to almost 1300 tasks) which was run over SQL Server 2005 engine (Microsoft, 2005).

Data Allocation and Efficient Availability

In order to test the efficiency of the PRG-based data allocation strategy, we have submitted the test workload according to different data placement configurations. The number of tasks that each node should execute depends on the data placement configuration and on the number of unavailable nodes.

In the first configuration, all nodes are on-line (ANOL). Then, we make an entire site off-line (site 2) and test three different placement configurations:

- *Full replication into a single node* (FRN) – data (*Lineitem* fragments) from nodes 1 and 2 of site 2 is replicated into node 1 of site 3.
- *Full replication into a single site* (FRS) – data (*Lineitem* fragments) from nodes 1 and 2 of site 2 are replicated into site 3. Data is partitioned between all the nodes from site 3.

Table 2. Measured Throughput - Percentage with respect to All Nodes On-Line configuration

Replica Placement Configuration	Measured Throughput (queries / minute)	Throughput percentage with respect to ANOL configuration
FRN	0.78	25.7%
FRS	1.58	52.3%
PRG	1.77	58.4%

- *Partitioned replica groups* (PRG) – *Lineitem* fragments from site 2 are balanced replicated over all available sites in the Grid.

For each configuration, we have measured throughput and mean response time. Tasks are allocated *in advance* to each on-line node in a round-robin strategy. Hence, when all nodes are on-line, each node executes 210 tasks (re-written queries).

In ANOL configuration (and with *in advance* scheduling), the entire workload is processed in almost 13.9 minutes (about 3 jobs per minute). Then, we have taken site 2 offline. It means that the online computing units represent almost 66.7% of those in ANOL configuration (without considering the scheduler node). Table 2 presents the measured throughputs in this new configuration and its percentage with respect to the one obtained in ANOL configuration according to the three considered data replication strategies.

The use of the PRG-based data replication strategy has lead to an acceptable drop in throughput. On the other hand, the other considered data replication strategies had lead to bad results (in FRN, a drop of 33.3% in the available process-

ing nodes caused a drop of almost 75% in the measured throughput). The good results from PRG are due to the load balancing level that is obtained in such configuration. Using PRG, each node executes 315 tasks; while in FRN a node executes 630 tasks and others execute 210 tasks, and in FRS the nodes from site 3 execute 840 tasks and the nodes from the other on-line processing site execute 420 tasks.

In the abovementioned tests, each job is transformed into several tasks that are allocated in a round-robin way to processing nodes. In such model, the drop in mean response time of submitted jobs had a behavior similar to the drop of the throughput level. Obtained results are represented in Table 3.

With all nodes on-line, the mean response time of the workload's queries was of about 454 seconds. When site 2 went off-line, the jobs' mean response time value has increased of almost 63% for PRG and of almost 235% for the FRN data replication configuration. Such high variation on response time was also due to load misbalancing. For instance, in the FRN configuration, the LBL metric value was 0.11, while in PRG configuration, it was of 0.96.

The obtained throughput and mean response

Table 3. Mean Job Response Time - Percentage with respect to All Nodes On-Line configuration

Replica Placement Configuration	Mean Response Time (seconds)	Mean response time percentage with respect to ANOL configuration
FRN	1,519.3	334.8%
FRS	837.9	184.6%
PRG	738.3	162.7%

Table 4. LBL value for several data placement and query scheduling configurations

Data Placement and Query Scheduling Model [3]	Load Balancing Level of the Configuration
ANOL with static scheduling	0.92
ANOL-DD	0.99
FRN with static scheduling	0.11
FRS with static scheduling	0.18
PRG with static scheduling	0.96
PRG-DD	0.99

time results for the several discussed configurations and that were presented in the previous tables show the importance of using a planned replication strategy for obtaining a highly available and efficient environment. The good results of the PRG-based replica allocation strategy show that this strategy is especially interesting for the Grid-based data warehouse.

But parallel query execution can be affected by several skew factors, including selectivity and heterogeneity skews (in fact, these two factors are the most relevant ones in PRG configuration, as different number of tuples result from each task execution and grid's nodes are heterogeneous). Therefore, the use of a dynamic query scheduling strategy that can deals with such skews may be useful. The results of experimental evaluation on the use of the demand-driven query scheduling policy are presented and discussed in the following subsection.

Dynamic Query Scheduling and Load Balancing

For each incoming job, there is no guarantee that generated tasks are all of the same size. Besides that, the computational environment of each grid site is usually heterogeneous. To choose a data allocation strategy that works together with a static query scheduling model and that can totally eliminate load misbalancing for any incoming workload (without knowing the workload in advance) and without using data movement during query execution is extremely difficult (if not impossible). Besides that, to do query movement during query execution in grid environment can highly degenerate performance (Ranganathan & Foster, 2004). Hence, even when all nodes are online, a dynamic query allocation policy is necessary to reduce load misbalancing and improve the system's performance.

Therefore, we have tested two more configurations, using the demand-driven task allocation strategy:

- *All nodes on-line with demand-driven scheduling* (ANOL-DD) – The demand-driven scheduling strategy is used with all sites on-line;
- *PRG-based replica allocation strategy with demand-driven scheduling* (PRG-DD) – The demand-driven query scheduling policy is used together with the PRG replica allocation strategy in a configuration with one processing site offline.

The following table presents the computed LBL values for all the evaluated configurations.

The high LBL values obtained in ANOL-DD and PRG-DD show the importance of using the dynamic demand-driven query scheduling policy. The success of such policies is based on its capabilities of assigning different number of tasks (of different sizes) to each node, reducing the

Figure 8. Number of tasks executed at each node: comparing static and dynamic scheduling

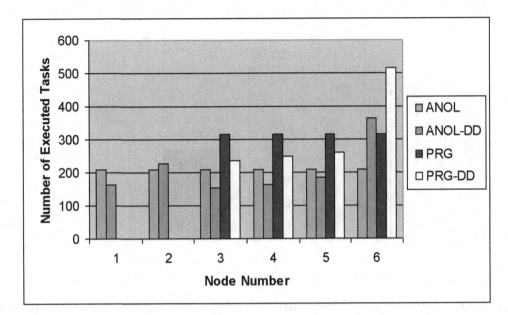

impact of data skews on performance (especially selectivity and heterogeneity skews).

In Figure 8, the number of tasks executed at each node for static and dynamic scheduling policies in the configurations with all nodes online and with one offline site is presented (nodes 1 and 2 belong to the offline site in PRG and PRG-DD configurations). Not only the dynamic scheduling policy assigned to each node a different number of tasks, but it has also assigned the highest number of tasks to the most powerful node.

The increase in the LBL level obtained with the use of demand-driven scheduling has caused benefits to the system's throughput and workload execution mean response time. The comparison between the measured throughput levels when using static and dynamic scheduling policies is presented in Figure 9. The use of dynamic scheduling has increased system's throughput in more than 10%.

An important improvement is also observed in mean response time (Figure 10): the reduction in mean response obtained when using dynamic

scheduling is greater than 20% in both ANOL and PRG configurations.

The abovementioned benefits that were obtained when using the demand-driven scheduling policy prove the importance of using a dynamic strategy to schedule query execution in the heterogeneous grid-based data warehouse.

CONCLUSION

The huge volumes of data that are currently being generated by global organizations must be transparently and efficiently queried by geographically distributed users. The use of distributed data warehouses may improve performance and reduce hardware requirements that would exist if a central site was used instead to store the entire database and to execute complex OLAP queries submitted by all users.

The Grid is the infra-structure that enables the use of distributed resources in order to provide a transparent access for the distributed grid-based data warehouse. But in order to obtain a

Figure 9. Throughput: comparing static and dynamic scheduling

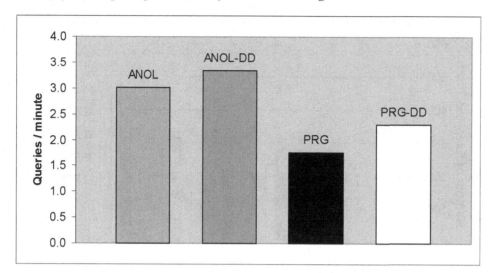

highly available and efficient environment, data placement and query scheduling must be well planned.

In this Chapter we presented the Grid-NPDW strategy to implement grid-based data warehouses. To provide efficient availability, we use a PRG-based data replication strategy, which replicates fragments of huge table across different sites. This increases data availability efficiently, by reducing the load misbalancing that would happen when a single node or site is used to replace other unavailable sites (or nodes), entirely processing large fact (and dimension) tables that should be processed by the unavailable processing elements.

Although, the use of the proposed data placement strategy reduces load misbalancing, it is still very susceptible to varying conditions when executing queries over the Grid, especially due to selectivity and heterogeneity skews. Hence, we use the PRG-replica placement strategy combined

Figure 10. Mean response time: comparing static and dynamic scheduling

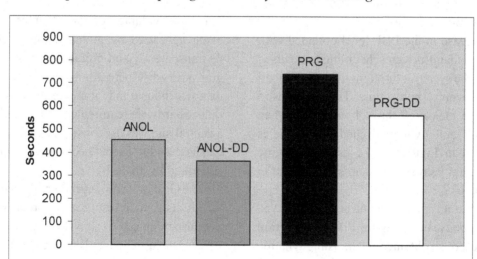

with a demand-driven dynamic query scheduling policy, which aims at maximizing resource utilization and reduces load misbalancing, thus improving the systems throughput and reducing the mean response time workloads' queries execution.

REFERENCES

Akal, F., Böhm, K., & Schek, H. (2002). OLAP query evaluation in a database cluster: A performance study on intra-query parallelism. In *Proceedings of the 6th East European Conference* (LNCS 2435, pp. 181-184).

Akinde, M. O., & Böhlen, M. H. (2001). Generalized MD-joins: Evaluation and reduction to SQL. In *Proceedings of the VLDB 2001 international Workshop on Databases in Telecommunications* (LNCS 2209, pp. 52-67).

Akinde, M. O., Böhlen, M. H., Johnson, T., Lakshmanan, L. V., & Srivastava, D. (2002). Efficient OLAP query processing in distributed data warehouses. In *Proceedings of the 8th international Conference on Extending Database Technology: Advances in Database Technology* (LNCS 2287, pp. 336-353).

Allcock, W., Bresnahan, J., Kettimuthu, R., & Link, M. (2005). The Globus striped GridFTP framework and server. In *Proceedings of the 2005 ACM/IEEE Conference on Supercomputing* (pp. 54-65).

Alpdemir, M., Mukherjee, A., Paton, N., Watson, P., Fernandes, A., Gounaris, A., & Smith, J. (2003). OGSA-DQP: A service-based distributed query processor for the Grid. In *Proceedings of UK e-Science All Hands Meeting*. EPSRC.

Baker, M., Buyya, R., & Laforenza, D. (2002). Grids and Grid technologies for wide-area distributed computing. *Software, Practice & Experience, 32*(15), 1437–1466. doi:10.1002/spe.488

Baralis, E., Paraboschi, S., & Teniente, E. (1997). Materialized views selection in a multidimensional database. In *Proceedings of the 23rd international Conference on Very Large Data Bases* (pp. 156-165).

Buyya, R., Abramson, D., & Giddy, J. (2000). Economy driven resource management architecture for computational power Grids. In *Proceedings of the 7th International Conference on Parallel and Distributed Processing Techniques and Applications (PDPTA2000)* (pp. 283-289).

Buyya, R., Abramson, D., & Giddy, J. (2000). Nimrod/g: An architecture of a resource management and scheduling system in a global computational Grid. In *Proceedings of the Fourth International Conference/Exhibition on High Performance Computing in the Asia-Pacific Region, 1* (pp. 283-289).

Cao, J., Spooner, D. P., Jarvis, S. A., & Nudd, G. R. (2005). Grid load balancing using intelligent agents. *Future Generation Computer Systems, 21*(1), 135–149. doi:10.1016/j.future.2004.09.032

Cao, J., Spooner, D. P., Jarvis, S. A., Saini, S., & Nudd, G. R. (2003). Agent-based Grid load balancing using performance-driven task scheduling. In *Proceedings of the 17th international Symposium on Parallel and Distributed Processing (IPDPS)*, (pp. 49).

Chaudhuri, S., & Dayal, U. (1997). An overview of data warehousing and OLAP technology. *SIGMOD Record, 26*(1), 65–74. doi:10.1145/248603.248616

Czajkowski, K., Foster, I. T., Karonis, N. T., Kesselman, C., Martin, S., Smith, W., & Tuecke, S. (1998). A resource management architecture for metacomputing systems. In *Proceedings of the Workshop on Job Scheduling Strategies For Parallel Processing* (LNCS 1459, pp. 62-82).

Foster, I., & Kesselman, C. (1997). Globus: A metacomputing infrastructure toolkit. *The International Journal of Supercomputer Applications, 11*(2), 115–128.

Foster, I., Kesselman, C., Nick, J., & Tuecke, S. (2002). The physiology of the Grid: An open Grid services architecture for distributed systems integration. In *Globus project tech report*.

Foster, I. T. (2001). The anatomy of the Grid: Enabling scalable virtual organizations. *In Proceedings of the 7ᵗʰ international Euro-Par Conference on Parallel Processing* (LNCS 2150, pp. 1-4).

Frey, J., Tannenbaum, T., Livny, M., Foster, I., & Tuecke, S. (2001). Condor-G: A computation management agent for multi-institutional Grids. In *Proceedings of the 10ᵗʰ IEEE international Symposium on High Performance Distributed Computing* (pp. 55).

Furtado, P. (2004). Workload-based placement and join processing in node-partitioned data warehouses. In *Proceedings of the 6ᵗʰ International Conference on Data Warehousing and Knowledge Discovery* (LNCS 3181, pp. 38-47).

Furtado, P. (2004). Experimental evidence on partitioning in parallel data warehouses. In *Proceedings of the 7ᵗʰ ACM international Workshop on Data Warehousing and OLAP* (pp. 23-30).

Furtado, P. (2005). Hierarchical aggregation in networked data management. In *Proceedings of the International Euro-Par Conference on Parallel Processing* (LNCS 3648, pp. 360-369).

Furtado, P. (2005). Replication in node partitioned data warehouses. In *Proceedings of the VLDB Workshop on Design, Implementation, and Deployment of Database Replication (DIDDR)*.

Gounaris, A., Smith, J., Paton, N., Sakellariou, R., Fernandes, A., & Watson, P. (2005). Adapting to changing resource performance in Grid query processing. In *Data Management in Grids* (DMG) (pp. 30-44).

Grimshaw, A. S., & Wulf, W. A., & CORPORATE The Legion Team. (1997). The Legion vision of a worldwide virtual computer. *Communications of the ACM, 40*(1), 39–45. doi:10.1145/242857.242867

Koenig, G., & Kale, L. (2007). Optimizing distributed application performance using dynamic Grid topology-aware load balancing. In *Proceedings of the 21ˢᵗ IEEE International Parallel and Distributed Processing Symposium (IPDPS 2007)* (pp. 1-10).

Krauter, K., Buyya, R., & Maheswaran, M. (2002). A taxonomy and survey of Grid resource management systems for distributed computing. In [SPE]. *Software, Practice & Experience, 32*(2), 135–164. doi:10.1002/spe.432

Lawrence, M., & Rau-Chaplin, A. (2006). The OLAP-enabled Grid: Model and query processing algorithms. In *Proceedings of the 20ᵗʰ international Symposium on High-Performance Computing in An Advanced Collaborative Environment* (pp. 4).

Lerner, A., & Lifschitz, S. (1998). A study of workload balancing techniques on parallel join algorithms. In *Proceedings of the International Conference on Parallel and Distributed Processing Techniques and Applications (PDPTA)*. (pp. 966-973).

Lima, A., Mattoso, M., & Valduriez, P. (2004). Adaptive virtual partitioning for OLAP query processing in a database cluster. In *Proceedings of the Brazilian Symposium on Databases (SBBD)* (pp. 92-105).

Microsoft. (2005). *Microsoft SQL server 2005 home page*. Retrieved November 2007, from http://www.microsoft.com/sql/

Nudd, G. R., Kerbyson, D. J., Papaefstathiou, E., Perry, S. C., Harper, J. S., & Wilcox, D. V. (2000). Pace--a toolset for the performance prediction of parallel and distributed systems. *International Journal of High Performance Computing Applications, 14*(3), 228–251. doi:10.1177/109434200001400306

O'Neil, P., & Graefe, G. (1995). Multi-table joins through bitmapped join indices. *SIGMOD Record, 24*(3), 8–11. doi:10.1145/211990.212001

Ranganathan, K., & Foster, I. (2004). Computation scheduling and data replication algorithms for data Grids. In *Grid Resource Management: State of the Art and Future Trends* (pp. 359-373). Amsterdam: Kluwer Academic Publishers.

Röhm, U., Böhm, K., & Schek, H. (2000). OLAP query routing and physical design in a database cluster. In *Proceedings of the 7th international Conference on Extending Database Technology: Advances in Database Technology* (LNCS 1777, pp. 254-268).

Smith, J., Gounaris, A., Watson, P., Paton, N. W., Fernandes, A. A., & Sakellariou, R. (2002). Distributed query processing on the Grid. In *Proceedings of the Third international Workshop on Grid Computing* (LNCS 2536, pp. 279-290).

Stöhr, T., Märtens, H., & Rahm, E. (2000). Multi-dimensional database allocation for parallel data warehouses. In *Proceedings of the 26th international Conference on Very Large Data Bases* (pp. 273-284).

Tannenbaum, T., Wright, D., Miller, K., & Livny, M. (2002). Condor: A distributed job scheduler. In *Beowulf Cluster Computing with Linux* (pp. 307-350).

Transaction processing council benchmarks. (2007). Retrieved November 2007, from http://www.tpc.org/

Walton, C. B., Dale, A. G., & Jenevein, R. M. (1991). A taxonomy and performance model of data skew effects in parallel joins. In *Proceedings of the 17th international Conference on Very Large Data Bases* (pp. 537-548).

Wehrle, P., Miquel, M., & Tchounikine, A. (2007). A Grid services-oriented architecture for efficient operation of distributed data warehouses on Globus. In *Proceedings of the 21st international Conference on Advanced Networking and Applications* (pp. 994-999). Washington, DC: IEEE Computer Society.

Yagoubi, B., & Slimani, Y. (2007). Task load balancing strategy for Grid computing. *Journal of Computer Science, 3*(3), 186–194.

ENDNOTES

[1]   Information about packets transferred from a given source to a given destination. This includes, for example, origin and destination IP, port and mask, besides the number of transferred packets and the total transferred bytes.

[2]   Remember that in NPDW large fact and dimension relations are partitioned and placed at different nodes.

[3]   ANOL and ANOL-DD are configurations where all nodes are online. In all other configurations, site 2 is offline. But comparing the LBL value of configurations with different number of nodes is possible, as the LBL metric is concerned about the utilization level of online nodes, no matter how many they are.

Section 4
Data Mining Techniques

Chapter 10
MOSAIC:
Agglomerative Clustering with Gabriel Graphs

Rachsuda Jiamthapthaksin
University of Houston, USA

Jiyeon Choo
University of Houston, USA

Chun-sheng Chen
University of Houston, USA

Oner Ulvi Celepcikay
University of Houston, USA

Christian Giusti
University of Udine, Italy

Christoph F. Eick
University of Houston, USA

ABSTRACT

Strong theoretical foundation and low computational complexity make representative-based clustering one of the most popular approaches for a clustering problem. Despite those superiorities, it presents two main drawbacks: the shape of clusters obtained is limited to convex shapes, and its performance is highly dependent on seeds initialization. To address these problems, the authors introduce MOSAIC, a novel agglomerative clustering algorithm, which greedily merges neighboring clusters maximizing a plug-in fitness function. The key idea is that by considering neighboring relationship computed using Gabriel Graphs among cluster, MOSAIC can derive non-convex shapes as the unions of small clusters previously generated by a representative-based clustering algorithm. The authors evaluate MOSAIC for traditional unsupervised clustering with k-means and DBSCAN, and also for supervised clustering. The experimental results show that compared to k-means stand-alone, their proposed post-processing techniques obtain higher quality clusters, whereas compared to DBSCAN results, MOSAIC is capable of identifying comparable arbitrary shape clusters, given a suitable fitness function. In addition, MOSAIC

DOI: 10.4018/978-1-60566-748-5.ch010

Copyright © 2010, IGI Global. Copying or distributing in print or electronic forms without written permission of IGI Global is prohibited.

can cope with problems of clustering on high dimensional data. The authors also claim that MOSAIC can be employed as an effective post-processing clustering algorithm to further improve the quality of clustering.

1 INTRODUCTION

Representative-based clustering methods work by initially selecting a set of representatives and assigning each object of the dataset to the closest representative. The most popular representative-based clustering algorithm is k-means, which uses centroids of clusters as representatives and iteratively updates both clusters and centroids until no change occurs and the best local configuration is reached. k-means is widely used because of its low computational complexity, $O(k \cdot t \cdot n)$ where k is the number of clusters, t is the number of iterations and n is the number of objects in the dataset. In spite of its fast computation, when using k-means we have to deal with three main problems. First, the number of clusters k has to be known prior to being used as a parameter. Second, the clusters obtained by using this technique are always convex and it is not possible to get good results when dealing with non convex shapes (Jiang, 2004) and third, the method is very sensitive to the initialization of representatives and also to the outliers.

Agglomerative hierarchical clustering (AHC) is one of the techniques capable of detecting clusters of arbitrary shapes (Tan, 2005, pp. 516-520). It merges the two closest clusters; because it does not consider any other merging candidates,

the search space is very narrow, which results in missing many high quality solutions. Moreover, the computational complexity of this technique is $O(n*n)$ or worse, therefore it is not applicable to very large datasets.

In this chapter, we propose a new technique combining advantages of the representative-based clustering and agglomerative clustering. This hybrid clustering algorithm makes use of an externally given fitness function in order to greedily merge neighboring clusters. The neighboring relationship is computed by using Gabriel Graphs (Gabriel, 1969), one of the most popular proximity graphs, and non-convex shapes are created by merging a set of small convex clusters that have been generated using a representative-based clustering algorithm, as illustrated in Fig. 1. The art of creating mosaics refers to the procedure that assembles small tiles in order to create a sophisticated drawing; in the same way our method, called MOSAIC, merges small convex clusters together in order to obtain better clusters having a non-convex shape where needed.

By using proximity graphs, MOSAIC is able to conduct a very wide search, which in turn results in obtaining higher quality clusters. Moreover, the computationally expensive agglomerative clustering step is not run for the whole dataset (n),

Figure 1. An illustration of MOSAIC's approach © 2007 Springer. Used with permission.

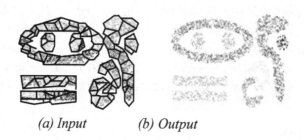

(a) Input   (b) Output

Figure 2. Pseudo code for MOSAIC © 2007 Springer. Used with permission.

1. Run a representative-based clustering algorithm to create a large number of clusters.
2. Read the representatives of the obtained clusters C_i.
3. Create a merge candidate relation using proximity graphs.
4. WHILE there are merge-candidates(C_i, C_j) left
    BEGIN
    Merge the pair of merge-candidates(C_i, C_j), that enhances fitness function q the most, into a new cluster C'.
    Update merge-candidates:
    Merge-Candidate(C', C) ⇔
    Merge-Candidate(C_i, C) ∨ Merge-Candidate(C_j, C)
    END
    RETURN the best clustering X found.

but only for the set of representatives (k) where $k \ll n$. In this way, the agglomerative technique is executed for usually less than 1,000 iterations, reducing the overall computational complexity. Our technique is highly generic and uses the following components: the representative-based clustering, the proximity graph and the cluster evaluation function, which can be replaced by any similar method.

Fig. 2 gives the pseudo code of the proposed MOSAIC algorithm. First MOSAIC obtains a set of cluster representatives from a representative-based clustering algorithm. Next, it finds a merge-candidate relation by using a proximity graph. After that, MOSAIC iteratively merges a pair of merging candidates, which maximizes the given fitness function q, and then incrementally updates the merge-candidate relation. The algorithm terminates if there is no merging candidate left, and returns the best clustering found.

In summary, main contributions presented in this research are:

*   A hybrid clustering algorithm that combines representatives-based clustering and agglomerative clustering is introduced.

*   The proposed technique is highly generic and not restricted to any representative clustering algorithms or fitness functions.
*   MOSAIC performs a wider search for merging candidates compared to traditional agglomerative clustering algorithms.
*   MOSAIC can be employed as a post-processing method to identify clusters with complex shapes.

The remainder of this work is organized as follows: in section 2 we provide details on MOSAIC and also explain cluster evaluation measures used in traditional and supervised clustering. The time complexity of MOSAIC is also analyzed. Section 3 reports the experimental evaluation of MOSAIC. Section 4 introduces the related work and in section 5 the conclusions are given.

2 POST-PROCESSING WITH MOSAIC

In this section, we provide more details on MOSAIC by first introducing Gabriel Graphs and other proximity graphs and their usage in agglomerative clustering. Then, we discuss clustering evaluation measures employed in our fitness

Figure 3. Pseudo code for constructing Gabriel graphs. © 2007 Springer. Used with permission.

Let $R = \{r_1, r_2, ..., r_n\}$, be a set of cluster representatives.

FOR each pair of representatives $(r_i, r_j) \in R^2$:

IF for each representative r_k, the following inequality holds

$$d(r_i, r_j) \le \sqrt{d^2(r_i, r_k) + d^2(r_j, r_k)}$$

where $k \ne i, j$ and $r_k \in R$,

THEN r_i and r_j are neighboring.

$d(r_i, r_j)$ denotes the distance of representatives r_i and r_j.

---

functions. Finally, we analyze the complexity of the MOSAIC.

2.1 Using Gabriel Graphs for Determining Neighboring Clusters

Given a set of objects, proximity graphs (Toussaint, 1980) are capable of representing neighboring relationships. In context of clustering Delaunay graph (DG) (Kirkpatrick, 1980) is one of the most popular choices employed to generate relationships of neighboring clusters. The shapes of these clusters can be produced using Voronoi cells which are dual to Delaunay graphs.

The algorithm used to generate the Delaunay graphs from a set of objects is called Delaunay triangulation (DT) (Okabe, 1992). High dimensional datasets are not suitable for Delaunay triangulation since its time complexity is proportional to the number of dimensions: $O(n^{d/2})$, where n is the number of graph vertices and d is the dimensionality of the dataset. In order to avoid this high computational complexity MOSAIC uses Gabriel graphs (GG) (Gabriel, 1969) instead, which is a sub-graph of the DG. In GG, two points are categorized as Gabriel neighbors if there is not another point in their diametric sphere. Since the percentage of the edges of a DG preserved in corresponding GG is very high, Gabriel graphs provide very good approximations of Delaunay graphs (Asano, 1990).

The time complexity to construct Gabriel graphs is $O(dn^3)$, but faster approximate algorithms that have lower time complexity of $O(dn^2)$) exist (Bhattacharya, 1981). The pseudo code of the algorithm to construct the Gabriel graph is shown in Fig. 3. MOSAIC first, constructs the Gabriel graph using the set of representatives, which in case of k-means corresponds to the cluster centroids, and then determines which of the initial clusters are neighboring using a boolean merge-candidate relation that is constructed using this graph.

Then, this merge-candidate relation is updated incrementally each time a merge of clusters is performed. The construction of Gabriel graph is illustrated in Fig. 4. In this figure, black polygons represent the clusters generated by the representative-based algorithm, red dots represent the cluster representatives, and yellow segments represent the neighboring relationship (e.g. Merge-Candidates)

2.2 Cluster Evaluation Measures for Traditional Clustering

In order to assess the quality of a clustering, many cluster evaluation measures have been developed in the literature (Tan, 2005, pp. 532-555). In this work, we utilize three popular cluster evaluation measures: Cohesion, Separation, and Silhouettes (Rousseeuw, 1987). Cohesion measures the tight-

Figure 4. Gabriel graph for clusters generated by a representative-based clustering algorithm

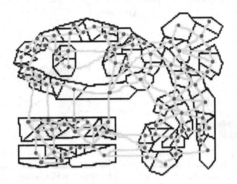

ness of a cluster while Separation measures how well-separated a cluster is from other clusters. The formula of both evaluation measures are defined as:

Let $O=\{o_1,...,o_n\}$ be the dataset to be clustered, d_{ij} be the distance between objects o_i and o_j, $X=\{C_1,...,C_k\}$ be a clustering of O with $C_i \subseteq O$ and $C_i \cap C_j = \varnothing$ for $i \neq j$ $Intra(X)$ be the number of intra-cluster distances and $Inter(X)$ be the number of inter-cluster distances in a clustering X,

$$Cohesion(X) = \frac{Sumintra(X)}{Intra(X)}$$

$$Separation(X) = \frac{Suminter(X)}{Inter(X)}$$

where,

$$Sumintra(X) = \sum_{i<j,\, o_i \text{ and } o_j \text{ belong to the same cluster}} d_{i,j}$$

$$Suminter(X) = \sum_{i<j,\, o_i \text{ and } o_j \text{ belong to different clusters}} d_{i,j}$$

On the other hand, Silhouettes considers both separation and cohesion and has been extensively used in clustering evaluation. The equation to estimate the Silhouette Coefficient s_i for each object o_i

belonging to cluster C_k is given in equation (1):

$$s_i = \frac{(a_i - b_i)}{\max(a_i, b_i)} \qquad (1)$$

where,

$$a_i = \min_m \left(\frac{1}{|C_m|} \sum_{o_j \in C_m} d_{ij} \right), \quad m \neq k \text{ and} \qquad (2)$$

$$b_i = \frac{1}{|C_k|} \sum_{o_j \in C_k} d_{ij}. \qquad (3)$$

In the equation (1), a_i represents the minimum of average dissimilarity of an object o_i compared to all objects o_j in other clusters. b_i represents the average dissimilarity of an object o_i to all other remaining objects within the same cluster. Since we are interested in measuring the entire clustering quality rather than quality of one object, we take the average of Silhouettes over whole dataset. So, the fitness function $q(X)$ that uses these values becomes:

$$q(X) = \frac{1}{n} \sum_{i=1}^{n} s_i \qquad (4)$$

where n represents the number of objects in a dataset and X is the dataset partition. We simply

Figure 5. Differences between traditional clustering and supervised clustering.

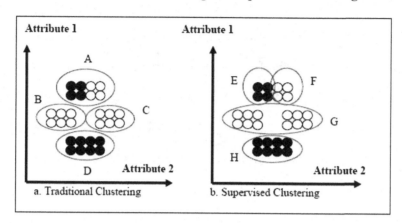

call this fitness function, Silhouettes through the rest of the chapter.

2.3 A Cluster Evaluation Measure for Supervised Clustering

Due to the fact that MOSAIC supports plug-in fitness functions, it can be used as a supervised clustering algorithm. In general, supervised clustering is applied to classified examples with the aim of producing clusters that have high probability density with respect to individual classes. Moreover, in supervised clustering, we also like to keep the number of clusters small, and examples are assigned to clusters using a notion of closeness with respect to a given distance function. Fig. 5 illustrates the differences between a traditional and a supervised clustering. Let us assume that the black examples and the white examples represent objects belonging to two different classes. A traditional clustering algorithm would, very likely, identify the four clusters depicted in Fig. 5 (a). This clustering would not be very attractive in the case of supervised clustering because cluster A has low purity of 50%, containing examples of two classes; moreover, the white examples are subdivided into two separate clusters B and C, although they are neighboring.

A supervised clustering algorithm that maximizes class purity, on the other hand, would split cluster A into two clusters E and F (Fig. 5 (b)). Another characteristic of supervised clustering is that it tries to keep the number of clusters low. Consequently, clusters B and C would be merged into a single cluster without compromising class purity while reducing the number of clusters.

In the experiments, we evaluate our post-processing technique using a reward-based fitness function. In particular, the quality $q(X)$ of a clustering X is computed as the sum of the rewards obtained for each cluster $c \in X$. Cluster rewards are computed as the product of interestingness of a cluster and the size of a cluster. More specifically, the evaluation function $q(X)$ is defined as follows:

$$q(X) = \sum_{c \in X} \mathrm{Re}\,ward(c) = \sum_{c \in X} \frac{i(c) \times \left(|c|\right)^{\beta}}{n^{\beta}}$$

with the interestingness $i(c)$ of a cluster c be defined as follows:

$$i(c) = \begin{cases} \left(\dfrac{(purity_Y(c) - hst)}{(1 - hst)}\right)^\eta & if \ purity_Y > hst \\[3ex] \left(\dfrac{(cst - purity_Y(c))}{cst}\right)^\eta & if \ purity_Y < cst \\[3ex] 0 & otherwise \end{cases}$$

where hst and cst are hotspot and coolspot purity thresholds, and $purity_Y(c)$ is the percentage of examples in cluster c that belong to the class of interest Y.

In general, we are interested in finding larger clusters if the larger clusters are at least equally as interesting as smaller clusters. Consequently, our evaluation scheme uses a parameter β with $\beta > 1$; that is, fitness value increases nonlinearly with cluster-size dependent on the value of β, favoring clusters with more objects. Selecting larger values for the parameter β usually results in a smaller number of clusters in the best cluster-ing X. The measure of interestingness i relies on a class of interest Y, and assigns rewards to regions in which the distribution of class Y significantly deviates from the prior probability of class Y in the whole dataset.

The parameter η determines how quickly the reward function grows to maximum reward of 1. If η is set to 1 it grows linearly, if it is set to 2, a quadratic function would be used that grows significantly slower initially. In general, if we are interested in giving higher rewards to purer clusters, it is desirable to choose large values for η: e.g. $\eta=8$.

To clarify the reward-based fitness function, we generate an example to illustrate the calculation as follows: Let us assume a clustering X that contains 1,000 examples has to be evaluated with respect to a class of interest "Poor". Suppose that the generated clustering X subdivides the dataset into three clusters c_1, c_2, c_3 with the following characteristics. $|c_1| = 250$, $|c_2| = 200$, $|c_3| = 550$;

$purity_{Poor}(c_1) = 130/250$, $purity_{Poor}(c_2) = 20/200$, $purity_{Poor}(c_3) = 50/550$. Moreover, the following parameters used in the fitness function are as follows: $\beta = 1.1$, $\eta=1$. A *coolspot* (cst=0.1) is defined as a cluster that contains less than 10% and a *hotspot* (hst=0.3) is a cluster that has more than 30% of instances of the class "Poor". Due to the settings clusters that contain between 10% and 30% instances of the class "Poor" do not receive any reward at all; therefore, no reward is given to cluster c_2 in the example. The remaining clusters received rewards because the distribution of class "Poor" in the cluster is significantly higher or lower than the corresponding threshold. Consequently, the reward for the first cluster c_1 is $11/35 \times (250)1.1$ since $purity_{Poor}(c_1) = 52\%$ is greater than hotspot which is 30%, $11/35$ is obtained by applying the function $purity_Y(c)$, thus we get $purity_{Poor}(c_1) = ((0.52-0.3)/(1-0.3)) \times 1 = 11/35$. Rewards of other clusters are computed similarly and the following overall reward for X is obtained:

$$q_{Poor}(X) = \frac{\dfrac{11}{35} \times 250^{1.1} + 0 + \dfrac{1}{11} \times 550^{1.1}}{1{,}000^{1.1}} = 0.115$$

2.4 Complexity

Our hybrid clustering algorithm operates in a time complexity that is a function of two compo-nents; the complexity of the representative-based clustering algorithm and the complexity of the agglomerative clustering. As mentioned before, the cost of constructing Gabriel Graph (GG) is $O(k^3)$ where k is the number of the representatives. The next step is to merge the k vertices of the GG. Because the Gabriel Graph is a connected subset of a Delaunay Graph which is a planar graph, the number of the edges e will have a value within the following interval: $k-1 \leq e \leq 3k-6$. This indicates that the number of edges is always linear to the number of vertices in the graph: $e=O(k)$. The merge-candidates are given by the edges of the Gabriel Graph; this means that, at each time, we have $O(k)$ merge-candidates. In each iteration, k is decreased by one. Therefore, $O(k-i)$ merge-candidates have to be evaluated at the ith iteration and the complexity of total fitness function evaluations can be represented as: $O(k-1)+O(k-2)+\ldots+1$ which adds up to $O(k^2)$. Considering all these, the time complexity for MOSAIC algorithm becomes $O(k^3+k^2 \cdot O(q(X)))$ where $O(q(X))$ represents the time complexity of the fitness function. The complexity of the MOSAIC algorithm can be reduced by computing the fitness value of a clustering incrementally, where previous fitness function values can be reused in merging steps instead of recalculating all the fitness values.

2.5 Incremental Update of Silhouette Function

In this section, a detailed description of the technique that can be used for incrementally updating the Silhouette function will be provided:

The Silhouette function is computed by using the following values for each object $o_i \in C_k$:

$$a_{i,m} = \frac{1}{|C_m|} \sum\nolimits_{o_j \in C_m} d_{i,j} \quad (3) \text{ and}$$

$$A_{i,j} = \left(\sum\nolimits_{o_m \in C_j} d_{i,m} \right)$$

where $d_{i,j}$ is the Euclidean distance between objects *i-th* and *j-th*.

Thus, at each merging step p, for each object o_i, we should compute each possible

$$B_{i,j} = \left(\sum\nolimits_{o_m \in C_j} 1 \right)$$

and then find out the minimum amongst them.

Since the procedure merges only two clusters at a time, not all the values a_i and b_i will be changed at each computational step p. If we more deeply analyze the way the Silhouette values change, we are able to detect two main cases, each one can be decomposed into two sub-cases:

1. Object o_i belongs to a cluster that has just been merged with another cluster.
2. Object o_i does not belong to a cluster that has been merged with another cluster during the computational step p.

Case 1:
This case is applied when the object $o_i \in C_k$ that we are taking into account belongs to a cluster which has just been merged by the merging procedure. This case must be divided in two sub-cases:

a. The cluster C_k has not been merged with the cluster that minimized the eq. (1) at the step $p-1$. Since the value of a_i is computed only by using objects belonging to external clusters, the cluster minimizing the eq. (1) remains the same, therefore, in this case $a_i(p) = a_i(p-1)$, where p is the current step of computation.

b. The cluster C_k has been merged with the cluster that minimized the eq. (1) at the step $p-1$. The value of a_i is computed using objects belonging to external clusters, but in this case the cluster minimizing the eq. (1) cannot remain the same, because it has just been merged with the cluster C_k. This means that at step p, the index of the cluster that minimizes eq. (1) is the second best value for the eq. (1) at the previous step: $a_i(p) = secondbest(a_i(p-1))$.

Case 2:

This case is applied when the object $o_i \in C_k$ that we are taking into account doesn't belong to one of the two clusters which have just been merged together by the merging procedure. Even this case must be divided in two sub-cases similarly to the case 1:

a. Let C_l and C_r be the two clusters that have just been merged and let q be the index of the cluster that minimized eq. (1) at step $p-1$ with $q \neq l, r$. In this case, the index of the cluster that minimizes the eq. (1) at step p must be chosen between index q (the previous best) and the index of the new cluster $(l+r)$, thus:

$a_i(p) = min(a_i(p-1), a_{i,l+r}(p-1))$ but it's easy to prove that:$a_i(p) = min(a_i(p-1), a_{i,l+r}(p-1)) = a_i(p-1)$.

b. Let C_l and C_r be the two clusters that have just been merged and let l or r the index of the cluster that minimized eq. (1) at step $p-1$. In this case, the cluster that minimized the eq. (1) at the previous step does not exist anymore, thus the index that minimizes the equation must be chosen between the previous second best value and the new cluster $C(l+r)$:

$a_i(p) = min(secondbest\ a_i(p-1), a_{i,l+r}(p))$

It is clear that this is the only case in which we have a computational complexity that is different from $O(1)$. Thus, in order to compute the complexity, we have to estimate the number of times this case occurs.

Now it remains to compute incrementally the value of b_i at each step p. In order to maintain such a value updated, without recomputing it every time, we can compute two matrices $(n \times k)$, where n is the number of objects and k the number of clusters such as:

$$\frac{A_{i,l} + A_{i,r}}{B_{i,l} + B_{i,r}} \text{ and } A_{i,l+r} = A_{i,l} + A_{i,r}.$$

If at step p, clusters C_l and C_r have been merged together, we can recompute all the new values of b_i (for each $i \in C_{l+r}$), simply by computing

$$A_{i,j} = \left(\sum_{o_m \in C_j} d_{i,m} \right).$$

In the end, an update of the two matrices must be performed in order to manage the new situation. Since cluster C_l and cluster C_r have been merged together and have become a single cluster C_{l+r}, we have to compute:

$$B_{i,j} = \left(\sum_{o_m \in C_j} 1 \right)$$

for each object o_i.

The same update has to be performed on the matrix B. This operation takes time equal to $O(n)$ where n is the cardinality of the set of objects o_i.

If we analyze the computational complexity, it is simple to see that the computation of a_i during MOSAIC's execution takes time $O(k \cdot n \cdot m)$, where k is the number of clusters, n the number of objects in the dataset and m the computational cost of the case 2b at each step p (this is the worst case because not always we have to perform the case 2b). For the computation of b_i, the greatest cost is due to the initialization of matrices A and B, which takes time equal to $O(n^2)$ because all distances between all the possible couples of objects must be computed.

Summarizing, the computational complexity of the Silhouette fitness function by using an incremental technique reduces to $O(k \cdot n \cdot m) + O(n^2)$. At this time we are exploring the possibility of computing $q(X)$ locally, in order to reduce the intrinsic computational complexity introduced by this fitness function.

3 EXPERIMENTS

We set up experiments that evaluate MOSAIC for traditional clustering and supervised clustering. In the traditional clustering experiment, clustering results generated by MOSAIC are compared with ones generated by DBSCAN and k-means. In the supervised clustering section, we demonstrate how MOSAIC is effective in discovering arbitrary-shaped clusters; MOSAIC is used as a post-processing algorithm to agglomerate initial clusters generated by Supervised Clustering with Evolutionary Computing algorithm (SCEC).

3.1 Experiments on Traditional Clustering

The MOSAIC algorithm with the Silhouettes fitness function is used in our experiments. The experimental results are compared to the ones obtained from DBSCAN and k-means[1]. Only partial results are presented due to the limitation of the space. More results and detailed discussions can be found in (Choo, 2007). Following datasets are used in our experiments:

1. **9Diamonds** (DMML Repository, 2007): 3,000 objects with 9 natural clusters
2. **Volcano** (DMML Repository, 2007): 1,533 objects

3. **Diabetes** (UCI Machine Learning Repository, 2007): 768 objects
4. **Ionosphere** (UCI Machine Learning Repository, 2007): 351 objects
5. **Vehicle** (UCI Machine Learning Repository, 2007): 8,469 objects

The platform for running experiments is a Dell Inspiron 600m laptop that was equipped with an Intel® Pentium(R) M 1.6GHz CPU and 512 MB of RAM.

Experiment 1: The experiment analyses Cohesion, Separation and Silhouettes over a MOSAIC run. The goal of this experiment is to understand how fitness with respect to the three fitness functions changes as MOSAIC merges clusters.

Discussion: Figure 6 depicts how Separation, Cohesion and Silhouettes evolve in one run of the post-processing algorithm for the 9Diamonds dataset. The top graph of the figure shows that as the number of clusters decreases, both Separation and Cohesion increase; the same pattern was observed for many other data sets. In other words, there is a trade off between the size of clusters, and Cohesion and Separation. In addition, Separation and Cohesion have a tendency to increase more quickly for small k values. On the other hand, we observed (Choo, 2007), that the Silhouettes curve takes many different forms for different datasets. As shown in the bottom graph

Figure 6. Evaluation graphs of clustering using Cohesion, Separation and Silhouettes

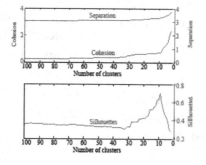

of the figure, the experimental result depicts a highest value of the Silhouette function when k reaches 9, which is number of *natural clusters* in the dataset.

Experiment 2: The experiment compares the clustering results of MOSAIC with the results of k-means where k=9.

Discussion: MOSAIC is capable of finding natural clusters as shown in Fig. 7 (c) using initial clusters generated by k-means shown in Fig. 7 (b). On the other hand, k-means fails to identify them correctly as depicted in Fig. 7 (a) due to the sensitivity problem of initial representative selection.

Experiment 3: The experiment compares MOSAIC and DBSCAN using 9Diamonds and Volcano datasets to illustrate the ability of arbitrary shape detection.

Discussion: It is a challenging task to tune-up proper values for the *MinPts* and ε which are the required parameters in order to run DBSCAN. Initially, we follow the procedure suggested in the original paper (Ester, 1996) to determine the right values of *MinPts* and ε. According to our investigation, using DBSCAN with the parameters determined by this method creates a single cluster for both datasets. Alternatively, an interactive procedure is created to decide parameters for DBSCAN; we initially randomly generate a few parameter settings, visualize clustering results generated by DBSCAN for the different parameter settings, obtain feedback from the user about clustering quality, and then generate further parameter settings based on the user's feedback. After a couple of iterations, DBSCAN with the new parameter settings produces better clustering results. Moreover, ε values are much smaller than those suggested in the original paper that analyzes the sorted k-dist graph. One of the best clustering results of the 9Diamonds dataset created by DBSCAN is shown in Fig. 7 (d); MOSAIC correctly identify the natural clusters of the given dataset whereas DBSCAN generates correct number of clusters with missing objects as outliers.

A significant characteristic of Volcano datasets is that it contains elongated patterns with different densities. It is of particular interest to identify these patterns. Generally DBSCAN and MOSAIC generates comparable clusters. For instance, Fig. 8 shows that MOSAIC is superior in identifying the elongated clusters on the left half of the visualization (Fig. 8 (a)). DBSCAN is, on the other hand, superior in detecting the elongated clusters in the upper right of the visualization (Fig. 8. (b)). However, neither DBSCAN nor MOSAIC can identify all the elongated patterns in the dataset.

Experiment 4: We compare MOSAIC with k-means using three high dimensional datasets: Vehicle, Ionosphere, and Diabetes. MOSAIC

Figure 7. Experimental results for the 9Diamonds dataset © 2007 Springer. Used with permission.

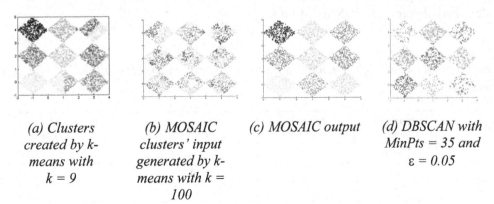

| (a) Clusters created by k-means with k = 9 | (b) MOSAIC clusters' input generated by k-means with k = 100 | (c) MOSAIC output | (d) DBSCAN with MinPts = 35 and ε = 0.05 |

Figure 8. Experimental results of MOSAIC and DBSCAN on Volcano dataset © 2007 Springer. Used with permission.

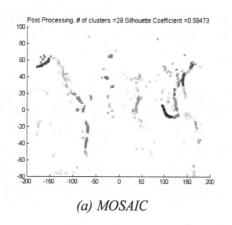

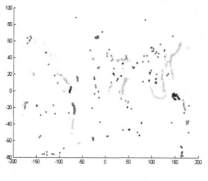

(a) MOSAIC   *(b) DBSCAN with MinPts = 5 and ε = 0.02*

uses 100 initial clusters created by *k*-means, and iteratively merges a pair of clusters until only two clusters left. We compare the quality of clusters using Silhouette; for MOSAIC the Silhouette values are averaged over the 98 iterations and for *k*-means the Silhouette values are averaged over 98 runs of *k*-means, where *k*=2, ..., 99. A summary of the results is presented in Table 1.

Discussion: It is clear from the above table that MOSAIC outperforms *k*-means on the Vehicle dataset. We also observe minor improvements of MOSAIC results for the Ionosphere and Diabetes datasets.

3.2 Supervised Clustering Experiments

In traditional clustering section, *k*-means is used to generate initial clusters for MOSAIC. In this

section, we also run a supervised clustering algorithm, namely SCEC, to generate a set of small input clusters for MOSAIC. SCEC (Eick, 2004) is a representative-based supervised clustering algorithm that employs evolutionary computing to seek for the "optimal" set of representatives by evolving population of solutions over a fixed number of generations. The size of the population is fixed to a predetermined number when running SCEC. The initial generation is created randomly. The subsequent generations are generated by applying three different genetic operators: *Mutation*, *Crossover*, and *Copy*, to members of the current generation that are selected based on the principles of survival of the fittest. Figure 9 shows a flowchart of the SCEC algorithm, whose key features include:

Table 1. Information for the high dimensional datasets and experimental results © 2007 Springer. Used with permission.

Dataset	Number of objects	Number of dimensions	Average Silhouette coefficient of *k*-means	Average Silhouette coefficient of MOSAIC
Vehicle	8,469	19	0.20013	0.37157
Ionosphere	351	34	0.2395	0.26899
Diabetes	768	8	0.23357	0.24373

Figure 9. Key features of the SCEC algorithm

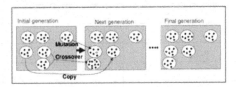

1. Chromosomal Representation: A solution consists of a set of representatives that are a subset of the examples to be clustered.

2. Genetic Operators:

   Mutation: replaces a representative by a non-representative.

   Crossover: take 2 "parent" solutions and creates an offspring as follows:

   A. Include all representatives that occur in both parents in the offspring

   B. Include representatives that occur in a single parent with a probability of 50%.

   Copy: Copy a member of the current generation into the next generation.

3. Selection: *K*-tournament selection is used to select solutions for generating the next generation through mutation, crossover, and copying. *K*-tournament randomly selects *K* solutions from the current population, and uses the solution with the highest $q(X)$ value to be added to the mating pool for the breeding of the next generation.

4. Transformation of the Chromosomal Representation into Clusters and Evaluation:

   A. Create clusters by assigning the remaining examples in the dataset to the closest representative.

   B. Evaluate the obtained clustering X using $q(X)$.

We set up two experiments that use the following datasets: an artificial dataset called **Binary Complex 8** (DMML Repository, 2007) consisting of 2,551 objects, **Binary Complex 9** (DMML Re- pository, 2007) containing 3,031 objects, **Earth- quakes 1%** (DMML Repository, 2007) containing 3,161 objects, **Volcano** (DMML Repository, 2007) containing 1,533 objects, **Arsenic 20%** (DMML Repository, 2007) containing 2,385 objects and **Diabetes** (UCI Machine Learning Repository, 2007) containing 768 objects. All of the tested datasets contain objects belonging to two different classes except Earthquakes 1%, which contains 3 classes. The common parameters for SCEC of both experiments are listed in Table 2. In this chapter, experiments on supervised clustering focus on discovering large size of high purity clusters. So we use the reward-based fitness function whose interestingness is the purity function as discussed in Section 2.3. The parameters settings for the fitness function are as follows: β=1.0001 and η=7—the parameters are chosen to instruct SCEC to produce a large number of initial clusters.

Experiment 5: The experiment evaluates post-processing SCEC clusters with MOSAIC for discovering arbitrary shape clusters for three two-dimensional datasets: Binary Complex 8, Binary Complex 9, and Earthquake (with sampling rate 1 percent) datasets. For MOSAIC we use β=1.3 and η=1 values in Earthquakes dataset experiments and β=3 and η=1 values in the other datasets experiments.

Discussion: The datasets contain clusters of varying shapes, density and distribution. We assert that MOSAIC is capable of merging neighboring clusters into larger continuous clusters while maintaining purity. The high purity and arbitrary shape clusters discovered by MOSAIC are displayed in Fig. 10. The clusters created by SCEC are shown on the middle panel, and the clusters on the right

Table 2. Parameters for SCEC

Dataset	Number of objects
Initial crossover rate	0
Initial mutation rate	0.95
Copy rate	0.05
Population size	400
Number of generations	1,500
K for tournament	2

are generated by MOSAIC. For Binary Complex 8 MOSAIC can merge the three red elongated clusters which belong to the same class. It can also agglomerate the two blue elongated shapes belonging to the same class. The green, black and yellow clusters are not further merged because there is no neighboring edge of Gabriel Graph connecting them. For Binary Complex 9, MOSAIC can merge the two cyan circles, merge the red ellipse cluster and a red C-shape cluster, merge the green elongated and half of another green C-shape cluster, and merge the remaining half of blue C-shape cluster and the blue question mark shape cluster. The 2 halves of C-shape cluster in green and blue are not merged together because there exists an intervening cluster, generated by SCEC, with a different majority class (the tiny red part at the middle of the 2 halves of C-shape cluster is agglomerated to the red C-shape cluster). Since Gabriel Graph only creates edges from the flawed cluster to them, MOSAIC does not merge because it is required to merges one half with the red C-shape cluster resulted in decreasing fitness value. For Earthquakes1% dataset, MOSAIC is able to form chain-like clusters. The clustering result on the rightmost is very comparable to original clusters residing on the leftmost. It also should be emphasized that MOSAIC can be employed as a post-processing clustering algorithm for any representative clustering algorithm to enhance the clustering result

Experiment 6: The empirical study conducts a qualitative analysis of MOSAIC and SCEC for different fitness parameter settings. We perform the qualitative analysis of the benefits of MOSAIC as a post-processing clustering algorithm for SCEC clusters, in terms of quality of cluster $q(X)$, the purity of clusters, and the number of clusters. The same fitness function used in Experiment 5 is also used in MOSAIC with 4 different parameter settings: (β=1.0001, η=7), (β=1.01, η=6), (β=1.3, η=1), (β=3, η=1).

Discussion: The experimental results listed in Table 3 indicate that this post-processing technique considerably improves the quality of SCEC clusters. We can conclude from the comparison between SCEC and MOSAIC that MOSAIC enhances or keeps the purity and the quality, and decreases the number of clusters on Binary Complex 8, Binary Complex 9, and Arsenic 20% datasets for all parameter settings. For the Volcano, Earthquake 1% and Diabetes datasets, post-processing improves the quality in most cases and reduces the number of clusters significantly when β is small. In general, the experimental results also convince us to use parameter β in clustering tasks; larger values for the parameter β usually result in a smaller number of clusters in the best clustering. From a quantitative point of view, Table 3 shows that the post-processing technique improves average purity by 2.8%, average cluster quality by 13.3% and decreases the average number of clusters by 51.4%.

Figure 10. Experimental results of SCEC and MOSAIC on Binary Complex 8, Binary Complex 9 and Earthquakes 1% datasets

Datasets	Original Clusters	Clusters generated by SCEC	MOSAIC result
Binary Complex 8	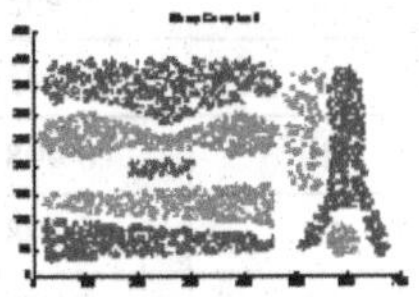	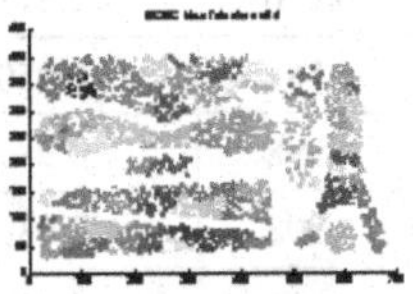	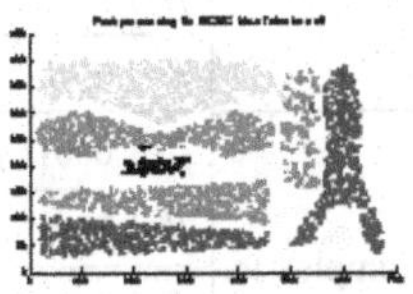
Binary Complex 9	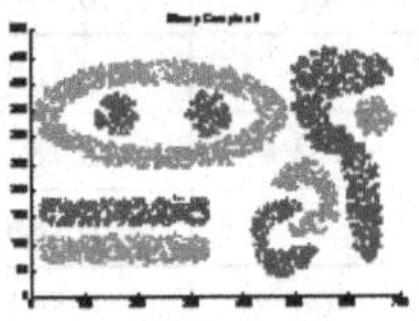	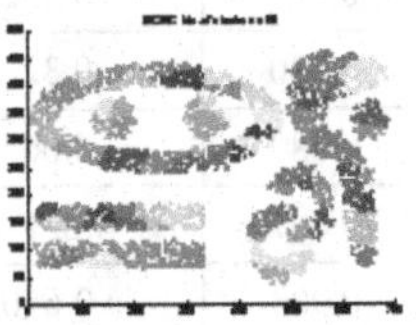	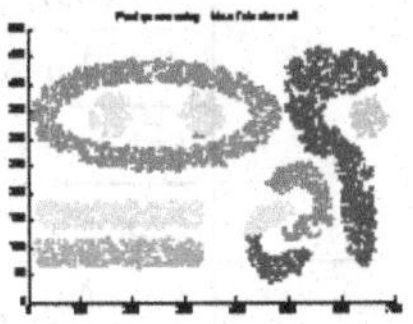
Earthquakes 1%	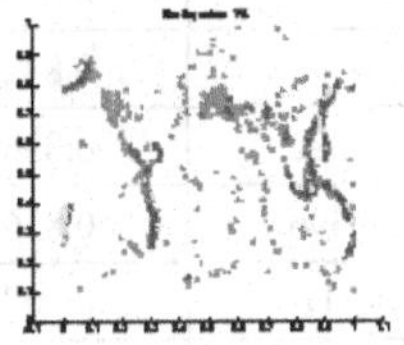	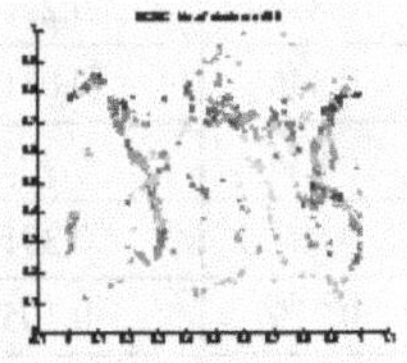	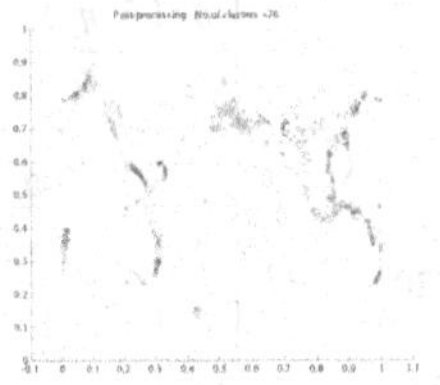

4 RELATED WORK

Many works in spatial domain address the potential of hierarchical clustering and incorporate it into automatic interpretation and analysis of spatial data. For instance, Anders (2003) developed a hierarchical clustering algorithm that employs various proximity graphs for automating cartography in different refinement levels. Jiang (2004) utilized dendrograms as visual support of generalization processes in GIS. In theory, agglomerative hierarchical clustering (AHC) is capable of detecting clusters of arbitrary shapes, which is an important task in spatial clustering. However, in practice, the use of AHC faces many limitations. First, it performs a very narrow search by only merging the two closest clusters without considering other merge candidates, and therefore it often misses high quality solutions. Second, its time complexity is equal to $O(n^2)$ or worse, which restricts its application to small and medium-sized data sets. Third, clusters obtained by AHC are not necessarily contiguous, as illustrated in Fig. 11: a hierarchical clustering algorithm that uses average linkage[2] would merge clusters C3 and C4, although the two clusters are not neighboring. This example emphasizes the need to prohibit merging of non-neighboring clusters in agglomerative clustering. Gao (2002) overcame the aforementioned problems by using Delaunay triangulation to identify the neighboring distance among instances before identifying clusters using Minimum Spanning Tree. Proximity graphs are also used in divisive clustering. The algorithm

Table 3. The qualitative and quantitative analysis of SCEC and MOSAIC

Dataset	Parameters	SCEC			MOSAIC		
		Purity	Quality	Clusters	Purity	Quality	Clusters
Binary Complex 8	β=1.0001, η=7	0.995	0.951	94	0.995	0.952	12
	β=1.01, η=6	0.990	0.901	90	0.995	0.940	12
	β=1.3, η=1	0.916	0.418	8	0.995	0.682	5
	β=3, η=1	0.886	0.050	4	0.995	0.115	5
Binary Complex 9	β=1.0001, η=7	0.998	0.989	80	0.998	0.989	9
	β=1.01, η=6	0.998	0.937	98	0.998	0.973	9
	β=1.3, η=1	0.937	0.339	22	0.998	0.607	8
	β=3, η=1	0.830	0.032	4	0.997	0.075	6
Volcano	β=1.0001, η=7	0.790	0.332	402	0.780	0.332	230
	β=1.01, η=6	0.780	0.322	402	0.780	0.316	230
	β=1.3, η=1	0.789	0.068	372	0.787	0.110	176
	β=3, η=1	0.607	4.65E-4	7	0.786	0.002	117
Earthquake 1%	β=1.0001, η=7	0.903	0.610	400	0.884	0.610	147
	β=1.01, η=6	0.895	0.575	404	0.884	0.599	147
	β=1.3, η=1	0.846	0.272	5	0.858	0.412	76
	β=3, η=1	0.846	0.061	4	0.842	0.141	34
Arsenic 20%	β=1.0001, η=7	0.836	0.402	392	0.836	0.402	172
	β=1.01, η=6	0.834	0.391	396	0.836	0.392	72
	β=1.3, η=1	0.779	0.105	11	0.808	0.253	90
	β=3, η=1	0.774	0.021	6	0.779	0.065	41
Diabetes	β=1.0001, η=7	0.770	0.315	94	0.742	0.315	17
	β=1.01, η=6	0.790	0.289	94	0.742	0.310	17
	β=1.3, η=1	0.740	0.228	5	0.753	0.208	9
	β=3, η=1	0.726	0.050	2	0.764	0.018	9
Average		0.844	0.361	141.5	0.868	0.409	68.75

requires only $O(n\log n)$. Beside agglomeration, Amoeba (Estivill-Castro, 2000) is a divisive clustering algorithm that also operates on proximity graphs with the same time complexity. After constructing a Delaunay graph for all instances, the algorithm recursively divides a cluster into sub-clusters by removing Delaunay edges whose distance exceed global mean distance.

An alternative clustering paradigm that enhances the performance of hierarchical clustering is hybrid clustering. The basic idea is to agglomerate a set of small clusters obtained by a partitioning algorithm to enhance the quality of the clustering. A simple example of hybrid clustering algorithms is CURE (Guha, 1998) that generates a set of representatives of initial clusters and agglomerates the closest pair of representatives. Another example is a combination of representative-based clustering and agglomerative clustering proposed by Lin (2002) and Zhong (2003); despite introducing different merging criteria, they still perform a narrow search considering a single pair of merge candidates. In the first phase, CHAMELEON employs a multilevel graph-partitioning

Figure 11. Merging elongated clusters

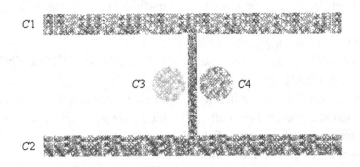

algorithm to generate initial clusters whereas MOSAIC employs a representative-based clustering algorithm to perform the same task. In the second phase, the CHAMELEON agglomerates multiple clusters, if any, maximizing relative interconnectivity and relative closeness, whereas MOSAIC agglomerates clusters maximizing an externally given fitness function. Nevertheless, MOSAIC, in contrast to the other algorithms, is superior when coping with real world problems. While other algorithms form clusters by restricting only intrinsic characteristics, MOSAIC is able to generate different clustering solutions with respect to the extrinsic characteristics defined by the plug-in fitness function. Surdeanu (2005) introduced another hybrid clustering approach that utilizes Expectation Maximization (EM) algorithm and agglomerative clustering.

Besides hierarchical clustering, density based clustering is a viable alternative for discovering arbitrary shape clusters (Ester, 1996; Sander, 1998; Kriegel, 2005; Hinneburg, 1998). However, the use of such density-based clustering algorithms is not trivial. Users must have background knowledge of density functions in order to tune the parameters effectively. Moreover, density-based clustering algorithms are not appropriate in clustering high dimensional data. Another problem is that different density-based algorithms have different assumptions on density of the data. The older generation of density based clustering algorithms like DBSCAN (Ester, 1996) assumes all clusters have similar density. The newer generation like LDBSCAN (Duan, 2007) considers the existence of varying densities in a dataset and alleviates this problem by introducing local density measures to handle this varying density.

A family of supervised clustering algorithms has been proposed by Eick, (2004, 2006) and Jiang (2007) that allow for plug-in fitness functions to be used by clustering algorithm to maximize these fitness functions and search for better clustering solutions. The family of supervised clustering algorithms consists of agglomerative-based, grid-based, representative-based and density-based clustering algorithms. Even though they are built generic enough for many data mining tasks, they are mainly used for the region discovery tasks (Ding, 2006; Ding, 2007; Ding, 2008).

5 CONCLUSION

This chapter introduces a novel agglomerative clustering algorithm, MOSAIC, that is capable of forming various aspects of arbitrary-shape clusters with respect to the extrinsic characteristics specified by domain people (or domain experts). MOSAIC comprises two phases: running a representative-based clustering algorithm to obtain initial clusters, and greedily merging neighboring clusters to maximize a fitness function. Even though MOSAIC is similar to agglomerative grid-based clustering algorithms in terms of micro-clusters employment and greedy aggregation of neighboring clusters, MOSAIC is superior because the shape of clusters that MOSAIC can detect are convex, whereas other algorithms are limited to discovering only rectangular shapes. Additionally, MOSAIC allows discovering of polygons of different sizes. MOSAIC provides significant benefits by allowing the use of any proximity graphs to generate clusters neighboring. Consequently, it provides wider search for merge candidates compared to traditional agglomerative clustering algorithms that only merge the "closest" clusters. On the other hand, users and domain experts are able to incorporate their interestingness to the anticipated clusters via plug-in fitness function.

We conducted both unsupervised and supervised clustering experiments to illustrate the capability of MOSAIC to handle various clustering tasks with respect to different plug-in fitness functions. For unsupervised clustering experiments, MOSAIC employing k-means in conjunction with Silhouettes function significantly improves cluster quality compared to employing k-means stand-alone. We also show that the cluster quality generated by MOSAIC and DBSCAN are comparable. However, MOSAIC is preferable because it requires the least human effort for parameter tuning; MOSAIC only requires a plug-in fitness function as a single input parameter, while DBSCAN requires a procedure to determine its parameters. The supervised clustering experiments reveal another advantage of MOSAIC: it can be applied as a post-processing algorithm. MOSAIC considerably improves the quality of SCEC clusters. The experimental results show that MOSAIC is able to obtain complex shape clusters in both artificial and real world datasets. Specifically, it can identify elongated clusters in the Earthquake dataset and clusters residing in another cluster in the Binary Complex 9 dataset. Such kinds of complex shape clusters are hardly identified by traditional clustering algorithms.

6 ACKNOWLEDGMENT

This research was supported in part by a grant from the Environmental Institute of Houston (EIH).

REFERENCES

Anders, K. H. (2003). A hierarchical graph-clustering approach to find groups of objects (Technical Paper). In *Proceedings of the ICA Commission on Map Generalization. Fifth Workshop on Progress in Automated Map Generalization*.

Asano, T., Ibaraki, T., Imai, H., & Nishizeki, T. (1990). Algorithms. In *Lecture Notes in Computer Science* (pp. 70-71). New York: Springer-Verlag.

Bhattacharya, B., Poulsen, R., & Toussaint, G. (1981). Application of proximity graphs to editing nearest neighbor decision rule. In *Proceedings of the International Symposium on Information Theory*.

Choo, J. (2007). Using proximity graphs to enhance representative-based clustering algorithms. Unpublished master's thesis, Department of Computer Science, University of Houston, TX.

Ding, W., Eick, C. F., Wang, J., & Yuan, X. (2006). A framework for regional association rule mining in spatial datasets. In B. Werner (Ed.), *Proceedings of the Sixth IEEE International Conference on Data Mining*, Hong Kong (pp. 851-856).

Ding, W., Eick, C. F., Yuan, X., Wang, J., & Nicot, J.-P. (2007). on regional association rule scoping. In *Proceedings of the International Workshop on Spatial and Spatio-Temporal Data Mining* (pp.595-600).

Ding, W., Jiamthapthaksin, R., Parmar, R., Jiang, D., Stepinski, T., & Eick, C. F. (2008). Towards region discovery in spatial datasets. In T. Washio, E. Suzuki, K. M. Ting, & A. Inokuchi (Eds.), *Advances in knowledge discovery and data mining* (LNCS 5012, pp. 88-99). Berlin, Germany: Springer.

Duan, L., Xu, L., Guo, F., Lee, J., & Yan, B. (2007). A local-density based spatial clustering algorithm with noise. *Information Systems, 32*(7), 978–986. doi:10.1016/j.is.2006.10.006

Eick, C. F., Vaezian, B., Jiang, D., & Wang, J. (2006). discovery of interesting regions in spatial datasets using supervised clustering. In *Proceedings of the Tenth European Conference on Principles and Practice of Knowledge Discovery in Databases: Vol. 4213* (pp. 127-138).

Eick, C. F., Zeidat, N., & Zhao, Z. (2004). Supervised clustering --- algorithms and benefits. In *Proceedings of the International Conference on Tools with AI (ICTAI).*

Ester, M., Kriegel, H. P., Sander, J., & Xu, X. (1996). Density-based spatial clustering of applications with noise. In *Proceedings of the International Conference on Knowledge Discovery and Data Mining.*

Estivill-Castro, V., & Lee, I. (2000). Amoeba: Hierarchical clustering based on spatial proximity using Delaunaty diagram. In *Proceedings of the Ninth International Symposium on Spatial Data Handling* (pp. 7a.26-7a.41).

Gabriel, K. R., & Sokal, R. R. (1969). A new statistical approach to geographic variation analysis. *Systematic Zoology, 18*, 259–278. doi:10.2307/2412323

Gao, D., Peuquet, D., & Gahegan, M. (2002). Opening the black box: Interactive hierarchical clustering for multivariate spatial patterns. In *Proceedings of the Tenth ACM International Symposium on Advances in Geographic Information Systems* (pp. 131-136).

Guha, S., Rastogi, R., & Shim, K. (1998). CURE: An efficient clustering algorithm for large databases. In *Proceedings of the International Conference of ACM SIGMOD on Management of Data* (pp. 73-84).

Hinneburg, A., & Keim, D. (1998). An efficient approach to clustering in large multimedia databases with noise. In *Proceedings of the International Conference on Knowledge Discovery in Data Mining.*

Jiang, B. (2004). Spatial clustering for mining knowledge in support of generalization processes in GIS. In *Proceedings of the ICA Workshop on Generalisation and Multiple Representation.*

Jiang, D., Eick, C. F., & Chen, C. S. (2007). on supervised density estimation techniques and their application to clustering. In *Proceedings of the Fifteenth ACM International Symposium on Advances in Geographic Information Systems.*

Karypis, G., Han, E. H., & Kumar, V. (1999). CHAMELEON: A hierarchical clustering algorithm using dynamic modeling. *IEEE Computer., 32*, 68–75.

Kirkpatrick, D. (1980). A note on Delaunay and optimal triangulations. *Information Processing Letters, 10*, 127–128. doi:10.1016/0020-0190(80)90062-9

Kriegel, H. P., & Pfeifle, M. (2005). Density-based clustering of uncertain data. In *Proceedings of the International Conference on Knowledge Discovery in Data Mining* (pp. 672-677).

Lin, C., & Chen, M. (2002). A robust and efficient clustering algorithm based on cohesion self-merging. In *Proceedings of the International Conference of Eighth ACM SIGKDD on Knowledge Discovery and Data Mining* (pp. 582-587).

Machine Learning Repository, U. C. I. (2007). Retrieved January 3, 2007, from http://www.ics.uci.edu/~mlearn/MLRepository.html

Okabe, A., Boots, B., & Sugihara, K. (1992). *Spatial tessellations: Concepts and applications of Voronoi diagrams*. New York: John Wiley & Sons.

Repository, D. M. M. L. (2007). *Data mining and machine learning group website*. Retrieved January 31, 2007, from http://www.tlc2.uh.edu/dmmlg/Datasets

Rousseeuw, P. J. (1987). Silhouettes: A graphical aid to the interpretation and validation of cluster analysis. *International Journal of Computational and Applied Mathematics*, *20*(1), 53–65. doi:10.1016/0377-0427(87)90125-7

Sander, J., Ester, M., Kriegel, H.-P., & Xu, X. (1998). Density-based clustering in spatial databases: The algorithm GDBSCAN and its applications. *International Conference on Data Mining and Knowledge Discovery*, *3*(3), 169-194.

Surdeanu, M., Turmo, J., & Ageno, A. (2005). A hybrid unsupervised approach for document clustering. In *Proceedings of the International Conference of Eleventh ACM SIGKDD on Knowledge Discovery in Data Mining* (pp. 685-690).

Tan, M., Steinbach, M., & Kumar, V. (Eds.). (2005). *Introduction to data mining*. Reading, MA: Addison Wesley.

Toussaint, G. (1980). The relative neighborhood graph of a finite planar set. In . *Proceedings of the International Conference of Pattern Recognition*, *12*, 261–268. doi:10.1016/0031-3203(80)90066-7

Zhong, S., & Ghosh, J. (2003). A unified framework for model-based clustering. *International Journal of Machine Learning Research*, *4*, 1001–1037. doi:10.1162/jmlr.2003.4.6.1001

ENDNOTES

[1] In general, we would have preferred to compare our algorithm also with CHAMELEON and DENCLUE. However, we sadly have to report that executable versions of these two algorithms no longer exist.

[2] Average linkage uses the average distance between the members of two clusters as its distance function.

Chapter 11
Ranking Gradients in Multi–Dimensional Spaces

Ronnie Alves
University of Nice Sophia-Antipolis, France

Joel Ribeiro
University of Minho, Portugal

Orlando Belo
University of Minho, Portugal

Jiawei Han
University of Illinois at Urbana-Champaign, USA

ABSTRACT

Business organizations must pay attention to interesting changes in customer behavior in order to anticipate their needs and act accordingly with appropriated business actions. Tracking customer's commercial paths through the products they are interested in is an essential technique to improve business and increase customer satisfaction. Data warehousing (DW) allows us to do so, giving the basic means to record every customer transaction based on the different business strategies established. Although managing such huge amounts of records may imply business advantage, its exploration, especially in a multi-dimensional space (MDS), is a nontrivial task. The more dimensions we want to explore, the more are the computational costs involved in multi-dimensional data analysis (MDA). To make MDA practical in real world business problems, DW researchers have been working on combining data cubing and mining techniques to detect interesting changes in MDS. Such changes can also be detected through gradient queries. While those studies have provided the basis for future research in MDA, just few of them points to preference query selection in MDS. Thus, not only the exploration of changes in MDS is an essential task, but also even more important is ranking most interesting gradients. In this chapter, the authors investigate how to mine and rank the most interesting changes in a MDS applying a TOP-K gradient strategy. Additionally, the authors also propose a gradient-based cubing method to evaluate interesting gradient regions in MDS. So, the challenge is to find maximum gradient regions (MGRs) that maximize the task of raking gradients in a MDS. The authors' evaluation study demonstrates that the proposed method presents a promising strategy for ranking gradients in MDS.

DOI: 10.4018/978-1-60566-748-5.ch011

Copyright © 2010, IGI Global. Copying or distributing in print or electronic forms without written permission of IGI Global is prohibited.

1 INTRODUCTION

The amount of data available in business data warehouses is increasing every day. To get interesting insights from those multi-dimensional databases is not a simple task. Since 1990s, several efforts were made in OLAP research area, making Multi-Dimensional data analysis (MDA) effective and real on several business applications. However, being effective does not imply being practical. In that time, DW researchers were concerned about how to deal with data cubes. Data cube is a multidimensional data structure from which one can dig interesting trends from DW. So, questions like how to build, how to explore, how to index, and how to maintain were in the agenda. Once the cube was available, business analysts could explore it, testing several what-if scenarios, and figuring out interesting business opportunities. Given that such inspection was usually carried out manually, it would be reasonable to mine interesting trends automatically, *e.g.*, by data cubing (Sarawagi, 1998; Sarawagi, 2000; Sathe, 2001).

Taking the "wave" of data mining methods in the last decade, a bunch of papers were written about combining cubing and mining, also called OLAPing, for getting better MDA over DWs (Imielinski, 2002; Dong, 2004; Sarawagi, 1998; Sarawagi, 2000; Sathe, 2001; Wang, 2006). Using those hybrid strategies, one can evaluate cube's dimensions and measures, not only before of after cubing, but even more sophisticated, while cubing. Those approaches are also called as change-based, exception-based or outlier-based methods.

Since data cube is usually big, independently of applying any of the current OLAPing methods, the amount of interesting patterns that could be brought out from them is still big too. Therefore, it is necessary to provide preference selection among those patterns, i.e., ranking most interesting patterns for further analysis. Ranking queries (Chang, 2000; Hristidis, 2001; Bruno, 2002) have been studied substantially by the information retrieval and database communities, and recently attracted attention of OLAP researchers (Xin, 2006a; Wu, 2008).

In this chapter, we present a new OLAPing method which combines efforts from both active research areas: OLAPing and Ranking. Our main goal is to mining the most interesting (TOP-K) changes in an MDS applying a gradient-based cubing strategy. The challenge is to find Maximum Gradient Regions (MGRs) that maximize the task of mining Top-K gradient cells. We also introduce several constraints related to mine TOP-K gradients that help us to mine the MDS efficiently. These constraints include support threshold (iceberg), closedness (that indicates the closed cells in the cube), spreadness (which measure the variability of gradient regions), gradient threshold (which focuses the search to most interesting changes in the MDS) and TOP-K (the number of interesting gradient cells to locate). Different from the previous studies, we call this strategy *Raking Gradient-Based Aggregation Mining*. Our solution to this problem consists of: 1) an efficient partitioning method based on gradient-regions, 2) an effective TOP-K gradient-cubing method which prunes non-gradient cells and also guides TOP-K search efficiently.

The chapter is organized as follows. In Section 2, we describe related works. In Section 3, we provide a short review of gradient queries. In Section 4, we formulate the Top-K gradient problem, presenting this type of *Rank-gradient query* through simple SQL-examples, followed by the proposed strategy in Section 5. A performance study is provided in Section 6. We conclude the work with a final discussion in Section 7.

2 RELATED WORK

The problem of mining changes of sophisticated measures in a MDS was first introduced by (Imielinski, 2002) as the cubegrade problem. The main idea is to explore how changes (*delta changes*) in a set of measures (*aggregates*) of interest are associated with changes in the underlying characteristics of sectors (*dimensions*). In (Dong, 2004), a method called *LiveSet-Driven* was proposed, leading to a more efficient solution for mining gradient cells. This is achieved by group processing of live probe cells and pruning of search space by pushing several constraints deeply. There are also other studies (Sarawagi, 1998; Sarawagi, 2000; Sathe, 2001) for mining interesting cells on data cubes. The idea of interestingness in these works is quite different from that explored by gradient-based ones. Instead of using a specified gradient threshold in relevance to the cells' ancestor, descendants, and siblings, it relies on the *statistical analysis* of neighborhood values of a cell to determine its interestingness (or also *outlyingness*).

These previous methods employ the idea of interestingness supported by either statistical or ratio-based approach. Such approaches still provide a large number of interesting cases to evaluate. In a real application scenario, one could be interested in exploring just a small number (best cases of *Top-K cells*) of gradient cells. There are several research papers on answering top-k queries (Chang, 2000; Hristidis, 2001; Bruno, 2002) on large databases, which could be used as baseline for mining Top-K gradient cells. However, the range of complex non-convex functions provided by the cube gradient model complicates the direct application of those traditional Top-K query methods. To the best of our knowledge, the problem of mining Top-K gradient cells in large databases is not well addressed yet. Even the idea of Top-K queries with Multi-Dimensional selection was introduced quite recently by (Xin, 2006a). In (Xin, 2007) is introduced a progressive and selective strategy for answering ad-hoc ranking functions. Another recent study on raking aggregates is presented by (Wu, 2008) where the query execution model follows a candidate generation and verification framework. In summary, ranking is applied over multidimensional aggregates. Furthermore, these models still rely on the computation of convex

functions, which cannot be applied to ratio-based functions like gradients. In this work we are interested in raking gradients where ranking is evaluated through ratio-based (gradient) function over multidimensional aggregates.

3 GRADIENT QUERIES

Gradient queries (or cubegrades) are basically cube statements that can be interpreted as "what if" formulae about how selected aggregates are affected by various cube modifications. It also can be viewed as a generalization of *association rules* (*Multi-Dimensional ones*). Possible cube operations include: cube specialization (roll-down), roll up and mutation. The roll up operation show how different measures are affected by cube generalization; mutations hypothetically change one of the attribute (dimension) values in the cube (for example change the location from Porto to Braga) and determine how different measures are affected by such an operation. Thus, gradient queries express how different subpopulations of the database are affected by different modifications to their definitions (see Figure 1). This delta change is measured by the way selected aggregates change in response to operations such as specialization (roll down), generalization (roll up) and mutation.

Particularly in (Imielinski, 2002), three types of gradient queries are presented:

- The **how** query: This query deals with how a delta change in a cube affects a certain measure? Does it go up or down? By how much? In the context of gradients and derivatives of functions, it would be analogous to the question of finding $\Delta f(x)$, given $x_{initial}$ and Δx.

- The **which** query: This type of query deals with finding cubes that have measures affected in a predefined way by the delta changes. This is analogous to the question

Figure 1. Cubegrade operations

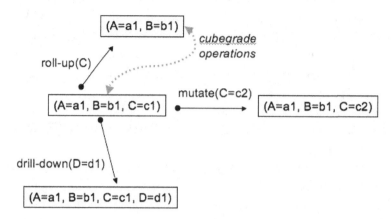

of finding $x_{initial}$, given the gradient, *i.e.*, both Δx and $\Delta f(x)$.

- The **what** query: This type of query deals with finding what delta-changes on cubes affect a given measure in a predefined manner. This is analogous to the question of finding $x_{initial}$ and Δx given $\Delta f(x)$.

In the rest of the chapter we focus on the "which" query as the basis query model for our TOP-K gradient-cubing strategy. In the next section we present an example (scenario of application) showing how "which" queries work, and furthermore, we demonstrate the importance of preference selection over gradient cells.

The query evaluation strategy used to find *cubegrades* is called as Grid-based pruning (GPB). Differently from other support pruning methods like Apriori, and BUC (Beyer, 1999), GPB evaluates pruning using several aggregating functions. To make this possible, several *monotonicity* studies are conducted. Query monotonicity is explored in the same fashion like frequent pattern sets, but it is deeply checked through a view monotonicity schema, (Imielinski, 2002). The final grid is then used to prune non-interesting cubegrades. GPB was devised to evaluate gradient queries, and not raking gradients. More recent works, such as *constrained gradients* (Dong, 2004), *closed gra-*

dients (Wang, 2006), *rank-cube* (Xin, 2006a), and *ARCube* (Wu, 2008) do not provide any preference selection over gradients in an MDS either.

4 PROBLEM FORMULATION

Given a base relation table R with categorical attributes $A_1, A_2, ..., A_n$ and real valued measures M_1, $M_2, ..., M_r$. We denote the categorical attributes as *selecting dimensions* and the measures as *raking dimensions*. A classical Top-K query specifies the selection condition over one or more categorical attributes, and evaluates a raking function "*f*" on a subset of one or more measure attributes (Chang, 2000; Hristidis, 2001). The result is an ordered set of K tuples according to the given raking condition. A relational Top-K query can be expressed as follows using the SQL-like notation:

Query-1

1: select top k * from R
2: where $A_1 = a_1$ and ...$A_n = a_j$
3: order by $f(M_1, ..., M_r)$ asc

On the other hand, one could be interested in evaluating the Top-K query above using a *Multi-Dimensional selection condition* (Xin, 2006a). A possible SQL-like notation would be:

Query-2

```
1: select top k * from (
2: select A₁, A₂,...,Aₙ,f(M₁,...,Mᵣ) from R
3: group by A₁, A₂,...,Aₙ
4: with cube) as T
5: where A₁ = a₁ and ...Aⱼ = aⱼ
6: order by T.f(M₁,...,Mᵣ) asc
```

One can see that different users may not only propose ad-hoc ranking conditions but also use different levels of data abstraction to explore interesting subsets (see Query-2). Actually, in many data applications, users may need to go through an exhaustive study of the data by taking a Multi-Dimensional analysis of the Top-K query results (Xin, 2006a).

Query-2 seems to be attractive and practical in many real applications, but it is also more complex than Query-1. The cube computation, line-2 through line-4, will provide all of the possible combinations of the selecting dimensions (*curse-of-dimensionality dilemma*) available in R, but these dimensions could also be constrained (line-5). Another way to constraint this Multi-Dimensional query is by rewriting Query-2, adding a HAVING condition within the GROUP BY aggregation. Even by using such query rewriting, to find the TOP-K gradients in Multi-Dimensional space also requires a special raking condition constraint not addressed yet by the current Top-K methods (Sarawagi, 2000; Hristidis, 2001; Bruno, 2002; Xin, 2006a; Wu, 2008).

We denote such ranking condition constraint as *raking gradient constraint*. Thus, the aggregating function in Query-2 is constrained by some properties, focusing the evaluation on particular gradient cells. Besides, the raking function in line 6 is a gradient function, which means that every aggregation cell should be tested against its neighborhood cells (mutation, generalization or specialization) (Imielinski, 2002), to see if it satisfies a gradient constraint such as $f(M_1,...,M_r) > 65\%$ (delta). This means that one would be interested in locating the

most interesting changes (TOP-K gradient cells) above this particular threshold. Even by using this threshold, one cannot afford to compute the whole cube to locate these cells. So, one alternative is to explore these TOP-K gradients while cubing. After rewriting Query-2, a possible SQL solution would be like Query-3:

Query-3

```
1:  select top k * from (// TOP-K gradient
    cells
2:  select A₁, A₂,...,Aₙ,f(M₁,...,Mᵣ) from R
3:  group by A₁, A₂,...,Aₙ // Partitioning gradi-
    ent regions
4:  with cube as T // Gradient-based cubing,
    aggregates interesting regions
5:  having f(M₁,...,Mᵣ) > min-delta) // Change
    threshold
5:  where A₁ = a₁ and ...Aⱼ = aⱼ // Probe cells to
    constraint gradient comparison
6:  order by T.f(M₁,...,Mᵣ) desc
```

Example 1. As an example of application, consider the following case of generating alarms for potential fraud situations on mobile telecommunications systems. Generally speaking, those alarms are generated when abnormal utilization of the system is detected, meaning that sensitive changes happened concerning the normal behavior. For example, one may want to see what are associated with significant changes of the average (w.r.t., the number of calls) in the Porto area on Monday compared against Tuesday, and the answer could be one in the form "*the average of number of calls for callings during working time in Campanha went up 55 percent, while those callings during night time in Bonfim went down 15 percent*". Expressions such as "callings during working time" correspond to cells in data cubes and describe sectors of the business modeled by the data cube. Given that the number of calls generated in a business day in Porto area is extremely large (hundred million calls); the fraud analyst would be interest to evaluate just the Top-10 higher changes in that scenario, specially those in Campanha area. Then the fraud analyst would be able to "*drillthrough*" most interesting customers.

The problem of mining Top-K cells with Multi-Dimensional selection conditions and raking gradients is significantly more expressive than the classical Top-K and cubegrade query. In this work, we are interested to mine best cases (Top-K cells) of Multi-Dimensional gradients in a MDS. Further we provide few definitions that help us to formalize the problem of *mining top-k gradient cells*.

A *cuboid* is a Multi-Dimensional summarization by means of aggregating functions over a subset of dimensions and contains a set of cells, called cuboid cells. A data cube can be viewed as a *lattice of cuboids*, which also integrates a set of cuboid cells. Data cubes are built from *relational base tables* (fact tables) from large data warehouses.

Definition 1 (**K-Dimensional Cuboid Cell**) In an n-dimension data cube, a cell $c = (i_1, i_2, \ldots, i_n: m)$ (where m is a measure) is called a k-dimensional cuboid cell (i.e., a cell in a k-dimensional cuboid), if and only if there are exactly k ($k \leq n$) values among $\{i_1, i_2, \ldots, i_n\}$ which are not * (i.e., all). If k = n, then c is a *base cell*. A base cell does not have any descendant. A cell c is an *aggregated cell* only when it is an ancestor of some base cell (i.e., where k < n). We further denote $M(c) = m$ and $V(c) = (i_1, i_2, \ldots, i_n)$.

Definition 2 (**Iceberg Cell**) A cuboid cell is called *iceberg cell* if it satisfies a threshold constraint on the measure. For example, an iceberg constraint on measure count is $M(c) \geq min\_supp$ (where *min_supp* is a user-given threshold).

Definition 3 (**Closed Cells**) Given two cells $c = (i_1, i_2, \ldots, i_n: m)$ and $c' = (i_1', i_2', \ldots, i_n': m')$, we denote $V(c) \leq V(c')$ if for each i_j (j = 1,\ldots,n) which is not *, $i_j' = i_j$. A cell c is said to be covered by another cell c' if for each c'' such that $V(c) \leq V(c'') \leq V(c')$, $M(c'') = M(c')$. A cell is called a *closed cuboid cell* if it is not covered by any other cells.

Definition 4 (**Matchable Cells**) A cell c is said to match a cell c' when they differ from each other in one, and only one, cube modification at time. These modifications could be: Cube *generalization/specialization* iff c is an *ancestor* of c' and c' a *descendant* of c; or *mutation* iff c is a sibling of c', and vice versa.

Definition 5 (**Probe Cells**) Probe cells (c_p) are particular cases of cuboid cells that are significant according to some muti-dimensional selection condition. This condition is more than a query constraint on base table's dimensions. For instance, in this work, the probe cells are those cells that are *iceberg closed cells*.

Definition 6 (**Gradient Cells**) A cell c_g is said to be gradient cell of a probe cell c_p, when they are matchable cells and their *delta change*, given by $\Delta g(c_g, c_p) \equiv (g(c_g, c_p) \geq \Delta_{min})$ is *true*, where ψ is a constant value and g is a *gradient function*.

Problem Definition. Given a base table *R*, iceberg condition *IC*, probe condition *PC*, and a minimum delta change Δ_{min}, the mining of *Top-k Multi-Dimensional Gradients* from *R* is: Find the most interesting (Top_K) gradient-probe pairs (c_g, c_p) such that $\Delta g(c_g, c_p)$ is *true*.

In this work we confine our discussion with average gradients ($1 - M(c_g)/M(c_p)$). Average gradients are effective functions for detecting interesting changes in Multi-Dimensional space, but they also pose great challenge to the cubing

Figure 2. It presents the distribution of aggregating values from a 2-D(x, y) cube.

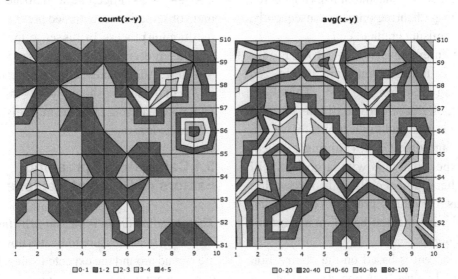

computation model (Dong, 2004). The first issue is that average is a *non-antimonotonic* function which complicates pruning efforts on data cubing (Han, 2001). The second issue is that by using average gradient as our *raking condition*, we have to be able to mine Top-K cells employing a *non-convex* function.

Example 2. Example of K-cuboid cells from Table 1 are $c1=(x1,y2,z3:1)$, $c2=(x1,*,*:2,5)$, $c3=(*,y1,z2:2.5)$, $c4=(x1,*,z1:4)$ and $c5=(*,*,z3:1)$. Lets say we have a $IC(ci>2)$, cells c5 and c1 are not an iceberg cell. The cell c5 is covered by c1, thus is a non-closed cell too. Lets say that applying the proposed strategy we set cell c2 as a probe cell. Thus, cell c2 is only matchable with c4, and this gradient is evaluated as 0.375.

5 RAKING GRADIENTS IN MDS

Before start the discussion about raking gradient cells in MDS, lets first look to Figure 2. This figure shows how aggregating values are distributed along cube's dimensions. The base table used

for cubing was generated according to a uniform distribution. It has 100 tuples, 2 dimensions (x, y) with cardinalities varying from 1 to 10, and a measure (m) varying from 1 to 100.

From Figure 2 we can see that different aggregating functions (Gray, 1997), (distributive and algebraic functions) will provide different density regions in data cubes. When searching for gradients, one may want to start this task by evaluating a cube region in which presents higher variance with respect to aggregating values. In Figure 2($avg(x-y)$) the central region corresponding to the rectangle $R1=\{[4, 6]: [6, 4]\}$ which covers all five *bins* $\{b_0=\{0-20\}, b_1=\{20-40\}, b_2=\{40-60\}, b_3=\{60-80\}, b_4=\{80-100\}\}$. If it is possible to identify such region, before cubing, i.e., during partitioning, chances are that the most interesting gradients will take place there. We denote those regions as *gradient regions(GR)*. The problem is that *average* is an algebraic function and it has a *spreading factor(SF)*, with respect to the distribution of aggregating values over the cube, unpredictable. Thus, there will be sets of possible gradient regions to looking for in the cube before selecting the most interesting gradient cells. Thus, the main challenge will rely in partitioning the base table in such way that maximizes this search for interesting gradient regions, and consequently, providing promising gradient cells.

Another interesting insight from Figure 2(*avg(x-y)*) is that gradients are maximized when walking from bins b_0 to b_4. Therefore, even if a region doesn't cover all bins but if at least has the lowest and highest ones; it should be a good candidate *GR* for mining gradient cells. We expect that *GRs* with largest *SF* will provide higher gradient cells. This observation motivates us to evaluate gradients cells by using a partitioning method based on a *gradient ascent approach*.

Gradient ascent is based on the observation that if the real-valued function $f(x)$ is defined and differentiable in a neighborhood of a point Y, $f(x)$ then increases fastest if one goes from Y in the direction of the gradient of f at Y, $\Delta f(Y)$. It follows that, if

$$Z = Y + \gamma \Delta f(Y) \qquad Eq.(1)$$

for, $\gamma > 0$ a small enough number, then $f(Y) \leq f(Z)$. With this observation, one could start with x_0 for a local maximum of f, and considers the sequence $x_0, x_1, x_2, \ldots$ such that

$$x_{n+1} = x_n + \gamma_n \Delta f(x_n), n \geq 0 \qquad Eq.(2)$$

We have $f(x_0) \leq f(x_1) \leq f(x_2) \leq \ldots$, so we expect the sequence (x_n) converge to the local maximum. Therefore, when evaluating a *GR* we first search for the *probe cells*, i.e. the highest closed cells on *GR+* (cells having aggregating values higher than the average in the "ALL" cuboid) and lowest ones on *GR-* (cells having aggregating values lower than the average in the "ALL" cuboid) and then we calculate its gradients from all possible *matchable cells*. Further we provide more details about the partitioning process.

To make possible gradient ascent traversal

through cube's lattice, one needs to incorporate the main observations mentioned previously into the partitioning process. In this sense, the lattice itself should represent gradient regions according to its *SF* value. Additionally, all *projected dimensions* (*GRs*) in the lattice should follow this spreading factor, i.e., starting from the most discriminating *GR* to the less one.

5.1 Calculating Spreading Factors of Gradient Regions

The spreading factor is measured by the variance. This statistical measure indicates how the values are spread around the expected value. From each *GR* we want to capture how large the differences are in a list of measures values $L_n=(M_1,\ldots,M_n)$ available from a base relation R. Thus, dimensions are projected onto cube's lattice according to this variation. This variation follows the following Equation for each *GR*:

$$sf(GR) = \frac{\sum (GR_{Ln} - avg(GR)^2}{n} \qquad Eq.(3)$$

where *GR* is a particular dimension value, *avg(GR)* is the average for that *GR partition*, and L_n and n are respectively the list of available measures (L_n) in *GR* and number of elements in this list. For large tables one could use a variation of Equation 3, using a sample rather than the population. In this sense one can replace n with $n-1$. After getting the *spreadness measure* for each gradient region we can rank them according to this measure. The intuition is that regions with highest spreadness values will present promising gradients values. The same behavior happens when projecting *GRs*.

Example 3. With Equation 3 we can compute de *SF* values and possible partitions (*GRs*) from Table 1. Thus for the dimension X, partitioning within x1, we have the following *GR*[x1] = {1,4}. Finally, we can raking

Figure 3. GR-tree and GR[x1] partition. Cells on italics are candidate gradient pairs.

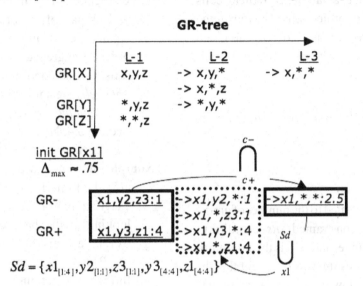

all partitions in the dimension X as follows $sf(x1) \gg sf(x2) \gg sf(x3)$.

5.2 Partitioning Gradient Regions

Once we have all *GRs* and its corresponding spreadness, the next step is partitioning table relation. The proposed ranking method generally relies on a three level framework. Thus, in the first two levels we focus on *ordering* and *partitioning*, and in the third one we do *Gradient-based aggregation* (*cubing*).

Level one. Given a particular descending order of all *GRs* available in a table relation *R*, we create a *GR-tree* (see Figure 3) that allows us to further traverse it (*DFS order*) and compute *K* gradient cells from *R*. To get better pruning of non-closed cells we also take a *Top-Down* approach, Xin, D et al. (2006b). In this step, we compute just the *GR-tree* first level (*L-1*), on each dimension, keeping only cells whose are closed ones. For each *GR* we also set a *meta-information bin* [agg$_{min}$; agg$_{max}$] containing the lower and upper *bin* boundaries (w.r.t. aggregating values). Each *GR* is also partitioned in two *GRs*, one *GR+* (covering cells having average higher than "ALL"), and the other one

GR- (covering cells having average higher than "ALL"). Finally we enumerate all possible set of dimension (*GR partitions*) values $Sd=\{d_1, d_2, \ldots, d_n\}$ which are directly identified by all closed cells on each *GR*. The *bin* boundaries are set for each dimension too. The number of elements in the *Sd* subset for each *GR* is obtained by:

$$Sd(GR) = \sum_{n=1}^{D} Card(GR_n) \qquad Eq.(4)$$

where *Card(GR)* correspond to the number of distinct elements on each dimension (D) in that *GR*.

Level two. Given all possible gradient regions and its associated *Sd* sets, we can enumerate all candidate *GR pairs* to project in order to find gradient cells. Additionally, to each pair we set an approximation, the maximum delta (Δ_{max}) that could be reached by doing that projection. Next, we can order all *GR pairs* according to this new information. The intuition is that projecting those *GRs* first will provide the highest gradient values. Consequently, it has a higher probability of evaluating K gradient cells on those first P' projections. The *maximum* number of projections P to evaluate given a set of *GRs* is evaluated through the following equation:

$$P(GR) \approx \binom{Card(GR) \times 2}{2} + Card(GR), (\Delta_{max}(GR) \geq \Delta_{min})$$

Eq.(5)

where $Card(GR)$ is related to the number of gradient regions in R, Δ_{max} constrained *GRs* according to its highest delta change, and Δ_{min} is the minimum delta change of interestingness (gradient threshold). Projections following particular combinations like $(GR+,GR-), (GR-,GR+), (GR-,GR-)$ and then $(GR+,GR+)$. Since projections must satisfy those delta changes, we focus on aggregating only those *GRs* that maximize the task of finding promising gradients. Given that the search space provided by $P(GR)$ will be quite large, and since we can find those K gradient cells on the first $P'(GR)$ projections, to smooth computational costs we must confine the minimum number of projections P' according to the next equation:

$$P'(GR) \approx \min\big(Card(P(GR)), \max(10, K \times K)\big)$$

Eq.(6)

where K is the number of gradients to locate.

Level three. In this level we aggregate *promising partitions* found in the previous levels and evaluates theirs *candidate probe cells* (cc_p). Candidate probe cells are those ones that are valid aggregating cells (intersecting $GR+$, $GR-$) while projecting the highest (K) cells in $GR+$ with the lowest (K) cell in the $GR-$. Once all $cc_p s$ are identified on that GR, we can enumerate possible *matchable cells* to evaluate its corresponding

gradients. This will provide us an order list gl with pair of cells to evaluate gradients. Again, we can make use of the (Δ_{max}), in order to aggregate only cells in gl which satisfies this condition. Further all *matchable cells* are aggregated using a *Gradient-based cubing* strategy. We go through it on Section 5.4. Next section, we explore *closedness measure* for getting closed cells.

Example 4. Lets use the same partition $GR[x1]$ from Example 3. The $Sd[x1] = \{x1,y2,z3,y3,z1\}$ subset is obtained by looking at the base cells from all TIDs $=\{1,4\}$ associated to $GR[x1]$ (see Table 2). Possible GR pairs (**Level two**) for further projections taking $GR[x1]$ are $\{(x1+:x1-),(x1+:y2-),..,(x1+:z1-),...\}$. This will also provide the following cells (**Level one**) $c1=<x1,y2,z3:1>$ in $GR-$ and $c2=<x1,y3,z1:4>$ in $GR+$. Those cells are also closed ones. For the $GR[x1]$ we can enumerate the probe cell (c_p) $c_p1=<x1,*,*:2.5>$ resulting from intersecting cells c1 and c2. Possible matchable cells (c_m) to c_p1 are $c_m1=<x1,y2,*:1>$, $c_m2=<x1,y3,*:4>$, $c_m3=<x1,*,z3:1>$ and $c_m4=<x1,*,z1:4>$. Since we keep *bins* for each dimension in GR, it is possible to evaluate *candidate gradient cells* before aggregating them. This will lead us to the following cells (**Level three**) $c_m1=<x1,y2,*:1>$ and $c_m3=<x1,*,z3:1>$, which express a $\Delta=60\%$ when compared with $c_p1=<x1,*,*:2.5>$. The total number of projection for Table 1 is 162. Assuming that we are searching for the Top-10 gradients with a $\Delta_{min}>55\%$, we then can confine our search to the first 100 projections ($P'(GR)=100$). Since the $\Delta_{min}>55\%$ and $\Delta_{max}[x1]=75\%$, hopefully we will find those Top-10 values by just evaluating the first $\binom{5}{2}$ projections of GR.

Table 1. Example of a base table R.

Tid	X	Y	Z	M
1	x1	y2	z3	1
2	x2	y1	z2	2
3	x3	y1	z2	3
4	x1	y3	z1	4

5.3 Evaluating Closed Cells through Closeness measure

To identify closed cells we make use of the *closed-ness measure* that is calculated according to the strategy proposed by (Xin, 2006b). It is also an algebraic measure and it can be computed based on two other measures, *representative tuple id* (distributive) and *closed mask* (algebraic). Next we describe each of the measures required to calculate closedness:

- **Representative tuple id** (R) of a cell is the smallest id of the tuples that aggregate to this cell. When this cell is empty (which means do not contain any tuple), the R is set to a NULL value.
- **Closed mask** (C) of cell contains D bits, where D is the number of dimensions in the original database. The bit is 1 only when all the tuples, which aggregated that cell, have the same value in the corresponding dimension. It is also evaluated according to the following equation.

$$C(S,d) = \prod_{i=1}^{k} C(S_i,d) \times Eq\left(\left|\left\{V\left(T(S_i),d\right), 1 \leq i \leq k\right\}\right|, 1\right)$$
Eq.(7)

Where, $|\{V(T(S_i),d), 1 \leq i \leq k\}|$ means the number of distinct values in the set $\{V(T(S_i),d), 1 \leq i \leq k\}$, and $Eq(x,y)$ is 1 if x equals to y, otherwise evaluates to 0. When S contains only one tuple is evaluated as 1 for all d. S_i are subsets of S, and $T(S_i)$ is the

representative tuple id for that subset.

- **All mask** (A) of a cell is a measure consisting of D bits, where D is the number of dimensions. The bit is 1 only when that cell has a star value (*) in the corresponding dimension.
- **Closedness**. Given a cells whose closed mask C and all mask is A, the closedness checking is defined as C&A, where & is a bitwise operation.

Example 5. Lets say that after cubing Table 1 we got a cell like (x1,*,z3). This cell has A=(0,1,0). Note that A is a property of the cell and can be calculated directly. If C(x1,*,z3)=(0,1,1), then its closedness value is (0,1,0).

5.4 Gradient-Based Cubing

Our cubing method follows *Frag-Cubing* approach (Li, 2004). We start by building *inverted indices* and *value-list indices* from the base relation R, and then assembling high-dimensional cubes from low-dimensional ones. For example, to compute the cuboid cell {x1, y3, *} from Table 1, we intersect the *tids* (see Table 2) of x1 {1, 4} and y3 {4} to get the new list of {4}.

A processing tree *GR-tree* following a Top-Down DFS traversal is used to aggregate potential *GRs*. We also calculate *spreadness* (*sf*, see Section 5.1) for all individual dimensions X, Y and Z, and consequently, all possible partitions from Table 1.

From Table 2 we can say that we have a total of nine *GRs* to grow.

Table 2. Inverted indices and spreadness for all partitions in Table 1.

Attr.Value	Tid.Lst	Tid.Sz	sf
x1	1, 4	2	2.25
x2	2	1	0
x3	3	1	0
y1	2, 3	2	0.25
y2	1	1	0
y3	4	1	0
z1	4	1	0
z2	2, 3	2	0.25
z3	1	1	0

The *GR-tree* will follow the order of X>>Y>>Z. Given that we want to find large gradients, those higher ones will take place on projecting *GRs* having higher spreading factors. Here comes the first heuristic for pruning (**p₁**, **pruning non-valid projections**). For example, a threshold constraint on a *GR* is $\Delta_{max} \geq \Delta_{min}$ (where Δ_{min} is a user-given threshold). Let's say that we are interested to search for gradients on *GRs* having a Δ_{min}>55%. From this constraint we only need to evaluate *GRs* and its projections satisfying this minimum delta value (looking at Δ_{max} for each *GR*). Cubing is carried out through projecting each *GR* from Table 2. An example with *GR*[x1] is presented in Figure 3.

After cubing those *candidate regions* from Table 2., it is possible now to mine the Top-K gradient cells from them. We also augment each *GR* pair with its respective *bin* [agg$_{min}$; agg$_{max}$] according to the minimum and maximum aggregating value on it, allowing also an approximation of the maximum delta value on each projection. With all those information we can make use of the second heuristic for pruning (**p₂**, pruning **non-valid probe cells**). Given that we have a gradient condition such as $\Delta_{min} \geq 65\%$, we can confine our search for the Top-K cells only for all probe cells in the *gl* list (see section 5.2, Level-three) that approximates a *GR* delta maximum closer to that delta minimum.

Even by using such constraint, the number of gradient pairs to evaluate is still large in x1. So, we must define our set of probe cells $c_p\{\}$ to rank. Remember the discussion about *gradient ascent*; by taking the local maximum (i.e., a cuboid cell having the highest aggregating value) from a particular *GR*, all matchable cells containing this local maximum will increase gradient factors (delta). Thus, our probe cells are given by the set of the maximum and minimum aggregating values (*GR+,GR-*) in that region, maximizing gradient search. For a cuboid cell to be eligible as a probe cell, it can be also a closed cell. For example, in Figure 3 the cuboid cell = {x1,y2,z3} is a closed cell on a *GR-*. Next, intersecting *GR+*[x1] and *GR-*[x1], will provide a candidate gradient cell = {x1,*,*}. Finally we select possible matchable cells by projecting this cell against the *Sd* subset of *GR*[x1]. For example, gradients cells in *GR*[x1] are evaluated by cells {{x1,y2,*};{x1,*,z3}} to {x1,*,*}.

Usually we will have several valid projections rather than in the previous example. Therefore, the final solution must take into account all valid projections before *raking Top-K cells*. Besides, after having calculated all local cells (by each projection), we continue searching for other valid gradient cells resulting from *matchable cells* (i.e., projecting probe cells from a GR_i over cuboid cells in GR_j). It is important to mention that one just needs to intersect cells from their *inverted indices* (Li, 2004). From the above discussion we summarize our Gradient-based cubing (TopK$_{gr}$-Cube) method as follows.

Pseudo Algorithm TopK$_{gr}$-Cube

<u>Input</u>: a table relation t_{rel}; an iceberg condition on average *min_avg*; a gradient constraint *min_delta*; the number of Top-K cells K

    <u>Output</u>: the set of gradient-cell pairs *TopK$_{gr}$*.
Method:

1.   Let ft_{rel} be the relation fact table
2.   Build inverted index, 1-D cuboids and *GR-tree*
3.   Call TopK$_{gr}$-Cube().

Procedure TopK$_g$-Cube(ft, Index, GR, min_avg, min_delta, K)
1: Get 1-D cuboids ordered by *spreadness*
//Level I: build *gradient regions*
2: For each maxCell in GR$_{tree}$ do {
//maxCell is a closed cell in GR$_{tree}$
1st level
3: maxCell' ← reorder dimension values of maximalCell
4:    if M(maxCell') < M(*)
     then Set GR⁻ ← maxCell' and their first descendents
     else Set GR⁺ ← maxCell' and their first descendents}
//Level II: rank *gradient regions*
5: For each GR$^{\{+,-\}}$ do {
6:    Set GRprojs ← valid projections of actual GR$^{\{+,-\}}$ with all others GRs$^{\{+,-\}}$ ordered by Δ_{max}} // apply **p1** if Δ_{max} < *min_delta*
//Level III: search gradients
7: For each GRproj of GRprojs do {
8:    Set TopK$_{pc}$ ← Top-K probe cells of the first region of GRproj //

Last-K if region is GR⁻
9:    Set LastK$_{pc}$ ← Last-K probe cells of the second region of GR-proj // Top-K if the first region is GR⁻
10:   For each probeCell1 of TopK$_{pc}$ do{
11:      For each probeCell2 of LastK$_{pc}$ do{
12:   Set probeGradient ← gradient of probeCell1 and probeCell2 // apply **p2** if probeGradient < *min_delta*
  // probeGradient is the maximum gradient by // comparing those matchable cells
13:        if probeCell1 and probeCell2 are matchable cells
       then Set TopK$_{pc}$ ← probeGradient
14:   Set TopK$_{pc}$ ← all gradients of all matchable cells cells of the intersection of both probeCell1 and probeCell2 GRs$_{tree}$
15:   if (TopK size == K) *min_delta* ← max(last value of TopK, *min_delta*)

5.5 Estimating Projections in TopK$_{gr}$-Cube with Non-Iceberg Dependence

Since we guide the whole search of gradients by exploring *spreadness* (*sf*) measure of gradient regions, we can also estimate the number of projections $P'GR$ to handle in order to identify the K gradients cells according to a minimum delta (Δ_{min}) from a relation R. Assuming that the firsts GR' are those ones with higher *spreadness*, and from which any projection GR'', is maximized through theirs maximum delta (Δ_{max}), we can calculate, approximately, the total number of projections (see Equation 6) by the following *boxplot-based equation*:

Table 3. The overall information of each dataset

Dataset	Tuples	Dims	Card*	M[min,max]
D1	5000	7	100	100,1000
D2	10000	10	100	100,1000
D3	20000	10	100	100,1000

$$GR_{\Delta max} = \begin{cases} GR_{75\%} = \dfrac{3 \times (Card(GR)) + 2}{4} \\ GR_{50\%} = \dfrac{(Card(GR)) + 1}{2} \\ GR_{25\%} = \dfrac{(Card(GR)) + 2}{4} \end{cases}, \ni sf(GR_{\Delta 75\%}) \ge sf(GR_{\Delta 50\%}) \ge sf(GR_{\Delta 25\%})$$

Eq. (8)

From Equation.8 we can define an upper bound limit to maximize gradient search. Different from a classical *box-plot*, those limits are on a reversal order:

$$\Delta_{upper} = \Delta(GR_{75\%}) + \left(\left(\Delta(GR_{75\%}) - \Delta(GR_{25\%}) \right) \times 1.5 \right)$$

Eq. (9)

By using this upper adjacent limit, we can say that any projection *GR''* that does not satisfy this upper bound constraint cannot provide highest gradients. While traversing *GR-tree* to locate gradients we may say that those initial partitions *TOP-K P(GR)*, more dense ones, will be locate from that left to the right of the tree.

6 PERFORMANCE STUDY

TopK$_{gr}$-Cube was coded with Java 1.5, and it was performed over synthetic datasets (see Table 3). These datasets were generated using the data generator described in (Dong, 2004; Han, 2001). All the experiments were performed on a 1.86GHz Pentium M with 256Mb of Java Virtual Machine (JVM) memory, running Windows XP Professional.

When running the next performance study, we confine our tests with TopK$_{gr}$-Cube to the following scenarios:

- *Scenario One*, (Figures 4, 6 and 7) we want to see the effects of using K and Δ_{min} parameters as main constraints for mining Top-K gradient cells. Given that on real applications we will be able to investigate a few examples, from those figures we can observe that the present strategy presents an interesting behavior when recovering small K (K<=100).

- *Scenario Two*, (Figure 5) we want to see the computational costs involved on each level of our strategy. The costs at each level are balanced when dealing with small K. For recovering more cells (K>100), more efforts on searching gradient cells (*Level-3*) are required which increases computational costs. As we expected *Level-3* poses more challenge for exploring new pruning studies.

- *Scenario Three*, (Figures 8 to 10) the pruning effects by using the heuristics used by our Top-K cubing method. Again, we can see that for recovering small K, both P1 and P2 poses good tradeoff between processed projections x pruned cells. P1 works better on very sparse databases, pruning efficiently non-valid projections. P2 increases the chances of finding good candidate probe cells in the very beginning of the process, pruning non-valid probe cells as soon as possible. This simple heuristic reduces the search space for evaluating candidate gradient pairs by at least one order of magnitude.

We can see through those performance figures that our method is a promising OLAPing method

Figure 4. Left: D1 Performance: Run.time(seconds) (Y-axis) x K effects (X-axis); Right: D1 Performance: Runtime(seconds) (Y-axis) x Δ_{min} effects (X-axis).

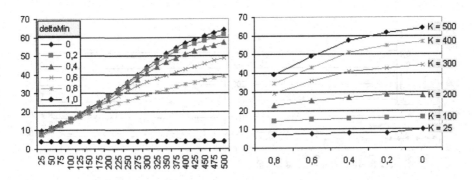

Figure 5. D1 TopK$_{gr}$-Cube levels: Impact(%) (Y-axis) x K effects (X-axis, bottom) and Δ_{min} effects (X-axis, top).

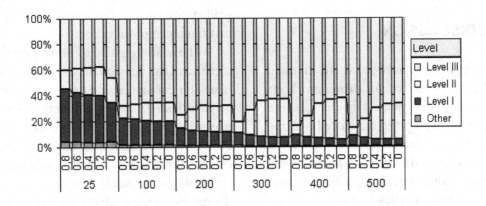

Figure 6. Left: D2 Performance: Runtime(seconds) (Y-axis) x K effects (X-axis); Right: D2 Performance: Runtime(seconds) (Y-axis) x Δ_{min} effects (X-axis).

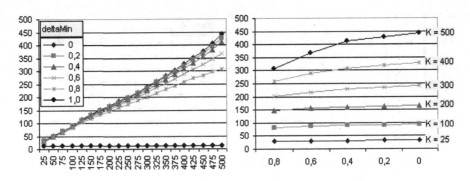

Figure 7. Left: D3 Performance: Runtime(seconds) (Y-axis) x K effects (X-axis); Right: D3 Performance: Runtime(seconds) (Y-axis) x Δ_{min} effects (X-axis)

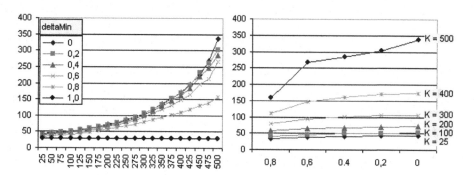

for raking gradients in a MDS, by applying a *Gradient-based cubing* strategy to retrieve Top-K gradient cells from a MDS.

7 FINAL DISCUSSION

In this chapter, we have proposed an effective and efficient OLAPing method for *raking gradients in MDS*. Gradients are interesting changes in a set of measures (aggregates) associated with the changes in the core characteristics of cube cells. We have also proposed a *Gradient-based cubing* strategy to evaluate interesting gradient regions in MDS. This strategy relies on cubing gradient regions presenting high *spreadness*. Thus, the main

challenge is to find *maximum gradient regions* (MGRs) that maximize the task of mining Top-K gradient cells. To do so, we devised a *gradient ascent* approach with a set of pruning heuristics guided by a specific *GR-tree* followed with new partitioning approach.

We have also verified by several performance scenarios that dense databases have workload issues on *cubing(Level-3)* and sparse databases on *partitioning(Level-2)*. Therefore, it would be reasonable to apply other soft constraints (Wang, 2006), on those databases, and thus, smoothing computational costs in both levels. Given that real applications usually provide sparse databases (Beyer, 1999), our method reduces computational cost by at least an order of magnitude. Additionally,

Figure 8. Left: Processed projections (Y-axis) x K effects (X-axis); Right: Impact of heuristic P1 on D1: Pruned projections(%) (Y-axis) x Δ_{min} effects (X-axis).

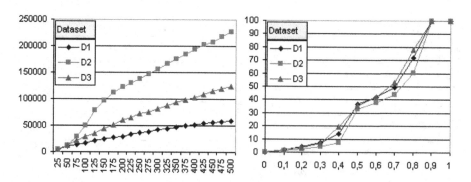

Figure 9. Impact of heuristic P2 on D1. Left: Processed Cells (Y-axis) x K effects (X-axis); Right: Processed Gradients (Y-axis) x K effects (X-axis).

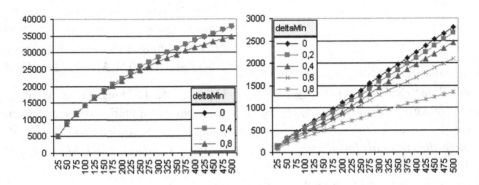

from a practical point of view, we demonstrated that the method is robust while retrieving small (10-25) *K* gradient cells.

Our performance study indicates that our strategy is effective and efficient on mining the most interesting gradients in MDS. To conclude this discussion we set the following topics as interesting issues for future research:

- *Top-K average pruning into GRs*. Although, we make pruning of *GRs* according to an iceberg condition. One can take advantage of Top-K average (Han, 2001), for cubing only *GRs* satisfying this condition. Furthermore, it would be interesting to use

the equation in Section 5.5 to couple with iceberg condition in order to explore monitonicity properties within the *spreadness measure*.

- *Looking ahead for Top-K gradients*. Given that $P_1 >> P_2 >> P_3$, it should be the case that by looking ahead for a gradient cell in projection P_2 will not generate gradients higher than that in P_1. This could be achieved by evaluating *delta maximums* for all next partitions. We also verified in the performance study that we can constraint the maximum number of projection by re-writing equation 6:

Figure 10. Impact of heuristic P2 on D3. Left: Processed Cells (Y-axis) x K effects (X-axis); Right: Processed Gradients (Y-axis) x K effects (X-axis).

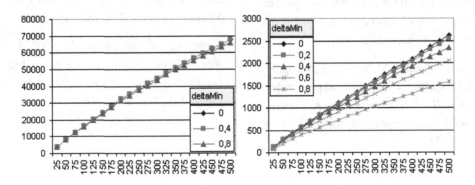

$$P_{\max}(GR) = \min\left(Card(P(GR)), \max(K \times K, \frac{X}{2})\right)$$

Eq. (10)

where X is the number of records in a table relation R. We split R on a *median basis*. Though, it is also possible to make use of Equation 8 applying quartiles instead.

Mining high-dimensional Top-K cells. The idea is to select small-fragments (Li, 2004), with some measure of interest, and then explore on-line query computation to mine high-dimensional Top-K cells. It would be interesting to evaluate the proposed strategy on *relational database engine*, and such small-fragments could be used to define proper *multi-dimensional query views*.

REFERENCES

Beyer, K., & Ramakrishnan, R. (1999). Bottom-up computation of sparse and iceberg CUBE. In *Proceedings of the International Conference on Management of Data (SIGMOD)*.

Bruno, N., Chaudhuri, S., & Gravano, L. (2002). Top-k selection queries over relational databases: Mapping strategies and performance evaluation. *ACM Transactions on Database Systems, 27*(2), 153–187. doi:10.1145/568518.568519

Chang, Y., Bergman, L., Castelli, V., Li, C.-S., Lo, M.-L., & Smith, J. R. (2000). Onion technique: Indexing for linear optimization queries. In *Proceedings of the International Conference on Management of Data (SIGMOD)*.

Dong, G., Han, J., Lam, J. M. W., Pei, J., Wang, K., & Zou, W. (2004). Mining constrained gradients in large databases. *IEEE Transactions on Knowledge Discovery and Data Engineering, 16*(8), 922–938. doi:10.1109/TKDE.2004.28

Gray, J., Chaudhuri, S., Bosworth, A., Layman, A., Reichart, D., & Venkatrao, M. (1997). Data cube: A relational aggregation operator generalizing group-by, cross-tab, and sub-totals. *Journal of Data Mining and Knowledge Discovery, 1*(1), 29–53. doi:10.1023/A:1009726021843

Han, J., Pei, J., Dong, G., & Wank, K. (2001). Efficient computation of iceberg cubes with complex measures. In *Proceedings of the International Conference on Management of Data (SIGMOD)*.

Hristidis, V., Koudas, N., & Papakonstantinou, Y. (2001). Prefer: A system for the efficient execution of multi-parametric ranked queries. In *Proceedings of the International Conference on Management of Data (SIGMOD)*.

Imielinski, T., Khachiyan, L., & Abdulghani, A. (2002). Cubegrades: Generalizing association rules. *Data Mining and Knowledge Discovery, 6*(3), 219–257. doi:10.1023/A:1015417610840

Li, X., Han, J., & Gonzalez, H. (2004). High-dimensional OLAP: A minimal cubing approach. In *Proceedings of the International Conference on Very Large Databases (VLDB)*.

Sarawagi, S., Agrawal, R., & Megiddo, N. (1998). Discovery-driven exploration of OLAP data cubes. In *Proceedings of the International Conference on Extending Database Technology (EDBT)*.

Sarawagi, S., & Sathe, G. (2000). i3: Intelligent, interactive investigaton of OLAP data cubes. In *Proceedings of the International Conference on Management of Data (SIGMOD)*.

Sathe, G., & Sarawagi, S. (2001). Intelligent rollups in multi-dimensional OLAP data. In *Proceedings of the International Conference on Very Large Databases (VLDB)*.

Wang, J., Han, J., & Pei, J. (2006). Closed constrained gradient mining in retail databases. *IEEE Transactions on Knowledge and Data Engineering, 18*(6), 764–769. doi:10.1109/TKDE.2006.88

Wu, T., Xin, D., & Han, J. (2008). ARCube: Supporting ranking aggregate queries in partially materialized data cubes. In *Proceedings of the International Conference on Management of Data (SIGMOD)*.

Xin, D., Han, J., & Chang, K. (2007). Progressive and selective merge: Computing top-k with ad-hoc ranking functions. In *Proceedings of the International Conference on Management of Data (SIGMOD)*.

Xin, D., Han, J., Cheng, H., & Xiaolei, L. (2006a). Answering top-k queries with multi-dimensional selections: The ranking cube approach. In *Proceedings of the International Conference on Very Large Databases (VLDB)*.

Xin, D., Shao, Z., Han, J., & Liu, H. (2006b). C-cubing: Efficient computation of closed cubes by aggregation-based checking. In *Proceedings of the 22nd International Conference on Data Engineering (ICDE)*.

ENDNOTE

* Those cardinalities provide very sparse data cubes, thus, poses more challenge to the Top-K cubing computation model.

Chapter 12
Simultaneous Feature Selection and Tuple Selection for Efficient Classification

Manoranjan Dash
Nanyang Technological University, Singapore

Vivekanand Gopalkrishnan
Nanyang Technological University, Singapore

ABSTRACT

Feature selection and tuple selection help the classifier to focus to achieve similar (or even better) accuracy as compared to the classification without feature selection and tuple selection. Although feature selection and tuple selection have been studied earlier in various research areas such as machine learning, data mining, and so on, they have rarely been studied together. The contribution of this chapter is that the authors propose a novel distance measure to select the most representative features and tuples. Their experiments are conducted over some microarray gene expression datasets, UCI machine learning and KDD datasets. Results show that the proposed method outperforms the existing methods quite significantly.

INTRODUCTION

It is no longer news that data are increasing very rapidly day-by-day. Particularly with Internet becoming so prevalent everywhere, the sources of data have become numerous. Data are increasing in both ways: dimensions or features and instances or examples or tuples, not all the data are relevant though. While gathering the data on any particular aspect, usually one tends to gather as much information as will be required for various tasks. One may not explicitly have any particular task, for example classification, in mind. So, it behooves for a data mining expert to remove the noisy, irrelevant and redundant data before proceeding with classification because many traditional algorithms fail in the presence of such noisy and irrelevant data (Blum and Langley 1997). As an example, consider microarray gene expression data where there are thousands of features (or genes) and only 10s of tuples (or sample tests). For example, Leukemia cancer data (Alon, Barkai et al. 1999) has 7129 genes and 72 sample tests. It has been shown that even with very few genes one can achieve the same or even better prediction ac-

DOI: 10.4018/978-1-60566-748-5.ch012

Copyright © 2010, IGI Global. Copying or distributing in print or electronic forms without written permission of IGI Global is prohibited.

curacy than whole data. Similarly not all sample tests are necessary for the classification task. In addition to this advantage, removing such noisy features and tuples improves the understanding of the user by bringing focus.

Thus, as a solution, in this chapter we study how to remove the noisy and irrelevant features and tuples while improving or at least not significantly reducing the prediction accuracy. This task is called "focusing" in this chapter, i.e, select the relevant features and tuples in order to improve the overall learning. In the literature many feature selection and tuple selection methods have been proposed (Dash and Liu 1997; Liu and Motoda 1998). Feature selection algorithms can be broadly grouped as wrapper and filter (Blum and Langley 1997; Kohavi and John 1997; Liu and Motoda 1998; Inza, Larranaga et al. 2004). In the wrapper method the classifier is used as an evaluation function to evaluate and compare the candidate feature subsets. In filter method evaluation of feature subsets is usually independent of the final classifier. In tuple selection, a broad category of methods let the learning algorithm to select the relevant tuples (Blum and Langley 1997; Liu and Motoda 2001; Fragoudis, Meretakis et al. 2002).

Contribution of this chapter is that we propose a distance measure to select representative features and tuples. Experimental results over several microarray datasets[1] and UCI machine learning repository datasets (Asuncion and Newman 2007) and UCI KDD archive (Hettich and Bay 1999) show that the proposed TwoWayFocused algorithm performs better than the existing feature selection methods.

The rest of the chapter is organized as follows. In the next section we briefly discuss the related work in feature selection and tuple selection for classification. In Section 3 we describe the distance measure, and then describe our proposed feature selection method for classification using the distance measure. In Section 4 we describe our proposed tuple selection method for classification using the distance measure. In Section 5 we describe how to handle different types of data such as binary, nominal, discrete, and continuous. Section 6 describes the empirical study where we show the comparison results between the proposed algorithm and some existing methods. The chapter concludes in Section 7.

RELATED WORK

We study the related work in feature selection and tuple selection. We will mainly draw our references from the work that has been done in the area of machine learning.

Feature Selection

Feature selection is defined by many authors by looking at it from different angles. A common definition is:Definition 1. The aim of feature selection is to choose a subset of features for improving prediction accuracy or decreasing the number of features without significantly decreasing prediction accuracy of the classifier built using only the selected features (John, Kohavi et al. 1994).

Ideally feature selection methods search through the subsets of features and try to find out the best one among the competing 2m subsets according to some evaluation criterion. Here m is the number of features. But this procedure is exhaustive and impractical even for moderate size m. Other methods are based on heuristic or random search. These methods need a stopping criterion to prevent an exhaustive search. So, a typical feature selection process consists of (a) search and generate procedure, (b) an evaluation function, (c) a stopping criterion, and (d) a validation function to validate the selected features (Dash and Liu 1997).

The evaluation function measures the goodness of a feature subset. It can either be wrapper (Kohavi and John 1997; Kim, Street et al. 2000) or filter (Liu and Setiono 1996; Hall 2000; Yu and

Liu 2003). The wrapper models use the prediction accuracy of a predetermined learning algorithm to determine the goodness of a feature subset. These methods are computationally expensive for data with large number of features (Kohavi and John 1997). The filter model separates feature selection from classifier learning and selects feature subsets that are independent of any learning algorithm. It relies on various measures of the general characteristics of the training data such as distance, information, dependency, and consistency (Dash and Liu 1997). Search is another key problem in feature selection. To balance the tradeoff of result optimality and computational efficiency, different search strategies such as complete, heuristic, and random search have been studied to generate candidate feature subsets for evaluation (Dash and Liu 1997). According to the availability of class labels, there are feature selection methods for supervised learning (Dash and Liu 1997; Yu and Liu 2003) as well as for unsupervised learning (Kim, Street et al. 2000; Dash, Choi et al. 2002). Feature selection has found success in many applications like text categorization (Yang and Pedersen 1997), image retrieval (Dy, Brodley et al. 2003), genomic microarray analysis (Xing, Jordan et al. 2001; Goh, Song et al. 2004; Yu and Liu 2004). The process of search and generate, and evaluate ends when a stopping criterion is satisfied. A stopping criterion can be (a) whether a predetermined number of features are selected, (b) whether a predetermined number of iterations reached, (c) whether optimal feature subset based on the evaluation function obtained, and so on. The feature selection process halts by outputting a selected subset of features to a validation procedure.

Representatives of wrapper model include (Xiong, Fang et al. 2001; Goh, Song et al. 2004). In (Xiong, Fang et al. 2001), Xiong et al. introduced a wrapper feature selection method, called SFS. It is essentially a heuristic search, in which the evaluation criterion is the accuracy of learning algorithms. The other method, which is proposed by Goh et al. in (Goh, Song et al. 2004), is a hybrid method that is a combination of filter and wrapper model. In the filter process, features are grouped based on their similarity using Pearson correlation coefficient, and then they are ranked according to the signal-to-noise ratio (SNR) and the feature with the highest value is chosen as the representative of its group. In the wrapper process, features are ranked according to their SNR value before being fed to a learning algorithm to find the subset with the highest prediction accuracy.

Traditional filter feature selection methods select features by ranking them according to informative characteristics, which form their relevance to class concept, and then pick the top-ranked features only (Golub, Slonim et al. 1999; Model, Adorjn et al. 2001). Research show that just combining highly relevant features in the final subset does not give the best prediction accuracy since many of them are redundant (Ding and Peng 2003), that is, their information about the class label is subsumed by others. Assessing the degree of redundancy of a feature against a subset is a highly complicated task. Some single-phase methods can remove redundant features but require the computational time of $O(m^2)$ (Ding and Peng 2003), where m is the number of features in the original data. It raises the need for multiple-phase algorithms, where the search space is significantly reduced in the first phase by a data reduction algorithm; next, the smaller search space is examined more closely in the second phase. To scale down the number of features, the widely-used technique is clustering. For example, in (Jaeger, Sengupta et al. 2003), similar groups of features are created by using a clustering technique, and then a test-statistic is applied for each group to select the final features. The shortcoming of clustering-based methods is that they depend on the clustering algorithm which is often influenced by noisy data. Other methods try to reduce the high number of features by using a simple random sampling technique (SRS) to quickly select initial features and then perform more detailed search over them (Liu and Setiono 1996; Dash and Liu 2003). It is known that SRS gives good representative samples when the sample size is moderate or large (Bronnimann, Chen et al. 2003). However, SRS is unable to maintain the underlying structure of the original dataset, when the sample size is small.

Tuple Selection

Similar to feature selection, there has been some work in tuple selection where the aim is to find informative and representative tuples to assist the learning task on hand. There are primarily three main reasons for performing tuple selection: (a) to reduce computation time by ignoring redundant tuples, (b) to reduce the cost of labeling as superfluous tuples are discarded, and (c) to increase the efficiency of the learning algorithm by focusing only on relevant and informative tuples. Approaches in tuple selection can be categorized as embedded methods where the process of tuple selection occurs within the inductive learning algorithm, and does not use classification algorithm as the evaluation function; or as wrapper methods where the tuple selection uses the classification algorithm as the evaluation function; or as filter methods where tuple selection is done in order to bring focus in the learning task. Examples of embedded methods for tuple selection include perceptron (Rosenblatt 1962), k-nearest neighbor (Cover and Hart 1967), heterogeneous probabilistic classifier (Lewis and Catlett 1994). Methods like (Rosenblatt 1962; Cover and Hart 1967), also called conservative algorithms, are based on the idea that they can learn only from tuples that cause misclassification, and hence ignore all tuples on which their classification is correct. In cases where there is an amount of uncertainty in class labels of the tuples, (Lewis and Catlett 1994) essentially overcomes the labeling cost by using an efficient probabilistic classifier to filter out tuples which are then fed to the C4.5 (Quinlan 1993) classifier. Some of the tuple selection methods based on the

wrapper approach are the windowing technique (Quinlan 1983; Schapire 1990). In (Quinlan 1983) a decision tree iteratively generated from a random set of misclassified tuples is used to classify the entire dataset. A boosting technique in (Schapire 1990) keeps changing the distribution of the training data to the learning algorithm to focus more on the misclassified data.

In this chapter we propose a filter feature selection and filter tuple selection algorithm.

Feature Selection

The proposed feature selection method is a two-phase algorithm where in the first phase we rank the features based on their relevance to the class label, and in the second phase we select from the top-ranking features in order to remove the redundant features. Before introducing the feature selection method, we briefly describe the notations and define a distance function used in the feature selection method.

Notations

Let the data D have n number of tuples and m denote the number of features. Let I be the set of tuples where I_i is the ith tuple for $i = 1, ..., n$. F be the set of features where f_j is the jth feature for $j = 1, ..., m$. C is the set of class labels. We will introduce other notations as and when they become necessary.

Histogram Based Distance Measure

The proposed TwoWayFocused method tries to find a small subset having -itemset frequencies that are close to those in the entire database. The distance or discrepancy of any subset S_0 of a superset S with respect to 1-itemset frequencies is computed by the L2-norm (Euclidean distance) as follows:

$$dist(S_0, S) = \sum (freq(A; S_0) - freq(A; S))^2$$

$$(1)$$

where A is an 1-itemset, and each element in subset S and S_0 is a set of items. Using this distance function we can compare two subsets S_1 and S_2 for their representative-ness of the superset S: if $dist(S_1, S) < dist(S_2, S)$, then arguably S_1 is a better representative of the whole set than S_2. In place of L2-norm, we can also use L1-norm (Manhattan distance) and L_∞-norm.

Without losing generality consider, for this subsection, that there are a set of transactions T and a set of items E where each transaction T_i is represented by a binary vector of length E. Values in T_i are either 0 or 1 depending on whether the corresponding item is present or absent in the transaction respectively. Represent by A any item in E. Then

$$freq(A; T) = \frac{num(A; T)}{|T|}$$

is the relative frequency of item A in the set T where $num(A; T)$ is the number of transactions in T that contain item A (i.e., for item A, $num(A; T)$ transactions in T have value 1 and $|T| - num(A; T)$ transactions have value 0). For all A in E, we can plot $freq(A; T)$ to generate the frequency histogram H_T.

Let $T1$ and $T2$ be two subsets of T where $T1 = T2$. We want to determine which of these two subsets is a better representative of T. Here, we define representative-ness in a broad sense. If T' is a representative of T then using T' one can carry out, with reasonable efficiency, the usual data exploration tasks including classification, clustering and association rule mining. One way of determining representative-ness is if the distance between the histograms for $T1$ and T is smaller than the distance between the histograms for $T2$ and T then it suggests that $T1$ may be a better representative of T than $T2$. It suggests that $T2$

contains more outlier transactions (i.e., transactions having items whose frequency is less than average item frequency) than $T1$. To be sure, one needs to compare the frequency histograms of 2-itemsets, 3-itemsets, and so on. But as our experiments suggest, often it is enough to compare the 1-itemset histograms. The proposed method, although based on 1-itemset histograms, can be easily extended to histograms of higher number of itemsets by simply adding them in constructing the histogram. On the flip side, when we consider histograms for higher itemsets, the computational cost increases very rapidly. In a way, one contribution of this chapter is to show convincingly that simply by considering histograms for 1-itemsets gives a fairly accurate measure of representative-ness. In the rest of the chapter we consider distances based on 1-itemset histograms.

Feature Ranking

In this section we show how the proposed distance function can be used to rank features based on their relevance. Relevance of a feature is defined in (John, Kohavi et al. 1994) as features whose removal would affect the original class distribution. In the previous section we showed that it is possible to compare two subsets for their representativeness of a superset. We extend this idea to compare individual features. Given that F is the total set of features, we can compare two features f_1 and f_2 as follows: if $dist(F - \{f_1\}, F) < dist(F - \{f_2\}, F)$ then f_2 is arguably better than f_1.

The idea is that if by removing feature f_1 distance of the resultant set $\{F - f2\}$ from the whole set F is greater than the distance of $\{F - f_1\}$ (after removing f_1) from the whole set F, then it indicates that f_2 is arguably a better representative of F than f_1. We can easily extend this idea to rank all the features. For each feature $f_j, j = 1, ..., m$, compute $dist(F - \{f_1\}, F)$. Features having larger distances are given higher ranks. In Equation 1 the frequencies are determined for 1-itemsets. To compute in a similar fashion data must be binary valued (i.e., 0 or 1). Later in Section 5, we describe how to deal with other types of data such as nominal, discrete, and continuous. As we are dealing with classification task, data has class labels. We can make use of class information simply by first separating the data into groups based on the class labels. Then we apply the ranking algorithms for each group of tuples. Next we add the ranks of each feature for all groups to find out the overall rankings. Ties are broken arbitrarily, i.e., if two features f_1 and f_2 have the same overall rank, then one of them is placed first and the other next to it. So, when we select a certain number of features, then we may select only f_1 not f_2. As our experiments show, this is a simple yet powerful way of utilizing the class information.

Feature Selection to remove Redundancy

After ranking the features we need to select a subset of features. The main goal here is to remove redundancy because while ranking the features we did not consider the fact that there may be redundant features.

In phase 2, we use a measure called inconsistency measure (Dash and Liu 2003) to remove redundancy. Inconsistency of a feature subset is measured by finding out how inconsistent it is vis-a-vis the class label. It is defined as follows.

1. A pattern is a part of a tuple without class label, i.e., given a feature subset consisting of two binary features, there can be maximum 4 patterns {0,0}, {0,1}, {1,0}, and {1,1}. A pattern is considered inconsistent if there exists at least two tuples such that they match all but their class labels; for example, an inconsistency is caused by tuples (0,1,1) and (0,1,0) where the bold-faced numbers are the class labels. In this example the first two numbers in each tuple constitute the pattern.

2. The inconsistency count for a pattern of a feature subset is the number of times the pattern appears in the data minus the largest number among different class labels. For example, let us assume for a feature subset S a pattern p appears n_p times out of which c_1 tuples have class label 1, c_2 tuples have class label 2, and c_3 tuples have class label 3, where $c_1 + c_2 + c_3 = n_p$. If c_3 is the largest among the three, the inconsistency count is $(n - c_3)$. Notice that the sum of all n_p s over different patterns p that appear in the data for the feature subset S is the total number of tuples n in the dataset, i.e., $\sum_p n_p = n$.

3. The inconsistency rate of a feature subset S, denoted by $I_R(S)$, is the sum of all the inconsistency counts over all patterns of the feature subset that appears in the data divided by n.

Although inconsistency measure can be used directly to remove the redundant features, in order to search through the feature space we need a more efficient mechanism than a simple exhaustive method. We propose to use forward selection algorithm. A forward selection algorithm works as follows. In the beginning the highest ranked feature (according to phase 1) is selected. Note that the phase 2 is invoked after phase 1 where features are ranked by the distance measure. Then if the task is to select $|S'|$ number of features we take 2 * $|S'|$ top-ranked features. Then we find out the best feature to add to the highest ranked feature by sequentially going through 2 * $|S'| - 1$ features. We compare the subsets by measuring their redundancy and relevance. Redundancy is measured by inconsistency rate, and relevance is measured by determining the correlation between the subset of features. and the class. We use mutual information to estimate the correlation. It is described as follows.

Mutual information: Let X and Y be two random variables with joint distribution p(x, y) and marginal distribution p(x) and p(y). The mutual information M(X; Y) is given as:

$$M(X;Y) = \sum_x \sum_y p(x,y) \log \frac{p(x,y)}{p(x)p(y)} \quad (2)$$

It can be seen that mutual information is conceptually a kind of "distance" between the joint distribution $p(x, y)$ and the product distribution $p(x) p(y)$. It measures how much knowing one of these variables reduces our uncertainty about the other. For example, if X and Y are independent i.e., $p(x, y) = p(x) p(y)$, then knowing X does not give any information about Y and vice versa, so their mutual information is zero. At the other extreme, if X and Y are identical then all information conveyed by X is shared with Y: knowing X determines the value of Y and vice versa. The larger value of M indicates variables are more dependent. Thus, mutual information is appropriate to measure the correlation between a feature and the class.

We combine these two measures, i.e., mutual information M, and inconsistency measure I_R as follows. As discussed initially S' is the highest ranked feature f_r, i.e., $S' = \{ f_r \}$. Suppose that at a certain stage we are considering feature f_j and we denote $S' = S' \cup \{ f_r \}$, then the next feature to be added to S' is

$$f^* = \arg\max_{f_j} (w_1 * M(f_j, C) + \frac{w_2}{I_R(S')}) \quad (3)$$

Our empirical experiments suggest that w_1 is 0.9 and w_2 is 0.2. The overall feature selection algorithm is as follows.

```
Algorithm for feature selection
Input: D, F , C, numSelFea /* C is
the set of different class labels*/
Output: Selected Features S'
    /* Initialization */
S' = φ ;
    for k =1, ..., |C|
```

```
        for j =1, ..., mdistance_k[j]=
rank_k[j]= -1;
        for j =1, ...,
moverallRank[j] = 0;
    /* Separate the tuples based on
class information */
    for k =1, ..., CD_k = set of all
tuples having class label C_k;
    /* Rank the features for each
class label */
    for k =1, ... |C|
    for each feature  f_j ∈ F, j = 1,...,m F'
= F - f_j ;
        distance_k[j]= dist(F', F );
        rank_k = sortInDescendingOrder
(distance_k);
    /* Produce overall ranking */
    for j =1, ..., m
    for k =1, ..., |C|
            overallRank[j] =
overallRank[j] + rank_k[j];
    /* Select the features */
    initialize S'' to the top ranked
(2 * numSelFea) features from over-
allRank;
    for j_1 =1, ..., numSelFea
f* = arg max_{f_j} (w_1 * M(f_j,C) + \frac{w_2}{I_R(S')})
        where j =1, ..., 2 * numSelF-
ea;
        S' = S' + {f*};
    return S';
```

In the above algorithm, the procedure *sortInDescendingOrder* (*distance*) sorts the distances produced by the removal of the corresponding feature. Note that rank 1 or the highest rank corresponds to the highest distance, and so on.

Tuple Selection

Each tuple in the set of tuples I is first of all ranked using the same method described for ranking of features. Distance is computed by removing each tuple I_i from I in turn for $i = 1, ..., n$, and finally sorting the distances in descending order in order to produce ranks of the tuples. The difference between feature selection and tuple selection is the manner in which they utilize the class information. Like feature selection, here we first separate out the tuples based on their class labels. In an experimental set up there is a training set and a testing set. So, the tuples in the training set are separated out based on the class labels whereas the test set is untouched. Next, like feature selection, we compute the distance of each tuple under each class label. But notice that, unlike feature selection where each class had all the features, in tuple selection that is not the case. The total number n of tuples are divided among C number of class labels. So, here we select a proportionate number of top-ranking tuples from each group and the combination of such top-ranking tuples are output as the selected tuples. The idea is that the final sample should have proportionate number of tuples from each class label. Ties in rankings are arbitrarily broken. The detailed algorithm is as follows.

```
Algorithm for tuple selection
Input: D, I, C, numSelectedTuples
Output: Selected Tuples I'
    /* Initialization */
```
$I' = \varphi$;
```
    for k =1, ..., |C|
        for i =1, ..., ndistance_k[i]=
rank_k[i]= -1;
    /* Separate the tuples based on
class information */
    for k =1, ..., |C|
        D_k = set of all tuples having
class label C_k;
    /* Rank the tuples for each
class label */
    for k = 1, ..., |C|
```
for each tuple $I_{k_i} \in I_k$, $i =1, ...,$

$nI_k' = I_k - I_{k_i}$;
```
                distance_k[i]=
dist(I_k',I_k);
                rank_k = sortInDescend-
ingOrder (distance_k);
    /* Select the tuples */
    /* determine proportion of tu-
ples for each class label */
    for k =1, ..., |C|
        n_k = number of tuples having
class label C_k ;
```
select top $(\frac{n_k}{n}$ * numSelectedTu-

ples) from $rank_k$;
```
        put them in I';
    return I';
```

Finally we propose a new algorithm called TwoWayFocused which denotes first applying feature selection followed by tuple selection. In order to compare we also propose OneWayFocused which denotes only feature selection without performing tuple selection.

Handling Different Data Types

In this section we describe how to apply the proposed focused classification method for different data types such as binary, nominal, discrete and continuous. In this section, for ease of understanding we consider the data to be a matrix of rows and columns where the task is to select a set of rows. This holds true (a) for feature selection where features are considered rows and tuples are considered as columns, and (b) for tuple selection where tuples are considered rows and features are considered columns. Note that the proposed distance function works for binary data only. So, for binary type of data there is no need to modify it. For nominal data type, it is converted to binary using the following technique. First of all, count the number of different nominal values that appear in a column l. If column l takes p different values, then we convert it to p binary columns $l_1, l_2, ..., l_p$.

Discrete and Continuous Data Types

If a column has continuous data type, it is discretized first of all. In the literature there are many discretization methods which can be broadly grouped as supervised and unsupervized depending on whether they use the class information. A good survey is available in (Liu, Hussain et al. 2002). In this work we use a simple and popular discretization method called '0-mean 1-sigma' where mean is the statistical mean μ of the values in a column f_j and sigma is the standard deviation σ of column f_j (Yu and Liu 2004). This discretization method assumes that μ is at 0. Each value in the column takes a new discretized value from the set 1, 2, 3 based on the following conditions. Any numerical value in the range $[\mu - \sigma, \mu + \sigma]$ is assigned the discrete value 2, numerical values in the range $[-\infty, \mu - \sigma]$ is assigned the discrete value 1, and numerical values in the range $[\mu + \sigma, +\infty]$ is assigned the discrete value 3. After discretization each column is converted to 3 columns. An original value v will be converted to a vector of 3 binary values which can be {100}, or {010}, or {001}.

If a column has discrete data type, it is treated as continuous data and is discretized using the same method described here.

Empirical Study

In this section we describe the experiments conducted to test our proposed algorithm. We mainly used two groups of datasets – group 1: UCI machine learning repository (Asuncion and Newman 2007) and UCI KDD archive (Hettich and Bay 1999), and group 2: gene expression microarray datasets[2] (Asuncion and Newman 2007). Although both groups of data are high-dimensional, the difference is that in group 1 (UCI repository) the number of tuples usually far exceed the number

of features, whereas for microarray data the number of features or genes are in thousands but the tuples or samples are in 10s. The two groups have a mixture of continuous and nominal data types, and different number of classes. In Table 1 we give a summary of the datasets used in the empirical study. First, in Section 6.1 we describe the existing methods that are selected to compare our proposed algorithm, in Section 6.2 we describe the framework for comparison study, and finally in Section 6.3 we give our comparison results and analyze these results.

Existing Methods

Existing methods are selected keeping in mind the various taks that we perform in our proposed algorithm, such as feature ranking, feature selection, and tuple selection. We select three methods: ReliefF, t-test, and RBF (Kira and Rendell 1992; Kononenko 1994; Jaeger, Sengupta et al. 2003; Yu and Liu 2004). RBF is selected because it is a recently proposed and very successful feature selection method. We selected t-test or F-test because it is a commonly used feature ranking method that usually works well. We selected ReliefF because (a) arguably it is the most robust feature ranking and selection method, and (b) it has tuple selection, using random sampling, incorporated inside.

Framework for Comparison

Comparison is done based on prediction accuracy and time of a decision tree classifier. We chose C4.5 (Quinlan 1993) to obtain the accuracy, and we use system time. We used the WEKA implementation of C4.5 (Witten and Frank 2005). We chose C4.5 because of its popularity particularly in showing good results over UCI datasets. Each data is divided into a training set and a testing set. We use 10-fold cross-validation for each experiment, i.e, 9 folds are used for training and one fold is used for testing. Note that feature selection, tuple

Table 1. Summary of Datasets

Title	Features	Tuples	Classes
UCI ML/KDD Repository			
Coil2000	85	5822	2
Promoters	57	106	2
Splice	60	3190	3
Musk2	166	6598	2
Isolet	617	1560	26
Multi Features	649	2000	10
Lung Cancer	56	32	3
Arrhythmia	279	452	16
Gene Expression Microarray Data			
Colon Cancer	2000	62	2
Leukemia	7129	72	2
Prostate Cancer	12600	136	2
Lung Cancer (μarray)	12533	181	2

selection, and training of C4.5 decision tree are all done using the 9 folds, and finally the prediction accuracy is tested using the last fold. That means, reported accuracy and time are average of 10 (for 10 folds) runs. All experiments are conducted in a system with configuration Pentium 4, 1.6 GHz and 512 MB RAM.

The proposed algorithm TwoWayFocused performs both feature selection (FS) and tuple selection (TS). We implemented two versions of the algorithm: (a) without TS (OneWayFocused) and (b) with TS (TwoWayFocused). Comparison is done with the three existing algorithms discussed in Section 6.1 which are ReliefF, t-test, and RBF. Among these three, ReliefF and t-test are feature ranking methods whereas RBF is a feature selection method. We compare TwoWayFocused and OneWayFocused with these three methods in two ways: (a) ReliefF and t-test rank the features; so we compare the four algorithms for various number of top-ranked features; the range of the number of top-ranked features vary across datasets because total number of features vary, and (b) RBF outputs a single subset S'; so we take $|S'|$ top-ranked features for TwoWayFocused and

OneWayFocused.

Both RBF and the proposed algorithms Two-WayFocused and OneWayFocused first discretize the data for feature selection. Then the original (numerical) data is used for training and testing the C4.5 classifier using the selected features.

RESULTS AND ANALYSIS

In Tables 2 and 3 we give the comparison results of feature ranking using four algorithms: TwoWay-Focused, OneWayFocused, ReliefF and t-test. In Table 4 we give the comparison results of feature selection using three algorithms: TwoWay-Focused, OneWayFocused and RBF. The best prediction accuracy for each data is high-lighted.

In ALL experiments over 12 datasets, for both feature ranking and feature selection, the highest prediction accuracy is obtained by either TwoWayFocused or OneWayFocused. In feature ranking (see Tables 2 and 3), TwoWayFocused outperforms the other three algorithms including OneWayFocused. Only in 8 out of 60 experiments (12 datasets times 5 tests) for feature ranking,

Table 2. Comparison results for feature ranking for UCI ML/KDD repository datasets

Datasets	Accuracy						Time (sec)
UCI ML/KDD Repository Datasets							
CoiL2000	#Features	30	40	50	60	70	6.37
	ReliefF	93.9	92.3	90.1	88.2	88.4	0.40
	t-test	94	93.4	89.5	86.7	88.9	1.20
	OneWayFocused	94.7	93.1	93.1	91.3	90	2.13
	TwoWayFocused	**95**	**94.6**	**94.1**	**93.2**	**92**	
Promoters	#Features	10	20	30	40	50	0.09
	ReliefF	75	51.9	66.4	66.2	70.9	0.06
	t-test	77.6	74.3	76	75.1	74.8	0.02
	OneWayFocused	**80.2**	**80.2**	**81.3**	79	79.2	0.02
	TwoWayFocused	79.3	80.2	80.1	**80.5**	**82.4**	
Splice	#Features	20	30	40	50	60	2.68
	ReliefF	85.4	86.7	84.2	87.7	89.1	3.25
	t-test	86.1	88.9	85.2	89.2	87.4	0.71
	OneWayFocused	87.2	90	88.3	90.3	91	0.98
	TwoWayFocused	**89.8**	**91.5**	**90.4**	**92.1**	**92.6**	
Musk2	#Features 60 70 80 90 100						18.6
	ReliefF	80.5	78.6	78.4	75.2	77.4	34.69
	t-test	80.6	79.5	77.2	76.3	79.7	2.20
	OneWayFocused	80.2	83.1	83.5	81.2	82.1	3.45
	TwoWayFocused	**82**	**85.2**	**84.9**	**84.9**	**85.8**	
Isolet	#Features	65	85	105	125	150	20.80
	ReliefF	65.4	67.4	71.8	69.1	74	28.52
	t-test	77.6	79.7	75.3	70.9	74.6	3.03
	OneWayFocused	81.5	81.9	**83.7**	80.8	**83**	4.14
	TwoWayFocused	**82.5**	**83.5**	82.4	**82.9**	81.9	
Multi-Features	#Features	50	100	150	200	250	22.48
	ReliefF	85.5	86.7	84.2	83.6	82.1	18.92
	t-test	92	92.1	90.3	89.7	87.5	1.78
	OneWayFocused	87.2	91	92.4	89.3	91.1	2.98
	TwoWayFocused	**93.1**	**93.1**	**92.9**	**91.7**	**93.8**	
Lung Cancer	#Features	20	25	30	35	40	0.06
	ReliefF	83.1	82.8	81.7	80.9	80.2	0.03
	t-test	80.2	79.3	79.3	78	77.6	0.01
	OneWayFocused	**83.2**	84.6	**85.9**	84	83.7	0.01
	TwoWayFocused	81.7	**85.3**	85.2	**85.8**	**84.5**	
Arrhythmia	#Features	30	50	70	90	110	2.76
	ReliefF	66.2	65	65.6	64.1	62	1.86
	t-test	60.8	59.5	58.3	57.9	58.2	0.03
	OneWayFocused	63.1	64.4	63.2	66.9	63.1	0.03
	TwoWayFocused	**67.9**	**65.8**	**65.7**	**68.8**	**66.3**	

OneWay-Focused is better than TwoWayFocused. Similarly, in feature selection (see Table 4), TwoWayFocused is better than RBF and OneWayFocused for 11 out of 12 datasets, and for the remaining one time, OneWayFocused is better than RBF and TwoWayFocused. The prediction accuracy results of TwoWayFocused and OneWayFocused are more stable than the other algorithms. The possible reason is that the proposed algorithms are able to select important set of features that is

Table 3. Comparison results for feature ranking for microarray data

Datasets		Accuracy					Time (sec)
	#Features	31	62	124	248	496	
Colon Cancer	ReliefF	80.5	78.8	74.1	75.7	75	3.50
	t-test	81.6	75.5	80.4	80.5	74.1	0.03
	OneWayFocused	81.6	80.4	80.2	82.7	77	0.05
	TwoWayFocused	**82.9**	**84.8**	**83.1**	82.7	**79.1**	0.06
	#Features	56	112	224	448	896	
Leukemia	ReliefF	83.2	85.5	84.6	85.6	81.7	13.20
	t-test	78.1	83.7	83.1	86.3	80.3	0.13
	OneWayFocused	84.5	87.7	93.7	92.9	84.1	0.30
	TwoWayFocused	**86.5**	**89.6**	**94.4**	**93.2**	**87.4**	0.42
	#Features	98	196	392	784	1568	
Prostate Cancer	ReliefF	91.1	87.1	85.3	84.2	82.9	71.50
	t-test	73.6	76.3	76.9	75.3	78.5	1.31
	OneWayFocused	**91.4**	88.9	90.1	89.4	87.6	0.95
	TwoWayFocused	89.8	**90.1**	**90.1**	**90.3**	**87.7**	1.14
	#Features	19	38	76	152	304	
Lung Cancer (μArray)	ReliefF	**95.6**	96.2	96.1	95.1	95.6	124.70
	t-test	81	83.9	82.8	89.2	91.7	1.52
	OneWayFocused	**95.6**	96.2	97.1	94.3	95.8	2.12
	TwoWayFocused	93.1	**97.6**	**97.4**	**95.3**	**96.4**	2.89

Table 4. Comparison results for feature selection

Datasets	#Selected Features	RBF		OneWayFocused		TwoWayFocused	
		Accuracy	Time	Accuracy	Time	Accuracy	Time
UCI ML/KDD Repository Datasets							
CoiL2000	5	93	1.59	93.5	1.23	**94.3**	0.78
Promoters	6	72.6	0.11	83.6	0.03	**84.1**	0.02
Splice	12	91.7	1.67	94.8	1.61	**95.2**	0.8
Musk2	2	83.8	4.99	85.5	3.23	**86.8**	1.9
Isolet	25	83.5	9.05	84	8.2	**85.7**	9.3
Multi-Features	47	93.7	29.56	93.6	23.57	**95.9**	24.23
Lung Cancer	4	84.5	0.01	**84.9**	0.01	82.8	0.01
Arrhythmia	5	70.4	0.04	71.6	0.03	**72.2**	0.02
Microarray Datasets							
Colon Cancer	4	85.3	0.23	91.2	0.06	**92.6**	0.87
Leukemia	4	88.9	1.17	94.4	0.23	**94.4**	0.31
Prostate Cancer	78	86.7	14.34	92.2	1.23	**93.3**	2.41
Lung Cancer (μarray)	1	97.2	17.48	97.2	2.98	**97.2**	3.76

much close to the optimal set.

Similarly for time, for both ranking and selection, the lowest execution time is reported by either TwoWayFocused or OneWayFocused except for 3 datasets. For these 3 datasets, t-test reported the lowest execution time.

To test whether the results obtained were significant enough statistically, we compared TwoWayFocused with ReliefF, t-test and RBF. We use one-tailed (upper tail) paired t-test between the accuracy of TwoWayFocused and the accuracy of an existing algorithm. For level of significance 5%, all values are significant, i.e., the null hypothesis of equality (i.e., TwoWayFocused and the existing algorithm has no significant difference in performance) is rejected in all tests. The p-values are quite significant in most cases (e.g., < 0.0005).

An interesting outcome of this empirical study is that although the number of tuples or sample tests for gene expression microarray data is quite small (e.g., Leukemia dataset has only 72 tuples), still tuple selection improves the prediction accuracy even after reducing the number of tuples by half. Until now researchers have not considered the idea that some tuples may be unnecessary or even detrimental for prediction accuracy for classification of microarray data. They had only focused on how to reduce the thousands of genes or features (e.g., Leukemia dataset has 7129 genes) to 10s of genes. This new found information is going to assist the biologist in their study of gene functionalities.

The results show that the proposed feature ranking method using the histogram distance measure is working well in selecting the relevant features. It shows that by measuring the 1-itemset frequencies and comparing different feature subsets based on these frequencies has good performance in removing irrelevant features. The leave-one-out principle used in feature ranking is working well to rank the features correctly. The key idea is that removal of a highly relevant feature will cause higher distance from the whole set of features, than a less relevant feature. The mutual informa-

tion method and the inconsistency count method used for feature selection is able to remove the redundant features correctly.

CONCLUSION AND FUTURE DIRECTIONS

In this chapter we proposed focused classification using feature selection and tuple selection. The novelty of the work is that a distance based ranking method based on frequency histogram is used both for feature selection and tuple selection. Although the ranking is based on 1-itemset frequencies, the results showed that for a wide range of datasets the performance is better than existing algorithms. Although it applies directly to binary or count data (transactional data), we have shown that by using discretization it is easily extended to continuous and nominal data types. After ranking the features, we use a redundancy removal method to remove the redundant features. Experiments are conducted over some UCI ML repository datasets, UCI KDD archive datasets, and gene expression microarray datasets. The proposed algorithm TwoWayFocused consistently outperformed the three chosen existing algorithms Relief, t-test, and RBF. Also, results over a range of selected features showed that TwoWayFocused and OneWayFocused produce very good prediction accuracy consistently. This shows that the ranking using the proposed distance measure is effective at least for these tested datasets.

Future directions include a comparison study between distance measure based on 1-itemset frequencies, and distance measure based on larger itemsets. We foresee a trade-off between prediction accuracy and computational efficiency where distance measure based on 1-itemset will be computationally quite efficient while compromising a little bit in prediction accuracy vis-a-vis the distance measure based on larger itemsets. The trade-off will probably vary with the type of data. If the data has too much correlation among features, then distance measure based on larger itemsets will probably give better prediction accuracy.

Another future direction is to compare the proposed tuple selection algorithm with boosting, and similar algorithms. There are many differences between boosting and the proposed tuple selection algorithm, but their goals are the same, i.e., to enhance classification accuracy. The proposed tuple selection algorithm is deterministic at its present state. So, an immediate study can be to compare whether efficiency of the classifier is better by choosing samples using the Boosting strategy where "hard" portions of the data are given more chances to be selected in each iteration, compared with the one-time selection of the tuples using the proposed algorithm.

Another line of research is to use the proposed distance measure in the context of streaming data. The proposed algorithm computes distance for each tuple independent of other tuples because it uses the frequency histogram to compute the distance. This is a very suitable characteristic to be used in streaming data environment. Finally, we are currently extending the proposed method to clustering. Clustering has no class information but still the preliminary results are very encouraging.

REFERENCES

Alon, U., Barkai, N., et al. (1999). Broad patterns of gene expression revealed by clustering analysis of tumor and normal colon tissues probed by oligonucleotide arrays. Proceedings of the National Academy of Sciences of the United States of America, 96(12), 6745–6750. PubMeddoi:10.1073/pnas.96.12.6745doi:10.1073/pnas.96.12.6745

Asuncion, A., & Newman, D. J. (2007). *UCI machine learning repository*. Retrieved from http://www.ics.uci.edu/~mlearn/MLRepository.html

Blum, A., & Langley, P. (1997). Selection of relevant features and examples in machine learning. Artificial Intelligence, 97, 245–271. doi:10.1016/S0004-3702(97)00063-5doi:10.1016/S0004-3702(97)00063-5

Bronnimann, H., Chen, B., et al. (2003). Efficient data reduction with EASE. In *Proceedings of the SIGKDD* (pp. 59-68).

Cover, T. M., & Hart, P. E. (1967). Nearest neighbor pattern classification. IEEE Transactions on Information Theory, 13(1), 21–27. doi:10.1109/TIT.1967.1053964doi:10.1109/TIT.1967.1053964

Dash, M., & Liu, H. (1997). Feature selection for classification. Intelligent Data Analysis, 1(1-4), 131–156. doi:10.1016/S1088-467X(97)00008-5doi:10.1016/S1088-467X(97)00008-5

Dash, M., & Liu, H. (2003). Consistency-based search in feature selection. Artificial Intelligence, 151(1-2), 155–176. doi:10.1016/S0004-3702(03)00079-1doi:10.1016/S0004-3702(03)00079-1

Dash, M., Choi, K., et al. (2002). Feature selection for clustering - a filter solution. In *Proceedings of the ICDM* (pp. 115-122).

Ding, C., & Peng, H. (2003). Minimum redundancy feature selection from microarray gene expression data. In *Proceedings of the CSB* (pp. 523-529).

Dy, J. G., Brodley, C. E., et al. (2003). Unsupervised feature selection applied to content-based retrieval of lung images. IEEE Transactions on Pattern Analysis and Machine Intelligence, 25(3), 373–378. doi:10.1109/TPAMI.2003.1182100doi:10.1109/TPAMI.2003.1182100

Fragoudis, D., Meretakis, D., et al. (2002). Integrating feature and instance selection for text classification. In *Proceedings of the SIGKDD* (pp. 501-506).

Goh, L., Song, Q., et al. (2004). A novel feature selection method to improve classification of gene expression data. In *Proceedings of the APBC* (pp. 161-166).

Golub, T. R., Slonim, D. K., et al. (1999). Molecular classification of cancer: Class discovery and class prediction by gene expression monitoring. Science, 286(5439), 531–537. PubMeddoi:10.1126/science.286.5439.531doi:10.1126/science.286.5439.531

Hall, M. A. (2000). Correlation-based feature selection for discrete and numeric class machine learning. In *Proceedings of the ICML* (pp. 359-366).

Hettich, S., & Bay, S. D. (1999). The UCI KDD archive. Retrieved from http://kdd.ics.uci.edu

Inza, I., Larranaga, P., et al. (2004). Filter versus wrapper gene selection approaches in DNA microarray domains. Artificial Intelligence in Medicine, 31(2), 91–103. PubMeddoi:10.1016/j.artmed.2004.01.007doi:10.1016/j.artmed.2004.01.007

Jaeger, J., Sengupta, R., et al. (2003). Improved gene selection for classification of microarrays. In *Proceedings of the Pacific Symposium on Biocomputing* (pp. 53-64).

John, G. H., Kohavi, R., et al. (1994). Irrelevant features and the subset selection problem. In *Proceedings of the ICML* (pp. 121-129).

Kim, Y. S., Street, W. N., et al. (2000). Feature selection in unsupervised learning via evolutionary search. In *Proceedings of the KDD* (pp. 365-369).

Kira, K., & Rendell, L. A. (1992). The feature selection problem: Traditional methods and a new algorithm. In *Proceedings of the AAAI* (pp. 129-134).

Kohavi, R., & John, G. H. (1997). Wrappers for feature subset selection. Artificial Intelligence, 97(1-2), 273–324. doi:10.1016/S0004-3702(97)00043-Xdoi:10.1016/S0004-3702(97)00043-X

Kononenko, I. (1994). Estimating attributes: Analysis and extensions of RELIEF. In *Proceedings of the ECML* (pp. 171-182).

Lewis, D. D., & Catlett, J. (1994). Heterogenous uncertainty sampling for supervised learning. In *Proceedings of the ICML* (pp. 148-156).

Liu, H., & Motoda, H. (Eds.). (1998). *Feature extraction, construction and selection: A data mining perspective*. Berlin, Germany: Springer.

Liu, H., & Motoda, H. (Eds.). (2001). *Instance selection and construction for data mining*. Berlin, Germany: Springer.

Liu, H., & Setiono, R. (1996). A probabilistic approach to feature selection - a filter solution. In *Proceedings of the ICML* (pp. 319-327).

Model, F., Adorjn, P., et al. (2001). Feature selection for DNA methylation based cancer classification. In *Proceedings of the ISMB (Supplement of Bioinformatics)* (pp. 157-164).

Quinlan, J. R. (1983). Learning efficient classification procedures and their application to chess end games. In *Machine Learning. An Artificial Intelligence Approach* (pp. 463-482).

Quinlan, J. R. (1993). *C4.5: Programs for machine learning*. San Francisco: Morgan Kaufmann.

Rosenblatt, F. (1962). *Principles of neurodynamics: Perceptrons and the theory of brain mechanisms*. Washington: Spartan Books.

Schapire, R. E. (1990). The strength of weak learnability. Machine Learning, 5, 197–227.

Witten, I. H., & Frank, E. (2005). *Data mining: Practical machine learning tools and techniques*. San Francisco: Morgan Kaufmann.

Xing, E. P., Jordan, M. I., et al. (2001). Feature selection for high-dimensional genomic microarray data. In *Proceedings of the ICML* (pp. 601-608).

Xiong, M., Fang, X., et al. (2001). Biomarker identification by feature wrappers. Genome Research, 11(11), 1878–1887. PubMed

Yang, Y., & Pedersen, J. O. (1997). A comparative study on feature selection in text categorization. In *Proceedings of the ICML* (pp. 412-420).

Yu, L., & Liu, H. (2003). Feature selection for high-dimensional data: A fast correlation-based filter solution. In *Proceedings of the ICML* (pp. 856-863).

Yu, L., & Liu, H. (2004). Redundancy based feature selection for microarray data. In *Proceedings of the SIGKDD* (pp. 737-742).

ENDNOTES

[1] Kent ridge biomedical dataset repository. http://sdmc.lit.org.sg/GEDatasets/Datasets.html

[2] Kent ridge biomedical dataset repository. http://sdmc.lit.org.sg/GEDatasets/Datasets.html

Section 5
Advanced Mining Applications

Chapter 13
Learning Cost–Sensitive Decision Trees to Support Medical Diagnosis

Alberto Freitas
CINTESIS – Center for Research in Health Information Systems and Technologies, Portugal
University of Porto, Portugal

Altamiro Costa-Pereira
CINTESIS – Center for Research in Health Information Systems and Technologies, Portugal
University of Porto, Portugal

Pavel Brazdil
LIAAD INESC Porto L.A. – Laboratory of Artificial Intelligence and Decision Support, Portugal
University of Porto, Portugal

ABSTRACT

Classification plays an important role in medicine, especially for medical diagnosis. Real-world medical applications often require classifiers that minimize the total cost, including costs for wrong diagnosis (misclassifications costs) and diagnostic test costs (attribute costs). There are indeed many reasons for considering costs in medicine, as diagnostic tests are not free and health budgets are limited. In this chapter, the authors have defined strategies for cost-sensitive learning. They have developed an algorithm for decision tree induction that considers various types of costs, including test costs, delayed costs and costs associated with risk. Then they have applied their strategy to train and to evaluate cost-sensitive decision trees in medical data. Generated trees can be tested following some strategies, including group costs, common costs, and individual costs. Using the factor of "risk" it is possible to penalize invasive or delayed tests and obtain patient-friendly decision trees.

INTRODUCTION

In medical care, as in other areas, knowledge is crucial for decision making support, biomedical research and health management (Cios, 2001). Data mining and machine learning can help in the process of knowledge discovery. Data mining is the non-trivial process of identifying valid, novel, potentially useful and ultimately understandable

DOI: 10.4018/978-1-60566-748-5.ch013

Copyright © 2010, IGI Global. Copying or distributing in print or electronic forms without written permission of IGI Global is prohibited.

patterns in data (Fayyad et al., 1996). Machine learning is concerned with the development of techniques which allow computers to "learn" (Tom Mitchell, 1997).

Classification methods can be used to generate models that describe classes or predict future data trends. It generic aim is to build models that allow predicting the value of one categorical variable from the known values of other variables. Classification is a common, pragmatic method in clinical medicine. It is the basis for determining a diagnosis and, therefore, for the definition of distinct strategies of therapy. In addition, classification plays an important role in evidence-based medicine. Machine learning systems can be used to enhance the knowledge bases used by expert systems as they can produce a systematic description of clinical features that uniquely characterize clinical conditions. This knowledge can be expressed in the form of simple rule or decision trees (Coiera, 2003).

A large number of methods have been developed in machine learning and in statistics for predictive modelling, including classification. It is possible to find, for instance, algorithms using Bayesian methods (naïve Bayes, Bayesian networks), inductive decision trees (C4.5, C5, CART), rule learners (Ripper, PART, decision tables, Prism), hiperplanes approaches (support vector machines, logistic regression, perceptron, Winnow), and lazy learning methods (IB1, IBk, lazy Bayesian networks, KStar) (Witten and Frank, 2005). Besides these base learner algorithms there are also algorithms (meta-learners) that allow the combination of base algorithms in several ways, using for instance bagging, boosting and stacking. There are a few examples that consider costs, using these techniques.

In fact, the majority of existing classification methods was designed to minimize the number of errors. Nevertheless, real-world applications often require classifiers that minimize the total cost, including misclassifications costs (each error has an associated cost) and diagnostic test

costs representing the costs of obtaining the value of given attributes. In medicine a false negative prediction, for instance failing to detect a disease, can have fatal consequences, while a false positive prediction can be, in many situations, less serious (e.g. giving a drug to a patient that does not have a certain disease). Each diagnostic test has also a cost and so, to decide whether it is worthwhile to pay the costs of tests, it is necessary to consider both misclassification and tests costs. There are many reasons for considering costs in medicine. Diagnostic tests, as other health interventions, are not free and budgets are limited.

Misclassification and test costs are the most important costs, but there are also other types of costs (Turney, 2000). Cost-sensitive learning (also known as cost-sensitive classification) is the area of machine learning that deals with costs in inductive learning.

The process of knowledge discovery in medicine can be organized into six phases (Shearer, 2000), namely the perception of the medical domain (business understanding), data understanding, data preparation, application of data mining algorithms (modeling), evaluation, and the use of the discovered knowledge (deployment). The data preparation (selection, pre-processing) is normally the most time consuming step of this process (Feelders et al., 2000). The work presented in this chapter is mostly related with the fourth phase, the application of data mining algorithms, particularly classification.

With this chapter we aim to enhance the understand of cost-sensitive learning problems in medicine and present a strategy for learning and testing cost-sensitive decision trees, while considering several types of costs associated with problems in medicine.

The rest of this chapter is organized as follows. In the next section we discuss the main types of costs. Then we review related work. After that, we discuss the evaluation of classifiers. Next, we explain our cost-sensitive decision tree strategy and, subsequently, we present some experimental results. Finally, we conclude and point out some future work.

TYPES OF COSTS

Turney (2000) presented a taxonomy for many possible types of costs that may occur in classification problems. Turney divides costs into cost of misclassification errors, cost of tests, cost of classifying cases (by an expert), cost of intervention, cost of unwanted achievements, cost of computation, cost of cases, cost of human-computer interaction, and cost of instability. In this enumeration, misclassification and test costs are on the most important ones. They will be discussed in more detail further on. With the proposed taxonomy, Turney expected contribute to the organization of the cost-sensitive learning literature.

Costs can be measured in many distinct units as, for instance, money (euros, dollars), time (seconds, minutes) or other types of measures (e.g., quality of life).

Misclassification Costs

A problem with *n* classes is normally characterized by a matrix $n \times n$, where the element in line *i* and column *j* represents the cost of classifying a case in class *i* being from class *j*. Usually the cost is zero when $i = j$. Typically, misclassification costs are constant, that is, the cost is the same for any instance classified in class *i* but belonging to class *j*. The traditional error rate measure can be defined by attributing the cost 0 when $i = j$ and 1 for all the other cells.

In some cases the cost of misclassification errors can be conditional, that is, it can be dependent of specific features or dependent on a moment in time. The cost of prescribing a specific drug to an allergic patient may be different than prescribing that drug to a non allergic patient.

The cost of misclassification can be associated with the particular moment it occurs. A medical device (with sensors) can issue an alarm when a problem occurs. In this situation, the cost is dependent simultaneously on the correctness of the classification and also on the time the alarm has been issued. That is, the alarm will only be useful if there is time for an adequate action (Fawcett and Provost, 1999). Misclassification costs can also be dependent on the classification of other cases. In the previous example, if one alarm is correctly and consecutively issued for the same problem, then the benefit of the first alarm should be greater than the benefit of the others.

Cost of Tests

In medicine the majority of diagnostic tests have an associated cost (e.g., an echography or a blood test). These costs can be highly distinct for different diagnostic tests (representing the costs of obtaining the value of given attributes).

The costs of tests may be constant for all patients or may change according to specific patient features. A bronchodilatation test, for instance, has a higher cost for children less than 6 years, which means that the feature age has influence on the cost of the test.

Medical tests can also be very distinct when considering their influence on the "quality of life". A range of tests are completely harmless for patients (e.g., obstetric echography), others can be dangerous and put patient's life at risk (e.g., cardiac catheterism), and some can be (only) uncomfortable (e.g., digestive endoscopy).

Some tests can be cheaper (and faster) when done together (in group) than when ordered individually and sequentially (e.g., renal, digestive and gynecological echography). Some tests can also have common costs that can be priced only once. Blood tests, for instance, share a common cost of collecting the blood sample. There is not only an economic reduction but also a non-economical reduction in the cost of "worry" of the patients.

A number of tests might depend of the results of some other tests (attributes). The attribute "age", for instance, may influence the cost of the bronchodilatation test. Some tests can have an increased price as result of secondary effects. Other tests can have patient-specific, time-dependent or emergency-dependent costs.

In general, tests should only be ordered if their costs are not superior to the costs of classification errors.

CURRENT COST-SENSITIVE APPROACHES

In supervised learning (learning by examples), the majority of the work is concerned with the error rate (or success rate).

Nevertheless, some work has been done considering non-uniform misclassification costs, that is, different costs for different types of errors (Breiman et al., 1984; Elkan, 2001). Other literature is concerned with the cost of tests, without taking into account misclassification costs (Núñez, 1991; Melville et al., 2005).

There is also some work concerned simultaneously with more than one type of costs, including the work of Turney (1995), Zubek and Dietterich (2002), Greiner et al. (2002), Arnt and Zilberstein (2004), and Ling et al. (Chai et al., 2004; Ling et al., 2004; Sheng et al., 2005; Sheng and Ling, 2005; Zhang et al., 2005; Ling et al., 2006). Turney (1995) was the first to consider both test and misclassification costs. Next, we give a brief overview of this work considering both costs.

Turney (1995) implemented the ICET system that uses a genetic algorithm for building a decision tree that minimizes test and misclassification costs. The ICET system was robust, but very time consuming.

Several authors formulated the problem with costs as a Markov decision process that has the disadvantage of being computationally expensive. Zubek and Dietterich (2002) used an optimal search strategy, while Arnt and Zilberstein (2004)

included a utility cost for the time needed to obtain the result of a test.

Greiner et al. (2002) analyzed the problem of learning cost-sensitive optimal active classifiers, using a variant of the probably-approximately-correct (PAC) model.

Chai et al. (2004) proposed a cost-sensitive naïve Bayes algorithm for reducing the total cost. Ling et al. (2004) proposed a decision tree algorithm that uses a cost reduction as a splitting criterion during training, instead of minimum entropy. After that Sheng et al. (2005) presented an approach where a decision tree is built for each new test case. In another paper, Sheng et al. (2005) proposed a hybrid model that results from the integration of a decision tree sensitive to costs with a naïve Bayes classifier. Zhang et al. (2005) compared strategies for checking if missing values should or not be obtained, and stated that for tests with high costs or high risk it should be more cost-effective not to obtain their values. Recently, Ling et al. (2006) updated their strategy for building cost-sensitive decision trees, with the inclusion of sequential test strategies.

Meta-Classifiers

In order to obtain cost-sensitive classifiers it is possible to manipulate either the training data or the outputs of the learned model by further processing. These types of algorithms are known as meta-classifiers (Vilalta and Drissi, 2002). In cost-sensitive learning, a meta-classifier converts a cost-insensitive learning algorithm into a cost-sensitive one. A meta-classifier pre processes the training data or post processes the output of a base classifier. They can be applied over (almost) any type of classifier and provide classifications modified to minimize misclassification error costs. This method is also known as cost-sensitive meta-learning.

Meta-classifiers can be divided into those that use sampling to modify the learning data and those that do not. Costing (Zadrozny et al., 2003) is an example of a meta classifier that uses sampling to produce a cost-sensitive classification from a cost-insensitive classifier. Costing is a technique based on cost-proportionate rejection sampling and ensemble aggregation. The other approach, without using sampling, can be further divided in three categories, specifically relabeling, trough the minimal expected cost (Viaene et al., 2004); weighting (Abe et al., 2004); and threshold adjusting (ShengVS and Ling, 2006). Relabeling can be applied to training data, as in MetaCost (Domingos, 1999), or to test data, as in CostSensitiveClassifier (Witten and Frank, 2005).

In the meta-classifier CostSensitiveClassifier two methods can be used make a classifier sensitive to misclassification costs. One of the approaches is to reweight training instances according to the total cost of each class (*reweighting*). The other approach is to adjust the model to predict the class with minimum expected misclassification cost, as a substitute to predicting the most frequent class (*relabeling*).

Meta-classifiers work over built classifiers, and so they can only consider misclassification error costs and do not have influence on the process of deciding which attribute to use in each node of the tree.

Cost-Sensitive Strategies

Generically, there are three main types of strategies for cost-sensitive learning: a strategy with the manipulation of the training data, a strategy with the manipulation of the outputs, and a strategy with the modification of the learning algorithm. This section will briefly explain these three strategies.

Cost-sensitive learning with the manipulation of training data – One common approach in cost-sensitive learning is to change the class distribution in order to minimize, in a specific way (increasing specificity or sensitivity), the costs with new instances. These changes aim to give each class a distribution proportional to its

importance (its cost). This process can be done by *stratification/rebalancing*, with the use of *undersampling* or *oversampling*. In a medical classification problem, to increase or reduce the number of positive cases of a specific disease is an example of this type of manipulation.

As mentioned in the previous section, the algorithm CostSensitiveClassifier (Witten and Frank, 2005) manipulates the training data in one of its approaches. Considering the total cost of each class, this algorithm assigns different weights to training instances (*reweighting*). MetaCost (Domingos, 1999) is also an example of an algorithm that manipulates the training data for making an arbitrary classifier sensitive to costs, with the classifier wrapped by a cost-minimizing procedure. MetaCost relabel training examples with their estimated minimal-cost classes and apply the error-based learner to the new training set.

Cost-sensitive learning with the manipulation of the outputs – For a given instance, many classification algorithms produce a probability estimate for each class, or can be modified to output class probabilities. In decision trees, the class distribution of examples in a leaf can be used to estimate the probability of each class for a particular instance. With the probabilities of each class it is then possible to modify the result of the classification, giving more (or less) weight to each class, i.e., adjusting to misclassification error costs (false negatives and false positives, in the case of a binary classification).

Cost-sensitive learning with the modification of the learning algorithm – Another approach to cost-sensitive learning is to internally modify the training algorithm to use information about costs when building the classifier. In decision trees, the classifier is built considering the measure information gain, as a tree-split criterion. This criterion can be modified, as we will see later.

EVALUATION OF CLASSIFIERS

In the area of medicine, we can find many different measures for the evaluation of classifiers performance, such as classification accuracy, sensitivity and specificity, and post-test probability (Lavrac, 1999). Some methods used to compare classifiers focus on problems with two classes only, or else the problem has to be transformed into a set of 2-class problems. The misclassification error rate (1 minus classification accuracy), ROC (Receiver Operating Characteristics) graphs, and the Area Under ROC Curve (AUC) are the most common.

ROC Graphs

Receiver Operating Characteristic (ROC) graph is a useful technique that enables to visualize and compare the performance of classifiers. ROC graphs have often been used in medical decision making (Swets et al., 2000), and recently they have been progressively adopted in the machine learning and data mining communities. In medicine, ROC graphs are used in the evaluation of diagnostic tests. ROC graphs have some qualities that make them especially useful in domains with unequal distribution of classes and different costs for misclassification errors.

ROC graphs are represented in two dimensions, with True Positive Rate (TP rate) plotted on the Y axis and False Positive Rate (FP rate) on the X axis. This allows to visualize the relation between the true positives and the false negatives, i.e., the relation between sensitivity (recall or TP rate) and specificity (FP rate = 1 – specificity).

The use of the single value — Area Under the Curve (AUC) — is usual when comparing several classifiers. This method has important statistical properties, namely it is equivalent to the Mann-Whitney-Wilcoxon (Hanley and McNeil, 1982) test, and is also closely related to the Gini index (Breiman et al., 1984). If we use just this criterion we may say that the larger the area (AUC), the better is the model.

ROC graphs are useful to compare and understand the relation between different classifiers, without considering class distribution or misclassification errors. For imprecise environments and in constant mutation (e.g., with variable misclassification costs), variants to this method can be used, such as the ROC Convex Hull (ROCCH) proposed by Provost and Fawcett (2001).

Cost-sensitive Evaluation of Classifiers

Several approaches exist for the cost-sensitive evaluation of classifiers. Margineantu and Dietterich (2000) proposed two statistical methods, one to construct a confidence interval for the expected cost of a single classifier, and another to construct a confidence interval for the expected cost difference of two classifiers. The basic idea behind these methods is to detach the problem of estimating probabilities for each cell in the confusion matrix from the problem of calculating the expected cost (a confusion matrix is a matrix where each column represents the instances in a predicted class and each row represents the instances in a real class).

Adams and Hand (1999) proposed a method, the LC index, which extends the work on ROC curves. In their work, they argued that normally there is no precise information about costs, and there is only an idea about the relation between one error (FN) and the other (FP) (for instance, FN can cost ten times more than FP). The proposed method maps the ratio of error costs on an interval between 0 and 1, and transforms ROC curves into parallel lines, showing dominant classifiers in specific regions of the interval. LC index is a measure of confidence that indicates whether a classifier is superior to another within an interval. LC index is only a measure of superiority, and does not express the differences between costs (Fawcett, 2004).

Cost Curves

Some of the limitations of ROC graphs can be surpassed through the use of cost curves (Drummond and Holte, 2000a). In fact, in a ROC graph, a single scalar performance measure cannot capture all aspects of the differences in the performance of two classifiers, including for instance a case where the costs of misclassification are much different between classes. Cost curves are more powerful for visualizing cost-sensitive classifiers performance as they are specifically designed for the specific performance measure "expected cost". In cost curves, a line is associated to each classifier showing how the classifier performance varies with changes in class distribution and misclassification costs. Cost curves include the majority of ROC graphs qualities and, additionally, they support the visualization of specific performance assessment that cannot be easily done with ROC graphs (Drummond and Holte, 2006). Among those types of performance assessment, cost curves permit the visualization of confidence intervals for a classifier performance and the statistical significance of the difference between the performances of two classifiers.

A simple classifier, or a confusion matrix, is represented by a point (FP, TP) in the ROC space. In the cost space this point is represented by a line joining the points (0, FP) and (1, FN). A set of points in ROC space is a set of lines in the cost space. While a ROC curve is defined by a set of connected ROC points, the cost curve is defined by the set of cost lines. Additional and detailed information about cost curves can be found in Witten and Frank (2005) or Drummond and Holte (2006).

A COST-SENSITIVE STRATEGY: TAKING RISK INTO ACCOUNT

Next, we briefly describe our strategy for implementing a cost-sensitive decision tree. Our aim

was to implement a tool for building decision models sensitive to costs, namely test costs, misclassification costs and other types of costs (Freitas, 2007).

We opted to use decision trees because they have several interesting characteristics for health professionals. They are easy to understand and use, and also present an intuitive and appealing structure. Their structure is congruent with decision making methods that physicians normally use in their daily routine, when trying to determine which is the best diagnostic test or the best treatment for a patient (Grobman and Stamilio, 2006).

We have modified the J48 version of the C4.5 algorithm (Quinlan, 1993) to contemplate costs and, consequently, to generate cost-sensitive decision trees. Specifically we used the J48 class, implemented in the open source package for data mining Weka (Witten and Frank, 2005).

Cost Function

We have adapted the decision tree splitting criteria to incorporate costs. Instead of information gain (or gain ratio), we have used the idea that is often exploited in management, namely a ratio of benefits (good informativity) to costs. Specifically we have adopted the following cost function:

$$\frac{\Delta I_i}{\left(C_i \phi_i\right)^\omega}.$$

where ΔI_i is the information gain (or gain ratio) for attribute i, C_i is the cost of attribute (diagnostic test) i, φ_i is the factor of "risk" associated with attribute (test) i, and ω is the cost scale factor.

When building a tree, for each node, the algorithm will select the attribute that maximizes the defined heuristic for the cost function. The cost function does not consider misclassification costs, as these costs do not have influence on the decision tree splitting criteria (Drummond and Holte, 2000b).

Attributes without cost, as age and gender, are assigned the value cost 1. Attributes with higher costs lead to lower values of the cost function and consequently have lower chances to be selected.

The factor of "risk" was introduced to enhance the effect of cost C_i. This factor was introduced to penalize attributes that might be invasive, can cause discomfort and disturb, or could somehow contribute to lower patient's quality of life (e.g., the invasive test "coronary angiography"). The value 1 means absence of this influence and is equivalent to a completely innocuous test, while values higher than 1 mean that undesirable influence exists. Higher factors lead to lower values of the cost function and therefore to lower chance for the particular attribute to be selected.

If both test cost and factor of "risk" are equal to one, then their effect is neutral and so the cost function represents the traditional information gain function. The cost of the attribute can be adjusted in two ways. It can be increased or decreased considering the inoffensiveness of the test (factor of "risk"), or it can be modified by the cost scale factor ω. This factor is a general parameter that is equally applied to all tests, reducing or increasing the influence of costs in attribute selection.

The factor of "risk" can also be used to penalize delayed tests. A longer test can have consequences on the patient's quality of life and may increase other costs, as those related to staff, facilities and increased length of stay. If we have a choice between two similar tests, one longer than the other, it makes sense that the faster one is preferred. Hence, considering the average length of tests, an adjustment can be made by the factor of "risk".

The cost scale factor ω regulates the influence of costs, as it can make trees more (or less) sensitive to costs. This factor may also be used to adjust the cost function to the used scale. An inexpensive test, such as "age", has the same cost in any scale (value 1). But tests with real costs have clearly different values in different scales. If some test, e.g. test of attribute "A", costs 10 in the Euro scale then it costs 1000 in the centime scale, that is, the ratio between the tests "age" and "A" is 1 to 10 in the Euro scale and 1 to 1000 in the other scale. To avoid that a change in the scale could benefit some attributes, it is important to adjust it with the cost scale factor.

For a cost scale factor ω of 0 the costs are not considered, as the denominator of the cost function becomes 1. This situation is equivalent to considering the original information gain. With an increase in the cost scale factor, the costs of tests will have more influence and less expensive tests will be preferred. The cost scale factor typically will be between 0 and 1.

For making our model sensitive to misclassification costs, we used a meta-learner implemented in Weka, CostSensitiveClassifier (Witten and Frank, 2005).

Decision Tree Test and Usage Strategies

After building cost-sensitive models, we need to conduct evaluation before using them. The test strategy can consider the cost of a test individually or in a group. Within groups of tests it is possible to distinguish between (i) tests ordered simultaneously or (ii) tests with a common cost.

Regards the first strategy, there may be a difference between the cost of a group of tests and the sum of individual tests costs. Many medical tests do not have an immediate result and therefore it is also important to consider the length of time for the group in opposition to the total of the lengths of the individual tests. When a medical doctor follows a given decision tree he must opt either for a group of tests or only for a single test. If he orders a group of tests, then the cost considered will be the group cost, even if some tests in the group are not used.

In the other situation—(ii) tests with a common cost—it is possible to separate out a common cost for a group of tests. In a group of blood tests, for instance, the cost of collecting blood represents a common cost for all tests in the group. Only the first test of the group will be priced for the common cost.

Delayed tests are considered in the training phase of the decisions tree. Longer tests will, therefore, have tendency to be scheduled only after shorter ones.

Individual Costs

Our strategy also allows (a) to consider specific patient characteristics, (b) to modify test costs in situations where their values are already known (due to previous tests), and (c) to consider availability and length of some tests.

As for (a), the cost of each test can be conditional and depend on the characteristics of the patient. That is, it is possible to have a variable cost associated with specific characteristics of the patient. As seen before, the age can change the cost of the test "bronchodilatation" (it is higher for children less than 6 years). The comorbidity index of a patient is another example, as it can influence the cost of some tests and, therefore, could be used to adjust the cost of the test. For a specific test, different patients may require additional tests, consequently with an increase in costs.

Regards (b), in some circumstances, some tests may have been obtained previously and so their original costs should not be considered again. Consequently, we adopt another approach for building trees where, for each new instance (patient), tests with known values are considered without additional cost or "risk". For each new vector of distinct costs a new decision tree is built.

As for (c), resources are not infinite and in practice may not always be available. A specific test may be conditional on the availability of a medical device in a specific time period. In these cases, it is possible to exclude that test and build a new tree. Optionally, it is possible to increase the factor of "risk" of that test, decreasing its probability of being selected. As the availability is not constant over time, this problem should be analyzed for

each case (patient). This is a circumstantial cost and not a cost intrinsic to the patient.

EXPERIMENTAL RESULTS

In this section we present some experimental results. We have tested our cost-sensitive decision tree approach with several datasets, including the Pima Indians Diabetes.

Pima Indians Diabetes

The Pima Indians Diabetes dataset1 contains 768 instances and the class assumes 2 values, "healthy" (500 instances) or "diabetes" (268 instances). The test costs of all attributes (numeric) are shown in Table 1 and the cost matrix is in Table 2.

Tests "glucose tolerance" and "serum insulin" are not immediate and have a distinct cost (other attributes have a symbolic cost of $1). Moreover they share a common cost, $2.1, from collecting blood. As these attributes are not immediate, when using the tree it is necessary to decide if both tests should be ordered together (in group) or not.

We varied the cost scale factor ω from 0.0 to 1.0 and induced decision trees. We evaluated them using 10-fold cross-validation. After that, we considered cost zero for cases classified correctly and varied misclassification costs, from $10 to $1,000, with equal costs for false negative (FN) and false positives (FP). In Table 3 we present the results of the evaluation of five decision trees for that range of misclassification costs. Notice that for a cost scale factor equal to zero, the model is equal to the one obtained by the original J48 algorithm (J48 is an implementation of the traditional C4.5 decision tree learner).

In Table 4, we considered different FN and FP costs, with a variable cost ratio. In this case, we can see that for low misclassification costs (less than or equal to $150) best results occur with cost scale factor equal to 1.0. For high misclassification costs, the model obtained with cost scale factor

Table 1. Attribute costs for Pima Indians Diabetes.

Test	Cost ($)	Group cost ($)
a. Number of times pregnant	1	
b. Glucose tolerance test	17.61	b + e = 38.29
c. Diastolic blood pressure	1	
d. Triceps skin fold thickness	1	
e. Serum insulin test	22.78	b + e = 38.29
f. Body mass index	1	
g. Diabetes pedigree function	1	
h. Age (years)	1	

Table 2. Cost matrix for Pima Indians Diabetes.

		Prediction	
		Healthy	**Diabetes**
Reality	**healthy**	$ 0	FP cost
	diabetes	FN cost	$ 0

equal to 0.0 (original J48) achieves better results, but only with slight differences. These results are similar to the previous ones, obtained with equal FN and FP costs.

In this example, for low misclassification costs, the best results have been obtained for a cost scale factor between 0.5 and 1.0. In these situations, average costs are much lower when compared with original J48. For high misclassification costs, compared to test costs, best results occur with cost scale factor equal to 0.0 (J48) and 0.1, but without substantial differences for the other models.

As misclassification costs rise, test costs tend to be negligible. That is, for sufficiently higher

Table 3. Average misclassification and attribute costs in the evaluation of 5 decision trees, for a range of misclassification costs (with FN cost equal to FP cost) and cost scale factors; 95% confidence intervals are included.

	Cost scale factor ω				
FN / FP cost	**0.0**	**0.1**	**0.2**	**0.5**	**1.0**
$10	23.4 ± 0.53	21.9 ± 0.57	19.5 ± 0.66	**6.4 ± 0.44**	**5.7 ± 0.35**
$20	26.0 ± 0.79	24.5 ± 0.81	22.2 ± 0.89	**9.5 ± 0.73**	**8.8 ± 0.68**
$50	33.8 ± 1.67	32.4 ± 1.67	30.6 ± 1.75	**19.0 ± 1.69**	**18.4 ± 1.66**
$100	46.9 ± 3.20	45.5 ± 3.21	44.4 ± 3.30	**34.7 ± 3.33**	**34.2 ± 3.31**
$200	73.1 ± 6.31	71.8 ± 6.31	72.2 ± 6.45	**66.2 ± 6.62**	**66.0 ± 6.61**
$500	**151.6 ± 15.7**	**150.8 ± 15.7**	**155.4 ± 16.0**	160.8 ± 16.5	161.3 ± 16.5
$1,000	**282.5 ± 31.2**	**282.3 ± 31.3**	**294.0 ± 31.8**	318.3 ± 33.0	320.2 ± 33.0
Accuracy (%):	73.8	73.7	72.3	68.5	68.2

Table 4. Average costs in the evaluation of 2 decision trees, for a range of misclassification costs (with FN cost different from FP cost) and cost scale factor (csf ω) 0.0 and 1.0.; 95% confidence intervals are included.

FN/FP ratio	FN ($)	FP ($)	csf ω = 0.0	csf ω = 1.0
1/10	10	100	34.3 ± 2.37	**17.3 ± 2.35**
10/1	100	10	36.0 ± 2.52	**22.6 ± 2.75**
3/1	150	50	47.9 ± 3.78	**37.2 ± 4.12**
1/3	50	150	46.0 ± 3.58	**31.3 ± 3.59**
½	500	1,000	**212.2 ± 24.58**	**225.8 ± 25.20**
2/1	1,000	500	**221.9 ± 25.67**	**255.7 ± 28.09**

misclassification costs and when considering equal cost for false negatives and false positives, a higher accuracy rate corresponds to a lower average cost.

In figure 1 we can see an example of a decision tree for cost scale factor ω = 0.5 and costs of $200 for both FP and FN. Comparing with the tree obtained for cost scale factor ω = 0, that is, without considering costs, this is a much simpler tree and with lower average costs.

In this evaluation we have also distinguished between individual and group costs, and realized that results considering group costs always had higher average costs. This occurred because the serum insulin test, which shares group costs with the glucose tolerance test, only intermittently appeared in the decision trees and, therefore,

there was an extra imputed cost that was used sporadically or not at all. Table 5 shows comparative results for the evaluation of five models, considering group costs.

Considering the Factor of "Risk"

To illustrate differences in the utilization of a cost-sensitive decision tree considering group costs and the factor of "risk", we applied our strategy to artificial data for a cardiac disease (Appendix A). This dataset has 40 cases and includes 3 independent attribute and a class indicating whether the disease is present or not, with 24 cases with class "No" and 16 with class "Yes".

We associated a factor of risk to each attribute, in order to distinguish between attributes

Figure 1. Decision tree for csf = 0.5 and costs for FP and FN = $200.

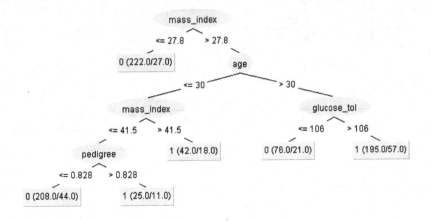

*Table 5. Average costs in the evaluation of 5 decision trees, for a range of misclassification costs (FN cost equal to FP cost) and cost scale factors, and considering **group costs**; 95% confidence intervals included.*

FN / FP cost	Cost scale factor ω				
	0.0	0.1	0.2	0.5	1.0
$10	40.9 ± 0.34	39.1 ± 0.74	34.8 ± 1.12	7.7 ± 0.63	6.2 ± 0.37
$20	43.5 ± 0.65	41.7 ± 0.94	37.6 ± 1.29	10.9 ± 0.87	9.4 ± 0.69
$50	51.4 ± 1.58	49.6 ± 1.75	45.9 ± 2.02	20.3 ± 1.77	18.9 ± 1.67
$100	64.5 ± 3.13	62.8 ± 3.26	59.7 ± 3.48	36.1 ± 3.38	34.8 ± 3.32
$200	90.6 ± 6.25	89.1 ± 6.35	87.5 ± 6.58	67.6 ± 6.65	66.6 ± 6.62
$500	169.2 ± 15.6	168.0 ± 15.7	170.7 ± 16.1	162.1 ± 16.5	161.9 ± 16.5
$1,000	300.0 ± 31.2	299.5 ± 31.3	309.3 ± 31.9	319.7 ± 33.0	320.8 ± 33.0
Accuracy (%):	73.8	73.7	72.3	68.5	68.2

more or less invasive to the patient, with a larger value meaning more discomfort/risk (Table 6). We also defined costs for misclassification errors (Table 7).

This example includes costs for individual tests and costs for groups of tests to be used when applying a decision tree. In our test strategy it is possible that a group of attributes have common or reduced costs when ordered in group. Suppose that attributes "Cholesterol" and "ECG" have a common preparation cost. That common cost should be priced only once, to the first test

ordered in the group. If the common cost is, for instance 5, then "cholesterol" test cost will be priced 10 if ordered first and 5 otherwise, i.e., after "ECG" has been carried out. Similarly, "ECG" test will cost 20 if ordered first or 15 if ordered later. In both situations the cost of the two tests sums 25.

Classification costs can be divided into costs for correct decisions and costs for incorrect decisions (misclassification costs). In this example the cost for a correct decision is 0, while for a misclassification error it can assume a high value;

Table 6. Cardiac disease test costs.

Test	Values	Cost	Group cost	F.Risk φ
ECG	Normal, Irregular	20	} 25	2
Cholesterol	Low, Medium, High	10		1
Exercise test	Positive, Negative	40	-	4

Table 7. Classification costs.

Actual class	Predicted class	Cost
No	No	0
No	Yes	100
Yes	No	300
Yes	Yes	0

Figure 2. Regular decision tree (not cost-sensitive).

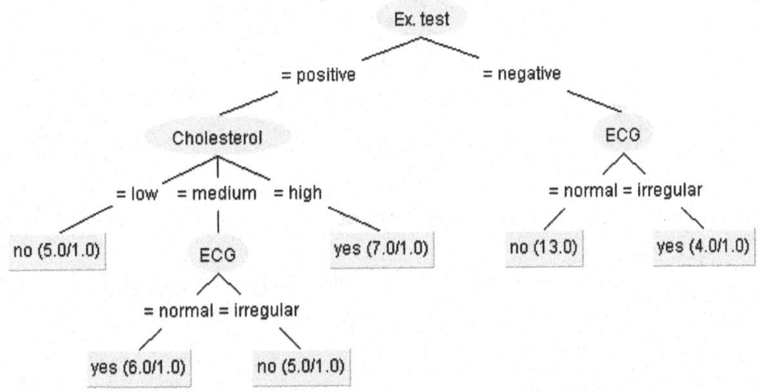

in this case 100 for false positives and 300 for false negatives (Table 7).

Prediction using J48

Figure 2 shows the decision tree for cardiac disease, built using J48, i.e., without considering costs. The accuracy is 87.5%. In the evaluation of this tree, using test costs and misclassification costs, the total cost for the 40 cases was 3,290 (3,500 if group tests were included), leading to an average cost of 82.25 (87.5).

Cost-Sensitive Prediction

In a subsequent study we have considered the costs of tests (attributes) in the process of inducing the decision tree. As result, the decision tree (Figure 3) is clearly different from the previous one, since the test "cholesterol" is at the top. This test is less expensive than the "exercise test" which was at the top of the previous (non cost-sensitive) decision tree. When evaluating the tree on the 40 cases, we can see that for the J48 tree all the 40 cases were tested for "cholesterol" as it is the main attribute of the tree, while in the latter tree only 16 cases were tested for this attribute.

In the evaluation of this cost-sensitive decision tree the global cost was 2,540 (the same cost when considering group costs), with an average cost of 63.5 (equal value when considering group costs), that is, an average reduction of 18.75 (24)

was obtained when comparing with the previous model. The accuracy remained 87.5%.

Cost-Sensitive Prediction, Considering both Test Costs and Factors of Risk

At this step, we used the factors of risk defined in Table 6 where, specifically, attribute "cholesterol" has neutral influence, "ECG" has some influence (factor of risk φ equal to 2) and "exercise test" has more influence (factor of risk φ equal to 4). Figure 4 shows the decision tree built using both attribute costs and factors of risk. Note that "exercise test" is only ordered after the other two tests.

Using test and misclassification costs defined previously, the total cost is 2,640 for individual test costs and 2,440 for group tests costs. On average the cost is 66 (61 for group costs). With this adjustment of the factor of risk, which is related to the quality of life, the individual cost is on average increased by 2.5 when comparing with the previous model. Group costs are lower than in the previous model (63.5) because, at this time, both attributes ("cholesterol" and "ECG") are priced and tested. The accuracy of this decision tree is 85%.

Sensitivity Analysis of the Cost Model

In this stage we aimed to analyze the cost sensitivity for each attribute, that is, to identify significant

Figure 3. Cost-sensitive decision tree.

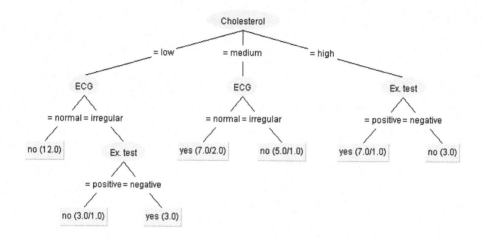

or insignificant impact of each attribute on model output (attributes with high or low influence). Table 8 (and Figure 5) shows average costs for all attributes and various subsets obtained by excluding one attribute at a time. The model without "exercise test" has accuracy lower than the model with all attributes but it is characterized also by a substantial reduction in the average cost. To compare these differences in costs we used the non-parametric Wilcoxon Signed Ranks Test for related samples (Wilcoxon, 1945) (Tables 9). Additionally, as the number of cases is relatively

small and data is sparse, we calculated significance levels using Monte Carlo method.

These results confirm that costs from the model with all attributes are significantly lower than costs from models without either the attribute "ECG" or without attribute "cholesterol". But, when comparing with the model without attribute "exercise test", there is no statistically significant difference. If the attribute costs were considered irrelevant the model with all attributes would be the best option as it achieves higher accuracy than the other models.

Figure 4. Decision tree considering both attribute costs and factors of risk.

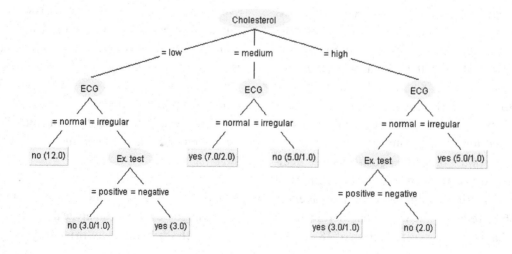

Table 8. Average costs (±95% CI for mean).

Attributes	Average cost	Accuracy (%)
All	61.00 ± 23.2	85.0
Without "ECG"	90.75 ± 28.8	75.0
Without "cholesterol"	76.00 ± 13.0	72.5
Without "exercise test"	48.75 ± 18.4	77.5

Figure 5. Average costs with 95% confidence interval for mean

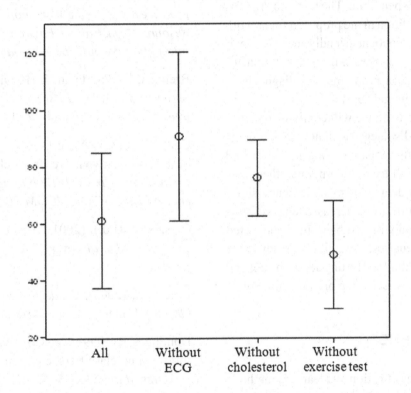

CONCLUSION

In this chapter we have presented approaches to build cost-sensitive decision trees, considering different aspects of attribute test costs, which include economic and non-economical costs. Our framework integrates also a cost-sensitive meta-learner applicable in situations where misclas-

Table 9. Wilcoxon Signed Ranks Test statistics

		W/o ECG – All	W/o Chol – All	W/o Ex Test – All
p (Wilcoxon)		0.003	0.000	0.525
p (Monte Carlo)		0.003	0.000	0.543
99% Conf. Int.	Lower	0.001	0.000	0.530
	Upper	0.004	0.000	0.555

sifications costs are different. Results show that it outperforms the traditional, non cost-sensitive, decision tree. We can clearly see that, in inductive learning, it is important to consider several types of costs as they can lead to substantial savings in the end.

As technologies became more expensive, it is even more rational to consider different costs involved. A big challenge is to have better healthcare using less expenditure. The factor of "risk" is an important addition in the proposed framework as we can induce patient-friendly models. Decision trees represent a natural representation for many classification problems (for diagnosis or prognosis) that include costs.

In our future work we will continue to evaluate the proposed strategy, with new experiments on other datasets prepared using real data and real costs. We will try to incorporate other costs associated with delayed tests, emergency situations, staff, facilities, and increased length of stay. The cost function will also be refined and tested for different scenarios. We will also study other methods for building and testing decision trees and in particular a cost-sensitive pruning strategy.

FUTURE TRENDS

In the future, classification and learning methods should be focused on the integration of different costs in medicine. For instance, in clinical decision support systems various health-related quality of life costs (Guyatt et al., 1993) and other costs related to diagnostic tests should be progressively considered when building and testing classification models. New strategies for urgent situations which require obtaining attribute test results, costs with staff and facilities, and other time-related costs, should also be considered.

REFERENCES

Abe, N., Zadrozny, B., & Langford, J. (2004). An iterative method for multi-class cost-sensitive learning. In *Proceedings of the 10ᵗʰ ACM SIGKDD International Conference on Knowledge Discovery and Data Mining (KDD'04)* (pp. 3-11).

Arnt, A., & Zilberstein, S. (2004). Attribute measurement policies for cost-effective classification. In *Proceedings of the Workshop Data Mining in Resource Constrained Environments, 4ᵗʰ SIAM International Conference on Data Mining*.

Breiman, L., Freidman, J. H., Olshen, R. A., & Stone, C. J. (1984). *Classification and regression trees*. Belmont, CA: Wadsworth.

Chai, X., Deng, L., Yang, Q., & Ling, C. X. (2004). Test-cost sensitive naive Bayes classification. In *Proceedings of the 4ᵗʰ IEEE International Conference on Data Mining (ICDM'2004)*.

Cios, K. J. (Ed.). (2001). *Medical data mining and knowledge discovery*. New York: Physica-Verlag.

Coiera, E. (2003). *Guide to health informatics* (2ⁿᵈ ed.). London: Hodder Arnold.

Domingos, P. (1999). MetaCost: A general method for making classifiers cost-sensitive. In *Proceedings of the 5ᵗʰ ACM SIGKDD International Conference on Knowledge Discovery and Data Mining (KDD-99)* (pp. 155-164).

Drummond, C., & Holte, R. C. (2000a). Explicitly representing expected cost: An alternative to ROC representation. In *Proceedings of the 6ᵗʰ ACM SIGKDD International Conference on Knowledge Discovery and Data Mining (KDD 2000)* (pp. 198-207).

Drummond, C., & Holte, R. C. (2000b). Exploiting the cost (in)sensitivity of decision tree splitting criteria. In *Proceedings of the 17ᵗʰ International Conference on Machine Learning (ICML)* (pp. 239-246).

Drummond, C., & Holte, R. C. (2006). Cost curves: An improved method for visualizing classifier performance. *Machine Learning, 65*, 95–130. doi:10.1007/s10994-006-8199-5

Elkan, C. (2001). The foundations of cost-sensitive learning. In *Proceedings of the 17ᵗʰ International Joint Conference on Artificial Intelligence (IJ-CAI'01)* (pp. 973-978).

Fawcett, T. (2004). *ROC graphs: Notes and practical considerations for researchers* (Tech. Rep.). HP Laboratories, Palo Alto, CA.

Fawcett, T., & Provost, F. (1999). Activity monitoring: Noticing interesting changes in behavior. In *Proceedings of the 5ᵗʰ ACM SIGKDD International Conference on Knowledge Discovery and Data Mining (KDD-99)* (pp. 53-62).

Fayyad, U. M., Piatetsky-Shapiro, G., Smyth, P., & Uthurusamy, R. (Eds.). (1996). *Advances in knowledge discovery and data mining.* Cambridge, MA: AAAI/MIT Press.

Feelders, A., Daniels, H., & Holsheimer, M. (2000). Methodological and practical aspects of data mining. *Information & Management, 37*, 271–281. doi:10.1016/S0378-7206(99)00051-8

Freitas, J. A. (2007). *Uso de técnicas de data mining para análise de bases de dados hospitalares com finalidades de gestão.* Unpublished doctoral dissertation, University of Porto, Portugal.

Greiner, R., Grove, A. J., & Roth, D. (2002). Learning cost-sensitive active classifiers. *Artificial Intelligence, 139*(2), 137–174. doi:10.1016/S0004-3702(02)00209-6

Grobman, W. A., & Stamilio, D. M. (2006). Methods of clinical prediction. *American Journal of Obstetrics and Gynecology, 194*(3), 888–894. doi:10.1016/j.ajog.2005.09.002

Guyatt, G. H., Feeny, D. H., & Patrick, D. L. (1993). Measuring health-related quality of life. *Annals of Internal Medicine, 118*(8), 622–629.

Hanley, J. A., & McNeil, B. J. (1982). The meaning and use of the area under a receiver operating characteristic (ROC) curve. *Radiology, 143*(1), 29–36.

Lavrac, N. (1999). Selected techniques for data mining in medicine. *Artificial Intelligence in Medicine, 16*, 3–23. doi:10.1016/S0933-3657(98)00062-1

Ling, C. X., Sheng, V. S., & Yang, Q. (2006). Test strategies for cost-sensitive decision trees. *IEEE Transactions on Knowledge and Data Engineering, 18*(8), 1055–1067. doi:10.1109/TKDE.2006.131

Ling, C. X., Yang, Q., Wang, J., & Zhang, S. (2004). Decision trees with minimal costs. In *Proceedings of the 21ˢᵗ International Conference on Machine Learning (ICML).*

Melville, P., Provost, F., Saar-Tsechansky, M., & Mooney, R. (2005). Economical active feature-value acquisition through expected utility estimation. In *Proceedings of the 1ˢᵗ International Workshop on Utility-Based Data Mining (UBDM'05)* (pp. 10-16).

Mitchell, T. (1997). *Machine learning.* Boston, MA: McGraw Hill.

Núñez, M. (1991). The use of background knowledge in decision tree induction. *Machine Learning, 6*, 231–250.

Provost, F., & Fawcett, T. (2001). Robust classification for imprecise environments. *Machine Learning, 42*(3), 203–231. doi:10.1023/A:1007601015854

Quinlan, J. R. (1993). *C4.5: Programs for machine learning.* San Francisco: Morgan Kaufmann Publishers.

Shearer, C. (2000). The CRISP-DM model: The new blueprint for data mining. *Journal of Data Warehousing, 5*(4), 13–22.

Sheng, S., & Ling, C. X. (2005). Hybrid cost-sensitive decision tree. In *Proceedings of the 9th European Conference on Principles and Practice of Knowledge Discovery in Databases (PKDD)*.

Sheng, S., Ling, C. X., & Yang, Q. (2005). Simple test strategies for cost-sensitive decision trees. In *Proceedings of the 16th European Conference on Machine Learning (ECML)* (pp. 365-376).

Sheng, V. S., & Ling, C. X. (2006). Thresholding for making classifiers cost-sensitive. In *Proceedings of the 21st National Conference on Artificial Intelligence (AAAI-06)*.

Swets, J. A., Dawes, R. M., & Monahan, J. (2000). Better decisions through science. *Scientific American, 283*(4), 82–87.

Turney, P. (1995). Cost-sensitive classification: Empirical evaluation of a hybrid genetic decision tree induction algorithm. *Journal of Artificial Intelligence Research, 2*, 369–409.

Turney, P. (2000). Types of cost in inductive concept learning. In *Proceedings of the Workshop on Cost-Sensitive Learning at the 17th International Conference on Machine Learning (WCSL at ICML-2000)* (pp. 15-21).

Viaene, S., Derrig, R. A., & Dedene, G. (2004). Cost-sensitive learning and decision making for Massachusetts PIP claim fraud data. *International Journal of Intelligent Systems, 19*, 1197–1215. doi:10.1002/int.20049

Vilalta, R., & Drissi, Y. (2002). A perspective view and survey of meta-learning. *Artificial Intelligence Review, 18*, 77–95. doi:10.1023/A:1019956318069

Wilcoxon, F. (1945). Individual comparisons by ranking methods. *Biometrics, 1*, 80–83. doi:10.2307/3001968

Witten, I. H., & Frank, E. (2005). *Data mining: Practical machine learning tools and techniques* (2nd ed.). San Francisco: Morgan Kaufmann.

Zadrozny, B., Langford, J., & Abe, N. (2003). Cost-sensitive learning by cost-proportionate example weighting. In *Proceedings of the 3rd IEEE International Conference on Data Mining (ICDM'03)*.

Zhang, S., Qin, Z., Ling, C. X., & Sheng, S. (2005). "Missing is useful": Missing values in cost-sensitive decision trees. *IEEE Transactions on Knowledge and Data Engineering, 17*(12), 1689–1693. doi:10.1109/TKDE.2005.188

Zubek, V. B., & Dietterich, T. G. (2002). Pruning improves heuristic search for cost-sensitive learning. In *Proceedings of the 19th International Conference of Machine Learning (ICML)* (pp. 27-35).

KEY TERMS AND DEFINITIONS

Classification: Technique used to predict group membership for data instances (e.g.: decision trees, neural networks)

Cost-Sensitive Learning: the sub-area of Machine Learning concerned with the questions of non-uniformity in costs.

Decision Tree: A predictive model; a mapping from observations about an instance to conclusions about its target class.

Error Rate: The rate of errors made by a predictive model (1 – accuracy).

False Negative: An instance belonging to the class positive and is classified as negative (in a classification problems with two classes).

False Positive: An instance belonging to the class negative and is classified as positive (in a classification problems with two classes).

Machine Learning: The study of computer algorithms that improve automatically through experience; a field of science and technology concerned with building machines that learn.

Model: A description that acceptably explains and predicts relevant data, and is normally much smaller than the data itself

ENDNOTE

[1]   UCI Repository of Machine Learning Databases, ftp://ftp.ics.uci.edu/pub/machine-learning-databases/

APPENDIX A. ARTIFICIAL DATA FOR CARDIAC DISEASE

Table 10.

ECG	cholesterol	Exercise test	Cardiac disease
Normal	Low	Positive	No
Normal	Medium	Positive	No
Normal	High	Positive	No
Irregular	High	Negative	No
Normal	Low	Negative	No
Normal	Low	Negative	No
Normal	Low	Negative	No
Normal	Low	Negative	No
Normal	Low	Negative	No
Normal	High	Negative	No
Normal	Medium	Negative	No
Normal	High	Negative	No
Normal	Low	Negative	No
Normal	Low	Negative	No
Normal	Low	Negative	No
Normal	Low	Negative	No
Normal	Low	Positive	No
Irregular	Low	Positive	No
Irregular	Low	Positive	No
Irregular	Medium	Positive	No
Irregular	Medium	Positive	No
Irregular	Medium	Positive	No
Irregular	Medium	Positive	No
Irregular	Medium	Positive	Yes
Irregular	High	Positive	Yes
Irregular	High	Positive	Yes
Irregular	High	Positive	Yes
Irregular	Low	Positive	Yes
Irregular	Low	Negative	Yes
Irregular	Low	Negative	Yes
Irregular	Low	Negative	Yes
Irregular	High	Positive	Yes
Normal	High	Positive	Yes
Normal	High	Positive	Yes
Normal	Medium	Positive	Yes
Normal	Medium	Positive	Yes
Normal	Medium	Positive	Yes

ECG	cholesterol	Exercise test	Cardiac disease
Normal	Medium	Positive	Yes
Normal	Medium	Positive	Yes

Chapter 14

An Approximate Approach for Maintaining Recent Occurrences of Itemsets in a Sliding Window over Data Streams

Jia-Ling Koh
National Taiwan Normal University, Taiwan

Shu-Ning Shin
National Taiwan Normal University, Taiwan

Yuan-Bin Don
National Taiwan Normal University, Taiwan

ABSTRACT

Recently, the data stream, which is an unbounded sequence of data elements generated at a rapid rate, provides a dynamic environment for collecting data sources. It is likely that the embedded knowledge in a data stream will change quickly as time goes by. Therefore, catching the recent trend of data is an important issue when mining frequent itemsets over data streams. Although the sliding window model proposed a good solution for this problem, the appearing information of patterns within a sliding window has to be maintained completely in the traditional approach. For estimating the approximate supports of patterns within a sliding window, the frequency changing point (FCP) method is proposed for monitoring the recent occurrences of itemsets over a data stream. In addition to a basic design proposed under the assumption that exact one transaction arrives at each time point, the FCP method is extended for maintaining recent patterns over a data stream where a block of various numbers of transactions (including zero or more transactions) is inputted within a fixed time unit. Accordingly, the recently frequent itemsets or representative patterns are discovered from the maintained structure approximately. Experimental studies demonstrate that the proposed algorithms achieve high true positive rates and guarantees no false dismissal to the results yielded. A theoretic analysis is provided for the guarantee. In addition, the authors' approach outperforms the previously proposed method in terms of reducing the run-time memory usage significantly.

DOI: 10.4018/978-1-60566-748-5.ch014

Copyright © 2010, IGI Global. Copying or distributing in print or electronic forms without written permission of IGI Global is prohibited.

1. INTRODUCTION

The strategies for mining frequent itemsets in static databases have been widely studied over the last decade such as the Apriori (Agrawal & Srikant, 1994), DHP (Park, Chen, & Yu, 1995), and FP-growth (Han et al., 2004) algorithms. Recently, the data stream, which is an unbounded sequence of data elements generated at a rapid rate, provides a dynamic environment for collecting data sources. It is considered that the main restrictions of mining data streams include scanning data in one pass and performing the mining process within a limited memory usage.

Since it is not feasible to store the past data in data streams completely, a method for providing approximate answers with accuracy guarantees is required. The hash-based approach was proposed in (Jin et al., 2003), in which each item in a data stream owns a respective list of counters in a hash table, and each counter may be shared by more than one item. A new novel algorithm, called hCount, was provided to maintain frequent items over a data stream and support both insertion and deletion of items with a less memory space. Lossy-counting is the representative approach for mining frequent itemsets from data streams (Manku & Motwani, 2002). Given an error tolerance parameter ε, the Lossy-counting algorithm prunes the patterns with supports being less than ε from a pool of monitored patterns such that the required memory usage is reduced. Consequently, the frequency of a pattern is estimated by compensating the maximum number of times that the pattern could have occurred before being inserted into the the pool of monitored patterns. It is proved that no false dismissal occurs with Lossy-counting algorithm. Moreover, for each pattern, the error rate of its estimated frequency is guaranteed not to exceed a given error tolerance parameter.

Although the restriction of memory usage was considered in the two works introduced previously, time sensitivity is another important issue when mining frequent itemsets from data streams. It is likely that the embedded knowledge in a data stream will change quickly as time goes by. In order to catch the recent trend of data, the estDec algorithm (Chang & Lee, 2003) decayed the old occurrences of each itemset as time goes by to diminish the effect of old transactions on the mining result of frequent itemsets over a data steam. The above approach provided time-sensitive mining for long-term data. However, in certain applications, it is interested only the frequent patterns discovered from the recently arriving data within a fixed time period. Under the assumption that exact one transaction arrives at each time unit, the sliding window method (Chang & Lee, 2004) defined the current sliding window to consist of the most recently coming w transactions in a data stream according to a given window size w. Consequently, the recently frequent itemsets were defined to be the frequent itemsets mined from the current sliding window. In addition to maintain the occurrence for the new transaction, the oldest transaction has to be removed from the maintained data structure when the window is sliding. However, all the transactions in the current sliding window need to be maintained in order to remove their effects on the current mining result when they are beyond the scope in the window.

In (Lin et al., 2005), a time-sensitive sliding window approach was also proposed for mining recently frequent itemsets within the current sliding window in a data stream. However, a general assumption that a block of various numbers of transactions (zero or more transactions) is inputted into the data stream at each time unit was adopted. Accordingly, the recently frequent itemsets were discovered from the most recent w blocks of transactions. For each block of transactions, the frequent itemsets in the block were found and all possible frequent itemsets in the sliding window were collected in a PFP (Potential Frequent-itemset Pool) table. For each newly inserted pattern, the maximum number of possible lost counts was estimated. Moreover, a discounting table was constructed to provide approximate counts of the expired data items. However, as the minimum support threshold is reduced, the number of frequent itemsets in a basic block will increase dramatically. Because of the increasing cost of table maintenance, the memory usage of PFP table will increase such that the execution efficiency of the algorithm goes down.

We propose a data representation method, named frequency changing point (FCP), for monitoring the recent occurrence of itemsets over a data stream to prevent from storing the whole transaction data within the sliding window (Koh & Shin, 2006). The effect of old transactions on the mining result of recently frequent itemsets is diminished by performing adjusting rules on the monitoring data structure. We also extend the FCP algorithm (Koh & Don, 2007) for solving the same problem considered in (Lin et al., 2005). Accordingly, the recently frequent itemsets or representative patterns are discovered from the maintained structure approximately. Experimental studies demonstrate that the proposed algorithms achieve high true positive rates and guarantees no false dismissal to the results yielded. A theoretic analysis is provided for the guarantee. In addition, our approach outperforms the previously proposed method in terms of reducing the run-time memory usage significantly.

This chapter is organized as follows. The related terms used in this chapter are defined in Section 2 first. The provided data structures for monitoring recent patterns over two different forms of data streams are shown in Section 3 and Section 4, respectively. In Section 5, the proposed algorithm for discovering recently representative patterns from the maintained structure is introduced. The performance evaluation on the proposed algorithms and related works is reported in Section 6. Finally, in Section 7, we conclude this chapter.

2. PRELIMINARIES

Let $I = \{i_1, i_2, ..., i_m\}$ denote the set of items in the specific application domain and a transaction be composed of a set of items in I. A basic block is a set of transactions arriving within a fixed unit of time. A data stream, $DS = [B_1, B_2, ..., B_t)$, is an infinite sequence of basic blocks, where each basic block $B_i = \{T_{i1}, T_{i2}, ..., T_{ij}\}$ is associated with an time identifier i and t denotes the time identifier of the latest basic block arriving currently. A special case of data steams supposes that there is exact one transaction in each basic block, which is adopted in the sliding window method (Chang & Lee, 2004) and named a data stream of transaction sequence in the following. Given a time interval $[i,j]$, $DS[i,j]$ denotes the multi-set of transactions collected from basic blocks in DS from time i to j. Under a predefined window size w, the current transaction window at time t, denoted as CTW_t, corresponds to $DS[t-w+1, t]$. The time identifier of the first basic block in CTW_t is denoted as CTW_t^{first}, that is $t-w+1$. Let $|DS[i,j]|$ denote the number of transactions in $DS[i,j]$. Therefore, $|CTW_t|$, equal to $|DS[CTW_t^{first}, t]|$, denote the number of transactions within current sliding window at time t.

An itemset (or a pattern) is a set consisting of one or more items in I, that is, a non-empty subset of I. If itemset e is a subset of transaction T, we call T contains e. Given a time interval $[i,j]$, the number of transactions in $DS[i,j]$ which contain e is named the support count of e in $DS[i,j]$, denoted as $C[i,j](e)$. The support of e in $DS[i,j]$, denoted as $Sup[i,j](e)$, is obtained from $C[i,j](e)/|DS[i,j]|$. Given a user specified minimum support threshold between 0 and 1, denoted as S_{min}, an itemset e is called a frequent itemset in $DS[i,j]$ if $Sup[i,j](e) \geq S_{min}$. Otherwise, e is a infrequent itemset in $DS[i,j]$. Under the predefined window size w, $Sup[CTW_t^{first}, t](e)$ is called the recent support of e, which is denoted as $Rsup_t(e)$. An itemset e is called a recently frequent itemset in DS if $Rsup_t(e) \geq S_{min}$. Otherwise, e is a recently infrequent itemset in DS.

Figure 1. An example of sliding window with size 5

Time	1	2	3	4	5	6	7	...
Basic block	B_1	B_2	B_3	B_4	B_5	B_6	B_7	
Itemsets	{bdef}	{f} {abe}	{abef}	{ch} {bef}	{b}	{abef}	{bf} {ab} {bf}	...

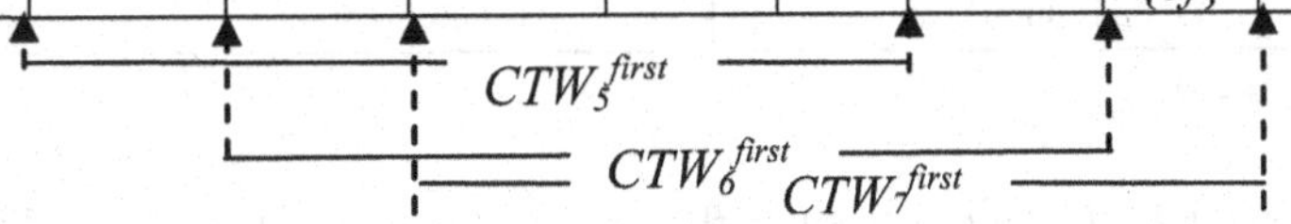

$$CTW_5^{first}$$
$$CTW_6^{first} \quad CTW_7^{first}$$

The processing of the sliding window approach (Chang & Lee, 2004) is characterized into two phases: window initialization phase and window sliding phase. The window initialization phase is activated when the current transaction window (sliding window) is not full. In this phase, the occurrences of patterns in a newly coming transaction have to be maintained. After the window has become full, the window sliding phase is activated. In addition to maintain the occurrences for the transactions in the newly coming basic block, the oldest basic block has to be removed from the window. As the example shown in Figure 1, the window sliding phase is activated at time 6. Basic block B_6 is inserted into and B_2 is removed from CTW_5^{first} to form CTW_6^{first}.

3. PATTERNS MONITORING OVER A DATA STREAM OF TRANSACTION SEQUENCE

3.1 FCP Monitoring Data Structure

A most compact method to represent the occurrences of a pattern p is to keep its first appearing time in the data stream, denoted as $p.t_s$, and an accumulated count of the pattern, denoted as $p.f$. Accordingly, $Rsup_t(p)$ is obtained from $p.f /\|DS[CTW_t^{first}, t]\|$ if $p.t_s$ is within current transaction window. Otherwise, $Rsup_t(p)$ is estimated by the support of p in $DS[p.t_s, t]$. Let $Est\_Rsup_t(p)$

denote the estimated recent support of p at time t. Accordingly, $Rsup_t(p)$ is obtained according to the following formula.

$$Rsup_t(p) = p.f /\|DS[CTW_t^{first}, t]\| \text{ if } p.t_s \geq CTW_t^{first}$$
; ---- <1>

$$= Est\_Rsup_t(p) = p.f / \|DS[p.t_s, t]\| \text{ otherwise.}$$

In a data stream of transaction sequence, the formula is simplified to be:

$$Rsup_t(p) = p.f /w \text{ if } p.t_s \geq CTW_t^{first} ; ---- <2>$$

$$= Est\_Rsup_t(p) = p.f / (t - p.t_s + 1) \text{ otherwise.}$$

However, if $p.t_s$ is far earlier than CTW_t^{first}, it is possible that the estimated support does not stand for the recent support of pattern p accurately. For analyzing the possible situations, the cases that whether a pattern p is frequent in $DS[p.t_s, CTW_t^{first}-1]$, in $DS[CTW_t^{first}, t]$, and in $DS[p.t_s, t]$ are illustrated as shown in Table 1.

In either Case 1 or Case 4, whether p is frequent in CTW_t (that is $DS[CTW_t^{first}, t]$) is consistent with the result shown in $DS[p.t_s, t]$. However, according to Case 2 and Case 3, to decide whether p is frequent in CTW_t according to its support in $DS[p.t_s, t]$ may cause false alarm and false dismissal, respectively. In Case 2, the false alarm occurs due to the distribution of p becomes sparser in CTW_t. The recent support of p in CTW_t is estimated

Table 1. The case analysis of frequent/infrequent during different time intervals for a pattern p

Interval	$DS[p.t_s, CTW_t^{first}-1]$	$DS[CTW_t^{first}, t]$	$DS[p.t_s, t]$
Case 1	p is frequent	p is frequent	p is frequent
Case 2	p is frequent	p is infrequent	p is frequent or infrequent
Case 3	p is infrequent	p is frequent	p is frequent or infrequent
Case 4	p is infrequent	p is infrequent	p is infrequent

according the count in $DS[p.t_s, t]$ such that p is evaluated to be recently frequent incorrectly. Similarly, in Case 3, the false dismissal occurs because a frequent pattern p in CTW_t is judged to be infrequent wrongly if p appears sparsely in $DS[p.t_s, CTW_t^{first}-1]$.

According to the cases discussed above, it is a critical point to set a new accumulated count of a pattern p when the appearing frequency of p becomes infrequent. Let t' denote the last time identifier when a pattern p appeared previously. As defined in Section 2, there is exact one transaction arriving in a data stream of transaction sequence. If p appears at current time t and $(t-t') > (1/S_{min})$, it is induced that p becomes infrequent in $DS[t', t-1]$ and t is named a *frequency changing point*(FCP) of p.

In the monitoring data structure, for an itemset p, each entry maintains a 6-tuple $(p, t_s, f, t_e, C_d, Rqueue)$ as described as follows:

(1) p: the corresponding itemset;
(2) t_s: the starting time of support count accumulation for p; initially, it is set to be the identifier of the basic block when p was inserted into the data structure;
(3) f: the support count of p in $DS[t_s, t]$;
(4) t_e: the time identifier of the latest basic block which contains p;
(5) C_d: the support count of p in $DS[t_s, t_e-1]$;
(6) $Rqueue$: a queue consists of a sequence of $(ct_1, ac_1), (ct_2, ac_2), ..., (ct_n, ac_n)$ pairs, in which the time identifier ct_i is a frequency changing point of p for i=1,...,n. Besides, ac_1 denotes the support count of p in $DS[t_s,$

$ct_1-1]$ and ac_i denotes the support count of p in $DS[ct_{i-1}, ct_i-1]$ for i=2,...,n.

In the following, $p.X$ is used to denote the X field in the entry of pattern p.

The frequency changing points of a pattern p are used to be the boundaries of intervals for accumulating the support counts of p. In our approach, when $p.t_s$ is beyond the corresponding time interval of CTW_t, $p.t_s$ will be adjusted to be a frequency changing point of p as approaching CTW_t^{first} as possible. The detail will be introduced in the nest subsection.

3.2 Maintenance of FCP Monitoring Data Structure

In the window initialization phase, a new transaction is appended into the FCP monitoring data structure (FCP_MDS). The maintained information of a pattern includes its frequency changing points and the accumulated support counts between the changing points. The corresponding pseudo code is shown in Figure 2.

In the window sliding phase, in addition to perform procedure AppendNew(), it is necessary to examine the starting time of support count accumulation for each monitored pattern. For a pattern p, the following cases are possible if $p.t_s$ is less than CTW_t^{first}.

(1) $p.Rqueue$ is empty: It implies that p remains a frequent itemset during its accumulation interval as Case 1 enumerated in Table 1. To judge whether p is a recently frequent

Figure 2. The pseudo code of procedure AppendNew ().

```
Procedure AppendNew()
  {If the record of p is in FCP_MDS
      { p.f= p.f+1;
        If t-p.te > (1/Smin)  /* t is a frequency changing point */
        {let n denote the number of elements in p.Rqueue ;  n=n+1;
         ctn=t, acn= (p.f- 1)- p.Cd;
         enqueue (ctn, acn) into p.Rqueue;
         p.Cd= p.f - 1; }
       p.te =t;}
      else { p.f=1; p.ts= t ; p.te= t; p.Cd=0; p.Rqueue=null;
        insert p into FCP_MDS;}}
```

pattern according to $Est\_Rsup_t(p)$, no false dismissal will occur. Accordingly, it is not necessary to reset $p.t_s$ in this situation.

(2) *p.Rqueue* is not empty: There is one or more frequency changing points of p occurring during its accumulation interval. In this case, the frequency changing points in *p.Rqueue* are checked one by one to reset $p.t_s$. Let (ct, ac) denote the first pair in *p.Rqueue*. It is applicable to reset $p.t_s$ in the following three conditions:

(2-1) The frequency changing point $ct \leq CTW_t^{first}$: it implies that the support count accumulated in ac is beyond the scope of CTW_t. Moreover, ct approaches CTW_t^{first} more than $p.t_s$ does.

(2-2) The frequency changing point $ct > CTW_t^{first}$ and $ac=1$: it implies that the occurring of p before ct is at $p.t_s$ only. Thus, the first appearing time of p within CTW_t is ct.

(2-3) The frequency changing point $ct > CTW_t^{first}$ and $ac>1$: Let t_e' denote the previous time point when p appears before ct. Although the value of t_e' is not maintained, the largest value of t_e' could be estimated from ct and $p.t_s$. Since ct is a frequency changing point, it is implied that $(ct - t_e') > 1/S_{min}$. That is, $t_e' < (ct - 1/S_{min})$. Moreover, ac keeps the support count accumulated in $DS[p.t_s, ct-1]$ and no frequency changing point occurs in this period.

In other words, the interval of every two adjacent appearing time in the ac times of occurring must be less than or equal to $1/S_{min}$. Thus, $t_e' \leq p.t_s + (ac-1) \times (1/S_{min})$ and $t_e' < p.t_s + (ac-1) \times (1/S_{min})+1$ is derived. By combining these two inequalities, the largest value of t_e', denoted as $t_e'\_max$, is derived to be $\min((ct - 1/S_{min}), p.t_s + (ac-1) \times (1/S_{min})+1)-1$. If $t_e'\_max$ is less than CTW_t^{first}, it implies that ct is the first time p appears within CTW_t.

When satisfying each one of the situations enumerated above, the changing point pair (ct, ac) is dequeued from *p.Rqueue*, the starting time $p.t_s$ is reset to be ct; and accumulated support counts $p.f$ and $p.C_d$ are modified accordingly. The corresponding procedure AdjustStart() is shown in Figure 3.

For each pattern p with $p.t_s$ being less than CTW_t^{first}, the adjusting method removes the period, in which p tends to become infrequent from the accumulation period, until $p.t_s$ is equal to CTW_t^{first} (condition 2-1) or $p.t_s$ is set to be the first appearing time of p within CTW_t (condition 2-2 and condition2-3). The situation that $p.t_s$ and $p.f$ are not adjusted occurs only when $ct > CTW_t^{first}$, $ac>1$, and $t_e'\_max \geq CTW_t^{first}$. In this case, p is frequent in $[p.t_s, CTW_t^{first})$ because there is not any frequency changing point appearing between $p.t_s$ and ct. When judging whether p is frequent

Figure 3. The pseudo code of procedure AdjustStart().

```
Procedure AdjustStart()
{For each p in FCP_MDS
 { If p.t_s < CTW_t^first
       Adjust = True;
   While (Adjust ∧ p.Rqueue≠null) {
     Get the first pair (ct, ac) from p.Rqueue;
          If (ct ≤ CTW_t^first)
          Else if ((ct > CTW_t^first )∧( ac=1))
        Else {t_e'_max = min((ct -1/S_min), p.t_s+ (ac-1)×(1/S_min)+1)-1;
          If (t_e'_max ≥ CTW_t^first) Adjust = False;}
          If (Adjust) {Dequeue (ct, ac) from p.Rqueue;
                      p.t_s = ct; p.f= p.f-ac; p.C_d= p.C_d-ac ;}
     }/*end while */
 }/*end for */
}
```

in CTW_t according to $Est\_Rsup_t(p)$, even though false alarm may occur, it is certain that no false dismissal will occur.

Moreover, it is indicated that a pattern p does not appear in CTW_t if $p.f$ becomes 0 or t_e is less than CTW_t^{first}. Therefore, such a pattern is pruned to prevent from storing the unnecessary patterns in the monitoring data structure. At any time whenever needing to enumerate recently frequent itemsets, all the patterns in the structure are examined to discover the patterns p with $Rsup_t (p) \geq S_{min}$.

[Example 1]

Table 2 shows an example of a data stream of transaction sequence. Suppose S_{min} is set to be 0.5 and window size w is 10. The process of constructing the monitoring data structure of frequency

changing points is described as the following.

From time point t_1 to t_4, there is not any frequency changing point occurring for those monitored patterns. The constructed monitoring data structure at t_4 is shown in Figure 4(a). After that, time t_5 is a frequency changing point of a and ab. Therefore, the changing point entry (5,2) is appended into $a.Rqueu$ and $ab.Rqueue$, respectively. The resultant monitoring data structure is shown in Figure 4(b).

Continuing the similar process, the resultant monitoring data structure at t_{10} after the patterns in T_{10} has been inserted into the data structure is shown in Figure 4(c). The process starting at t_{11} changes into the window sliding phase. For any monitored pattern p, the values of $p.t_s$ and $p.f$ are going to be adjusted if $p.t_s$ is less than CTW_t^{first}. For example, after T_{12} is inserted, the content in

Table 2. An example of a data stream of transaction sequence

Time	1	2	3	4	5	6	7	8	9	10	11	12	13	14	15
Transaction	T_1	T_2	T_3	T_4	T_5	T_6	T_7	T_8	T_9	T_{10}	T_{11}	T_{12}	T_{13}	T_{14}	T_{15}
Itemset	ab	ab	d	a	ab	ac	ae	ac	e	ae	ad	b	ae	b	ae

Figure 4. The process of constructing the monitoring data structure of Example 1

time: t_4

p	t_s	f	t_e	C_d	Rqueue
a	1	3	4	0	{}
b	1	2	2	0	{}
ab	1	2	2	0	{}
d	3	1	3	0	{}

$CTW_4=\{T_1\sim T_4\}$

(a) input transaction T_4

time: t_5

p	t_s	f	t_e	C_d	Rqueue
a	1	4	5	0	{}
b	1	3	5	2	{(5,2)}
ab	1	3	5	2	{(5,2)}
d	3	1	3	0	{}

$CTW_5=\{T_1\sim T_5\}$

(b) input transaction T_5

time: t_{10}

p	t_s	f	t_e	C_d	Rqueue
a	1	8	10	0	{}
b	1	3	5	2	{(5,2)}
ab	1	3	5	2	{(5,2)}
d	3	1	3	0	{}
c	6	2	8	0	{}
ac	6	2	8	0	{}
e	7	3	10	0	{}
ae	7	2	10	1	{(10,1)}

$CTW_{10}=\{T_1\sim T_{10}\}$

(c) input transaction T_{10}

time: t_{12}

p	t_s	f	t_e	C_d	Rqueue
a	1	9	11	0	{}
b	1	4	12	3	{(5,2),(12,1)}
ab	1	3	5	2	{(5,2)}
d	3	2	11	1	{(11,1)}
c	6	2	8	0	{}
ac	6	2	8	0	{}
e	7	3	10	0	{}
ae	7	2	10	1	{(10,1)}
ad	11	1	11	0	{}

$CTW_{12}=\{T_3\sim T_{12}\}$

(d) input transaction T_{12}(before adjustment)

p	t_s	f	t_e	C_d	Rqueue
a	1	9	11	0	{}
b	5	2	12	1	{(12,1)}
ab	5	1	5	0	{}
d	3	2	11	1	{(11,1)}
c	6	2	8	0	{}
ac	6	2	8	0	{}
e	7	3	10	0	{}
ae	7	2	10	1	{(10,1)}
ad	11	1	11	0	{}

$CTW_{12}=\{T_3\sim T_{12}\}$

(e) input transaction T_{12}(after adjustment)

p	t_s	f	t_e	C_d	Rqueue
a	1	10	13	0	{}
b	5	2	12	1	{(12,1)}
ab	5	1	5	0	{}
d	11	1	11	0	{}
c	6	2	8	0	{}
ac	6	2	8	0	{}
e	7	4	13	3	{(13,3)}
ae	7	3	13	2	{(10,1)(13,1)}
ad	11	1	11	0	{}

$CTW_{13}=\{T_4\sim T_{13}\}$

(f) input transaction T_{13}

time: t_{15}

p	t_s	f	t_e	C_d	Rqueue
a	1	11	15	0	{}
b	12	2	14	0	{}
d	11	1	11	0	{}
c	6	2	8	0	{}
ac	6	2	8	0	{}
e	7	5	15	3	{(13,3)}
ae	7	4	15	2	{(10,1)(13,1)}
ad	11	1	11	0	{}

$CTW_{15}=\{T_6\sim T_{15}\}$

(g) input transaction T_{15}

the monitoring data structure is shown in Figure 4(d). Among the monitored patterns, both $b.t_s$ and $ab.t_s$ are less than CTW_{12}^{first}, and their corresponding *Rqueues* are not empty. By satisfying the third case among the three conditions of adjustment, the changing point entry (5,2) is removed from $b.Rqueues$, $b.t_s$ is adjusted to be 5 and $b.f= b.f$-2. Similarly, $ab.t_s$ is set to be 5 and $ab.f= ab.f$-2. The obtained result is shown in Figure 4(e).

At time t_{13}, it is a frequency changing point of patterns e and ae. Besides, $d.t_s$ is adjusted to be 11 as shown in Figure 4(f). After T_{15} is inserted at time t_{15}, the information of pattern b is adjusted. Then pattern ab is removed because the last time it appeared is out of the range of CTW_{15}. The resultant monitoring data structure is shown as Figure 4(g).

From the result shown in Figure 4(g), the recent supports of a, b, d, c, ac, e, ae, and ad are estimated to be 0.73(11/15=0.73), 0.2(2/10=0.2), 0.1(1/10=0.1), 0.2(2/10=0.2), 0.2(2/10=0.2), 0.5(5/10=0.5), 0.4(4/10=0.4), and 0.1(1/10=0.1), respectively. The discovered recent frequent patterns are {a} and {e}.

4. PATTERNS MONITORING OVER A GENERAL DATA STREAM

4.1 Modified Summarization Record

In a general data stream, the numbers of transactions in basic blocks are various. It is not trivial to get the number of transactions arriving within a period of time. Furthermore, a pattern p may appear more than once in a basic block. Therefore, the data structure for monitoring the recent appearances of patterns is modified accordingly.

First, the definition of a frequency changing point of a pattern p is modified. Let t_l denote the first time identifier when a pattern p appeared. The earliest time identifier t', where $t' > t_l$, p appears in $B_{t'}$, and $Sup[t_l, t'-1](p) < S_{min}$, is named a frequency changing point(FCP) of p. If a frequency

changing point of p has ever occurred, t_l is set to be the latest frequency changing point of p.

For a pattern p, its record in the monitoring data structure is extended into an 8-tuple (p, t_s, f, f_c, t_e, t_{pre}, C_d, $Rqueue$) as the following to represent the summarization of p's occurrences.

(1) p: the corresponding itemset;
(2) t_s: the starting time of support count accumulation for p; initially, it is set to be the identifier of the basic block when p was inserted into the data structure;
(3) f: the support count of p in $DS[t_s, t]$;
(4) f_c: the support count of p in B_t;
(5) t_e: the time identifier of the latest basic block which contains p;
(6) t_{pre}: the latest time identifier which is a frequency changing point of p;
(7) C_d: the support count of p in $DS[t_s, t_{pre}-1]$;
(8) $Rqueue$: a queue consists of a sequence of (ct_1, ac_1), (ct_2, ac_2), ..., (ct_n, ac_n) pairs, in which the time identifier ct_i is a frequency changing point of p for i=1,...,n. Besides, ac_1 denotes the support count of p in $DS[t_s, ct_1-1]$ and ac_i denotes the support count of p in $DS[ct_{i-1}, ct_i-1]$ for i=2,...,n.

By comparing with the 6-tuple provided in the previous section, the extending part of the 8-tuple includes f_c for counting the support of p in B_t and t_{pre} for checking the modified definition of a frequency changing point.

For compressing the FCP monitoring data structure provided in our approach, a FP-tree-like structure named *pattern summarization tree (PS-tree)*, is adopted to organize the summarization records of itemsets which appear in current transaction window. However, to prevent from two scans over the data set, the items in a transaction are sorted according to their alphanumeric order instead of their frequency-descending order. Moreover, an array named *TranArray* is constructed to maintain the number of transactions in each basic block for the recent ($w+w/2$) blocks which is used

Figure 5. The pseudo codes of PS-tree maintenance

```
Procedure PS-tree_maintenance()
{
  TranArray and PS-tree are initialized;
  While (B_t is inputed){
    New_block_insert(B_t);
    For each node N in the PS-tree
    { Let p denote the associated items in N;
    If (t > w) /* sliding the window */
      If (p.t_e < CTW_t^{first}) Remove_itemset(PS-tree);
      Else If (p.t_s < CTW_t^{first}) Reset_start_time(PS-tree);
    If (p.f_s≠t and p.f≠0)
      Check_change_point(PS-tree);}/* end For */
    TranArray_update(TranArray);
    t=t+1; }/* end While */
}
```

to compute the total number of transactions within a given time interval for estimating the recent supports of a pattern. At time t, the number of transactions in basic blocks B_j $((CTW_t^{first}-w/2) \leq j \leq t)$ is stored in $TranArray[t-j]$.

4.2 Maintenance of PS-tree

On the whole, there are four sub-tasks for maintaining the PS-tree structure: (1) insert transactions in the new basic block into PS-tree, (2) eliminate the expired count of patterns, (3) check and record frequency changing points of patterns, and (4) update *TranArray*. The pseudo codes of the whole process are shown in Figure 5.

First, each transaction T in the newly inputted basic block is inserted into the *PS-tree*. The PS-tree is a trie structure, so there is one node constructed for representing each common prefix of patterns. For each prefix-subset p of T, if the corresponding node exists in the PS-tree, $p.f$, $p.f_c$, and $p.t_e$ in the node are updated accordingly. Otherwise, a new node for storing the summarization record of p with initial setting is constructed.

In the window sliding phase, for each monitored pattern p in the *PS-tree*, it is necessary to eliminate the expired count from the summarization information of p additionally. It is indicated that a pattern p does not appear in CTW_t if $p.t_e$ is less than CTW_t^{first}. Therefore, such a pattern is pruned to prevent from maintaining the unnecessary information. Moreover, similar to the process over a data stream of transaction sequence, it is necessary to adjust the starting time of support count accumulation for a pattern p as the following cases if $p.t_s$ is less than CTW_t^{first}.

(1) $p.Rqueue$ is empty: it is not necessary to adjust $p.t_s$.

(2) $p.Rqueue$ is not empty: The frequency changing points of p are checked one by one to adjust $p.t_s$ to be a frequency changing point of p as approaching CTW_t^{first} as possible. Let (ct, ac) denoted the first frequency changing point pair got from $p.Rqueue$. It is applicable to adjust $p.t_s$ in the following three conditions:

Table 3. An example of a general data stream

Time	1	2	3	4	5	6	7	8	9	10	...
Basic block	B_1	B_2	B_3	B_4	B_5	B_6	B_7	B_8	B_9	B_{10}	...
Transactions	{ab} {a} {a}	{b} {c} {c}	{ab}	{a}	{a} {b}	{c} {cd} {c} {cd}	{a} {b}		{a}	{cd}	...

(2-1) $ct \leq CTW_t^{first}$: it implies that ct approaches CTW_t^{first} more than $p.t_s$ does.

(2-2) $ct > CTW_t^{first}$ and $ac=1$; it implies that the first appearing time of p within CTW_t is ct.

(2-3) $ct > CTW_t^{first}$ and $ac>1$: Let t_e' denote the previous time point when p appears before ct. Let X denote the support count of p in $B_{te'}$. The maximum value of t_e', denoted by Max_t_e', must satisfy $(ac-X)/|DS[t_s, Max\_t_e'-1]| \geq S_{min}$ and $(ac-X)/|DS[t_s, Max\_t_e']| < S_{min}$ because there is not any frequency changing point occurring from $p.t_s$ to t_e'. Since the support count of p in $B_{te'}$ is not maintained, an upper bound of Max_t_e', denoted by $UB\_Max\_t_e'$, is estimated by $ac/|DS[t_s, UB\_Max\_t_e'-1]| \geq S_{min}$ and $ac/|DS[t_s, UB\_Max\_t_e']| < S_{min}$. If $UB\_Max\_t_e'$ is less than CTW_t^{first}, according to **[Theorem1]** shown below, it is indicated that all the possible value of t_e' must be less than CTW_t^{first}. Therefore, ct is the first time p appears within CTW_t.

[Theorem 1] It is given that $(ac-X)/|DS[t_s, Max\_t_e'-1]| \geq S_{min}$ and $(ac-X)/|DS[t_s, Max\_t_e']| < S_{min}$. If $ac/|DS[t_s, UB\_Max\_t_e'-1]| \geq S_{min}$ and $ac/|DS[t_s, UB\_Max\_t_e']| < S_{min}$, $UB\_Max\_t_e'$ is an upper bound of Max_t_e'.

[Prove] If $UB\_Max\_t_e' < Max\_t_e'$, it was implied that $UB\_Max\_t_e' \leq Max\_t_e'-1$. It is also implied that $|DS[t_s, UB\_Max\_t_e']| \leq |DS[t_s, Max\_t_e'-1]|$. Thus, we can get $S_{min} > ac/|DS[t_s, UB\_Max\_t_e']| \geq ac/|DS[t_s, Max\_t_e'-1]| \geq S_{min}$. It is a contradiction to induce $S_{min} > S_{min}$. Therefore, $UB\_Max\_t_e' \geq Max\_t_e'$ is proved. In other words, $UB\_Max\_t_e'$ is an upper bound of Max_t_e'.

When satisfying any one of the situations enumerated above, the (ct, ac) pair is removed from $p.Rqueue$, the starting accumulation time $p.t_s$ is adjusted to be ct; and accumulated support counts $p.f$ and $p.C_d$ are modified accordingly.

Moreover, for each pattern p monitored in the *PS-tree*, if p appears in current basic block ($p.f_c > 0$) and has ever appeared in any previous basic block ($p.t_s < t$), whether current time t is a frequency changing point of p is checked. If t is certified to be a frequency changing point of p, a frequency changing point pair (ct, ac) is inserted into $p.Rqueue$, where $ct=t$ and $ac=((p.f - p.f_c)-p.C_d)$. Besides, $p.t_{pre}$ and $p.C_d$ are updated to be t and $(p.f - p.f_c)$, respectively. After the checking, $p.f_c$ is reset to be 0.

Finally, after the previous three subtasks are finished. The data in *TranArray* is updated according to the number of transactions in current basic block.

[Example 2]

Table 3 shows an example of a general data stream. Suppose S_{min} is set to be 0.5 and window size w is 4. The process of constructing the *PS-tree* is described as the following.

From time point t_1 to t_2, there was not any frequency changing point occurring for the monitored patterns. The constructed *PS-tree* and *TranArray* at t_2 are shown in Figure 6(a). For simplifying the figures, the header table and the links connecting the nodes with same items are not shown in the figure. After processing B_3, time point t_3 is a frequency changing point of ab. Therefore, the changing point entry (3,1) is appended into $ab.Rqueue$. Besides, $ab.C_d$ is set to be $ab.f - ab.f_c$ =1, and $ab.t_{pre}$ is set to be 3. Accordingly, the resultant monitoring data structure is shown in Figure 6(c).

Continuing the similar process, the resultant monitoring data structure at t_5 after inserting the patterns in B_5 into the data structure is shown in Figure 6(d). Then the value of $ab.t_s$ is adjusted because $ab.t_s$ is less than $CTW_5^{first}(=2)$. According to the first frequency changing point pair of ab, $(3,1)$, which satisfies the first case of adjustment, $ab.t_s$ is reset to be 3, $ab.f$ is updated to be 1, and the pair is removed from $ab.Rqueue$ as the result shown in Figure 6(e). After recording the frequency changing point pair, $(5,1)$, of b, the result is shown in Figure 6(f). Figure 6(g) shows the result after inserting the transactions in basic block B_6. Since the first frequency changing point pair of b satisfies the second case of adjustment, $b.t_s$ and $b.f$ are adjusted to be 5 and 1, respectively. Moreover, $c.Rqueue$ is updated as Figure 6(h) shows. At time point t_7, the value of $ab.t_e$ is 3 (shown in Figure 6(i)) which less than $CTW_7^{first}(=4)$. It is indicated that all the occurrences of ab are out of the range of current transaction window. Thus, the node of ab is removed from the *PS-tree* as the result shown in Figure 6(j).

In spite of no transaction being inputted at t_8, by satisfying the third case among the three conditions of adjustment, $c.t_s$ is adjusted to be 6 and $c.f$ is reset to be 6. The obtained result is shown in Figure 6(k), which shows the *PS-tree* correctly catches the recent occurrences of the patterns b, c, d, and cd in the current transaction window. The estimated recent support of pattern a is higher than its real recent support (2/8). However, after B_{10} is processed at time t_{10}, the summarization record of a is adjusted as the monitoring data structure shown in Figure 6(l). Therefore, the estimation error of a is compensated after adjusting $a.t_s$.

5. RECENTLY REPRESENTATIVE PATTERNS MINING

Based on the maintained *PS-tree* structure, we modified the TD-FP Growth algorithm (Wang, et. al, 2002) to find all the patterns p with $Rsup_t(p) \geq S_{min}$ whenever needed. However, the sheer size of mining results is another challenge in frequent-pattern mining. In many cases, in addition to memory requirement and execution efficiency, a high minimum support threshold may discover only commonsense patterns but a low one may generate an explosive number of output patterns, which severely restricts its usage. To solve this problem, the closed frequent itemsets (Pei, Han, & Mao, 2000) provided a lossless compression of the whole collection of patterns; however, its compression power is limited. For providing a general method for high-quality compression, the distance measure between two frequent itemsets was defined in (Xin, et. al, 2005) to find a representative pattern for each cluster of patterns. Two greedy algorithms, named RPglobal and RPlocal, respectively, were proposed. The RP-global algorithm applied the greedy method to find representative patterns among the discovered frequent itemsets. For providing a scalable method, the RPlocal algorithm found the representative patterns locally during the process of pattern-growth. In this section, we will introduce how to apply the idea of RPlocal algorithm (Xin, et. al, 2005) to discover recently representative patterns from the maintained PS-tree.

For any two patterns p_r and p, let $T(p)$ and $T(p_r)$ denote the sets of transactions which contain p and p_r, respectively. By extending the definition of pattern distances proposed in (Xin, et. al, 2005), if p_r is a proper subset of p, the distance between p and p_r in CTW_t is defined to be:

$$RD(p,p_r) = 1 - \frac{|T(p) \cap T(p_r)|}{|T(p) \cup T(p_r)|} = 1 - \frac{|T(p_r)|}{|T(p)|} = 1 - \frac{Rsup_t(p_r)}{Rsup_t(p)}$$

Figure 6. The maintenance of the monitoring data structure.

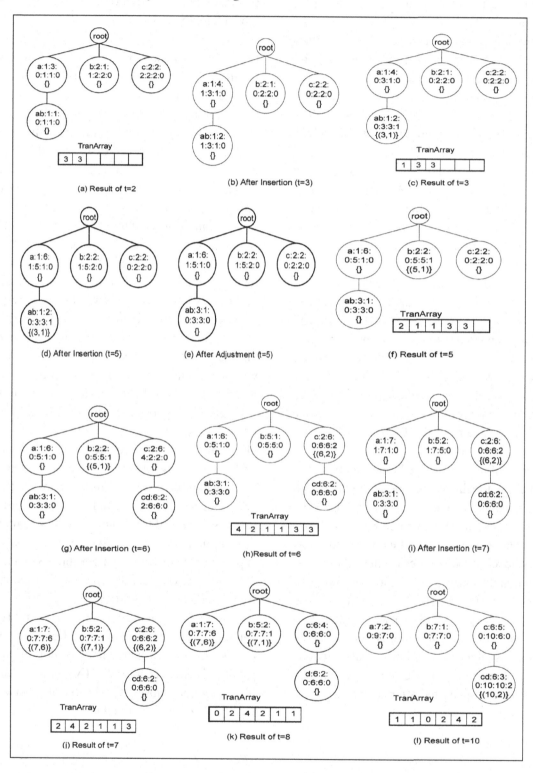

where T(p) and T(p$_r$) denote the set of transactions containing p and p$_r$, respectively.

Otherwise, RD(p, p_r) = ∞. If RD(p, p_r) is less than a given δ value, it is called that p_r δ-covers p and p is δ-covered by p_r in CTW_t . A recently frequent pattern p is named a *recently representative pattern* if p is not δ-covered by any recently frequent itemset.

The TD-FP Growth algorithm adopts a depth-first approach to perform pattern-growth. During the mining process, our approach constructs a *RP-tree* (Representative Pattern tree) to maintain the discovered representative patterns. The *RP-tree* is a trie structure, where each node contains a (p, sup) pair to denote a representative pattern p and its recent support, respectively. A pattern p can be decided whether it is a representative pattern only when no more frequent pattern is grown from p or all the patterns grown from p have been decided. Therefore, a *RP-stack* is used to maintain those patterns which have not been certified to be representative patterns yet. There are five fields in each entry of *RPstack*:

(1) p: the itemset;
(2) sup: the recent support of p;
(3) *covered*: whether p is δ-covered by other patterns;
(4) *cover_pattern*: the known maximum pattern which δ-covers p;
(5) *cover_RP*: the known maximal representative pattern which δ-covers p.

For a newly discovered recently frequent itemset p, each pattern p' in *RP-stack* is a prefix of p. If p' has not been δ-covered by a representative pattern and it is δ-covered by p, p'.covered is set to be 1. Besides, the pattern in p'.cover_pattern is replaced by p if p is larger than the original one.

In addition, the *RP-tree* is searched to find the representative patterns which δ-cover p. If more than one representative pattern δ-covers p, let p_r denote the maximum pattern among these satisfying patterns. Accordingly, p.covered is set

to be 2 and p_r is stored in p.cover_RP.

When the process of generating patterns grown from p is complete, the record of p is popped from *RP-stack*. According to the value stored in p.covered, whether p is a representative pattern is certified according to the following three cases:

(1) p.covered=2: there is a representative pattern δ-covers p, *thus,* p is not a representative pattern.
(2) p.covered=1: p is δ-covered by the pattern p' stored in p.cover_patter. If p' is found in the RP-tree, p is not a representative pattern because it is δ-covered by a representative pattern. Otherwise, p is certified to be a representative pattern and is inserted into the RP-tree.
(3) p.covered=0: there is not any pattern found to δ-cover p. Pattern p is certified to be a representative pattern and is inserted into the RP-tree.

6. PERFORMANCE STUDY

In the following two subsections, the performance studies for the proposed FCP method over the data streams of transaction sequence and the general data streams are introduced, respectively (Koh & Shin, 2006; Koh & Don, 2007).

6.1 Performance Study over a Data Stream of Transaction Sequence

The proposed FCP patterns monitoring method over a data stream of transaction sequence (FCP algorithm in short) and Sliding Window method (SW algorithm in short) (Chang & Lee, 2004) are implemented using Visual C++ 6.0. The TD_FP_Growth algorithm (Wang et al., 2002) is applied to discover recently frequent patterns from the FCP monitoring data structure.

In our approach, to prevent the monitoring data structure from glowing over time, the patterns

Table 4. The FDR and FAR values of the mining results

Time Point	200K	400K	600K	800K	1000K
FDR(%)	0	0	0	0	0
FAR(%)	0.4589	0.4713	0	0.1665	0.2862
ASE(%)	0.032	0.0323	0.0103	0.0206	0.0198

with recent supports less than the error tolerance parameter ε are pruned. Accordingly, the formula for getting $Rsup_t(p)$ is modified as the following for compensating the possible removed counts.

$$Rsup_t(p) = (p.f + \lfloor (p.t_s - CTW_t^{first}) \times \varepsilon \rfloor)/w \text{ if } p.t_s \geq CTW_t^{first} ; \text{ ---- <3>}$$

$$= Est\_Rsup_t(p) = p.f / (t - p.t_s + 1) \text{ otherwise.}$$

The experiments have been performed on a 3.4GHz Intel Pentium IV machine with 512 megabytes main memory and running Microsoft XP Professional. Moreover, the datasets are generated from the IBM data generator (Agrawal & Srikant, 1994), where each dataset simulates a data stream with a transaction coming within each time unit. In the first part of experiments, the false dismissal rates/false alarm rates are measured to indicate the effectiveness of the proposed method. Furthermore, the execution time and memory usage is measured in the second part of experiments to show the efficiency of FCP algorithm by comparing with the ones of SW algorithm.

[Experiment 1-1] To evaluate the effectiveness of FCP algorithm, an experiment is performed on the dataset T5.I4D1000K with window size w=20000, S_{min}=0.01, and ε=0.005. In this experiment, FCP algorithm is performed to maintain the monitoring data structures. Besides, TD_FP-Growth algorithm is performed once every 200K time points to find recently frequent itemsets. By comparing the mining results with the frequent itemsets found by Apriori

Algorithm on the corresponding CTW_t, the false dismissal rate (FDR), false alarm rate (FAR), and average support error (ASE) of the algorithm are measured.

The results shown in Table 4 illustrates that all the recently frequent patterns are discovered and no false dismissal occurs in FCP algorithm. Besides, it is reported that the false alarm rate of FCP algorithm is below 0.5%. The *average support error* defined in (Manku & Motwani, 2002) is also used to model the relative accuracy of the proposed method. The results show that ASE ($R_{FCP}|R_{Apriori}$) keeps under 3×10^{-5} in different time points.

[Experiment 1-2] In this experiment, FCP and SW algorithms are compared on their accumulated execution time (including the time of maintaining patterns and mining) and maximum memory usage used for maintaining the monitored patterns. This experiment is performed on the dataset T5.I4D1000K with S_{min} =0.01 and ε=0.005. When the window size is varied from 10000, 20000, to 30000, the results of accumulated execution time and maximum memory usage are shown in Figure 7(a) and 7(b), respectively. Although the accumulated execution time increases as window size grows, the efficiency of FCP algorithm is comparable to the one of SW algorithm. In contrast with SW algorithm, the memory usage of FCP is significantly reduced without being sensitive to the window size. Moreover, it verifies that FCP

Figure 7. The execution time and memory usage of FCP and SW algorithms

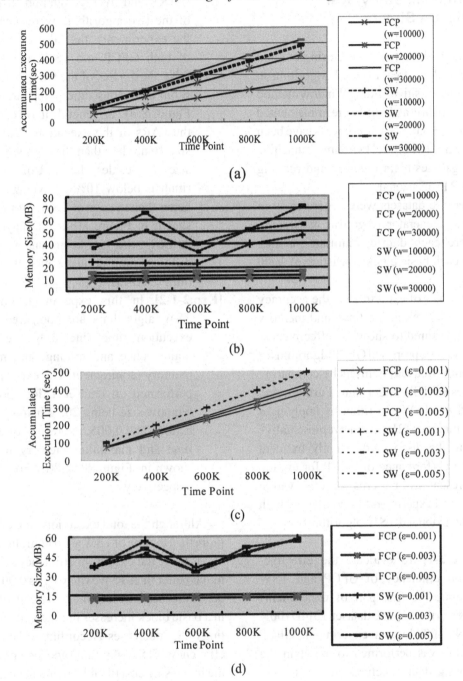

(a)

(b)

(c)

(d)

is feasible for the streaming environment with a limited memory. By varying the setting of ε, Figure 7(c) and 8(d) show the results of accumulated execution time and maximum memory usage, respectively. It is indicated that the execution time of FCP is not sensitive to ε. In addition, the maximum memory usage of FCP keeps steady, which is limited within 15 MB.

6.2 Performance Study over a General Data Stream

The proposed FCP patterns monitoring method over a general data stream (GFCP algorithm in short) and Time-sensitive Sliding Window method (TSW in short) (Lin et al.,2005) were implemented using Visual C++ 6.0. The experiments have been performed on a 3.4GHz Intel Pentium IV machine with 1G megabytes main memory and running Microsoft XP Professional.

Moreover, the datasets were generated from the IBM data generator (Agrawal & Srikant, 1994), where each dataset simulates a data stream with each basic block consisting of 1000 transactions.

In the first part of experiments, the accuracy of mining results, execution time, and memory usage were measured to show the effectiveness and efficiency of the proposed GFCP algorithm for mining recently frequent itemsets by comparing with the ones of TSW algorithm. Furthermore, we extended the TSW algorithm by applying a local greedy method [12] to extract representative patterns from the discovered recently frequent itemsets. The performance of GFCP for mining recently representative patterns was observed in the second part of experiments by comparing with the one of the extended TSW algorithm.

[Experiment 2-1] To evaluate the effectiveness and efficiency of GFCP and TSW algorithms, the first part of experiments were performed on the dataset T5I4D100K with |N|=100. In this experiment, GFCP algorithm was performed to maintain the monitoring data structures. Besides, TD_FP-Growth algorithm was performed once every 10 time points to find recently frequent itemsets.

[Exp.2-1-1] By comparing the mining results with the frequent itemsets found by Apriori algorithm on the corresponding CTW_t, the false dismissal rate (FDR), false alarm rate

(FAR), and average support error (ASE) of the two algorithms were measured. In the experiments, the false dismissal rates of both GFCP and TSW are zeros. The false alarm rates of the two proposed algorithm at various time points are shown in Figure 8(a). In general, it is reported that the FARs of the executions with window size 40 are less than the ones with window size 20. Besides, the FAR of GFCP algorithm is below 10% on average, which is better than the one of TSW. From the result shown in Figure 8(b), one may note that $ASE(R_{GFCP}|R_{Apriori})$ keeps under 25×10^{-3} at different time points, which is about one third of $ASE(R_{TSW}|R_{Apriori})$.

[Exp.2-1-2] In this experiment, GFCP and TSW algorithms are compared on their execution time (including the time of maintenance and mining) and maximum memory requirement. The experiment was performed on dataset T5I4D1000K with window size being 20. When S_{min} is set to be 0.01 and 0.005, the results of execution time and maximum memory usages are shown in, Figure 8(c), 8(d), 8(e), and 8(f), respectively.

Although the total execution time of GFCP is more than the one of TSW algorithm slightly when S_{min} is 0.01, the execution efficiency of GFCP is much better than TSW when S_{min} is 0.005. This is due to the fact that the number of frequent itemsets in a basic block increases dramatically as the setting of S_{min} decreases. Accordingly, the execution efficiency of TSW algorithm goes down because of the increasing cost of table maintenance. Regarding GFCP algorithm, little difference of maintenance time is observed between the two different settings of S_{min}. In addition, the effect of changing S_{min} on the mining time of GFCP is not significant. It should be noted that GFCP has better efficiency than TSW as S_{min} is smaller. By discarding the mining time, the maintenance time of GFCP is much less than the execution time of TSW. These results suggest that, if it is not necessary to get mining results at any time, GFCP algorithm is a very efficient method for monitoring patterns in a data stream to discover recently frequent itemsets on demand. Furthermore, in contrast with TSW, the memory usage of GFCP is not sensitive to the setting of S_{min}, which also keeps stable at different time points. These results clearly demonstrate that GFCP is feasible for the streaming environment with a limited memory.

[**Experiment 2-2**] In order to evaluate the GFCP algorithm and extended TSW algorithm for mining recently representative patterns, the execution time and maximum memory usage were measured for different settings of S_{min}. The experiment was performed with window size w=20 and δ=0.2. By varying the setting of S_{min} to be 0.01, 0.005, and 0.001, Figure 8(g) and 8(h) show the results of execution time and maximum memory usage, respectively. The result shown in Figure 8(g) is in general agreement with the one of [Exp.2-1-2]. Especially, when S_{min} is set to be 0.001, the execution time of GFCP is 600 sec. less than the one of extended TSW at most, which demonstrates the scalability of our approach. Clearly visible in Figure 8(h) is that the maximum memory usage of extended TSW increases as S_{min} decreases. On the other hand, as a smaller S_{min} is set, the amount of frequency changing points maintained in the FP-tree is decreased. This is the

7. CONCLUSION

The sliding window approach proposes a good solution for providing time-sensitive mining of frequent itemsets in data streams. In this chapter, a pattern summarization data structure based on the frequency changing point representation is provided to represent the occurrences of patterns over a data stream. The effect of old transactions on the mining result of recently frequent itemsets is diminished by performing adjusting rules on the monitoring data structure without needing to keep the whole transactions in the current sliding window physically. From the monitoring data structure, the recently frequent patterns are discovered efficiently at any time. Furthermore, to avoid generating redundant information in the mining results, the idea of local greedy method is applied to discover the recently representative patterns from the monitoring data structure.

The experimental results demonstrate that both the proposed FCP and GFCP algorithms achieve high accuracy for approximating the supports of recently frequent patterns and guarantees no false dismissal occurring. The maintaining process of the proposed monitoring data structures are very quick under various parameters setting. Furthermore, the memory requirement of our approach is significantly reduced by comparing with the one of the related works. These results suggest that, if it was not necessary to get mining results at any time, the frequency changing point method is a very efficient scheme for monitoring patterns in a data streaming environment with a limited memory to discover recently frequent patterns on demand.

REFERENCES

Agrawal, R., & Srikant, R. (1994). Fast algorithms for mining association rules. In *Proceedings of the International Conference on Very Large Data Bases.*

Chang, J. H., & Lee, W. S. (2003). Finding recent frequent itemsets adaptively over online data streams. In *Proceedings of the 9th ACM International Conference on Knowledge Discovery and Data Mining.*

Figure 8. The execution time and memory usage of GFCP and TSW algorithms reason for the maximum memory usage of GFCP under S_{min} =0.001 is only 1/60 of the one required by TSW.

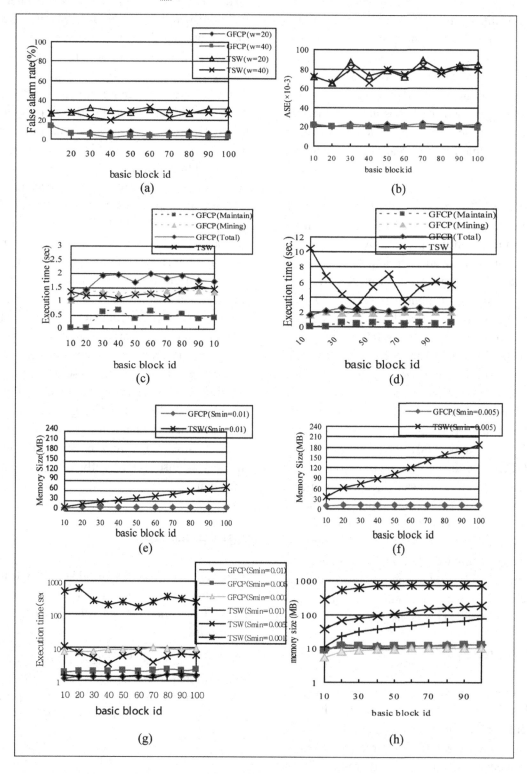

Chang, J. H., & Lee, W. S. (2004). A sliding window method for finding recently frequent itemsets over online data streams. *Journal of Information Science and Engineering, 20*, 753–762.

Han, J., Pei, J., Yin, Y., & Mao, R. (2004). mining frequent patterns without candidate generation: A frequent-pattern tree approach. *Data Mining and Knowledge Discovery, 8*(1), 53–87. doi:10.1023/B:DAMI.0000005258.31418.83

Jin, C., Qian, W., Sha, C., Yu, J. X., & Zhou, A. (2003). Dynamically maintaining frequent items over a data stream. In *Proceedings of the 12th ACM International Conference on Information and Knowledge Management.*

Koh, J. L., & Don, Y.-B. (2007). mining frequent approximately representative itemsets on data streams. In T. Washio, et al. (Eds.), *Proceedings of the 2007 International Workshop on High Performance Data Mining and Applications (PAKDD 2007)* (LNAI 4819, pp. 231-243). Berlin, Germany: Springer-Verlag.

Koh, J. L., & Shin, S. N. (2006). An approximate approach for mining recently frequent itemsets from data streams. In *Proceedings of the 8th International Conference on Data Warehousing and Knowledge Discovery.*

Lin, C. H., Chiu, D. Y., Wu, Y. H., & Chen, A. L. P. (2005). Mining frequent itemsets from data streams with a time-sensitive sliding window. In *Proceedings of the SIAM International Conference on Data Mining.*

Manku, G. S., & Motwani, R. (2002). Approximate frequent counts over data streams. In *Proceedings of the 28th International Conference on Very Large Database.*

Park, J. S., Chen, M. S., & Yu, P. S. (1995). An effective hash-based algorithm for mining association rules. In *Proceedings of the ACM SIGMOD International Conference on Management of Data.*

Pei, J., Han, J., & Mao, R. (2000). CLOSET: An efficient algorithm for mining frequent closed itemsets. In *Proceedings Of the ACM SIGMOD Workshop on Research Issues in Data Mining and Knowledge Discovery.*

Wang, K., Tang, L., Han, J., & Liu, J. (2002). Top down FP-growth for association rule mining. In *Proceedings of the 6th Pacific Area Conference on Knowledge Discovery and Data Mining.*

Xin, D., Han, J., Yan, X., & Cheng, H. (2005). Mining compressed frequent-pattern sets. In *Proceedings of the International Conference on Very Large Data Bases (VLDB'05).*

Chapter 15
Protocol Identification of Encrypted Network Streams

Matthew Gebski
National ICT Australia and University of New South Wales, Australia

Alex Penev
National ICT Australia and University of New South Wales, Australia

Raymond K. Wong
National ICT Australia and University of New South Wales, Australia

ABSTRACT

Traffic analysis is an important issue for network monitoring and security. The authors focus on identifying protocols for network traffic by analysing the size, timing and direction of network packets. By using these network stream characteristics, they propose a technique for modelling the behaviour of various tcp protocols. This model can be used for recognising protocols even when running under encrypted tunnels. This is complemented with experimental evaluation on real world network data.

INTRODUCTION

Computer security and intrusion detection are important problems in computer science that have no optimal solutions, and improvements on existing techniques are frequently published. One interesting area is that of misuse detection, wherein we attempt to identify inappropriate behavior and use of a system by its users (whether legitimate or not). With the increase in importance of the web over the past 10 years, so too has there been an increase in the number of ways that system resources can be abused. For instance, users may abuse their privileges by tunneling or using a proxy for P2P file sharing application over HTTP or SSH so that it appears to be a different activity.

This chapter looks at the problem of identifying the protocol of a network stream for which very little information is available. Unlike most previous approaches, the approach outlined here restricts itself to using only the timing, size and direction of packets and assumes that their content is scrambled. There are numerous scenarios where the amount of information for identification is limited to these attributes. For example, a proxy tunnel can be used to run an instant messenger chat application, yet the actual packets that identify the traffic as a chat protocol are enveloped inside the SSH stream and

DOI: 10.4018/978-1-60566-748-5.ch015

Copyright © 2010, IGI Global. Copying or distributing in print or electronic forms without written permission of IGI Global is prohibited.

encrypted. Tunnels and proxies are sometimes used to secretly run potentially-inappropriate activities in the workplace, such as file-sharing, IRC and instant messengers, and to circumvent a company's firewall in accessing blocked websites (e.g. webmail).

When the underlying protocol is scrambled and sent through a tunnel or proxy protocol, the only information the local routers can observe is the timing, size and direction of the packets. If the inner packet headers were available then identifying the protocol would be a trivial task. However, we restrict ourselves only to surface-level information.

Our aim is to develop a model based on the traffic structure that is visible externally and use it to train protocol profiles. A new (and unknown) stream can then be matched against these profiles. Suspicious connections that are identified as an inappropriate protocol can then simply be flagged for an administrator to investigate further. The presented approach constructs a bipartite graph to model the incoming and outgoing packets, a feature present in virtually all network traffic. In this graph, edges between nodes are the likelihoods of encountering a certain packet (size, timing, direction) after another. We can then classify a stream as a particular protocol with a confidence score by finding particular subsequences of packets that are indicative of a known protocol.

The contributions of this chapter are:

- An approach for discrimination of network protocols that is suitable for encrypted traffic.
- An improved model which provides higher accuracy and facilitates analysis of multiple protocol steams in one session.
- Analysis of accuracy and running time on real-world network data.
- A data set comprising 50,000 unique connections for several common protocols.

BACKGROUND

While there are many commercial and academic tools available for monitoring computer systems, many of these are rule-based and require a large amount of human effort to precisely specify what constitutes acceptable behavior and use of a system. As such, current attention is on developing techniques and tools that facilitate a more-automated approach.

In this context, we are not actively trying to prevent unauthorized access and as such there is a difference to the related problem of *intrusion detection*. However, intrusion detection systems use only rudimentary protocol identification techniques. The main IDSs such as Snort (Roesch, 1999) define the protocol of a stream based on the connection ports (McAfee, 2008) and (Enterasys Networks Incorporated, 2008), (Paxson, 1999).

Instead, we concentrate on determining if actions performed by the user, whether authorized or not, appear acceptable. This can still relate to unauthorized access because a malicious party that gains access to a system may use the compromised machine for inappropriate. This activity should be flagged, even for a legitimate user.

Related to protocol identification is the area of *misuse detection* (Kumar & Spafford, 1994), (Shavlik & Shavlik, 2004), (Maxion & Townsend, 2002), which involves determining if the actual user of a computer system matches the owner of the account being used. Misuse detection via analysis of user commands is in some ways similar to protocol identification: arbitrary observed sequences (shell commands versus packets) are compared against known behavioral models. Research by Lane & Brodley considered an instance-based learning approach (Lane & Brodley, Approaches to on-line learning and concept drift for user identification in computer security, 1998), (Lane & Brodley, Temporal sequence learning and data reduction for anomaly detection, 1999). Further work was done on misuse detection by Sequeira & Zaki with the ADMIT system (Sequeira & Zaki,

2002). ADMIT clustered related sequences and classified commands by the distance to the appropriate cluster. More recently, Gebski & Wong suggested modeling commands as a tree (Gebski & Wong, 2005). Each command was linked with previous commands based on the number of commands entered in between. Scoring was performed by comparing incoming tokens against the tree. Once misuse is detected, it may then be suitable to present the user with a form of secondary authentication (Pusara & Brodley, 2004).

Originally, protocols were identified by their known ports numbers, but this may be circumvented. The main IDSs such as Snort (Roesch, 1999) define the protocol of a stream based on the connection port (Enterasys Networks Incorporated, 2008), (McAfee, 2008), (Paxson, 1999). More advanced protocol identification was considered by Early, Brodley & Rosenberg using neural networks (Early, Brodley, & Rosenberg, 2003). They made use of the SYN, ACK, FIN, and PSH flags in the TCP frames as the basis for construction of C5.0 decision trees. Empirically, their approach was shown to perform acceptably: accuracy was worst for SMTP, which was still correctly classified 82% of the time. Unfortunately, TCP headers are not available in tunneled streams because the packets of the underlying 'true' protocol are scrambled and placed inside a different packet. It is not clear how their approach would perform in this case. Other techniques include decision trees (Tan & Collie, 1997) and in (Dreger, Feldmann, Mai, Vern, & Sommer, 2006), packet level analysis as part of their ongoing NIDS system.

More recently, Wright et al. considered protocol identification for scrambled streams with time and size information available (Wright, Monrose, & Masson, 2004). Their technique used Hidden Markov Models similar to those used for protein sequence alignment. Each state corresponded to a symbol, with probability distribution based on the position in the sequence. Two parallel chains of states were used to discriminate between client-server and server-client streams. Protocols

such as AIM and HTTP achieved 80% accuracy, while SMTP and FTP were closer to 60%. For SSH and Telnet, the technique performed poorly (20-40%).

Additional work related to encrypted data includes web-page classification over SSL. Sun et al. constructed signatures of HTTPS websites using the count and sizes of the external HTTP objects that they referenced, such as images and scripts (Sun, Simon, Wang, Russell, Padmanabhan, & Qiu, 2002). For static pages, up to 80% of sites were correctly identified. However, dynamic pages were "non-identifiable" due to the changing counts and sizes of external referenced objects. Consequently, their technique is not applicable to protocol identification because there are no objects being referenced, and even two identical TCP requests may fluctuate in terms of both size and timing due to retransmissions and network unpredictability.

APPROACH

Preliminaries

We assume that we are dealing with sets of incoming/outgoing sequences comprising tuples of attributes that summarize a packet. Each tuple has the form *<time, size, direction>*. All three of these are trivially observable without needing to inspect the payload.

We will use S to denote a session with S_{out} and S_{in} beings its outgoing and incoming packets. For simplicity and clarity we ignore the *ACK* acknowledgement packets, although our model can be adjusted to accommodate their existence.

For the purpose of training the protocol profiles, the source and destination hosts and ports are used to correctly label the streams under their protocol. In the test set, this information is ignored from the packet headers (assumed scrambled) and only the timing and size are used.

Figure 1. Two examples of real network traffic

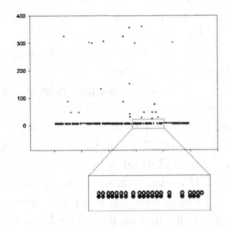

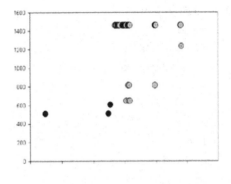

(a) An example of HTTP traffic   **(b) An example of MSN traffic**

Our aim is to determine the protocol τ being used for the transmission of a given session S; in the case where multiple protocols are present, we want to determine the set of these protocols, $\{\tau_1, \tau_2, ...\}$.

Model

The assumption made regarding packet flow is that server replies are logically related to client requests, or in other words, the ordering of packets is important. Using this, the sequences S_{out} and S_{in} form a flow of forward/backward packet pairs. Physically, the first value of these pairs corresponds to a request made from the client machine while the second corresponds to a response from the remote server. If a burst of many packets in a row are emitted from one end without an interruption from the other end, they are combined into a single node in S_{out} (or S_{in}). This happens quite often when the request or response is larger than the Maximum Transmission Unit (MTU) and the data is broken up into multiple packets.

For a protocol such as HTTP, a request for an image may be quite small (e.g. "GET http://www.url.com/pic.jpg HTTP/1.0") while the response

that actually contains the image may be hundreds of kilobytes. This exchange would involve hundreds of packets, but in our model will be represented as two nodes. We can see this behavior clearly in Figure 1a, where the vertical axis is packet size and the horizontal is the flow of time.

Naturally, we observe different behavior for other protocols. Traffic for the MSN Messenger protocol typically contains a periodic keep-alive of 6 bytes (with an 8 byte response), as shown in Figure 1b. Such idiosyncratic behavior is our best means of identifying protocols using our limited information. Algorithm 1: Bipartite graph construction

```
1) Nodes_out = Ø
2) Nodes_in = Ø
3) N = Create a new node
4) for ρ ∈ S
5)     if ρ ∈ S_out
6)         if q ∈ S_in
7)             N = Create a new node
8)             Add packet ρ to node N
9)             Add an edge between N
and N_PrevOut
10)        else
```

```
11)          Add packet ρ to node
N
12)    else if ρ ∈ S_in
13)        if q ∈ S_out
14)            N = Create a new node
15)            Add packet ρ to node
N
16)            Add an edge between N
and N_Prev
17)        else
18)            Add packet ρ to node
N
19)    q = ρ
```

With a time-flow in mind, a bipartite graph is constructed to represent each session. We use two sets of nodes, $\in S_{in}$ and $\in S_{out}$ to represent the outgoing and incoming nodes. Multiple packets in time without an interruption are combined into one node to represent a single abstract packet, as shown in Algorithm 1.

The packet ρ is the packet currently under consideration. We determine if it is an outgoing or incoming node and then create an edge to the appropriate node in S_{out} by considering the last observed node q. If q was on the other side of the bipartite graph to ρ, we create a new node and link it to the previous nodes.

Should we combine successive packets into a single node? Consider an uninterrupted sequence of packets (r_i, r_{i+1}, ..., r_{i+n}) which is a subsequence of S. If we do not want to represent (r_i ... r_{i+n}) using one node, there are two options. The first is to create a node for each packet with an edge between pairs of successive packets. The alternative is to again create multiple nodes, but instead of a single edge between r_{i+1} and r_i, an edge is created between all node pairs in the subsequence. Both methods give a finer-grained representation of the stream because we know how many packets were involved in the reply.

But in reality, TCP/IP packets do not necessarily arrive in the same order as how they were

transmitted, so it makes sense to group large bursts of uninterrupted activity into a single node and bypass any problems or inconsistencies in their ordering.

Post constructions, we now have a graph that represents interactions for a protocol τ. We are then able to determine how relevant particular interactions are in defining τ. For example, multiple edges from large outgoing transmissions to small incoming transmissions may suggest BitTorrent is being used to distribute files. However, merely knowing that there are connections between given transmission sizes are not adequate on their own. Ideally, we wish to know which particular transmission combinations are the most relevant. This is done by weighting and scoring the subsequences based on their likelihood of occurring.

Weighting

After the construction of the bipartite graph, edges are weighted to reflect varying strengths of relationships between different request/response pairs for a given protocol.

There are two cases of interest:

- Given an outgoing node N_{out} of size $N_{out}.s$, we want to determine the likelihood of receiving return information (that is, an incoming node) with packets of size $N_{in}.s$. An example of where this would be useful is for HTTP: the request is often relatively small while the reply is larger.

- Given an outgoing node N_{out} and corresponding return packet, we wish to be able to represent if either more packets are likely to be transmitted or if N_{out} is likely to be the last. For instance, HTTP sessions are typically very short while protocols such as MSN and BitTorrent often have longer sessions.

For the first of these cases, the weights are determined based on the outgoing packet size and the return sizes. For each outgoing packet size seen during training, we consider the likelihood of receiving each of the corresponding return sizes. Let us denote R_s as the set of outgoing nodes with byte size S. Then we compute the set $R_{in} = \{ N_{in} \mid N_{\downarrow} in^{\uparrow}$ has an edge to a node in $R_s \}$ for any given S. The weight for a return packet of size s' having transmitted a packet of size S is

$$W\left(s, s'\right) = \frac{(count(s') \times \left[R_{\downarrow} in^{\uparrow}\right]_{\downarrow}^{\uparrow} (-1))}{\left[argmax\right]_{\downarrow} (r \in R_{\downarrow} in^{\uparrow})^{\uparrow} (count(s') \times \left[\mid R_{\downarrow} in^{\uparrow}\mid\right]_{\downarrow}^{\uparrow} (-1)))}$$

That is, the weights are the ratio to the previous number of observations for that packet size to the maximum number of observed packets. In the case of a particular s' following a particular S very often, other s' will receive low weights. In the case where a given transmission size takes many values for its reply, there will be little contribution in the overall score for the stream. (We additionally consider $\overline{R_{in}}$ and $\sigma(R_{in})$, as described below.)

There are a number of reasons why the scores produced by this weighting system are useful. First, if we have a large spread of values, $\sigma(R_{in})$ will be large; the spread of relevant values which s' takes that result in a good score will also be large. This happens in the HTTP image example. We would expect a reasonably high variance for the replies in addition to a mean higher than the request size. In contrast, MSN sessions will often have small outgoing packets for keep-alive messages along with small replies. The ratio of $\left(\mid S_{\downarrow} in^{\uparrow}\mid\right) / \left(\mid S_{\downarrow} out^{\uparrow}\mid\right)$ is close to 1 and variance is small. In this case, if s' is very far from $\overline{R_{in}}$ it will be marked as being not very relevant to this protocol.

Using the MSN protocol as an example, we will have a reasonably large set for R_6. The set R_{in}

will comprised many items for $s'=8$ in addition to a smaller number of other sizes. The weights for $\tau = MSN$, $W(6,8)$ will now be reasonably large, indicating that this packet sequence is very characteristic of $\tau = MSN$.

Protocol Identification

As with the model construction, we focus on the outgoing and incoming transmissions comprising a network stream, each of which is represented as a *<time, size, direction>* tuples. Once we isolate the individual request and response pairs, we match each against the previously observed outgoing nodes. For each matching node, we weight the pair currently considered by the likelihood of it being from protocol profile τ. Once the current pair has been scored, we consider the following pair, and as well as calculating its score, we also examine the likelihood of its size (given the current pair).

The score for a whole session is:

$$scores(S) = \frac{1}{\mid Pairs \mid} \sum_{p_i \in Pairs} W\left(p_i.0, p_i.1\right) \times W\left(p_i, p_j\right)$$

where *Pairs* is the set of outgoing-incoming node pairs created by building the bipartite graph with no outgoing-outgoing edges (i.e. the set of request/ response pairs) and $p.O$ and $p.I$ correspond to the sizes of the outgoing and incoming nodes. Finally, W corresponds to the likelihood of an outgoing packet of the size of $p.O$ following the previous outgoing packet. That is, the score is the average score obtained by weighting each node based on the request/response sizes and the size of the following/previous nodes.

To further this, we also consider the likelihood of later packets occurring given the current packet. Consider our MSN example. It is common for the the keep-alive to be followed by an automatic response. On occasion, a message from the user may be received instead of the keep-alive's 8-byte response. This is not necessarily typical of the protocol, and because it is a rare event, we do not want it to heavily affect the profile. By looking ahead at future packet pairs, we can determine whether this is a usual occurrence and moderate the weights accordingly. We can think of this as a 'smoothing' effect of the observations that will reduce the significance of anomalous packets.

Binning

The technique for scoring does not take into account sizes that have not been observed during training the profiles. However, it is likely that some packets in the test data will have unseen sizes.

This is less of an issue when we consider encrypted streams for smaller sizes, because the process of encryption results in the size of the data being padded to cipher block sizes. As such, any packet will be rounded up with the same effect as in binning. For large nodes that were composed of a run of several packets, binning to a nearby round number will improve the match rate and accuracy. For example, if the training data for HTTP has a 125KB image and the testing data has a 127KB image, we can consider them as equal-sized nodes by binning them to a size of (say) 128KB.

The main disadvantage of binning occurs for protocols that behave in a similar manner and have similar transmission sizes, where the loss of information in the precise sizes would make it harder to differentiate between some protocol sequences.

Multiple Streams

In addition to single-protocol sessions, we test our approach on sessions in which two unknown protocols are interwoven. In some cases, there may be data from more than a single application or protocol being sent through the tunnel. A user may combine data from multiple original streams to create a composite stream, such that all data are

sent and received at the same visible endpoints. To a packet sniffer, interwoven streams are indistinguishable and we would be incorrect to claim that a packet is related to what follows it in sequence because it may come from the other protocol(s). Algorithm 2. Identifying multiple protocols

```
1) τ is the primary protocol for S
2) for each pair p in Nodes:
3)     S_pÄ = score of p for τ.
4)     for τ' ≠ τ
5)         S_pÄ = score of p for τ'
6)         if S_pÄ > m% and S_pÄ < n%
7)             remove p from Nodes
8) Calculate τ', the second protocol
present in S
9) Return τ'
```

Our approach to identify multiple protocol is shown in Algorithm 2, a multi-pass over the stream. We first determine one protocol that best matches the session. This is done by scoring the session for each protocol profile and then using the highest score. Once assigned an initial protocol τ, we score each node pair for τ and for all other protocols τ'. m and n represent the minimum and maximum associations required respectively for a pair p such that it is from τ as opposed to all other potential protocols τ'. Following the identification of p being part of protocol τ, we remove it from S to allow determination of following protocols. After removing all such pairs that appear to be characteristic of τ alone, the single-pass approach is run again to look for a second protocol.

EXPERIMENTAL RESULTS

Data Sets

Our experimental data has been collected from a small group of users over a number of months. TCP packets were captured using Ethereal[1]. The raw network logs were mined to extract the individual connection streams of various protocols. The size and direction of packets were trivially observable. The protocol field and port numbers were used to label the streams with the correct protocol. This information was used for training the profiles and labeling the correct answers, but not for identification calculations.

Sessions were stripped of all 0-length payload packets (usually ACKs), and sessions with fewer than 8 packets were discarded. There are approximately 15000 BitTorrent, 150 MSN, 80 SSH, 1000 SSL and 8000 HTTP streams, in addition to 16000 SSH intrusion attempts.

Often the MSN sessions ran for many hours (and in some cases days), which resulted in relatively few but long connections. The BitTorrent connections exhibited the largest variety in values. Many connections were short formalities for the purposes of bookkeeping or handshaking, but there were also many that involved large data transfers lasting for hours.

To simulate encryption, packet sizes were rounded up to the next multiple of 16 bytes. Protocol profiles were trained using unpadded streams, but testing and identification was performed on both padded and unpadded streams.

To simulate multiple protocols being tunneled through the same stream, sessions were randomly chosen from two different single protocols and merged into an interwoven session. The timing of sessions was adjusted to ensure that both protocols' packets overlapped. A total of 10,000 such streams were synthesized for each protocol pair.

The data used for these experiments is made publicly available and can be downloaded online. It has been preprocessed in the manner described above reduce its size, and has been obfuscated for privacy reasons.

Raw Data

We begin by considering how our identification technique performs on standard data using only the time, size and direction of packets. Table 1 shows that the approach has reasonable performance. A high threshold was required for a confident match, and HTTP and MSN received the lowest accuracy (when forced into a class, both score above 90%). It is interesting to note that the BitTorrent picks up a reasonably high percentage of SSH streams. This is due to both having small outgoing transmissions with an extremely large range of incoming transmission sizes. For the same reason, some short MSN sessions with a very high amount of activity were classified as BitTorrent.

Table 2 shows the accuracy of the approach on the standard data with more protocols included. Accuracy is high for all protocols. The primary source of confusion was BitTorrent, which picked up some MSN and SSH sessions due to its high spread of values. Only GMail had lower than 85% accuracy, but almost all of its misidentified streams were identified as HTTP instead.

Simulated Encryption

Following our experiments on the raw network data, we consider the performance on connections with packet sizes rounded to simulate the effect of cipher blocks. All packet sizes were padded to the next multiple of 16 bytes.

We would expect a reduction in the quality of classification as we are reducing the amount of information available. In particular, we would expect this where there exists a strong correlation between specific outgoing and incoming sizes. However, where there is ambiguity for the raw data, we may expect a slight increase in the quality. For example, HTTP requests are often similar---but not identical---in size due to variations in the lengths of URLs.

The most pronounced reduction in quality in Table 3 were BitTorrent packets, which were most commonly confused with SSH. This was for the same reason as the standard data. For MSN, there was a 13% increase in the accuracy compared to the unpadded data, likely because the slight varia-

Table 1. Results for standard data using only packet size/time/direction

Protocol	BitTorrent	HTTP	MSN	SSH	No Conf.
BitTorrent	**95.0%**	0.1%	0.5%	0.0%	4.4%
HTTP	0.3%	**3.1%**	0.0%	0.0%	36.6%
MSN	6.6%	0.0%	**67.1%**	0.0%	26.3%
SSH	12.5%	0.0%	0.0%	**87.5%**	0.0%

tions in message lengths were now smoothed and equalized while the keep-alive remained a useful identifying feature because of their timing and small size.

The bottom half of Table 2 includes GMail and SSL as protocols. The most notable difference over the results shown in Table 3 is the slight decrease in the accuracy for SSH.

Multiple Streams

We consider the effect of having multiple protocols present in the one stream (Table 4). This may occur if protocols are purposefully tunneled through a single proxy or if the system is unable to differentiate between the streams. We create the multiple stream datasets by randomly choosing

sessions for each protocol and combining them together. Combined sets were created from both the padded and non-padded streams, and accuracy is generally close to 70%.

The final set of experiments incorporate a number of failed SSH connections from unauthorized parties hoping to gain access to our network. There were 12465 such attempts, most of them likely to have been automated. Detecting such connections can identify which network or which individual external machines are continuously trying to access our network, and they can be consequently blocked (in case they ever succeed).

Table 5 shows the confusion matrix with these intrusion attempts included. Virtually all attempts were correctly identified because they have a consistent behavior. Failed SSH logins

Table 2. Top half is the confusion matrix for standard data, bottom for padded data.

Protocol	BitTorrent	GMail	HTTP	MSN	SSH	SSL	No Conf.
BitTorrent	**90.5%**	0.0%	4.6%	1.7%	2.5%	0.0%	0.6%
GMail	0.0%	**73.5%**	25.5%	0.0%	0.0%	0.0%	1.1%
HTTP	1.0%	2.4%	**88.8%**	0.0%	0.0%	0.0%	7.8%
MSN	4.6%	0.0%	1.2%	**87.2%**	0.0%	0.0%	6.9%
SSH	7.2%	0.0%	3.0%	0.0%	**85.8%**	0.4%	4.6%
SSL	2.1%	0.0%	0.0%	0.0%	0.1%	**95.8%**	3.0%
Protocol	BitTorrent	GMail	HTTP	MSN	SSH	SSL	No Conf.
BitTorrent	**84.6%**	0.0%	3.3%	2.4%	9.4%	0.2%	0.0%
GMail	0.0%	**87.0%**	13.0%	0.0%	0.0%	0.0%	0.0%
HTTP	0.7%	0.9%	**87.8%**	0.1%	0.0%	0.3%	10.2%
MSN	18.3%	0.0%	1.4%	**80.3%**	0.0%	0.0%	0.0%
SSH	14.3%	0.0%	0.0%	0.0%	**85.7%**	0.0%	0.0%
SSL	0.0%	0.0%	4.0%	0.0%	0.3%	**93.7%**	2.0%

Table 3. Results for padded data using only packet size/time/direction

Protocol	BitTorrent	HTTP	MSN	SSH	No Conf.
BitTorrent	**84.8%**	3.3%	2.4%	9.5%	0.0%
HTTP	0.8%	**88.9%**	0.1%	0.0%	10.2%
MSN	18.3%	1.4%	**80.3%**	0.0%	0.0%
SSH	4.3%	0.0%	0.0%	**95.7%**	0.0%

Table 4. Results for interwoven streams

Protocol	BT-HTTP	BT-MSN	BT-SSH	HTTP-MSN	HTTP-SSH	Other
BT-HTTP	**64.9%**	1.5%	3.6%	6.2%	2.1%	21.9%
BT-MSN	4.4%	**73.0%**	0%	2.3%	2.1%	18.2%
BT-SSH	0.0%	0%	**71.3%**	0.6%	4.2%	23.9%
HTTP-MSN	6.0%	0.3%	7.6%	**70.7%**	0.9%	14.4%
HTTP-SSH	3.8%	3.2%	0%	6.3%	**65.3%**	21.4%

and very short SSH sessions were sometimes misidentified as intrusion attempts, but the large majority of regular SSH sessions were still correctly identified.

Varying Training Information

The sensitivity of the approach regarding how much of the dataset is used for training the profiles in shown in Figure 2. There is a dramatic increase in accuracy for both SSH and MSN as more sessions are used for training, which is a direct result of the comparatively small number of unique sessions in the data set for those two protocols.

The most likely explanation for the decrease in BitTorrent accuracy in the padded data is that when few streams were used for training, BitTorrent acted as a 'catch-all' protocol due to its high variance. Consequently, some other protocol sessions were misidentified as BitTorrent and nearly every BitTorrent connect was correctly identified. When a more substantial number of sessions from the other protocols such as MSN were considered for training, some BitTorrent streams containing packet sequences typically associated with those protocols were now misidentified and its overall accuracy dropped.

Table 5. Results for block-padded packets and intrusion attempts

Protocol	SSH	BT	MSN	HTTP	GMail	SSH Intr.
SSH	**82.6%**	4.3%	0.0%	0.0%	0.0%	13.0%
BT	5.9%	**78.4%**	12.0%	3.3%	0.2%	0.1%
MSN	0.0%	2.0%	**95.9%**	0.0%	2.0%	0.0%
HTTP	1.0%	16.6%	0.0%	**79.2%**	3.0%	0.0%
GMail	0.0%	0.0%	0.0%	17.4%	**82.5%**	0.0%
SSH Intr.	0.0%	0.0%	0.0%	0.0%	0.0%	**99.9%**

Figure 2. Varying the size of training data

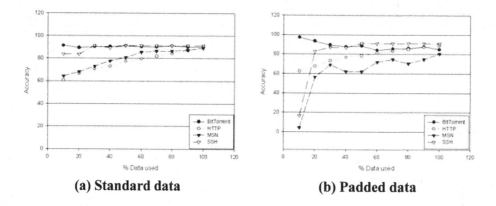

(a) Standard data   **(b) Padded data**

Running Time

Figure 3a shows the time required to construct the protocol profiles as the number of sessions and packets used was increased. The complexity is close to linear. The total amount of time required for nine million packets was under 12 minutes. The average time per connection was 0.02s using a Python implementation.

Figure 3b shows the time required for classification. Each line represents a different size protocol profile model: the lowest is constructed using 20% of the data, the next 60% and the largest

100%. Again, performance is close to linear and the implementation handled about 150 streams per second on a regular desktop.

DISCUSSION

There are other areas besides protocol identification where a similar approach can be used. For example, consider the problem of a bank determining the occupation of its customers by using only the regularity of income payments and their amounts; clients with similar jobs could receive

Figure 3. Effect of varying training data available

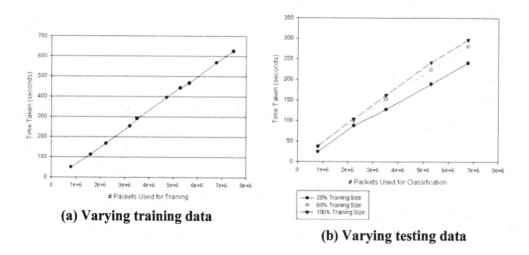

(a) Varying training data

(b) Varying testing data

similar-sized payments at similar intervals.

While the presented approach is effective in determining the underlying protocol of a network stream, it is possible that an adversary may be aware that protocol identification is taking place. As a result, they may take steps to attempt to circumvent or fool the system. We now consider possible actions they may take.

The easiest approach would be to pad all packets to a fixed size such that there is no distinction by packet size. This can be further combined with artificially delaying or tweaking the timing of the transmissions. Although this requires a fair bit of effort on behalf of the adversary, it would make it impossible for the approach to match the stream against the known protocol profiles because both the size and timing information has been changed.

However, a stream with consistent block sizes will not match any known protocol and will be flagged as such. A trivial analysis of this stream will indicate something abnormal is occurring.

A slightly more sophisticated circumvention would be to randomize the timing, size and ordering of packets. Ordering would not significantly affect our approach because multiple packets are condensed into one node, but size manipulation will certainly affect the results. Similar to the above scenario, if a user's traffic consistently does not match any protocol profile then it may be flagged as suspicious anyway.

The real difference between randomisation and maximum padding of the packet sizes occurs when the randomised sizes are similar to those of a known protocol. In this case, rather than being marked as unknown, we will receive a false positive leading us to believe that the network activity is in fact permissible (assuming the assigned protocol is permissible).

An advanced adversary may go one step further. Rather than simply randomising or padding transmissions, they may attempt to disguise any transmissions as another protocol. This can be done by monitoring a legitimate application and replacing the packet payloads. This becomes incredibly difficult to detect with our approach as we are now completely unable to distinguish any information about the underlying protocol.

In fact, even if we have access to the entire packet information, it is difficult to detect abuse performed in this manner. An adversary may construct packets with the same internal information and send these to legitimate looking destinations on the `correct' ports. It is only by performing analysis on the packet payload and noticing the encrypted message that we are able to determine that the protocol is different from what can be inferred externally.

CONCLUSION

This chapter looked at a simple machine learning approach for protocol identification in network streams that have been encrypted, such that the only information available for identifying the underlying protocol of a connection was the size, timing and direction of packets.

The approach makes efficient use of the request/response nature of most network protocols to identify common patterns and the general trend of outgoing/incoming transmissions and train protocol profiles. These are then matched against an unknown stream to determine the most likely protocol.

We have shown experimentally that this approach is both efficient in terms of running time and accuracy. This holds even when multiple protocols are present in the one network stream. Overall, the experiments show that it is possible to pinpoint potentially inappropriate activities for a workplace, institution or research center, such as using BitTorrent, GMail or MSN, and not confuse them with other common protocols such as HTTP and SSL.

REFERENCES

Dreger, H., Feldmann, A., Mai, M., Vern, P., & Sommer, R. (2006). Dynamic application-layer protocol analysis for network intrusion detection. In *USENIX-SS'06: Proceedings of the 15th conference on USENIX Security Symposium* (p. 18). Vancouver, Canada: USENIX Association.

Early, J., Brodley, C., & Rosenberg, C. (2003). Behavioral Authentication of server flows. In *ACSAC '03: Proceedings of the 19th Annual Computer Security Applications Conference* (p. 46). Washington, DC: IEEE Computer Society.

Enterasys Networks Incorporated. (2008). *Enterasys dragon*. Retrieved from http://www.enterasys.com/products/ids/

Gebski, M., & Wong, R. (2005). Intrusion detection via analysis and modelling of user commands. In *Proceedings of the 7th International Conference Data Warehousing and Knowledge Discovery (DaWaK)* (pp. 388-397). Copenhagen, Denmark: Springer.

Kumar, S., & Spafford, E. H. (1994). A pattern matching model for misuse intrusion detection. In *Proceedings of the 17th National Computer Security Conference* (pp. 11-21).

Lane, T., & Brodley, C. (1998). Approaches to on-line learning and concept drift for user identification in computer security. In *KDD '98: Proceedings of the 1998 ACM SIGKDD international conference on Knowledge discovery and data mining* (pp. 259-263). New York: ACM Press.

Lane, T., & Brodley, C. (1999). Temporal sequence learning and data reduction for anomaly detection. *ACM Transactions on Information and System Security, 2*(3), 295–331. doi:10.1145/322510.322526

Maxion, R. A., & Townsend, T. N. (2002). Masquerade detection using truncated command lines. In *DSN '02: Proceedings of the 2002 International Conference on Dependable Systems and Networks* (pp. 219-228). Washington, DC: IEEE Computer Society.

McAfee. (2008). *IntruShield network IPS application*. Retrieved from http://www.networkassociates.com/

Paxson, V. (1999). Bro: A system for detecting network intruders in real-time. *Computer Networks, 31*(23-24), 2435–2463. doi:10.1016/S1389-1286(99)00112-7

Pusara, M., & Brodley, C. E. (2004). User re-authentication via mouse movements. In *VizSEC/DMSEC '04: Proceedings of the 2004 ACM workshop on Visualization and data mining for computer security* (pp. 1-8). Washington, DC: ACM Press.

Roesch, M. (1999). Snort - lightweight intrusion detection for networks. In *LISA '99: Proceedings of the 13th USENIX conference on System administration* (pp. 229-238). Seattle, WA: USENIX Association.

Sequeira, K., & Zaki, M. (2002). ADMIT: Anomaly-based data mining for intrusions. In *Proceedings of the eighth ACM SIGKDD international conference on Knowledge discovery and data mining* (pp. 386-395). Edmonton, Canada: ACM Press.

Shavlik, J., & Shavlik, M. (2004). Selection, combination, and evaluation of effective software sensors for detecting abnormal computer usage. In *KDD '04: Proceedings of the 2004 ACM SIGKDD international conference on Knowledge discovery and data mining* (pp. 276-285). Seattle, WA: ACM Press.

Sun, Q., Simon, D. R., Wang, Y.-M., Russell, W., Padmanabhan, V. N., & Qiu, L. (2002). Statistical identification of encrypted Web browsing traffic. In *Proceedings of the IEEE Symposium on Security and Privacy* (pp. 19-30). Washington, DC: IEEE Computer Society.

Tan, K. M., & Collie, B. S. (1997). Detection and classification of TCP/IP network services. In *ACSAC '97: Proceedings of the 13th Annual Computer Security Applications Conference* (p. 99). Washington, DC: IEEE Computer Society.

Wright, C., Monrose, F., & Masson, G. M. (2004). HMM profiles for network traffic classification. In *VizSEC/DMSEC '04: Proceedings of the 2004 ACM workshop on Visualization and data mining for computer security* (pp. 9-15). Washington, DC: ACM Press.

ENDNOTE

[1]   http://www.ethereal.com

Chapter 16
Exploring Calendar–Based Pattern Mining in Data Streams

Rodrigo Salvador Monteiro
COPPE / UFRJ – Brazil

Geraldo Zimbrão
COPPE / UFRJ – Brazil

Holger Schwarz
IPVS - University of Stuttgart – Germany

Bernhard Mitschang
IPVS - University of Stuttgart – Germany

Jano Moreira de Souza
COPPE / UFRJ – Brazil

ABSTRACT

Calendar-based pattern mining aims at identifying patterns on specific calendar partitions. Potential calendar partitions are for example: every Monday, every first working day of each month, every holiday. Providing flexible mining capabilities for calendar-based partitions is especially challenging in a data stream scenario. The calendar partitions of interest are not known a priori and at each point in time only a subset of the detailed data is available. The authors show how a data warehouse approach can be applied to this problem. The data warehouse that keeps track of frequent itemsets holding on different partitions of the original stream has low storage requirements. Nevertheless, it allows to derive sets of patterns that are complete and precise. Furthermore, the authors demonstrate the effectiveness of their approach by a series of experiments.

INTRODUCTION

Calendar-based schemas (Li, Y. et al., 2001) (Ramaswamy, S. et al., 1998) were proposed as a

DOI: 10.4018/978-1-60566-748-5.ch016

semantically rich representation of time intervals and used to mine temporal association rules. An example of a calendar schema is (year, month, day, day_period), which defines a set of calendar patterns, such as every morning of January of 1999 (1999, January, *, morning) or every 16th day of January

Copyright © 2010, IGI Global. Copying or distributing in print or electronic forms without written permission of IGI Global is prohibited.

of every year (*, January, 16, *). In the research field of data mining, frequent itemsets derived from transactional data represent a particularly important pattern domain due to their large applicability (Boulicaut, J., 2004). Association rule mining is the most recognized application of frequent itemsets (Agrawal, R. et al., 1993). Other examples are generalized rule mining (Mannila, H., & Toivonen, H., 1996) and associative classification (Liu, B. et al., 1998). The combination of the rich semantics of calendar-based schemas with frequent itemset mining, namely calendar-based frequent itemset mining, corresponds to the first step of various calendar-based pattern mining tasks, e.g., calendar-based association rules. An example of calendar-based association rules provided in Li, Y. et al. (2001) is that eggs and coffee are frequently sold together in morning hours. Considering the transactions at the all-day granule would probably not reveal such a rule and its implicit knowledge.

Recent applications, such as network traffic analysis, web click stream mining, power consumption measurement, sensor network data analysis, and dynamic tracing of stock fluctuation are some examples where a new kind of data arises, the so called data stream. A data stream is continuous and potentially infinite. Mining calendar-based patterns in data streams is a difficult task described in the following statement:

Problem Statement: Let D be a transactional dataset provided by a data stream. Let X be a set of ad-hoc calendar-based constraints and T the subset of transactions from D satisfying X. The frequency of an itemset I over T is the number of transactions in T in which I occurs. The support of I is the frequency divided by the total number of transactions in T. Given a minimum support σ, the set of calendar-based frequent itemsets is defined by the itemsets with support $\geq \sigma$ over the set of transactions T.

Some examples of calendar-based constraints are: weekday in {Monday, Friday}; day_period = "Morning"; holiday = "yes"; etc. The calendar

partitions that will reveal interesting temporal patterns are not known a priori and at each point in time only a subset of the detailed data is available in a window based on the most recent data.

Existing approaches cannot solve the above problem because either they require all transactions to be available during the calendar-based mining task or they do not provide enough flexibility to consider a calendar-based-subset of the data stream transactions. In order to flexibly derive patterns based on calendar features in data streams, we need some kind of summary for previous time windows. As the calendar partitions that will be interesting for analysis are not known in advance, it is not obvious how to build and store such a summary.

CONTRIBUTIONS

The focus of DWFIST (Monteiro, R. S. et al., 2005) is on presenting the model of a data warehouse that keeps track of frequent itemsets holding on disjoint sets of the original transactions. We call each of these disjoint sets a partition. For each partition, the data warehouse stores all itemsets that are frequent in this partition.

In this chapter, we discuss how to apply DWFIST in a data stream scenario leveraging calendar-based pattern mining capabilities. One partition represents a period of one hour for example. The partitions may be freely combined in order to retrieve the frequent itemsets holding on any set of partitions. A temporal dimension on the data warehouse represents the calendar features, such as year, month, holiday, weekday, and many others. The main contributions of this chapter are as follows:

- Explain the structure of a data warehouse that supports calendar-based frequent itemset mining.
- Show that we can guarantee the completeness of the retrieved frequent itemsets and

that the pattern retrieval from the data warehouse is efficient and precise.

- Show how the required staging area tasks can cope with tight time constraints imposed by the data stream scenario.
- Show that the storage requirements of the data warehouse are kept at a manageable level, i.e., they are kept low compared to the size of the input stream.

Our approach does not propose a new algorithm for mining frequent itemsets directly on streams. Instead, we rely on existing algorithms to perform regular frequent itemset mining on small batches of the stream data, and provide means to flexibly combine the frequent itemsets of different batches. Instead of devising new data structures, the DWFIST approach is a database centered approach thus it benefits from database index structures, query optimization, storage management facilities and so on. These are vital features because the data warehouse of frequent itemsets potentially comprises a large, but manageable, volume of data. In addition, the approach can be implemented using conventional commercial databases.

The remainder of this chapter is organized as follows. First, related work is listed and the DWFIST approach is presented. Then, we discuss the use of DWFIST in a data stream scenario and show how to retrieve calendar-based frequent itemsets. Finally, the experimental results and the conclusions are presented.

Related Work

This section covers the major related work grouped into three topics: calendar-based mining; stream mining; and pattern storage and pattern management.

In order to discover temporal association rules, the work in Özden, B. et al. (1998) states very clearly the problem of omitting the time dimension. It is assumed that the transactions in the database are timestamped and that the user specifies a time interval to divide the data into disjoint segments, such as months, weeks, days, etc. Cyclic association rules are defined as association rules with a minimum confidence and support at specific regular time intervals. A disadvantage of the cyclic approach is that it does not deal with multiple granularities of time intervals. An example of a calendar pattern that cannot be represented by cycles is the simple concept of the first working day of every month. Ramaswamy, S. et al. (1998) introduces the notion of calendar algebra, which basically defines a set of time intervals. Each time interval is a set of time units, e.g. days. A rule is called calendric if it has the minimum support and confidence over every time unit in the calendar. A disadvantage of this approach is that the user must have prior knowledge about the temporal patterns in the transactional database to define the calendars. The work in Li, Y. et al. (2001) tries to overcome this problem by mining the calendars. Calendar schemas, as the example given in the introduction, are used to specify the search space for different possible calendars. The rules mined by such algorithms are presented together with their mined calendars. All these approaches perform a calendar-based frequent itemset mining step. However, they require the transactions to be available during the calendar-based mining task, which excludes these approaches from being applied to mine data streams and thus they cannot be used to solve our problem.

The focus in data stream mining has been on stream data classification and stream clustering. Only recently, mining frequent counts in streams gained attention. An algorithm to find frequent items using a variant of classic majority algorithm was developed simultaneously by Demaine, E. D. et al. (2002) and Karp, R. M. et al. (2003). A framework to compute frequent items and itemsets was provided in Manku, G., & Motwani, R. (2002). The presented algorithm, called Lossy Counting, mines frequent patterns in data streams by assuming that patterns are measured from the start of the stream up to the current moment.

Lossy Counting considers always the whole stream and does not provide flexibility to mine the frequent itemsets holding on a subset of the stream. Closer to our focus, the work presented in Giannella, C. et al. (2003) proposes a new model for mining frequent patterns from data streams, the FP-Stream. This model is capable of answering user queries considering multiple time granularities. A fine granularity is important for recent changes whereas a coarse granularity is adequate for long-term changes. FP-Stream supports this kind of analysis by a tilted-time window, which keeps storage requirements very low but prevents calendar-based pattern analysis. An example of a tilted-time window (in minutes) is 15, 15, 30, 60, 120, 240, 480, etc. It is possible to answer queries about the last 15 minutes or the last 4 hours (15+15+30+60+120 minutes), but it is not possible to answer queries about last Friday or every morning, for example. The lack of a uniform partitioning prevents calendar-based pattern analysis.

Regarding pattern storage and pattern management, Kimball, R., & Ross, M. (2002) presents an approach for market basket analysis storing the frequency counts in a fact table. Frequency counts for every pair of items that appear together in any transaction are stored. The number of possible combinations grows exponentially with the number of items. The information about all combinations is likely to require more storage than the original transactions, which is infeasible for data streams. Furthermore, it only handles itemsets with two items thus it is not possible to derive association rules involving three or more items. The PANDA project (2005) studies the state-of-the-art in pattern management and explores novel theoretical and practical aspects of a Pattern Base Management System. It deals with patterns in a broad sense, considering no predefined pattern types. The main focus lies in devising a general and extensible model for patterns. Specific calendar-based pattern mining issues are not considered in this project.

Requirements

The information stored in the Data Warehouse of Frequent Itemsets must be sufficient for answering queries that request patterns holding on some subset of the transactions in data sources. In other words, it must be possible to specify constraints on features of the original transactions when retrieving patterns. For each itemset retrieved from the data warehouse it must be possible to retrieve its frequency count over the subset of original transactions being queried. Whenever the exact frequency is not known, it must be possible to provide an approximate answer. Moreover, it must be possible to guarantee that the result of the query is complete, i.e., there is no pattern holding on the queried subset of transactions that is not retrieved when querying the data warehouse. Figure 1 sketches the retrieval of patterns from the data warehouse of frequent itemsets.

Another important requirement refers to the feasibility of coping with the tight time constraints imposed by data streams. The data warehouse of frequent itemsets is partitioned into disjoint sets of transactions. To cope with data stream requirements, we have to compute the frequent itemsets holding on one partition before the next partition is ready to be processed. We also have to consider the load process of the data warehouse. The periodicity of this load process must be completely independent from the time granularity and should be set to meet analysis requirements and availability.

The DWFIST Approach

The DWFIST approach (Data Warehouse of Frequent ItemSets Tactics) aims at providing a skilful environment to explore and analyze patterns based on frequent itemsets on transactional data. Figure 2 presents the major components of this approach.

The *pre-processing and loading step* is composed of three tasks: gather the transactions into

Figure 1. Pattern retrieval from the Data Warehouse of Frequent Itemsets

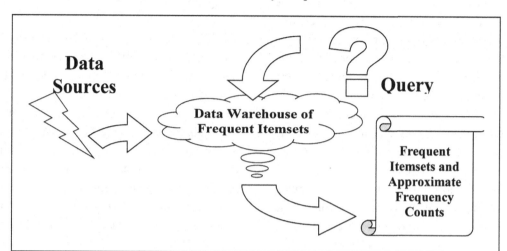

disjoint sets (partitions) according to a pre-defined criteria; mine the frequent itemsets holding on a partition using a pre-defined mining minimum support; and load the mined frequent itemsets into the data warehouse.

The *Data Warehouse of Frequent Itemsets* (referenced throughout this chapter simply as DW) is the main component of the approach. It stores and organizes the frequent itemsets into partitions. The role of the *Basic Frequent Itemset*

Retrieval Capabilities component is to retrieve a set of frequent itemsets holding on some user-specified set of DW partitions with a user-defined minimum support. The *Frequent Itemset Based Pattern Mining Engine* generates patterns that can be obtained from frequent itemsets. Association rules (Agrawal, R. et al., 1993) and Boolean rules (Mannila, H., & Toivonen, H., 1996) are two examples of such patterns. Depending on the pattern, user-defined parameters can be provided, e.g.,

Figure 2. Components of the DWFIST approach

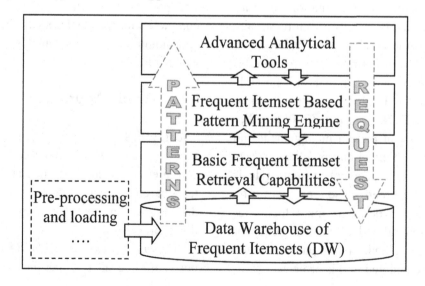

Figure 3. Partition Mining Properties Dimensional Schema

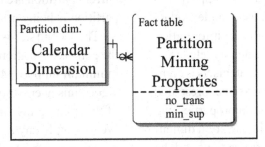

minimum confidence for association rules. The *Advanced Analytical Tools* component comprises analysis and exploration tools that can be built on top of the other components.

The main goals of the DWFIST approach are: (1) provide flexible pattern retrieval capabilities without requiring access to the detailed original data; (2) define a standardized logical view upon which analytical tools can be independently developed; and (3) use a conceptual view for pattern analysis that is familiar to business professionals.

The first goal listed above is the key feature for leveraging calendar-based pattern mining in data streams. In this chapter, we retain our discussion to this issue and thus we will not further discuss the Frequent Itemset Based Pattern Mining Engine and Advanced Analytical Tools components.

A Sample Data Warehouse of Frequent Itemsets

The sample data warehouse shown in Figures 3 and 4 is sufficient to discuss all major aspects related to calendar-based mining in data streams. It has one partition dimension and one item dimension.

Partition dimensions organize the space of the original transactions into disjoint sets. In our example, we use a calendar dimension with a basic granularity of 1 hour. This means that each tuple in the calendar dimension represents a period of 1 hour, e.g., "02/15/2005 [08:00AM, 09:00AM]", "02/15/2005 [09:00AM, 10:00AM]", and so on. Of course, additional calendar information has to be stored, like the period of the day (morning, afternoon, …), weekday, holiday (yes, no) and any other calendar unit that represents an aggregation of the basic granularity. This basic granularity also sets the criteria for gathering the transactions in the pre-processing step.

The item dimensions provide additional in-

Figure 4. Frequent Itemset Count Dimensional Schema

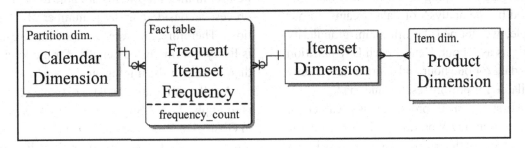

formation about the items that may appear in a transaction. In our example, we use a single product dimension. Examples of additional information are: description, department, category, etc.

A data warehouse of frequent itemsets is composed of two fact tables. The first one, presented in Figure 3, stores some partition properties and thus has relationships only with partition dimensions. It stores the number of transactions and the minimum support used for the frequent itemset mining task per calendar granule (1 hour). The second fact table, presented in Figure 4, stores the frequency count for each set of products mined as frequent in a specific calendar granule (1 hour). Figure 4 also presents an itemset dimension that works as a bridge table between the multivalued dimension (Kimball, R., & Ross, M., 2002) and the fact table.

This sample data warehouse of frequent itemsets tracks the frequent sets of products per hour. This also defines the minimum granularity of analysis. The minimum granularity in our example, i.e., one hour, makes it impossible to analyze time intervals shorter than one hour. On the other hand, all possible combinations of one-hour periods can be analyzed. These combinations based on calendar-terms specify a set ρ of DW partitions.

Time Constraint Issues in Pre-processing and Loading Steps

As far as we are able to pre-process and load the data of one DW partition before the next one is available, we are coping with the time constraints imposed by the analysis of data streams. In our example, we defined the minimum granularity of analysis as 1 hour. Hence, each DW partition covers data for one hour and a one-hour window is available for pre-processing and load.

The first step in pre-processing is to gather the transactions into DW partitions. This is straightforward because the partitioning is usually based on a timestamp. While the transactions of the current partition are being gathered, the previous partition is being mined and loaded.

The second step is to mine frequent itemsets on the gathered partition using a pre-defined mining minimum support. Many frequent itemset mining algorithms were proposed since the statement of this mining task in Agrawal, R. et al. (1993). We can apply any efficient algorithm in our pre-processing step. The efficiency of this step mainly depends on the mining minimum support and the number of transactions.

Finally, the frequent itemsets are loaded into the DW. This step mainly comprises the insertion of new frequent itemset frequency counts and the creation of new dimension tuples. An important property of the load step is that the time required is proportional to the number of frequent itemsets to be loaded and not to the number of transactions of one partition. Furthermore, an increase in the number of transactions for a frequent itemset mining task using a fixed minimum support does not represent a proportional increase in the number of frequent itemsets. In most cases, the number of frequent itemsets tends to stabilize or even decrease.

The definition of the minimum granularity of analysis plays a central role for coping with time constraints. First, it defines the time window available for processing. Second, an increase in the time window makes the task of the load step easier and the task of the mining step harder. The task of the mining step gets harder because a bigger window means a potentially higher number of transactions. Fortunately, current frequent itemset mining algorithms are able to efficiently process a considerable large number of transactions. Therefore, an increase in the time window is likely to bring more benefits for the load step than losses for the mining step.

An alternative approach for extreme scenarios is to apply the FP-Stream framework presented in Giannella, C. et al. (2003) to perform our mining task. This framework uses the FP-Growth algorithm (Han, J. et al., 2000) to mine frequent itemsets on batches of transactions from a data stream. It allows to answer queries such as "retrieve the frequent itemsets holding on the transactions of the last 15 minutes" or "retrieve the frequent itemsets holding on the transactions of the last 4 hours" on a stream. The important feature of this framework is that the required processing time is independent from the period being queried. This means that using this framework it is possible to increase the time window without increasing the time required for the mining step. The disadvantage of applying this framework is that it introduces an error in the frequency counts. This additional error has to be considered when computing the frequency upper bound during the retrieval from the data warehouse.

Storage Requirement Issues

An important observation regarding storage requirements is that the size of DW increases in a lower rate compared to the size of the considered input stream. The reasoning that supports this assertion is twofold. First, the frequent itemsets require less storage space than the original data stream transactions. Second, the reuse of information stored in the dimensions reduces the storage requirements.

Nevertheless, it is important to make a remark here. Dense correlated databases may produce a large number of frequent itemsets. An extensive amount of work has focused on condensed representations of frequent itemsets aiming at representing a set of frequent itemsets in a compact way. The DWFIST approach allows for the use of condensed representations to describe the frequent itemsets holding on each partition. In this work, we do not apply any condensed representations because we understand that using regular frequent itemsets imposes a more difficult scenario for streams, as we have to deal with a larger amount of data. In this sense, coping with stream requirements using regular frequent itemsets suggests that at least the same is achievable with condensed

representations.

A similar discussion on adjusting the minimum granularity of analysis presented in the previous section applies to storage requirements issues. In an analogous way, the storage requirements are proportional to the number of frequent itemsets being stored.

Calendar-based Frequent Itemset Retrieval

Along this section, we present how frequent itemsets can be retrieved from the DW and how calendar-based features are supported. Moreover, we address completeness and precision issues. We define the task of retrieving frequent itemsets from a DW as follows:

Frequent Itemset Retrieval Task: Given a set of DW partitions ρ and a query minimum support σ_q, retrieve the set Φ composed of the frequent itemsets with support $\geq \sigma_q$ over the set of transactions represented by ρ. The set Φ must contain also information on the frequency over ρ for each frequent itemset. The following function signature represents this task:

Formula 1: $\varphi = FI\_retrieval\left(\rho, \sigma_q\right)$ (1)

Let us now consider an individual itemset I over a set of DW partitions ρ. The itemset I may have been mined as frequent for a subset of ρ, which we call ρ_{known}, while considered infrequent for the complementary subset of partitions $\rho - \rho_{known}$. Over the subset $\rho - \rho_{known}$ the frequency of I is unknown. Therefore, it is not possible to retrieve the exact frequency count of I over ρ. Nevertheless, the unknown frequency is bounded and we are able to provide a frequency interval based on lower and upper bounds.

Property 1. (Disjoint partitions): The DW partitions represent completely disjoint sets of transactions and thus the frequency counts of a specific itemset can be summed over any set of partitions.

The frequency lower bound (LBF) is simply calculated by summing the known frequencies over ρ_{known}. In our example, these frequencies are represented by the attribute *frequency_count* in the Frequent Itemset Frequency fact table. Considering f a function that returns the frequency count of I on an individual DW partition ρ_i, the LBF of an itemset I over ρ is:

Formula 2: $\quad \text{LBF}\left(I,\rho\right) = \displaystyle\sum_{\rho_i \in \rho_{known}} f\left(I,\rho_i\right) \qquad (2)$

The upper bound is based on the following property:

Property 2 (Error upper bound): Given $|\rho_i|$ the number of transactions in partition ρ_i and σ_{mi} the minimum support (%) used for mining on partition ρ_i, the product $|\rho_i|\sigma_{mi}$ provides a strict upper bound on the number of missed frequencies over partition ρ_i. Moreover, a strict error upper bound UBe_ρ for a set of DW partitions ρ is provided by simply summing the upper bounds of the individual partitions:

Formula 3: $\quad \text{UBe}_\rho = \displaystyle\sum_{\rho_i \in \rho} \left|\rho_i\right| \sigma_{mi} \qquad (3)$

In the special case where σ_{mi} is constant over ρ we have:

Formula 4:

$$\text{UBe}_\rho = \sum_{\forall \rho_i \in \rho}\left|\rho_i\right| \sigma_{mi} = \sigma_m \sum_{\forall \rho_i \in \rho}\left|\rho_i\right| = \sigma_m\left|\rho\right|$$
$$(4)$$

The frequency upper bound (UBF) is computed by summing the error upper bound over $\rho - \rho_{known}$ and the frequency lower bound. Formally, it is expressed by:

Formula 5:

$$\text{UBF}(I,\rho) = \text{LBF}(I,\rho) + \text{UBe}_{\rho - \rho_{known}} \qquad (5)$$

In our example, $|\rho_i|$ and σ_{mi} are represented by the attributes *no_trans* and *min_sup* in the Partition Mining Properties fact table. As the exact frequency count of the itemsets may be unknown, we must retrieve the set Φ using the approximate information provided by the frequency intervals [LBF(I, ρ), UBF(I, ρ)]. We include an itemset I in Φ if its *support* $\geq \sigma_q$ considering the itemset frequency upper bound over ρ, i.e., if UBF(I,ρ) $\geq$ $|\rho|\sigma_q$. Therefore, it is possible to report itemsets in Φ that would not be reported if the same frequent itemset mining task could be performed on the original transactions. We address this problem as a precision issue in a later section. Another important issue is the possibility of missing frequent itemsets holding on the original transactions. The completeness of the set Φ retrieved from the DW is discussed in the section on completeness and precision as well.

Retrieving Calendar-based Frequent Itemsets from the DW

In this section, we show how to derive calendar-based frequent itemsets from the DW by means of SQL queries. The Calendar Dimension provides attributes representing different calendar features. In our example, an attribute *day_period* in the calendar dimension may classify the periods of 1 hour into morning, afternoon, evening and dawn. Let us discuss how the frequent itemsets retrieval task for the morning period would be performed. In this case, ρ is the set of DW partitions representing the morning period. Considering our sample data warehouse, Property 1 tells us that we can sum the frequencies of a specific itemset over any calendar partition represented in the Calendar Dimension. Equation (2) uses this property to compute the frequency lower bound. Figure 5 presents a query that retrieves the itemsets and their lower bound frequency counts considering the morning period.

Based on Property 2 we can compute two kinds of error upper bounds for the frequency

Figure 5. Frequency lower bound query

```
Select
  FMF.itemset_id,
   sum(FMF.frequency_count) as LB_Frequency
From Calendar_Dimension CD,
    Frequent_Itemset_Frequency FMF
Where CD.CD_id = FMF.CD_id and
      CD.day_period = 'Morning'
Group by FMF.itemset_id
```

counts, namely a global error upper bound and an itemset-specific error upper bound. The global error upper bound computes a single error margin for all itemsets over a set of DW partitions. The itemset-specific error upper bound computes an error margin for each individual itemset over a set of DW partitions. The first is easier to compute while the second is more precise.

A global error upper bound for our example is obtained computing equation (3) for all partitions related to the morning period (ρ). Figure 6 presents the corresponding query.

In order to compute the itemset-specific error upper bound using equation (5), for each itemset, we need the error upper bound for the set of partitions where the frequency of the itemset is unknown ($\rho - \rho_{known}$). The reasoning is that as far as the itemset frequency is known for a partition there is no reason to consider the error related to that partition. Based on a relational database, it is more efficient to compute this error upper bound related to the partition with unknown frequencies in two steps: (1) compute the error upper bound related to the partitions where the itemset frequency is known (ρ_{known}) and (2) subtract it

from the global error upper bound. The query presented in Figure 7 computes for each itemset the error related to the partitions where the itemset frequency is known (ρ_{known}).

A query minimum support (σ_q) must be specified for retrieval. By doing so, the answer must comprise the itemsets considered as frequent according to the query minimum support provided. The queries presented in Figures 5, 6 and 7 can be executed one after the other and have their results combined considering a query minimum support but, this task can also be computed by one single query. Figure 8 presents such a query for our example. This query implements the function signature presented in equation (1).

As the retrieved itemset frequencies are represented by intervals, we can only discard an itemset when its frequency interval lies completely below the specified threshold. Some important questions arise immediately at this point: (1) Which range of query minimum support can be supported by the DW as it does not contain complete information about the original transactions?; (2) Is it possible to guarantee that we are retrieving all the frequent itemsets holding on the original data?; and (3)

Figure 6. Global error upper bound query

```
Select
  sum(PMP.no_trans*PMP.min_sup) as Global_Error
From Calendar_Dimension CD,
    Partition_Mining_Properties PMP
Where CD.CD_id = PMP.CD_id and
      CD.day_period = 'Morning'
```

Figure 7. Itemset-specific error upper bound query

```
Select
  FMF.itemset_id,
  sum(PMP.no_trans*PMP.min_sup) as Known_Part_Error
From Calendar_Dimension CD,
     Frequent_Itemset_Frequency FMF,
     Partition_Mining_Properties PMP
Where CD.CD_id = PMP.CD_id and
      CD.CD_id = FMF.CD_id and
      CD.day_period = 'Morning'
Group by FMF.itemset_id
```

How close is the answer provided by the DW to the real set of frequent itemsets holding on the original transactions?. We address these issues in the following sections.

Completeness and Precision

We consider the frequent itemset retrieval task as defined before. For the sake of simplicity and without loss of generality, we assume that a constant minimum support σ_m was used for mining during the pre-processing step of all partitions ρ_i

belonging to ρ. If this is not the case, we can simply assume σ_m as the maximum σ_{mi} used for all ρ_i.

The following property states for which values of σ_q it is possible to guarantee that we are not missing frequent itemsets holding on the original data.

Property 3 (Completeness): Let I be an itemset with frequency greater or equal to UBe_ρ and σ_q a query minimum support. The frequency of I is known for at least one partition ρ_i belonging to ρ, otherwise this itemset would have an error greater or equal to the strict error upper bound. A

Figure 8. Single query for frequent itemset retrieval over the morning period

```
Select
  S.itemset_id,
  S.LB_Frequency,
  ( S.LB_Frequency +
    G.Global_Error +
    S.Known_Part_Error) as UB_Frequency
From ( Select
        FMF.itemset_id,
        sum(FMF.frequency_count) as LB_Frequency,
        sum(PMP.no_trans*PMP.min_sup) as Known_Part_Error,
      From Calendar_Dimension CD,
           Frequent_Itemset_Frequency FMF,
           Partition_Mining_Properties PMP
      Where CD.CD_id = PMP.CD_id and
            CD.CD_id = FMF.CD_id and
            CD.day_period = 'Morning'
      Group by FMF.itemset_id) S,
      ( Select
          sum(PMP.no_trans) as Total_no_trans,
          sum(PMP.no_trans*PMP.min_sup) as Global_Error
        From Calendar_Dimension CD,
             Partition_Mining_Properties PMP
        Where CD.CD_id = PMP.CD_id and
              CD.day_period = 'Morning') G
Where ( S.LB_Frequency +
        G.Global_Error +
        S.Known_Part_Error) >=
      ( G.Total_no_trans * :query_minimum_support )
```

query minimum support σ_q requests all itemsets with minimum frequency of $|\rho|\sigma_q$. Therefore, if the minimum frequency defined by σ_q is greater or equal to the strict error upper bound then the result is complete. Formally:

Formula 6:

$$\text{UBe}_\rho = |\rho|\sigma_m \leq |\rho|\sigma_q \quad \therefore \quad \sigma_m \leq \sigma_q \qquad (6)$$

Hence, using a query minimum support greater or equal to the mining minimum support is a sufficient condition to guarantee the completeness of the answer.

We address the precision of the result according to two aspects: false positives and frequency interval tightness. The first aspect relates to false positives, i.e., itemsets that are reported to be frequent although their real frequencies lie below the specified threshold. Such false positives are likely to appear because the frequency retrieved from the DW is an approximate frequency count. Nevertheless, we discovered an interesting property of such itemsets:

Property 4 (local frequent itemset): As far as the completeness is guaranteed, a false frequent itemset reported as frequent, due to the approximate count, for a query minimum support σ_q over a set of DW partitions ρ is guaranteed to be a σ_q-frequent itemset over the subset of partitions from ρ where its frequency is known.

Proof: Let I be a false frequent itemset reported as frequent for a query minimum support σ_q over a set of DW partitions ρ. Also, let ρ_{known} be the subset of partitions on ρ where the frequency of I is known, F_I the frequency of I over ρ_{known}, $|\rho_{known}|$ the number of transactions over ρ_{known} and $\text{UBe}_{(\rho-\rho kown)}$ the itemset-specific error upper bound for I over ρ. The following equation expresses the property we want to guarantee:

$$\frac{F_I}{|\rho_{known}|} \geq \sigma_q$$

In order to be reported as frequent, $F_I + \text{UBe}_{(\rho-\rho kown)}$ must be at least equal to $|\rho|\sigma_q$, therefore:

$$F_I \geq |\rho|\sigma_q - \text{UBe}_{(\rho-\rho known)}$$

The itemset-specific error upper bound $\text{UBe}_{(\rho-\rho kown)}$ can be expressed as $(|\rho| - |\rho_{known}|)\sigma_m$:

$$F_I \geq |\rho|\sigma_q - (|\rho| - |\rho_{known}|)\sigma_m$$

Substituting F_I in the property we want to guarantee:

$$\frac{|\rho|\sigma_q - (|\rho| - |\rho_{known}|)\sigma_m}{|\rho_{known}|} \geq \sigma_q$$

$$|\rho|\sigma_q - (|\rho| - |\rho_{known}|)\sigma_m \geq |\rho_{known}|\sigma_q$$

$$-(|\rho| - |\rho_{known}|)\sigma_m \geq |\rho_{known}|\sigma_q - |\rho|\sigma_q$$

Multiplying by minus one (-1):

$$(|\rho| - |\rho_{known}|)\sigma_m \leq |\rho|\sigma_q - |\rho_{known}|\sigma_q$$

$$(|\rho| - |\rho_{known}|)\sigma_m \leq (|\rho| - |\rho_{known}|)\sigma_q$$

$$\sigma_m \leq \sigma_q$$

The same condition to guarantee the completeness of the result is a sufficient condition for Property 4.

The above property tells us that the additional reported itemsets are indeed itemsets that present a frequent behavior on a subset of the current calendar being analyzed and thus are probably worth of a more detailed analysis. A simple coverage measure related to the number of partitions where the itemset frequency is known can aid the analyst to separate the itemsets that present a high coverage rate for the current calendar being analyzed from the locally frequent ones (low coverage rate). A simple count statement on the query presented in Figure 8 can easily compute this measure.

The second important aspect of precision relates to frequency interval tightness. In order to discuss this aspect we introduce a relative error measure:

Frequency Relative Error: Given an exact frequency count F_I and an approximation F_I' with an error ε equals to $|F_I - F_I'|$, the frequency relative error (FRE) is defined as:

Formula 7: $\quad \text{FRE} = \dfrac{\varepsilon}{F_I'}$ $\qquad$ (7)

The frequency relative error quantifies the size of the error with respect to the approximate frequency count.

Property 5 (Worst-case Frequency Relative Error): Considering a frequent itemset retrieval task and using as frequency approximation the middle point of the frequency interval, the worst-case for the frequent relative error is given by:

Formula 8:

$$\text{Worst\_case\_FRE} = \dfrac{\sigma_m}{2\left(\sigma_q - 0.5\sigma_m\right)} \qquad (8)$$

Proof: The error upper bound UBe_ρ corresponds to the maximum length of the frequency interval. Using the middle point of the frequency interval as the frequency approximation, the maximum ε is half of UBe_ρ. Also, F_I' is at least $(|\rho|\sigma_q - 0.5\text{UBe}_\rho)$ in order to be considered frequent. Therefore, the worst-case for the frequent relative error is:

$$\dfrac{\text{UBe}_\rho}{2\left(|\rho|\sigma_q - 0.5\text{UBe}_\rho\right)}$$

Substituting UBe_ρ using equation (4):

$$\dfrac{|\rho|\sigma_m}{2\left(|\rho|\sigma_q - 0.5|\rho|\sigma_m\right)} \doteq \dfrac{|\rho|\sigma_m}{2|\rho|\left(\sigma_q - 0.5\sigma_m\right)} = \dfrac{\sigma_m}{2\left(\sigma_q - 0.5\sigma_m\right)}$$

This provides the worst-case in equation (8).

∎

For $\sigma_q = \sigma_m$ equation (8) results in 100% and it decreases as the value of σ_q increases moving away from σ_m.

The above property provides a precision guarantee for the frequency count of itemsets retrieved

from the DW. As an example, consider a set of partitions in which a mining minimum support of 0.1% is used. If we request the frequent itemsets using a query minimum support of 0.3%, equation (8) tell us that the worst-case frequency relative error is 20%. The completeness of the result is guaranteed as well because the query minimum support (0.3%) is greater than the mining minimum support (0.1%). Equation (8) can also be used to govern the choice of the mining minimum support. If we expect to retrieve frequent itemsets using a query minimum support of $S\%$ and want to guarantee a worst-case frequency relative error of $E\%$, equation (8) can be applied to compute a suitable mining minimum support.

Experimental Results

We performed a series of experiments to evaluate the issues discussed in this chapter. We focus on measurements related to pre-processing and load time, data warehouse storage requirements, and the precision of the sets of frequent itemsets retrieved from the DW. All experiments were performed on a PC Pentium IV 1.2 GHz with 768 MB of RAM. We used Oracle 10g to implement a data warehouse identical to the example presented here. The only aspects worth mentioning of the applied physical design are: (1) the use of bitmap indexes for joins between dimensions and fact tables, and (2) the use of a 1MB extent for the frequent itemset frequency fact table.

The stream data was created using the IBM synthetic market-basket data generator that is managed by the Quest data mining group. Two data streams were generated both representing a period of one week. The first data stream (Stream1) has 60 million transactions, 1000 distinct items and an average of 7 items per transaction. The transactions of the first data stream were uniformly distributed over 168 one-hour partitions (1 week). This data stream does not present strong calendar pattern behavior. The second data stream (Stream2) was created in two steps. First, a dataset was created

Figure 9. Pre-processing and load time

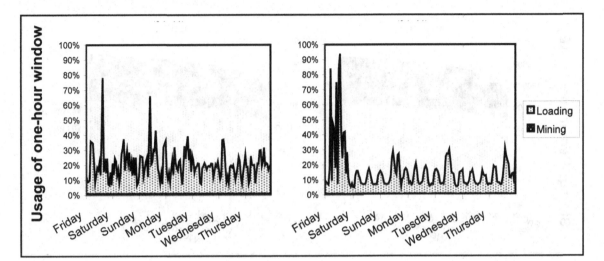

with 50 million transactions, 1000 distinct items and an average of 7 items per transaction. Second, another dataset with 10 million transactions, 1500 distinct items and an average of 7 items per transaction was created. The 50M-transactions dataset was uniformly distributed over 140 one-hour partitions and the 10M-transactions dataset over 28 one-hour partitions. Finally, the 28 one-hour partitions of the 10M-transactions dataset were associated to the morning period (08:00AM until 12:00PM) over the weekdays, and also to the period from 08:00AM to 17:00PM excluding lunch (12:00PM until 13:00) on the Saturday. The 140 one-hour partitions of the 50M-transactions were associated to the remaining slots completing a week. This second data stream presents strong calendar behavior over the morning period and on Saturday due to the additional items on the 10M-transactions dataset.

The pre-processing and load times are presented in Figure 9. In these two graphs the Y axis represents the percentage of the one-hour window that was required for processing whereas the X axis represents the one-hour partitions. The pre-processing step covers the frequent itemset mining based on an optimized implementation of FP-Growth (Han, J. et al., 2000) described in

Grahne, G., & Zhu, J. (2003). We used a mining minimum support of 0.1% for all one-hour partitions. As this task was performed in less than one minute for all partitions, it appears only as a thin layer at the bottom of the graphs. Figure 9 shows that for most of the partitions pre-processing and loading is completed in less than 30% of the available time window. Even for the rare partitions with peek processing time, the pre-processing is completed within the one-hour window.

Figure 10 presents the storage requirements comparing the sizes of the streams with the corresponding DW. It is clear that the storage requirements for the streams quickly reach unmanageable levels. For our examples, only one week already represents 2 GB. On the other side, the size of the DW increases at a lower rate and is orders of magnitude lower than the size of the source data stream. For both examples, the DW size did not reach 20 MB including indexing structures.

The loading step is performed by a package implemented in Oracle PL/SQL. For each one-hour partition, it first inserts a new tuple in the Calendar Dimension and in the Partition Mining Properties fact table. The latter one stores the minimum support used for mining (0.1%) and the number of transactions on the stream over the

Figure 10. Storage Requirements

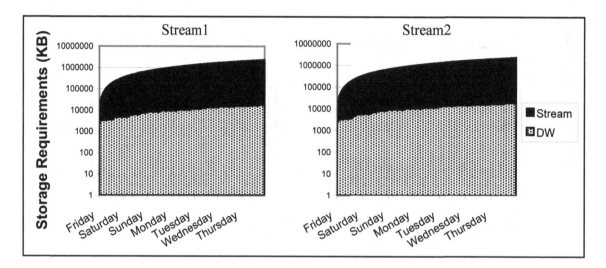

corresponding period. Afterwards, each itemset mined as frequent in the pre-processing step is loaded with its frequency count. For each itemset, the package checks if it already exists in the Itemset Dimension. For those that already exist, inserting a new tuple in the Frequent Itemset Frequency fact table is sufficient. Otherwise, a new tuple in the Itemset Dimension is required before inserting the new fact. Also, the items belonging to the new itemset that are new for the Product Dimension must be created. Finally, the items are associated to the new itemset (through an NxM relationship table).

The detailed analysis of the loading step reveals that it is mainly influenced by three factors: (1) the number of itemsets being loaded, (2) the number of new itemsets being created, and (3) the need for extending the physical storage area. The processing peeks of Figure 9 result from such an extension of the physical storage area. As the data warehouse dimensions are initially empty, many new itemsets have to be created while loading the first partitions. The highest processing peeks in Figure 9 are related to periods where the three factors present a negative influence.

Considering the above discussion, it is not likely that all three factors will negatively influence

the load processing of a small number of consecutive periods. For example, consecutive periods normally should not require an extension of the physical storage area. Moreover, if they happen to do, it is most likely that the size of the extent is not properly set. This suggests that it should be possible to compensate some processing peeks out of the window within a few consecutive periods. This would lead to a less conservative definition of the minimum granularity of analysis. Of course, an increase in the storage requirements, due to the need of a buffer to keep the itemsets with a delayed load, must also be considered.

The last part of our experiments presents measurements related to the precision of the set of frequent itemsets retrieved from the DW. We retrieved frequent itemsets for three different calendars: whole Saturday (00:00 to 24:00); Monday, Wednesday and Friday from 08:00 to 17:00; and morning periods of weekdays (08:00 to 12:00). These calendars are related to the strong calendar behavior introduced in Stream2 in different ways. "Saturday" comprises 24 partitions from which 8 come from the 10M-transactions dataset. "Monday, Wednesday and Friday from 08:00 to 17:00" presents 12 out of 27. "Morning periods of weekdays" is related only to partitions from the

10M-transactions dataset. They were defined in order to measure in Stream2 the effect of a strong calendar behavior on the precision of the result. We also executed the same queries on Stream1, which does not present a calendar behavior. The results on Stream1 provide a basis for isolating the effects of a strong calendar behavior from the regular error introduced by the use of an approximation.

The precision of the retrieved set of frequent itemsets is measured according to two aspects: number of false positives and frequency relative error. In order to obtain these measurements, we performed a regular frequent itemset mining task for each query directly on the corresponding stream transactions. The answer retrieved from the DW was compared with the exact answer.

As the results for the three queries on Stream1 presented the same behavior, we present only the results for one of them in Figure 11. The difference between the two bars on the left graph corresponds to the number of false positives. Note that with a query minimum support slightly greater than the mining minimum support (0.1%) it is already possible to retrieve the exact set of frequent itemsets. The graph on the right of Figure 11 presents the frequency relative error measurements. The Worst-case corresponds to the value obtained applying equation (8). The Maximum DW and Average DW are computed calculating the error as the

difference between the approximate frequency and the frequency upper bound thus corresponding to the tightness of the frequency interval. The Maximum Real and Average Real use the error as the difference between the approximate frequency and the exact frequency retrieved directly from the stream. The error drops quickly to zero for query minimum support values slightly greater than the mining minimum support.

Figure 12 presents the same graphs for the three queries executed on Stream2. Once again, for values of the query minimum support slightly greater than the mining minimum support the result already presents a good precision. For example, with a query minimum support of 0.12% the Average DW frequency relative error already drops below 10%. It is especially important to observe the low values of the Average DW. As it does not require knowledge about the exact real frequency it represents the average precision guarantee that will be provided for a user querying the DW. Also, the query for the morning period of weekdays presents the same behavior as the queries executed on Stream1. This allows us to come to an interesting conclusion: excluding the query minimum support values that are too close to the mining minimum support, the error of the result is exclusively due to some calendar behavior on some subset of the partitions being queried. Furthermore, Property 4 tells us that this

Figure 11. Precision measurements on Stream1

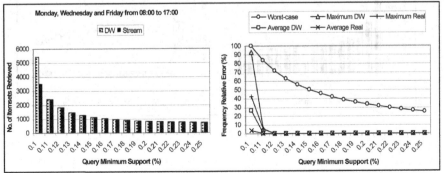

Figure 12. Precision measurements on Stream2

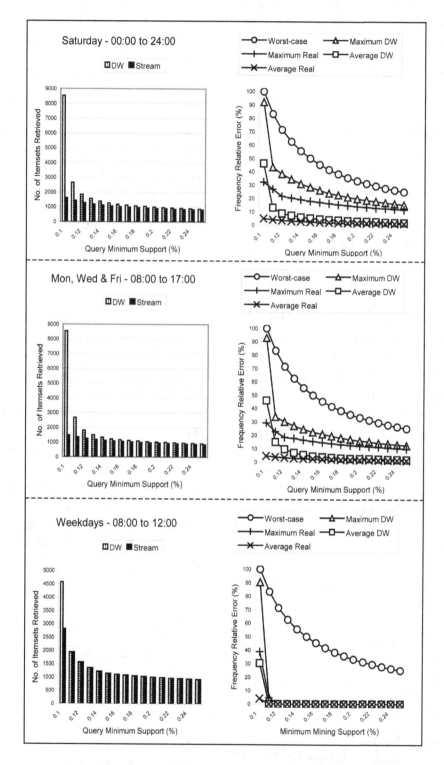

frequent behavior on some subset of the partitions being queried is at least as strong as the patterns we are requesting.

CONCLUSION

In this chapter, we presented how a data warehouse approach can be applied to leverage calendar-based pattern mining in data streams. We showed how the framework of the DWFIST approach can cope with tight time constraints imposed by data streams, keep storage requirements at a manageable level and, at the same time, support calendar-based frequent itemset mining.

Current frequent itemset mining algorithms can cope with data stream time constraints when processing size-limited batches of transactions. For the loading step, three major factors were pointed out as influencing the load time: the number of itemsets being loaded, the number of new itemsets being created, and the need for extending the physical storage area. The minimum granularity of analysis, parameters of the data warehouse (e.g. mining minimum support) and parameters of the database (e.g. extent size) provide ways to tune the load performance.

The storage requirements are directly related to the number of frequent itemset frequencies being stored. The minimum granularity of analysis and the mining minimum support play an important role. The proper setting of these parameters allows to keep the storage requirements at manageable levels.

We provided a sufficient condition for the completeness of the set of frequent itemsets retrieved from the DW. Furthermore, we addressed the precision issue regarding two aspects, namely the number of false positive frequent itemsets and the tightness of the frequency interval retrieved from the DW for each frequent itemset. The analysis revealed that the false positive frequent itemsets present a local frequent property thus presenting a potential interesting calendar behavior worth of a detailed analysis. A simple coverage measure can be applied to extract the local frequent itemsets. Additionally, we presented a theoretical worst-case bound for the relative error of the itemset frequency retrieved from the DW.

The precision of different sets of frequent itemsets retrieved from the DW was measured. The number of false positives decreases rapidly as the query minimum support moves away from the mining minimum support. Moreover, the tightness of the frequency interval presented an average behavior much better than the theoretical worst-case.

REFERENCES

Agrawal, R., Imielinski, T., & Swami, A. (1993). Mining association rules between sets of items in large databases. In *Proceedings of the 1993 ACM SIGMOD International Conference* (pp. 207-216).

Boulicaut, J. (2004). Inductive databases and multiple uses of frequent itemsets: The cInQ approach. In R. Meo, et al. (Eds.), *Database support for Data Mining Applications* (LNCS 2682, pp. 3-26).

Demaine, E. D. L'opez-Ortiz, A., & Munro, J. I. (2002). Frequency estimation of Internet packet streams with limited space. In *Proceedings of the 10ᵗʰ Annual European Symposium on Algorithms*.

Giannella, C., Han, J., Pei, J., Yan, X., & Yu, P. S. (2003). Mining frequent patterns in data streams at multiple time granularities. In H Kargupta, et al. (Eds.), *Data mining: Next generation challenges and future directions*. Cambridge, MA: AAAI/MIT Press.

Grahne, G., & Zhu, J. (2003). Efficiently using prefix-trees in mining frequent itemsets. In *Proceeding of the First IEEE ICDM Workshop on Frequent Itemset Mining Implementations*, Melbourne, FL.

Han, J., Pei, J., & Yin, Y. (2000). Mining frequent patterns without candidate generation. In *Proceeding of the 2000 SIGMOD Conference*, Dallas, Texas (pp. 1-12).

Karp, R. M., Papadimitriou, C. H., & Shenker, S. (2003). A simple algorithm for finding frequent elements in streams and bags. *ACM Transactions on Database Systems, 28*(1), 51–55. doi:10.1145/762471.762473

Kimball, R., & Ross, M. (2002). *The data warehouse toolkit: The complete guide to dimensional modelling* (2nd ed.). New York: John Wiley & Sons.

Li, Y., Ning, P., Wang, X. S., & Jajodia, S. (2001). Discovering calendar-based temporal association rules. In *Proceeding of the International Symposium on Temporal Representation and Reasoning* (pp. 111-118).

Liu, B., Hsu, W., & Ma, Y. (1998). Integrating classification and association rule mining. In *Proceedings of the KDD'98* (pp. 80-86). New York: AAAI Press.

Manku, G., & Motwani, R. (2002). Approximate frequency counts over data streams. In *Proceedings of the VLDB Conference* (pp. 346-357).

Mannila, H., & Toivonen, H. (1996). Multiple uses of frequent sets and condensed representations. In *Proceedings of the KDD'96* (pp. 189-194). Portland, OR: AAAI Press.

Monteiro, R. S., Zimbrão, G., Schwarz, H., Mitschang, B., & Souza, J. M. (2005). Building the data warehouse of frequent itemsets in the DWFIST approach. In *Proceedings of the 15th Inernational. Symposium on Methodologies for Intelligent Systems*, Saratoga Springs, NY.

Özden, B., Ramaswamy, S., & Silberschatz, A. (1998). Cyclic association rules. In *Proceedings of the 14th International Conference on Data Engineering* (pp. 412-421).

PANDA Project. (2005). Retrieved from http://dke.cti.gr/panda/

Ramaswamy, S., Mahajan, S., & Silberschatz, A. (1998). On the discovery of interesting patterns in association rules. In *Proceedings of the VLDB Conference* (pp. 368-379).

Compilation of References

Aalst, W. M. P. van der, & Hee, K., van. (2002). *Workflow management: Models, methods, and systems (cooperative information systems)*. Cambridge, MA: The MIT Press.

Abe, N., Zadrozny, B., & Langford, J. (2004). An iterative method for multi-class cost-sensitive learning. In *Proceedings of the 10th ACM SIGKDD International Conference on Knowledge Discovery and Data Mining (KDD'04)* (pp. 3-11).

Abelló, A., Samos, J., & Saltor, F. (2001). Understanding facts in a multidimensional object-oriented model. In *Proceedings of the 4th ACM international workshop on Data Warehousing and OLAP* (pp. 32-39). New York: ACM Press.

Abelló, A., Samos, J., & Saltor, F. (2002). On relationships offering new drill-across possibilities. In D. Theodoratos (Ed.), *Proceedings of the DOLAP* (pp. 7-13). New York: ACM.

Abidi, S. S. R., & Abdigi, S. R. (2001). A case of supplementing evidence base medicine with inductive clinical knowledge: Towards technology enriched integrated clinical evidence system. In *Proceedings of the 14th IEEE Symposium on Computer-Based Medical Systems, (CBMS'2001)*, Bethesda, MD, USA. Washington, DC: IEEE.

AERZTE_ZEITUNG. (2005). *Briten stellen auf elektronische patientenakten um.*

Agrawal, R., & Srikant, R. (1994). Fast algorithms for mining association rules. In *Proceedings of the International Conference on Very Large Data Bases.*

Agrawal, R., Grandison, T., Johnson, C., & Kiernan, J. (2007). Enabling the 21st century health care information technology revolution. *Communications of the ACM, 50*(2), 34–42. doi:10.1145/1216016.1216018

Agrawal, R., Imielinski, T., & Swami, A. (1993). Mining association rules between sets of items in large databases. In *Proceedings of the 1993 ACM SIGMOD International Conference* (pp. 207-216).

Agrawal, S., Chaudhuri, S., & Narasayya, V. R. (2000). Automated selection of materialized views and indexes in SQL databases. In *Proceedings of the 26th International Conference on Very Large Data Bases (VLDB 00)*, Cairo, Egypt (pp. 496-505).

Agresti, A. (2002). *Categorical data analysis* (2nd ed.). New York: John Wiley & Sons.

Ahmadi, S.-A., Sielhorst, T., Stauder, R., Horn, M., Feussner, H., & Navab, N. (2006). Recovery of surgical workflow without explicit models. In *Proceedings of the Medical Image Computing and Computer-Assisted Intervention (MICCAI 2006)* (pp. 420-428). Berlin, Germany: Springer.

Akal, F., Böhm, K., & Schek, H. (2002). OLAP query evaluation in a database cluster: A performance study on intra-query parallelism. In *Proceedings of the 6th East European Conference* (LNCS 2435, pp. 181-184).

Akinde, M. O., & Böhlen, M. H. (2001). Generalized MD-joins: Evaluation and reduction to SQL. In *Proceedings of the VLDB 2001 international Workshop on Databases in Telecommunications* (LNCS 2209, pp. 52-67).

Copyright © 2010, IGI Global, distributing in print or electronic forms without written permission of IGI Global is prohibited.

Akinde, M. O., Böhlen, M. H., Johnson, T., Lakshmanan, L. V., & Srivastava, D. (2002). Efficient OLAP query processing in distributed data warehouses. In *Proceedings of the 8th international Conference on Extending Database Technology: Advances in Database Technology* (LNCS 2287, pp. 336-353).

Akinde, M. O., Böhlen, M. H., Johnson, T., Lakshmanan, L. V., & Srivastava, D. (2003). Efficient OLAP query processing in distributed data warehouses. *Information Systems, 28*(1-2), 111–135. doi:10.1016/S0306-4379(02)00051-0

Al-Kahtani, M. A., & Sandhu, R. (2000). Access control meets public key infrastructure, or: Assigning roles to strangers. In *Proceedings of the 2000 Symposium on Security and Privacy.*

Al-Kahtani, M. A., & Sandhu, R. (2003). Induced role hierarchies with attribute-based RBAC. In *Proceedings of the SACMAT'03*, Como, Italy. New York: ACM Press.

Allcock, W., Bresnahan, J., Kettimuthu, R., & Link, M. (2005). The Globus striped GridFTP framework and server. In *Proceedings of the 2005 ACM/IEEE Conference on Supercomputing* (pp. 54-65).

Alon, U., Barkai, N., et al. (1999). Broad patterns of gene expression revealed by clustering analysis of tumor and normal colon tissues probed by oligonucleotide arrays. Proceedings of the National Academy of Sciences of the United States of America, 96(12), 6745–6750. PubMeddoi:10.1073/pnas.96.12.6745doi:10.1073/pnas.96.12.6745

Alpdemir, M., Mukherjee, A., Paton, N., Watson, P., Fernandes, A., Gounaris, A., & Smith, J. (2003). OGSA-DQP: A service-based distributed query processor for the Grid. In *Proceedings of UK e-Science All Hands Meeting.* EPSRC.

Anahory, S., & Murray, D. (1997). *Data warehousing in the real world: A practical guide for building decision support systems.* Reading, MA: Addison-Wesley Longman Publishing.

Anders, K. H. (2003). A hierarchical graph-clustering approach to find groups of objects (Technical Paper). In *Proceedings of the ICA Commission on Map Generalization. Fifth Workshop on Progress in Automated Map Generalization.*

Arge, L., de Berg, M., Haverkort, H., & Yi, K. (2004). The priority r-tree: A practically efficient and worst case optimal r-tree. In *Proceedings of the Dagstuhl Seminar.*

Arnt, A., & Zilberstein, S. (2004). Attribute measurement policies for cost-effective classification. In *Proceedings of the Workshop Data Mining in Resource Constrained Environments, 4th SIAM International Conference on Data Mining.*

Asano, T., Ibaraki, T., Imai, H., & Nishizeki, T. (1990). Algorithms. In *Lecture Notes in Computer Science* (pp. 70-71). New York: Springer-Verlag.

Asuncion, A., & Newman, D. J. (2007). *UCI machine learning repository.* Retrieved from http://www.ics.uci.edu/~mlearn/MLRepository.html

Audiimoolam, S., Nair, M., Gaikwad, R., & Qing, C. (2005, February 7). The role of clinical pathways in improving patient outcomes. Retrieved July 18, 2007, from http://www.healthsolve.com.au/wp-content/uploads/2008/05/role-of-clinical-pathways.pdf

Baker, M., Buyya, R., & Laforenza, D. (2002). Grids and Grid technologies for wide-area distributed computing. *Software, Practice & Experience, 32*(15), 1437–1466. doi:10.1002/spe.488

Banek, M., Tjoa, A. M., & Stolba, N. (2006). Integrating different grain levels in a medical data warehouse federation. In A. M. Tjoa & N. Tho (Ed.), *Proceedings of the DaWaK* (pp. 185-194). Krakow, Poland: Springer.

Baralis, E., Paraboschi, S., & Teniente, E. (1997). Materialized views selection in a multidimensional database. In *Proceedings of the 23rd international Conference on Very Large Data Bases* (pp. 156-165).

Bebel, B., Eder, J., Koncilia, C., Morzy, T., & Wrembel, R. (2004). Creation and management of versions in multiversion data warehouse. In *Proceedings of the 19th ACM Symposium on Applied Computing (SAC 04)*, Nicosia, Cyprus (pp. 717-723).

Beckmann, N., Kriegel, H. P., Schneider, R., & Seeger, B. (1990). The R*-tree: An efficient and robust method for points and rectangles. In *Proceedings of the 1990 ACM SIGMOD International Conference on Management of Data* (pp. 322-331).

Bellahsène, Z. (2002). Schema evolution in data warehouses. *Knowledge and Information Systems, 4*(3), 283–304. doi:10.1007/s101150200008

Bellatrèche, L., Giacometti, A., Marcel, P., Mouloudi, H., & Laurent, D. (2005). A personalization framework for OLAP queries. In *Proceedings of the 8th ACM International Workshop on Data Warehousing and OLAP (DOLAP 05)*, Bremen, Germany (pp. 9-18).

Ben Messaoud, R., Boussaid, O., & Rabaseda, S. (2006). Efficient multidimensional data representations based on multiple correspondence analysis. In *Proceedings of the Twelfth ACM SIGKDD International Conference on Knowledge Discovery and Data Mining (KDD 2006)*, Philadelphia, Pennsylvania, USA (pp. 662-667). New York: ACM Press.

Ben Messaoud, R., Rabaseda, S., Boussaid, O., & Bentayeb, F. (2004). OpAC: A new OLAP operator based on a data mining method. In *Proceedings of the 6th International Baltic Conference on Databases and Information Systems (DB&IS04)*, Riga, Latvia.

Bentayeb, F., Favre, C., & Boussaid, O. (2008). A user-driven data warehouse evolution approach for concurrent personalized analysis needs. *Journal of Integrated Computer-Aided Engineering, 15*(1), 21–36.

Berger, S., & Schrefl, M. (2006). Analysing multidimensional data across autonomous data warehouses. In A. M. Tjoa & N. Tho (Ed.), *Proceedings of the DaWaK* (pp. 120-133). Krakow, Poland: Springer.

Berger, S., & Schrefl, M. (2008). From federated databases to a federated data warehouse system. In *Proceedings of the HICSS*. Kona, Hawaii: IEEE Computer Society.

Bernardino, J., Furtado, P., & Madeira, H. (2002). DWS-AQA: A cost effective approach for very large data warehouses. In M. A. Nascimento, T. M. Özsu, & O. R. Zaïane (Eds.), *Proceedings of the IDEAS* (pp. 233-242). Washington, DC: IEEE Computer Society.

Beyer, K., & Ramakrishnan, R. (1999). Bottom-up computation of sparse and iceberg CUBE. In *Proceedings of the International Conference on Management of Data (SIGMOD)*.

Beyer, M., Kuhn, K. A., Meiler, C., Jablonski, S., et al. (2004). Towards a flexible, process oriented IT architecture for an integrated healthcare network. In *Proceedings of the 2004 ACM Symposium on Applied Computing, Special Track on Computer Applications in Health Care (CAHC)*, Nicosia, Cyprus (pp. 264-271). New York: ACM Press.

Bhagwat, D., Chiticariu, L., Tan, W.-C., & Vijayvargiya, G. (2004). An annotation management system for relational databases. In *Proceedings of the 30th VLDB International Conference on Very Large Databases*, Toronto, Canada (pp. 900-911).

Bhagwat, D., Chiticariu, L., Tan, W.-C., & Vijayvargiya, G. (2005). An annotation management system for relational databases. *The VLDB Journal, 14*(4), 373–396. doi:10.1007/s00778-005-0156-6

Bhatnagar, N., Juliano, B. A., & Renner, R. S. (2007). Data annotation models. In *Proceedings of the 3rd ICICIS International Conference on Intelligent Computing and Information Systems*, Cairo, Egypt.

Bhatnagar, N., Juliano, B. A., & Renner, R. S. (2007). Data annotation models and annotation query language. In *Proceedings of the ICKM International Conference on Knowledge Mining*, Bangkok, Thailand (pp. 440-445).

Bhattacharya, B., Poulsen, R., & Toussaint, G. (1981). Application of proximity graphs to editing nearest neighbor decision rule. In *Proceedings of the International Symposium on Information Theory*.

Binh, N. T., Tjoa, A. M., & Mangisengi, O. (2003). Meta-cube XTM: A multidimensional metadata approach for Semantic Web warehousing systems. In Y. Kambayashi, M. M. Mohania, & W. Wöss (Eds.), *Proceedings of the DaWaK* (pp. 76-88). Berlin, Germany: Springer.

BIOPATTERN. (2007). *BIOPATTERN network of excellence*. Retrieved August 20, 2007, from http://www.biopattern.org

Bishop, Y. M. M., Fienberg, S. E., & Holland, P. W. (1975). *Discrete multivariate analysis*. Cambridge MA: The MIT Press.

Blaschka, M. (1999). FIESTA: A framework for schema evolution in multidimensional information systems. In *Proceedings of the 6th Doctoral Consortium*.

Blaschka, M., Sapia, C., & Höfling, G. (1999). On schema evolution in multidimensional databases. In *Proceedings of the 1st International Conference on Data Warehousing and Knowledge Discovery (DaWaK 99)*, Florence, Italy (LNCS 1676, pp. 153-164).

Bliujute, R., Saltenis, S., Slivinskas, G., & Jensen, C. (1998). Systematic Change Management in dimensional data warehousing. In *Proceedings of the 3rd International Baltic Workshop on Databases and Information Systems*, Riga, Latvia (pp. 27-41).

Blum, A., & Langley, P. (1997). Selection of relevant features and examples in machine learning. *Artificial Intelligence*, 97, 245–271. doi:10.1016/S0004-3702(97)00063-5doi:10.1016/S0004-3702(97)00063-5

BMJ. (2007). *The British Medical Journal*. Retrieved September 19, 2007, from http://www.bmj.com/

Body, M., Miquel, M., Bédard, Y., & Tchounikine, A. (2002). A multidimensional and multiversion structure for OLAP applications. In *Proceedings of the 5th ACM International Workshop on Data Warehousing and OLAP (DOLAP 02)*, McLean, Virginia, USA (pp. 1-6).

Boulicaut, J. (2004). Inductive databases and multiple uses of frequent itemsets: The cInQ approach. In R. Meo, et al. (Eds.), *Database support for Data Mining Applications* (LNCS 2682, pp. 3-26).

BPMN. (2006, February). *BPMN (Business Process Modeling Notation) 1.0: OMG Final Adopted Specification*. Retreived from http://www.bpmn.org

Breiman, L., Freidman, J. H., Olshen, R. A., & Stone, C. J. (1984). *Classification and regression trees*. Belmont, CA: Wadsworth.

Briggs, B. (2005). Decision support software matures. *Health Data Management*.

Britt, P. (2005, November 1). A warehouse of opportunity. *Finance Tech*. Retrieved September 24, 2007, from http://www.financetech.com/showArticle.jhtml?articleID=173402279

Brobst, S., & Rarey, J. (2001). The five stages of an active data warehouse evolution. *Teradata Magazine*.

Bronnimann, H., Chen, B., et al. (2003). Efficient data reduction with EASE. In *Proceedings of the SIGKDD* (pp. 59-68).

Brunneder, W. (2008). *Parsing and transformation of SQL-MDi queries in federated data warehouses* (In German). Linz, Austria: Johannes Kepler University.

Bruno, N., Chaudhuri, S., & Gravano, L. (2002). Top-k selection queries over relational databases: Mapping strategies and performance evaluation. *ACM Transactions on Database Systems*, 27(2), 153–187. doi:10.1145/568518.568519

Bundesgesetz. (2004). 179. Bundesgesetz, Gesundheitsreformgesetz 2005, 7. Unterabschnitt, § 84a. (5). Bundesgesetztblatt für die Republik Österreich, Teil I: 12.

Burgert, O., Neumuth, T., Gessat, M., Jacobs, S., & Lemke, H. U. (2007). Deriving DICOM surgical extensions from surgical workflows. *Medical Imaging 2007: PACS and Imaging Informatics*, 8(35), 651604.1-651604.11.

Burgert, O., Neumuth, T., Lempp, F., Mudunuri, R., Meixensberger, J., & Strauß, G. (2006). Linking top-level ontologies and surgical workflows. *International Journal of Computer Assisted Radiology and Surgery*, 1(1), 437–438. doi:10.1007/s11548-006-0032-x

Buyya, R., Abramson, D., & Giddy, J. (2000). Economy driven resource management architecture for computational power Grids. In *Proceedings of the 7th International Conference on Parallel and Distributed Processing Techniques and Applications (PDPTA2000)* (pp. 283-289).

Buyya, R., Abramson, D., & Giddy, J. (2000). Nimrod/g: An architecture of a resource management and scheduling system in a global computational Grid. In *Proceedings of the Fourth International Conference/Exhibition on High Performance Computing in the Asia-Pacific Region, 1* (pp. 283-289).

Cabanac, G., Chevalier, M., Chrisment, C., & Julien, C. (2007). Collective annotation: Perspectives for information retrieval improvement. In *Proceedings of the 8th RIAO International Conference on Information Retrieval and its Applications*, Pittsburgh, PA, USA. Retrieved from http://riao.online.fr/papers/99.pdf

Cabibbo, L., & Torlone, R. (1998). A logical approach to multidimensional databases. In *EDBT'98: Proceedings of the 6th International Conference on Extending Database Technology* (Vol. 1377, pp. 183-197). Berlin, Germany: Springer.

Cabibbo, L., & Torlone, R. (2004). On the integration of autonomous data marts. In *Proceedings of the SSDBM* (pp. 223-234). Washington, DC: IEEE Computer Society.

Cabibbo, L., & Torlone, R. (2005). Integrating Heterogeneous Multidimensional Databases. In J. Frew (Ed.), *Proceedings SSDBM* (pp. 205-214). IEEE Computer Society.

Cao, J., Spooner, D. P., Jarvis, S. A., & Nudd, G. R. (2005). Grid load balancing using intelligent agents. *Future Generation Computer Systems, 21*(1), 135–149. doi:10.1016/j.future.2004.09.032

Cao, J., Spooner, D. P., Jarvis, S. A., Saini, S., & Nudd, G. R. (2003). Agent-based Grid load balancing using performance-driven task scheduling. In *Proceedings of the 17th international Symposium on Parallel and Distributed Processing (IPDPS)*, (pp. 49).

Cariou, V., Cubillé, J., Derquenne, C., Goutier, S., Guisnel, F., & Klajnmic, H. (2007). Built-in indicators to automatically detect interesting cells in a cube. In *Proceedings of the 9th International Conference on Data Warehousing and Knowledge Discovery (DaWaK 2007)*, Regensburg, Germany (pp. 123-124). Berlin, Germany: Springer.

Cariou, V., Cubillé, J., Derquenne, C., Goutier, S., Guisnel, F., & Klajnmic, H. (in press). Built-in indicators to discover interesting drill paths in a cube. In *Proceedings of the*

10th International Conference on Data Warehousing and Knowledge Discovery (DaWaK2008), Torino, Italy.

Carner®. (2007). *An introduction to the evidence based decision support center (EBDSC)*. Retrieved September 26, 2007, from http://www.cerner.com/public/filedownload.asp?LibraryID=12130

Caron, E. A. M., & Daniels, H. A. M. (2007). Explanation of exceptional values in multi-dimensional business databases. *European Journal of Operational Research*. doi:.doi:10.1016/j.ejor.2007.04.039

Carpani, F., & Ruggia, R. (2001). An integrity constraints language for a conceptual multidimensional data model. In *Proceedings of the 13th International Conference on Software Engineering & Knowledge Engineering (SEKE 01)*, Buenos Aires, Argentina (pp. 220-227).

Castellanos, M., & Casati, F. (2005). Is there anything new about business process intelligence? [panel]. In *ICDE 2005: Proceedings of the 21st International Conference on Data Engineering* (pp. 1141-1141). Los Alamitos, CA: IEEE Computer Society.

CEBM. (2004). *Why the sudden interest in EBM?* Retrieved July 18, 2007, from http://www.cebm.utoronto.ca/intro/interest.htm

Chai, X., Deng, L., Yang, Q., & Ling, C. X. (2004). Test-cost sensitive naive Bayes classification. In *Proceedings of the 4th IEEE International Conference on Data Mining (ICDM'2004)*.

Chang, J. H., & Lee, W. S. (2003). Finding recent frequent itemsets adaptively over online data streams. In *Proceedings of the 9th ACM International Conference on Knowledge Discovery and Data Mining*.

Chang, J. H., & Lee, W. S. (2004). A sliding window method for finding recently frequent itemsets over online data streams. *Journal of Information Science and Engineering, 20*, 753–762.

Chang, Y., Bergman, L., Castelli, V., Li, C.-S., Lo, M.-L., & Smith, J. R. (2000). Onion technique: Indexing for linear optimization queries. In *Proceedings of the International Conference on Management of Data (SIGMOD)*.

Chaudhuri, S., & Dayal, U. (1997). An overview of data warehousing and OLAP technology. *SIGMOD Record, 26*(1), 65–74. doi:10.1145/248603.248616

Chen, C. H. (2002). Generalized association plots: Information visualization via iteratively generated correlation matrices. *Statistica Sinica, 12*, 7–29.

Chen, Q. (1999). *Mining exceptions and quantitative association rules in OLAP data cube*. Unpublished doctoral dissertation, School of Computing Science, Simon Fraser University, British Columbia, Canada.

Chirkova, R. (2002). The view selection problem has an exponential bound for conjunctive queries and views. In *Proceedings of the ACM Symposium on Principles of Database Systems 2002.*

Chirkova, R., Halevy, A., & Suciu, D. (2001). A formal perspective on the view selection problem. In *Proceedings of the International Conference on Very Large Database Systems 2001.*

Chiticariu, L., Tan, W.-C., & Vijayvargiya, G. (2005). DBNotes: A post-it system for relational databases based on provenance. In *Proceedings of the ACM SIGMOD International Conference on Management of Data,* Baltimore, MD, USA (pp. 942-944).

Choo, J. (2007). Using proximity graphs to enhance representative-based clustering algorithms. Unpublished master's thesis, Department of Computer Science, University of Houston, TX.

Cios, K. J. (Ed.). (2001). *Medical data mining and knowledge discovery*. New York: Physica-Verlag.

Clifton, C., Doan, A., Elmagarmid, A., Kantarcioglu, M., et al. (2004). Privacy-preserving data integration and sharing. In *Proceedings of the DMKD'04,* Paris, France. New York: ACM.

Cochrane_Collaboration. (2007). *Cochrane centres.* Retrieved July 18, 2007, from http://www.cochrane.org/contact/entities.htm

Cochrane_Library. (2007). *Evidence for healthcare decision-making.* Retrieved July 18, 2007, from http://www.theCochraneLibrary.com

Codd, E. F. (1985). How relational is your database management system? *Computerworld.*

Codd, E. F., Codd, S. B., & Salley, C. T. (1993). *Providing OLAP (on-line analytical processing) to user-analysts: An IT mandate* (Tech. Rep.). E. F. Codd & Associates.

Coiera, E. (2003). *Guide to health informatics* (2nd ed.). London: Hodder Arnold.

Cong, G., Fan, W., & Geerts, F. (2006). Annotation propagation revisited for key preserving views. In *Proceedings of the 15th ACM CIKM International Conference on Information and Knowledge Management,* Arlington, VA, USA (pp. 632-641).

Cover, T. M., & Hart, P. E. (1967). Nearest neighbor pattern classification. *IEEE Transactions on Information Theory, 13*(1), 21–27. doi:10.1109/TIT.1967.1053964doi:10.1109/TIT.1967.1053964

Craig, J. C., Irwig, L. M., & Stockler, M. R. (2001). Evidence-based medicine: Useful tools for decision making. *The Medical Journal of Australia, MJA, 174,* 248–253.

Critchlow, T., Ganesh, M., & Musick, R. (1998). Automatic generation of warehouse mediators using an ontology engine. In *Proceedings of the 5th International Workshop on Knowledge Represenation Meets Databases (KRDB '98),* Seattle, Washington, USA. Retrieved from http://www.CEUR-WS.org

Czajkowski, K., Foster, I. T., Karonis, N. T., Kesselman, C., Martin, S., Smith, W., & Tuecke, S. (1998). A resource management architecture for metacomputing systems. In *Proceedings of the Workshop on Job Scheduling Strategies For Parallel Processing* (LNCS 1459, pp. 62-82).

Darmont, J., Bentayeb, F., & Boussaid, O. (2007). Benchmarking data warehouses. *International Journal of Business Intelligence and Data Mining, 2*(1), 79–104. doi:10.1504/IJBIDM.2007.012947

Dash, M., & Liu, H. (1997). Feature selection for classification. *Intelligent Data Analysis, 1*(1-4), 131–156. doi:10.1016/S1088-467X(97)00008-5doi:10.1016/S1088-467X(97)00008-5

Dash, M., & Liu, H. (2003). Consistency-based search in feature selection. *Artificial Intelligence*, 151(1-2), 155–176. doi:10.1016/S0004-3702(03)00079-1doi:10.1016/S0004-3702(03)00079-1

Dash, M., Choi, K., et al. (2002). Feature selection for clustering - a filter solution. In *Proceedings of the ICDM* (pp. 115-122).

Dayal, U., Hsu, M., & Ladin, R. (2001). Business process coordination: State of the art, trends, and open issues. In *VLDB 2001: Proceedings of the 27th International Conference on Very Large Data Bases* (pp. 3-13). San Francisco, CA: Morgan Kaufmann Publishers Inc.

dbMotion. (2005). *The dbMotion™ solution* [white paper].

Demaine, E. D. L'opez-Ortiz, A., & Munro, J. I. (2002). Frequency estimation of Internet packet streams with limited space. In *Proceedings of the 10th Annual European Symposium on Algorithms*.

Dhamankar, R., Lee, Y., Doan, A., Halevy, A., & Domingos, P. (2004). iMAP: Discovering complex semantic matches between database schemas. In *Proceedings of the SIGMOD* (pp. 383-394). Paris, France: ACM.

Ding, C., & Peng, H. (2003). Minimum redundancy feature selection from microarray gene expression data. In *Proceedings of the CSB* (pp. 523-529).

Ding, W., Eick, C. F., Wang, J., & Yuan, X. (2006). A framework for regional association rule mining in spatial datasets. In B. Werner (Ed.), *Proceedings of the Sixth IEEE International Conference on Data Mining*, Hong Kong (pp. 851-856).

Ding, W., Eick, C. F., Yuan, X., Wang, J., & Nicot, J.-P. (2007). On regional association rule scoping. In *Proceedings of the International Workshop on Spatial and Spatio-Temporal Data Mining* (pp.595-600).

Ding, W., Jiamthapthaksin, R., Parmar, R., Jiang, D., Stepinski, T., & Eick, C. F. (2008). Towards region discovery in spatial datasets. In T. Washio, E. Suzuki, K. M. Ting, & A. Inokuchi (Eds.), *Advances in knowledge discovery and data mining* (LNCS 5012, pp. 88-99). Berlin, Germany: Springer.

Docobo®. (2006). doc@HOME. Retrieved August, 16, 2007, from http://www.docobo.co.uk/products_docathome.htm

Dodds, D., Hasan, H., & Gould, E. (1999). Relational versus multidimensional databases as a foundation for online analytical processing. In *IRIS 22: Proceedings of the 22nd Information Systems Research Seminar in Scandinavia* (pp. 281-288).

Domingos, P. (1999). MetaCost: A general method for making classifiers cost-sensitive. In *Proceedings of the 5th ACM SIGKDD International Conference on Knowledge Discovery and Data Mining (KDD-99)* (pp. 155-164).

Dong, G., Han, J., Lam, J. M. W., Pei, J., Wang, K., & Zou, W. (2004). Mining constrained gradients in large databases. *IEEE Transactions on Knowledge Discovery and Data Engineering*, 16(8), 922–938. doi:10.1109/TKDE.2004.28

Dong, G., Han, J., Lam, J., Pei, J., & Wang, K. (2001). Mining multi-dimensional constrained gradients in data cubes. In *Proceedings of the 27th Very Large Data Bases conference, (VLDB2001)*, Roma, Italy.

Donovan, M. (2005). *Real-time connections*. Retrieved September 25, 2007, from http://www.teradata.com/t/page/131974/index.html

Dowsey, M. M., Kilgour, M. L., & Santamaria, N. M. (1999). A clinical pathway reduced length of stay, time to ambulation, and complications after hip and knee arthroplasty. *The Medical Journal of Australia*, 170, 59–62.

Dreger, H., Feldmann, A., Mai, M., Vern, P., & Sommer, R. (2006). Dynamic application-layer protocol analysis for network intrusion detection. In *USENIX-SS'06: Proceedings of the 15th conference on USENIX Security Symposium* (p. 18). Vancouver, Canada: USENIX Association.

Drummond, C., & Holte, R. C. (2000). Explicitly representing expected cost: An alternative to ROC representation. In *Proceedings of the 6th ACM SIGKDD International Conference on Knowledge Discovery and Data Mining (KDD 2000)* (pp. 198-207).

Drummond, C., & Holte, R. C. (2000). Exploiting the cost (in)sensitivity of decision tree splitting criteria. In *Proceedings of the 17ᵗʰ International Conference on Machine Learning (ICML)* (pp. 239-246).

Drummond, C., & Holte, R. C. (2006). Cost curves: An improved method for visualizing classifier performance. *Machine Learning*, *65*, 95–130. doi:10.1007/s10994-006-8199-5

Duan, L., Xu, L., Guo, F., Lee, J., & Yan, B. (2007). A local-density based spatial clustering algorithm with noise. *Information Systems*, *32*(7), 978–986. doi:10.1016/j.is.2006.10.006

Duftschmid, G., Dorda, W., & Gall, W. (2003). MAGDA-LENA versus HIPAA: Two national frameworks for healthcare data exchange. In *Proceedings of the a-telemed 2003* (pp. 25-33).

Dutch_DPA. (2006). *Handling of your medical data*. Retrieved August 29, 2007, from http://www.dutchdpa.nl/documenten/en_inf_subj_Handling_Medical_Data.shtml

Dy, J. G., Brodley, C. E., et al. (2003). Unsupervised feature selection applied to content-based retrieval of lung images. IEEE Transactions on Pattern Analysis and Machine Intelligence, 25(3), 373–378. doi:10.1109/TPAMI.2003.1182100doi:10.1109/TPAMI.2003.1182100

Early, J., Brodley, C., & Rosenberg, C. (2003). Behavioral Authentication of server flows. In *ACSAC '03: Proceedings of the 19ᵗʰ Annual Computer Security Applications Conference* (p. 46). Washington, DC: IEEE Computer Society.

Eavis, T., & Cueva, D. (2007). A Hilbert Space compression architecture for data warehouse environments. In *Proceedings of the International Conference on Data Warehousing and Knowledge Discovery* (pp. 1-12).

Eavis, T., & Cueva, D. (2007). The LBF R-tree: Efficient multidimensional indexing with graceful degradation. In *Proceedings of the International Database Engineering & Applications Symposium* (pp. 241-250).

Eckhardt, A. (2000). *Data abuse and what can be done to prevent it*. The Patient in the Data Network.

EHCRSupA. (2007). *Introduction to ENV 13606 version 1.0*. Retrieved September 27, 2008, from http://www.chime.ucl.ac.uk/work-areas/ehrs/EHCR-SupA/13606v1_8/sld003.htm

eHealth. (2006). *Impact of emerging ICT on patient safety*. Retrieved September 27, 2007, from http://www.ehealth-for-safety.org/workshops/bio_medical%202006/bio_medical_index.html

Eichelberg, M., Aden, T., Riesmeier, J., & Dogac, A. (2005). A survey and analysis of electronic health care record standards. *ACM Computing Surveys*, *37*(4), 277–315. doi:10.1145/1118890.1118891

Eick, C. F., Vaezian, B., Jiang, D., & Wang, J. (2006). discovery of interesting regions in spatial datasets using supervised clustering. In *Proceedings of the Tenth European Conference on Principles and Practice of Knowledge Discovery in Databases: Vol. 4213* (pp. 127-138).

Eick, C. F., Zeidat, N., & Zhao, Z. (2004). Supervised clustering --- algorithms and benefits. In *Proceedings of the International Conference on Tools with AI (ICTAI)*.

Elkan, C. (2001). The foundations of cost-sensitive learning. In *Proceedings of the 17ᵗʰ International Joint Conference on Artificial Intelligence (IJCAI'01)* (pp. 973-978).

Elsevier. (2007). *The Lancet*. Retrieved September 19, 2007, from http://www.thelancet.com/

Elsmari, R., & Navathe, S. (2004). *Fundamentals of database systems*. Reading, MA: Addison Wesley.

Enterasys Networks Incorporated. (2008). *Enterasys dragon*. Retrieved from http://www.enterasys.com/products/ids/

Espil, M. M., & Vaisman, A. A. (2001). Efficient intensional redefinition of aggregation hierarchies in multidimensional databases. In *Proceedings of the 4ᵗʰ ACM International Workshop on Data Warehousing and OLAP (DOLAP 01)*, Atlanta, Georgia, USA (pp. 1-8).

Ester, M., Kriegel, H. P., Sander, J., & Xu, X. (1996). Density-based spatial clustering of applications with noise. In *Proceedings of the International Conference on Knowledge Discovery and Data Mining*.

Estivill-Castro, V., & Lee, I. (2000). Amoeba: Hierarchical clustering based on spatial proximity using Delaunaty diagram. In *Proceedings of the Ninth International Symposium on Spatial Data Handling* (pp. 7a.26-7a.41).

EU. (1995). EU data protection directive. *Official Journal of the European Communities, 31*.

Faloutsos, C., & Kamel, I. (1993). On packing R-trees. In *Proceedings of the second international conference on Information and knowledge management* (pp. 490-499).

Faloutsos, C., & Kamel, I. (1994). Hilbert R-tree: An improved R-tree using fractals. In *Proceedings of the 20th Annual Conference on VLDB* (pp. 500-509).

Faloutsos, C., & Roseman, S. (1989). Fractals for secondary key retrieval. In *Proceedings of the Eighth ACM SIGACT-SIGMOD-SIGART Symposium on Principles of Database Systems (PODS)* (pp. 247-252).

Favre, C., Bentayeb, F., & Boussaid, O. (2007). Dimension hierarchies updates in data warehouses: A user-driven approach. In *Proceedings of the 9th International Conference on Enterprise Information Systems (ICEIS 07)*, Funchal, Madeira, Portugal (pp. 206-211).

Favre, C., Bentayeb, F., & Boussaid, O. (2007). Evolution of data warehouses' optimization: A workload perspective. In *Proceedings of the 9th International Conference on Data Warehousing and Knowledge Discovery (DaWaK 07)*, Regensburg, Germany (LNCS 4654, pp. 13-22).

Fawcett, T. (2004). *ROC graphs: Notes and practical considerations for researchers* (Tech. Rep.). HP Laboratories, Palo Alto, CA.

Fawcett, T., & Provost, F. (1999). Activity monitoring: Noticing interesting changes in behavior. In *Proceedings of the 5th ACM SIGKDD International Conference on Knowledge Discovery and Data Mining (KDD-99)* (pp. 53-62).

Fayyad, U. M., Piatetsky-Shapiro, G., Smyth, P., & Uthurusamy, R. (Eds.). (1996). *Advances in knowledge discovery and data mining*. Cambridge, MA: AAAI/MIT Press.

Feelders, A., Daniels, H., & Holsheimer, M. (2000). Methodological and practical aspects of data mining. *Information & Management, 37*, 271–281. doi:10.1016/S0378-7206(99)00051-8

Ferraiolo, D. F., Kuhn, D. R., & Chandramouli, R. (2003). Access control policy, models, and mechanisms - concepts and examples. In *Role-based access control* (pp. 27-49). Norwood, MA: Artech House.

Ferrell, K. (2007). *Continental Airlines - landing the right data*. Retrieved September 25, 2007, from http://www.teradata.com/t/page/133723/index.html

Foshay, N., Mukherjee, A., & Taylor, A. (2007). Does data warehouse end-user metadata add value? *Communications of the ACM, 50*(11), 70–77. doi:10.1145/1297797.1297800

Foster, I. T. (2001). The anatomy of the Grid: Enabling scalable virtual organizations. *In Proceedings of the 7th international Euro-Par Conference on Parallel Processing* (LNCS 2150, pp. 1-4).

Foster, I., & Kesselman, C. (1997). Globus: A metacomputing infrastructure toolkit. *The International Journal of Supercomputer Applications, 11*(2), 115–128.

Foster, I., Kesselman, C., Nick, J., & Tuecke, S. (2002). The physiology of the Grid: An open Grid services architecture for distributed systems integration. In *Globus project tech report*.

Fragoudis, D., Meretakis, D., et al. (2002). Integrating feature and instance selection for text classification. In *Proceedings of the SIGKDD* (pp. 501-506).

Franconi, E., & Sattler, U. (1999). A data warehouse conceptual data model for multidimensional aggregation. In *DMDW'99: Proceedings of the International Workshop on Design and Management of Data Warehouses* (Vol. 19, pp. 13.1-13.10). Retrieved from http://www.CEUR-WS.org

Freitas, J. A. (2007). *Uso de técnicas de data mining para análise de bases de dados hospitalares com finalidades de gestão.* Unpublished doctoral dissertation, University of Porto, Portugal.

Frey, J., Tannenbaum, T., Livny, M., Foster, I., & Tuecke, S. (2001). Condor-G: A computation management agent for multi-institutional Grids. In *Proceedings of the 10th IEEE international Symposium on High Performance Distributed Computing* (pp. 55).

Furtado, P. (2004). Experimental evidence on partitioning in parallel data warehouses. In *Proceedings of the 7th ACM international Workshop on Data Warehousing and OLAP* (pp. 23-30).

Furtado, P. (2004). Workload-based placement and join processing in node-partitioned data warehouses. In *Proceedings of the 6th International Conference on Data Warehousing and Knowledge Discovery* (LNCS 3181, pp. 38-47).

Furtado, P. (2005). Hierarchical aggregation in networked data management. In *Proceedings of the International Euro-Par Conference on Parallel Processing* (LNCS 3648, pp. 360-369).

Furtado, P. (2005). Replication in node partitioned data warehouses. In *Proceedings of the VLDB Workshop on Design, Implementation, and Deployment of Database Replication (DIDDR).*

Gabriel, K. R., & Sokal, R. R. (1969). A new statistical approach to geographic variation analysis. *Systematic Zoology, 18,* 259–278. doi:10.2307/2412323

Gaede, V., & Gunther, O. (1998). Multidimensional access methods. *ACM Computing Surveys, 30*(2), 170–231. doi:10.1145/280277.280279

Gallo, J. (2002). Operations and maintenance in a data warehouse environment. *DM Review Magazine.* Retrieved from http://www.dmreview.com/article sub.cfm?articleId=6118

Gao, D., Peuquet, D., & Gahegan, M. (2002). Opening the black box: Interactive hierarchical clustering for multivariate spatial patterns. In *Proceedings of the Tenth ACM International Symposium on Advances in Geographic Information Systems* (pp. 131-136).

Gebski, M., & Wong, R. (2005). Intrusion detection via analysis and modelling of user commands. In *Proceedings of the 7th International Conference Data Warehousing and Knowledge Discovery (DaWaK)* (pp. 388-397). Copenhagen, Denmark: Springer.

Geerts, F., Kementsietsidis, A., & Milano, D. (2006). MONDRIAN: Annotating and querying databases through colors and blocks. In *Proceedings of the 22nd IEEE ICDE International Conference on Data Engineering,* Atlanta, GA, USA (pp. 82).

Ghozzi, F., Ravat, F., Teste, O., & Zurfluh, G. (2003). Constraints and multidimensional databases. In *Proceedings of the 5th International Conference on Enterprise Information Systems (ICEIS 03),* Angers, France (pp. 104-111).

Giannella, C., Han, J., Pei, J., Yan, X., & Yu, P. S. (2003). Mining frequent patterns in data streams at multiple time granularities. In H Kargupta, et al. (Eds.), *Data mining: Next generation challenges and future directions.* Cambridge, MA: AAAI/MIT Press.

Gingras, F., & Lakshmanan, L. V. (1998). nD-SQL: A multi-dimensional language for interoperability and OLAP. In A. Gupta, O. Shmueli, & J. Widom (Eds.), *Proceedings of the VLDB* (pp. 134-145). San Francisco: Morgan Kaufmann.

Giovinazzo, W. A. (2000). *Object-oriented data warehouse design: Building a star schema.* Upper Saddle River, NJ: Prentice Hall PTR.

Goh, L., Song, Q., et al. (2004). A novel feature selection method to improve classification of gene expression data. In *Proceedings of the APBC* (pp. 161-166).

Goldstein, J., Ramakrishnan, R., & Shaft, U. (1998). Compressing relations and indexes. In *Proceedings of the Fourteenth International Conference on Data Engineering* (pp. 370-379).

Golfarelli, M., & Rizzi, S. (1998). A methodological framework for data warehouse design. In *DOLAP '98:*

Proceedings of the 1ˢᵗ ACM International Workshop on Data Warehousing and OLAP (pp. 3-9). New York: ACM Press.

Golfarelli, M., & Saltarelli, E. (2003). The workload you have, the workload you would like. In *Proceedings of the 6ᵗʰ ACM International Workshop on Data Warehousing and OLAP (DOLAP 03)*, New Orleans, Louisiana, USA (pp. 79-85).

Golfarelli, M., Maio, D., & Rizzi, S. (1998). Conceptual design of data warehouses from E/R schemes. In *Proceedings of the 31ˢᵗ HICSS Annual Hawaii International Conference on System Sciences*, Hawaii, USA (pp. 334).

Golfarelli, M., Maio, D., & Rizzi, S. (1998). The dimensional fact model: A conceptual model for data warehouses. *International Journal of Cooperative Information Systems, 7*(2/3), 215–247. doi:10.1142/S0218843098000118

Golomb, S. W. (1966). Run-length encodings. *IEEE Transactions on Information Theory, 12*(3), 399–401. doi:10.1109/TIT.1966.1053907

Golub, T. R., Slonim, D. K., et al. (1999). Molecular classification of cancer: Class discovery and class prediction by gene expression monitoring. Science, 286(5439), 531–537. PubMeddoi:10.1126/science.286.5439.531doi:10.1126/science.286.5439.531

Gorenberg, M., Marmor, A., & Rotstein, H. (2005). Detection of chest pain of non-cardiac origin at the emergency room by a new non-invasive device avoiding unnecessary admission to hospital. *Emergency Medicine Journal, 22*, 486–489. doi:10.1136/emj.2004.016188

Gounaris, A., Smith, J., Paton, N., Sakellariou, R., Fernandes, A., & Watson, P. (2005). Adapting to changing resource performance in Grid query processing. In *Data Management in Grids* (DMG) (pp. 30-44).

Grahne, G., & Zhu, J. (2003). Efficiently using prefix-trees in mining frequent itemsets. In *Proceeding of the First IEEE ICDM Workshop on Frequent Itemset Mining Implementations*, Melbourne, FL.

Gray, J., Bosworth, A., Layman, A., & Pirahesh, H. (1996). Data cube: A relational aggregation operator generalizing group-by, cross-tab, and sub-totals. In *Proceedings of the Twelfth International Conference on Data Engineering* (pp. 152-159).

Gray, J., Chaudhuri, S., Bosworth, A., Layman, A., Reichart, D., & Venkatrao, M. (1997). Data cube: A relational aggregation operator generalizing group-by, cross-tab, and sub-totals. *Journal of Data Mining and Knowledge Discovery, 1*(1), 29–53. doi:10.1023/A:1009726021843

Gregoratos, G., Cheitlin, M. D., & Conill, A. (1998). ACC/AHA guidelines for implantation of cardiac pacemakers and antiarrhythmia devices: Executive summary. *Circulation, 97*, 1325–1335.

Greiner, R., Grove, A. J., & Roth, D. (2002). Learning cost-sensitive active classifiers. *Artificial Intelligence, 139*(2), 137–174. doi:10.1016/S0004-3702(02)00209-6

Grigori, D., Casati, F., Castellanos, M., Dayal, U., Sayal, M., & Shan, M.-C. (2004). Business process intelligence. *Computers in Industry, Special Issue on Process/Workflow Mining, 53*(3), 321-343.

Grimshaw, A. S., & Wulf, W. A., & CORPORATE The Legion Team. (1997). The Legion vision of a worldwide virtual computer. *Communications of the ACM, 40*(1), 39–45. doi:10.1145/242857.242867

Grobman, W. A., & Stamilio, D. M. (2006). Methods of clinical prediction. *American Journal of Obstetrics and Gynecology, 194*(3), 888–894. doi:10.1016/j.ajog.2005.09.002

Guha, S., Rastogi, R., & Shim, K. (1998). CURE: An efficient clustering algorithm for large databases. In *Proceedings of the International Conference of ACM SIGMOD on Management of Data* (pp. 73-84).

Gupta, H., & Mumick, I. (2005). Selection of views to materialize in a data warehouse. [TKDE]. *Transactions of Knowledge and Data Engineering, 17*(1), 24–43. doi:10.1109/TKDE.2005.16

Gupta, H., Harinarayan, V., Rajaraman, A., & Ullman, J. (1997). Index selection for OLAP. In *Proceedings of the*

Thirteenth International Conference on Data Engineering (pp. 208-219).

Guttman, A. (1984). R-trees: A dynamic index structure for spatial searching. In *Proceedings of the 1984 ACM SIGMOD international conference on Management of data* (pp. 47-57).

Guyatt, G. H., Feeny, D. H., & Patrick, D. L. (1993). Measuring health-related quality of life. *Annals of Internal Medicine, 118*(8), 622–629.

GVG©. (2004). *Pseudonymisierung/anonymisierung.* Aktionsforum Telematik im Gesundheitswesen.

Gyssens, M., & Lakshmanan, L. V. S. (1997). A foundation for multi-dimensional databases. In *Proceedings of the 23rd VLDB International Conference on Very Large Databases*, Athens, Greece (pp. 106-115).

Hahn, C., Warren, S., & Loudon, J. (n.d.). Retrieved from http://cdiac.esd.ornl.gov/cdiac/ndps/ndpo26b.html

Halevy, A. Y. (2001). Answering queries using views: A survey. *The VLDB Journal, 10*(4), 270–294. doi:10.1007/s007780100054

Halevy, A. Y., Rajaraman, A., & Ordille, J. J. (2006). Data integration: The teenage years. In U. Dayal, K.-Y. Whang, D. B. Lomet, G. Alonso, G. M. Lohman, M. L. Kersten, et al. (Eds.), *Proceedings of the VLDB* (pp. 9-16). New York: ACM.

Hall, C. (2004, June). Business process intelligence. *BP-Trends Newsletter.* Retrieved from http://www.bptrends.com/publicationfiles/06%2D04%20NL%20BPI%20-%20Hall%20PH-2.pdf

Hall, M. A. (2000). Correlation-based feature selection for discrete and numeric class machine learning. In *Proceedings of the ICML* (pp. 359-366).

Han, J. (1997). OLAP mining: An integration of OLAP with data mining. In *Proceedings of the 1997 IFIP Conference on Data Semantics (DS-7)*, Leysin, Switzerland (pp. 1-11).

Han, J., & Kamber, M. (2001). *Data mining: Concepts and techniques.* San Francisco: Morgan Kaufman Publishers.

Han, J., Pei, J., & Yin, Y. (2000). Mining frequent patterns without candidate generation. In *Proceeding of the 2000 SIGMOD Conference*, Dallas, Texas (pp. 1-12).

Han, J., Pei, J., Dong, G., & Wank, K. (2001). Efficient computation of iceberg cubes with complex measures. In *Proceedings of the International Conference on Management of Data (SIGMOD).*

Han, J., Pei, J., Yin, Y., & Mao, R. (2004). Mining frequent patterns without candidate generation: A frequent-pattern tree approach. *Data Mining and Knowledge Discovery, 8*(1), 53–87. doi:10.1023/B:DAMI.0000005258.31418.83

Hanley, J. A., & McNeil, B. J. (1982). The meaning and use of the area under a receiver operating characteristic (ROC) curve. *Radiology, 143*(1), 29–36.

Hao, M. C., Keim, D. A., Dayal, U., & Schneidewind, J. (2006). Business process impact visualization and anomaly detection. *Information Visualization, 5*, 15–27. doi:10.1057/palgrave.ivs.9500115

Harinarayan, V., Rajaraman, A., & Ulman, J. (1996). Implementing data cubes efficiently. In *Proceedings of SIGMOD 1996.*

Hashmi, N., Myung, D., Gaynor, M., & Moulton, S. (2005). A sensor-based, Web service-enabled, emergency medical response system. In *Proceedings of the EESR '05: Workshop on End-to-End, Sense-and-Respond Systems, Applications and Services*, Seattle, WA. New York: ACM.

Haslhofer, B. (2006). A service oriented approach for integrating metadata from heterogeneous digital libraries. In *Proceedings of the 1st International Workshop Semantic Information Integration on Knowledge Discovery (SIIK 2006)*, Yogyakarta, Indonesia. Austrian Computer Society.

Hauptverband. (2007). *Österreichische sozialversicherung.* Retrieved September 27, 2007, from http://www.sozialversicherung.at

Hein, A., Nee, O., Willemsen, D., Scheffold, T., et al. (2006). SAPHIRE - intelligent healthcare monitoring based on semantic interoperability platform - the home-care scenario. In *Proceedings of the European Conference on eHealth 2006*, Fribourg, Switzerland (pp. 191-202).

Heitmann, K. U. (2006). Kommunikation mit HL7 version 3 – aspekte der interoperabilität im gesundheitswesen. *Datenbank Spektrum, (17)*, 12-16.

Hettich, S., & Bay, S. D. (1999). The UCI KDD archive. Retrieved from http://kdd.ics.uci.edu

Hilbert, D. (1891). Ueber die stetige abbildung einer line auf ein flchenstck. *Mathematische Annalen, 38*(3), 459–460. doi:10.1007/BF01199431

Hinneburg, A., & Keim, D. (1998). An efficient approach to clustering in large multimedia databases with noise. In *Proceedings of the International Conference on Knowledge Discovery in Data Mining.*

HIPPA. (1996). *HIPPA.ORG*. Retrieved September 27, 2007, from http://www.hipaa.org/

HIR-group. (2006). *Health informatics research*. Retrieved September 26, 2007, from http://www.cit.uws.edu.au/hir/

HL7. (2007). *Health level seven*. Retrieved September 26, 2007, from http://www.hl7.org

Holland, J. H., Holyoak, K. J., Nisbett, R. E., & Thagard, P. R. (1986). *Induction: Processes of inference, learning, and discovery*. Cambridge, MA: MIT Press.

Hristidis, V., Koudas, N., & Papakonstantinou, Y. (2001). Prefer: A system for the efficient execution of multi-parametric ranked queries. In *Proceedings of the International Conference on Management of Data (SIGMOD).*

Huang, Y., Jing, N., & Rundensteiner, E. (1997). Spatial joins using r-trees: Breadth first traversal with global optimizations. In *Proceedings of the VLDB* (pp. 322-331).

Huffman, D. (1952). A method for the construction of minimum redundancy codes. *Proceedings of the Institute of Radio Engineers, 40*(9), 1098–1101.

Hurtado, C. A., & Mendelzon, A. O. (2001). Reasoning about summarizability in heterogeneous multidimen-sional schemas. In J. Van den Bussche, & V. Vianu (Eds.), *Proceedings of the ICDT* (pp. 375-389). Berlin, Germany: Springer.

Hurtado, C. A., & Mendelzon, A. O. (2002). OLAP dimension constraints. In *PODS 2002: Proceedings of the 21st ACM Symposium on Principles of Database Systems* (pp. 169-179).

Hurtado, C. A., Gutiérrez, C., & Mendelzon, A. O. (2005). Capturing summarizability with integrity constraints in OLAP. *ACM Transactions on Database Systems, 30*(3), 854–886. doi:10.1145/1093382.1093388

Hurtado, C. A., Mendelzon, A. O., & Vaisman, A. A. (1999). Maintaining data cubes under dimension updates. In *Proceedings of the 15th International Conference on Data Engineering (ICDE 99)*, Sydney, Australia (pp. 346-355).

Hurtado, C. A., Mendelzon, A. O., & Vaisman, A. A. (1999). Updating OLAP dimensions. In *Proceedings of the 2nd ACM International Workshop on Data Warehousing and OLAP (DOLAP 99)*, Kansas City, Missouri, USA (pp. 60-66).

Hüsemann, B., Lechtenbörger, J., & Vossen, G. (2000). Conceptual data warehouse design. In *DMDW'2000: Proceedings of the 2nd International Workshop on Design and Management of Data Warehouses at CAiSE'00* (Vol. 28, pp. 6.1-6.11). Retrieved from http://www.CEUR-WS.org

IHE. (2006, June). *IHE cardiology technical framework year 2: 2005-2006. Volume I: Integration profiles*. Retrieved August 26, 2007, from http://www.ihe.net/Technical_Framework

IHE. (2007). *IHE changing the way healhtcare connects*. Retrieved September 27, 2007, from http://www.ihe.net/

IHE. (2007). *IHE connectathons present a unique testing opportunity*. Retrieved September 26, 2007, from http://www.ihe.net/Connectathon/

IHE. (2007). *IHE in Europe 2007*. Retrieved September 27, 2007, from http://ihe.univ-rennes1.fr/europe2007/

Imielinski, T., Khachiyan, L., & Abdulghani, A. (2002). Cubegrades: Generalizing association rules. *Data Mining and Knowledge Discovery, 6*(3), 219–258. doi:10.1023/A:1015417610840

Infoway, C. H. (2007). *Transforming health care.* Retrieved September 20, 2007, from http://www.infoway-inforoute.ca/

Infoway, C. H. (2007). *Advancing Canada's next generation of healthcare.* Retrieved October, 11, 2007, from http://www.infoway-inforoute.ca/en/pdf/Vision_2015_Advancing_Canadas_next_generation_of_healthcare.pdf

Inmon, W. (2005). *Building the data warehouse* (4th ed.). New York: John Wiley & Sons.

Inmon, W. H. (1992). *Building the data warehouse.* New York: John Wiley & Sons.

Inmon, W. H. (2002). *Building the data warehouse* (3rd ed.). Hoboken, NJ: John Wiley & Sons.

InterfaceWare. (2007). *HL7 standard.* Retrieved from http://www.interfaceware.com/manual/hl7.html

Inza, I., Larranaga, P., et al. (2004). Filter versus wrapper gene selection approaches in DNA microarray domains. Artificial Intelligence in Medicine, 31(2), 91–103. PubMeddoi:10.1016/j.artmed.2004.01.007doi:10.1016/j.artmed.2004.01.007

ISO. (1992). ISO/IEC 9075:1992: Information technology -- database languages -- SQL.

Jaeger, J., Sengupta, R., et al. (2003). Improved gene selection for classification of microarrays. In *Proceedings of the Pacific Symposium on Biocomputing* (pp. 53-64).

Jagadish, H. (1990). Linear clustering of objects with multiple attributes. *SIGMOD Record, 19*(2), 332–342. doi:10.1145/93605.98742

JAMA. (2007). *The Journal of the American Medical Association.* Retrieved September 19, 2007, from http://jama.ama-assn.org/

Jank, E., Rose, A., Huth, S., Trantakis, C., Korb, W., & Strauss, G. (2006). A new fluoroscopy based navigation system for milling procedures in spine surgery. *International Journal of Computer Assisted Radiology and Surgery, 1*(Supplement 1), 196–198.

Jannin, P., Raimbault, M., Morandi, X., Riffaud, L., & Gibaud, B. (2003). Model of surgical procedures for multimodal image-guided neurosurgery. *Computer Aided Surgery, 8*(2), 98–106. doi:10.3109/10929080309146044

Jiang, B. (2004). Spatial clustering for mining knowledge in support of generalization processes in GIS. In *Proceedings of the ICA Workshop on Generalisation and Multiple Representation.*

Jiang, D., Eick, C. F., & Chen, C. S. (2007). on supervised density estimation techniques and their application to clustering. In *Proceedings of the Fifteenth ACM International Symposium on Advances in Geographic Information Systems.*

Jin, C., Qian, W., Sha, C., Yu, J. X., & Zhou, A. (2003). Dynamically maintaining frequent items over a data stream. In *Proceedings of the 12th ACM International Conference on Information and Knowledge Management.*

Jindal, R., & Acharya, A. (2004). *Federated data warehouse architecture, Wipro Technologies* [white paper]. Retrieved September 19, 2007, from http://hosteddocs.ittoolbox.com/Federated%20data%20Warehouse%20Architecture.pdf

Jobson, J. D. (1991). *Applied multivariate data analysis. Volume I: Regression and experimental design.* New York: Springer Verlag.

John, G. H., Kohavi, R., et al. (1994). Irrelevant features and the subset selection problem. In *Proceedings of the ICML* (pp. 121-129).

Kalnis, P., Mamoulis, N., & Papadias, D. (2002). View selection using randomized search. *Data & Knowledge Engineering, 42*(1). doi:10.1016/S0169-023X(02)00045-9

Kalra, D., Singleton, P., Ingram, D., & Milan, J. (2004). Security and confidentiality approach for the clinical e-science framework (CLEF). *HealthGrid, 44*(2), 193–197.

Kamber, M., Han, J., & Chiang, J. (1997). Metarule-guided mining of multi-dimensional association rules using data cubes. In *Proceedings of the 3rd International Conference on Knowledge Discovery and Data Mining (KDD 1997)*, Newport Beach, CA, USA (pp. 207-210). Menlo Park, CA: The AAAI Press.

Karenos, K., Samaras, G., Chrysanthis, P., & Pitoura, E. (2004). Mobile agent-based services for view materialization. *ACM SIGMOBILE Mobile Computing and Communications Review, 8*(3).

Karlo, H., & Mihail, M. (1999). On the complexity of the view-selection problem. In *Proceeding of PODS 1999*.

Karp, R. M., Papadimitriou, C. H., & Shenker, S. (2003). A simple algorithm for finding frequent elements in streams and bags. *ACM Transactions on Database Systems, 28*(1), 51–55. doi:10.1145/762471.762473

Karypis, G., Han, E. H., & Kumar, V. (1999). CHAMELEON: A hierarchical clustering algorithm using dynamic modeling. *IEEE Computer., 32*, 68–75.

KBV. (2006). *xDT - synonym für elektronischen datenaustausch in der arztpraxis*. Retrieved September 27, 2007, from http://www.kbv.de/ita/4274.html

KFF. (2006). *Comparing projected growth in health care expenditures and the economy*. Retrieved October 22, 2007, from http://www.kff.org/insurance/snapshot/chcm050206oth2.cfm

Kim, H. J., Lee, T. H., Lee, S. G., & Chun, J. (2003). Automated data warehousing for rule-based CRM systems. In *Proceedings of the 14th Australasian Database Conference, Database Technologies (ADC 03)*, Adelaide, Australia (pp. 67-73).

Kim, K. (2005). Clinical data standards in health care: Five case studies. *ihealh reports*.

Kim, S., & Cha, S. (1998). Sibling clustering of tree-based indexes for efficient spatial query processing. In *Proceedings of the ACM Intl. Conf. Information and Knowledge Management* (pp. 322-331).

Kim, W., & Seo, J. (1991). Classifying schematic and data heterogeneity in multidatabase systems. *IEEE Computer, 24*(12), 12–18.

Kim, Y. S., Street, W. N., et al. (2000). Feature selection in unsupervised learning via evolutionary search. In *Proceedings of the KDD* (pp. 365-369).

Kimball, R. (1996). *The data warehouse toolkit: Practical techniques for building dimensional data warehouses*. New York: John Wiley & Sons, Inc.

Kimball, R. (2002). *The data warehouse toolkit: Practical techniques for building dimensional data warehouses* (2nd ed.). New York: John Wiley & Sons.

Kimball, R., Reeves, L., Ross, M., & Thornthwaite, W. (1998). *The data warehouse lifecycle toolkit: Expert methods for designing, developing and deploying data warehouses*. Hoboken, NJ: John Wiley & Sons.

Kira, K., & Rendell, L. A. (1992). The feature selection problem: Traditional methods and a new algorithm. In *Proceedings of the AAAI* (pp. 129-134).

Kirkgoze, R., Katic, N., Stolba, M., & Tjoa, A. M. (1997). A security concept for OLAP. In *Proceedings of the 8th International Workshop on Database and Expert System Application 1997* (pp. 619-626). Washington, DC: IEEE Computer Press.

Kirkpatrick, D. (1980). A note on Delaunay and optimal triangulations. *Information Processing Letters, 10*, 127–128. doi:10.1016/0020-0190(80)90062-9

Koenig, G., & Kale, L. (2007). Optimizing distributed application performance using dynamic Grid topology-aware load balancing. In *Proceedings of the 21st IEEE International Parallel and Distributed Processing Symposium (IPDPS 2007)* (pp. 1-10).

Koh, J. L., & Don, Y.-B. (2007). mining frequent approximately representative itemsets on data streams. In T. Washio, et al. (Eds.), *Proceedings of the 2007 International Workshop on High Performance Data Mining and Applications (PAKDD 2007)* (LNAI 4819, pp. 231-243). Berlin, Germany: Springer-Verlag.

Koh, J. L., & Shin, S. N. (2006). An approximate approach for mining recently frequent itemsets from data streams. In *Proceedings of the 8th International Conference on Data Warehousing and Knowledge Discovery*.

Kohavi, R., & John, G. H. (1997). Wrappers for feature subset selection. Artificial Intelligence, 97(1-2), 273–324. doi:10.1016/S0004-3702(97)00043-Xdoi:10.1016/S0004-3702(97)00043-X

Kononenko, I. (1994). Estimating attributes: Analysis and extensions of RELIEF. In *Proceedings of the ECML* (pp. 171-182).

Kotidis, Y., & Roussopoulos, N. (1999). Dyna-Mat: A dynamic view management system for data warehouses. *SIGMOD Record*, 28(2), 371–382. doi:10.1145/304181.304215

Krauter, K., Buyya, R., & Maheswaran, M. (2002). A taxonomy and survey of Grid resource management systems for distributed computing. In [SPE]. *Software, Practice & Experience*, 32(2), 135–164. doi:10.1002/spe.432

Krenn, F. (2006). *IT-platforms help to improve efficiency in health care*. Retrieved September 27, 2007, from www.ehealth-bg.org/images/Siemens_Franz%20 Krenn_1.ppt

Kriegel, H. P., & Pfeifle, M. (2005). Density-based clustering of uncertain data. In *Proceedings of the International Conference on Knowledge Discovery in Data Mining* (pp. 672-677).

Kumar, S., & Spafford, E. H. (1994). A pattern matching model for misuse intrusion detection. In *Proceedings of the 17th National Computer Security Conference* (pp. 11-21).

Lakshmanan, L., Pei, J., & Zhao, Y. (2003). QC-trees: An efficient summary structure for semantic OLAP. In *Proceedings of the 2003 ACM SIGMOD international conference on Management of data* (pp. 64-75).

Lampson, B. W. (1974). Protection. *ACM Operating Systems*, 8(1), 18–24. doi:10.1145/775265.775268

Lane, T., & Brodley, C. (1998). Approaches to on-line learning and concept drift for user identification in computer security. In *KDD '98: Proceedings of the 1998 ACM SIGKDD international conference on Knowledge discovery and data mining* (pp. 259-263). New York: ACM Press.

Lane, T., & Brodley, C. (1999). Temporal sequence learning and data reduction for anomaly detection. *ACM Transactions on Information and System Security*, 2(3), 295–331. doi:10.1145/322510.322526

Lavrac, N. (1999). Selected techniques for data mining in medicine. *Artificial Intelligence in Medicine*, 16, 3–23. doi:10.1016/S0933-3657(98)00062-1

Lawrence, M., & Rau-Chaplin, A. (2006). Dynamic view selection for OLAP. In *Proceedings of the 8th International Conference on Data Warehousing and Knowledge Discovery (DaWaK 06)*, Krakow, Poland (LNCS 4081, pp. 33-44).

Lawrence, M., & Rau-Chaplin, A. (2006). The OLAP-enabled Grid: Model and query processing algorithms. In *Proceedings of the 20th international Symposium on High-Performance Computing in An Advanced Collaborative Environment* (pp. 4).

Lechtenbörger, J. (2001). Data warehouse schema design (Doctoral dissertation, Westfälische Wilhelms-Universität Münster). *Dissertations in database and information systems, 79*.

Lenz, H.-J., & Shoshani, A. (1997). Summarizability in OLAP and statistical data bases. In *SSDBM 1997: Proceedings of the 9th International Conference on Scientific and Statistical Database Management* (pp. 132-143).

Lenzerini, M. (2002). Data integration: A theoretical perspective. In L. Popa (Ed.), *Proceedings of PODS* (pp. 233-246). New York: ACM.

Lerner, A., & Lifschitz, S. (1998). A study of workload balancing techniques on parallel join algorithms. In *Proceedings of the International Conference on Parallel and Distributed Processing Techniques and Applications (PDPTA)*. (pp. 966-973).

Leutenegger, S., Lopez, M., & Eddington, J. (1997). STR: A simple and efficient algorithm for R-tree packing. In *Proceedings of the Thirteenth International Conference on Data Engineering* (pp. 497-506).

Lewis, D. D., & Catlett, J. (1994). Heterogenous uncertainty sampling for supervised learning. In *Proceedings of the ICML* (pp. 148-156).

Li, X., Han, J., & Gonzalez, H. (2004). High-dimensional OLAP: A minimal cubing approach. In *Proceedings of the International Conference on Very Large Databases (VLDB)*.

Li, Y., Ning, P., Wang, X. S., & Jajodia, S. (2001). Discovering calendar-based temporal association rules. In *Proceeding of the International Symposium on Temporal Representation and Reasoning* (pp. 111-118).

Lima, A., Mattoso, M., & Valduriez, P. (2004). Adaptive virtual partitioning for OLAP query processing in a database cluster. In *Proceedings of the Brazilian Symposium on Databases (SBBD)* (pp. 92-105).

Lin, C. H., Chiu, D. Y., Wu, Y. H., & Chen, A. L. P. (2005). Mining frequent itemsets from data streams with a time-sensitive sliding window. In *Proceedings of the SIAM International Conference on Data Mining*.

Lin, C., & Chen, M. (2002). A robust and efficient clustering algorithm based on cohesion self-merging. In *Proceedings of the International Conference of Eighth ACM SIGKDD on Knowledge Discovery and Data Mining* (pp. 582-587).

Lin, F., Chou, S., Pan, S., & Chen, Y. (2000). Mining time dependency patterns in clinical pathways. IN *Proceedings of the 33rd Hawaii International Conference on System Sciences*.

Ling, C. X., Sheng, V. S., & Yang, Q. (2006). Test strategies for cost-sensitive decision trees. *IEEE Transactions on Knowledge and Data Engineering, 18*(8), 1055–1067. doi:10.1109/TKDE.2006.131

Ling, C. X., Yang, Q., Wang, J., & Zhang, S. (2004). Decision trees with minimal costs. In *Proceedings of the 21st International Conference on Machine Learning (ICML)*.

Litwin, W., Mark, L., & Roussopoulos, N. (1990). Interoperability of multiple autonomous databases. *ACM Computing Surveys, 22*(3), 267–293. doi:10.1145/96602.96608

Liu, B., Hsu, W., & Ma, Y. (1998). Integrating classification and association rule mining. In *Proceedings of the KDD'98* (pp. 80-86). New York: AAAI Press.

Liu, H., & Motoda, H. (Eds.). (1998). *Feature extraction, construction and selection: A data mining perspective*. Berlin, Germany: Springer.

Liu, H., & Motoda, H. (Eds.). (2001). *Instance selection and construction for data mining*. Berlin, Germany: Springer.

Liu, H., & Setiono, R. (1996). A probabilistic approach to feature selection - a filter solution. In *Proceedings of the ICML* (pp. 319-327).

Liu, Z., Chrysanthis, P., & Tsui, F. (2004). A comparison of two view materialization approaches for disease surveillance system. In *Proceedings of SAC 2004*.

Lo, M., & Ravishankar, C. (1995). Towards eliminating random I/O in hash joins. In *Proceedings of the Twelfth International Conference on Data Engineering* (pp. 422-429).

Loos, C. (2006). *E-health with mobile Grids: The Akogrimo heart monitoring and emergency scenario* [white paper].

Luján-Mora, S., Trujillo, J., & Song, I. Y. (2002). Multidimensional modeling with UML package diagrams. In *Proceedings of the 21st International Conference on Conceptual Modeling (ER 2002)* (pp. 199-213). Berlin, Germany: Springer Verlag.

Luján-Mora, S., Trujillo, J., & Song, I.-Y. (2006). A UML profile for multidimensional modeling in data warehouses. *Data & Knowledge Engineering, 59*(3), 725–769. doi:10.1016/j.datak.2005.11.004

Machine Learning Repository, U. C. I. (2007). Retrieved January 3, 2007, from http://www.ics.uci.edu/~mlearn/MLRepository.html

Maislinger, L. (2009). *Grafisches Werkzeug zur Integration von Data Marts* (in German). Linz, Austria: Johannes Kepler University.

Malan, D., Jones, T., Welsh, M., & Moulton, S. (2004). CodeBlue: An ad hoc sensor network infrastructure for emergency medical care. In *Proceedings of the International Workshop on Wearable and Implantable Body Sensor Networks, BSN 04*.

Malinowski, E., & Zimányi, E. (2006). Hierarchies in a multidimensional model: From conceptual modeling to logical representation. *Data & Knowledge Engineering, 59*(2), 348–377. doi:10.1016/j.datak.2005.08.003

Mangisengi, O., Essmayr, W., Huber, J., & Weippl, E. (2003). XML-based OLAP query processing in a federated data warehouse. In *Proceedings of the ICEIS*, (pp. 71-78).

Manku, G. S., & Motwani, R. (2002). Approximate frequent counts over data streams. In *Proceedings of the 28th International Conference on Very Large Database.*

Mannila, H., & Toivonen, H. (1996). Multiple uses of frequent sets and condensed representations. In *Proceedings of the KDD'96* (pp. 189-194). Portland, OR: AAAI Press.

Mansmann, S., & Scholl, M. H. (2007). Empowering the OLAP technology to support complex dimension hierarchies. *International Journal of Data Warehousing and Mining, 3*(4), 31–50.

Mansmann, S., & Scholl, M. H. (2008). Extending the multidimensional data model to handle complex data. *Journal of Computer Science and Engineering, 1*(2).

Mansmann, S., Neumuth, T., & Scholl, M. H. (2007). Multidimensional data modeling for business process analysis. In *ER 2007: Proceedings of the 26th International Conference on Conceptual Modeling* (pp. 23-38). Berlin, Germany: Springer.

Mansmann, S., Neumuth, T., & Scholl, M. H. (2007). OLAP technology for business process intelligence: Challenges and solutions. In *DaWaK'07: Proceedings of the 9th International Conference on Data Warehousing and Knowledge Discovery* (pp. 111-122). Berlin, Germany: Springer.

Marshall, C. C. (1998). Toward an ecology of hypertext annotation. In *Proceedings of the 9th ACM HYPERTEXT International Conference on Hypertext and Hypermedia*, Pittsburgh, PA, USA (pp. 40-49).

Matoušek, P. (2003). Verification of business process models (Doctoral dissertation, VŠB - Technická Univerzita Ostrava). In *Kolekce vysoko kolských kvalifikačních prací zpracovaných do konce 1. pololetí 2006.* VŠB-TUO.

Maxion, R. A., & Townsend, T. N. (2002). Masquerade detection using truncated command lines. In *DSN '02: Proceedings of the 2002 International Conference on Dependable Systems and Networks* (pp. 219-228). Washington, DC: IEEE Computer Society.

McAfee. (2008). *IntruShield network IPS application.* Retrieved from http://www.networkassociates.com/

Melville, P., Provost, F., Saar-Tsechansky, M., & Mooney, R. (2005). Economical active feature-value acquisition through expected utility estimation. In *Proceedings of the 1st International Workshop on Utility-Based Data Mining (UBDM'05)* (pp. 10-16).

Mendelzon, A. O., & Vaisman, A. A. (2000). Temporal queries in OLAP. In *Proceedings of the 26th International Conference on Very Large Data Bases (VLDB 00)*, Cairo, Egypt (pp. 242-253).

Microsoft. (2005). *Microsoft SQL server 2005 home page.* Retrieved November 2007, from http://www.microsoft.com/sql/

Mitchell, T. (1997). *Machine learning.* Boston, MA: McGraw Hill.

Model, F., Adorjn, P., et al. (2001). Feature selection for DNA methylation based cancer classification. In *Proceedings of the ISMB (Supplement of Bioinformatics)* (pp. 157-164).

Monteiro, R. S., Zimbrão, G., Schwarz, H., Mitschang, B., & Souza, J. M. (2005). Building the data warehouse of frequent itemsets in the DWFIST approach. In *Proceedings of the 15th Inernational. Symposium on Methodologies for Intelligent Systems*, Saratoga Springs, NY.

Moon, B., Jagadish, H., Faloutsos, C., & Saltz, J. (2001). Analysis of the clustering properties of the Hilbert space-filling curve. *Knowledge and Data Engineering, 13*(1), 124–141. doi:10.1109/69.908985

Morineau, A. (1984). Note sur la caractérisation statistique d'une classe et les valeurs-test. *Bulletin technique Centre Statistique Informatique Appliquées, 2*(1-2), 20-27.

Moron, M. J., Casilari, E., Luque, R., & Gazquez, J. A. (2005). A wireless monitoring system for pulse-oximetry sensors. In *Proceedings of the 2005 Systems Communications (ICW'05)* (pp. 79-84).

Morzy, T., & Wrembel, R. (2003). Modeling a multiversion data warehouse: A formal approach. In *Proceedings of the 5th International Conference on Enterprise Information Systems (ICEIS 03)*, Angers, France (pp. 120-127).

Morzy, T., & Wrembel, R. (2004). On querying versions of multiversion data warehouse. In *Proceedings of the 7th ACM International Workshop on DataWarehousing and OLAP (DOLAP 04)*, Washington, Columbia, USA (pp. 92-101).

Münchenberg, J., Brief, J., Raczkowsky, J., Wörn, H., Hassfeld, S., & Mühling, J. (2000). Operation planning of robot supported surgical interventions. In *IROS 2000*. Washington, DC: IEEE. *Proceedings of Intelligent Robots and Systems, 1*, 547–552.

Muth, P., Wodtke, D., Weißenfels, J., Weikum, G., & Kotz-Dittrich, A. (1998). Enterprise-wide workflow management based on state and activity charts. In *Workflow management systems and interoperability* (Vol. 164, pp. 281-303). Berlin, Germany: Springer.

National_Research_Council. (1997). *For the record: Protecting electronic health information*. Washington, DC: The National Academies Press.

Nestorov, S., & Jukic, N. (2003). Ad-hoc association-rule mining within the data warehouse. In *Proceedings of the 36th Hawaii International Conference on System Sciences (HICSS-36)*.

Neumuth, T., Schumann, S., Strauß, G., Jannin, P., Meixensberger, J., & Dietz, A. (2006). Visualization options for surgical workflows. *International Journal of Computer Assisted Radiology and Surgery, 1*(1), 438–440.

Neumuth, T., Strauß, G., Meixensberger, J., Lemke, H. U., & Burgert, O. (2006). Acquisition of process descriptions from surgical interventions. In *DEXA 2006: Proceedings of the 17th International Conference on Database and Expert Systems Applications* (pp. 602-611). Berlin, Germany: Springer.

Neumuth, T., Trantakis, C., Eckhardt, F., Dengl, M., Meixensberger, J., & Burgert, O. (2007). Supporting the analysis of intervention courses with surgical process models on the example of fourteen microsurgical lumbar discectomies. *International Journal of Computer Assisted Radiology and Surgery, 2*(Supplement 1), 436–438.

Ng, W., & Ravishankar, C. V. (1997). Block-oriented compression techniques for large statistical databases. *IEEE Transactions on Knowledge and Data Engineering, 9*(2), 314–328. doi:10.1109/69.591455

Nguyen, T. M., Schiefer, J., & Tjoa, A. M. (2005). Sense & response service architecture (SARESA): An approach towards a real-time business intelligence solution and its use for a fraud detection application. In *Proceedings of the 8th ACM international workshop on Data warehousing and OLAP (DOLAP '05)*, Bremen, Germany (pp. 77-86). New York: ACM Press.

NHS. (2005, June). *The spine*. Retrieved September 15, 2007, from http://www.connectingforhealth.nhs.uk/resources/comms_tkjune05/spine_factsheet.pdf

NHS. (2007). *Connecting for health*. Retrieved September 15, 2007, from http://www.connectingforhealth.nhs.uk/

Nudd, G. R., Kerbyson, D. J., Papaefstathiou, E., Perry, S. C., Harper, J. S., & Wilcox, D. V. (2000). Pace--a toolset for the performance prediction of parallel and distributed systems. *International Journal of High Performance Computing Applications, 14*(3), 228–251. doi:10.1177/109434200001400306

Núñez, M. (1991). The use of background knowledge in decision tree induction. *Machine Learning, 6*, 231–250.

Nuseibeh, B., & Easterbrook, S. (2000). Requirements engineering: A roadmap. In *Proceedings of the ICSE* (pp. 35-46). New York: ACM Press.

O'Neil, P., & Graefe, G. (1995). Multi-table joins through bitmapped join indices. *SIGMOD Record, 24*(3), 8–11. doi:10.1145/211990.212001

O'Neil, P., & Quass, D. (1997). Improved query performance with variant indexes. *SIGMOD Record, 26*(2), 38–49. doi:10.1145/253262.253268

Okabe, A., Boots, B., & Sugihara, K. (1992). *Spatial tessellations: Concepts and applications of Voronoi diagrams*. New York: John Wiley & Sons.

Open_Clinical. (2006). *Knowledge management for medical care*. Retrieved September 27, 2007, from http://www.openclinical.org/clinicalpathways.html

openEHR. (2007). *The openEHR foundation*. Retrieved September 27, 2007, from http://www.openehr.org

Özden, B., Ramaswamy, S., & Silberschatz, A. (1998). Cyclic association rules. In *Proceedings of the 14th International Conference on Data Engineering* (pp. 412-421).

Özsu, T. M., & Valduriez, P. (1999). *Principles of distributed database systems* (2nd ed.). Upper Sadle River, NJ: Prentice Hall.

Padoy, N., Horn, M., Feußner, H., Berger, M.-O., & Navab, N. (2007). Recovery of surgical workflow: A model-based approach. In *CARS 2007: Proceedings of the 21st International Congress and Exhibition on Computer Assisted Radiology and Surgery*. Berlin, Germany: Springer.

Pagel, B., Six, H., & Winter, M. (1995). Window query-optimal clustering of spatial objects. In *Proceedings of the fourteenth ACM SIGACT-SIGMOD-SIGART symposium on Principles of database systems* (pp. 86-94).

Palpanas, T., & Koudas, N. (2005). Using datacube aggregates for approximate querying and deviation detection. *IEEE Transactions on Knowledge and Data Engineering, 17*(11), 1–11. doi:10.1109/TKDE.2005.187

PANDA Project. (2005). Retrieved from http://dke.cti.gr/panda/

Papastefanatos, G., Kyzirakos, K., Vassiliadis, P., & Vassiliou, Y. (2005). Hecataeus: A framework for representing SQL constructs as graphs. In *Proceedings of the 20th International Workshop on Exploring Modeling Methods for Systems Analysis and Design (EMMSAD 05), in conjunction with the 17th International Conference on Advanced Information Systems Engineering (CAiSE 05)*, Porto, Portugal.

Papastefanatos, G., Vassiliadis, P., & Vassiliou, Y. (2006). Adaptive query formulation to handle database evolution. In *Proceedings of the 18th International Conference on Advanced Information Systems Engineering (CAiSE 06), CAiSE Forum*, Luxembourg, Grand-Duchy of Luxembourg.

Park, J. S., Chen, M. S., & Yu, P. S. (1995). An effective hash-based algorithm for mining association rules. In *Proceedings of the ACM SIGMOD International Conference on Management of Data*.

Patient Care Technologies®, I. (n.d.). *Well@home device*. Retrieved August 16, 2007, from http://www.ptct.com/wah_device.html

Paxson, V. (1999). Bro: A system for detecting network intruders in real-time. *Computer Networks, 31*(23-24), 2435–2463. doi:10.1016/S1389-1286(99)00112-7

Peano, G. (1890). Sur une courbe, qui remplit toute une aire plane. *Mathematische Annalen, 36*(1), 157–160. doi:10.1007/BF01199438

Pedersen, T. B., & Jensen, C. S. (2001). Multidimensional database technology. *IEEE Computer, 34*(12), 40–46.

Pedersen, T. B., Jensen, C. S., & Dyreson, C. E. (2001). A foundation for capturing and querying complex multidimensional data. *Information Systems, 26*(5), 383–423. doi:10.1016/S0306-4379(01)00023-0

Pei, J., Han, J., & Mao, R. (2000). CLOSET: An efficient algorithm for mining frequent closed itemsets. In *Proceedings Of the ACM SIGMOD Workshop on Research Issues in Data Mining and Knowledge Discovery*.

Peralta, V., Illarze, A., & Ruggia, R. (2003). On the applicability of rules to automate data warehouse logical design. In *Proceedings of the 15th International Conference on Advanced Information Systems Engineering (CAiSE 03), CAiSE Workshops*, Klagenfurt, Austria.

Perreault, L. E., & Metzger, J. B. (1999). A pragmatic framework for understanding clinical decision-support. *Journal of Healthcare Information Management, 13*(2), 5–21.

Phipps, C., & Davis, K. C. (2002). Automating data warehouse conceptual schema design and evaluation. In *DMDW'2002: Proceedings of the 4th International Workshop on Design and Management of Data Warehouses* (Vol. 58, pp. 23-32). Retrieved from http://www.CEUR-WS.org

PIPEDA. (2006). *Pipeda info*. Retrieved February 10, 2006, from http://www.pipedainfo.com/

Pommerening, K., & Reng, M. (2004). Secondary use of the EHR via pseudonymisation. *Studies in Health Technology and Informatics, 103*, 441–446.

Pourabbas, E., & Rafanelli, M. (2000). Hierarchies and relative operators in the OLAP environment. *SIGMOD Record, 29*(1), 32–37. doi:10.1145/344788.344799

Provost, F., & Fawcett, T. (2001). Robust classification for imprecise environments. *Machine Learning, 42*(3), 203–231. doi:10.1023/A:1007601015854

Pusara, M., & Brodley, C. E. (2004). User re-authentication via mouse movements. In *VizSEC/DMSEC '04: Proceedings of the 2004 ACM workshop on Visualization and data mining for computer security* (pp. 1-8). Washington, DC: ACM Press.

Qi, J., Jiang, Z., Zhang, G., Miao, R., & Su, Q. (2006). A surgical management information system driven by workflow. In *SOLI '06: Proceedings of the IEEE International Conference on Service Operations and Logistics, and Informatics* (pp. 1014-1018). Washington, DC: IEEE.

Quinlan, J. R. (1983). Learning efficient classification procedures and their application to chess end games. In *Machine Learning. An Artificial Intelligence Approach* (pp. 463-482).

Quinlan, J. R. (1993). *C4.5: Programs for machine learning*. San Francisco: Morgan Kaufmann Publishers.

Ramaswamy, S., Mahajan, S., & Silberschatz, A. (1998). On the discovery of interesting patterns in association rules. In *Proceedings of the VLDB Conference* (pp. 368-379).

Ranganathan, K., & Foster, I. (2004). Computation scheduling and data replication algorithms for data Grids. In *Grid Resource Management: State of the Art and Future Trends* (pp. 359-373). Amsterdam: Kluwer Academic Publishers.

Ravat, F., Teste, O., & Tournier, R. (2007). OLAP aggregation function for textual data warehouse. In *Proceedings of the 9th ICEIS International Conference on Enterprise Information Systems*, Funchal, Ravat, F., Teste, O., Tournier, R., & Zurfluh, G. (2008). Algebraic and graphic languages for OLAP manipulations. *International Journal of Data Warehousing and Mining, 4*(1), 17–46.

Ray, G., Haritsa, J. R., & Seshadri, S. (1995). Database compression: A performance enhancement tool. In *Proceedings of the International Conference on Management of Data (COMAD)*.

Regenstrief_Institute. (2007). Logical observation identifiers names and codes (LOINC®). Retrieved September 20, 2007, from http://www.regenstrief.org/medinformatics/loinc/

Reijers, H. A. (2003). *Design and control of workflow processes: Business process management for the service industry* (Vol. 2617). Berlin, Germany: Springer.

Repository, D. M. M. L. (2007). *Data mining and machine learning group website*. Retrieved January 31, 2007, from http://www.tlc2.uh.edu/dmmlg/Datasets

RESolutionLtd. (2007). *Resolution xCase™*. Retrieved September, 25, 2007, from http://www.xcase.com/

Rindfleisch, T. (1997). Privacy, information technology and healthcare. *Communications of the ACM, 40*(8), 92–100. doi:10.1145/257874.257896

Rissanen, J. (1976). Generalized Kraft inequality and arithmetic coding. *IBM Journal of Research and Development, 20*(3), 198–203.

Rizzi, S., & Golfarelli, M. (2006). What time is it in the data warehouse? In *Proceedings of the 8th International Conference on Data Warehousing and Knowledge Discovery (DaWaK 06)*, Krakow, Poland (LNCS 4081, pp. 134-144).

Rizzi, S., Abelló, A., Lechtenbörger, J., & Trujillo, J. (2006). Research in data warehouse modeling and design: Dead or alive? In I.-Y. Song & P. Vassiliadis (Eds.), *Proceedings of the DOLAP* (pp. 3-10). New York: ACM.

Roesch, M. (1999). Snort - lightweight intrusion detection for networks. In *LISA '99: Proceedings of the 13th USENIX conference on System administration* (pp. 229-238). Seattle, WA: USENIX Association.

Röhm, U., Böhm, K., & Schek, H. (2000). OLAP query routing and physical design in a database cluster. In *Proceedings of the 7th international Conference on Extending Database Technology: Advances in Database Technology* (LNCS 1777, pp. 254-268).

Rosenblatt, F. (1962). *Principles of neurodynamics: Perceptrons and the theory of brain mechanisms*. Washington: Spartan Books.

Rossgatterer, T. (2008). Entwicklung eines Query Prozessors in einem Föderierten Data Warehouse System (in German). Linz, Austria: Johannes Kepler University.

Rousseeuw, P. J. (1987). Silhouettes: A graphical aid to the interpretation and validation of cluster analysis. *International Journal of Computational and Applied Mathematics, 20*(1), 53–65. doi:10.1016/0377-0427(87)90125-7

Roussopoulos, N., & Leifker, D. (1985). Direct spatial search on pictorial databases using packed R-trees. *SIGMOD Record, 14*(4), 17–31. doi:10.1145/971699.318900

Roussopoulos, N., Kotidis, Y., & Roussopoulos, M. (1997). Cubetree: Organization of the bulk incremental updates on the data cube. In *Proceedings of the 1997 ACM SIGMOD international conference on Management of data* (pp. 89-99).

Sackett, D. L., Rosenberg, W. M., Gray, J. A., & Haynes, R. B. (1996). Evidence-based medicine: What it is and what it isn't. [editorial]. *BMJ (Clinical Research Ed.), 312*(7023), 71–72.

Sander, J., Ester, M., Kriegel, H.-P., & Xu, X. (1998). Density-based clustering in spatial databases: The algorithm GDBSCAN and its applications. *International Conference on Data Mining and Knowledge Discovery, 3*(3), 169-194.

Sapia, C., Blaschka, M., Höfling, G., & Dinter, B. (1999). Extending the E/R model for the multidimensional paradigm. In *ER 1998: Proceedings of the Workshops on Data Warehousing and Data Mining* (pp. 105-116).

Sarawagi, S. (1999). Explaining differences in multidimensional aggregates. In *Proceedings of the 25th International Conference On Very Large Databases (VLDB1999)*, Edinburgh, Scotland, UK.

Sarawagi, S. (2000). User-adaptive exploration of multidimensional data. In *Proceedings of the 26th International Conference On Very Large Databases (VLDB2000)*, Cairo, Egypt.

Sarawagi, S., & Sathe, G. (2000). i3: Intelligent, interactive investigaton of OLAP data cubes. In *Proceedings of the International Conference on Management of Data (SIGMOD)*.

Sarawagi, S., Agrawal, R., & Megiddo, N. (1998). Discovery-driven exploration of OLAP data cubes. In *Proceedings of the International Conference on Extending Database Technology (EDBT)*.

Sartipi, K., Yarmand, M. H., & Down, D. G. (2007). Mined-knowledge and decision support services in electronic health. In *Proceedings of the International Workshop on Systems Development in SOA Environments*. Washington, DC: IEEE Computer Society.

Sathe, G., & Sarawagi, S. (2001). Intelligent rollups in multidimensional OLAP data. In *Proceedings of the 27th International Conference on Very Large Databases (VLDB2001)*, Roma, Italy.

Schanner, A. (2006, September). *NÖ am weg zur elektronischen gesundheitsakte*. Retrieved September 20, 2007, from http://www.lknoe.at/

Schapire, R. E. (1990). The strength of weak learnability. Machine Learning, 5, 197–227.

Schuerenberg, B. K. (2003). Clearing the hurdles to decision support. *Health Data Management*.

SCIPHOX. (2006). *Dokumenten-kommunikation im gesundheitswesen*. Retrieved September 27, 2007, from http://sciphox.hl7.de/ueber_uns/flyerallgemein.pdf

Sellis, T., Roussopoulos, N., & Faloutsos, C. (1987). The R+-tree - a dynamic index for multidimensional objects. In *Proceedings of the 13ᵗʰ International Conference on Very Large Data Bases* (pp. 507-518).

Sequeira, K., & Zaki, M. (2002). ADMIT: Anomaly-based data mining for intrusions. In *Proceedings of the eighth ACM SIGKDD international conference on Knowledge discovery and data mining* (pp. 386-395). Edmonton, Canada: ACM Press.

Sharp, A., & McDermott, P. (2001). *Workflow modeling: Tools for process improvement and application development*. Norwood, MA: Artech House, Inc.

Shavlik, J., & Shavlik, M. (2004). Selection, combination, and evaluation of effective software sensors for detecting abnormal computer usage. In *KDD '04: Proceedings of the 2004 ACM SIGKDD international conference on Knowledge discovery and data mining* (pp. 276-285). Seattle, WA: ACM Press.

Shearer, C. (2000). The CRISP-DM model: The new blueprint for data mining. *Journal of Data Warehousing, 5*(4), 13–22.

Sheng, S., & Ling, C. X. (2005). Hybrid cost-sensitive decision tree. In *Proceedings of the 9ᵗʰ European Conference on Principles and Practice of Knowledge Discovery in Databases (PKDD)*.

Sheng, S., Ling, C. X., & Yang, Q. (2005). Simple test strategies for cost-sensitive decision trees. In *Proceedings of the 16ᵗʰ European Conference on Machine Learning (ECML)* (pp. 365-376).

Sheng, V. S., & Ling, C. X. (2006). Thresholding for making classifiers cost-sensitive. In *Proceedings of the 21ˢᵗ National Conference on Artificial Intelligence (AAAI-06)*.

Sheth, A. P., & Larson, J. A. (1990). Federated database systems for managing distributed, heterogeneous, and autonomous databases. *ACM Computing Surveys, 22*(3), 183–236. doi:10.1145/96602.96604

Sismanis, Y., Deligiannakis, A., Roussopoulos, N., & Kotidis, Y. (2002). Dwarf: Shrinking the PetaCube. In *Proceedings of the 2002 ACM SIGMOD Conference* (pp. 464-475).

Smith, J., Gounaris, A., Watson, P., Paton, N. W., Fernandes, A. A., & Sakellariou, R. (2002). Distributed query processing on the Grid. In *Proceedings of the Third international Workshop on Grid Computing* (LNCS 2536, pp. 279-290).

Smith, M. (2002, December, 5). Business process intelligence. *Intelligent Enterprise*. Retrieved from http://www.intelligententerprise.com/021205/601feat2 1.jhtml

SNOMED. (2007). *Systematized nomenclature of medicine (SNOMED)*. Retrieved September 20, 2007, from http://www.snomed.org/

Song, I.-Y., Rowen, W., Medsker, C., & Ewen, E. F. (2001). An analysis of many-to-many relationships between fact and dimension tables in dimensional modeling. In *DMDW'01: Proceedings of the 3ʳᵈ International Workshop on Design and Management of Data Warehouses* (Vol. 39, pp. 6.1-6.13). Retrieved from http://www.CEUR-WS.org

Spronk, R. (2007). *The spine, an English national programme*. Retrieved September 15, 2007, from http://www.ringholm.de/docs/00970_en.htm

SRS. (n.d.). *SRS glossary: Definitions of scoliosis terms*. Retrieved from from http://www.srs.org/patients/glossary.asp

Stefanovic, N., Han, J., & Koperski, K. (2000). Object-based selective materialization for efficient implementation of spatial data cubes. *IEEE Transactions on Knowledge and Data Engineering, 12*(6). doi:10.1109/69.895803

Stöhr, T., Märtens, H., & Rahm, E. (2000). Multi-dimensional database allocation for parallel data warehouses. In *Proceedings of the 26ᵗʰ international Conference on Very Large Data Bases* (pp. 273-284).

Stolba, N., & Schanner, A. (2007). eHealth integrator - clinical data integration in lower Austria. In *Proceedings of the Third International Conference on Computational Intelligence in Medicine and Healthcare (CIMED 2007)*, Plymouth, England.

Stolba, N., & Tjoa, A. M. (2006). An approach towards the fulfilment of security requirements for decision support systems in the field of evidence-based healthcare. In *Proceedings of the Knowledge Rights - Legal, Societal and Related Technological Aspects (KnowRight2006)*, Vienna; Austria (pp. 51-59). Austrian Computer Society.

Stolba, N., & Tjoa, A. M. (2006). The relevance of data warehousing and data mining in the field of evidence-based medicine to support healthcare decision making. In *Proceedings of the International Conference on Computer Science (ICCS 2006)*, Prague, Czech Republic.

Stolba, N., Banek, M., & Tjoa, A. M. (2006). The security issue of federated data warehouses in the area of evidence-based medicine. In *Proceedings of the First International Conference on Availability, Reliability and Security (ARES 2006)*, Vienna, Austria (pp. 329-339). Washington, DC: IEEE Computer Society Press.

Stolba, N., Nguyen, T. M., & Tjoa, A. M. (2007). Towards a data warehouse based approach to support healthcare knowledge development and sharing. In *Proceedings of the 2007 Information Resources Management Association (IRMA) International Conference*, Vancouver, Canada. Hershey, PA: Idea Group Publishing.

Stolba, N., Nguyen, T. M., & Tjoa, A. M. (2007). Towards sustainable decision-support system facilitating EBM. In *Proceedings of the 29th Annual International Conference of the IEEE Engineering in Medicine and Biology Society (EMBC 2007)*, Lyon, France.

Stolba, N., Tjoa, A. M., Mueck, T., & Banek, M. (2007). Federated data warehouse approach to support the national and international interoperability of healthcare information systems. In *Proceedings of the 15th European Conference on Information Systems (ECIS 2007)*, St. Gallen, Switzerland.

Strategis. (2005). *PIPEDA Overview*. Retrieved August, 29, 2007, from http://privacyforbusiness.ic.gc.ca/epic/site/pfb-cee.nsf/en/hc00005e.html

STRING-Kommission. (2000). *Rahmenbedingungen für ein logisches österreichisches Gesundheitsdatennetz (MAGDA-LENA), Teil 2: Hauptteil, Version 2.0.*

Sun, L., Hu, P., Goh, C., Hamadicharef, B., et al. (2006). Bioprofiling over Grid for early detection of dementia. In *Proceedings of the 1st international conference on Scalable information systems (INFOSCALE '06)*, Hong Kong. New York: ACM Press.

Sun, Q., Simon, D. R., Wang, Y.-M., Russell, W., Padmanabhan, V. N., & Qiu, L. (2002). Statistical identification of encrypted Web browsing traffic. In *Proceedings of the IEEE Symposium on Security and Privacy* (pp. 19-30). Washington, DC: IEEE Computer Society.

Surdeanu, M., Turmo, J., & Ageno, A. (2005). A hybrid unsupervised approach for document clustering. In *Proceedings of the International Conference of Eleventh ACM SIGKDD on Knowledge Discovery in Data Mining* (pp. 685-690).

Swets, J. A., Dawes, R. M., & Monahan, J. (2000). Better decisions through science. *Scientific American, 283*(4), 82–87.

SYBASE. (2007). *Elisa mobiilsideteenused. Customer success story.* Retrieved September 25, 2007, from http://www.sybase.com/detail?id=1040227

SYBASE. (2007). *China Telecom. Customer success story.* Retrieved September 25, 2007, from http://www.sybase.com/detail?id=1036771

Symmetry_Corporation. (2007). *ADAPT*. Retrieved September 19, 2007, from http://www.symcorp.com/

Tan, K. M., & Collie, B. S. (1997). Detection and classification of TCP/IP network services. In *ACSAC '97: Proceedings of the 13th Annual Computer Security Applications Conference* (p. 99). Washington, DC: IEEE Computer Society.

Tan, M., Steinbach, M., & Kumar, V. (Eds.). (2005). *Introduction to data mining*. Reading, MA: Addison Wesley.

Tan, W.-C. (2003). Containment of relational queries with annotation propagation. In *Proceedings of the 9th DBPL International Workshop on Database and Programming Languages*, Potsdam, Germany (LNCS 2921, pp. 37-53).

Tannenbaum, T., Wright, D., Miller, K., & Livny, M. (2002). Condor: A distributed job scheduler. In *Beowulf Cluster Computing with Linux* (pp. 307-350).

Taweel, A., Rector, A., Kalra, D., Rogers, R., et al. (2004). CLEF – joining up healthcare with clinical and post-genomic research. In *Proceedings of the HEALTH-CARE COMPUTING* (pp. 203-212). British Computer Society.

Teradata. (2003, October). *ONE GmbH. Industry solutions > communications.* Retrieved September 25, 2007, from http://www.teradata.com/t/pdf.aspx?a=83673&b=107494

Teradata. (2004, July). *Office Depot. Industry solutions > retail*. Retrieved September 25, 2007, from http://www.teradata.com/t/pdf.aspx?a=83673&b=166244

Teradata. (2006, April). *Teradata solutions methodology.* Retrieved September 24, 2007, from http://www.teradata.com/t/pdf.aspx?a=83673&b=92291

Theodoratos, D., & Bouzeghoub, M. (2000). A general framework for the view selection problem for data warehouse design and evolution. In *Proceedings of the 3rd ACM International Workshop on Data Warehousing and OLAP (DOLAP 00)*, Washington, Columbia, USA (pp. 1-8).

Theodoratos, D., & Sellis, T. (1999). Dynamic data warehouse design. In *Proceedings of DaWaK 1999*.

Theodoratos, D., & Sellis, T. (2000). Incremental design of a data warehouse. *Journal of Intelligent Information Systems, 15*(1), 7–27. doi:10.1023/A:1008773527263

Theodoratos, D., & Xu, W. (2004). Constructing search spaces for materialized view selection. In *Proceedings of the 7th ACM international workshop on Data warehousing and OLAP 2004*.

Theodoratos, D., Ligoudistianos, S., & Sellis, T. (2001). View selection for designing the global data warehouse. *Data & Knowledge Engineering, 11*(39).

Theodoridis, Y., & Sellis, T. (1996). A model for the prediction of R-tree performance. In *Proceedings of the 15th ACM Symposium on Principles of Database Systems (PODS)* (pp. 161-171).

Thomsen, E. (2002). *OLAP solutions -- building multidimensional information systems* (2nd ed.). New York: John Wiley & Sons.

Torlone, R., & Panella, I. (2005). Design and development of a tool for integrating heterogeneous data warehouses. In A. M. Tjoa, & J. Trujillo (Ed.), *Proceedings of the DaWaK* (pp. 105-114). Berlin, Germany: Springer.

Toussaint, G. (1980). The relative neighborhood graph of a finite planar set. In . *Proceedings of the International Conference of Pattern Recognition, 12*, 261–268. doi:10.1016/0031-3203(80)90066-7

Transaction processing council benchmarks. (2007). Retrieved November 2007, from http://www.tpc.org/

Tryfona, N., Busborg, F., & Christiansen, J. G. B. (1999). starER: A conceptual model for data warehouse design. In *DOLAP '99: Proceedings of the 2nd ACM International Workshop on Data Warehousing and OLAP* (pp. 3-8). New York: ACM Press.

Tsui, F.-C., Espino, J. U., Dato, V. M., & Gestelnad, P. H. (2003). Technical description of RODS: A real-time public health surveillance system. [JAMIA]. *Journal of the American Medical Informatics Association, 10*(5), 399–408. doi:10.1197/jamia.M1345

T-Systems. (2007). *Innovatives design.* Retrieved September 20, 2007, from http://www.t-systems.at/

Turney, P. (1995). Cost-sensitive classification: Empirical evaluation of a hybrid genetic decision tree induction algorithm. *Journal of Artificial Intelligence Research, 2*, 369–409.

Turney, P. (2000). Types of cost in inductive concept learning. In *Proceedings of the Workshop on Cost-Sensitive Learning at the 17th International Conference on Machine Learning (WCSL at ICML-2000)* (pp. 15-21).

Uni_Münster. (2001). *Medizincontrolling/DRG research group.* Retrieved September 20, 2007, from http://drg.uni-muenster.de/de/behandlungspfade/cpathways/clinicalpathways_reisebericht.php

Vassiliadis, P., & Sellis, T. K. (1999). A survey of logical models for OLAP databases. *SIGMOD Record, 28*(4), 64–69. doi:10.1145/344816.344869

Vassiliadis, P., Papastefanatos, G., Vassiliou, Y., & Sellis, T. (2007). Management of the evolution of database-centric information systems. In *Proceedings of the 1st International Workshop on Database Preservation (PresDB 07)*, Edinburgh, Scotland, UK.

Vetterli, T., Vaduva, A., & Staudt, M. (2000). Metadata standards for data warehousing: Open information model vs. common warehouse metamodel. *SIGMOD Record, 29*(3), 68–75. doi:10.1145/362084.362138

Viaene, S., Derrig, R. A., & Dedene, G. (2004). Cost-sensitive learning and decision making for Massachusetts PIP claim fraud data. *International Journal of Intelligent Systems, 19*, 1197–1215. doi:10.1002/int.20049

Vilalta, R., & Drissi, Y. (2002). A perspective view and survey of meta-learning. *Artificial Intelligence Review, 18*, 77–95. doi:10.1023/A:1019956318069

W3C. (2004, Febrauary 10). *OWL Web ontology language overview.* Retrieved July 18, 2007, from http://www.w3.org/TR/owl-features/

W3C. (2004). *Resource description framework (RDF).* Retrieved July 18, 2007, from http://www.w3.org/RDF/

W3C. (2007, June 14). *SPARQL query language for RDF.* Retrieved July, 18, 2007, from http://www.w3.org/TR/rdf-sparql-query/

Walters, T. (2003). *TELE.RING dialing up customized services.* Retrieved September 25, 2007, from http://www.teradata.com/t/page/114954/index.html

Walton, C. B., Dale, A. G., & Jenevein, R. M. (1991). A taxonomy and performance model of data skew effects in parallel joins. In *Proceedings of the 17th international Conference on Very Large Data Bases* (pp. 537-548).

Wang, J., Han, J., & Pei, J. (2006). Closed constrained gradient mining in retail databases. *IEEE Transactions on Knowledge and Data Engineering, 18*(6), 764–769. doi:10.1109/TKDE.2006.88

Wang, K., Tang, L., Han, J., & Liu, J. (2002). Top down FP-growth for association rule mining. In *Proceedings of the 6th Pacific Area Conference on Knowledge Discovery and Data Mining.*

Wehrle, P., Miquel, M., & Tchounikine, A. (2007). A Grid services-oriented architecture for efficient operation of distributed data warehouses on Globus. In *Proceedings of the 21st international Conference on Advanced Networking and Applications* (pp. 994-999). Washington, DC: IEEE Computer Society.

Westmann, T., Kossmann, D., Helmer, S., & Moerkotte, G. (2000). The implementation and performance of compressed databases. *SIGMOD Record, 29*(3), 55–67. doi:10.1145/362084.362137

WfMC. (1999, February). *Terminology & glossary.* Retrieved from http://www.wfmc.org/standards/docs/TC-1011 term glossary v3.pdf

White, B. (2004). *Making evidence-based medicine doable in everyday practice.* American Academy of Family Physicians, Family Practiced Management.

Wikimedia Commons. (2007). *Category: Vertebra.* Retrieved from http://commons.wikimedia.org/wiki/Category:Vertebra

Wikipedia. (2007). *Randomized controlled trial.* Retrieved July 18, 2007, from http://en.wikipedia.org/wiki/Randomized_controlled_trial

Wikipedia. (2007). *Data protection act.* Retrieved August 29, 2007, from http://en.wikipedia.org/wiki/Data_Protection_Act

Wikipedia. (2007). *Personal information protection and electronic documents act.* Retrieved August 29, 2007, from http://en.wikipedia.org/wiki/Personal_Information_Protection_and_Electronic_Documents_Act

Wikipedia. (2007). *Directive 95/46/EC on the protection of personal data.* Retrieved August, 29, 2007, from http://en.wikipedia.org/wiki/Directive_95/46/EC_on_the_protection_of_personal_data#Scope

Wikipedia. (2007). *Pseudonymity.* Retrieved August, 30, 2007, from http://en.wikipedia.org/wiki/Pseudonymity

Wikipedia. (2007). *Dementia*. Retrieved September 20, 2007, from http://en.wikipedia.org/wiki/Dementia

Wilcoxon, F. (1945). Individual comparisons by ranking methods. *Biometrics, 1*, 80–83. doi:10.2307/3001968

Witten, I. H., & Frank, E. (2005). *Data mining: Practical machine learning tools and techniques* (2nd ed.). San Francisco: Morgan Kaufmann.

Witten, I. H., & Frank, E. (2005). *Data mining: Practical machine learning tools and techniques*. San Francisco: Morgan Kaufmann.

Wright, C., Monrose, F., & Masson, G. M. (2004). HMM profiles for network traffic classification. In *VizSEC/DMSEC '04: Proceedings of the 2004 ACM workshop on Visualization and data mining for computer security* (pp. 9-15). Washington, DC: ACM Press.

Wu, M., & Buchmann, B. (1998). Encoded bitmap indexing for data warehouses. In *Proceedings of the Fourteenth International Conference on Data Engineering* (pp. 220-230).

Wu, T., Xin, D., & Han, J. (2008). ARCube: Supporting ranking aggregate queries in partially materialized data cubes. In *Proceedings of the International Conference on Management of Data (SIGMOD)*.

Wu, W., & Ozsoyoglu, Z. (2005). Rewriting XPath queries using materialized views. In *Proceedings of VLDB 2005*.

Wyatt, J. C., & Spiegelhalter, D. J. (1991). Field trials of medical decision-aids: potential problems and solutions. In *Proceedings of the Annual Symposium Computer Applications in Medical Care* (pp. 3-7).

Xin, D., Han, J., & Chang, K. (2007). Progressive and selective merge: Computing top-k with ad-hoc ranking functions. In *Proceedings of the International Conference on Management of Data (SIGMOD)*.

Xin, D., Han, J., Cheng, H., & Xiaolei, L. (2006). Answering top-k queries with multi-dimensional selections: The ranking cube approach. In *Proceedings of the International Conference on Very Large Databases (VLDB)*.

Xin, D., Han, J., Yan, X., & Cheng, H. (2005). Mining compressed frequent-pattern sets. In *Proceedings of the International Conference on Very Large Data Bases (VLDB'05)*.

Xin, D., Shao, Z., Han, J., & Liu, H. (2006). C-cubing: Efficient computation of closed cubes by aggregation-based checking. In *Proceedings of the 22nd International Conference on Data Engineering (ICDE)*.

Xing, E. P., Jordan, M. I., et al. (2001). Feature selection for high-dimensional genomic microarray data. In *Proceedings of the ICML* (pp. 601-608).

Xiong, M., Fang, X., et al. (2001). Biomarker identification by feature wrappers. Genome Research, 11(11), 1878–1887. PubMed

Yagoubi, B., & Slimani, Y. (2007). Task load balancing strategy for Grid computing. *Journal of Computer Science, 3*(3), 186–194.

Yang, J., Karlapalem, K., & Li, Q. (1997). Algorithms for materialized view design in data warehousing environment. In *Proceedings of the Intl. Conference on Very Large Database Systems 1997*.

Yang, Y., & Pedersen, J. O. (1997). A comparative study on feature selection in text categorization. In *Proceedings of the ICML* (pp. 412-420).

Yu, L., & Liu, H. (2003). Feature selection for high-dimensional data: A fast correlation-based filter solution. In *Proceedings of the ICML* (pp. 856-863).

Yu, L., & Liu, H. (2004). Redundancy based feature selection for microarray data. In *Proceedings of the SIGKDD* (pp. 737-742).

Yu, S., Atluri, V., & Adam, N. (2005). Selective view materialization in a spatial data warehouse. In *Proceedings of Data Warehouse and Knowledge Discovery (DaWak 2005)*.

Zadrozny, B., Langford, J., & Abe, N. (2003). Cost-sensitive learning by cost-proportionate example weighting. In *Proceedings of the 3rd IEEE International Conference on Data Mining (ICDM'03)*.

Zhang, S., Qin, Z., Ling, C. X., & Sheng, S. (2005). "Missing is useful": Missing values in cost-sensitive decision trees. *IEEE Transactions on Knowledge and Data Engineering, 17*(12), 1689–1693. doi:10.1109/TKDE.2005.188

Zhong, S., & Ghosh, J. (2003). A unified framework for model-based clustering. *International Journal of Machine Learning Research, 4*, 1001–1037. doi:10.1162/jmlr.2003.4.6.1001

Zhu, H. (1998). *On-line analytical mining of association rules.* Unpublished doctoral dissertation, Simon Fraser University, Burnaby, British Columbia V5A 1S6, Canada.

Ziv, J., & Lempel, A. (1977). A universal algorithm for sequential data compression. *IEEE Transactions on Information Theory, 23*(3), 337–343. doi:10.1109/TIT.1977.1055714

Zubek, V. B., & Dietterich, T. G. (2002). Pruning improves heuristic search for cost-sensitive learning. In *Proceedings of the 19ᵗʰ International Conference of Machine Learning (ICML)* (pp. 27-35).

About the Contributors

Tho Manh Nguyen received his PhD in Information Systems from the Vienna University of Technology in September 2005 and currently keeps a Postdoctoral Research Fellowship. He has been awarded Microsoft Student Travel Awards, IBM Europe Student Event Recognition, and Outstanding Students Award, Best Paper Award at the 4th IEEE International Conference On Computer Sciences Research; Innovation And Vision For The Future (RIVF 2006), Best Paper Award at the Information Resources Management Association (IRMA) International Conference in 2007. He is PC member and organizer numbers of international conferences and workshops such as DaWaK, DAWAM, ARES, SIIK, CONFENIS etc and has several publications in international conferences and journals in the field of data warehousing and knowledge discovery. His research areas of interest include Data Warehousing, Data Mining and Knowledge Discovery, Business Intelligence Systems, Grid-based Knowledge discovery, Service-Oriented Computing, Ontology and Semantic Management.

* * *

Nabil R. Adam is a professor of Computers and Information Systems, and the founding director of the Rutgers University Center for Information Management, Integration and Connectivity (CIMIC). He received his Ph.D. in Engineering from Columbia University. Dr. Adam has published numerous technical papers in such journals as IEEE Transactions on Software Engineering, IEEE Transactions on Knowledge and Data Engineering, ACM Computing Surveys, Communications of the ACM, Journal of Management Information Systems, and International Journal of Intelligent and Cooperative Information Systems. Dr. Adam is the co-founder and the Executive-Editor-in-Chief of the International Journal on Digital Libraries and serves on the editorial board of a number of journals including Journal of Management Information Systems, the Journal of Electronic Commerce, and the Journal of Electronic Commerce Research and Applications.

Ronnie Alves received his PhD in Computer Science from the University of Minho at Braga, Portugal, in April 2008. While pursuing his PhD studies, he also served as a Visiting Researcher in the Data Mining Group (at DAIS Lab in the University of Illinois at Urbana-Champaign, USA) led by Professor Dr. Jiawei Han and in the Bioinformatics Research Group (at Pablo de Olavide University - Sevilla, Spain) led by prof. Dr. Jesus Aguilar. He has also served in several program committees of international conferences and workshops. His research interests include databases, data mining, data cubing, and its application on business and scientific data analysis. Currently he is a post-doc Researcher in the Virtual Biology Lab at the Institute of Signaling Developmental Biology and Cancer at Nice.

Copyright © 2010, IGI Global, distributing in print or electronic forms without written permission of IGI Global is prohibited.

Vijayalakshmi Atluri is currently a professor in the Management Science and Information Systems Department, and research director for the Center for Information Management, Integration and Connectivity (CIMIC) at Rutgers University, NJ, USA. She received her B.Tech. in Electronics and Communications Engineering from Jawaharlal Nehru Technological University, Kakinada, India, M.Tech. in Electronics and Communications Engineering from Indian Institute of Technology, Kharagpur, India, and PhD in Information Technology from George Mason University, USA. Dr. Atluri's research interests include information systems security, databases, workflow management, spatial databases, multimedia and distributed systems. She has published over 100 technical papers in the refereed journals and conference proceedings in these areas and is the co-author of the book, Multilevel Secure Transaction Processing, Kluwer Academic Publishers (1999).

Orlando Belo is an associate professor in the Department of Informatics at Minho University, Portugal. He is also a member of the Computer Science and Technology Center in the same university, working in areas like Data Warehousing Systems, OLAP, and Data Mining. His main research topics are related with data warehouse design, implementation and tuning, ETL services, and distributed multidimensional structures processing. During the last few years he was involved with several projects in the decision support systems area designing and implementing computational platforms for specific applications like fraud detection and control in telecommunication systems, data quality evaluation, and ETL systems for industrial data warehousing systems.

Fadila Bentayeb has been an associate professor at the University of Lyon 2, France since 2001. She is a member of the Decision Support Databases research group within the ERIC laboratory. She received her PhD degree in computer science from the University of Orléans, France in 1998. Her current research interests regard database management systems, including the integration of data mining techniques into DBMSs and data warehouse design, with a special interest for schema evolution, analysis personalization, XML and complex data warehousing, benchmarking and optimisation techniques.

Stefan Berger is a research and teaching assistant at the Department of Business Informatics – Data and Knowledge Engineering, University of Linz, Austria and PhD student in Computer Science. He received his Magister degree from the University of Linz in 2004. His research activity is focused on data warehousing, conceptual modeling of databases and data warehouses, distributed OLAP query processing and integration of heterogeneous multi-dimensional data.

Omar Boussaid is a full professor in computer science at the School of Economics and Management of the University of Lyon 2, France. He received his PhD degree in computer science from the University of Lyon 1, France in 1988. Since 1995, he is the director of the Master Computer Science Engineering for Decision and Economic Evaluation of the University of Lyon 2. He is a head of the Decision Support Databases research group within the ERIC Laboratory. His main research subjects are data warehousing, multidimensional databases and OLAP. His current research concerns complex data warehousing and mining, XML warehousing, combining OLAP and data mining, and the use of ontologies within complex data warehousing.

Pavel Bernard Brazdil got his PhD degree from the University of Edinburgh in 1981. Since 1998 he is full professor at Faculty of Economics. Currently he is the Coordinator of R&D Unit LIAAD (earlier known as group NIAAD of LIAAC, founded in 1988). Pavel Brazdil is known for his activities in Machine Learning, Data Mining, Metalearning, Adaptive Modeling, Text Mining and various applications in Economic Modeling, Medicine and Bioinformatics. He has participated in two international projects and acted as a technical coordinator of one of them (METAL). Besides he has participated in various international research networks. Pavel Brazdil has supervised 9 PhD students all of whom have completed their studies while 2 others are in progress. He has organized more than 10 international conferences / workshops and participated in many program committees (including 14 different editions of ECML). He is a co-author of one book published in 2008 (on Metalearning) and has (co-)edited 4 other books published by major publisher. Besides he has published more than 120 articles. Out of these 16 are referenced on ISI and 28 on ISI Proceedings / DBLP. The publications have attracted more than 110 citations.

Oliver Burgert is head of the research group "Scientific Methods" at the Innovation Center Computer Assisted Surgery (ICCAS), which is part of the medical faculty of the University of Leipzig. He studied Computer Science at the University of Karlsruhe (TH), Germany. After that he worked as a research scientist in the "Collaborative Research Fund: Information Technology in Medicine" (SFB 414), and other medical simulation and planning projects in CMF, heart, and neurosurgery. His research at ICCAS includes modular surgical assist systems (Therapy Imaging and Model Management System (TIMMS)), surgical workflows, ontologies, and Surgical DICOM. His overall aim is to help surgeons to operate more safely and with higher efficiency by using modern informatics techniques.

Guillaume Cabanac is a PhD candidate in Computer Science, Université de Toulouse 3 – Paul Sabatier, France. He is part of the Information Systems team at the Toulouse Computer Science Laboratory (IRIT, UMR 5505 CNRS). His research mainly concerns how people daily use digital documents in organizations. Guillaume's recent works addressed how the common annotation practice may unify and improve organizational members' document-related activities. For more information, please visit http://www.irit.fr/~Guillaume.Cabanac.

Véronique Cariou is an assistant professor at the Statistics, Sensometrics and Chemometrics Laboratory from ENITIAA, a National Graduate Institute For Food Industries. She received a PhD in computer sciences in 1998 at the University of Paris-IX Dauphine where she was involved in the European project SODAS on symbolic data analysis. She has worked at Electricité de France Research and Development Centre as a research engineer for five years. Her research interests include multidimensional databases and statistics with applications in food industries, especially sensometrics and chemometrics.

Oner Ulvi Celepcikay got his bachelor degree in Electrical Engineering in 1997 from Istanbul University, Istanbul, Turkey. He is a PhD candidate in the Computer Science Department at University of Houston where he also acquired his MS Degree in 2003. He had worked at University of Houston Educational Technology Outreach (ETO) Department from 2003 to 2005. He has been the president of Cosmos Foundation which opens and operates charter schools and he now oversees the operation of foundation's current 19 schools. He has worked on various projects and developed number of Technology and GT courses. He has published number of papers in his research fields including cluster analysis, multivariate statistical analysis, and spatial data mining. He served as session chair in International Conference on Multivariate Statistical Modeling & High Dimensional Data Mining in 2008 in Kayseri, Turkey and has been serving as as a non-pc reviewer in many conferences.

Chun-Sheng Chen was born in 1974 in Taiwan. He earned his master degree in Mining, Metallurgy and Materials Science at National Cheng Kung University (Taiwan) in 1998. He received his master degree in computer science in 2005 and is now a PhD student in computer science at the University of Houston, Texas. His research interests include data mining and knowledge discovery in spatial dataset, cluster analysis machine learning and artificial intelligence. He has published papers in his area of interest and served as a reviewer for many scientific conferences. He also served as a volunteer staff for the 2005 IEEE ICDM Conference, November 2005, Houston, Texas.

Max Chevalier is an associate professor in computer science at the University Paul Sabatier of Toulouse III (France) since 2002. His research addresses user centered approaches in information systems like personalization, recommender systems, visual information retrieval interface and social computing. He conducts research on these topics at the Toulouse Computing Research Laboratory (IRIT - UMR 5505). For more information, please visit http://www.irit.fr/~Max.Chevalier.

Jiyeon Choo graduated with a bachelor degree in Home Economics at Duksung Women's University in Seoul, Korea. She graduated with a master degree in Computer Science at the University of Houston in 2007. She served as a researcher for the Data Mining & Machine Learning Group at the University of Houston. She has published works in the area of data mining, cluster analysis, and knowledge discovery. She has worked as a Software developer for three years in Seoul, Korea. Currently, she is working as a Software Engineer at Hewlett-Packard.

Rogério Luís de Carvalho Costa is a PhD student at the University of Coimbra – Portugal. He teaches undergraduate curricula at Pontifícia Universidade Católica do Rio de Janeiro (PUC-Rio) - Brazil. His research interests include data warehousing, parallel and distributed database systems, self-tuning and bioinformatics.

Altamiro Costa-Pereira, MD, got the PhD degree from the University of Dundee in 1993. Currently he is full professor at FMUP and director of the Department of Biostatistics and Medical Informatics. He is also coordinator of the research unit CINTESIS and director of two master programs (Master in Medical Informatics, Master in Evidence and Decision Making in Healthcare) and one PhD program (Doctoral Program in Clinical and Health Services Research). Since 1999, he has been an independent expert, acting as evaluator, at the European Commission. He is author of more than two hundred publications, including fifty indexed by the ISI, which attracted more the 300 citations.

Jérôme Cubillé is a research engineer at the Division Research and Development of Electricité de France. He is a survey statistician, graduated from ENSAE - Paris Tech (National School of Statistics and Economic Administration). He is an expert in sample designs and multivariate data analysis. He has been working for thirteen years, applying his skills in a wide range of studies, most related to electricity residential sector knowledge. He also teaches in vocational courses as in prestigious university-level French colleges.

David Cueva received a Masters in Computer Science degree in 2007 from Concordia University in Montreal, Canada. In his Masters thesis he investigated a datawarehouse compression algorithm using an n-dimensional Hilbert curve. He had previously obtained an Engineering in Informatics Systems from Escuela Politecnica Nacional in Quito, Ecuador. His research interests include datawarehousing, database architecture and parallel algorithms. David currently works at SAP Labs Canada, an advanced development facility of SAP AG, the third largest software company in the world.

Manoranjan Dash is at present an assistant professor in School of Computer Engineering, Nanyang Technological University, Singapore. His main research topic are machine learning and data mining with their applications in multimedia, microarray gene expression data, and streaming data. He has more than 40 refereed papers in journal and conferences in major conferences and journals, such as KDD, DMKD, AI, ICDM, ACM Transactions on Multimedia Computing Communications and Applications, ACM Journal of Data and Information Quality, IEEE Transactions on SMC, Pattern Recognition, and ECML. He has been in the program committee of major conferences such as KDD, AAAI, and SIAM SDM. He is an editorial board member of International Journal of Theoretical and Applied Computer Science (IJTACS).

Jano Moreira de Souza is a professor of Computer Science at the Graduate School of Engineering (COPPE) and Mathematics Institute of the Federal University of Rio de Janeiro (UFRJ) (Brazil). His area of specialization is Databases, and he is involved in research in fields such as CSCW, Decision Support Systems, Knowledge Management and GIS. Professor de Souza received his bachelor's degree in Mechanical Engineering (1974) and his master's degree (1978) in System Engineering from the Federal University of Rio de Janeiro (Brazil), and his PhD in Information Systems (1986) from the University of East Anglia (England).

Christian Derquenne is a senior researcher at Electricité de France R&D. He received PhD in Statistics. His main researches are Categorical Data Analysis, Generalized Linear Models, Structural Equations Modelling, Bayesian Networks, Clustering Methods, Robust Regression, Combining Data from Different Sources Methods, Goodness of Fit Tests. He wrote more than sixty publications and congress communications. His actual main applications are on customers satisfaction and loyalty, forecasting of phone calls. He is also a Statistics teacher in different Statistical Schools and Universities. Vice-Secretary of the Statistical French Society, Elected Member of the International Statistical Institute (ISI), President of the French Members Group of ISI, expert for the French Research Agency and Member of Scientific Council of the KXEN Society.

Yuan-Bin Don received the BS and MS degrees in information and computer education from National Taiwan Normal University, Taiwan, Republic of China, in 2004 and 2006, respectively. He joined Info Explorer Inc. in 2008 as an associate engineer. His current work is about MMCS system and IBM Informix.

Todd Eavis is an assistant professor at Concordia University in Montreal, Canada. He received his PhD from Dalhousie University in Halfiax and was a NSERC Postdoctoral Fellow at Carelton University in Ottawa. His research interests include Online Analytical Processing, multi-dimendional indexing, parallel databases, and DBMS architectures. Dr. Eavis currently holds a Concordia University Research Chair in Parallel Data Warehousing.

Christoph F. Eick received a PhD degree from the University of Karlsruhe in Germany in 1984. Currently, he is an associate professor in the Department of Computer Science at the University of Houston. His research interests include data mining, machine learning, evolutionary computing, knowledge-based systems, databases and artificial intelligence. He published more than 90 refereed papers in these areas. He currently serves on the program committees of various data mining conferences.

Cécile Favre is currently a lecturer in computer science at the University of Lyon 2, France. She is a member of the Decision Support Databases research group within the ERIC laboratory. She received her MSc degree in Knowledge Discovery in Databases in 2003 and her PhD in Computer Science in 2007, both from the University of Lyon 2. After working on integrating data mining techniques into DBMSs, her current research interests now relate to data warehouse design and evolution, especially analysis personalization and integration of users' knowledge in data warehouses.

Alberto Freitas received the MSc and PhD degrees from the University of Porto (Portugal) in 1998 and 2007, respectively. He is member of the Faculty of Medicine of University of Porto (FMUP), in the Department of Biostatistics and Medical Informatics. He is also member of CINTESIS (Centre for Research in Health Technologies and Information Systems), a research unit recognized and supported by the Portuguese Foundation for Science and Technology (FCT) [POCTI/0753/2004] and hosted by FMUP. His research interests include health information systems and data mining.

Pedro Furtado is assistant professor and senior researcher at the University of Coimbra, where he teaches both undergraduate and postgraduate curricula. His research interests include data warehousing, parallel and distributed database systems, performance and scalability, distributed data intensive systems. He received a PhD in computer science from the University of Coimbra - Portugal in 2000.

Matthew Gebski recently completed his PhD at the University of New South Wales and National ICT Australia as a member of data base group, where he was on postgraduate and research awards. His interests are in data mining with a particular focus on outlier and anomaly detection for security related tasks such as fraud detection and network security. He is also interested in information retrieval and document management. Outside of work, he likes water fights and skiing.

Christian Giusti was born in 1978 in Udine (Italy). He graduated magna cum laude in Computer Science in 2004 and now he is a PhD Candidate in Computer Science at University of Udine. His research interests include computer vision and image recognition, image processing, pattern classification, neural networks, cluster analysis and everything that is concerned with artificial intelligence. He also performs activity of reviewer for many scientific journals and conferences.

Vivekanand Gopalkrishnan has over 14 years of research and development experience in industry and academia. He is currently an assistant professor in School of Computer Engineering at Nanyang Technological University, Singapore. His work is broadly in databases, datawarehousing and currently in data mining. His present focus is in real-time data warehousing, and in applying data mining techniques in three main domains: media (semantics, querying and indexing), finance (portfolio management, derivatives pricing and risk assessment), and biology (comparative genomics and microscopy images). Dr.

Vivekanand is an Associate Editor for The International Journal of Distance Education Technologies (JDET), and has been a PC member of several conferences including WISE and EDOC.

Sabine Goutier is a research engineer at the Division Research and Development of Electricité de France, the French energy supplier and electricity producer. She received a joined Master in Statistics and Econometrics in 2001 at Universities of Toulouse 1 and 3. Her research activities are now focused on long-run risk, and flexibility introduction (wind, energy storage, demand response) in generation fleet including information systems and multidimensional databases. She also teaches Data Mining methods at Universities of Paris 7 and Paris 2.

Françoise Guisnel is a research engineer at Electricité de France R&D since 1982. She graduated from Ecole des Mines de Paris in 1982. She has first worked on different projects concerned by numerical simulation in acoustics and mechanics, using finite element methods and studying mesh algorithms. She spent some years working on virtual reality simulators for the maintenance of nuclear plants. Since 2003, she has managed different EDF R&D projects dealing with business intelligence and information systems (data warehouses, OLAP, OLAP mining…). She is currently working in the EDF R&D project dealing with data streams, to handle the evolutions of information systems expected in EDF.

Jiawei Han is a professor in the Department of Computer Science at the University of Illinois. He has been working on research into data mining, data warehousing, stream data mining, spatiotemporal and multimedia data mining, biological data mining, social network analysis, text and Web mining, and software bug mining, with over 350 conference and journal publications. He has chaired or served in over 100 program committees of international conferences and workshops. Jiawei has received three IBM Faculty Awards, the Outstanding Contribution Award at the 2002 International Conference on Data Mining, ACM Service Award (1999) and ACM SIGKDD Innovation Award (2004), and IEEE Computer Society Technical Achievement Award (2005). He is an ACM Fellow (2004). His book "Data Mining: Concepts and Techniques" (Morgan Kaufmann) has been used popularly as a textbook.

Rachsuda Jiamthapthaksin graduated her bachelor degree in Computer Science in 1997 and graduated with Honors in master degree in Computer Science, Dean's Prize for Outstanding Performance, in 1999 from Assumption University, Bangkok, Thailand. She was a faculty in Computer Science department, Assumption University during 1997-2004. She is now a PhD candidate in Computer Science at University of Houston, Texas. She has published papers in the area of her research interests including intelligent agents, fuzzy systems, cluster analysis, data mining and knowledge discovery. She has served as a non-pc reviewer in many conferences and served as a volunteer staff in an organization of the 2005 IEEE ICDM Conference, November 2005, Houston, Texas.

Henri Klajnmic is a research engineer at Electricité de France R&D since 1974 in the Commercial Innovation and Market Analysis Department. He studied computing science at the National Polytechnical Institute of Toulouse and applied statistics and mathematics at the University Pierre and Marie Curie in Paris. His main interests are statistical modelling, extreme value analysis and data mining.

Jia-Ling Koh received the BS degree in computer science from National Chiao-Tung University, Taiwan, Republic of China, in 1991, and the MS and PhD degrees in computer science from the National

Hsing-Hua University, Taiwan, in 1993 and 1997, respectively. She joined National Taiwan Normal University, Taiwan, as an assistant professor in 1997, and became an associate professor in the department of computer science and information engineering in 2001. Her current research interests include multimedia information retrieval and data mining.

Svetlana Mansmann received a Diploma in International Economic Relations from the Belarusian State University, Belarus, in 1999, and the M.Sc. degree in information engineering from the University of Konstanz (Germany) in 2003. She recently completed a Ph.D. degree in computer science, also at the University of Konstanz. She is currently working as a research assistant in the Databases and Information Systems Group at the University of Konstanz. Previous research fields are decision support systems and e-Government. Recent publications focus on data warehousing and OLAP, multidimensional data modeling, business process intelligence, and visual exploration of multidimensional data. She received a Best Paper Award of ICECE 2005 (International Conference on Engineering and Computer Education) and Top 10 Best Papers Award of DaWaK 2006 and DaWaK 2007 (International Conference on Data Warehousing and Knowledge Discovery). Mrs. Mansmann has been an associate member of the Graduate College "Explorative Analysis and Exploration of Large Information Spaces" at the University of Konstanz (Germany) since 2004.

Bernhard Mitschang is a professor for Database and Information Systems at Stuttgart University. He received the Ph.D. degree (Dr.-Ing.) in Computer Science from the University of Kaiserslautern in 1988. From 1994 to 1998 he was a professor at the Technische Universität München. From 1989 to 1990 he was on leave to IBM Almaden Research Center, San Jose, CA as a visiting scientist. His research interests are database management systems, including object-oriented support, semantic modelling, query languages, optimization and parallelism, and application-oriented areas like middleware and component technology, engineering information systems, and knowledge base management systems.

Rodrigo Salvador Monteiro is a researcher at the Federal University of Rio de Janeiro (Brazil). His area of specialization is Databases, and he is involved in research in fields such Spatial Databases, GIS, Data Mining, Data Warehouse and MDA. Dr. Monteiro received his bachelor's degree (2000) in Computer Science and his master's degree (2001) in Computer Science from the Federal University of Rio de Janeiro (Brazil). In 2004/2005 Dr. Monteiro was a Ph.D. Sandwich student at the University of Stuttgart (Germany) and received his Ph.D. (2005) in Computer Science from the Graduate School of Engineering (COPPE) at the Federal University of Rio de Janeiro (Brazil).

Thomas Neumuth is group leader of the working group, "Workflow and Knowledge Management" at the Innovation Center Computer Assisted Surgery (ICCAS) at the University of Leipzig, Germany. From 1997 to 2004 he studied Electrical Engineering Management and Automation Engineering at the University of Applied Sciences Leipzig. From 2005 to 2007, he was research fellow for the research field of Surgical Workflows. Since 2007, he is the leader of the group Workflow and Knowledge Management and has submitted his PhD thesis on Surgical Process Modeling in Medical Engineering. ICCAS is an interdisciplinary cooperation between the disciplines surgery, computer science and medical engineering. ICCAS focuses on outstanding and internationally competitive research in Computer Assisted Surgery and aims to attract young scientists as well as to transfer the innovative research findings into companies to create innovative products for the operating room of the future.

Alex Penev is currently a PhD student at the University of New South Wales, Australia, and received a BE (Software Engineering) there in 2005. For the past few years he has been part of the database group at NICTA, a large national research and commercialisation centre that has partnerships with many universities and provides resources to PhD students. Alex's interests include information retrieval and data mining, particularly any web-related problems or technologies related to those fields.

Franck Ravat obtained his PhD in computer science from the University of Toulouse III in France, with a thesis on distributed databases in 1996. He also obtained a habilitation on decision support systems based on data warehouses and multidimensional data marts. His current research interests include all aspects of data warehouse architecture, design and languages. His publications appear in major national and international conferences or journals, for which he also serves as reviewer. Since 1997, Dr. Franck Ravat is a permanent Associate Professor at the University of Toulouse I and director of the Master IGSI, which is specialized on information systems. He currently teaches Information Systems, Databases, Decision Support System architectures and Data Warehousing.

Joel Ribeiro is a MSc student in the Department of Informatics at the University of Minho, Portugal. He has been finishing his thesis based in Top-K Multidimensional Gradients. While pursuing his Master degree, he had also worked on research and industrial projects related to OLAP and data mining, having published a few papers on international conferences and workshops. In a near future, he will be a PhD candidate at the Eindhoven University of Technology, conducting his research in the Process Mining area

Matthias Röger received his M.Sc. degree (Dipl.-Inform. (FH)) in business informatics from the University of Applied Sciences in Konstanz (Germany) in 2005 and a MSc degree in information engineering from the University of Konstanz (Germany) in 2008. During his studies he worked on the project "Data Warehouse for Surgical Workflow Analysis" as a student assistant in the Databases and Information Systems Group at the University of Konstanz, which also became the topic of his Master thesis. Since 2008, he works as a Consultant for Business Intelligence at the NOVO Business Consultants AG, Berne, Switzerland.

Marc H. Scholl received his MSc degree (Dipl.-Inform.) and PhD degree (Dr.-Ing.) both in computer science from the Technical University of Darmstadt, Germany, in 1982 and 1988, respectively. He is currently a full Professor of Computer Science at the University of Konstanz, Germany. During the years 1998-2004 he served as Vice-President of the University, responsible for the information infrastructure. Previous positions held include an associate professorship at the University of Ulm, Germany (1992-94) and an assistant professorship ("Oberassistent") at ETH Zurich, Switzerland (1989-92). Current research topics include XML and databases, query processing & optimization, DBMS architecture, digital libraries, data warehouse applications and interfaces for decision support and e-Government applications. Prof. Scholl is a member of IEEE Computer Society, ACM and ACM SIGMOD, EDBT (currently EDBT President), the ICDT Council, and the German Computer Society (GI).

Michael Schrefl received his Dipl.-Ing. degree and his Doctorate from Vienna University of Technology, Vienna, Austria, in 1983 and 1988, respectively. During 1983–1984 he studied at Vanderbilt University, USA, as a Fulbright scholar. From 1985 to 1992 he was with Vienna University of Technology. During

1987–1988, he was on leave at GMD IPSI, Darmstadt, where he worked on the integration of heterogeneous databases. He was appointed Professor of Information Systems at Johannes Kepler University of Linz, Austria, in 1992, and professor in Computer and Information Science at University of South Australia in 1998. He currently leads the Department of Business Informatics – Data and Knowledge Engineering at University of Linz, with projects in data warehousing, workflow management, and web engineering. M. Schrefl is a member of ACM and IEEE Computer Society.

Holger Schwarz received his PhD in Computer Science from the Universität Stuttgart in 2002 where he currently works as senior researcher and lecturer. His main scientific interests cover data warehousing, data mining and online analytic processing as well as optimization technologies for database management systems and data-intensive workflows.

Shu-Ning Shih received the BS degree in computer science from Soochow University, Taiwan, Republic of China, in 2002 and the MS degree in information and computer education from National Taiwan Normal University, Taiwan, in 2005. She works in FIH Co. Ltd now and her main task is to do researches on mobile terminal products.

Nevena Stolba received her PhD in Information Systems from Vienna University of Technology in 2007. She has several publications in international conferences in the field of data warehousing and knowledge discovery. Currently, she is working as a data warehouse specialist with Teradata Austria. She has been awarded Best Paper Award at Information Resources Management Association (IRMA) International Conference in 2007 and Consulting Excellence Award of the NCR in 2000. Her research area of interest includes data warehousing and business intelligence systems in the field of evidence-based medicine and health care in general.

Olivier Teste obtained his PhD in computer science from the University of Toulouse III, France, with a thesis on data warehouse modeling in 2000. Since 2001, he is associate professor at the University of Toulouse, teaching Database Systems, Data Warehousing and Programming Languages. His research interests include all aspects related to data warehousing, in particular multidimensional modeling, OLAP querying and XML document warehousing. He serves in program committees of several national and international conferences. He has published over 40 papers in international and national conferences.

A Min Tjoa since 1994 is director of the Institute of Software Technology and Interactive Systems at the Vienna University of Technology. He is currently also the head of the Austrian Competence Center for Security Research. He received his PhD in Engineering from the University of Linz, Austria in 1979. He was Visiting Professor at the Universities of Zurich, Kyushu and Wroclaw (Poland) and at the Technical Universities of Prague and Lausanne (Switzerland). From 1999 to 2003 he was the president of the Austrian Computer Society. He is member of the IFIP Technical Committee for Information Systems and vice-chairman of the IFIP Working Group on Enterprise Information Systems (WG 8.9). He has served as chairman of several international conferences including the IEEE Int. Conf. on Distributed Computing Systems (ICDCS), European Software Engineering Conference (ESEC), ACM SIGSOFT Symposium on the Foundations of Software Engineering (FSE), the International Conference on Database and Expert Systems Applications (DEXA), the International Conference on Electronic Commerce and Web Technologies (ECWeb). He is Honorary Chairman of the International Conference on Very

Large Databases (VLDB 2007). His current research focus areas are e-Commerce, Data Warehousing, Grid Computing, Semantic Web, Security, and Personal Information Management Systems. He has published more than 150 peer reviewed articles in journals and conferences. He is author and editor of 15 books.

Raymond Wong is a Project Leader at NICTA leading the universal storage scheme project. He is also an associate professor of Computer Science and Engineering at the University of New South Wales, Sydney, Australia. Dr. Wong has more than ten years of research and development experience in the areas of database systems, XML processing, and mobile technologies. He has published more than 100 research articles in these areas.

Songmei Yu is currently an assistant professor in the Computer Information Systems department at Felician College, Lodi, NJ, USA. She received her PhD from Rutgers University in Information Technology, MS in Computer Science from State University of New York at Stony Brook, and Bachelor of Engineering from Chengdu University of Science and Technology, China. Dr. Yu's major research interests are in Web mining, data warehouse and knowledge retrieval areas.

Geraldo Zimbrão is a professor of Computer Science at the Graduate School of Engineering (COPPE) and Mathematics Institute of the Federal University of Rio de Janeiro (UFRJ) (Brazil). His area of specialization is Databases, and he is involved in research in fields such Spatial and Temporal Databases, Data Mining, Business Rules and GIS. Professor Zimbrão received his bachelor's degree in Computer Science (1992) and his master's degree (1993) in Applied Mathematics – Computer Algebra from the Federal University of Rio de Janeiro (Brazil), and his PhD in Computer Science (1999) from the Federal University of Rio de Janeiro (Brazil).

Index

Copyright © 2010, IGI Global, distributing in print or electronic forms without written permission of IGI Global is prohibited.